TAX POLICY IN OECD COUNTRIES
Choices and Conflicts

"The view [that a link exists between science and ethics] is open to two objections. First, it seems improbable that science can alleviate conflicts by settling debates in areas outside its specific jurisdiction. Second, it appears that not all conflicts are results of clashes between incompatible assertions."

Anatol RAPOPORT,

Forward to *Fights, games and debates*, 1960.

TAX POLICY IN OECD COUNTRIES
Choices and Conflicts

K.C. Messere

IBFD Publications BV

Amsterdam

IBFD Publications BV
P.O. Box 20237
1000 HE Amsterdam
The Netherlands
Tel. +31 (0)20 626 77 26
Fax +31 (0)20 622 86 58
Telex 13217 intax nl

ISBN 90-70125-64-1
NUGI 696

PREFACE

This book is about the domestic tax policy choices of OECD[1] governments over the last two or three decades, the decisions that have been taken and the reasons why they have been taken. It seeks also to identify predominant trends and similarities or differences between countries or groups of countries.

International factors are referred to only insofar as they influence or constrain country choices. There may be a second volume which would cover the international dimension including such issues as co-ordination versus competition, capital import and capital export neutrality, developments in the European Community, border tax adjustments, double taxation and transfer pricing issues, international tax avoidance and evasion etc., but for the time being this is not clear. In addition, whilst many of the topics discussed are also of relevance to countries outside the OECD area, the practices of such countries are rarely referred to.

The kind of issues that this book discusses are OECD governments' tendencies to increase, stabilise or reduce tax levels, to change or not change relative reliance on different kinds of tax revenues and which of the multitude of different options they have favoured with regard to designing or changing particular kinds of tax as well as to reforming their tax systems more fundamentally. The period covered is mostly 1965 to 1992 with emphasis on more recent years, but occasionally reference is made to choices over the last hundred years as well as to what might be expected to happen in the future.

The intention is to address not only tax specialists, but also general readers with an interest in tax policy issues. In accordance with this intention, discussion of public finance theory and the nuts and bolts of tax administration is reduced to a minimum. Some technical expressions or abbreviations have to be used and these are defined or described where this seems most appropriate. In addition, a general glossary of terms and expressions is provided at the beginning of the Appendix to this volume.

1. Countries in the Organisation for Economic Co-operation and Development are, as at March 1993, Australia, Austria, Belgium*, Canada, Denmark*, France*, Finland, Germany*, Greece*, Iceland, Ireland*, Italy*, Japan, Luxembourg*, the Netherlands*, New Zealand, Norway, Portugal*, Spain*, Sweden, Switzerland, Turkey, the United Kingdom* and the United States. Those marked with an asterisk are also Members of the European Community.

PREFACE

CONTENTS

(a more detailed breakdown of contents is provided at the beginning of most chapters)

LIST OF TABLES

LIST OF CHARTS

INTRODUCTION

The book is divided into three parts. Part I deals with tax developments usually between 1965 and 1992, or in the case of tax revenue statistics usually between 1965 and 1989, the latest years for which firm data are available as at June 1992. Chapter 1 concentrates on the recent wave of tax reforms that began in 1984, but also surveys earlier years and discusses what tax reforms might occur during the nineties. Chapters 2 to 4 deal with the questions of the magnitude of tax revenues and the sources from which they have been raised in OECD countries. Chapter 2 provides a first summary of the results together with various possible factors which could account for them. Chapter 3 reproduces in greater detail data on OECD country tax levels and tax structures in 1989 and between 1965 and 1989, though a postscript provides total tax receipts to GDP ratios for 1990, with estimates for 1991. Chapter 4 compares developments in various groups of countries, as a substitute for looking more intensively at developments within each OECD country, which would require a book twice as long as this.

Part II of the book discusses some analytical and general tax policy questions, which usually apply to more than one kind of tax. In particular the conflict between the ability to pay or accretion principle (those who can pay more should pay more) and the benefit principle (those who benefit most should contribute most) and the conflict between tax interventionism and tax neutrality in its various senses frequently arises. Chapter 5 self-indulgently but briefly, takes time out to record some of the author's frustrations with the irrationality which permeates tax policy discussions and the literature, usually due to the misuse of language. Chapter 6 discusses in more detail what seem to be two of the most important conflicts of tax policy: higher expenditures versus lower taxes and tax expenditures versus direct expenditures. Chapter 7 discusses the relationship between tax policy and economic and social policy in the areas of household savings, income distribution and energy and environmental policy. Chapters 8 and 9 deal respectively with the various ways in which OECD governments finance social welfare programmes and local government expenditures.

Part III, which constitutes by far the largest part of the book, examines the policy choices confronted by governments in designing or changing all the major kinds of tax. The introduction or modification of any kind of tax raises a multitude of policy, legal, administrative and technical issues. In keeping with the aims indicated above this survey of particular kinds of tax is confined to those policy issues likely to be of most interest to the general reader. Operationally this means concentrating the discussion on those choices which could have an impact on economic efficiency or on horizontal or vertical equity. The technique that is generally adopted is first to identify what the main policy choices are, second to discuss the arguments for or against various possible solutions and third to indicate usually by comparative tables, the choices of OECD governments and how they have changed over the last twenty-five years. Having discussed the advantages and disadvantages of various choices, I have usually left evaluation of them to the reader but when holding strong views I have expressed them.

Insofar as there are deep books and wide books, the foregoing remarks indicate that this one is intended to be in the latter category. Nevertheless, to keep it within manageable length, it has been necessary to make selections on the statistical comparisons to be undertaken and the issues to be covered. To some extent, reasons for the statistical selections are explained, but it is more difficult to make the distinction between major policy issues to be included and others to be excluded, beyond such generalities that academic issues regarding non-existent taxes along with details of administrative procedures are hardly discussed, however important they may be in looking at fiscal policy in all its dimensions. On the other hand, something needs to be said about such widely-discussed but non-existent taxes as progressive expenditure taxes and cash-flow corporation taxes and also about some of the important administrative choices in designing a value added tax.

The fascination of tax policy, and why one can work on it for a lifetime without getting too bored, is that it relates to so many other aspects of life, not only economic policy and legal complexities, but also, for example, logic and linguistic analysis, political theory, psychological attitudes and their manipulation by politicians. Tax policy choices also involve conflict, trade-offs, resort to second, third or fourth best choices. Finally, as subsequently noted, at this theoretical and speculative level, the relationship between tax and death has been commented on from Pliny the Younger to Benjamin Franklin, and the relationship between tax and sin from St. Thomas Aquinas to the November 1992 Catholic Church Catechism. On a more practical level, tax policy impinges on a variety of social and economic concerns, which is why it is sometimes relevant to provide statistical information on such diverse matters as (inter alia) saving patterns, energy prices and the consumption of cigarettes.

I should mention that between 1971 and 1991 I was Head of the Fiscal Affairs Division of the Organisation for Economic Co-operation and Development (henceforth OECD) since this book uses various published OECD reports to which I contributed in my professional capacity; it uses also material from various articles that I have written in a personal capacity, sometimes in collaboration with S. Cnossen, J. Nørregaard or J. Owens. A large proportion of the bibliography at the end of the book is devoted to OECD literature, because the OECD's Fiscal Affairs Committee has examined almost all the issues discussed in this book, and the empirical data provided are mostly based on those supplied and verified by members of that Committee and its Working Parties. The material has also been discussed not only among the national civil servants that constitute the Committee and its Working Parties, but also with representatives of business, industry and trade unions. A number of public finance academics have contributed to the drafting of many of OECD published reports, as have representatives from other international organisations such as the International Monetary Fund and the Commission of the European Communities. Input has also been provided by research institutes such as the Brookings Institution in Washington, the International Bureau of Fiscal Documentation in Amsterdam and the Institute of Fiscal

Studies in London. To a large extent this book aims at providing a synthesis of a number of these separately published OECD reports together with other material not covered by them.

This book reproduces a mass of facts about country practices, of which I hope and believe at least 95 per cent are accurate. But these "facts" are provided as an indication of governments' policy choices at a particular point in time and for three different kinds of reasons should not necessarily be assumed to represent current country positions: first, government practices change, and the information provided may not always represent the most recent position; second, spatial constraints require simplification and there are all kinds of caveats, exceptions and reservations, not always indicated in the tables provided; third, even in my privileged position in the OECD it was not always easy to know what was the real situation on certain matters of fact in particular countries, since different information would occasionally be provided by different informants, and to establish unequivocally what was the real situation was sometimes impossible before it was time to go to press.

Because of my OECD connection, I have been asked why I preferred to write about domestic tax rather than international tax issues, given the growing interdependence of national economies and the growing importance of international regional groupings. There are many reasons. First, the OECD Committee on Fiscal Affairs examines not only international co-operation, for example to reduce international double taxation and tax evasion and avoidance but also compares country tax practices, together with why they were adopted and how they might change, and I have always found this latter aspect of the work the more interesting. Secondly, immediately after my retirement from the OECD in January 1991, I became a Member of the Ruding Committee whose mandate was to make recommendations to the EC Commission on the future of business taxation in the single market and this involved examining a number of international tax considerations. It would not have been easy simultaneously to discuss these questions with my colleagues on the Committee and reach conclusions for a book. Third, domestic tax policy does represent an almost self-contained topic of great interest and I strongly disagree with the fashionable view that international considerations are going to dominate domestic tax policy decisions, for while this may happen in limited areas, (e.g. rate lowering and base broadening of personal and corporate income taxes) there is little evidence that international pressures for conformity have so far played a major part in most tax policy choices of national governments who are generally free, subject to domestic constraints, to pursue their own preferences, and I believe that this will continue to be the case during the next decade.

Lastly, I should like to convey my thanks to a number of people who have contributed directly or indirectly to this book. Evidently none of them are committed to agreement with anything that is said. I wish especially to thank Richard Bird and Sijbren Cnossen who have commented on most of the chapters of this book, provided valuable input and frequently pointed out where I had gone wrong as well as indicating further avenues to explore. Their welter of (sometimes conflicting) advice made my task much more interesting and has greatly improved the original drafts. I am much indebted to John Nørregaard who provided helpful suggestions on a number of chapters. I am also most grateful to Rijkele Betten, Patricia Ellman and Marcel Poelmeijer of the IBFD staff for the considerable amount of work they have undertaken in improving the accuracy and presentation of this book.

Thanks are also due to Jeffrey Owens for his comments on Chapter 9, as well as for his contributions to a number of articles which we have written together and which have provided input for Chapters 2, 4 and 10E4; to David Jones and Jack Short for their comments on Chapters 7D and 7E; and to Donal de Buitleir and Malcolm Gammie for their comments on Chapter 12.

The indirect influences on this book through my contacts with civil servants and the business community at the OECD, with public finance academics at the International Institute of Public Finance and with tax lawyers and accountants at the International Fiscal Association are too numerous to mention. I would like to single out three good friends, where past collaboration has affected the contents of this book. The first is Jørgen Lotz; since around 1969-70 we developed together what was to become a few years later, with some modifications, the OECD classification of taxes which enabled revenue statistics to be provided for the first time on an internationally comparable basis in reasonably disaggregated form, and the resulting annual OECD publication *Revenue Statistics in OECD Countries* is much quoted in this book. Second, is the late Jack Wiseman, who was the guru of the OECD Fiscal Affairs Division from its creation in 1971 until the late seventies and who was one of the major creators of the average production worker (APW) whose tax/benefit position is referred to in Chapter 10. Third, is the late Joseph Pechman with whom I frequently discussed tax policy between the mid-seventies and late eighties. He invited me to provide an overview to a 1987 Brookings Institution Conference on World Tax Reform and part of this overview has been incorporated into the first chapter of this book.

At the technical level I am most grateful to Edel McManus for creating and checking numerous statistical tables and verifying much of the first hundred pages, to Ken and Marie-Laurence Smith for processing the bulk of the book in a very efficient way and to Verity Russell for supplying most of the Appendix. Their good humour in coping with my bad hadwriting helped a lot, as did the friendliness of Hubert Hamaekers and all his colleagues at the International Bureau of Fiscal Documentation who were involved in the production of this book.

Warmest thanks of all go to Brunehilde Lequesne Messere, for many years my motivating force, to whom this book is dedicated.

PART I
TAX DEVELOPMENTS IN OECD COUNTRIES BETWEEN 1965 AND 1992

Chapter 1
An introduction to the recent wave of tax reforms

A. Summary of longer-term developments

1. Outside the tax world

Over the last forty years there have been major changes in the economic, social and technological environment of OECD countries, and many of them have provoked changes in governments' tax policies. These include:

- a continuing change since the late forties in the composition of the labour force, over which time, two-earner couples have become the norm rather than the exception;
- the transition from uninterrupted full-employment expansionary economies between 1955 and around 1975 to fluctuation since then with high inflation and unemployment rates often prevalent;
- the two oil shocks during the early seventies and late seventies to early eighties and the discovery of North Sea oil;

- changing family patterns since the early seventies with the growth of informal unions and one-parent families;
- changing demographic patterns, where the proportion of the non-productive elderly will continue to increase into the 21st century;
- a sharp decline in government and private savings between the late seventies and late eighties;
- a continuing improvement in technology, including the development in the late eighties of the general use of pocket computers;
- a growing concern since the mid-eighties with environmental problems;
- a growing internationalisation of economies since the mid-eighties, as exemplified especially by the European Community's single market and the North American free trade agreement;
- a growing demand for greater local autonomy at sub-national levels of government, of which Catalonia, Quebec and Scotland provide examples.
- the unification of Germany, the retreat from Communism, and the breakup to varying degrees of what was Czechoslovakia, the Soviet Union and Yugoslavia.

2. Within the tax world

Since 1945 when the second world war ended there have been three major waves of tax reforms. The first was the widespread growth of payroll taxes on employees, employers and the self-employed to finance social security benefits. This first wave occurred generally before 1965 and so is not commented on in this chapter, though their continual growth is discussed elsewhere. The second wave was the move to value added taxation, which occurred in half of the 24 OECD countries between 1967 and 1975 and in another seven between 1985 and 1991. This second wave is discussed in Chapter 13 on consumption taxation rather than in this chapter. The third wave of tax reforms which occurred between 1984 and 1992 was the drastic reduction in almost all OECD countries in rates of personal and corporate income taxes, accompanied almost universally by a widening of the personal income tax base and usually by a widening of the corporate income tax base. This third wave of tax reforms is discussed in this chapter, and in more detail in Chapters 10 (personal income taxes) and 12 (corporate income taxes).

Outside these major changes it is simpler to avoid defining what constitutes a "tax reform" as distinct from minor adjustments to the tax system, for different sets of people have different criteria and motives for making this distinction. For example, politicians may wish to take a high-profile approach and call a minor operation a major tax reform or a low-profile approach and call a major tax reform a minor adjustment; tax practitioners may focus on the numbers of winners and losers and, accordingly, the practical consequence for their own work in judging whether a change in tax legislation merits being described as a tax reform; the criteria of academics is likely to be whether or not there are major structural changes to the tax system. Accordingly "tax reform" is used here to cover all major changes to the tax legislation recently undertaken and which may be taken in the near future.

A number of government statements and reports of tax reform commissions have given similar answers at more than one level of generality on why tax systems need reforming. The broad objectives of tax reform are – in no special order of importance – simplicity, transparency, economic efficiency, the improvement of horizontal (no longer vertical) equity, along with that ever-conflicting pair, the promotion of economic and social goals and the achievement of tax neutrality, the latter now predominating except in certain sensitive areas. Other statements relate to more specific goals such as improving the labour supply, encouraging private saving and reducing the attractions of the underground economy. More specifically, governments go straight ahead to the methods that they think will achieve some of these objectives, such as cutting statutory rates of personal and corporate income taxes, broadening the tax base of these income taxes and moving from income and payroll to consumption taxation.

In the past the consensus seems to have been that in good economic times (for example, the sixties and early seventies), it is not worth undertaking tax reform because potential winners will not react and the potential losers will be resentful enough to vote out the government introducing such tax reforms. Nevertheless, there may be other reasons for undertaking a particular tax reform, and the move to a value added tax by twelve of the twenty four OECD countries between 1965 and 1975 was possibly more far-reaching than anything they did subsequently by way of tax reform. Again, during the seventies, when inflation was continuous and growth was gradually lessening, little major tax reform occurred, though certain issues were addressed. In particular, most governments felt compelled to offset, at least partially, fiscal drag from the income tax, whether by discretionary measures or indexation. Also, in a number of countries the growth of two-earner families led to a change from joint taxation to separate taxation, or at least the option for such. Since that change led to a tax gain for higher-earning couples, many governments gave aid to parents outside the tax system or replaced tax allowances by tax credits.

During the eighties, when the levels of growth, employment, and inflation were lower and voters' perceptions have been that tax systems are unfair, inefficient and unnecessarily complicated, governments have been persuaded that tax reform may be a vote winner rather than a vote loser. Among other factors helping to account for the recent unprecedented wave of tax reforms are: the fact that because of declining fiscal drag due to lower rates of inflation and increasing avoidance through moonlighting and use of tax shelters, governments found it too difficult to increase personal income tax receipts, for most of them the most important source of government revenues; reforms in the mid-eighties in the United States and a few other countries resulting in the cutting of income tax rates and widening the base compelled most other countries to follow suit for competitive reasons; tax reform commissions have learnt from each other and persuaded their government of the distorting effects of their current tax systems.

Section B of this chapter looks at the problems governments have addressed and consists of two catalogues: first, a list of discontents with present tax systems; second, a list of arguments for and against moving from income (and payroll) taxes to consumption taxes. There are various problems in improving tax systems such as conflicting objectives (Section C), political and implementational problems (Section D) and various constraints on *radical* tax reform (Section E). Solutions adopted since the mid-eighties are summarised in Section F, and Section G suggests tax reforms that might occur in the nineties.

Throughout this chapter tax reform is discussed in the context of (more or less) revenue neutrality. Chapter 6 especially, and Chapters 2 to 4 refer to whether the tax take and government intervention in the economy is likely to increase, decrease, or remain much as it is at present.

B. Problems addressed since the mid-eighties

1. A list of discontents

Tax problems vary from country to country on certain issues. To take two examples of such diversity: first a number of governments have used tax incentives to increase saving at the expense of borrowing but in Japan it was felt that the tax system favoured savings too much; second, though a number of countries have announced an intention to rely more greatly on consumption taxes and less on income taxes, such a shift in the tax mix would seem inappropriate in a country like France with a heavy consumption tax and low income tax.

However, despite such country variations, the criticisms of their tax systems have been common to most countries. First, they are too complex for taxpayers to understand, and for the tax authorities to operate them efficiently. This increases government administrative and taxpayers' compliance costs as well as opening the way to sophisticated tax-avoidance schemes. (When in 1789, a year before his own death, Benjamin Franklin wrote: "In this world nothing can be said to be certain except death and taxes", he could not be expected to be aware of the potentialities of the tax avoidance industry, to say nothing of tax fraud.)

Second, the distribution of the personal income tax burden is unfair. Individuals with similar tax capacity pay markedly different amounts of tax. This conflicts with the principle of horizontal equity, generates resentment on the part of taxpayers and undermines tax morality.

Third, high marginal rates of tax distort economic decisions. Taxpayers may be encouraged to work less or to enter the underground economy. Moreover, high statutory rates do not even succeed in the objective of taxing higher incomes at higher rates, since use of tax loopholes enables effective high rates to be avoided in practice.

Fourth, capital income may in fact be even negatively taxed in some countries, where there is unlimited deductibility for interest payments, with the consequence that income tax schedules may even be regressive at the highest income levels.

Fifth, corporate tax structures encourage firms to undertake investments and to restructure their balance sheets for tax rather than economic reasons. The quality of capital formation may be adversely affected and scarce resources misallocated.

Sixth, large differences between personal and corporate tax rates may encourage firms to incorporate or not to incorporate simply to save tax.

Seventh, discrimination against dividends favours debt as a means of financing new investment to the detriment of economic efficiency.

Eighth, the tax systems of most OECD countries encourage borrowing at the expense of saving and discriminate arbitrarily between the different forms of savings.

2. Changing the tax mix

Changing the tax mix, usually from income taxation to value added taxation is an issue that has been much discussed in many countries but until 1989, leaving aside countries introducing VAT during the eighties, this has happened to any significant extent only in the United Kingdom.

The main arguments that have been put forward in favour of a move from income taxes towards consumption taxes are:

i) *Improved incentives to save*. The switch will reduce the difference between the pre-and-post tax return to saving that encourages taxpayers to consume rather than save.
ii) *Less easy to avoid*. Earners may believe they pay too much income tax compared with people receiving fringe benefits and those in a position to exploit tax shelters and loopholes or to make tax-free capital gains or to enter the underground economy.
iii) *Less easy to evade*. Though evasion does occur under VAT, especially in the service sector, there is an impression that the proportion of revenue lost is less than that under income taxes (e.g. the 1983 French Conseil des Impôts report on VAT).
iv) *Greater revenue buoyancy under conditions of non-inflationary growth*. If taxpayer resistance to the income tax is increasing, broad-based consumption taxes may prove a more buoyant source of revenue.
v) *Lower administrative costs*. Little empirical evidence is available, but some estimates suggest a lower cost per dollar of revenue collected for VAT than for the personal income tax.
vi) *Potentially more efficient instrument for macro-economic policy*. Changes in consumption tax rates are likely to have a greater and more rapid influence on aggregate consumer demand than changes in other taxes.

The main criticisms put forward against an increased reliance on general consumption taxes or introducing such a tax are:

i) *Price levels*. Though it is now more frequently believed that increases in personal income taxes are eventually shifted into higher prices through higher wages, it would seem likely that a revenue equivalent increase in a general consumption tax would be shifted into prices to a greater extent and more quickly – with inflationary consequences.

ii) *General consumption taxes are less progressive than income taxes.* Empirical data support the view that the burden of consumption taxes tends to be less progressive than that of the personal income tax.

iii) *Taxpayer resistance.* Because of the magnitude of compliance costs perceived as being associated especially with a VAT, taxpayer resistance may be high, as had been evidenced by some business representations against VAT both in countries having VAT (Norway) and in those contemplating its adoption (Canada and Japan). Similar objections were raised by the Australian business community when the introduction of a retail sales tax was contemplated.

iv) *Consumption patterns may be distorted.* Whilst these taxes are in principle neutral, in most countries exemptions from the tax base, taxation of intermediate goods and multi-rate systems all introduce distortions in consumer spending patterns.

v) *The cost of introducing a general consumption tax.* For countries not actually having a broad-based consumption tax, the introduction of such a tax can take a number of years and may require a large increase in the administrative costs of government and the compliance costs of traders.

The effect on incentives to work as a result of a move from income taxes towards consumption taxes is debatable. Some have argued that a switch from income taxes to consumption taxes will favourably influence the work-leisure trade-off, thereby encouraging greater work effort, especially if effective marginal rates of income tax plus social security tax are high. Others argue that consumption taxes effectively tax labour income, since a general consumption tax does not have an effect upon income that is saved currently, and is therefore economically equivalent to a tax on wages. Thus, consumption taxes affect the work-leisure trade-off in a similar way to an income tax. According to this latter view, a revenue-neutral switch from an income tax to a consumption tax requires higher effective marginal tax rates on wages, thereby discouraging work effort.

In a number of countries the desirability of relying less on social security contributions and more on general consumption taxes to finance social security revenues has also been considered and a number of the arguments referred to in the foregoing paragraphs are also relevant to this issue. An additional argument in favour of such a substitution is that it would be unlikely to have any regressive effects since social security contributions are probably at least as, if not more regressive, than general consumption taxes, and also that employers' contributions may have deterrent effects on employers taking on labour, especially low-paid and part-time labour; another argument against such a substitution is that in a number of countries social security contributions may be viewed by both employers and employees as a quasi-insurance which at the same time may render them more acceptable than other taxes and help to keep a brake on public expenditure.

The question has also been raised whether under present border tax adjustment arrangements, increased reliance on consumption taxes might improve a country's international competitiveness. However, a consensus seems to have emerged that this is not an important issue, especially in these days of flexible exchange rates.

C. Conflicting objectives

As indicated by its sub-title, a major theme of this book is that the objectives of tax policy frequently conflict and a change in tax provisions to promote one objective may have secondary effects which can either help or hinder other objectives. Many examples of such conflicts are discussed in greater detail in subsequent chapters and the following paragraphs only list a few of them in general terms.

At the most general level the main function of taxation is to provide revenues to finance public expenditures, but concessions to meet social and economic policy objectives may clash with this aim by reducing tax yields. There may also be conflicts between equity and efficiency objectives, or between economic efficiency and simplicity, in that a particular measure which promotes one of these objectives may have detrimental effects on the other.

Another conflict of tax policy is how far the tax system should reflect the taxpayers' ability to pay (accretion principle) and how far the benefits the taxpayer receives (benefit principle). Generally, tax systems take account of both, progressive personal income taxes fulfilling the first function and social security contributions and sometimes local property taxes and user charges the latter. A related conflict is that the earmarking of taxes for particular kinds of expenditures contributes to the benefit principle but may reduce economic efficiency objectives in adversely affecting governments' macroeconomic control. Also related is the conflict between macroeconomic central control and local accountability in deciding to what extent governments at subordinate levels of government should have control of tax revenues as discussed in Chapter 9.

"Vertical equity", or the equitable differential tax treatment of taxpayers having different levels of income and/or capital, often conflicts with economic efficiency and administrative efficiency. For example, tax reliefs to encourage economic objectives are apt to conflict with the principle of vertical equity, since concessions for such purposes tend to benefit least the lower income groups and whilst a single rate value added tax has everything to be said for it from the point of view of efficiency, it makes the system somewhat more regressive than a multi-rate VAT (see Chapter 13). More important is the conflict in the income tax system between rate progressivity, which aims at vertical equity and all the disadvantages of progressivity summarised by R. Mathews (1984) as:

> Nearly every major problem that arises in formulating and implementing taxation policy results from this single cause – the progressive (Australian) income tax. Problems of dealing with income splitting, taxing fluctuating incomes, taxing superannuation benefits, measuring tax allowances, indexing for inflation, integrating personal and company taxes, taxing capital and windfall gains, administering and collecting taxes (including arranging for source deductions), reducing economic disincentives and inhibiting incentives to avoid and evade tax would be greatly alleviated, and in some cases would disappear altogether under a flat-rate or linear income tax.

As already noted in the recent wave of tax reforms the progressivity of the rate schedules has been much reduced, or in some cases even eliminated. The consequent loss of vertical equity has been offset by increasing the income level at which income tax becomes payable and reducing tax loopholes which benefit most higher income groups, but because of the complexity of the trade-offs involved, it is not easy to evaluate how the totality of these income tax changes has affected income distribution. A related conflict is between those who see the tax system playing a part in redistributing income and alleviating poverty and those who see such goals more efficiently achieved outside the tax system by reduction in primary (before tax) income differentials or through government expenditures on welfare benefits (see Chapter 7C). Here it may be remarked that how far it is reasonable to neglect taxation as an instrument for redistributing income and alleviating poverty depends to a large extent on how far taxing and spending decisions are integrated. Such integration seems easiest in small industrialised countries like New Zealand and those in Scandinavia, which helps to explain why these countries have been able to apply a very high single rate VAT on nearly all goods and services, whereas this has not been found acceptable in other countries.

There may also be a conflict between transparency and flexibility. Many consider that in a democracy transparency should be paramount but others may take the view, more cynically or pragmatically, that certain desirable goals like fiscal consolidation or macroeconomic stability may be achievable only by taking advantage of taxpayers' illusions. This is one feature in the debate on government aid through the tax system discussed in more detail in Chapter 6C: its relative non-transparency is cited as a reason by some for supporting it and by others for opposing it. Also for many years governments have benefited from taxpayers' illusions that their income tax bill does not increase when rates and allowances are unchanged, even though there are limits to these illusions as when fiscal drag is due primarily to inflation: transparency suggests indexing rates and allowances to prevent this whereas flexibility suggests the contrary (see Chapter 10 D5 for a discussion of this issue). The virtue of transparency may also be questioned on another level. Transparency has to be relative and in practice the transparency is for the minority, mostly higher income groups, who attentively read about tax developments.

The economic objectives which tax reliefs are intended to promote may also conflict. For example, tax reliefs to promote savings, may distort saving patterns by encouraging institutional investment to the detriment of what may be more economically-productive investments.

Another conflict is that between the macroeconomic objectives of governments at federal or central government levels and the demand for local accountability at subordinate levels of government in the allocation of revenues (see Chapter 9).

Finally, the multiple effects of particular changes in tax provisions may provide reinforcement of, or conflict between, government objectives. For example, widening the tax base could meet the twofold objective of making the system seem fairer to taxpayers and enabling rates to be lowered, or pollution taxes may promote both environmental and revenue-raising goals in each case providing a re-enforcement effect: in contrast a policy of not adjusting income tax thresholds for inflation may promote, on the one hand, the intended effect of increasing revenues and, on the other, unintended effects in relation to the unemployment and poverty trap, taxpayer discontent and administrative problems in coping with the increased number of taxpayers who drift into the tax net.

D. Political problems in implementing tax reform

Countries have taken very different routes to overcome the political and pressure group resistance to major tax reform.

The separation of powers prevalent in the *United States* led to numerous tax reform proposals (including two from the Administration, one from the Senate and one from the House of Representatives) so very different from each other that at one point major tax reform seemed doomed. However, the 1986 reform prevailed in the end due to the coalition of a President and important members of Congress of diverse views strongly in favour of tax reform, together with the broad perception that a transfer of income tax burdens from individuals to corporations along with a large reduction in rates of tax would reduce the power of individual and corporate pressure groups to retain their tax privileges and would prove popular among voters. The United States' success set in train what has been called the "fascination" or "imitation" effect and many other countries followed the United States route.

For example, the United States rate lowering and base broadening more or less compelled *Canada* to follow suit. The Canadian government also wished to replace the inefficient federal manufacturing sales tax by a value added tax. The first half of the proposal, relatively uncontroversial, was announced by the government soon after the United States tax reform and put into effect quite quickly. The second half involving complex questions of federal/provincial tax powers was discussed extensively, and it was not until 1991 that a federal VAT was introduced.

In *Australia* with its relatively short (three-year) election period, action was pursued urgently in order to carry out the tax reform before the next election. A national taxation summit was called and agreement was obtained in 1985 within a few months on drastic changes to the personal and corporate income tax but not on the replacement of the wholesale sales tax by a more neutral general consumption tax.

In *Japan* the government made a number of attempts at income tax reform on the lines of that carried out in other OECD countries but each time the proposals were withdrawn because of the opposition to the introduction of VAT. Only after a compromise which reduced the VAT rate to 3 per cent was that reform eventually undertaken in 1989.

Of the non-European OECD countries, conditions for fundamental tax reform were most favourable in *New Zealand*, partly because its relative smallness created fewer administrative constraints, partly because its reliance on income tax was far greater than in any OECD country and this created evident inefficient allocation of resources and horizontal inequities, and partly because there was an enthusiastic tax reformer as Minister of Finance. After a carefully planned publicity campaign, a comprehensive reform of personal and corporate income taxes was obtained on the lines of those in other countries, and also a single rate VAT on a wider base than that of any other OECD country.

For most of the last twenty-five years, the *United Kingdom* government has had a clear majority in Parliament and, whilst putting out discussion papers to get public reactions to its proposed tax reforms, has had less need than a number of other European countries to achieve a consensus with opposition political parties before enacting tax reform legislation. The near doubling of the VAT rate in 1979 and the 1984 reduction of the corporate tax rates combined with base widening and subsequent reductions of personal income tax rates provide examples. Other more eccentric examples rendered possible by this executive power are discussed in Chapters 4F and 9E7 and 9F.

Germany with its coalition government announced a gradual long-term programme of income tax reform (in the same direction as other countries) and political discussion during the late eighties focused on whether or not the timetable should be accelerated.

In *Belgium, Denmark, the Netherlands, Norway and Sweden*, tax reform commissions made various proposals during the late eighties and early nineties and the tendency has been to try to obtain a consensus both between different political parties and between different groups (business, trade unions, economists).

These somewhat simplified descriptions of developments in certain countries show that there is much variation between countries in the degree to which public opinion has to be prepared and a consensus obtained to implement tax reforms successfully. Also of practical relevance to the success of tax reforms are the views of the government (especially the Minister of Finance, or equivalent) and top civil servants concerned with tax policy and tax administration, their respective personalities and the "power" relationship between them, i.e. whose will is more likely to prevail in the event of disagreement. Of course this will vary as between countries and over time within any country. Other things being equal (which they rarely are) the tax administrator will prefer a no-change policy, since any major tax reform involves a great increase in the work of the department – already likely to be understaffed – to cope with the necessary transitional adjustments, to introduce the legislation and administrative instructions, to train staff and inform the public if a new tax is to be introduced, to re-deploy staff if a tax is to be abolished. Politicians forming a government do not have this constraint and may desire tax reform if they think it will be a vote-winner in the next election or, if newly elected, to fulfil some previous promise to the voters (e.g. to introduce or abolish a net wealth tax). There may also be a conflict between civil servants, with tax administrators more aware of the resource costs and tax policy makers of the potential economic advantages of a particular tax reform.

E. Constraints on radical tax reform

In addition to some of the constraints already mentioned on any kind of tax reform there are other limitations on radical tax reform, or a major change to the tax structure. Existing modern tax systems are extremely complex and to dismantle them in favour of some totally different form of taxation would be to introduce an administrative nightmare, even apart from the transitional difficulties in moving towards such new forms of taxation. In addition, a whole series of international agreements have been built up on the basis of the present tax system, which for the purposes of such agreements comprises in all OECD countries a personal and corporate income tax and specific and general indirect consumption taxes. It is difficult to imagine what international rules could emerge in a world where economies are increasingly interdependent if one or a few countries went in for major radical reform.

All this has not prevented public finance experts designing new kinds of taxes for the consideration of policy makers and governments and if the area of impact is sufficiently circumscribed they may even succeed (cf. later remarks in Chapter 4 on the British selective employment and poll taxes). There is no need in the context of this book to comment on what might be called the metaphysics of tax policy as exemplified by such approaches as optimal tax theory or public choice theory as serious guides for improving real world tax systems, though for a readable demolition of optimal taxation as a guide to tax policy, the reader is referred to A. Tait (1989). However, mention should perhaps be made of one kind of tax which does not actually exist in OECD countries, not only because it has a long intellectual ancestry going back to John Stuart Mill, as well as currently being preferred by many, or possibly even most public finance academics, but has even been recommended by tax reform commissions in Ireland, Sweden, the United Kingdom and the United States, either to replace or to supplement the personal income tax. This is the progressive expenditure tax, also variously called "lifetime income tax" "consumer income tax", "personal consumption tax". The base of such a tax would be consumer expenditures (represented by total income plus gifts and bequests minus savings), and a progressive rate schedule would be applied to this base. Its proponents frequently, but not necessarily, assume that a progressive expenditure tax would be accompanied by an annual net wealth tax (see Chapter 11) and a cash flow corporation tax (see Chapter 12).

The relative merits and disadvantages of comprehensive personal income taxes and progressive expenditure taxes is a fascinating topic on which much has been written, but since for the reasons already mentioned, it is unlikely that any OECD government is going seriously to consider the adoption of a progressive expenditure tax in the foreseeable future, it is not a policy option within the scope of this book. However, it seems worth mentioning here that though a direct expenditure tax (supplemented by a cash flow corporate tax and a tax on bequests) from a theoretical point of view neatly encourages savings while preserving redistribution objectives, in practice it would pose all kinds of practical problems, such as transitional adjustments, defining the scope of the savings to be deducted, control of aged emigrants wishing to escape the bequest tax and the renegotiation of tax treaties with countries with classical income taxes. Also such a tax seems superfluous when value added taxes provide a perfectly good way of taxing consumption, and it is probably not coincidental that advocacy for a direct expenditure tax comes mostly from the United States, which at federal level lacks a general consumption tax.

It should also be added that in the real world personal income taxes are hybrid taxes on income and consumption since savings are largely excluded from the income tax base, as discussed in detail in Chapter 10, which leads to an endorsement of the conclusion of Aaron, Galper and Pechman (1988) who said that:

> The papers in this book do not add up to a call for either an income tax or a consumption tax. They are inspired by the realization that while advocates of either pure approach to taxation may pave the way for a superior tax system some time in the future, the tax debate today and in the years immediately ahead will address how to balance conflicting tax principles, drawn in

part from the norms of income taxation, in part from the norms of consumption taxation, and in part from concerns over non-tax problems. Tax analysts interested in contributing to that debate must come to terms with this fact. They should recognize that recommendations for perfecting pure forms of taxation may well be inferior advice for improving a hybrid tax system. Of equal importance, they may be politically irrelevant.

F. Solutions adopted during the eighties

The move to value added taxation is commented on in Chapter 13 and this section deals only with recent and projected reforms to the personal and corporate income tax which are summarised in general terms in Tables 1.1 and 1.2 and discussed in more detail in Chapters 10 and 12.

Changes to the personal income tax generally contain the following features:

a) *Widening the tax base*. For example, it may be extended to include capital gains, fringe benefits, sickness and unemployment benefits, and to eliminate deductibility of certain interest payments, social security contributions and local taxes.
b) *Rate restructuring*. Almost all tax reforms provide for a substantial lowering of the top schedule rates of tax, rate flattening and a reduction in the number of tax brackets.
c) *More equal treatment of different sources of income*. Under many tax systems the tax paid depends upon the source of income. Different rates and allowances may apply as between earned and unearned income; capital gains are usually treated more favourably than other sources of income, etc. Some tax reforms have removed these differences to provide a more neutral tax treatment of income from different sources though others have created new differentials (See Chapter 10A).

Reforms of the corporate income tax generally have the following characteristics:

a) *A removal or reduction of tax incentives which bias investment decisions*. Most corporate tax systems contain a variety of investment incentives (investment tax credits; regional allowances, etc.) and in almost all systems tax depreciation substantially exceeds economic depreciation. Reforms have generally eliminated special investment incentives, removed many tax shelters relating to property investment and particular industries and moved tax depreciation nearer to economic depreciation.
b) *A reduction of the statutory rate of tax*. Irrespective of whether the tax base has been widened, rates have been reduced in nearly all countries (see Table 1.2).
c) *A variation of the relative burden on retained and distributed profits*. The general tendency has been to reduce or remove the tax prejudice against distributed profits but in a few countries the move has been in the opposite direction.

G. Possible tax reform for the nineties

Despite the spate of major tax reforms since the mid-eighties, tax reform for the time being shows no signs of abating. To some extent tax reform provides its own momentum for further reform. Australia and the United States are among the countries who have noted that the investigations into their tax systems and the reforms required further, if less extensive, tax reform as exemplified by the long and complicated United States "Technical Corrections Act". Nevertheless, there remain a number of reasons for assuming that the pace of tax reform will slow down in the nineties. Above all, business requires a stable tax environment and governments have to be convinced that voters will be in favour of further tax reform, and also there still remains disagreement over the precise economic and distributive effects of tax systems and on their impact on work incentives and investment decisions. In addition, tax systems are complex and to change them drastically and quickly arouses opposition from many groups concerned that their own special tax advantages may be withdrawn. Widening the tax base by the removal of tax expenditures tends to alienate well-organised groups of taxpayers (e.g. farmers, house owners, insurance companies), whilst the majority of taxpayers who would benefit from such reforms tend to be less vocal. Finally, there are practical and administrative constraints on tax reform. For example, the introduction of a new tax and a substantial change in collection methods may take a number of years and possibly require a large increase in tax officials and/or extensive education of taxpayers.

Nevertheless, there remains some important tax reform issues which it could be expected that a number of OECD governments will address during the nineties.

- A first area is the provision of a more equal treatment of different saving instruments. Tax factors continue to influence the ways in which households save. In particular, saving for retirement, for home purchase and in the form of life insurance are heavily subsidised by the tax system. Saving in the form of equities of certain kinds is also provided with a favourable treatment in some countries, but is mostly disadvantaged. A number of governments have recently been evaluating critically the cost and effectiveness of these tax subsidies.
- Second, a reduction of the tax bias in favour of borrowing may be expected. Many tax systems provide an incentive to borrow, because the interest on such borrowings is deductible from income subject to tax. This may adversely influence the level of saving. The experience of the few countries (e.g. Denmark) which have reduced this bias suggests that the level of household indebtedness can be lowered quite rapidly.
- Third, there may be a reduction of the influence of taxation on investment decisions. Whilst major improvements have been made in providing a "level playing field" for investment decisions, there remain a large number of tax incentives intended to influence these decisions. Certain sectors (e.g. shipping) have even obtained new tax subsidies in recent years. An elimination or phasing-out of tax subsidies which have either fulfilled their original purpose or which are promoting an inefficient allocation of capital may be expected.
- Fourth, and related to the first three, governments may review their relative tax treatment of earned income and income from capital.

- A fifth area of tax-induced distortions is in the structure of labour markets. Income tax and social security contribution structures are far from neutral towards different segments of the labour market. The participation of women in the economy is in some countries encouraged and in others discouraged by income tax structures; part-time work is generally penalised by ceilings on social security contributions; the zero or near zero threshold for payroll taxes may provide a disincentive to take on new labour. At a more general level, for equity as well as incentive reasons, greater attention may be paid to these structural distortions and to ensuring greater coordination between, or even integration of, income tax and social security contribution systems.
- Sixth, environment and especially energy taxes may become more important as revenue raisers (see Chapter 7).
- Seventh, the balance of taxing power between federal/central and subordinate levels of governments may change (see Chapter 9).
- Eighth, changing the tax mix is still on the agenda of a number of countries and the 1991 Swedish tax reform is likely to shift the burden from income tax to VAT.
- Lastly, tax harmonisation proposals, especially in the field of consumption tax and corporate taxation, by the European Community may compel tax changes during the nineties in the twelve OECD countries already Members of the European Community, as well as a number of other European countries that may well be joining (e.g. Austria, Finland, Iceland, Norway, Sweden and Switzerland).

Table 1.1: Personal income tax changes and proposals between 1986 and 1992 relating to base and rate schedule[1] (federal/central government only)

Country	Base broadening	Reduction of top and high rates[2]	Fewer brackets	Some details of changes
Australia	1989	1987 1989 1990	1987 1989	Inclusion of capital gains and separate tax on fringe benefits
Austria	1989 1991	1989 1991	1989	Limitation on deductibility of entertainment expenses
Belgium	1989 1990	1988 1990	1990	
Canada	1988	1988	1988	Elimination of tax expenditures. Taxing capital gains as ordinary income (1988)
Denmark		1987		Introduction of supplementary income tax on wider base (1987)
Finland	1989 1990	1989 1990 1991	1989	Fringe benefits, limitations and mortgage interest deduction, abolition of bond interest exemption and earned income allowance (1989)
France		1987 1988 1989		
Germany		1990		
Greece	1988	1988	1988	
Iceland	1988	1988	1988	Adoption of flat rate tax
Ireland	1989	1989 1990 1991		Restriction on mortgage relief interest
Italy	1989 1991	1989	1989	Introduction of capital gains tax. Limitations on mortgage relief and entertainment expenses
Japan		1988 1989	1988 1989	
Netherlands	1989 1990	1990	1990	Limitations on deductions
New Zealand	1987 1988 1989	1987 1988 1989	1987 1989	Separate tax on fringe benefits
Norway	1987 1992	1987 1988 1989 1992	1987 1988 1989 1992	Increase in imputed rental income. Increase of supplementary income tax on wider base (1988-90)
Portugal	1989	1989	1989	Move from a schedular to global system
Spain		1989	1989	Increased threshold and new zero rate (1987)
Sweden	1990 1991	1987 1988 1989 1990 1991	1987 1991	Separate taxation of earned income (1991)
United Kingdom		1988	1988	Limitations on company tax-free cars and entertainment expenses
United States	1987	1987	1987	Increased threshold (1987). Switch from zero rate to basic allowance (1987). Introduction of alternative minimum tax (1987)

1. As far as is known, no major changes have taken place or been proposed in Luxembourg, Switzerland and Turkey.

2. First positive rate is increased in many of these countries, see Table 10.11.

Various sources.

Table 1.2: Corporate income tax changes and proposals between 1986 and 1992 relating to base and rate schedule (federal/central government only)

Country	Base broadening	Reduction of rates	Others
Australia	1988	1988	Removal of various incentives in 1988 and in 1991
Austria	1989	1989	Removal of various incentives in 1989
Belgium	1989	1989	
Canada	1988	1988	
		1991	
Denmark	1990	1990	
		1991	
		1992	
Finland	1989	1990	Limits to incentives in 1989-1990. Introduction of imputation system in 1990
		1991	
France		1989	Introduction of new incentives relating to new firms in 1989 and to firms which reduce the working hours of their personnel in 1990.
		1990	
		1992	Introduction of 34 per cent tax on long-term financial capital gains (other than savings)
Germany		1990	Limits to regional incentives in 1988
Greece		1988	
Ireland	1990	1988	
		1989	
Italy		1989	
Japan		1988	Introduction of a special corporate tax from April 1992
		1989	
		1990	
Luxembourg		1987	
		1988	
		1989	
		1990	
Netherlands	1988	1988	
New Zealand		1988	
Norway	1992	1992	
Portugal	1989	1989	Removal of various incentives in 1989
Spain			Limits to investment credit in 1989
Sweden	1989	1989	
	1991	1991	
United Kingdom	1986	1986	Reduction in rate for small companies in 1986, in 1987 and 1988
	1987	1990	
		1991	
United States	1987	1987	Removal of various incentives and introduction of the new branch tax in 1987

1. As far as is known no major changes have been made or proposed in Iceland, Luxembourg, Switzerland and Turkey.
Various sources.

Chapter 2
A first general survey of tax revenue developments in OECD countries

A. Introduction

Valid international comparisons of tax levels and tax structures presuppose standardised definitions of what counts as a tax and how different kinds of tax should be classified. In the early seventies a standardised international classification of taxes was established by the OECD in cooperation with the International Monetary Fund (henceforth IMF) and data based on this classification have been published annually since 1973 under the title *Revenue Statistics of OECD Member Countries* (henceforth OECD RS). The 1991 edition covering the period 1965 to 1989 with provisional results for 1990 provides the data source for nearly all of the tax revenue statistics provided in this book.

The OECD classification of taxes which is reproduced as Table 2.1 is accompanied by an interpretative guide to ensure international uniformity in resolving such questions as what counts as a tax rather than a user charge or other non-tax revenue and under which heading of the classification should revenues from each country's taxes be shown. The main principle of the classification is that taxes are primarily classified according to the base on which they are levied (income and profits, payroll, property, goods and services etc.) and in some cases according to who pays the tax (households, incorporated enterprises, businesses) and that the earmarking of taxes for particular kinds of expenditure does not affect classification. The one exception is that a special heading is provided for compulsory payments to governments earmarked for social security expenditures.

Section B presents some first results and points to certain generalisations that they suggest. Section C tries to provide provisional explanations of tax revenue developments by looking first at what would happen to the revenues of various kinds of taxes if governments made no legislative changes, second, at some of the reasons which might prompt governments to make or not to make such legislative changes, third, at new tax handles available to governments and, fourth, at residual factors which could frustrate governments' intentions. Section D correlates countries' total tax ratios in 1989 with other non-fiscal data (GDP per capita) and with particular total tax ratios to see if any interesting explanatory factors arise but mostly they do not. Finally Section E provides a warning note by drawing attention to some of the main limitations on international comparability of countries' tax levels and structures. An Annex to Section E of this chapter describes some of the more technical and methodological aspects of the limitations on international comparisons of tax levels and tax structures.

This is perhaps a convenient place to draw attention to a few expressions which are used extensively in this and the next two chapters; they are:

> *"Tax level" and "Total tax ratio"* – Tax ratio is the criterion by which tax levels are measured and refers to the ratio of total tax receipts to gross domestic product (GDP) at market prices.
>
> *"Income tax ratio" and "Social security ratio" etc.* – The ratio of income tax receipts, receipts from social security receipts etc. to GDP at market prices.

Table 2.1: The OECD classification of taxes

1000	**Taxes on income, profits and capital gains**			
	1100	Taxes on income, profits and capital gains of individuals		
		1110	On income and profits	
		1120	On capital gains	
	1200	Corporate taxes on income, profits and capital gains		
		1210	On income and profits	
		1220	On capital gains	
	1300	Unallocable as between 1100 and 1200		
2000	**Social security contributions**			
	2100	Employees'		
	2200	Employers'		
	2300	Self-employed or non-employed		
	2400	Unallocable as between 2100, 2200 and 2300		
3000	**Taxes on payroll and workforce**			
4000	**Taxes on property**			
	4100	Recurrent taxes in immovable property		
		4110	Households	
		4120	Other	
	4200	Recurrent taxes on net wealth		
		4210	Individual	
		4220	Corporate	
	4300	Estate, inheritance and gift taxes		
		4310	Estate and inheritance taxes	
		4320	Gift taxes	
	4400	Taxes on financial and capital transactions		
	4500	Other non-recurrent taxes on property		
		4510	On net wealth	
		4520	Other non-recurrent	
	4600	Other recurrent taxes on property		
5000	**Taxes on goods and services**			
	5100	Taxes on production, sale, transfer, leasing and delivery of goods and rendering of services		
		5110	General taxes	
			5111	Value added taxes
			5112	Sales taxes
			5113	Other general taxes on goods and services
		5120	Taxes on specific goods and services	
			5121	Excises
			5122	Profits of fiscal monopolies
			5123	Customs and imports duties
			5124	Taxes on exports
			5125	Taxes on investment goods
			5126	Taxes on specific services
			5127	Other taxes in international trade and transactions
			5128	Other taxes on specific goods and services
		5130	Unallocable as between 5110 and 5120	
	5200	Taxes on use of goods, or on permission to use goods or perform activities		
		5210	Recurrent taxes	
			5211	Paid by households in respect of motor vehicles
			5212	Paid by others in respect of motor vehicles
			5213	Other recurrent taxes
		5220	Non-recurrent taxes	
	5300	Unallocable as between 5100 and 5200		
6000	**Other taxes**			
	6100	Paid solely by business		
	6200	Paid by other than business or unidentifiable		

Source: Revenue Statistics of OECD Member Countries 1965-1990 (OECD 1991) (henceforth OECD RS, with relevant year indicated).

"Tax structure", "Tax mix" and "Tax share" – Each of these expressions refers to the relative importance of receipts from particular kinds of tax in total tax receipts.

"Tax profile" – A more general expression to cover both tax levels and tax structures.

"Excises etc." – Refers not only to 5121 (excises) but to all the subheadings of 5120.

Although comparisons of tax levels and structures are designed to answer two separate questions (how much tax revenues and what tax mix, respectively), data on tax structures could be simply derived from those on tax levels by some multiplication and division. It would accordingly be superfluous to reproduce all the information twice and more detailed comparisons are confined to tax level data. However, it is useful for a number of reasons to have some separate information on tax structures. If total tax receipts rather than GDP at market prices is chosen as the denominator, trends as between different kinds of tax are more clearly revealed, not only because the numbers are larger, but because trends in particular tax ratios can conceal trends in the relative share of receipts from particular taxes in total tax revenue. For example, though the unweighted average corporation tax ratio increased slightly between 1965 and 1989 and that of the property tax remained stable, the share of receipts from both these kinds of tax decreased as a percentage of total tax receipts; and while the unweighted average of employees' social security ratio increased, its share of total tax receipts remained stable. Also, tables solely on tax levels would obscure country choices on their tax mix, since Denmark and Sweden would appear near the top and Turkey and the United States near the bottom of most particular tax ratios, simply because of the extreme difference in their total tax ratios.

B. Some generalisations

Tables 2.2 and 2.3 present some results in very summary form. Even without the more detailed data provided in Chapters 2 and 3 they suggest a number of generalisations.

a) *Major sources of revenue*. Table 2.3 shows that though most countries levy many different kinds of taxes, over the last three decades around 85 per cent of revenues usually come from three sources - personal income taxes, social security contributions and consumption taxes. A few countries, however, have a relatively high reliance on corporation income taxes and property taxes which, if added to the three taxes referred to above, brings their average overall share of total tax revenues to over 96 per cent in nearly all OECD countries. Where the money has been coming from in the past is of evident relevance to what is likely to happen in the future.

b) *Trends in total tax ratios*. There are fluctuations from year to year in the ratio of total tax revenues to GDP in most countries, but in all countries it was higher in 1989 than in 1965, the earliest year for which data are available on an internationally comparable basis. The total tax ratio has generally continued to increase, though much less rapidly in more recent years (see Table 2.2 and also Table 3.4).

c) *Timing of increases in total tax ratios*. Table 2.2 shows that the extent and timing of increases in total tax ratios varies greatly from country to country.

d) *Total tax ratios and form of government.* For the most part, among industrialised countries, federal countries tend to have the lowest total tax ratios (Australia, Switzerland, the United States) and they tend to increase the least (Germany, the United States). Of the ten countries that currently have the highest total tax ratios, only Austria in eighth place has a federal form of government.

e) *Developments in the tax mix.* While country variations are plentiful the unweighted OECD average shows an enormous move away from consumption taxes to income taxes and social security contributions between 1965 and 1975, but relatively little change since 1975.

Table 2.2 : Receipts from total taxes and the main taxes as a percentage of GDP at market prices, 1965, 75, 82, 89

Country[1]	**Total taxes**				**Personal income taxes (1100)**				**Corporate income taxes (1200)**				**Employees' social security taxes (2100)**			
	(1)				(2)				(3)				(4)			
	65	75	82	89	65	75	82	89	65	75	82	89	65	75	82	89
Sweden	35	44	49	56	17	20	20	22	2	2	2	3	1	–	–	–
Denmark	30	42	44	50	12	23	24	26	1	1	1	2	1	0	1	1
Netherlands	33	44	45	46	9	12	11	10	3	3	3	3	5	7	8	9
Norway	33	45	48	45	13	14	12	13	1	1	8	2	–	2	3	4
Belgium	31	42	46	44	6	13	16	14	2	3	3	3	3	4	5	5
France	34	37	43	44	4	4	5	5	2	2	2	2	2	3	5	6
Luxembourg	30	39	41	42	8	11	11	10	3	6	6	7	4	4	5	5
Austria	35	39	41	41	7	8	10	8	2	2	1	1	4	4	5	6
New Zealand	25	31	35	40	10	17	21	18	5	4	3	4	–	–	–	–
Finland	29	35	34	38	11	17	16	18	2	1	2	2	–	–	–	–
Germany	32	36	37	38	8	11	11	11	2	2	2	2	4	5	6	6
Italy	25	26	34	38	3	4	9	10	2	2	3	4	n.a.	2	2	2
Ireland	26	31	37	38	4	8	11	12	2	1	2	1	1	2	2	2
United Kingdom	30	36	39	36	9	13	11	10	2	2	4	4	2	2	3	3
Canada	25	32	33	35	6	11	12	13	4	4	2	3	0	1	1	2
Portugal	18	25	31	35	n.a.	n.a.	n.a.	5	n.a.	n.a.	n.a.	1	2	3	3	3
Spain	14	19	26	34	2	3	5	8	1	1	1	3	1	2	3	2
Iceland	28	31	32	34	5	6	n.a.	8	0	1	n.a.	1	–	–	–	–
Greece	22	25	33	33	1	2	5	4	0	1	1	1	3	3	5	5
Switzerland	21	30	31	32	6	11	11	11	1	2	2	2	1	3	3	3
Japan	18	21	27	31	4	5	7	8	4	4	5	7	1	2	3	3
Australia	23	28	30	30	8	12	13	13	4	3	3	4	–	–	–	–
United States	26	29	30	30	8	9	11	11	4	3	2	3	2	3	3	3
Turkey	15	21	22	29	4	7	9	7	1	1	3	2	0	1	1	2
OECD unweighted average	27	33	36	38	7	10	12	11	2	2	3	3	n.a.[3]	n.a.[3]	n.a.[3]	n.a.[3]
OECD Europe unweighted average	27	34	38	40	7	10	12	11	2	2	3	3	n.a.[3]	n.a.[3]	n.a.[3]	n.a.[3]

Table 2.2(cont.): Receipts from total taxes and the main taxes as a percentage of GDP at market prices, 1965, 75, 82, 89

Country	Employers' social security taxes (2200)				General consumption taxes (5110)				Excises etc (5120)				Property taxes (4000)			
	(5)[2]				(6)				(7)				(8)			
	65	**75**	**82**	**89**	**65**	**75**	**82**	**89**	**65**	**75**	**82**	**89**	**65**	**75**	**82**	**89**
Sweden	3	8(2)	13(1)	14(2)	4	5	6	8	7	5	5	5	1	1	1	2
Denmark	0	0	1	0	3	7	10	10	9	6	6	6	2	2	2	2
Netherlands	4	8	8	7	4	6	7	7	5	3	3	3	1	1	1	2
Norway	3	8	7	8	7	9	9	9	6	7	7	7	1	1	1	1
Belgium	6	9	8	9	7	7	7	7	4	4	4	3	1	1	1	1
France	9(2)	11(1)	12(1)	12(1)	8	9	9	8	5	3	3	4	1	1	2	2
Luxembourg	6	6	6	6	4	5	5	6	3	3	4	4	2	2	2	3
Austria	4(3)	5(3)	7(3)	7(2)	6	8	8	9	6	5	4	4	1	1	1	1
New Zealand	–	–	–	(1)	2	3	4	8	5	4	4	4	3	3	3	3
Finland	1(2)	3(1)	3	3	6	6	7	9	7	5	6	5	1	1	1	1
Germany	5	7	7	7	5	5	6	6	5	4	3	3	2	1	1	1
Italy	n.a.	10	9	9	3	4	5	5	6	4	3	4	2	1	1	1
Ireland	1	3	3	3	1	5	7	8	11	9	9	8	4	3	1	2
United Kingdom	2	4	3	3	2	3	5	6	8	5	5	5	4	4	5	5
Canada	1	2	2	3	5	4	4	5	4	4	5	4	3	3	3	3
Portugal	2	5	5	6	2	3	5	7	8	7	8	8	1	1	1	0
Spain	3	7	9	9	3	3	3	6	3	2	2	4	1	1	1	1
Iceland	2(0)	1(1)	n.a.	1(1)	5	9	n.a.	12	12	10	n.a.	6	1	2	n.a.	3
Greece	3	3	5	4(1)	2	5	5	9	7	6	8	6	2	2	1	1
Switzerland	2	3	3	3	2	2	3	3	4	3	3	2	2	2	2	3
Japan	2	3	4	4	–	–	–	1	5	3	4	2	1	2	2	3
Australia	(1)	(2)	(2)	(2)	2	2	2	3	5	5	6	4	3	2	2	3
United States	2	4	5	5	1	2	2	2	4	3	2	2	4	4	3	3
Turkey	1	1	2	2	–	–	–	5	8	8	6	2	2	1	1	1
OECD unweighted average	n.a.[3]	n.a.[3]	n.a.[3]	n.a.[3]	3	5	5	6	7	5	5	3	3	3	3	3
OECD Europe unweighted average	n.a.	n.a.	n.a.	n.a.	4	5	6	7	6	5	5	5	2	2	1	2

1. Countries ranked according to 1989 total tax ratio.
2. Figures in brackets in column (5), refer to payroll taxes on employers that equal 1 per cent or more of GDP.
3. The unweighted OECD average for all social security contributions (2000) was: 65: 5 per cent; 75: 7 per cent; 82: 9 per cent; 89: 9.5 per cent.

n.a. = not available – = non-existent.

Source: OECD RS 1991. For references to titles of tax see Table 2.1.

Table 2.3: Receipts from particular taxes as a percentage[1] of total tax receipts, 1965, 75, 82, 89

Country	Income taxes (1000)				Social security contributions (2000)				Consumption taxes (5000)				Property taxes (4000)			
	65	75	82	89	65	75	82	89	65	75	82	89	65	75	82	89
Australia	51	56	55	57	–	–	–	–	35	29	32	28	11	9	7	9
Austria	25	26	26	24	25	28	32	33	37	34	31	32	4	3	3	3
Belgium	28	39	42	38	31	32	30	34	37	26	26	25	4	2	2	3
Canada	39	47	44	47	6	10	12	13	41	42	33	29	13	9	9	9
Denmark	46	59	56	59	5	1	3	2	41	34	37	33	8	6	4	4
Finland	44	53	51	50	3	9	9	8	43	34	38	38	4	2	2	4
France	16	18	18	17	34	41	43	44	38	33	30	29	4	3	4	5
Germany	34	35	34	35	27	33	36	36	33	27	27	26	6	4	3	3
Greece	9	13	18	18	32	29	34	32	49	47	41	45	10	10	4	3
Iceland	21	23	n.a.	27	8	3	n.a.	3	63	63	n.a.	55	4	5	n.a.	8
Ireland	26	30	34	35	6	14	15	14	53	46	46	44	15	10	4	5
Italy	18	21	35	37	34	46	36	33	39	29	25	27	7	3	3	2
Japan	44	45	45	49	22	29	30	28	26	17	15	13	8	9	9	10
Luxembourg	36	43	43	41	32	29	28	26	25	21	22	24	6	5	6	8
Netherlands	36	35	31	29	31	38	41	41	29	24	24	26	4	2	3	4
New Zealand	60	66	69	58	–	–	–	–	28	24	23	32	11	9	8	8
Norway	43	34	42	33	12	25	21	27	41	38	35	36	3	2	2	3
Portugal	25	17	23	26	22	35	28	26	44	41	43	45	5	2	1	1
Spain	24	22	26	33	28	47	46	35	41	24	22	29	6	6	4	4
Sweden	55	50	44	43	12	19	28	26	31	24	24	24	2	1	1	3
Switzerland	38	44	42	40	22	29	31	33	30	20	20	19	9	7	7	9
Turkey	30	42	53	31	6	9	14	16	54	41	27	25	10	7	5	2
United Kingdom	37	44	38	39	15	17	17	18	33	25	29	31	14	13	13	13
United States	46	44	45	44	16	25	28	29	22	18	17	16	15	13	10	10
OECD unweighted average	35	38	40	38	18	23	24	23	38	31	29	30	8	6	5	6
OECD Europe unweighted average	31	34	36	35	21	26	27	26	40	33	30	32	7	5	4	5

1. To nearest percentage point.
n.a. = not available – = non-existent.
Source: OECD RS 1991.

C. Some explanatory factors

At this point in the book a number of particular factors are suggested as explanations for developments in tax levels and structures, under the headings: the effect of automatic tax elasticities; government reasons for offsetting or reinforcing these effects; newly available tax handles for governments; factors over which governments have little control. A discussion of more general theoretical explanations is provided in Chapter 6B2.

1. The effect of automatic tax elasticities

Artificially isolating developments on the revenue side, a first step would be to see what happens if governments refrained from changing rates, allowances, introducing indexation provisions, etc. In these circumstances, particular tax ratios will be affected by such factors as demographic changes in the taxpaying population, changes in income distribution and above all by changes in price inflation and real growth, which will have the following effects on the automatic elasticities of tax receipts:

Personal income tax ratios will increase with inflation and real growth. Because of the progressivity of tax schedules, taxpayers will move into higher rate brackets and those with incomes previously too low to pay tax will be brought into the tax net (so-called bracket creep). Also the real value of allowances will be eroded by inflation. These effects are variously referred to as fiscal drag, or the built-in flexibility or high elasticity of the personal income tax.

Social security ratios decrease with inflation, since in most countries there is a ceiling on earnings subject to contributions and once this ceiling is passed the marginal rate of contributions is zero and the average rate begins to fall. If the government does not increase these ceilings in line with inflation, their yield will fall in real terms, but in some countries contributions are indexed and since ceilings tend to be above average earnings, the automatic decrease is likely to be relatively small.

General consumption tax ratios will remain broadly unaffected by inflation, since they are based on the value of goods and services, but increased growth could have a positive effect through greater consumption.

Excise ratios will decrease with inflation. Because they are levied mostly on the weight of tobacco, strength of alcohol, volume of petrol, etc., it needs an increase in the rate to maintain their yield in real terms in times of inflation.

Property tax ratios will also decrease, if governments do not revalue land and buildings to take account of inflation.

2. Government reasons for offsetting or reinforcing automatic effects

a) *Political preferences.* Political attitudes will influence government views on the size of government, the desired level of taxation and the taxes preferred. For example, right of centre governments have generally tended to favour less government intervention, lower taxes and consumption taxes rather than income taxes, whereas left of centre governments have tended to favour increasing the size of government, accepting that this may require higher taxes and especially higher income taxation.

b) *Cultural differences.* Left and right are relative terms and in most European industrialised countries, there has been a political consensus for a welfare-state economy, which has been less the case, for example, in Japan, Switzerland and the United States.

c) *The inertia factor.* Tax changes imply winners and losers. Since the latter are more likely to be resentful of changes than the former are grateful, losers are more likely to form pressure groups to urge inaction. In addition, governments have many things to occupy them and in the absence of pressures for tax change may be content to avoid major tax reforms. Leaving aside moves to value added tax, this seems to have happened in most OECD countries between 1965 and 1984, the tax reform explosions since then having been commented on earlier in Chapter 1.

d) *Avoidance of uncertainty.* Some governments may avoid frequent changes because of the importance they attach to maintaining a stable fiscal environment for business. Table 2.2 suggests that Austria, Germany and Switzerland are among such countries.

e) *Government perceptions.* Voters' attitudes to particular kinds of taxes and their preferences as between lower taxes and higher benefits are also likely to be explanatory factors. Perceptions about levies earmarked for social security are especially relevant here. In addition, to have a high tax ratio in the high growth days may have been regarded then as a sign of caring generosity, but nowadays of profligacy. Governments seeking re-election are likely to pay attention to predominant taxpayer attitudes. Such attitudes may be affected by the social cohesion within a country and degree of integration of taxing and spending decisions. Such cohesion appears to occur most clearly in the small industrialised countries of North Europe where tax ratios are highest.

3. Newly available tax handles for governments

Over the last three decades governments have acquired a number of tax handles which help to explain the increase in total tax ratios. They may be divided into:

a) *Technical improvements.* Among these have been withholding tax at source, better exchanges of information within government departments and between tax administrations across frontiers, better accounting systems in the private sector and the growing availability of pocket computers for audit purposes.

b) *The growing use of value added taxation* which is capable of providing more revenue for governments than other kinds of general consumption tax (see Chapter 13).

4. Factors over which governments may have little short-term control

a) *Economic conditions.* The difference in the development of tax ratios between 1965 and 1975 and 1975 and 1988, as shown by Table 2.2 can be explained in part by the different economic conditions, particularly in the more industrialised countries. Between 1965 and 1975 economic conditions were generally buoyant, but afterwards high inflation was followed by a period of low growth and high unemployment. In more recent years with real incomes sometimes declining, it has become particularly difficult to increase personal income tax ratios.

b) *Composition of the labour force.* The lower the percentage of employees in relation to the percentage of self-employed such as farmers, artisans, liberal professions, the more difficult it is to raise large amounts of revenue from a broad-based income tax, and countries like France and Greece and until recently Ireland, Italy, and Spain have accepted a low personal income tax ratio.

c) *Constitutional set-up.* As observed earlier, federal states tend to have lower tax ratios perhaps because each level of government has access to a more limited range of taxes and may find it more difficult to raise the taxes under their control. This constraint may be reinforced by separation of powers as between the executive and legislature (the United States). Of relevance, too, is the relative strength of the executive and legislature, the size and cohesion of the parliamentary majority, and the (likely) period between parliamentary elections.

d) *Efficacy of the tax administration.* In nearly all OECD countries this has greatly improved over the last two decades and this is certainly an important cause of the general increase in total tax ratios. On the other hand, lack of trained personnel and computer facilities has probably prevented such growth in some countries. Another brake is provided by the greater sophistication of the tax avoidance industry.

e) *International economic integration.* Governments of countries with small relatively open economies are often obliged for competitive reasons to follow the lead of other countries (e.g. the United Kingdom and the United States reduction of income tax rates in the mid-eighties was followed shortly after by most OECD countries), and the half of the 24 OECD countries, which are also members of the European Community, have to modify part of their tax system to conform to EC Directives. However, there is not much evidence to suggest that until now increasing economic integration has had much effect on the tax ratios and the tax mix of OECD countries.

f) *Unforeseen factors and mistakes.* There are always explanations for changes in tax ratio developments which governments could not be expected to foresee, such as the recent oil shocks. Also forecasting errors concerning the results of legislative changes frequently occur, for example, because macroeconomic assumptions about rates of growth or inflation turn out to be inaccurate, or because taxpayers' behavioural reactions to changes in legislation in terms of investment, savings and consumption were not as anticipated. Consequently, anticipated revenues are often over- or underestimated and these mistakes can be one explanatory factor in tax ratio developments.

D. Fishing expeditions

Since so many factors are likely to influence tax levels and structures, it is doubtful whether many important correlations are likely to be found between tax levels and structures and other phenomena like rates of growth, or inflation, or GDP per capita, or even if they were found that this would have much significance in terms of causal linkage. In the 1960s this was less evident and the IMF tax effort literature showed that among OECD as well as developing countries, there was, for example, a high correlation between GDP per capita and total tax and income tax ratios. Thus R. Goode (1968) was able then to conclude:

> The tendency for higher income countries to impose relatively heavier direct taxes may be due not so much to income differences as to a positive correlation between per capita income and other social and economic conditions that facilitate the use of direct taxes. In other words, per capita income may be a proxy for the characteristics that actually make direct taxes acceptable and effective. These characteristics include a high level of literacy, wide use of standard accounting methods, effective public administration, and political stability.

Now that countries like Ireland, Portugal and Spain have a higher total tax ratio than those of Japan and the United States, this generalisation clearly no longer holds, even if it is true (see Chart 2.1) that there remains a high correlation between the income tax <u>share</u> and GDP per capita.

Various fishing expeditions (mostly unpublished) were carried out in OECD and IMF during the seventies and eighties to apply regression analysis to see if statistically and explanatory significant correlations emerged between tax levels and tax structures on the one hand, and the kinds of variables referred to above on the other, but nothing of great interest emerged. As an illustrative example, Chart 2.2 is provided to show the absence of much correlation between total tax ratios and GDP per capita.

Another set of fishing expeditions has attempted to correlate tax phenomena and has been designed to answer two sets of questions. The first is, are there competing sources of tax revenue so that governments having a high tax type A ratio are obliged in practice to have a low total tax type B ratio? The second is, assuming that a government wishes to increase its total tax ratio which particular tax ratio(s) does experience suggest that governments have to increase?

With regard to the first question, two potentially competing tax ratios would be that of a) personal income tax and social security contributions and b) general and specific consumption taxes. Chart 2.3 shows a clear negative correlation between personal income tax and social security ratios in that in two-thirds of OECD countries with an above average ratio in one of these levies this is accompanied by a below average ratio in the other. [If the income tax ratio had been correlated with employees' contributions, the results (not reproduced here) would have been a negative correlation of 18-6 instead of 16-8.] Concerning competition between general consumption taxes and excises, there are two conflicting factors: on the one hand countries relying heavily on general consumption taxes might be expected to dampen their reliance on excises (and conversely), but on the other hand, countries may have a traditional preference for relying greatly or negligibly on consumption taxes as a whole: the positive correlation between the two kinds of tax in Chart 2.4 indicates that the latter factor is predominant in most countries.

On the second question, that if governments wish to increase total tax ratios, on which kinds of tax should they concentrate, R. Goode (1981) took the view that the income tax was the most likely source and I contested this in Messere (1983) on the grounds that all the countries with high total tax ratios had high consumption tax ratios (and in particular high VAT ratios). My view appeared to be confirmed in *Taxing Consumption* (OECD 1988), Chart 2.1, page 42 (not reproduced here), which showed that in 1985 in 20 of the 23 OECD countries included, a high consumption tax ratio was associated with a high total tax ratio or a low consumption tax ratio with a low total tax ratio, Greece and Portugal (high consumption and low total) and Luxembourg (low consumption and high total) being the only exceptions. However, when one comes to 1989 there is little evidence of much difference between the three major sources of revenue as Charts 2.5, 2.6 and 2.7 illustrate. For each of the ratios of taxes on incomes and profits, on consumption and social security taxes, there is a correlation with total tax ratios for around two thirds of countries and an absence of correlation for the others.

These fishing expeditions are interesting to undertake but yield relatively little fish worth consuming. Different approaches to explaining developments in tax levels and structures are accordingly taken in the next two chapters.

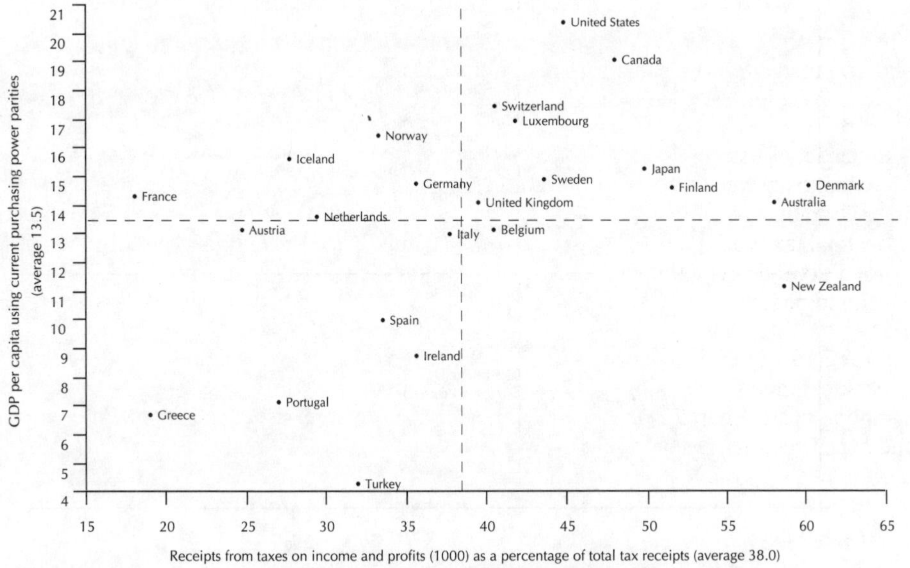

Chart 2.1: Presence of some correlation between personal and corporate income tax share and GDP per capita, 1989 (Source: OECD RS 1991.)

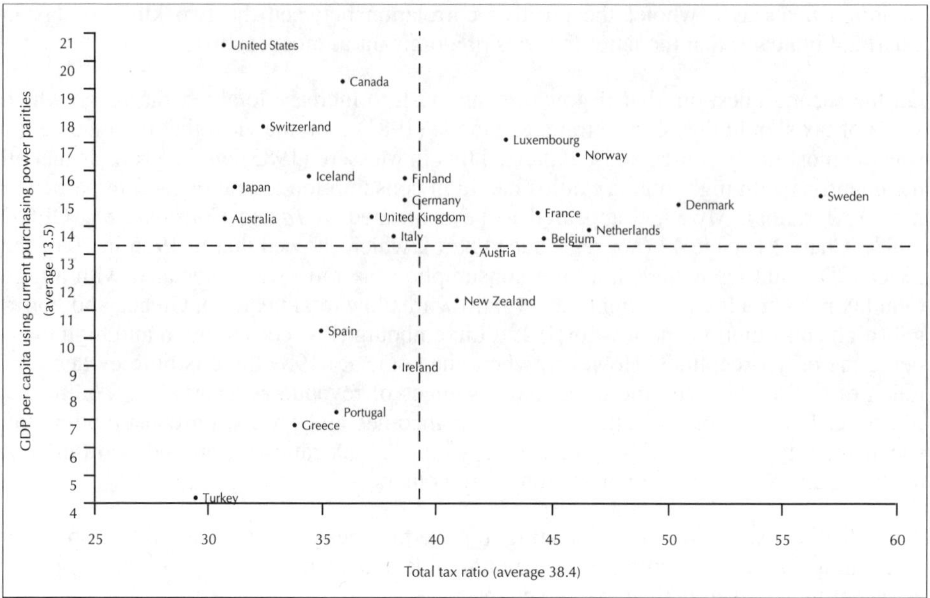

Chart 2.2: Absence of correlation between total tax ratios and GDP per capita, 1989 (Source: OECD RS 1991.)

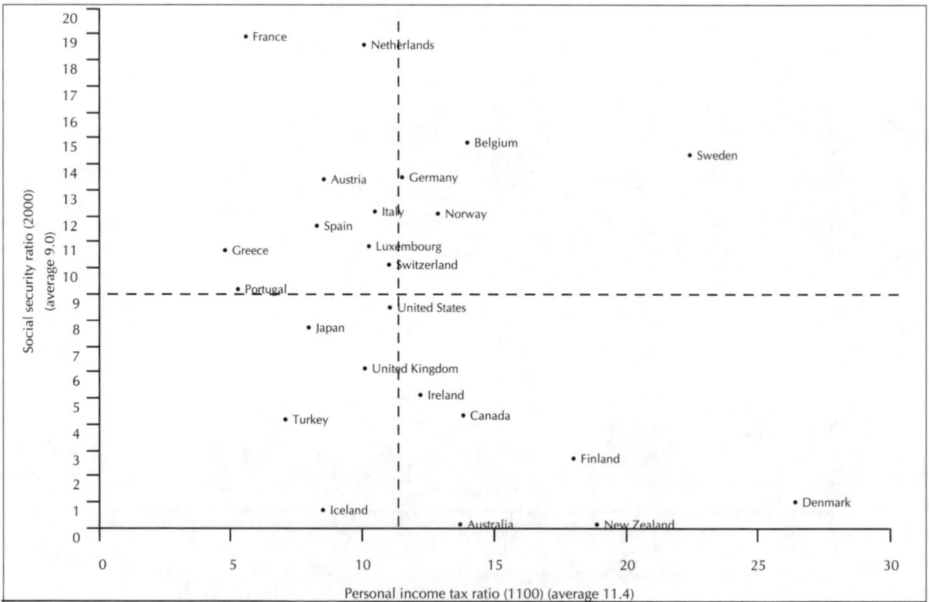

Chart 2.3: Presence of negative correlation between personal income tax and social security ratios, 1989 (Source: OECD RS 1991.)

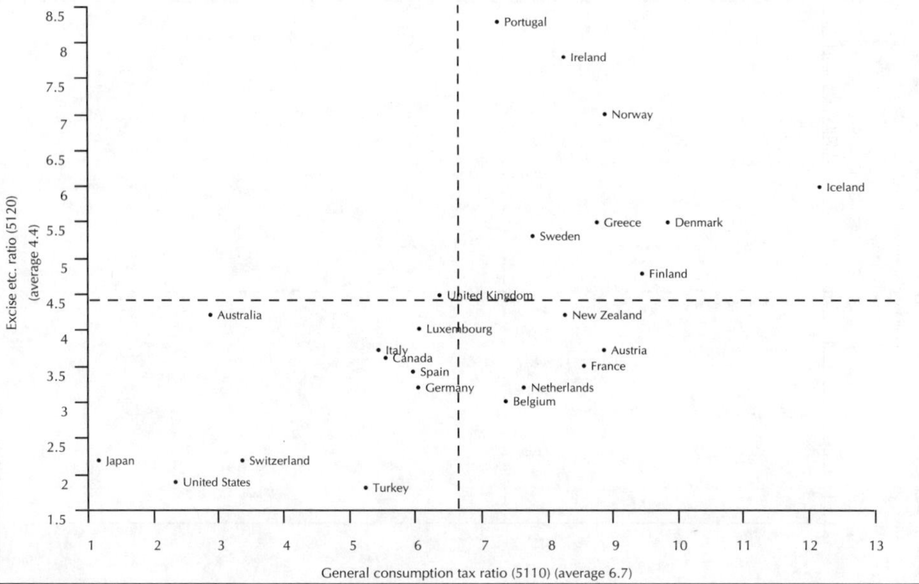

Chart 2.4: Presence of positive correlation between general and selective consumption tax ratios, 1989 (Source: OECD RS 1991.)

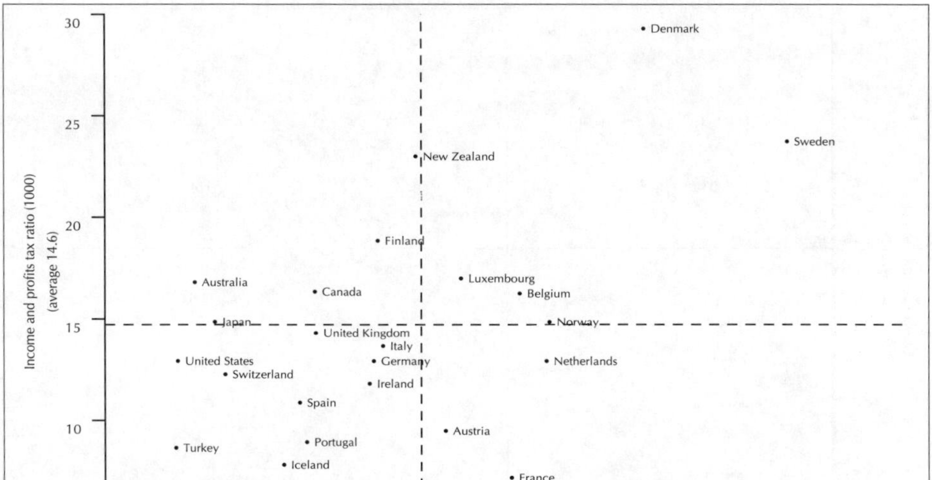

Chart 2.5: Presence of some positive correlation between income and profits taxes ratios and total tax ratios, 1989 (Source: OECD RS 1991.)

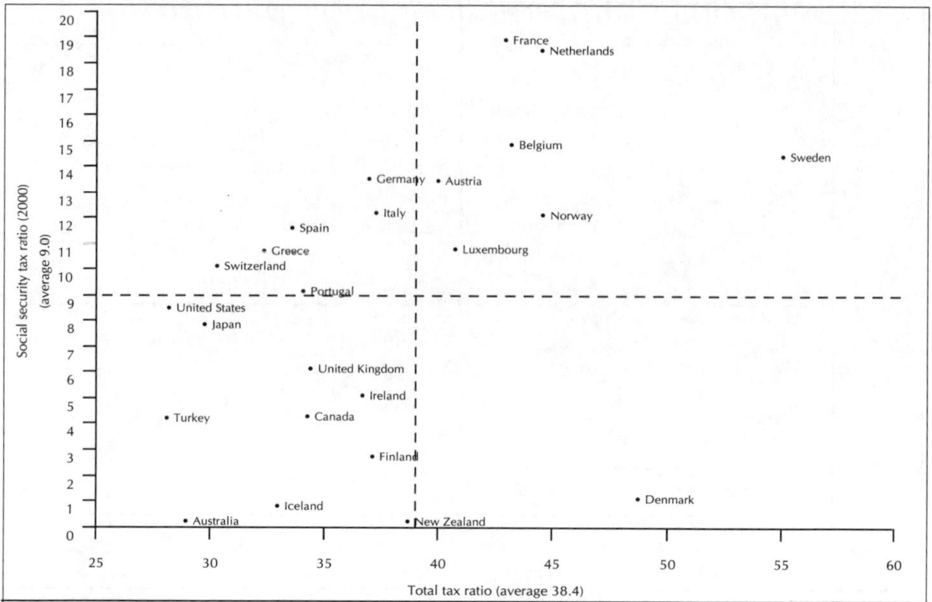

Chart 2.6: Presence of some positive correlation between social security ratios and total tax ratios, 1989 (Source: OECD RS 1991.)

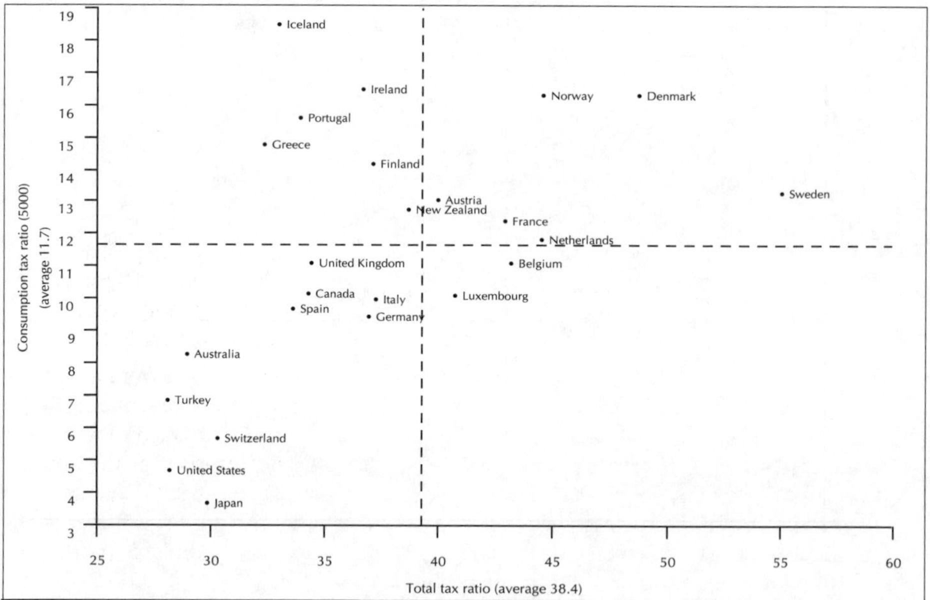

Chart 2.7: Presence of some positive correlation between consumption tax ratios and total tax ratios, 1989 (Source: OECD RS 1991.)

E. Limitations on international comparisons

The data based on the OECD/IMF classification provide the most disaggregated revenue statistics that exist, and as the results are systematically verified by the staff of OECD and IMF, they are also the most reliable. It is believed that these results which are summarised and analysed in the first three chapters of this book do provide useful insights into developments in tax levels and structures on a reasonably comparable basis between countries and unequivocally so within a particular country over time. That is the good news. The bad news is that there are many kinds of limitation on the use to which they may be put.

The main problem is that though the ratio of tax yields to some measurement of GDP or GNP is the only practicable way of making international comparisons of global tax levels, for a number of reasons these ratios cannot provide an unequivocal guide either to the level of government intervention in the economy or to the level of compulsory transfers from the private to the public sector. This section comments on some of them.

1. Various means of government intervention

In OECD countries, governments intervene in the economy in the following ways:

- Direct government expenditures. These may be financed by taxes, non-tax revenues or by borrowing.
- Tax expenditures. As discussed in the next sub-section, these are subsidy programmes implemented via the tax system which have the effect of reducing tax revenues below what they would otherwise have been.
- Government loan guarantees. These reduce the cost of borrowing below what it would otherwise be.
- An obligation on the private sector to collect compulsory levies for the provision of certain social security benefits. (Table 2.5 shows that amounts represent between 4 to 6 per cent of GDP in Finland, the Netherlands and Switzerland.)
- Other government regulatory activities which increase the costs of the private sector (e.g. environmental controls, marketing brands, banking regulations). These in substance impose levies or provide subsidies to the private sector and accordingly, though having no budgetary impact, may have economic effects similar to taxes.
- There are various means by which a government can extract revenue from a particular activity. If, for example, the government wishes to obtain more revenue from the activity of gambling it can do so either through the tax route (a tax on the betting stake or the net profits or gross turnover of the gambling enterprise) or the non-tax route of a State lottery: if it wishes to raise extra money from electricity consumption it can do so by an indirect tax or by the non-tax route of increasing the price of goods supplied by a nationalised industry and requiring that industry transfer part of the increased revenue to general government.

2. Relative reliance on tax expenditures and direct expenditures

Perhaps the most important international incomparability in quantitative terms in interpreting published tax burden comparisons is that one country may place a heavy reliance on tax expenditures – subsidies paid out via the tax system – whilst another may rely predominantly on direct expenditures to achieve similar policy goals. Other things being equal, the tax level of a country in the first category will be lower than that of a country in the second category, even if in the two cases, the level of government intervention in the economy and the resource cost are more or less the same. A conceptual complication is that there is room for disagreement on whether particular provisions, such as tax allowances for parents, or higher rates of valued added tax, should be regarded as a tax expenditure being a substitute for a direct expenditure or as an integral part of the tax structure. In any event, only about half of OECD countries can provide data on these tax expenditures and the data available are unlikely to be fully comparable on an international basis.

3. Taxes paid by government to itself

Taxes paid by government to itself constitute a relatively large and varying proportion of government receipts, taking the form either of payments from one level of government to another, for example local property taxes paid by central government, or of payments by the same level of government to itself, such as value added tax on purchases by central government. Two questions arise:

- Can the amounts of revenue in question be isolated and what is their relative importance?
- If identifiable, should they be included or excluded from tax yields?

With regard to the first question, it seems that the most important of these levies are social security contributions paid by government in their capacity as employers and the amounts involved can usually be identified. They can be very sizeable, amounting in the extreme case of Sweden to nearly 5 per cent of GDP (see Table 2.5). Few governments can identify the amounts of property or consumption taxes they pay to themselves: extrapolating from those that can, the amounts seem relatively slight in comparison to payments of social security contributions.

Opinions vary as to whether identifiable amounts of taxes paid by government to itself should be eliminated from tax receipts. The OECD has decided against elimination and the IMF for elimination (and this constitutes the only conceptual difference between the data provided by the two organisations). The argument for elimination is that if the intent is to provide data on the flow of cash payments to the government sector from the rest of the economy, then tax payments between different units of the same level of government and between different levels of government should be eliminated in the consolidation of the tax accounts of general government. On the other hand, if the aim of recording tax flows is to provide an insight into the value of government output in the context of the economy as a whole, it would be more appropriate to take into account payments by government to itself.

4. The underground economy

Activities carried out in the underground economy will largely be taken into account in GDP figures, but incomes from such activities by definition do not generate tax revenues. Though estimates of the size of the underground economy remain unreliable, it is probable that it varies considerably from country to country and this provides yet another reason why tax to GDP ratios cannot provide an unequivocal guide to relative tax burdens.

5. International incomparabilities in measuring tax levels

a) Problems with the denominator

Various arguments have been advanced for preferring Gross Domestic Product (GDP) or Gross National Product (GNP) and at factor costs or market prices. In practice, for most though not all countries, this choice does not have a large influence on relative tax ratios and this issue is, accordingly, not discussed here. OECD comparisons use GDP at market prices for the pragmatic reason that these data are the most easily and rapidly available. A more serious problem in using tax to GDP ratios is that they reflect movements in both tax receipts and GDP. In some countries, a large change in this ratio could be due to the fact that the GDP figure has been subject to a large revision, particularly as regards more recent years. (Italy and Luxembourg are two countries where GDP figures have been frequently revised.)

More importantly, it has been argued because of the deficiencies referred to above, GDP or GNP in their various forms are an inappropriate denominator and preference should be accorded to some other denominator such as total profits for the corporation tax and total private consumption for consumption taxes. Unfortunately, as indicated in an unpublished 1985 OECD study, it is impossible for technical reasons to achieve international comparability with corporate profits as the denominator. It is somewhat easier to provide roughly comparable data for total private consumption and Table 2.4 makes some comparisons for the earliest and latest available years between results using total private consumption and GDP at market prices as the denominator to measure the tax on goods and services ratio. It shows (reassuringly) that for most countries ranking order is barely affected or is even unaffected by the choice of the denominator, exceptions being Greece and Ireland for 1965 and Luxembourg for 1985.

b) Reliability of data

Though the country submissions are verified to ensure that country returns conform to the guidelines before the data are published, some countries are able to provide more reliable and disaggregated data than others and this is another factor affecting international comparability.

c) A partial quantification of certain international incomparabilities

As noted above, it is just not possible to quantify what is almost certainly the most important source of incomparability, that is, countries' different relative reliance on direct expenditures and tax incentives. However, J. Owens and myself (OECD 1987) provided a quantification of certain incomparabilities. These are reproduced in Table 2.5 which shows that:

- The relative reliance on compulsory social security contributions to the private sector and on revenues from fees, fines and sales differs significantly between countries.
- The importance of social security contributions and payroll taxes paid by government to itself also varies, reflecting the size of the public sector and the rates of employers' contributions.
- The adjustment of tax ratios for these variables would significantly change the ranking order of some countries. For example, the Netherlands and Switzerland would move up, whereas Canada and Sweden would move down, if the various factors referred to in Table 2.5 were taken into account.

Table 2.4: Receipts from taxes on goods and services as a percentage of:

	A. Total private consumption					B. GDP at market prices				
	1965	Rank	1985	Rank	85-65	1965	Rank	1985	Rank	85-65
Australia	13.2	(15)	16.7	(17)	3.5	8.1	(15)	9.8	(15)	1.7
Austria	21.9	(3)	24.4	(6)	2.5	13.0	(4)	13.8	(5)	0.9
Belgium	17.3	(10)	17.5	(14)	0.2	11.4	(7)	11.4	(12)	–
Canada	18.0	(9)	18.6	(13)	0.6	10.5	(10)	10.4	(13)	-0.1
Denmark	20.6	(5)	30.5	(3)	9.9	12.1	(6)	16.8	(3)	4.7
Finland	20.8	(4)	25.5	(5)	4.7	12.9	(5)	13.7	(6)	0.8
France	22.0	(2)	20.7	(9)	-1.3	13.4	(3)	13.4	(7)	–
Germany	18.6	(8)	17.1	(15)	-1.5	10.4	(11)	9.7	(16)	-0.7
Greece	14.8	(14)	23.4	(7)	8.6	10.7	(9)	15.2	(4)	4.5
Ireland	19.1	(7)	30.7	(2)	11.6	13.7	(1)	17.4	(2)	3.7
Italy	17.3	(11)	16.7	(15)	-0.6	9.3	(14)	8.8	(17)	-0.5
Japan	8.4	(21)	6.8	(22)	-1.6	4.8	(22)	3.9	(22)	-0.9
Luxembourg	13.0	(16)	20.8	(8)	7.8	7.5	(17)	10.2	(14)	2.7
Netherlands	16.0	(12)	19.7	(12)	3.7	9.5	(13)	11.6	(11)	2.1
New Zealand	10.7	(18)	13.4	(18)	2.7	6.9	(18)	8.0	(18)	1.1
Norway	24.3	(1)	36.9	(1)	12.6	13.6	(2)	17.9	(1)	4.3
Portugal	12.0	(17)	19.8	(11)	7.8	8.1	(15)	13.2	(9)	5.1
Spain	8.4	(21)	11.8	(19)	3.4	6.0	(20)	7.6	(19)	1.6
Sweden	19.7	(6)	26.0	(4)	6.3	11.0	(8)	13.3	(8)	2.3
Switzerland	10.5	(19)	9.8	(20)	-0.7	6.3	(19)	6.1	(20)	-0.2
United Kingdom	15.7	(13)	19.9	(10)	4.2	10.1	(12)	12.0	(10)	1.9
United States	8.7	(20)	7.8	(21)	-0.9	5.7	(21)	5.2	(21)	-0.5

Sources: For column A, *OECD National Accounts* 1989. For column B, OECD RS 1987.

Table 2.5: Some adjustment of tax levels for 1982 (Billions of national currency and as percentage of GDP)[1]

Country	Tax levels as defined by OECD		Compulsory social security contributions paid to private schemes		Fees, fines and sales as defined by IMF		Total (1)+(2)+(3)		Social security contributions & payroll taxes paid by government		Column (4) minus colum (5)	
	(1)		(2)		(3)		(4)		(5)		(6)	
Canada	127.3	(33.8)	–	–	1.4[2]	(0.4)	128.7	(34.2)	7.1	(1.9)	121.6	(32.3)
Finland	86.7	(35.4)	10.9	(4.4)	2.1[2]	(0.8)	99.7	(40.7)	–	–	–	–
France	1561.9	(43.8)	–	–	36.9	(1.0)	1598.8	(44.8)	66.6	(1.8)	1532.2	(43.0)
Germany	598.1	(37.4)	–	–	47.6	(2.9)	645.7	(40.3)	–	–	–	–
Italy	17682.9	(37.5)	–	–	420.0[3]	(0.9)	18102.9	(38.4)	–	–	–	–
Japan	7257.2	(27.1)	–	–	134.0[2]	(0.1)	7270.6	(27.2)	–	–	–	–
Netherlands	167.5	(45.4)	16.3	(4.4)	2.9[2]	(0.8)	186.7	(50.8)	3.8	(1.0)	182.9	(49.7)
Sweden	313.3	(49.9)	–	–	4.7	(0.7)	318.0	(50.7)	29.2	(4.7)	288.8	(46.0)
Switzerland	60.8	(31.0)	11.1	(5.7)	8.9	(4.5)	80.8	(41.2)	0.9	(0.4)	79.9	(40.8)
United Kingdom	108.2	(39.2)	–	–	5.2	(1.9)	113.4	(41.1)	2.6	(0.9)	110.8	(40.1)
United States	923.2	(30.5)	–	–	54.0	(1.8)	977.2	(32.3)	–	–	–	–
Source Tables	Table 3		Tables 61-83		Tables 149-171				Tables 84-106			

1. The figures in parenthesis are national currencies expressed as a percentage of GDP.
2. Central government only.
3. 1981.
– = not available.
Source: OECD RS 1985.

Chapter 3
Tax levels and tax structures in 1989 and changes since 1965

A. Tax levels and structures in 1989

Chart 3.1 summarises OECD countries' total tax ratios in 1989 and Chart 3.2 the share of total tax revenues from some of the main revenue sources in the same year. Charts 3.3 and 3.4 indicate the OECD unweighted average of the main tax ratios and their share in total tax revenues. The rest of this section seeks to illustrate in what particular ways OECD countries have conformed or deviated from these average tax ratios and shares in 1989.

Table 3.1 shows how far in 1989 particular countries deviate from the average both with respect to total and particular tax ratios. When corrective statistical formulae are applied (see bottom line) there is much less deviation from the average of total tax ratios, itself quite considerable, than from the average of particular taxes. Diversification is most pronounced for social security ratios, as it always has been in similar tests carried out for earlier years in the sixties, seventies and eighties. Some countries such as Canada, Germany, Italy, Luxembourg, Switzerland and the United Kingdom remain close to average for most particular tax ratios, whereas others such as Denmark (especially), France, Ireland, New Zealand and Sweden deviate considerably. (Similar tests for earlier years also show

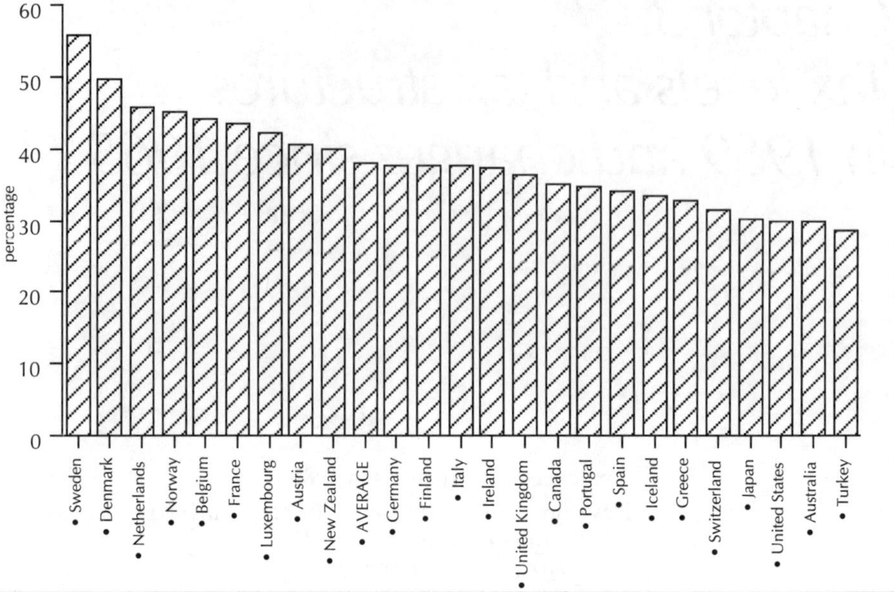

Chart 3.1: Total tax revenue as a percentage of GDP, 1989
(Source: OECD RS 1991.)

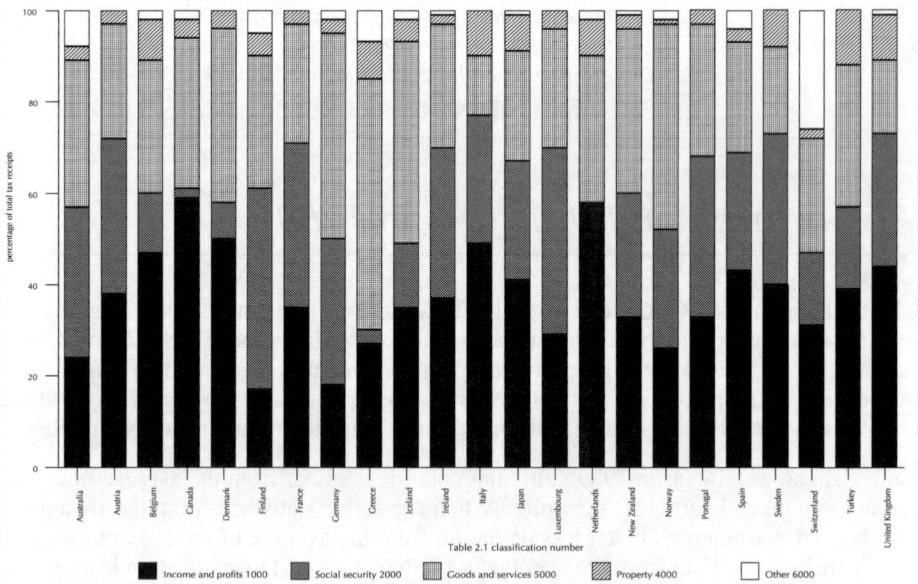

Chart 3.2: Tax structures according to main headings of OECD classification, 1989 (Source: OECD RS 1991.)

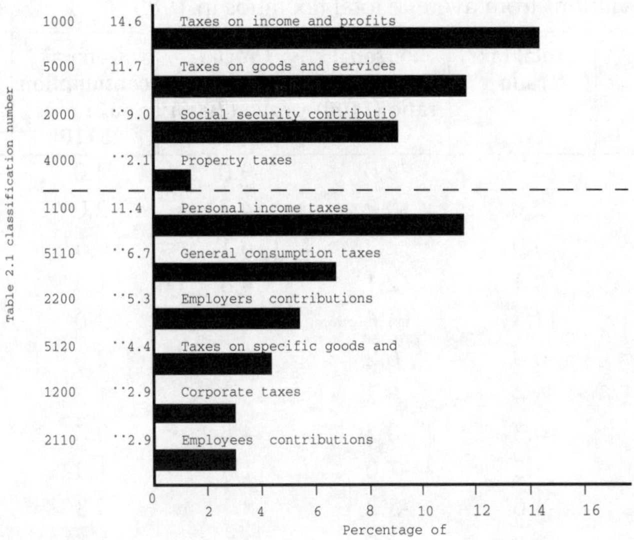

Chart 3.3: Unweighted average of main tax ratios, 1989 (Source: OECD RS 1991.)

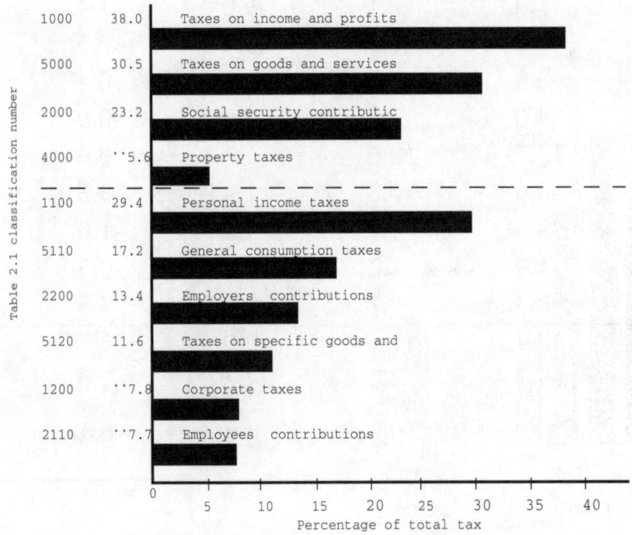

Chart 3.4: Unweighted average of main tax shares in total tax receipts, 1989 (Source: OECD RS 1991.)

Table 3.1: Deviations from average total tax ratios in 1989

	Total tax ratio	Personal income tax ratio (1100)	Social security tax ratio (2000)	General consumption tax ratios (5110)	Excises etc. ratio (5120)
Australia	-8.3	2.0	-9.0	-4.0	0.0
Austria	2.6	-3.2	4.7	2.0	-0.5
Belgium	5.9	2.2	6.1	0.5	-1.2
Canada	-3.1	2.1	-4.4	-1.3	-0.7
Denmark	11.5	14.6	-7.8	3.0	1.2
Finland	-0.3	6.2	-6.0	2.6	0.5
France	5.4	-6.2	10.2	1.7	-0.6
Germany	-0.3	-0.2	4.8	-0.8	-1.0
Greece	-5.2	-7.0	1.5	1.9	1.2
Iceland	-4.6	-3.2	-8.1	5.3	1.7
Ireland	-0.8	0.5	-3.6	1.4	3.5
Italy	-0.6	-1.3	3.5	-1.4	-0.5
Japan	-7.8	-3.8	-0.5	-5.7	-2.1
Luxembourg	4.0	-1.5	2.1	-0.8	-0.2
Netherlands	7.6	-1.7	9.9	0.8	-1.0
New Zealand	1.9	7.1	-9.0	1.4	0.0
Norway	7.1	1.1	3.4	2.0	2.7
Portugal	-3.3	-6.5	0.2	0.4	4.0
Spain	-4.0	-3.5	2.9	-0.9	-0.8
Sweden	17.7	10.6	5.7	0.9	1.0
Switzerland	-6.6	-0.8	1.4	-3.5	-2.1
Turkey	-9.4	-4.7	-4.5	-1.6	-2.5
United Kingdom	-1.9	-1.7	-2.6	-0.5	0.2
United States	-8.3	-0.7	-0.2	-4.5	-2.4
Average ratio	38.4	11.4	9.0	6.7	4.4
Mean absolute deviation (MAD)	5.3	3.8	4.7	2.0	1.3
MAD divided by average ratio	0.14	0.34	0.52	0.30	0.30

Source: OECD RS 1991.

Canada, Germany and Switzerland close to and Denmark, France and Sweden far from average.)

Table 3.2 identifies the extreme deviants from average tax ratios even if the range chosen to qualify as extreme has to be somewhat arbitrary. The results are sometimes different from those in Table 3.1, major deviations from an OECD average occurring most frequently in Australia, Iceland, New Zealand and Sweden, though this is largely because social security contributions do not exist or hardly exist in these four countries apart from large employers' contributions in Sweden. Table 3.3 uses a similar method to identify extreme deviants from an average 1989 tax structure. Only Canada has no such deviation though in another 10 countries the deviation is confined to the share of only one kind of tax: at the other extreme there are eight countries which diverge largely from the average share of three or four of the seven taxes considered.

Table 3.2: Exceptionally high[1] and low[2]/tax ratios in 1989

Particular tax receipts as a percentage of GDP at market prices (to nearest percentage point)

	Income tax ratio 1100	**Corporation tax ratio 1200**	**Employees' social security ratio 2100**	**Employers' social security ratio 2200**	**General Consumption tax ratio 5110**	**Excises tax ratio 5120**	**Property tax ratio 4000**	**Number of taxes where large differences from average**
OECD average	11	3	3	5	7	4	2	
Exceptional differences from average = + or – in percentage points	6	2	2	3	3	2	1	
Australia			(0)	(0)	(3)			3
Austria			6					1
Belgium				9				1
Canada								0
Denmark [3]	26			(0)				2
Finland [3]	18		(0)					2
France			6	12				2
Germany			6					1
Greece	(4)							1
Iceland[3]			(0)	(1)	12			3
Ireland						8		1
Italy				9				1
Japan		7			(1)			2
Luxembourg		7					4	2
Netherlands			9					1
New Zealand	18		(0)	(0)				3
Norway [3]						7		1
Portugal						8		1
Spain				9				1
Sweden[3]	22		(0)	14				3
Switzerland					(3)			1
Turkey								0
United Kingdom							5	1
United States					(2)			1

1. Without brackets.
2. With brackets.
3. A proportion of personal income tax receipts are earmarked for social security benefits and it is recalled that these are shown under 1100.

Source: OECD RS 1991.

Table 3.3: Exceptionally high[1] and low[2] sources of revenue in 1989

Particular tax receipts as a percentage of GDP at market prices (to nearest percentage point)

	Income tax ratio 1100	Corporation tax ratio 1200	Employees' social security ratio 2100	Employers' social security ratio 2200	General Consumption tax ratio 5110	Excises tax ratio 5120	Property tax ratio 4000	Number of taxes where large differences from average
OECD average	29	8	8	13	17	12	6	
Exceptional differences from average = + or – in percentage points	12	5	4	5	6	5	3	
Australia	45		(0)	(0)	(9)			4
Austria			14					1
Belgium				21				1
Canada								0
Denmark [3]	52		(2)	(0)				3
Finland [3]	46		(0)		24			3
France	(12)		13	27				3
Germany			16	19				2
Greece	(13)		15		26			3
Iceland [3]			(0)	(3)	35	18		4
Ireland						21		1
Italy				24			(2)	2
Japan		24			(3)		10	3
Luxembourg		18						1
Netherlands			19					1
New Zealand	46		(0)	(0)				3
Norway [3]							(1)	1
Portugal	(14)					24	(2)	3
Spain				27				1
Sweden [3]			(0)	25				2
Switzerland					(10)			1
Turkey							(2)	1
United Kingdom							13	1
United States					(7)		10	2

1. Without brackets.
2. With brackets.
3. A proportion of personal income tax receipts are earmarked for social security benefits and it is recalled that these are shown under 1100.

Source: OECD RS 1991.

B. Developments in total tax ratios between 1965 and 1989

1. Overall trends

Table 3.4, which reproduces Table 3 of OECD RS 1991, provides total tax ratios for all OECD countries and for all years between 1965-1989, with certain gaps for Iceland. It shows that total tax ratios have risen in all 24 OECD countries between 1965 and 1989, but that the amount of increase and its timing varies greatly from country to country. It shows also that for most, but not all countries, the increase took place in the first half of these 24 years and mostly but not everywhere it has slowed down since. For example, it can be seen from the table that there has actually been a decrease in total tax ratios between 1985 and 1989 in nine OECD countries and hardly any increase in another three.

Table 3.4: Total tax ratios 1965-89[1]

	1955[2]	1960[2]	1965	1966	1967	1968	1969	1970	1971	1972	1973	1974	1975	1976	1977
Australia	22.6	26.5	23.2	22.6	23.4	23.2	24.0	24.2	24.7	23.8	25.3	27.1	27.6	28.0	28.0
Austria	30.0	30.5	34.7	35.4	35.3	35.3	35.8	35.7	36.4	36.9	37.1	38.1	38.6	38.5	39.1
Belgium	24.0	26.5	31.2	33.3	34.0	34.8	35.0	35.7	36.7	37.0	38.0	38.9	41.8	42.2	43.8
Canada	21.7	24.2	25.4	27.0	28.2	29.0	31.2	31.3	30.7	31.2	30.8	33.2	32.4	31.8	31.1
Denmark	23.4	25.4	29.9	32.5	33.1	36.0	35.7	40.4	43.5	42.9	42.4	44.2	41.4	41.6	41.9
Finland	26.8	27.7	29.5	30.7	31.6	32.0	30.5	31.4	32.8	32.9	33.5	32.7	35.1	38.6	38.2
France	n.a.	n.a.	34.5	34.3	34.7	34.9	35.8	35.1	34.5	34.9	35.0	35.5	36.9	38.7	38.7
Germany	30.8	31.3	31.6	32.2	32.2	32.2	33.9	32.9	33.4	34.7	36.3	36.5	35.7	36.8	38.1
Greece	n.a.	n.a.	22.0	23.7	24.8	25.7	25.7	25.3	25.2	25.4	23.8	24.6	25.5	28.0	28.5
Iceland	n.a.	n.a.	27.8	n.a.	n.a.	n.a.	n.a.	28.5	n.a.	n.a.	n.a.	n.a.	31.4	n.a.	n.a.
Ireland	22.5	22.0	26.0	28.1	28.7	29.1	29.8	31.2	32.3	31.0	31.2	31.6	31.5	35.0	33.3
Italy	30.5	34.4	25.5	25.3	26.2	27.0	26.4	26.1	26.9	26.9	24.4	25.7	26.2	27.1	27.4
Japan	17.1	18.2	18.3	17.8	18.3	18.5	18.8	19.7	20.0	20.7	22.5	23.0	20.9	21.8	22.3
Luxembourg	n.a.	n.a.	30.4	30.1	30.8	29.7	29.6	30.2	32.9	32.7	33.1	33.9	39.2	39.1	42.6
Netherlands	26.3	30.1	33.2	34.7	35.7	36.4	36.7	37.6	39.4	40.3	41.8	42.3	43.7	43.4	44.0
New Zealand	26.8	27.3	24.7	25.6	25.4	25.2	25.2	27.4	27.5	27.3	28.6	31.4	31.3	31.0	33.4
Norway	28.3	31.2	33.3	34.6	36.6	37.7	39.1	39.3	42.4	44.9	45.3	44.8	44.9	46.2	47.3
Portugal	15.4	16.3	18.4	19.0	19.7	19.8	20.6	23.1	22.7	22.4	21.9	22.5	24.7	26.8	27.4
Spain	n.a.	n.a.	14.3	13.3	16.6	15.9	16.4	16.7	17.0	17.9	18.5	17.9	19.4	19.4	21.3
Sweden	25.5	27.2	35.2	36.0	36.9	39.0	40.1	40.0	40.8	42.2	41.4	42.6	43.6	47.9	50.2
Switzerland	19.2	21.3	20.7	21.5	21.6	22.6	23.7	23.8	23.5	23.9	26.3	27.3	29.6	31.3	31.6
Turkey	n.a.	n.a.	15.0	15.1	16.2	16.0	17.3	17.7	19.5	19.1	19.6	17.9	20.7	21.1	21.7
United Kingdom	29.8	28.5	30.4	31.6	32.9	34.5	36.1	36.9	34.8	33.3	31.3	34.9	35.5	35.3	34.7
United States	23.6	26.6	25.9	26.2	27.3	26.8	29.3	29.2	27.8	28.7	28.7	29.2	29.0	28.3	29.1
OECD unweighted average	n.a.	n.a.	26.7	27.4	28.3	28.8	29.4	30.0	30.7	30.9	31.2	32.0	32.8	33.8	34.5

Table 3.4(cont.): Total tax ratios 1965-89[1]

	1978	1979	1980	1981	1982	1983	1984	1985	1986	1987	1988	1989
Australia	26.8	27.5	28.5	29.3	29.6	28.5	30.0	30.0	30.6	30.8	30.3	30.1
Austria	41.4	41.0	41.2	42.5	41.2	41.1	42.4	43.1	43.1	42.6	42.0	41.0
Belgium	45.0	45.5	44.4	45.0	46.4	46.4	47.4	47.6	47.1	47.2	46.1	44.3
Canada	30.8	30.6	31.6	33.7	33.5	33.0	33.0	33.1	33.7	34.8	34.6	35.3
Denmark	43.4	44.5	45.5	45.3	44.5	46.5	47.6	49.0	50.8	51.5	51.1	49.9
Finland	35.1	33.3	33.0	34.6	34.1	34.0	35.6	37.0	38.5	35.9	37.8	38.1
France	38.6	40.2	41.7	41.9	42.8	43.6	44.6	44.5	44.0	44.5	43.9	43.8
Germany	37.9	37.7	38.0	37.6	37.4	37.3	37.5	38.0	37.6	37.7	37.4	38.1
Greece	28.8	30.1	28.4	28.8	32.7	33.9	34.9	35.1	37.0	37.5	34.8	33.2
Iceland	n.a.	n.a.	30.5	31.4	31.7	29.1	30.2	28.9	28.9	29.0	31.8	33.8
Ireland	31.5	31.2	34.0	35.2	36.8	38.3	39.2	38.2	39.1	39.3	41.2	37.6
Italy	27.4	26.6	30.2	31.4	33.7	35.8	34.8	34.4	36.1	36.3	37.0	37.8
Japan	24.0	24.4	25.4	26.2	26.6	27.0	27.1	27.6	28.4	29.7	30.3	30.6
Luxembourg	43.6	40.3	41.0	40.7	41.0	44.9	43.2	44.0	42.3	42.5	42.2	42.4
Netherlands	44.6	45.0	45.8	45.2	45.4	46.7	45.0	44.9	45.8	48.5	48.4	46.0
New Zealand	32.0	32.9	33.1	34.1	35.0	32.7	33.0	34.1	34.4	37.9	37.4	40.3
Norway	46.6	45.7	47.1	48.7	47.9	46.6	45.8	47.6	50.0	47.9	47.8	45.5
Portugal	26.4	26.0	28.7	30.4	31.1	32.9	32.2	31.6	33.4	31.5	34.6	35.1
Spain	22.6	23.1	23.8	25.2	25.5	27.6	28.9	28.8	30.6	32.6	32.9	34.4
Sweden	50.6	49.2	49.1	50.5	49.4	50.3	50.0	50.4	53.0	56.1	55.5	56.1
Switzerland	31.6	31.1	30.8	30.6	31.0	31.6	32.3	32.0	32.5	32.0	32.6	31.8
Turkey	21.3	20.8	21.7	23.4	22.4	20.7	17.3	19.7	22.8	24.1	22.8	29.0
United Kingdom	33.0	32.6	35.3	36.6	39.1	37.4	37.9	37.9	37.6	37.0	37.0	36.5
United States	29.0	29.0	29.5	30.0	29.9	28.4	28.4	29.2	28.9	30.2	29.8	30.1
OECD unweighted average	34.4	34.3	34.9	35.8	36.2	36.4	36.6	36.9	37.8	38.2	38.3	38.4

1. For 1990 figures and estimates for 1991 see Table 3.13 of this book.
2. Source of 1955 and 1960 is *Long-term trends in tax revenues of OECD Member Countries 1955-1980* (OECD 1981).
n.a. = not available.
Main source: Extract from Table 3 (OECD RS 1991).

Table 3.4 shows also that between 1965 and roughly 1975 to 1977 countries with high tax ratios were for the most part increasing them more rapidly than those with medium ratios, who were in turn increasing them more than those with the lowest ratios. Moreover, with a few exceptions, high, medium and low taxed countries could be identified by the following groupings:

a) high total tax ratios: most industrialised European countries (Austria, Belgium, Denmark, Finland, France, Germany, Luxembourg, the Netherlands, Norway, Sweden, the United Kingdom);

b) medium total tax ratios: non-European OECD countries excluding Japan (Australia, Canada, New Zealand, the United States) plus Iceland, Ireland, Italy and Switzerland;

c) low total tax ratios: less industrialised Europe (Greece, Portugal, Spain, Turkey) plus Japan.

Table 3.4 also provides total tax ratios for 1955 and 1960 for those countries for which data were available. It shows that for all countries the following categorisation (a) to (c) was equally the case in 1955, and that for most countries the generalisations about rates of increase in total tax ratios between 1955 and 1965 were consistent with what happened over the next decade.

Over the last fifteen years or so, this pattern has very much changed. Whilst some industrialised European countries have continued to increase their total tax ratio quite considerably, in others it became stable for many years or even declined over recent years. Apart from Japan and New Zealand, the non-European OECD countries have scarcely increased their total tax ratio between 1975 and 1989. In contrast, the lowest taxed countries of less industrialised Europe have increased their total tax ratio considerably. As a result, in recent years the total tax ratios of Greece, Portugal and Spain have come to exceed those of Australia, Switzerland and the United States.

Over nearly all this period the eight countries with the highest tax ratios[1] have been above the OECD average, and the nine countries with the lowest total ratios[2] have always been below the average but there has been much fluctuation among the middle seven: for example, Germany and the United Kingdom for most of the period were above the OECD average but are now below and New Zealand for most of the period was below the OECD average but is now above.

To return to Table 3.4 which provides all the data necessary to understand what has been happening to OECD total tax ratios between 1965 and 1989, it also shows that the average OECD total tax ratio barely changed between 1987 and 1989 and that for nearly all countries annual changes in total tax ratios were well under 1 percentage point. (Notable exceptions between 1987 and 1988 were a decline of around 3 percentage points in Greece and an increase of around the same amount in Iceland and Portugal, and between 1988 and 1989 a decline of around 4 percentage points in Ireland and an increase of around 6 percentage points in Turkey and 3 percentage points in New Zealand). An inspection of Table 3.4 indicates that annual changes in total tax ratios rarely exceed 3 percentage points and have never done so over the 1965-89 period in most OECD countries. When they do, it is frequently to correct a large move in the opposite direction. Provisional estimates provided for 1990 for 15 countries suggest that the average total tax ratio will not differ greatly from those in more recent years, most countries forecasting a decline of less than 0.5 percentage points.

1. Austria, Belgium, Denmark, France, Luxembourg, the Netherlands, Norway and Sweden.
2. Australia, Greece, Iceland, Japan, Portugal, Spain, Switzerland, Turkey and the United States.

Table 3.5 shows the highest total tax ratio of all OECD Member Countries, but as indicated in footnote 1 it should be read in conjunction with Table 3.13 which records more recent information.

Table 3.5: Amount and timing of highest tax ratio until 1989

Country	Highest total tax ratio until 1989[1]	Year highest total tax ratio reached
Australia	30.8	1987
Austria	43.1	1985 + 86
Belgium	47.6	1985
Canada	35.3	1989
Denmark	51.5	1987
Finland	38.2	1977
France	44.6	1984
Germany	38.1	1977 + 89
Greece	37.5	1987
Iceland	33.8	1989
Ireland	41.2	1988
Italy	37.8	1989
Japan	30.6	1989
Luxembourg	44.9	1983
Netherlands	48.5	1987
New Zealand	40.3	1989
Norway	50.0	1986
Portugal	35.1	1989
Spain	34.4	1989
Sweden	56.1	1989
Switzerland	32.6	1988
Turkey	29.0	1989
United Kingdom	39.1	1982
United States	30.2	1987

1. Table 3 of OECD RS (1992) shows that 1990 represented the highest total tax ratio ever in Canada, Italy, Japan, Sweden and Turkey (see Table 3.13 which includes substantial revision of the figure for Turkey for 1989).

Source: Tables 3 and 112 of OECD Revenue Statistics 1991 edition.

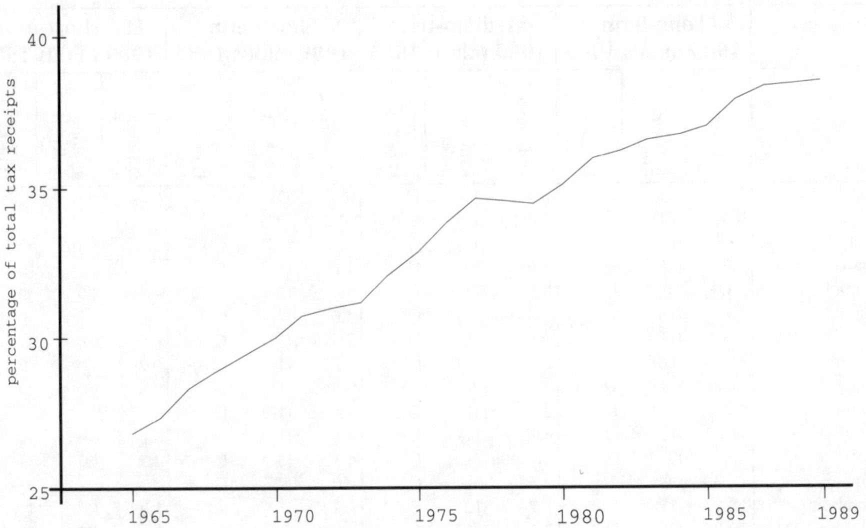

Chart 3.5: Unweighted total tax ratios of the 24 OECD countries between 1965 and 1989 (Source: OECD RS 1991.)

Chart 3.5 shows that apart from a slight decline in the years 1977 to 1979, the OECD average total tax ratio has increased every year since 1965, even if hardly at all since 1987.

Table 3.6. provides changes in total tax ratios over the long term (1965-1989), medium term (1975-1989) and short term (1982-1989). For all three periods considered, the same countries show the largest increases (Denmark, Sweden, New Zealand, Spain and Portugal) and also the smallest increases (the United Kingdom and the United States). A few other countries rarely change their ranking order according to the period (e.g. Ireland and Luxembourg are always 11th to 13th place), but in most the ranking order varies greatly according to the period chosen. A comparison of long-term and short-term increases, for example, shows Belgium falling from 6th to 22nd place, the Netherlands from 8th to 18th place and Norway from 11th to 23rd place, whereas Finland moves up from 18th to 7th place and Iceland from 23rd to 10th place. Table 3.6 is designed primarily to illustrate the convergence and divergence of total tax ratios, a topic discussed in the next sub-section .

Table 3.6: Convergence and divergence of total tax ratios[1] (in percentage points)

	Long-term 1989 minus 1965			Medium-term 1989 minus 1975			Short-term 1989 minus 1982			EEC short-term 1989 minus 1982		
	Difference	Ranking order	D or C	Difference	Ranking order	D or C	Difference	Ranking order	D or C	Difference	Ranking order	D or C
Australia	6.9	(19)	D	2.5	(15)	D	0.5	(17)	D			
Austria	6.3	(21)	C	2.4	(17)	C	-0.2	(21)	C			
Belgium	13.1	(6)	D	2.5	(15)	C	-2.1	(22)	C	-2.1	(10)	C
Canada	9.9	(16)	D	2.9	(14)	D	1.8	(10)	D			
Denmark	26.0	(3)	D	8.5	(7)	D	4.4	(5)	D	4.4	(2)	D
Finland	8.6	(18)	C	3.0	(13)	C	4.0	(7)	C			
France	9.3	(17)	C	6.9	(10)	D	0.5	(17)	C	0.5	(9)	C
Germany	6.5	(20)	C	2.4	(17)	C	0.7	(15)	C	0.7	(7)	D
Greece	11.2	(14)	D	7.9	(9)	C	0.5	(17)	D	0.5	(9)	D
Iceland	6.0	(23)	C	2.4	(17)	D	2.1	(10)	D			
Ireland	11.6	(13)	D	6.1	(11)	C	0.8	(13)	C	0.8	(6)	D
Italy	12.3	(9)	C	11.6	(3)	C	4.1	(6)	C	4.1	(3)	C
Japan	12.3	(9)	C	9.5	(5)	C	4.0	(7)	C			
Luxembourg	12.2	(11)	D	3.2	(12)	C	1.3	(12)	C	1.3	(5)	C
Netherlands	12.8	(8)	D	2.3	(21)	C	0.6	(18)	C	0.6	(8)	C
New Zealand	15.6	(4)	C	9.0	(5)	C	4.8	(4)	C			
Norway	12.2	(11)	D	0.6	(24)	C	-2.4	(23)	C			
Portugal	16.5	(5)	C	10.4	(4)	C	4.0	(7)	C	4.0	(4)	C
Spain	20.1	(2)	C	15.0	(1)	C	8.9	(1)	C	8.9	(1)	C
Sweden	20.9	(1)	D	12.5	(2)	D	6.7	(2)	D			
Switzerland	11.1	(15)	D	2.2	(20)	D	0.8	(13)	D			
Turkey	14.0	(6)	C	8.3	(8)	C	6.6	(3)	C			
United Kingdom	6.1	(22)	C	1.0	(23)	C	-2.6	(24)	C	-2.6	(12)	C
United States	4.2	(24)	D	1.1	(22)	D	0.2	(20)	D			
Average for earlier year	26.7			32.8			36.2			38.0		
Average 1989	38.4			38.4			38.4			39.9		
Difference	11.7			5.6			2.2			1.9		
Annual average difference	0.5			0.4			0.3			0.3		
Number of convergent countries			12			16			16			8
Number of divergent countries			12			8			8			4

1. Note: Convergence = H – or L +, Divergence = H + or L –, where:
H = Higher than average total tax ratio in earlier of two years compared.
L = Lower than average total tax ratio in earlier of two years compared.
\+ = Higher than average increase in total tax ratio over period compared.
– = Lower than average increase in total tax ratio over period compared.
Source: OECD RS 1990 and 1991 editions.

2. Convergence and divergence

Convergence occurs over a period of time, if the deviation of a country from the average OECD total tax ratio is less in the second year than the first and *divergence* occurs when the reverse is the case. In practice, convergence entails that *either* a country with a below average total tax ratio increases it by more than the average increase between the two periods *or* that a country with an above average ratio increases it by less than average: likewise, divergence occurs when above average country tax ratios increase the ratio by more than the average or below average country tax ratios increase it by less that the average. Trends in convergence and divergence regarding total tax ratios can give some indication as to whether governments which rely less on the public sector are compelled to catch up, or conversely, whether a particular attitude to public expenditure gathers momentum, so that spending-prone governments are compelled to spend even more and tax even more, while those governments relying more on the private sector continue to do so.

Table 3.6 provides a summary of the convergence and divergence of OECD countries over the three different periods and of EC countries over the short-term period only, because four countries joined the EC in the eighties. It should be recalled that the symbols C (convergence) and D (divergence) are used to cover both very extreme and very mild departures from a no-trend situation, so can give only a very rough guide to total tax ratio trends in this respect.

Before commenting on the results of Table 3.6, I refer to some earlier investigations on similar lines, for the extent of convergence and divergence of total tax ratios is a function of the years and countries compared.

R. Goode (1968) compared 16 OECD countries (not Australia, Finland, Ireland, Luxembourg, New Zealand, Portugal, Spain, Turkey) and concluded that the fact that the total tax ratios increased between 1955-57 and 1963-65 in all sixteen OECD countries, strongly suggests that some common influences must have been at work. Whatever these figures were, they did not operate to narrow differences among countries. Countries having relatively high or low ratios in 1955-57 tended to have relatively high or low ratios in 1963-64. In 1975, 1982 and 1983, I carried out similar tests published in IIPF Congress 1976 and Intertax 1985/8 comparing 15 countries for the periods 1965-72 and 1965-74 and in each case their total tax ratio converged in 6 and diverged in 9. A comparison of 17 OECD countries for 1965 and 1979 showed that the total ratio converged in 6 and diverged in 11. Finally, comparisons of 23 countries (all OECD countries except Iceland) for the period 1974-81 showed convergence in 11 and divergence in 12 countries.

On the basis of the results, I concluded in *Comparative Tax Studies* (1983) that it seemed more likely that spending-prone governments were obliged to spend and tax more rather than that there was some patching up mechanism, referring to S. Peltzman (1980) for corroboration on the spending side (see Chapter 6B2).

The results of Table 3.6 compel a revision of this opinion for more recent years, and show that the convergence of total tax ratios expected by many commentators over many years has at last begun to happen. (Compare 12C 12D for 1965 to 1989 and other similar results for earlier years with 16C 8D for both 1975-89 and 1982-89 or 8C 4D for the EC countries).

Another test, which confirms these recent results, is to compare the standard deviations from total tax ratios over different years. This test indicated that the standard deviation was 6.2 in 1965, 7.9 in 1980, 8.0 in 1985 and 6.8 in 1990. In other words, this test also indicates a growing variation between countries between 1965 and 1980 or 1965 and 1985, but that the variation has much decreased over recent years.

However, even though it no longer seems possible to refer in puzzlement to the persisting divergent trend in total tax ratios, there is little evidence that governments are greatly influenced by other governments in setting their total tax ratios. In other areas of taxation, as discussed in Chapters 1, 10 and 12 with regard to rate lowering and base broadening of income taxes, international considerations can exert a powerful influence towards conformity and convergence, but governments still seem to be relatively free from international pressures in arriving at their preferred total tax ratio.

3. Tax buoyancy ratios and marginal tax ratios

Use is made of tax buoyancy ratios and marginal tax ratios to separate out the effects of increases in total tax receipts from those in GDP. The tax buoyancy ratio is the ratio of the change in total tax receipts to the change in GDP, so that a ratio of more than 1 per cent indicates that total tax ratios have been growing faster than GDP. Marginal tax ratios indicate the fraction of the increase in GDP absorbed in taxes.

Table 3.7 provides some results over selected periods. Columns 4 and 8 data are not entirely comparable with those of the others, since there have been some revisions of the data for the earlier years and three-year averages and not specific years have been used in columns 4 and 8. However, as remarked earlier, the objective of these comparisons is to give a rough overall impression rather than great precision – which would take too much time. It is not the intention here to comment in any detail on the results, though some possible explanations for country differences are discussed in the next chapter. However, there follows a few comments on the data in this table.

First, there is no correlation between the ranking order in the four left- and four right-hand columns, but rather the contrary: countries like Japan, Portugal, Spain and Turkey which mostly have the highest tax buoyancy ratios have the lowest marginal tax ratios, whereas certain countries with the highest marginal tax ratios over the same periods have the lowest tax buoyancy ratios (e.g. Belgium and Norway). Second, a comparison of the first four columns shows that, while a few countries have the highest tax buoyancy ratios no matter what period is compared (e.g. Spain and Sweden) and others the lowest (e.g. the United Kingdom), for most countries the ranking order fluctuates considerably, reflecting the fact that large increases in total tax ratios as between countries occurs during different time periods. Third, apart from the very short term, as recorded in column (3), total tax ratios have always been growing faster than GDP: between 1985 and 1989 this, however, has not been the case in Austria, Belgium, France, Greece, Ireland, Luxembourg, Norway, Switzerland and the United Kingdom. Fourth, short-term changes in tax buoyancy ratios indicate sometimes violent contrasts with those of medium- or long-term (e.g. compare Greece and Iceland). Fifth, turning to marginal tax ratios, which for the most part are much less volatile than tax buoyancy ratios, the ranking order of columns (5) and (6) is almost identical to the ranking order of total tax ratios in 1989 (see Table 2.2), just as that in column (8) reflects the ranking order of total tax ratios in the late seventies. The short-term comparisons between 1985 and 1989 in column (7) sometimes

Table 3.7: Tax buoyancy and marginal tax ratios 1965-89, 1975-89, 1985-89

Country	Tax Buoyancy Ratios[1]								Marginal Tax Ratios[2]							
	1965-89 (a)	Ranking	1975-89 (a)	Ranking	1985-89 (a)	Ranking	Average 1965-67 minus average 1977-79 (b)	Ranking	1965-89 (a)	Ranking	1975-89 (a)	Ranking	1985-89 (a)	Ranking	Average 1965-67 minus average 1977-79 (b)	Ranking
	(1)		(2)		(3)		(4)		(5)		(6)		(7)		(8)	
Australia	1.31	(17)	1.12	(13)	1.01	(8)	1.28	(14)	30.5	(23)	30.7	(22)	30.3	(24)	31.0	(18)
Austria	1.21	(22)	1.10	(16)	0.75	(23)	1.24	(17)	42.1	(8)	42.5	(8)	32.4	(19)	42.5	(7)
Belgium	1.48	(11)	1.09	(20)	0.67	(24)	1.47	(4)	46.3	(5)	45.7	(5)	32.1	(20)	48.4	(5)
Canada	1.42	(15)	1.12	(13)	1.25	(9)	1.19	(22)	36.2	(15)	36.3	(17)	41.4	(9)	32.8	(15)
Denmark	1.73	(4)	1.29	(9)	1.08	(14)	1.44	(7)	51.8	(2)	53.2	(2)	53.0	(3)	46.3	(6)
Finland	1.31	(17)	1.11	(17)	1.09	(13)	1.22	(18)	38.6	(11)	38.9	(12)	40.4	(10)	38.2	(11)
France	1.29	(19)	1.25	(10)	0.94	(18)	1.20	(19)	44.6	(6)	46.0	(4)	41.7	(8)	41.8	(8)
Germany	1.26	(20)	1.12	(13)	1.02	(14)	1.28	(14)	39.7	(10)	40.1	(10)	38.6	(11)	40.9	(9)
Greece	1.52	(9)	1.33	(7)	0.89	(19)	1.31	(13)	33.5	(20)	33.9	(19)	31.2	(21)	28.9	(19)
Iceland	1.13	(24)	1.06	(21)	1.29	(7)	n.a.		33.8	(9)	33.8	(21)	37.1	(15)	n.a.	
Ireland	1.46	(12)	1.23	(11)	0.94	(18)	1.28	(14)	38.1	(13)	38.8	(13)	35.9	(16)	35.6	(12)
Italy	1.50	(10)	1.50	(3)	1.31	(6)	1.20	(19)	38.3	(12)	39.4	(11)	45.1	(6)	31.4	(17)
Japan	1.73	(4)	1.74	(2)	1.55	(2)	1.37	(10)	31.7	(21)	36.5	(10)	42.9	(7)	25.2	(21)
Luxembourg	1.44	(19)	1.12	(13)	0.86	(21)	1.85	(1)	43.9	(7)	43.8	(7)	37.8	(13)	57.0	(1)
Netherlands	1.45	(12)	1.10	(18)	1.21	(11)	1.35	(12)	48.3	(3)	48.1	(3)	54.6	(2)	50.5	(4)
New Zealand	1.65	(7)	1.30	(8)	1.42	(4)	1.37	(10)	40.3	(9)	40.9	(9)	48.6	(4)	33.6	(14)
Norway	1.40	(16)	1.02	(24)	0.79	(22)	1.45	(6)	46.6	(4)	45.7	(5)	37.6	(14)	50.6	(3)
Portugal	1.92	(2)	1.44	(4)	1.22	(10)	1.44	(7)	35.4	(10)	35.7	(18)	38.5	(12)	27.7	(20)
Spain	2.45	(1)	1.90	(1)	1.53	(3)	1.47	(4)	35.1	(17)	36.8	(14)	43.9	(5)	22.4	(22)
Sweden	1.65	(7)	1.38	(6)	1.39	(5)	1.56	(3)	58.2	(1)	60.2	(1)	69.9	(1)	56.9	(2)
Switzerland	1.68	(6)	1.14	(2)	0.97	(7)	1.84	(2)	34.8	(18)	33.9	(19)	31.1	(22)	39.2	(10)
Turkey	1.94	(3)	1.40	(5)	1.57	(1)	1.39	(9)	29.0	(24)	29.0	(24)	30.9	(23)	21.5	(23)
United Kingdom	1.22	(21)	1.04	(23)	0.88	(20)	1.10	(23)	37.0	(14)	36.8	(14)	33.4	(17)	35.1	(13)
United States	1.19	(23)	1.05	(22)	1.13	(2)	1.20	(18)	30.7	(22)	30.5	(23)	32.9	(18)	32.5	(16)

1. Percentage increase in taxes divided by percentage increase in GDP over the designated periods.

2. Increase in total tax receipts divided by increase in GDP expressed as a percentage for the designated periods.

Sources: (a) OECD RS 1991 (b) OECD RS 1981), reproduced from Messere (1983).

conform less to this picture (e.g. compare Spain and Austria in column (7) with columns (5) and (6)).

4. The future of total tax ratios

The survey in this section covering overall trends, convergencies and divergencies, tax buoyancy ratios and marginal tax ratios leads to perhaps the more interesting question of what is going to happen to total tax ratios during the nineties.

On this aspect, one may start with R. Goode (1981) who drew attention to many erroneous forecasts in the past when he said:

> A limit to taxation holds only for a particular place and time. The observation that the ratio of tax revenue to national income has risen in many countries over time without disastrous effects and that it differs greatly among countries at any given time compels acceptance of the relativist view. The increased availability of statistics and the publication of many historical studies and international comparisons have effectively discredited some earlier hypotheses about generally applicable limits. Among these hypotheses are the opinions of several eighteenth and nineteenth century writers that taxes amounting to 15 per cent of national income are excessive in all but the most exceptional circumstances and Colin Clark's generalisation advanced in 1945 and repeated as recently as 1977 that the safe limit of taxation in nontotalitarian countries in times of peace is about 25 per cent of net national income. In the mid-1970s the ratio of taxation to gross domestic product (GDP) or gross national product (GNP) ranged from 45 per cent or more in several countries in northwestern Europe to below 9 per cent in a number of less developed countries. Over the preceding decade or longer, tax ratios had been rising in most of the countries for which statistics are available.

During the late seventies and early eighties I went on record in various articles in forecasting that this rise in total tax ratios would continue, but in my most recent venture [Messere and Owens (1989)] became more cautious about predicting future developments in total tax ratios, saying:

> It is difficult to predict what will happen in the late eighties and beyond. Since 1984 a number of governments have announced their intention to reduce total tax burdens. Consequently, whereas in the past our papers have gone on record unambiguously in forecasting further increases in overall total tax ratios, we would prefer now in the changing climate, to remain agnostic about what might happen to these ratios over the next few years.

A forecast about what will happen to total tax ratios in the nineties is predominantly a forecast about future political attitudes, a matter discussed more extensively in Chapter 6B. On the one hand there is a trend towards privatisation and smaller government, on the other, a demand for increased government expenditure to cope with demographic changes and high unemployment levels as well as to improve the infrastructure for competitive reasons. During the eighties, a number of governments have avowedly supported the former approach, but in most OECD countries it has not taken the form of a decline in total tax ratios. A pendulum theory towards tax/expenditure decisions would suggest that in the post-Reagan, post-Bush era the United States for a start may be expected to increase total tax ratios and Germany may have to do so to meet the costs of its unification. Canada and Japan (Japan albeit very modestly) have recently adopted value added taxes, and if experience is any guide adoption of value added taxes should lead to increases in total tax ratios (see Chapter 13). Whilst a number of small countries both with high (Denmark, the Netherlands, Sweden) and low GDP per capita (Ireland, Portugal) may be expected, after their large expansion of total tax ratios in the eighties, to slow down or even reverse this increase, there would seem grounds for predicting a modest increase in total tax ratios in most of the larger OECD countries over the next decade. However, with so many countries currently in recession, it seems quite likely that during the next two or three years overall total tax ratios will follow the pattern of the late seventies and slightly fall.

C. Developments in the tax ratios of the main revenue sources between 1965 and 1989

This section is confined to developments in the tax ratios of the three main revenue raisers [taxes on income and profits (heading 1000 of Table 2.1), social security contributions (heading 2000) and taxes on goods and services (heading 5000) and the main subdivisions thereof], revenue developments in the less important capital taxes and taxes on immovable property being discussed in Chapters 11 and 14 respectively.

1. Developments within the main revenue sources

Taxes on income and profits comprise personal income taxes together with the much less important taxes on the profits of unincorporated enterprises (1100) and corporate tax (1200). The ratio of 1100 taxes varied from 4 per cent to 24 per cent in 1989 whereas the ratio of 1200 taxes exceeded 4 per cent only in Japan, Luxembourg and the United Kingdom. It should, however, be mentioned that the distinction between the two kinds of tax is not always clear-cut in view of their frequent interaction in the taxation of distributed profits and the various borderline cases referred to at the end of the Annex to Chapter 2E. Relative revenue yields in different countries from these two kinds of taxes are also influenced by the relative prevalence of incorporated enterprises in comparison to unincorporated and this may have little or nothing to do with tax considerations, even if in a number of countries there is a tax incentive to incorporate or not to incorporate. For example, it is understood that the large number of small incorporated firms is probably the main explanatory factor for the high corporation tax ratio in Japan and that, greater prevalence of incorporation in the United Kingdom is also an explanatory factor for why its corporation tax ratio is so much higher than that of Germany. Also there may be some competition between 1100 and 1200 taxes in that business pressures for reduction mainly focus on 1200 taxes and households' pressures on 1100 taxes. An interesting recent example of such competition was the 1986 United States tax reform where the avowed intention was to move the income tax burden away from individuals towards business, the 1200 ratio in the United States having dropped from 3.0 to 2.0 between 1980 and 1985. In practice, the United States corporate tax ratio did pick up to 2.6 per cent in 1989 but there was no reduction in its personal income tax ratio.

Within social security contributions – the main distinction is between those paid by employees (2100) and those paid by employers (2220), a distinction discussed more fully

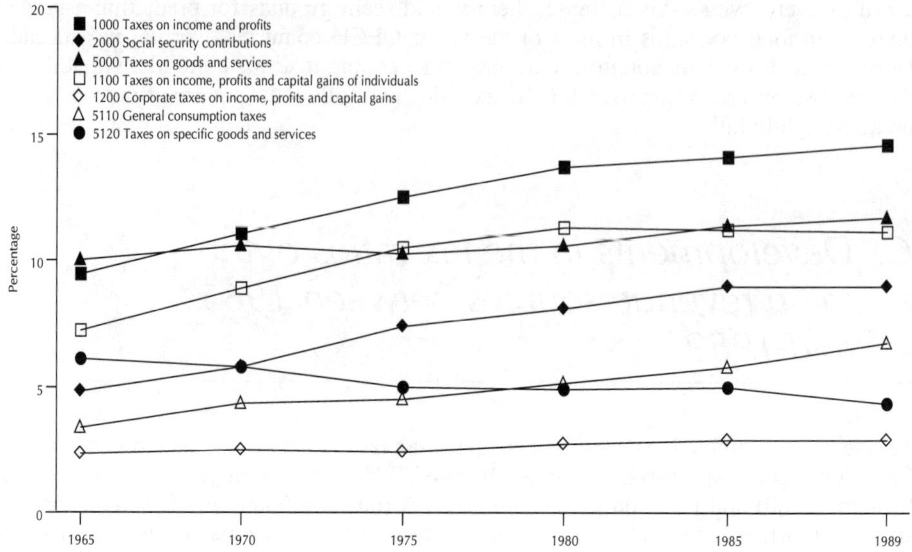

Chart 3.6: Unweighted average of the tax ratios of the main revenue sources between 1965 and 1989 (Source: OECD RS 1991.)

in Chapter 8. Here it is noted that the employers' ratio has always been greater in most OECD countries and especially so in Belgium, France, Italy, Norway, Spain and Sweden. Only in Denmark, Greece and the Netherlands (no longer) is the employees' ratio (slightly) higher and only in Switzerland are the two ratios equal. Since 1975 the tendency has been for the employees' ratio to increase slightly more in relative terms than that of the employers, for in 1975 the unweighted average of the employers' ratio was about twice that of the employees whereas in 1990 it was 1.8 times the former, but in absolute terms the average employers' ratio increased by 0.7 during that period, and the employees' ratio by 0.6.

Among the third main category of revenue raisers, taxes on goods and services, the main distinction is between general consumption taxes (5110) and excises etc. (5120). As Chart 3.6 shows, there has been a considerable increase in the overall general consumption tax ratio, whereas the excise etc. tax ratio is the only major tax ratio to have declined since 1965. In 1965 the unweighted average of the general consumption tax ratio represented just over half of that of the excise etc. ratio (0.56) whereas in 1989 it was more than one and a half times that of the latter. The reason for the increase in general consumption tax ratios is much bound up with the move to value added taxation, discussed in more detail in Chapter 13. Countries with VAT have generally increased its rate and widened its base, and most of those without an important broad-based general consumption tax have tried to introduce one and as at 1989 only Australia, Japan, Switzerland and the United States lack a general consumption tax ratio of 4 per cent or more. The decline of the excise etc. tax ratio can be attributed to two main factors. First, something like 65 to 70 per cent of excises etc. revenues are derived from various taxes on alcoholic drinks, tobacco and motoring (on hydrocarbon oils and the vehicles) which are based mainly on measures unrelated to value such as strength of alcohol, weight of tobacco and volume of hydrocarbon oils, and in times of inflation the value in real terms of revenues from such taxes decreases in the absence of rate increases ('so-called negative fiscal drag' or 'fiscal boost'). Such rate increases are politically unpopular because they contribute to inflationary pressures and are not appreciated by consuming voters who are apt to think in terms of nominal rather than real prices. Second, excises etc. comprise import duties which on average accounted for 15 per cent of receipts from taxes on goods and services in 1965 but only 5.4 per cent in 1988, as a result of the various GATT negotiations on tariffs and the emergence of free trade regional groupings such as the European Community. There are other factors accounting for the decline in the excise ratio such as the reduced consumer expenditures over the period on tobacco especially and on alcohol to some extent and also in some countries, such as Greece and Japan, the introduction of value added tax was accompanied by a phasing-out of selective consumption taxes.

2. Developments between the major revenue sources

There has been much diversity in the movement of countries' particular tax ratios over the last eighteen years with relatively little change in some countries and violent changes in others (e.g. the Irish general consumption tax ratio changed from 1 per cent to 8 per cent and the Swedish employers' social security ratio from 3 per cent to 14 per cent, in each case from one of the lowest to one of the highest in the OECD area.) The mainstream trend is that between 1965 and 1975 there was in most OECD countries a considerable increase in the personal income tax and/or social security ratio, accompanied by a scarcely changing tax ratio of taxes on goods and services. After the mid-seventies, however, in many countries growth in the personal income tax and social security ratios became sluggish, whereas general consumption tax ratios tended more and more to increase. Thus, the general trend away from consumption taxes to income and payroll taxes, which had in fact been occurring ever since 1955, came gradually to a halt in the mid-to late seventies, and in some countries (Denmark, Finland, New Zealand, the United Kingdom) the trend has been reversed.

Between 1975 and 1985, the tax ratios of the three main revenue sources grew more or less equally and between 1985 and 1989 they have stagnated more or less equally. Overall only the general consumption tax ratio has grown to any extent since 1985 and this has been offset by a decline in the overall excise etc. ratio which after remaining stable at 5 per cent between 1975 and 1985 had fallen to 4.4 per cent by 1989.

The main trend between 1965 and the mid-seventies and its cessation thereafter is not difficult to explain. In the years of rapid growth and increasing real incomes taxpayers were prepared to accept higher taxation of these incomes as the fairest way of financing the growing welfare State. However, once real incomes ceased to grow or even fell, and fiscal drag was almost entirely due to inflation which itself became very high, taxpayers' illusions ceased and voters, successfully in most countries, demanded that measures should be taken to offset fiscal drag. Another explanation may be provided for the rise and more recent levelling-off of the social security ratio, of which on average nearly two thirds is paid by employers. In times of full employment, employers' payroll taxes have a lot to be said for them. They are easy to collect, easy to vary for conjunctural purposes and they are relatively acceptable to most voters. However, once unemployment levels become high, which in itself automatically slows the growth of such revenues, these levies are seen as a disincentive to taking on labour and again political pressure to reduce them comes into play. When personal income tax and social security revenues were flowing in effortlessly, governments did not have to take the politically unpopular decision of raising rates of consumption taxes. Since the mid-seventies when income and payroll taxes ceased to be buoyant, governments had to increase consumption tax revenues by raising rates and widening the tax base.

3. Convergence and divergence

Whereas an analysis of convergence and divergence of total tax ratios throws light on governments' tax/expenditure policies as a whole over time, an analysis of the convergence and divergence of particular tax ratios poses the question can governments continue to rely more and more on those taxes which have brought them most revenues in the past and/or to continue to neglect those revenue sources which they have neglected in the past (divergence), or are they obliged to diversify their sources of revenue towards an OECD average (convergence)?

Table 3.8 summarises the results of tests taken over various years and covering many different periods to measure the convergence and divergence of particular tax ratios. This sub-section follows the pattern of the discussion of convergence and divergence of total tax ratios earlier in this chapter. It is again recalled that the number of convergent and divergent countries provides only a very rough guide to trends, because it does not distinguish between drastic and mild convergence or divergence. To some extent Table 3.9 remedies this by identifying major examples of convergence and divergence between 1965 and 1989, 1975 and 1989 and 1982 and 1989.

In all the cases summarised in Table 3.8 divergence predominates among social security ratios, but less so since 1982 than in earlier years. Social security ratios have been increasing considerably in almost all countries, but by more in those countries where they were above average in the earlier of the two years compared. The excise etc. ratio represents the exact opposite trend, convergence predominating in all but one (case 3) of the eight comparisons. The excise ratio has declined or remained stable in nearly all countries over the periods covered, but has generally declined most in what were the highest excise ratio countries in the earlier year.

With regard to the other three ratios the proportion of convergent to divergent countries varies according to the countries and periods compared but mostly does not stray far from an equal number of convergent and divergent countries.

As already mentioned, since four of the twelve EC countries joined in the eighties separate comparisons for EC countries are made only for the short-term 1982-89 period and the results are somewhat surprising. A comparison of lines 6a) and 6b) of Table 3.8 indicates that there is much more convergence among EC countries than among OECD countries as a whole with regard to personal income tax, social security and excise etc. ratios, but much less convergence with regard to corporate income and general consumption tax ratios.

Table 3.8: Summary table of convergence and divergence of particular tax ratios between various countries[1] and over various periods

			Personal Income Tax Ratios			Corporate Tax Ratios			Social Security Ratios			General Consumption Tax Ratios			Excises etc. Tax Ratios		
			C	**D**	**= or n.a.**	**C**	**D**	**= or n.a.**	**C**	**D**	**= or n.a.**	**C**	**D**	**= or n.a.**	**C**	**D**	**= or n.a.**
1.	1965-74	15 OECD Countries	7	8	0	n.a.	n.a.	n.a.	4	10	1	8	7	0	11	4	0
2.	1965-81	23 OECD Countries	13	9	1	n.a.	n.a.	n.a.	9	13	1	15	8	0	14	9	0
3.	1974-81	23 OECD Countries	13	9	1	n.a.	n.a.	n.a.	8	15	0	7	15	1	10	13	0
4.	1965-89	All OECD Countries	7	15	2	10	11	3	6	18	0	10	14	0	16	8	0
5.	1975-89	All OECD Countries	12	11	1	11	10	3	7	17	0	10	14	0	12	10	2
6.	1982-89	a) All OECD Countries	10	11	3	10	10	4	8	12	4	14	9	1	12	10	2
		b) 12 EC Countries	8	3	1	3	7	2	5	7	0	6	5	1	8	3	1

1. Line 1 is taken from Messere (1978) and lines 2 and 3 from Messere (1985), where Iceland is the OECD country excluded. The 15 countries considered in line 1 are Australia, Austria, Belgium, Canada, Denmark, France, Germany, Ireland, Italy, Japan, Netherlands, Norway, Sweden, the United Kingdom and the United States. Lines 4, 5 and 6 have been prepared for this book.

C = Convergent D = Divergent = No trend n.a. = not available.

Source: various editions of OECD RS.

Table 3.9: Summary of long-term, medium-term and short-term convergence and divergence of particular tax ratios

	1100 Personal income tax ratios			1200 Corporate tax ratios			2000 Social security ratios			5110 General consumption ratios			5120 Excises etc. ratios			1982-89 convergence and divergence of EC countries				
	1965-89	1975-89	1982-89	1965-89	1975-89	1982-89	1965-89	1975-89	1982-89	1965-89	1975-89	1982-89	1965-89	1975-89	1982-89	1100	1200	2000	5110	5120
Australia	D	D	D	C	C	D	D	D	D	D	D	D	C	C	D					
Austria	D	D	D	D	D	C	D	D	C	C	C	C	D	D	C					
Belgium	D	C	C	C	C	C	D	D	D	C	C	C	C	C	C	C	C	D	C	D
Canada	D	D	D	C	C	C	D	D	C	D	D	C	C	D	C					
Denmark	D	D	D	C	C	C	D	D	D	D	D	C	C	D	C	D	C	D	C	=
Finland	D	C	D	D	D	D	D	D	D	D	D	D	C	=	D					
France	D	D	C	=	=	=	D	D	D	C	C	C	C	C	C	C	D	D	C	C
Germany	C	C	C	D	=	C	D	D	D	C	D	C	C	C	C	C	D	D	D	D
Greece	D	C	C	C	C	C	C	D	C	D	D	D	C	D	D	C	D	C	D	C
Iceland	D	C	n.a.	D	D	n.a.	D	D	n.a.	D	D	n.a.	C	C	n.a.					
Ireland	C	C	C	D	D	D	D	D	D	C	D	C	C	C	C	C	D	D	D	C
Italy	C	C	C	D	D	D	C	C	D	D	D	D	D	C	D	C	D	D	D	C
Japan	D	C	C	D	D	D	C	C	C	D	D	D	D	D	D					
Luxembourg	D	D	C	D	D	D	C	C	C	D	D	D	C	C	D	C	D	C	=	C
Netherlands	C	D	D	D	C	D	D	D	=	D	C	C	C	C	C	D	=	C	C	C
New Zealand	D	D	C	C	C	D	D	D	=	C	C	C	C	C	C					
Norway	C	C	D	C	C	C	D	C	D	C	C	C	D	D	D					
Portugal	n.a.	n.a.	n.a.	n.a.	n.a.	n.a.	C	C	C	C	C	C	D	D	D	n.a.	n.a.	C	C	D
Spain	C	C	C	C	C	C	D	D	C	D	C	C	C	C	C	C	C	C	C	C
Sweden	D	D	D	D	D	C	D	D	D	D	D	C	D	D	D					
Switzerland	D	D	=	=	D	C	D	D	D	D	D	D	C	D	C					
Turkey	D	D	D	C	C	D	D	C	C	C	C	C	D	C	D					
United Kingdom	C	C	D	D	D	D	D	D	D	C	C	D	C	=	C	D	D	D	D	C
United States	=	C	D	C	C	C	C	C	C	D	D	D	D	D	=					
Number of Convergent	7	12	10	10	11	11	6	7	9	10	10	14	16	12	12	8	3	5	6	8
Number of divergent	15	11	11	11	10	10	18	17	12	14	14	9	8	10	10	3	7	7	5	3
No trend or data unavailable	2	1	3	3	3	3	0	0	3	0	0	1	0	2	2	1	2	0	1	1

C = Convergent D = Divergent = No trend n.a. = not available.

Source: OECD RS 1990 and 1991.

Table 3.9 indicates which countries are convergent and which divergent over the three periods considered. These results are derived from data published in OECD RS 1991, though 1982 published data is taken from OECD RS 1990.

Table 3.10: Largest shifts in tax levels, 1965-89, 1975-89, 1982-89

Figures represent later period minus earlier period tax ratio to nearest percentage point[1]

	Long-term 1989 minus 1965			Medium-term 1989 minus 1975			Short-term 1989 minus 1982		
Personal income tax ratio	Denmark	14	D	Italy	6	C	New Zealand	-3	C
	New Zealand	9	D	Spain	5	C	Spain	3	C
	Canada	8	C	Ireland	4	C			
Corporate income tax ratio	Luxembourg	4	D	Japan	3	D	Norway	-6	C
	Japan	3	D	Italy	2	C	Japan	2	D
				United Kingdom	2	0	Spain	2	C
Employees' social security ratio	Netherlands	4	D	France	2	D	No change of more than 1 percentage point		
	Norway	4	C	Greece	2	D			
	France	3	D						
Employers' social security ratio	Sweden	11	D	Sweden	6	D	No change of more than 1 percentage point		
	Spain	6	D	Spain	2	D			
	Norway	4	D						
General consumption tax ratio	Denmark	7	C	New Zealand	5	C	Turkey	5	C
	Iceland	7	D	Turkey	5	C	New Zealand	4	C
	Ireland	7	C				Portugal	3	C
	Portugal	7	C						
Excises etc. ratio	Iceland	-6	C	Turkey	-7	C	Turkey	-4	C
	Turkey	-6	C	Iceland	-4	C	Spain	2	C
	Ireland	-4	C				Greece	-2	C

1. Thus there were no major shifts in tax ratios in Australia, Austria, Belgium, Finland, Germany, Switzerland and the United States, but many in Spain (6), Turkey (5) and New Zealand (4).

C = Convergent D = Divergent 0 = No trend.

Source: OECD RS 1990 and 1991.

D. Developments in the tax mix between 1965 and 1989

Though developments in the tax mix to some extent mirror those in tax ratios, there are significant differences (compare Tables 3.10 and 3.12).

Table 3.11 and Chart 3.7 show how the unweighted OECD average regarding reliance on the main sources of revenue has changed over the period. Table 3.11 makes it clear that *on average* the major changes in tax structures took place between 1965 and 1975 and

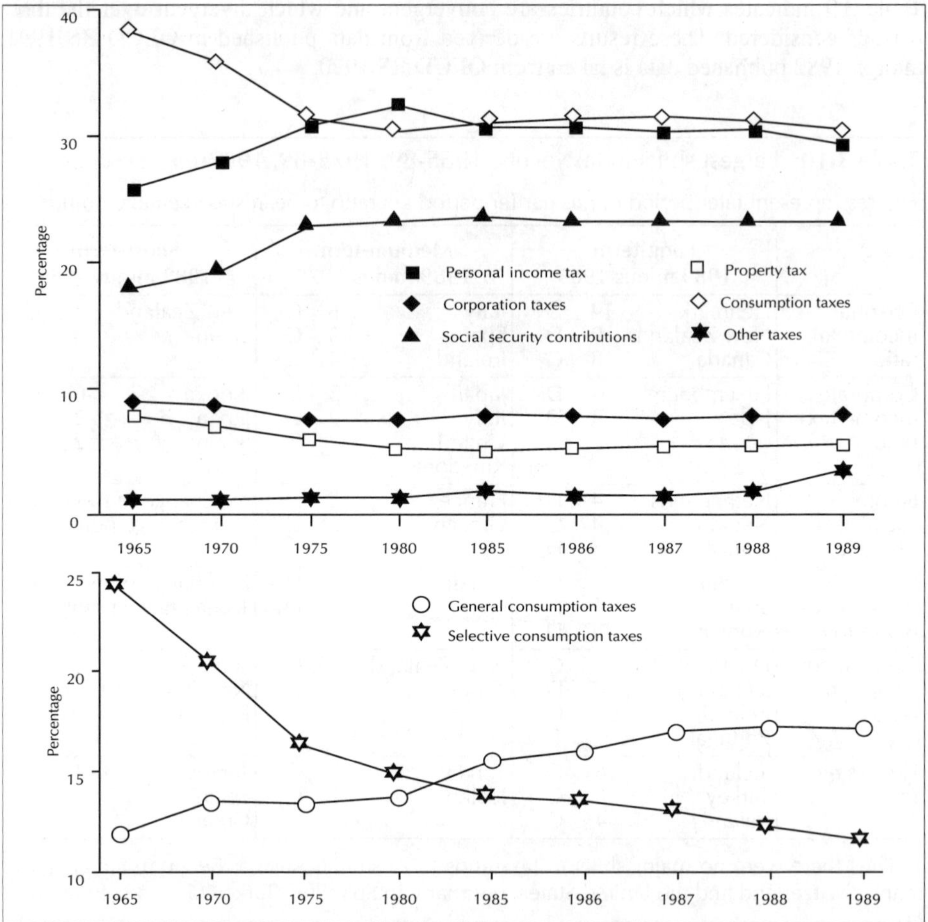

Chart 3.7: Unweighted average of receipts from the main revenue sources to total tax receipts between 1965 and 1989 (Source: OECD RS 1991.)

also that these changes constituted mainly a shift away from excises and property taxes towards personal income taxes and social security contributions. Since 1975 shifts in the average tax mix have been mostly very slight and have occurred mainly within the consumption tax share, general consumption tax receipts, mostly value added taxes, increasing their share at more or less the same rate that the receipts from excises etc. have fallen.

Naturally, these averages conceal many differences among countries and Table 3.12 identifies those countries where there has been major shifts in relative reliance on these various sources. Despite quite large changes in the tax structures of a number of countries, for the most part there is little change over the short term, medium term or long term between countries' extreme reliance on particular sources of revenue. For example, no matter which of the periods are considered, the Nordic countries and New Zealand rely most and France and Greece least on the personal income tax as a source of revenue. More is said about similarities and differences in the tax structures of particular countries in Chapter 4, but Table 3.12 already gives an indication of those countries which have frequently made sweeping changes to their tax structures and those which have not, as well as identifying those countries where changes in tax structures have been the largest..

Table 3.11: Changes in the unweighted OECD average of particular tax shares in total tax revenues, 1965, 1975, 1982, 1989 (particular tax receipts as percentage of total tax receipts)

	1965	1975	1982	1989	Long-term difference (1989 minus 1965)	Medium-term difference (1989 minus 1975)	Short-term difference (1989 minus 1982)
1000 Income taxes	35	38	40	38	3	-2	-2
Personal	26	31	33	29	4	-1	-3
Corporation	9	8	8	8	-1	0	0
2000 Social security	18	23	25	23	5	0	-2
Employees'	6[1]	7[1]	8[1]	8[1]	2	1	0
Employers'	10[1]	14[1]	14[1]	13[1]	3	-1	-1
5000 Consumption taxes	38	31	29	31	-7	0	2
General	12	13	13	17	5	4	4
Excises	24	16	14	12	-24	-4	-2
4000 Property taxes	8	6	5	6	-2	0	1
Total	99	98	99	98			

1. Estimates. Also note that that 1 000, 2 000, and 5 000 are more than the sum of their components in this table (see Table 1.1). Also numbers are not always consistent due to rounding up.
Source: OECD RS 1990 and 1991.

Table 3.12: Largest shifts in tax structures, 1965-89, 1975-89, 1982-89 (Figures represent later period share minus earlier period share in total receipts to nearest percentage point[1])

	Long-term 1989 minus 1965		**Medium-term 1989 minus 1975**		**Short-term 1989 minus 1982**	
Personal income tax share	Italy	16	Italy	12	Turkey	-16
	Canada	15	UK	-11	New Zealand	-14
	Ireland	15	Turkey	-10	Belgium	-5
Corporation income tax share	N.Zealand	-12	UK	6	Norway	-11
	US and Canada	-7	Canada	-5	Japan	4
	Luxembourg	7	Italy and Japan	4	Spain	4
Employees' social security share	Norway	9	France	4	Spain	-5
	France	6	Norway	4	Norway	4
	US	5	Portugal	-4		
Employers' social security share	Sweden	16	Italy	-13	Spain	-9
	US	7	Spain	-12	Belgium	4
	Norway	7	Sweden	7		
Property tax share	Ireland	-10	Greece	-6	Turkey	-3
	Turkey	-8	Ireland	-5	Australia	2
					Luxembourg	2
					Sweden	2
	Greece	-6	Turkey	-5		
General consumption tax share	Portugal	20	Turkey	18	Turkey	18
	Iceland	19	N.Zealand	11	Greece	12
	Turkey	18	Portugal	9	New Zealand	9
Excises etc. share	Turkey	-47	Turkey	-34	Turkey	-20
	Iceland	-27	Iceland	-16	Greece	-8
	Ireland	-22	Ireland	-9	Australia	-7

1. Thus there were no major shifts in the tax mix of Austria, Denmark, Finland and Germany but many in Turkey (11), Ireland (5), Norway (5), Greece (4) and Italy (4).

Source: OECD RS 1990 and 1991.

E. Postscript: total tax ratios in 1990 and estimates for 1991

Data for 1990 became available in OECD RS 1992 after this book was at the print stage, so there is not the possibility of reproducing these data, let alone commenting on them. However, in view of the general interest in total tax ratios, Table 3.13 provides them for 1990 with provisional estimates, as well as revisions of total tax ratios for the years 1987, 1988 and 1989. The table also illustrates (see last two columns) trends in total tax ratios between 1989 and 1991.

A comparison of the revised 1989 data with the new 1990 results shows little change in total tax ratios for most countries. Only in Greece with more than three percentage points increase and in Turkey with more than two percentage points are fluctuations greater than two percentage points. Changes of between one and two percentage points occurred upwards in Canada, Italy and Luxembourg and downwards in Denmark and New Zealand.

One's first impression of the comparisons between 1990 relatively firm figures and 1991 provisional figures (doubtless to be revised) is that the recent stagnation of unweighted average total tax ratios is likely to continue, for there have been very heavy decreases in a few countries (5.2 percentage points in Sweden, 2.9 in Belgium and 1.1 in Germany, despite revenues from additional Länder). In contrast, Canada, Italy and Turkey will have their highest ever total tax ratio in 1991. Otherwise movements in total tax ratios between 1990 and 1991 never exceeded one percentage point, in an upward direction in Portugal, Ireland and Norway and in a downward direction in Finland.

As regards the revisions for 1987, 1988 and 1989, it is normally the case that in recent years a number of countries have had to modify both total tax receipts and GDP figures, though almost invariably this affects total tax ratios by less than half a percentage point and more often by 0.1 or 0.2 of a percentage point and for a number of countries not at all. The main exeption is Luxembourg, where over the years there has been more than one vacillation as to what should be included in GDP and the latest change has increased the total tax ratio by more than seven percentage points, unfortunately rendering invalid what was written at an earlier date in Chapter 4D. The only other revision amounting to one percentage point or more of the tax ratio occurred exclusively in 1989, where OECD RS 1992 reduces the RS 1991 figures by 4.8 percentage points in Turkey and by 1.0 percentage point in both Iceland and New Zealand. One consequence of these revisions is that between 1988 and 1989 the unweighted total tax ratio declined by 0.2 percentage points. This was the first and only decline since 1978 to 1979 (also 0.2 per cent) since the series began in 1965.

OECD RS 1992 observed:

> Prior to 1990, the figures for Luxembourg did not correspond to those published by the OECD National Accounts, since imputed bank services provided to non-residents were not deducted. The new figures do correspond to those in the OECD National Accounts, however, and this explains the increase in total tax revenues as a percentage of GDP not only for 1990, but also for all previous years, as compared to the figures given in the past years' editions of this publication.

Table 3.13: Total tax ratios, 1987–1991 with revisions for 1987 to 1989

country	1987	1988	1989	1990	1991	1991 provisional minus 1990	1990 minus 1989
Australia	31.1	30.5	30.4	30.8	n.a.	n.a.	+0.4
Austria	42.3	42.1	41.2	41.6	42.0	0.4	+0.4
Belgium	47.7	46.3	44.6	44.9	42.0	–2.9	+0.3
Canada	34.7	34.5	35.4	37.1	39.4	+2.3	+1.7
Denmark	51.5	51.7	50.4	48.6	48.2	–0.4	–1.8
Finland	35.9	37.8	37.4	38.0	37.2	–0.8	+0.6
France	44.5	43.8	43.7	43.7	43.9	+0.2	0.0
Germany	38.0	37.7	38.3	37.7[1]	36.6	–1.1	–0.6
Greece	37.3	34.7	33.3	36.5	n.a.	n.a.	+3.2
Iceland	29.3	32.0	32.8	32.6	32.5	–0.1	–0.2
Ireland	38.9	40.6	37.0	37.2	37.9	+0.7	+0.2
Italy	36.3	37.0	37.9	39.1	40.5	+1.4	+1.2
Japan	29.7	30.3	30.7	31.3	n.a.	n.a.	+0.6
Luxembourg	50.1	49.7	48.8	50.3	n.a.	n.a.	+0.6
Netherlands	48.5	48.4	45.8	45.2	47.2	+2.0	+1.5
New Zealand	37.9	37.2	39.3	38.2	n.a.	n.a.	–1.1
Norway	47.9	47.8	46.0	46.3	47.0	+0.7	+0.3
Portugal	31.5	34.6	35.1	34.6	35.5	+0.9	–0.5
Spain	32.5	32.7	34.6	34.4	34.6	+0.2	–0.2
Sweden	56.1	55.5	56.0	56.9	51.7	–5.2	+0.9
Switzerland	32.0	32.6	31.7	31.7	31.4	–0.3	0.0
Turkey	24.1	22.8	25.4	27.8	30.0	+2.2	+2.4
United Kingdom	37.1	37.3	37.0	36.7	36.2	–0.5	–0.3
United States	30.2	29.4	29.6	29.9	n.a.	n.a.	+0.3
OECD unweighted average:	38.5	38.6	38.4	38.8	n.a	n.a	n.a

1. Includes new Länder revenues for the second half of the year. If these were excluded the figure would be 36.3, a drop of two percentage points from 1989.

n.a. = not available.

Source: OECD RS 1992.

As already noted this has the effect of increasing Luxembourg's total tax ratios for the past years by more than 7 percentage points and has also an effect on the unweighted annual total tax ratio. Since these unweighted total tax ratios have been commented on in this chapter and they effect the unweighted total tax ratio by more than 0.1 percentage point since 1976, corrected figures are now provided.

	1976	1977	1978	1979	1980	1981	1982	1983	1984	1985	1986	1987	1988	1989
RS 1991	33.8	34.5	34.4	34.3	34.9	35.8	36.2	36.4	36.6	36.4	37.8	33.2	33.3	38.4
RS 1992	34.0	34.7	34.7	34.5	35.2	36.0	36.5	36.7	36.8	37.2	38.0	38.5	38.6	38.4

This may provoke the reaction that if a change in calculating GDP in such a small country as Luxembourg can so disturb a time series, why use unweighted averages at all? In addition it has been argued that *weighted* averages better reflect economic realities. There are two reasons why despite their limitations, *unweighted* averages are preferred over weighted averages as a rough guide to tax trends. First, from a technical point of view the arithmetic is simpler and with weighted averages different results emerge according to the method of weighting chosen; second, unweighted averages provide a better guide to the trends in a number of disparate countries, for to take an extreme example, because of the preponderance of the United States and Japan in OECD economies, a weighted average would suggest that VAT played a small role in OECD taxation but since nearly all other OECD countries have important VAT revenues, the use of weights would give a misleading picture of OECD country choices.

Finally, a reminder should be given that the commentary in Chapters 2, 3 and 4 refers always to the data in OECD RS 1991 and never to the data in OECD RS 1992.

Chapter 4
Some country comparisons of tax revenue developments between 1965 and 1989

A. Introduction

The tax revenue developments within any country can be adequately explained only by a detailed survey of all the relevant historical, economic and political considerations within such a country. To do this for the 24 OECD countries would require a lengthy book in itself. As a somewhat superficial compromise this chapter attempts to provide some explanations of tax revenue developments usually by comparing what has happened in selected groups of countries and 19 of the 24 OECD countries are covered in this way.

No comment is made in this chapter on the remaining five OECD countries (Austria, Finland, Iceland, Luxembourg, Turkey) though it may be observed that even if its total tax ratio is higher, the tax profile of Austria is not dissimilar to that of Germany, especially regarding the stability of its tax structure since 1975.

B. The five non-European OECD countries plus Switzerland

Except for Japan, these six countries have had roughly similar total tax ratios over the period between 1965 and 1982 (always well below the OECD average) and except in New Zealand the greater part of this increase occurred in the late sixties and early seventies and it was due (entirely in Australia and New Zealand and mostly in Canada, Switzerland and the United States) to increases in the personal income tax ratio. In Japan the total tax ratio barely changed between 1965 and 1975 and though it increased between 1975 and 1982 it remained well below that of the other countries in this group. Between 1982 and 1989 the total tax ratio has remained almost static in Australia, Canada, Switzerland and the United States but has increased considerably in Japan, which has now more or less the same total tax ratio as the other countries in this group. In New Zealand the total tax ratio also increased between 1982 and 1989 and in 1989 exceeded an OECD average thus becoming significantly higher than those of the other countries in this group.

These six countries have had a very similar tax structure for most of the period between 1965 and 1989. All six countries rely heavily on personal and corporation income taxes and property taxes and, except in the United States in most recent years, much below average reliance on social security contributions which do not even exist in Australia and New Zealand. Except recently in New Zealand, reliance on consumption taxes is also much below average and excises usually continue to raise greater yields than general consumption taxes, which is not the case in other countries.

C. Five Southern European countries: France, Greece, Italy, Portugal and Spain

Though France and Italy are more industrialised than Greece, Portugal and Spain, they have a number of characteristics in common which are reflected in their tax structures. The relatively large number of people who are self-employed or are in the agricultural sector implies a relatively low reliance on the personal income tax, and a relaxed attitude to smoking and drinking has resulted in a relatively low reliance on excises, even though petrol is heavily taxed in all five countries. As a consequence, revenue comes mostly from social security contributions (especially the employer's share) and general consumption taxes. Another aspect which these five countries have in common is that in contrast to those OECD countries considered in the last group, the big increase in total tax ratios has usually occurred since the mid-seventies, these ratios having remained relatively stable between 1965 and 1975 (see Table 3.4). In most recent years total tax ratios have continued to rise in Italy, Portugal and Spain, have remained relatively stable in France and have declined in Greece.

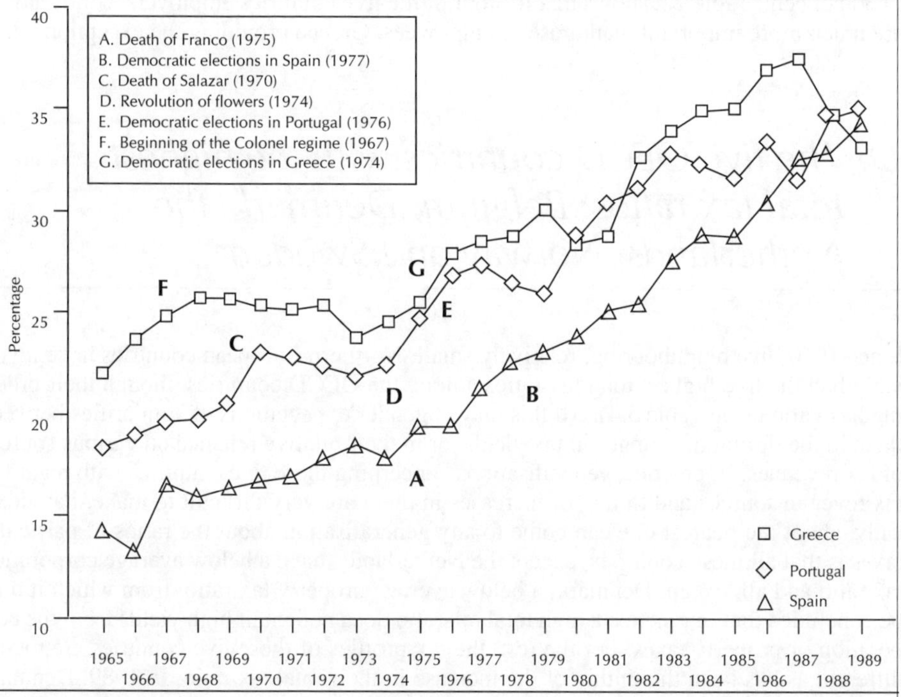

Chart 4.1: Political events as a partial explanation of changes in total tax ratios in Greece, Portugal and Spain, 1965-83

Chart 4.1 suggests that the rapid rises in total tax ratios in Greece, Portugal and Spain were due in part to the change to democratic regimes, after the periods marked G, D and B on the chart, especially in view of their stagnancy before this period. A priori one would expect that such changes would accompany a demand for increased social expenditures (entailing increased revenues) and increases in income taxes as a means of providing these revenues in the least regressive way. The trends displayed in Table 2.2 corroborate this hypothesis.

Table 2.3 shows that for all years and in all these countries, the personal income tax share is well below average, even though between 1974 and 1982, it grew considerably in Greece, Italy and Spain and by more than the OECD average. The share of corporation income tax is also well below the OECD average except in Italy. The share of social security contributions and general consumption taxes is greater than the OECD average for all these countries except that the share of general consumption tax is slightly below average in Italy. The increase over the period in the social security share was generally larger than the overall trend as was the fall in the share of consumption taxes, the consumption tax share remaining stable only in Portugal. The decline in the share of consumption taxes between 1965 and 1982 in Spain is particularly striking – around 20 percentage points, but following the introduction of VAT by 1988 it had increased from around 22 per cent to 30 per cent. Table 2.2 shows that for four of the five countries employers' contributions are much more important than those of employees, Greece providing the exception.

D. The five OECD countries with the highest total tax ratios: Belgium, Denmark, the Netherlands, Norway and Sweden

Since 1970, five neighbouring, relatively small, Northern European countries have invariably had the five highest total tax ratios among the OECD countries, though their ordering has varied (see Table 3.4). All this may engender expectations of similarities between them in the timing of changes in tax yields, or in their relative reliance on various sources of tax revenues. In practice, generalisations concerning these five countries with regard to tax revenue sources and timing of increases in them are very difficult to make. Paradoxically, about the nearest one can come to any generalisation about the ratios of particular taxes is that all these countries, except the Netherlands, have a below average corporation tax ratio and all, except Denmark, a below average property tax ratio, from which it may be concluded that in practice a high total tax ratio does not entail high yields from the corporation or property taxes. For the rest, the tax profiles of these five countries are totally different as has been the timing of the increase in their total tax ratio. In 1989, Denmark had the highest personal income tax and general consumption tax ratios of any OECD country, the Netherlands the highest employees' social security ratio, Sweden the highest employers' social security ratio and Norway the highest excise ratio , except for Ireland and Portugal.

Whilst the increase of the total tax ratio of the five countries between 1965 and 1975 was not dissimilar (annual average growth of 0.9 to 1.2 percentage points compared to an OECD average growth of 0.6 percentage points), since then growth patterns have been very different. Possibly the greatest increase ever in OECD total tax ratios was that in Denmark between 1965 and 1971 which changed from 30 per cent to 43 per cent, mainly because of an increase in the income tax ratio, due to fiscal drag and a change in collection methods. This large increase was followed by the indexation of the income tax system, the formation and growth of an anti-tax party, and a stabilisation of the total tax ratio, which was not much higher in 1982 than in 1971.

Between 1975 and 1982 there were large increases in the total tax ratios of Belgium and Sweden, moderately large increases in that of Denmark and Norway, and somewhat less in that of the Netherlands. These varying increases in the total tax revenue were due to increases in different sources of revenue: in Belgium it was the personal income tax, in Denmark the general consumption tax, in the Netherlands employees' social security contributions, in Norway corporation tax (North Sea oil) and in Sweden employers' social security contributions.

Since 1982 there has been a very large increase in the total tax ratio of Denmark and Sweden, hardly any change in the Netherlands and a decline in Belgium and Norway. Except in the case of Denmark where most of the increase was due to higher personal income tax receipts, changes in particular tax ratios were relatively slight except for a heavy decline in Norway's corporation tax ratio and a not insignificant decline in Belgium's personal income tax ratio. In 1982 Norway's corporate tax ratio was by far the highest in the OECD area but by 1989 it was only just above the OECD average (due to the decline of North Sea oil).

In most recent years there have been major tax reforms in all of these five countries, but most of them will probably not have much effect on tax ratios and structures, but one which will certainly affect tax structures is the partial integration of the personal income tax and social security contributions in the Netherlands.

E. Two disparate European countries: Germany and Ireland

In contrast to the five Northern European countries discussed in sub-section D, there is no reason to expect that the large federal Germany and the small unitary Ireland would have much in common with regard to their tax profiles and developments in them over the last twenty-five years, and in fact they do not. The contrast is chosen to illustrate the different paths that governments may follow with regard to relative stability and volatility.

German tax levels and structures have remained remarkably stable since 1975. Since the German total tax ratio peaked in 1977 at 38.1 per cent it has never fallen below 37.3 per cent, a stability which is only to be found elsewhere in OECD countries in Switzerland and the United States. Likewise, since 1975, the income tax share has remained in the region of 33 to 35 per cent, the social security share between 34 and 37 per cent and the consumption tax share between 25 and 27 per cent. Such long-term stability of tax structures is also rarely to be found in OECD countries. One possible explanation for this stability is that business and industry interests may have a stronger influence on government fiscal policy in Germany than in most other countries and business prefers tax stability; a second is that the revenue sharing formulae between the federal government and the länder (see Chapter 9) may inhibit major changes in tax structures.

In contrast tax levels and structures in Ireland have been remarkably volatile, as illustrated in a number of tables in Chapter 3 as well as the charts for Germany and Ireland at the end of this chapter. To cite a few examples:

- The total tax ratio increased from 26.0 in 1965 (below the OECD average) to 41.5 in 1988 (well above the OECD average) but fell back to 37.8 in 1989 (around the OECD average).
- The general consumption tax ratio increased from 1.5 per cent in 1985, (well below the OECD average) to 8.1 in 1989, (well above the OECD average).

- The social security ratio has almost doubled over this period though remaining below the OECD average.
- The property tax ratio fell from 3.9 in 1965 (about twice the OECD average) to 1.8 per cent (below the OECD average).
- The corporate income tax and ratio has also significantly declined from 2.4 per cent in 1965 (above the OECD average) to 1.3 in 1989 (well below the OECD average).
- The excise etc. ratios declined even more drastically from 11.3 in 1965 to 7.9 per cent in 1989, whilst remaining well above the OECD average.

The immediate cause of these fluctuations can be easily identified (e.g. taking advantage of fiscal drag and extending the income tax coverage as regards the personal income tax ratio and share, rate reductions and tax incentives as regards corporate tax, the move from a flat rate to an ad valorem on social security, the abolition of a household property tax, the introduction of first a supplementary general retail tax and then a value added tax). The underlying reasons for all these changes require a deeper analysis not undertaken here.

F. The United Kingdom: a special case

The main reason for treating the United Kingdom as a special case is that it would seem that, excluding the move away from dictatorships in certain southern European countries referred to in sub-section C, political preferences would seem to have played a more important, though by no means decisive, role here in tax level and tax structural developments than in most OECD countries. (The assumption is that the left (Labour) government would prefer higher total tax ratios and a higher personal income tax share, and that a right (Conservative) government would prefer the contrary.)

Chart 4.2 shows that as regards total tax ratios, expected political preferences prevailed between 1965 and 1974 and between 1982 and 1989, but not between 1974 and 1982. Thus, the total tax ratio consistently increased between 1964 and 1970 under the two Labour governments and consistently decreased under the 1970-74 Conservative government. Though it started to increase again under the 1974-79 Labour government, since 1975 exactly the reverse has happened: the ratio went consistently down between 1975 and 1979 and consistently up between 1979 and 1982 under the Conservative government. Since 1982 the ratio has declined. Thus apparent political preferences were overridden by other factors between 1975 and 1982.

On tax structures, the presumed preference of the Conservative government for less reliance and for Labour governments for greater reliance on the personal income tax obtained during the period 1965 to 1970 and throughout the eighties, but during the seventies such presumed preferences were overridden by other factors, as Chart 4.2 also indicates. Thus the greatest increase in the personal income tax share occurred during the Conservative 1970-74 administration, the greatest decrease during the 1974-79 Labour administration.

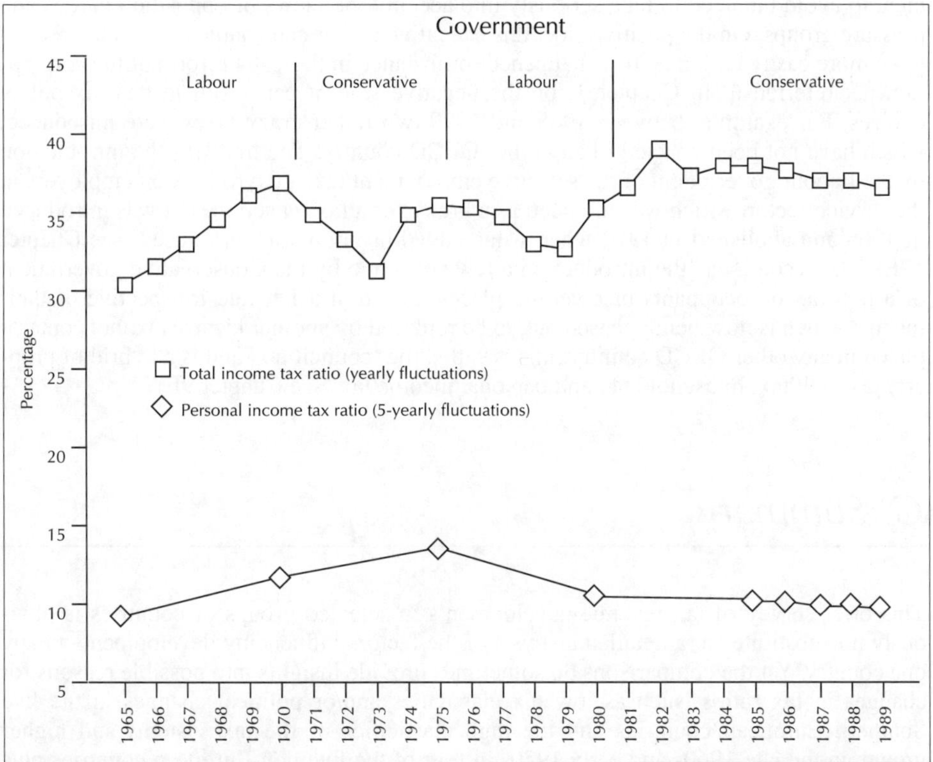

Chart 4.2: United Kingdom total tax and personal income tax ratios correlated with changes of government

It would seem that between 1970 and 1974 the factors already referred to which were conducive to a rise in total tax ratios generally and personal income tax ratios in particular outweighed any political preferences. Between 1976 and 1979 income policies were being applied in the United Kingdom in an attempt to moderate inflation and this included government commitments to limit income tax increases – then by far the most important source of United Kingdom revenue – in return for restraints in wage increases. The 1979 Conservative government had as a priority objective a reduction of the borrowing requirement and, in addition to the availability of new sources of revenue from North Sea oil, nearly doubled the rate of value added tax as part of its policy to move from income to consumption taxation and increased the unearmarked payroll tax. Taking changes in total tax ratios in the United Kingdom as a whole during the period 1965-89 (though doubtless there are other explanatory factors), it would seem that political preferences played a major part during the first ten and the last six years and economic constraints during the middle period.

Another feature of the United Kingdom is the relative strength of the executive in relation to the legislature with regard to fiscal policy choices. This is probably the result of the first past the post electoral system, not offset by any separation of powers, which usually, though not invariably, has provided the government with a parliamentary majority sufficient to avoid the need to take seriously into account the views of opposition parties and pressure groups. On the positive side, this executive power can enable rational tax reform to be more easily undertaken, as happened for instance in the 1984 reform of the corporation tax referred to in Chapter 1: on the negative side, it can result in bad tax policy choices. For example, between 1965 and 1990 two rather crazy taxes were introduced, which have not been enacted in any other OECD country. The first was the introduction by the Labour government of the selective employment tax, a payroll tax on employers in the service sector, which was intended as a proxy for a tax on services: it was introduced in 1966 and abolished in 1972 when value added taxation was introduced (see Chapter 12E). The second was the introduction a few years ago by the Conservative government of a poll tax on occupants of dwelling places, levied at a flat rate irrespective of their income which is now being phased out, to be replaced by another bizarre tax, not contemplated in any other OECD country: this is called the 'council tax' and is a hybrid of property tax, poll tax, household tax and personal income tax (see Chapter 9E).

G. Summary

This brief survey of tax revenue developments in selected groups of countries is obviously no substitute for a detailed analysis of the factors influencing developments in any one country. Yet the comparisons do sometimes provide insights into possible reasons for changes in tax ratios, such as low tax elasticities and/or political changes in the five Southern European countries and the high elasticities of the tax systems and higher growth in the late 1960s and early 1970s in four of the five non-European countries plus Switzerland. On the other hand the differences in total tax ratios, and reliance on different tax sources among the smaller, highest taxed, Northern European countries means that conclusions have to be of a negative nature, that is, if you want to have, or avoid, a high total tax ratio, there is no obvious way of going about it. The contrasting development in Germany and Ireland provides a reminder of the fact that governments have very different priorities as regards how much revenue to raise, the ways in which to raise it and the relative importance of fiscal stability and fiscal innovation. The United Kingdom scenario provides a different kind of reminder: that the political preferences of a government may be an important, but not always decisive factor in tax revenue developments and that executive power can breed strange fiscal mutations.

H. Charts illustrating countries' tax structures

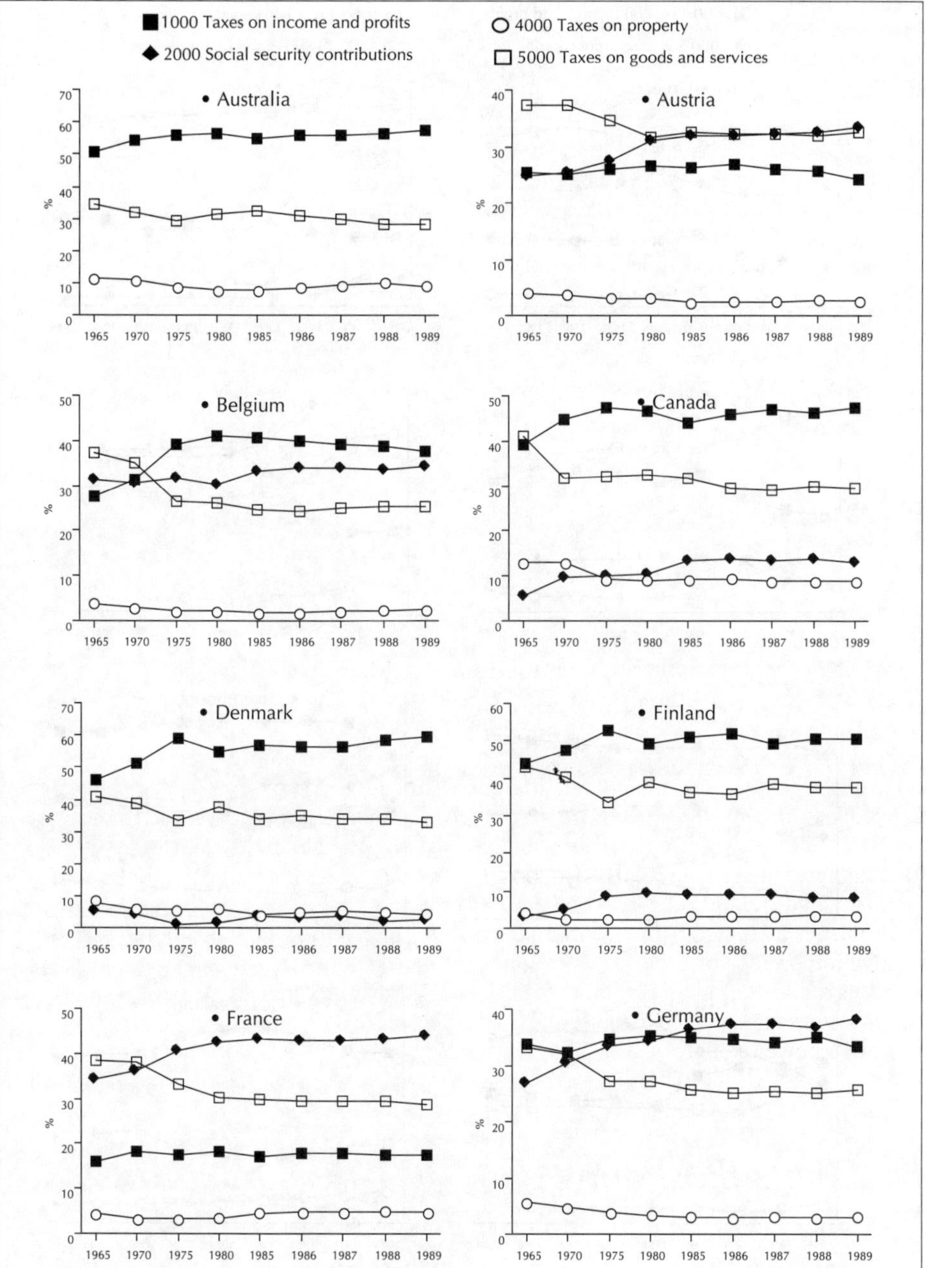

Chart 4.3: Tax structures in OECD countries between 1965 and 1989 (receipts as percentage of total tax revenue)

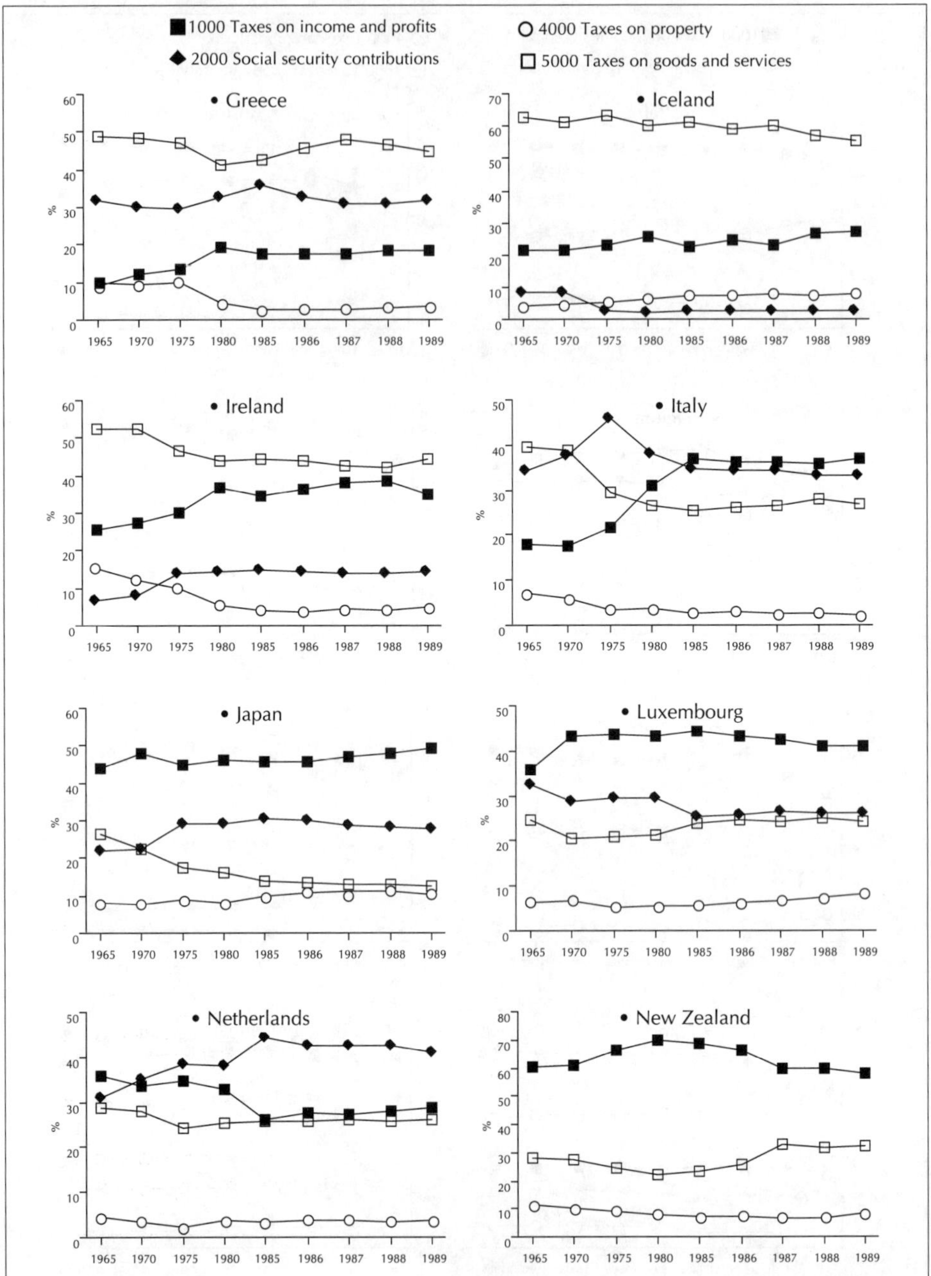

Chart 4.3(cont.): Tax structures in OECD countries between 1965 and 1989 (receipts as percentage of total tax revenue)

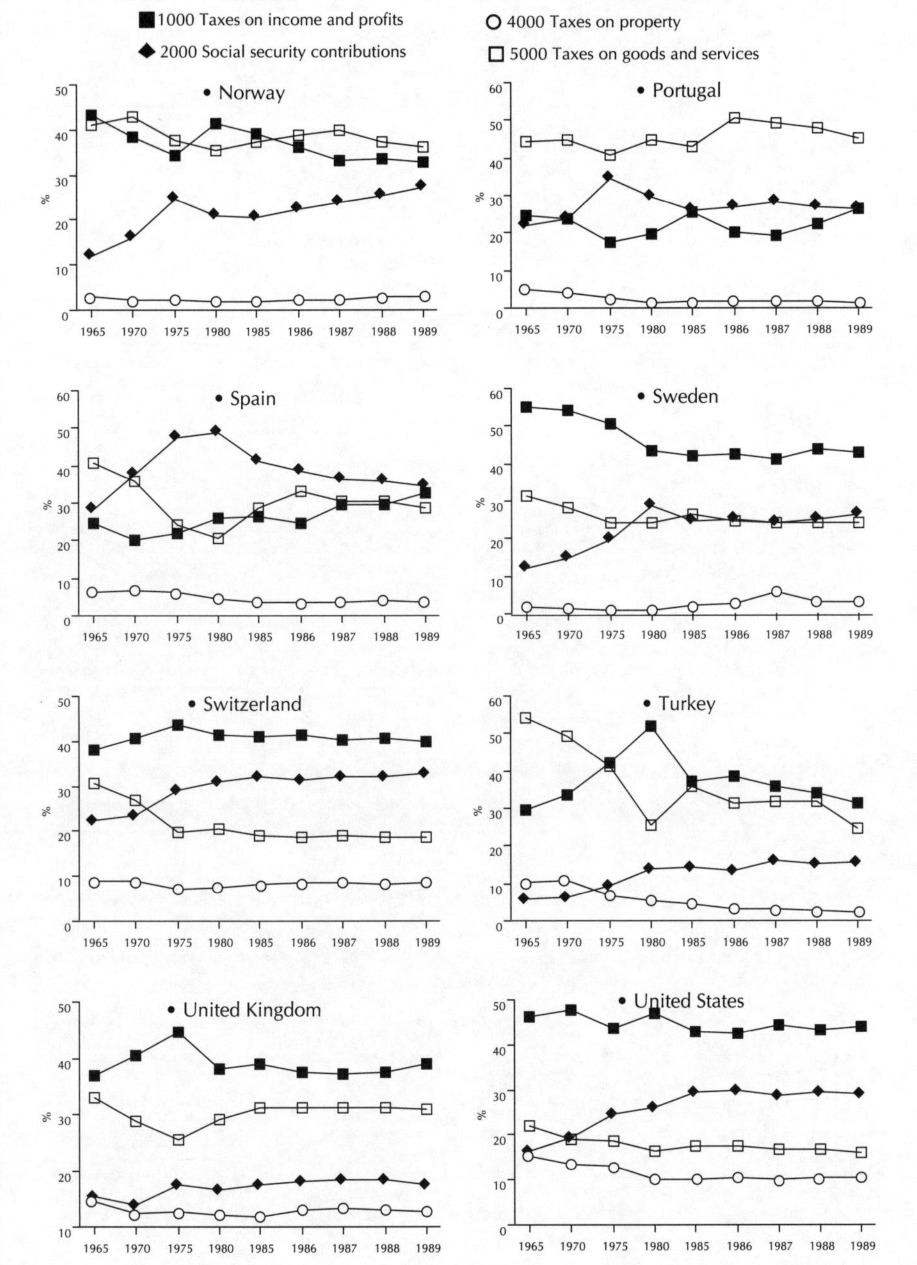

Chart 4.3(cont.): Tax structures in OECD countries between 1965 and 1989 (receipts as percentage of total tax revenue) (Source: OECD RS 1991.)

PART II
SOME ANALYTICAL AND POLICY ISSUES

Chapter 5 Irrationalities

A. Summary

As in other areas where value-judgments and emotions are involved (e.g. aesthetics, ethics, politics, psychology) irrationality permeates public finance literature and discussions of tax policy issues, and frequently this is because terms and expressions are used in an inconsistent or ambiguous way. The objective of this chapter is to identify some of these ambiguities and confusions, so that the reader will be in a better position to evaluate the arguments in favour or against various courses of action that are discussed in the remaining chapters of this book.

Although accusations are made, culprits are not identified: there are so many, that it would be invidious and unfriendly to cite examples, and in case I sound too complacent I admit to having been such a culprit myself on more than one occasion. The reasons why irrationality is so prevalent are evidently outside the scope of this book, but for those who wish to examine the question further, I mention persuasive definitions (Stevenson 1945), mistakes in the logical geography of concepts (Ryle 1949), the emotion of conflict (Rapoport 1960) and psychological reasoning difficulties (Wason and Johnson-Laird 1972)[1].

1. For more on persuasive definitions see Section C of this chapter and for further reading see Section (2) (Chapter 5) of the Bibliography in the Appendix.

Section B describes some systematic ambiguities arising from the fact that, although tax objectives are capable of being defined in objective terms, some of these goals are in practice interpreted subjectively according to particular commentators' value-judgments. Section C deals with a more debased form of ambiguity, debased because whether or not intentional, it has propaganda impact, and for this reason is referred to for dramatic effect as "newspeak ambiguity" after George Orwell's 1949 novel *Nineteen eighty-four*, even if "persuasive definitions" (Stevenson 1945) would have been a more rational title. Section D refers to some examples of "arbitrary ambiguity" which arise either because its perpetrators have wanted one term or expression to mean too much or because they have failed to appreciate important differences, but unlike "newspeak ambiguity" no propaganda is involved. Section E refers to the fact that the immediate "impact" of a tax increase on the persons who pay it is usually different from its ultimate "incidence" on the persons who bear it in the longer term in the form of lower profits, lower earned income or higher prices. The difference between "impact" and "incidence" is sometimes relevant, sometimes irrelevant, to the issues being discussed and presuppositions about the degree and timing of tax shifting sometimes require to be made explicit if dialogue is to be meaningful. Finally, Section F lists some tax illusions which may be held at various times and to varying extent both by governments and taxpayers, and which may have an influence on decisions taken.

B. Systematic ambiguity

It may be difficult to give an unequivocal meaning to some of the goals of tax reform, because they may be seen from many points of view, their interpretation may depend on value judgments and there is no unanimity on whether tax policy should be promoting any of these goals. Some of these main tax objectives are discussed in the following paragraphs.

Tax neutrality is generally seen as a situation where economic decisions are unaffected or minimally affected by tax factors. (It is also often used as a synonym for the achievement of a 'level playing field' meaning that one group of taxpayers is not advantaged or disadvantaged as a result of the system but this is strictly a question of horizontal equity). However, whenever one enters a particular area of taxation, neutrality is seen to be multifacetted and consequently ambivalent: to take three concrete examples:

- Neutrality for gainfully employed wives means something different according to whether their tax treatment is compared to that of their husbands, single women or married women outside the labour force, and tax neutrality towards the decision for a second spouse to take up paid labour normally differs from tax neutrality towards two partners getting married (see Chapter 10E3);
- In the context of the taxation of enterprises and their shareholders, statutory rates of corporate and personal income taxes as well as those on capital gains, together with indexation provisions and the treatment of the tax base are all relevant towards vari-

ous kinds of tax neutrality (a) between debt and equity capital; (b) between self-financing by enterprises and new share issues; (c) between unincorporated and incorporated enterprises (see Chapter 12D);

- Tax neutrality towards international flows of capital, services and technology is generally broken down into CEN (capital export neutrality) and CIN (capital import neutrality). Whilst some tax changes will promote both CEN and CIN, others will promote CEN to the detriment of CIN or CIN to the detriment of CEN (an issue not within the scope of this book).

Horizontal equity or the equitable tax treatment of persons with the same level of income and/or capital who differ in other relevant respects is also an ambiguous goal in that measures which promote horizontal equity between two categories of taxpayers may create inequities with a third category. The relative tax treatment of single persons, one-earner couples and two-earner couples, as discussed in Chapter 10E3, provides a case in point, and the relative treatment of occupants of dwelling places as between tenants, mortgaged and unmortgaged owners in respect of the tax treatment of interest deductions and imputed rent provides another.

Economic efficiency can be seen either as avoiding distortions in the allocation of resources through taxation so that market forces may prevail (neutrality approach) or as encouraging an improvement in the allocative function of markets by providing tax incentives to invest or to operate in particular kinds of ways (interventionist approach) or, as invariably is the case in practice, some mixture of these two approaches.

Simplification may be sought in various ways, e.g. by reducing the number of tax brackets and tax reliefs, fuller integration of the income tax and social welfare systems, changing collection methods. The effects of any such simplifications may be various. Reducing the number of rates, for example, may make the system seem simpler without having much operational effect. Changing the collection method may make the system simpler for tax administrations but more complicated for taxpayers, or simpler for one class of taxpayer but more complicated for another. For example, withholding income tax at source simplifies the task of tax administrations, but creates more work for employers, while self-assessment systems also simplify the task of tax administrators but not that of taxpayers generally. In addition, moves towards a simpler system may require transitional measures, which could render the system more complicated for a number of years.

C. Newspeak ambiguity and persuasive definitions

The language of "Newspeak" is described in full in the Appendix to Orwell's novel *Nineteen eighty-four* and three respective slogans from the Ministry of Truth are "war is peace: freedom is slavery: ignorance is strength". Newspeak in the tax propaganda literature takes the form of using an expression with a well understood factual meaning and some normative impact in a different or even opposite sense of its normal meaning to take advantage of its favourable or unfavourable normative connotation. Some newspeak expressions have become so much part of the technical tax jargon that quite expert public finance commentators have failed to appreciate that they are using such expressions in several quite incompatible ways and in a propagandistic sense.

One relatively naive use of newspeak is to sweeten the introduction of a potentially unpopular new tax by misnaming it. Already cited have been examples from the United Kingdom where an unearmarked payroll tax was called a "national insurance surcharge" and a poll tax was called a "community charge". This does little harm because it is evidently in the realm of political propaganda and in democracies opposition parties are able to identify such mis-descriptions.

More pernicious is the use of expressions with a normative flavour in several different senses to provide a pseudo-argument for or against certain tax policy choices. Two such expressions that are frequently misused in this way are "economic double taxation" (bad) and "tax neutrality" (good). The expression "economic double taxation" does have a legitimate use in the context of international double taxation to distinguish the case where *economically related* entities are subject to similar taxes by two different tax jurisdictions from that where the *same* entity is so subject (*juridical* double taxation). However, the expression is also variously used in the tax literature (a) to describe the situation that distributed profits may be subject to both corporation tax and personal income tax (b) as a synonym for the non-neutralities that arise between the tax treatment of debt, self-financing and new equities and/or between incorporated and unincorporated enterprises, of which economic double taxation in sense (a) is one, but not the only or even principal cause, or (c) as a synonym for certain causes of non-neutralities, in sense (b) such as the tax treatment of capital gains or the non-alignment of statutory rates of personal and corporate income taxes. When such an expression is used (often by the same writer) in so many different incompatible senses, it is evident that it has no rational but only a rhetorical function.

Persuasive definitions are also used to take over the favourable connotation of "tax neutrality" in order to equate it with particular kinds of tax non-neutrality. The conjuring trick takes the following form: a particularly favoured kind of tax interventionism promotes economic efficiency, and since tax neutrality also promotes economic efficiency, this particular interventionism is *really* tax neutrality. Another form of this propaganda is used in the environment literature, where tax interventionism is redefined to cover only interventionism benefitting particular groups of taxpayers, and since tax measures to achieve environmental objectives benefit the community as a whole, they are alleged not to conflict with the principle of tax neutrality. All these kinds of arguments are designed to obscure the very important conflict between "tax neutrality" in its normal sense and "tax interventionism" referred to on numerous occasions in subsequent chapters. In the present Orwellian context "tax neutrality is economic efficiency" is akin to "war is peace", "freedom is slavery" and "ignorance is strength", irrespective of whether one believes that as a general rule tax neutrality is more likely than tax interventionism to promote economic efficiency.

D. Arbitrary ambiguity

Without conscious or unconscious propaganda intent the same terms and expressions are frequently overworked to describe more than one situation, or used in different senses to conceal differences. The term "integration" is used in a variety of senses to cover everything from the conversion of the personal and corporate income tax into one single tax [as recommended by the 1966 Canadian Royal Commission (Carter) Report] to any measure of any kind which reduces the combined amount of personal and corporate tax on distributed profits. Other terms and expressions in the discussion of corporate tax systems are also used ambiguously and artificially, as summarised in the Annex to Chapter 12D. In the consumption tax field "sales taxes" sometimes means any general consumption tax, sometimes only single stage taxes, and "turnover tax" sometimes means any general consumption tax, sometimes only multi-stage taxes, and sometimes only cascade taxes. Also, the different kinds of possible value added taxes are described differently in different books (Chapter 13 deals with these terminological ambiguities in the consumption tax area). Other examples could be cited, but the obvious point that is being made is that imprecise or varying terminology begets confusion.

E. The relevance of tax shifting

There are many specific issues where unavowed assumptions are being made, but which may not be shared among discussants and because discussants are unaware of this their dialogue may be short of meaningful. One problem is that results will frequently differ according to assumptions about to what extent tax increases are shifted into lower profits, or lower wages and salaries or higher prices, how long the shifting will take and what would be the relative effect on profits, wages and salaries and prices if taxes were decreased. A second problem is what is the relevance of shifting to the issues that are being discussed? To take two contrasting examples: it is generally agreed that the shifting of the corporation tax has little, if any, relevance to the question of what is the optimal corporate tax system to adopt; at the other extreme, according to shifting assumptions, taxes on household buildings and land may be seen as very regressive or alternatively proportional or even mildly progressive (see Chapter 14C4 and 5) and this may be an important issue in determining the extent to which property taxes should be used to finance local government expenditures.

F. Tax illusions

The foregoing sections of this chapter suggest that all is not clear in tax policy discussions. There are also additional reasons for believing that taxpayers (and others) may be subject to illusions. Whether it is more important to stress that one can't fool all the people all the time or that one can fool most of the people for much of the time is something on which public finance commentators differ. This is an area in which illusions and attitudes intermix, and it is often not entirely clear, for example, whether taxpayers really are being fooled by governments into unknowingly paying more tax than they would wish, or whether they are willing to be taxed more because they want governments to spend more.

One example of the mixture of illusion and attitudes has already been cited in Chapter 3 in relation to fiscal drag and the income tax. Under withholding systems, taxpayers may look directly at their net of tax pay and, if that is increasing as a result of economic growth, be unaware that their income tax bill has increased (illusion), or if aware, be happy to forgo some of the increase in favour of improvements to social and economic welfare programmes (attitude). As remarked earlier, these illusions or attitudes were probably the main cause of the heavy increase in personal income tax ratios throughout the sixties and early seventies and its cessation thereafter when net income ceased to increase greatly in real terms and inflation became the main component of fiscal drag. Once this happened the illusion was untenable, and attitudes changed. On the other hand, it is still probably true that offsetting negative fiscal drag by increases in rates of taxes on alcoholic drinks and cigarettes is regarded by most taxpayers as a tax increase, because illusions are more likely to occur when the nominal tax take, or more precisely the price of commodities, becomes higher. What is relevant to tax choices is not only illusions and attitudes, but also taxpayer behaviour. As G. Schmölders (1977) put it in the context of work effort responses to taxation: "Attitudes had been defined as a readiness to respond in a particular way to a stimulus. The response however might be mainly (or only) a readiness to express disapproval or grumble. It might not be the readiness to change one's behaviour."

Illusions probably still widely persist among taxpayers with regard to social security contributions, which help to make increases in contributions more acceptable than increases in other taxes, for here there is an admixture of two kinds of illusion: first, there is the "insurance illusion" that the taxpayers' benefits to be received later will necessarily relate to their contributions; second, there is the "shifting illusion" that the taxpayers may well not realise that their employers' contributions are likely to be paid largely through lower wages and salaries (see Chapter 8 for more details).

Two other examples of the exploitation by governments of tax illusions, discussed more fully in the next chapter, are in their apparent invitations to voters for a free fiscal lunch. The first is the non-costing of tax incentives, which was generally prevalent before the mid-seventies and the second is deficit financing which passes the bill to the next generation. Both examples appear to offer a combination of lower taxes and higher expenditures.

Chapter 6 Tax policy and public sector developments

A. Introduction and summary

It is alleged by many economists that to tax at all is to create deadweight losses by reducing the optimum allocation of resources, even though such an assertion would hold good only if all resources in the absence of government intervention were allocated in perfectly competitive markets and without negative externalities. Such economists consider that the best tax systems are those which least affect economic and social decisions such as where to invest, whether or not to get married, to take up paid employment, etc., and since in their opinion taxation necessarily distorts, the lower the tax burden the better. This view presupposes that governments are unlikely to improve on market forces in terms of economic efficiency and/or equity, so that their role in the economy should be kept to the necessary minimum. In practice, all governments have intervened in the economy to varying, and usually growing degrees, over the last eighty years, both through direct expenditures and through the tax system (henceforth tax expenditures). The appropriate size of the public sector and the desirable degree of government intervention in the economy are essentially questions of political preferences and economic fashion, and as such, outside the scope of this book. However, these questions do raise general tax policy issues which are the subject of this chapter.

Section B deals with the choice between higher government spending and lower taxes (taking into account the government borrowing or the deferred taxation option), but primarily from the point of view of the effect on tax policy choices. The main question addressed is how far are governments influenced in their decisions by their need to meet demands for increased expenditures from their voters, or on the contrary, how far, is it the demand of voters for no or small increases in their tax burden that has to constrain the growth of government expenditures? Evidently there is an interplay in all countries between the two sets of decisions, though especially in certain larger countries such as the United Kingdom and the United States, where the spending decisions and taxing decisions go through different procedures, there may be no coherent overall tax/spending programme.

In Chapter 1C something like twenty separate factors were suggested as possible explanations for developments in total tax ratios over the last two or three decades under the headings of automatic tax elasticities, government reasons for offsetting or reinforcing the effects of automatic tax elasticities, newly available tax handles for governments and factors over which governments may have little control. No attempt was made in that chapter to discuss the numerous theories that have been advanced to explain what has happened in the past or to offer plausible predictions about what is likely to happen in the future. Indeed, the impression was deliberately left that because possible explanatory causes were so numerous and of so many different kinds, and that because there were so many differences between countries and within particular countries over time, no single general theory was likely to provide an adequate overall interpretation of what has happened or what might happen in the future.

However, because there have been a number of common developments in the OECD area and a number of general theories have been advanced by public finance economists to explain such developments, which may have had an influence on policy makers, it does seem appropriate to refer briefly to some of them, which is what this section tries to do. Nevertheless, first thoughts remain last thoughts. This brief survey suggests that there is no single theory capable of explaining the diversity of past public sector developments, nor of convincingly predicting future developments, even if some of them provide some insight into what has happened in certain countries over certain periods and suggest what might be expected to happen in the near future. Longer-term developments in total tax ratios and the size of the public sector are likely to be determined predominantly by exogenous factors, such as reactions of governments to demographic and environmental changes, the increasing interdependence of world economies and future developments in the single European market where there are conflicting demands for greater harmonisation and greater independence not only at central but also at local government level.

Section C is devoted mainly to discussing the relative advantages and disadvantages of the various means of government intervention in subsidising or penalising particular activities, regions, categories of taxpayer. This involves drawing attention to the conceptual problem of what should count as a tax expenditure and the measurement problem of how to cost the amounts of tax expenditures, but because these problems are largely of a methodological and technical nature they are mainly set out in the Annex to this chapter. However, Table 6.4 concludes the chapter with an overview of the tax relief and expenditure accounts in selected countries.

Of more policy interest is the fact that whilst until the mid-seventies the costing of tax expenditures was confined to the introduction or modification of particular tax reliefs, nowadays nearly all OECD countries cost the totality of tax expenditures and in many of them governments are under a legal obligation to do so on an annual basis. This was largely because governments became increasingly aware, at a time when they first felt the need to constrain the growth of government expenditures as a result of declining economic growth, that they required a better knowledge in quantitative terms of the loss of government revenues resulting from tax expenditures (or what were sometimes called off-budget activities to indicate that they were not subject to normal budgetary controls). Many tax concessions had been incorporated in governments' tax systems over several decades and most of them remained unnoticed even if they no longer had any rationale. Moreover, the general absence of co-ordination of tax expenditures and direct expenditures to achieve similar (sometimes even conflicting) economic or social objectives made little sense. The overall costing of tax expenditures whether through consolidated tax expenditure budgets (as in some countries) or through listing the cost of each particular tax expenditure (as in others), which has taken place during the late seventies and eighties, should have facilitated rational decision-making and enabled improved budgetary control, whatever may have happened in practice.

B. Higher government spending versus lower taxes

1. Historical perspectives

In the mid-thirteenth century, St. Thomas Aquinas said in answering the question whether it was possible for robbery to take place without sin that it could "when a sovereign ruler levies taxes in accordance with the demands for justice to promote the general welfare". F. Grapperhaus (1989), my source for this quotation, regards it as expressing ambivalence towards taxation which may be seen as a (not necessarily unjustifiable) limitation on private ownership rights and of course the justification may not be unrelated to the amount of tax demanded. Catholic ambivalence continues in modern times since [according to Webber and Wildavsky (1989, p. 549)] the official Vatican newspaper *L'Osservatore Romano* recently declared that tax evasion was not a sin, but the November 1992 Catholic Church Catechism has declared that tax evasion is a sin.

From time to time over the last thousand years taxes in general and increases in them in particular have been found unacceptable by taxpayers and have even contributed to rebellions, regicides and revolutions, as for example in England, France and the United States. Between 1880 and 1980 taxes have considerably increased in all OECD countries mostly with little taxpayer resistance. Over the last decade or so – the period varies from country to country – taxpayer resistance has become much stronger, with the consequence that increases in taxation have slowed down in a number of OECD countries and have been replaced by decreases in others (see Chapters 3B4 and 3E). This section examines theories that have been advanced to explain past choices made between lower taxes and higher government expenditures and the guidance that they could give on the direction of future choices.

2. Explanatory theories for past developments

As in many areas of discourse, analytical and normative explanations are not rigorously distinguished and preferred analytical explanations tend to conform to political and moral preferences. The left prefer demand side explanations as exemplified by A. Wagner's Law of 1883 that it is the need for higher public sector expenditure, especially on social welfare, that governs and should govern the level of total tax ratios: the right prefer supply side public choice explanations, as developed by J. Buchanan in the United States and A. Peacock and J. Wiseman in the United Kingdom, that voter preferences should determine tax levels and that without the downward pressure by taxpayers "voting with their feet", the interest of "Leviathan" as represented by the interests of bureaucrats will inexorably and irrationally increase tax burdens. Another way of characterising these two approaches is the "State rules citizen" and "citizen over State" view (S. Cnossen, 1988).

The analysis of the public choice school concerning the triangular relationship between the bureaucracy, governing politicians and the voting public seems empirically flawed, at least with regard to what happens between bureaucracy and governments in most OECD countries. There is no monolithic bureaucracy searching for higher taxation and government expenditures. Reflecting the views of their political masters, civil servants in spending departments (health, education, pensions, transport, etc.) will be advocating greater expenditures, but in practice they usually have less power than civil servants in revenue departments who will veto these demands unless their own political masters agree to them, whether because they think that such increased expenditures will help to win the next election or whether because they happen to believe that this is the most valid policy option. The Leviathan myth, as Thomas Hobbes, its genial progenitor well realised, is designed as propaganda to frighten the masses and to provide adrenalin for conservatives, or as R. Bird (1991) more delicately puts it: "The more drastic propositions sometimes associated with this school of thought seem overdone."

Another reason for rejecting this Leviathan myth, which will be obvious to anyone who has observed government at work, is that there is no predetermined monolithic government view on any tax choice. All is worked out by compromises and trade-offs between conflicting pressure groups among the bureaucrats, the private sector and the politicians. The rest of Part II provides concrete examples. For example, in the next chapter, conflicting choices are discussed on how best to achieve desired objectives with regard to composition and levels of household savings, income distribution and energy, transport and environmental policy. In each of these cases there are differences among government officials as well as the private sector, about what should be the goals to be pursued and what are the best means to pursue them. The Leviathan myth implausibly characterises the pluralistic society which exists in the real world.

Yet another point is that taxpayers' choice between lower taxes versus higher expenditures rarely occurs, outside Switzerland, at central government level. In most OECD countries, though the appropriate level of taxation and government expenditure may be a major issue in central governments elections, it is never the only one, and in practice voters normally have the choice between a package of policies and personalities and there is little that the majority of voters can do if the tax/expenditure/borrowing solution adopted by an incoming government turns out differently from what they would have wished. Even where it is generally agreed that this choice played a major part in voters' decisions as in the April 1992 United Kingdom election, most commentators have taken the view that it was not the predominant reason for the Conservative victory. (It did, however, bear out the cynical observation that when asked for their views, many voters will altruistically opt for higher expenditures, but, when actually voting, support the political party promising lower taxes). It is also relevant that in many countries there is an implicit or explicit consensus among the most important political parties that increases in tax burdens should be severely limited and this is what generally happens in practice in such countries. Even in countries where there has been general enthusiasm for improving the welfare state, there are limits to taxpayers' tolerance of increases in taxation. An extreme example reported in Chapter 4D was the case of Denmark where there was an all-time record increase in total tax ratios in the late sixties and early seventies which was followed by the formation of an influential anti-tax party and the stabilisation of the total tax ratio for ten years. (However, old habits took over and the increase during most of the eighties in the Danish total tax ratio was among the highest in OECD countries.)

The supply side analysis by Peacock and Wiseman in 1957 which argued that heavy increases in total tax ratios would be accepted by taxpayers only in times of revolution, wars and other major social upheavals, but could not be sustained in other "normal" times, provided a convincing partial explanation of changes in the size of the public sector in the period before they were writing and also of such changes since 1985. Nevertheless, even though they allowed for moderate increases in total tax ratios as a result of automatic tax elasticities and taxpayers' illusions, such a theory could hardly explain the massive increase in the public sector that occurred in nearly all OECD countries between 1955 and 1985. The theories of A. Wagner and subsequent demand side theorists provide a more convincing explanation of developments over this period. Between 1955 and around 1975 there was economic growth and increased standards of living in most industrialised countries and a corresponding readiness of taxpayers to accept more tax burdens to contribute to a better welfare state. Though from around 1975, following the first oil shock, economic growth slackened, it took another ten years for the tax backlash to manifest itself in most industrialised OECD countries. Such factors, already referred to in Chapter 2, as the positive automatic elasticities of the most important taxes, plus the new tax handles, plus increased borrowing, plus greater technical efficiency in tax administrations, plus the increasing use of tax expenditures, all facilitated the growth of the public sector in most OECD industrialised countries.

Supply side theories have provided a more convincing explanation than demand side theories of developments since 1985. But as R. Bird (1991) argues, the constraint on public growth is probably due to disenchantment with government spending programmes resulting from the stagnation of middle-class incomes, which itself led to calls for smaller government and privatisation, first in the United Kingdom and United States and, more recently, in nearly all OECD industrialised countries.

The "inertia theory", as developed especially by R. Rose (1985), takes the view that both governments and taxpayers have a common interest in leaving things alone: if not too oppressed, taxpayers prefer the old taxes that they have lived with and do not wish for radical changes, and governments too prefer, other things being equal, a quiet life on the tax reform front, taking the plausible view that voters who may gain from tax returns are less likely to change their voting patterns than those who lose. However, voter discontent or government perceptions of it may overcome inertia, as illustrated by the recent wave of income tax reforms, as may also governments' eagerness to utilise a new tax handle like VAT, however hostile the initial reactions of voters. It is probably more appropriate to regard inertia as one of many influences on public sector developments than as a major determinant.

Another interesting theory, which seems better to explain developments between 1965 and 1985 than in more recent years, is that formulated by S. Peltzman (1980) that reduced inequality of income stimulates growth of government. The greater the inequality between taxpayers in a prior period, the less they are inclined to support redistributative spending in a later period, or conversely, "the counter-intuitive result that on balance, more equality breeds a political demand for still more income equalisation runs through virtually all our data". As noted in Chapter 2, Peltzman's findings on expenditure trends were corroborated by the predominant divergence of total tax ratios that astonished many of us over many years as we read about the increasingly global economy. However, since around 1985, convergence has predominantly taken over from divergence on the tax side and presumably also on the spending side.

One question that arises is whether there is any causal link between the wave of reforms to the personal and corporate income taxes that have occurred in nearly all OECD countries since the mid-eighties and the stagnation of total tax ratios in most of them since then. Though these reforms were generally intended to be, and were mostly revenue neutral, it seems unlikely that the reforms themselves were responsible for the stagnation of total tax ratios. As already indicated, lower economic growth and higher unemployment levels are more likely to be responsible for this stagnation. The demand for greater tax neutrality and international competition, following from the rate reductions of personal and corporate income tax in the United Kingdom and United States, are mainly responsible for the income tax reforms in many other countries.

3. The deficit financing option

Another factor in interpreting the past and forecasting the future of developments in total tax ratios is the extent to which governments feel able and are willing to fund expenditures by borrowing, leaving it for future generations to pay the bill so incurred. Whilst it is generally accepted that in the short term such deficits may be a valid way of boosting economies during a period of recession, there is virtual unanimity among all commentators that in the longer term deficit financing is both irrational and immoral. Even self-declared fiscal conservatives such as C. McLure (1988) have gone on record as preferring tax increases to continuing fiscal deficits in the United States, and S. Cnossen (1988), in the same volume in the European Community context, provides a John the Baptist style warning that: "We are living through the Dies Irae of public finance and it is going to be a long reckoning!"

Table 6.1 shows that between 1974 and 1982 nearly all OECD governments used the deficit financing option and some very heavily. Over the eighties there was a steady fall in budget deficits in most countries[1], but as Table 6.2 shows this fall has come to an end since 1989, and in most countries the situation is likely to worsen in 1992 with little improvement foreshadowed in 1993. Most OECD governments have gone on record as deploring this situation, but seem to have subscribed to St. Augustine's[2] "Give me chastity and continency, but not yet".

Table 6.1: Trends in general government net lending in selected OECD countries, 1960-1982 (Percentage of nominal GDP)

	Average 1960-1966	Average 1967-1973	Average 1974-1982
Australia	1.5	1.7	-1.1
Austria (1964-1982)	1.2	0.6	-2.1
Canada	-0.8	0.8	-2.0
Denmark (1971-1982)	n.a.	4.3	-2.3
Finland	2.3	3.9	2.1
France	0.5	0.5	-1.1
Germany	1.2	-0.1	-3.2
Iceland (1960-1980)	3.2	0.9	-0.1
Ireland (1970-1981)	n.a.	-3.6	-9.7
Italy	-1.8	-4.5	-9.6
Japan (1970-1980)	n.a.	1.0	-3.6
Luxembourg (1960-1980)	n.a.	2.7	2.0
Netherlands (1960-1979)	-0.6	-0.4	-2.0
Norway	3.9	4.4	3.6
Portugal (1960-1976)	-0.2	1.3	-4.7
Spain (1964-1981)	-0.2	0.4	-1.1
Sweden	3.3	4.2	-0.8
United Kingdom	-1.1	-0.5	-3.8
United States	0.2	-0.5	-1.6

n.a. = not available.
Source: *OECD, Annual National Accounts,* taken from P. Saunders and F. Klau (OECD Economic Studies, Spring 1985).

1. Webber and Wildavsky (1988) note (pages 556-7) that reducing the budget deficit was the (achieved) objective of at least 18 OECD countries at various periods between 1975 and 1986, no reference in that book being made to Greece, Iceland, Ireland, Luxembourg, New Zealand and Turkey.
2. Also figures just published in Table 8 of *OECD Economic Outlook no. 52* (December 1992), but not reproduced here, indicate that all OECD countries except Japan, are expected to remain in deficit in 1994.

Table 6.2 : General government financial balances[1], 1986-1993
Surplus (+) or deficit (-) as a percentage of nominal GNP/GDP

	1986	1987	1988	1989	1990	1991	1992	1993
United States[2]	-3.4	-2.5	-2.0	-1.6	-2.5	-3.0	-3.8	-2.7
Japan[3]	-0.9	+0.5	+1.5	+2.4	+3.1	+2.4	+1.9	+1.8
Germany[3]	-1.3	-1.9	-2.1	+0.2	-1.8	-2.9	-3.4	-3.3
France	-2.7	-1.9	-1.7	-1.1	-1.4	-2.1	-2.3	-2.3
Italy	-11.6	-11.0	-10.7	-9.9	-10.9	-10.2	-11.3	-10.8
United Kingdom	-2.3	-1.2	+1.2	+1.2	-0.7	-1.7	-4.6	-5.2
Canada	-5.4	-3.8	-2.6	-3.1	-3.8	-5.5	-4.6	-3.2
Total of above countries[4]	-3.2	-2.3	-1.6	-0.9	-1.6	-2.3	-3.0	-2.5
Australia	-1.8	-0.2	+1.5	+1.6	+1.4	-2.2	-4.0	-2.7
Austria	-3.7	-4.3	-3.0	-2.7	-2.1	-2.3	-2.0	-2.1
Belgium	-9.0	-7.2	-6.4	-6.3	-5.3	-6.0	-5.5	-5.0
Denmark	+3.4	+2.4	+0.6	-0.5	-1.4	-2.0	-2.1	-1.1
Finland	+0.8	-1.5	+1.3	+2.9	+1.4	-5.0	-7.7	-6.3
Greece	-12.6	-12.3	-13.8	-17.7	-18.6	-17.1	-14.5	-12.3
Ireland[3]	-11.5	-9.1	-4.9	-1.8	-2.0	-1.9	-1.9	-2.5
Netherlands	-6.1	-6.5	-5.1	-5.1	-5.3	-2.7	-3.4	-2.7
Norway	+5.9	+4.8	+2.7	+1.6	+2.6	-0.5	-2.9	-2.8
Spain	-6.0	-3.2	-3.2	-2.8	-4.0	-4.4	-4.9	-3.9
Sweden	-1.3	+4.3	+3.5	+5.5	+4.1	-1.5	-4.1	-4.8
Total of above smaller countries[4]	-3.6	-2.3	-1.9	-1.7	-2.1	-3.6	-4.4	-3.8
Total of above European countries[4]	-4.0	-3.5	-3.0	-2.2	-3.3	-4.0	-4.9	-4.8
Total of above OECD countries[4]	-3.2	-2.3	-1.7	-1.0	-1.7	-2.4	-3.2	-2.6

1. On an SNA basis except for the United States, the United Kingdom, Australia, Greece and Sweden, where the data are based on national methods.

2. Excludes capital outlays for the Resolution Trust Corporation (RTC).

3. Percentage of nominal GNP.

4. 1987 GDP weights and exchange rates.

Source: Table 8 of *OECD Economic Outlook no. 51* (OECD June 1992).

4. Tax levels and taxpayers' perceptions

a) Tax visibility and taxpayers' surplus

The greater the visibility of a tax the more unpopular it is likely to be. It is impossible to disguise the visibility of some taxes such as those on death or immovable property. Taxpayers are aware that they are paying income tax and social security contributions, but may not notice how much if, as in nearly all OECD countries, they are withheld at source. Though the introduction of pay-as-you-earn for income tax was taken on efficiency grounds, it lessens the transparency of the tax and thereby illustrates the conflicts governments may have between the transparency and acceptability of taxation: their choice between these two objectives may depend on whether they wish to increase or decrease taxes and government expenditures. An amusing example that I encountered in the sixties when working on border tax adjustments was that in some countries there was a legal obligation on traders to indicate the amount of general consumption tax in the price charged to purchasers and in other countries there was a legal obligation not to indicate it.

How willing taxpayers are to pay more taxes depends on how satisfied they are with the way governments spend the moneys so raised. Of course this will vary among taxpayers, but it can be assumed that most taxpayers will favour increased real expenditure on health, education and recreation. R. Bird (1982) constructed an index of tax visibility and taxpayers' surplus in Canada for the years 1947 to 1977 and found that taking the year 1947 to be 100 the index of tax visibility had risen to 177 but the index of taxpayers' surplus, measured by the increase in real expenditure on health, education and recreation, had risen only to 115. He took this to be a major factor in taxpayers' complaints about growing taxation.

b) *Fiscal justice*

The willingness of taxpayers to take the higher tax/greater government spending route will evidently be influenced by how far they regard the operation of the tax system as relatively fair and this will depend upon both the tax provisions themselves and the way in which they are administered.

J. Lucas (1980) observed in his chapter on fiscal justice:

> Tax law, like other forms of law, depends on being generally accepted for its being generally observed. Although some taxes can be exacted in the teeth of public opposition, just as some criminal statutes can be enforced on an unwilling public – and it is a counsel of fiscal expediency to choose levies that can be adequately exacted with a minimum of co-operation – public support for a tax is invaluable, and its absence in the long run fatal. Nobody likes paying taxes, but if the tax, and the tax system generally, is just, few people will go so far as to evade them, and those who do will keep quiet about it. If, however, either a particular impost or the whole system is unjust, those who are being done down by it will not see any reason why they should not escape, by any effective stratagem, being mulcted. First avoidance, then evasion, will become respectable and widespread. And, as we shall see later, once people begin to think that others are not paying their share, they will resent being dunned themselves. There is then a widespread collapse of confidence in the tax system, with taxes being regarded as the arbitrary impositions of rapacious tax-gatherers, which everyone should do his utmost to fend off, ending with a general collusion on the part of the public to defeat the requisitions of the public fisc. The only reliable protection against avoidance and evasion is public opinion and private conscience, and therefore, even if our ultimate concern were only that of expediency, justice would still be, fiscally speaking, the best policy.

c) *Public relations*

Lucas describes the limit case of a particular tax or whole tax system perceived as unjust, which has rarely happened in OECD countries, although he did forecast quite precisely what was to happen to the British poll tax seven or eight years later. The more general situation is reflected by the growing effort of OECD governments over recent years to persuade their taxpayers that the tax system and the way it is operated are mainly fair and to invite their co-operation in improving its fairness. As OECD 1990 puts it:

> Many countries are seeking to improve the service provided to the taxpayer, in part because modern tax systems require increased co-operation from the taxpayers if they are to operate efficiently and also as a result of changing attitudes towards the role of the tax administration vis-à-vis the taxpayer. This co-operation is more likely to be forthcoming if there is mutual trust between the taxpayer and the administration and if the taxpayers' rights are clearly set out and protected.

The details of these "massaging" techniques for improving tax compliance go beyond the scope of this book, but Table 6.3 which reproduces the contents of OECD 1990 indicates the kinds of action involved. The relevance of all this to the present discussion is that even in countries where tax compliance is regarded as high, it is generally believed that improved tax compliance would considerably increase total tax ratios without any changes to the tax law or alternatively allow existing yields to be maintained even if tax rates were reduced.

5. Predicting future developments

Some attempts have already been made in Chapters 2 and 3 to predict what will happen to total tax ratios in the short to medium term where it was forecast that they are likely to continue to rise gently during the nineties in most countries, but probably not between 1991 and 1993 because of the general economic recession.

Over the longer term, a reading of the articles in *Tax policy in the twenty-first century* by so many experts has to daunt any confident speculation. The nearest that one finds to unanimity is that the future of personal income tax revenues does not look too bright with what V. Tanzi describes as the atomisation of productive processes, or make your own shoes etc. at home, which renders also the possibility of greater VAT evasion. On the other hand, the information powers of the fisc continue to increase both at the domestic and at the international level, which may balance out revenue losses through tax evasion. The aging of the population is going to influence matters in one way or another: the old have the power of the ballot box as well as greater influence on government decisions, but as the young have increasingly to subsidise the old there could well be a young taxpayers' revolution. A number of plausible hypotheses are put forward by various contributors to *Tax policy in the twenty-first century*, but confident predictions as to whether the tax take and government expenditures will increase or decrease relative to where we are now are invariably lacking. There is a pertinent comment from R. Bird who, adopting what he called a rear-window approach, noted that the enormous increase in total tax ratios between 1937 and 1987 was generally matched by an equally enormous increase between 1887 and 1937. But like other contributors he wisely hedges his bets saying:

> The great growth of the public sector throughout the industrialised world during the past 100 years... is surely one of the most striking phenomena of the 20th century. The question of whether this prolonged period of growth, has now come to an end, as many seem to assume, is critically important to all those concerned with social and economic matters, including tax policy.

He concludes this article by saying that "... 'may you live in interesting times' is said to have been an ancient Chinese curse...". I suggest that the pace and nature of future tax

Table 6.3: Table of contents of *Taxpayers' rights and obligations* (OECD 1990)

policy changes in various countries will, in the end, be governed primarily by how "interesting their future turns out to be" – which in a sense echoes the views of Peacock and Wiseman (1957) cited above.

C. Tax expenditures versus direct expenditures

1. The concept of tax expenditures

In the late sixties and early seventies there was much debate between S. Surrey, who was above all responsible for developing the concept of "tax expenditures" and B. Bitker who was sceptical about the useability or usefulness of such a concept, a debate excellently summarised by C. Shoup (1975). Following Surrey's book *Pathways to tax reform: the concept of tax expenditures* in 1973 and the introduction of consolidated tax expenditure accounts in Germany and the United States shortly afterwards, most OECD governments came to agree that the concept was both useable and useful as an aid for rational decision-making and government control. However, whilst all countries agreed that information on tax reliefs was necessary to make rational policy choices, there remained differences of views about how this information should be made available and about the practical feasibility of incorporating such information into consolidated tax expenditure accounts.

The somewhat technical definitional and measurement problems are discussed in the annex to this section and here it is sufficient to say that "tax expenditures" are defined in various ways in terms of departures from a "norm", "benchmark", "basic or generally accepted" tax structure and the expression "tax expenditures" was chosen in part to emphasise their similarity to direct expenditure programmes in that they are alternative ways of achieving the same kinds of economic and social objectives, and in part to indicate that they should be subject to similar budgetary control procedures as direct government expenditures.

In the early seventies other writers such as M. Weidenbaum (1970) preferred the expression "tax aids" to "tax expenditures" to stress the fact that though there were obvious parallels between expenditures through the tax and through the transfer systems, there were also some important and less obvious differences. This terminological dispute also reflected to some extent a difference of view between those who considered that the onus was on those advocating expenditures through the tax system (a view tended to be taken by Surrey), and those who considered that the choice between subsidising any particular activity or group of people through the tax or the transfer systems should be considered on its own merits. Because the political impetus behind the costing of tax subsidies was to subject them to normal budgetary control and because Surrey was the generally accepted pioneer of such analysis, since the mid-seventies, the expression "tax expenditures" has been universally adopted and is accordingly used in this section.

Tax expenditures can take many different forms and R. Bird (1980) has produced a useful taxonomy and analysis of them. It is beyond the scope of this book to discuss these differences, but many practical examples are noted in subsequent chapters (e.g. Chapter 7D)

2. Arguments for and against the use of tax expenditures

a) General considerations

The underlying assumption in this sub-section is that governments have decided on what should be the approximate amount of their expenditures and the question to be resolved is how much should be done through tax expenditures and how much through direct expenditures. In most countries nowadays this is a reasonably realistic assumption, since tax expenditures are as, or almost as, transparent as direct expenditures. However, for most of the last three decades this has not been the case in most OECD countries. Before tax expenditures were increasingly brought under budgetary control, they provided a means, not so much for governments systematically to increase public expenditure, but rather to provide sweeteners to powerful pressure groups, who first obtained their tax subsidy and then were able to retain it because it was well hidden. Such tax subsidies frequently offended not only against horizontal and vertical equity, but also against economic efficiency and in the United States these unfortunate aspects of tax expenditures were considerably reduced in two stages: first S. Surrey and associates were the driving force in persuading the government to make the cost of tax expenditures transparent as from 1975 and then J. Pechman and associates provided the intellectual stimulus for the 1986 Tax Reform which abolished or reduced many of the worst of them.

However, even in the bad old days when nobody knew how much governments were spending and redistributing income (regressively) through expense-related tax expenditures, a quite convincing rationale could be made for their selective use. Such a rationale was provided by S. Steinmo (1986), who focused on the Swedish experience with tax expenditures. Five quotations from that important but relatively unknown article are now made to indicate that the choice between tax expenditures and direct expenditures remains an important tax policy issue:

> "Most criticisms of tax expenditures are in fact criticisms of poorly designed tax expenditures and should not be put forward as critiques of the instruments themselves. To the extent that the critique of tax expenditures in the United States is generalizable, it is more appropriately directed toward the political process that poorly uses these tax instruments rather than the products of this process. It is the American policy process to which reformers should direct their attention. Indeed, it is interesting to note the similarity between the liberal critique of tax expenditures, which argues that these tools are so often misused that they should simply be kept off the budget, and the conservative attack on state welfare programs, which argues that many (or most) direct expenditure programs are poorly designed and therefore should be cut back."

> "The Swedish authorities have opened a series of very deep "loopholes", or tax expenditures, in which capitalists are able to hide a significant share of their profits from tax authorities. In contrast to most tax expenditures in America, especially for corporate capital, these fiscal incentives are widely seen to have contributed to the broadly approved socioeconomic objectives of growth stability and high employment. Thus, by many measures these tax incentives in

Sweden can be viewed as quite successful. However, if one were to apply the standards of judgment implied in the American critique of tax expenditures, one would almost certainly doom them as inappropriate, wasteful, and unfair."

"What has gone wrong? If tax expenditures are good, then why aren't more of them better? Here one can see tax expenditures as a more generalized political phenomenon. Tax expenditures worked in Sweden when they were discretionary, when central elites used them to favor some particular segment in society in the short run for the benefit of the whole in the longer run. This discretion depended on a degree of autonomy from social and political interests on the part of the political elite elected to represent those interests. As that autonomy diminished – as the center became less able to overrule the short-term demands of their constituency – the policy instruments that once successfully promoted the general welfare became overused and ultimately wasted. The instruments, then, became the subject of new criticisms because they no longer achieved the goals they were originally designed to achieve."

"The tax measures discussed in this paper are intellectually fascinating precisely because they stand out as such inegalitarian measures in a highly egalitarian society. Swedish policymakers possess other fiscal instruments, such as the wealth tax, through which they can redistribute income and wealth in society. Social Democratic elites interviewed for this study, however, firmly believed that the most important forces which have contributed to income equalization in Sweden have been high growth, full employment, and the generous social welfare programs for which Sweden is so famous. Rather than use corporate taxation as another means of squeezing the rich, corporate tax policy has instead been used as an instrument of government economic policy. Tax expenditures have been an essential element of that policy."

"The other major lessons that can be drawn from this case study are directed toward the criterion and assumptions used to evaluate these policy instruments. First, to be effective as instruments of economic policy, tax expenditures should be unequally distributed and economically nonneutral. This, of course, is not to suggest that possessing these characteristics will inherently make them useful. Second, even if tax expenditures do not "induce" a particular activity, it may be acceptable to discriminate in favor of some types of firms over others simply because they engage in certain activities. Tax expenditures are a means, but not the only means, through which this type of subsidy can take place. Finally, if expenditures are to be effective policy tools, they must be used sparingly. As the tax code becomes more crowded with various special incentives, the marginal effect of each is minimized. In other words, a small number of very deep loopholes for the few is more effective than lots of shallow loopholes for the many. "

b) *Transparency and budgetary control*

The use of tax expenditures makes it easier for governments to stay within their spending limits because they are recorded as potential revenue losses rather than expenditure increases. Moreover, since government intervention is frequently measured by total tax receipts and government expenditures as a percentage of GDP, one way to get these ratios down without actually changing government intervention in the economy is to convert a transfer payment into a tax expenditure equivalent, or alternatively to classify some "mongrel cases" such as non-wastable tax credits or premiums paid through the tax system (see Annex to Chapter 2E) as tax expenditures rather than as transfer payments in the government accounts. Moreover, the lack of regular review of these tax expenditures compared with that of direct expenditures may from one point of view be seen as preserving their stability and from another of making it more difficult to abolish tax expenditures that have outlived their usefulness (e.g. those given to subsidise declining industries such as shipbuilding) which in turn impedes structural adjustment goals. The conflict between flexibility and transparency, already discussed in Chapter 1 is doubtless the main factor influencing attitudes towards the viability of tax expenditures, but there are others.

c) Other differences between tax and direct expenditures

Effects on revenues. In the longer run an increase in either direct expenditures or tax expenditures requires increased taxation or increased borrowing. In the short run an increase in direct expenditures does not affect total tax ratios whereas an increase in tax expenditures reduces total tax ratios.

Predictability of tax revenues. The costs of a tax expenditure may be more difficult to estimate than an equivalent direct expenditure programme because the value of the subsidy to taxpayers will change as effective rates of tax change, so that an increase in income tax rates will generally increase the value of a tax expenditure, and because sometimes there will be no costs (e.g. when enterprises make no profits).

Recipients of benefits. Apart from the relatively rare case of non-wastable tax credits, tax expenditures benefit only those paying taxes, which is not normally the case with direct expenditures.

Automaticity of benefits. Tax expenditures are usually provided automatically and direct expenditures usually require a claim. This means that the take-up ratios of tax expenditures is likely to be higher and the benefits received more rapidly.

Administrative cost. It would seem likely, though by no means necessary, that tax expenditures will be cheaper to administer than direct expenditures. Relative costs are likely to vary from project to project and country to country depending upon institutional structure and on the nature of the tax system.

d) Some additional advantages of tax expenditures

Tax expenditures may be seen as more flexible than direct expenditures, first because they allow the individual or firm to determine how much the particular activity is to be supported and secondly because of the variety of instruments which may be used. For example, if it is wished to encourage investment by profitable firms a tax allowance enables such firms to gain most; if it is wished to provide assistance to those with low income, this can be done by non-wastable tax credits.

A point made by C. Shoup (1975) is that a tax expenditure decentralises decision-making in a way that may be desirable. Contributions to religious bodies provide an example, where the taxpayer alone decides which religious body is to be given government money, thus relieving legislators of the delicate and perhaps socially divisive task of allocating government money between several candidates.

e) Some additional disadvantages of tax expenditures

Modifications to the tax system to influence specific economic or social objectives may have a number of secondary effects, which governments have to take into account (for example, on government revenues, prices, payment levels, income distribution and international competitiveness) both in the short and longer term. While this may also be true of direct subsidies, it is usually less difficult in the latter case to evaluate the results.

The widespread use of tax expenditures increases the complexity of the tax system and obscures the difference between actual and potential revenue collections. This may make it difficult for governments, the legislature, and the public generally to recognise the overall impact of tax expenditures on the tax system. A proliferation of tax expenditures could also overburden the assessment process.

Tax expenditures can sometimes be utilised for tax avoidance purposes by adapting them for purposes for which they were never intended (e.g. tax subsidies for manufacturing have been used for leasing).

Apart from non-wastable tax credits, which may be considered as essentially direct expenditures that use the tax system as a delivery mechanism, tax expenditures cannot relieve poverty and are in practice mostly regressive.

f) Ambivalent conclusions

Rationality suggests that as matters now stand, with many tax expenditures almost as transparent and subject to budgetary control as direct expenditures, there is little point in generalising about the relative merits of tax expenditures and direct expenditures as a means of implementing government policies. Conclusions depend, amongst other things, on the goals of the programme, the type of tax expenditure and direct expenditure used, the characteristics of the income tax system and on the administrative structure which exists in a given country. Under certain circumstances a tax expenditure may be preferable; under others a direct expenditure. Conflicts between competing goals occur: a tax expenditure may theoretically be less equitable but in practice it may be administratively convenient; a direct expenditure may be more effective in alleviating poverty but may reach fewer of the eligible claimants.

It would seem appropriate to examine whether each expenditure project, on the basis of the criteria referred to above, is best financed through tax expenditures or direct expenditures, or some mixture of the two. One example of such an examination is provided in Chapter 10E4 in a discussion of how parents may best be aided through the tax/transfer system. However, it is not possible to cover the enormous number of areas where the choice between tax expenditures and direct expenditures or a mixture of the two occur once governments have decided that they should subsidise, for example, agriculture, charities, culture, education, health, regional policy, research and development, retirement schemes, savings, small and medium enterprises and transport.

One can make certain generalisations. For example, small and medium enterprises generally make little taxable profit in their first years and what profit they do make is often paid out in wages and salaries, so that direct subsidies or low-interest loans would appear to be a more effective means than tax expenditures of subsidising them. It is also probably true that some kinds of tax expenditures are better than others. The cost of a reduced rate of personal or corporate income tax for certain activities or certain groups of taxpayers may be difficult to calculate and difficult for political reasons to withdraw, even if no longer justifiable on economic grounds and the same goes for many concessions affecting the corporate income tax base, especially if given through depreciation allowances. On the other hand, tax credits, being flat amounts, are easy to cost and can be as transparent as direct expenditures.

Finally, the conclusion that each case should be considered on its own merits does not imply disagreement with the opinion of various commentators from C. Shoup (1975) to the Ruding Committee (1992) that on balance direct expenditures are likely to be preferable to tax expenditures in most instances. Nor does it call into question the findings of various surveys which have suggested that the cost of corporate income tax expenditures in terms of revenue forgone *frequently* exceeds the amount of investment induced which probably also applies to the cost of many direct expenditures.

Table 6.4: A brief overview of tax relief and expenditure accounts in selected countries

	First application	Statutory obligation	Coverage	Contents	Classification	Quantification	Measurement concept
Australia	1981-2 budget statement	No	Federal income, sales and payroll taxes	160 tax expenditures and description of objectives	By functional category	Periodic evaluation. No aggregation	Mixed: revenue forgone and revenue gain, accrual figures
Austria	1979 annual subsidy report	Yes	Federal government taxes	Detailed analysis of main subsidies and link with expenditures	By type of tax, function and beneficiary	Annual evaluation and aggregation	Revenue forgone, accrual figures
Canada	1979 Budget presentation. Regular updates	No	Federal individual and corporate income taxes and sales and excise taxes	220 tax expenditures. Data plus description of major provisions	By objective, beneficiary and type of tax	Periodic evaluation. No aggregation	Revenue forgone, accrual figures
France	1981 law; annual report appears in "Ways and Means" Annex to project law	Yes	Direct and indirect taxes of the State	350 tax expenditures. Analytical data description of major provisions	By objective, beneficiary and type of tax	Annual evaluation. No aggregation	Revenue gain, cash figure
Germany	1959 first publication. 1967 law required biennial reports on direct and tax subsidies	Yes	All Federal taxes and some Länder taxes	Detailed analysis of 122 tax expenditures and link with direct expenditures	By objective, beneficiary and type of tax	Biennial evaluation. Aggregation by sector of overall economy	Revenue forgone, accrual figures
Ireland	1981 Annual Revenue Commissioners' Report	No	Central Government personal and corporate income tax	Listing and evaluation of main tax reliefs	By type of tax	Annual evaluation. No aggregation	Revenue forgone, accrual figures
Portugal	1980	No	Income taxes only	Listing of evaluation of certain reliefs	By type of relief and tax	Annual evaluation. No aggregation	Revenue forgone, accrual figures
Spain	1978 law. Annual submission to Parliament	Yes	Direct and indirect taxes of Central Government	Listing of main tax expenditures	By type of tax and function	Annual evaluation. Aggregation	Revenue gain, cash figure
United Kingdom	1979 first report in this area. Listing of all tax relief in annual White Paper	No	Direct taxes of Central Government	Analysis of over 100 tax reliefs. Data plus description of major provisions	By type of tax	Annual evaluation where data available. No aggregation	Revenue forgone, accrual figures
United States	1968 annual expenditure budget. 1974 law required annual report in the Federal Budget	Yes	Federal personal and corporate income tax	Analysis of 87 tax expenditures. data plus description of major provisions	By type of tax and by functional areas	Annual evaluation of individual items. Aggregation	Outlay equivalence, and revenue forgone. accrual figures

Source: *Tax expenditures: a review of the issues and country practices* (OECD 1984).

Chapter 7
Some economic and social issues

A. Summary

This chapter covers five areas of economic and social policy where tax decisions may play or be seen to play an important part. The rationale for treating these five disparate topics in one chapter is that each of them provides an example of conflicting policy objectives which have been high on the political agenda of many OECD countries. Also each of them involves more than one kind of tax, so that they cannot be conveniently fitted into Chapters 10 to 14 which deal in detail with country practices regarding one particular kind of tax. Finally, each provides a concrete illustration of those objectives on which tax policy can apparently have an influence such as equity and allocative efficiency, as distinct from those where the impact of tax policy choices is likely to be much more uncertain, for example, on economic growth, macroeconomic stability and balance of payments improvements.

Section B deals with the relationship between taxation and household savings. The level of saving, especially in a country with a relatively closed economy, may affect the rate of capital formation of economic growth and the standard of living. Table 7.1 shows that in nearly all countries there was a substantial fall during the first half of the eighties in all the three components of saving (private household, private corporate and government) and that in nearly all countries private household savings are by far the most important component of total national savings. There remains disagreement among commentators on how far taxation can influence the level of household savings, but virtual unanimity that tax provisions have in an arbitrary and irrational way influenced the composition of household savings, and not in the direction of promoting either equity or economic efficiency.

Section C discusses taxation and income distribution or income redistribution. Whatever views are held on whether taxation is, should be, or even could be an appropriate instrument for income redistribution, in the real world this question invariably arises through the political process if governments wish to modify the personal income tax, property taxes or consumption taxes. This section briefly surveys some general aspects of this problem, as well as describing some work done by the OECD in this area.

Section D deals with taxation and energy policy. Nowadays this is seen primarily in the context of environmental concerns, but in the seventies and the early eighties energy policy was dominated by the sharp increases in the price of imported crude oil following the two oil shocks of 1973 and 1979. In those days tax interventionism was much more fashionable than it is now, and as the oil crises were of central concern to government policy-making, taxation was used by nearly all OECD governments as a major means of influencing the demand and supply of energy. This section surveys developments in taxation and energy policy over the last two decades with special emphasis on measures taken between 1973 and 1981 to influence taxpayer behaviour.

Section E refers to the influence of taxation in promoting environmental objectives which has become a major policy issue only in recent years. Lip-service has been paid for many years to the polluter pays principle, but especially because pollution crosses frontiers, few countries have been prepared to put themselves at an international competitive disadvan-

Table 7.1: Private and government net saving as a percentage of GDP, 1976-1980 and 1981-1985

	1976-1980					**1981-1985**				
	Household and non profit institutions	Corporate and quasi-corporate	Total private sector	Government savings	Total savings	Household and non-profit institutions	Corporate and quasi-corporate	Total private sector	Government savings	Total savings
Australia	8.0	-0.1	7.9	-1.0	6.9	7.3	-2.7	4.6	-1.7	2.9
Belgium	12.5	0.8	13.3	-2.6	10.7	11.6	1.3	12.9	-7.5	5.4
Canada	8.1	5.6	13.7	-0.7	13.0	10.1	2.7	12.8	-3.6	9.2
Finland	2.7	1.8	4.5	5.0	9.5	2.7	4.1	6.8	2.7	9.5
France	9.3	0.3	9.6	1.7	11.3	8.0	-1.5	6.5	-0.6	5.9
Germany	7.3	1.8	9.1	1.9	11.0	5.3	2.2	7.5	1.0	8.5
Italy	17.5	-0.2	17.3	-4.8	12.5	15.3	-0.2	15.1	-7.3	7.8
Japan	15.0	2.3	17.3	2.1	19.4	11.8	2.3	14.1	3.2	17.3
Netherlands	8.6	2.7	11.3	1.0	12.3	9.9	3.4	13.3	-1.5	11.8
Sweden	2.2	1.7	3.9	3.5	7.4	0.8	5.3	6.1	-1.3	4.8
United Kingdom	5.7	2.6	8.3	-1.2	7.1	5.2	2.3	7.5	-1.6	5.9
United States	6.2	7.4	8.6	-1.1	7.5	5.9	1.7	7.6	-3.7	3.9
Average	8.6	1.8	10.4	0.3	10.7	7.8	1.7	9.5	-1.8	7.7

Source: *United Nations National Accounts Statistics: Main aggregate and detailed tables, 1985* (United Nations 1987) taken from R. Smith (1989).

tage by imposing pollution taxes of any importance when their neighbours do not. The growing influence of the ecological lobby and the European Commission on these matters suggests that this may be one area for tax reform over the next two decades. This section discusses some aspects of taxation changes in the past that have had some positive environmental effects, even if taken for other motives, such as to raise revenues and to influence the demand and supply of energy, as well as looking at the possibilities for an internationally coordinated carbon tax.

Section F very briefly refers to the taxation of small to medium enterprises (henceforth SME's). How to define SME's is not discussed, but if one adopts the definition in Chapter 3 of the Ruding Report that SME's are firms with fewer than 500 employees (irrespective of their legal form) they account for 95 per cent of EC Community businesses and provide two thirds of employees in the Community – about 60 per cent in manufacturing and over 75 per cent in services. Government intervention or non-intervention, whether through taxation or otherwise, has become a major policy issue in most OECD countries as well as in the EC Commission and the problems these choices and conflicts raise are very much akin to others discussed in this and the previous chapter. One difference lies in the fact that unless governments make special provisions for SME's, there is likely to be tax discrimination against them of the following kinds:

- Their compliance costs in meeting the demands of tax administrations for documentation, invoices and other kinds of information in respect of income and value added tax are likely to be higher than those for larger enterprises who would anyway usually be keeping detailed records for their own purposes.
- If subject to the same statutory rate of personal or corporate income tax as larger firms, the *effective* rate of SME's is likely to be higher, since they generally have fewer possibilities of taking advantage of tax expenditures and other tax provisions which reduce effective rates, for example, depreciation allowances and tax credits under imputation systems.

B. Taxation and household savings

1. Tax and non-tax influences

Taxation may have an influence on the savings behaviour of households at four different stages. First, there is the tax treatment of the interest on borrowing necessary to acquire an asset, since such interest may be totally, partially or not at all deductible from income, subject to the personal income tax. At a second stage, the *acquisition* of different savings instruments may increase or decrease tax liabilities of various kinds (e.g. taxes on financial and capital transactions and other stamp duties) as well as varying the amounts of relief from the personal income tax, the amounts of which usually depend on the nature of the asset required, something which generally varies a lot between contributions to private retirement schemes, home ownership and financial assets, as well as between subcategories of these three main categories. (For example, among financial assets there is likely to be different tax treatment as between equities, government bonds, other bonds, life assurance, bank deposits, institutional investments in pension funds, investments in new financial instruments such as junk bonds.) At a third stage, the holding or ownership of an asset may attract net wealth and other capital and property taxes, as well as taxes on imputed rent. At a final stage the disposal of the asset may attract capital gains tax or other taxes on financial and capital transactions.

BUT Evidently, the savings behaviour of households is also influenced by a number of factors having little or nothing to do with taxation, such as the demographic and income distribution composition of the population, the level of inflation and interest rates, the level of social welfare programmes and the relative weight placed upon security of capital and the desire to make a big gain. However, it is generally believed that tax considerations have had and still have, a considerable impact on taxpayers' choice of savings instruments and more doubtfully that taxation may also have an influence on the level of household savings.

2. Tax distortions to savings patterns

For many years the tax systems of most OECD countries have subsidised borrowing at the expense of saving and have treated the different forms of saving unevenly, generally discriminating against investment in equities and encouraging investment in home ownership and contributions to insurance and private retirement schemes. These points are illustrated by two short quotations which, though directed respectively at Ireland and the United Kingdom, certainly also apply to a number of other countries.

> The level of savings in Ireland is inadequate. Penal taxes are imposed on certain forms of saving and borrowing is heavily subsidised. Incentives are provided for people to save through pension funds and insurance policies but not in other ways, with the result that the supply of capital for risk investment is reduced. Incentives are available for people to invest in housing. These are not related to housing needs. As a result too much investment goes into certain types of housing and the price for building land is forced up. (Report by the 1984 Irish Commission on incentives.)
>
> The pattern of fiscal discrimination described is arbitrary in its effects between people saving through different institutions in different assets and at times of differing inflation. The principles underlying the privileges granted to certain assets and the penalties applied to others are obscure and confused; indeed in most cases it is clear that the discrimination is entirely accidental rather than the object of conscious policy. (J. Hills, 1984.)

3. Some policy issues

For a number of reasons it is not easy to generalise about what is the appropriate differential income tax treatment between the different forms of saving and borrowing. First, this may vary not only between countries but over time within each country according to what are the paramount social and economic objectives. Second, the privileged or non-privileged tax treatment of borrowing for the acquisition of assets and of the various forms of saving may each have its own rationale which may or may not be relevant in the light of changing social and economic conditions. Third, in practice, governments have to start with systems that actually exist with all that this implies in terms of the constraints referred to in Chapter 1D (winners and losers and pressure group resistance to losses of tax privileges) so that the theoretically ideal tax treatment of the different forms of saving may differ from the treatment which it is feasible to adopt in practice. The fact that these tax privileges will often have been capitalised in higher prices – especially of dwelling places – has to be taken into account when changes are proposed, since complicated horizontal equity issues are raised, for example, as between those who have already bought their home, those who are in the process of doing so and those who hope to do so in the future.

Two more general issues are whether tax deductibility of interest should be affected by the purpose for which the borrowing is made and what should be the relative tax treatment of savings through financial institutions and direct investment in equities.

As regards borrowing, most countries take the view that interest payments should be deductible from any income associated with it, but not deductible when there is no associated income. Thus, most countries allow deductibility of interest on borrowing for the purpose of one's own business but do not allow deductibility of interest on borrowing for the purchase of consumer goods. A few countries, however, make no distinction between the various purposes for which the borrowing is made, allowing the same degree of deductibility in all cases. This is possibly based on the principle that neutrality should prevail as between deductibility of interest from income subject to tax, irrespective of the purpose for which the loan is acquired, or on the consideration that, if a distinction were made, deductible loans would in any event be diverted to expenditures which were non-deductible, or that it is difficult to verify how borrowed money is in fact used. However, tax deductibility of interest for consumer credit clearly encourages borrowing to the detriment of saving and for that reason has in recent years been abolished in Ireland, New Zealand and the United States.

The other issue is the desirability of providing income tax incentives to taxpayers to place their funds with institutional investment (pension funds, insurance companies, etc.) in excess of the incentives given for direct investment in equities. It is argued that this may discourage risk-taking, because such institutions are generally reluctant to provide venture capital to newly-established small companies, which (though opinions are by no means unanimous on this point) have been considered as being in the forefront of technological developments and providing large employment opportunities. However, it is doubtful whether the removal of these tax privileges will lead to a change in the investment behaviour of small savers, who may well be more concerned with the security of their investment than with making a big gain.

4. Summary of issues and possible tax reforms

A distinction should be made between the possible influence of the existing tax regime on savings levels and the possibility of influencing such levels by changing the tax regime. On the first issue V. Tanzi (1988) divided countries into those with the most and those with the least generous provisions for interest deductions from income subject to personal income tax and found that the savings rate from the second group was on average almost three times that for the first group during the period 1974 to 1985. In particular, he noted that the Northern European countries plus the United States have been particularly generous, and that it is in these countries that the savings rate was especially low.

Much scepticism has been expressed on inducing a sustainable increase in household saving rates by increasing tax incentives. The problem was well expressed by B. Bosworth (1984).

> Government can increase private saving incentives either by reducing taxation of the income from capital or by providing tax benefits tied to current saving. Both of these measures increase the effective after-tax rate of return. But these tax incentives generate both income and substitution effects that pull in opposite directions and the net effect on the saving behaviour of the individual much less the economy is indeterminate on *a priori* grounds. A reduction in the tax on the income from capital has an incentive effect of encouraging individuals to reduce their current consumption to take advantage of the higher after-tax return on saving – in effect, lowering the price of future consumption (the substitution effect). On the other hand, the increased lifetime income that will be earned on previously planned saving as a result of lower tax rates encourages higher current as well as future consumption (the income effect). This has not been an easy question for the empirical studies to resolve.

According to the Danish authorities, the 1987 tax reform was designed *inter alia* to increase household savings and did so by around 1.5 percentage points between 1987 and 1989, but since 1989 this increase has not been entirely sustained and was due mainly to a substantial decrease in the rates of net wealth tax on individuals and tax on capital from income, which at the same time reduced the tax bonus for borrowing. As R. Smith (1989) noted:

> Because there are no clear guidelines on how to alter the rate of private saving, tax reform appears to have given very limited attention to the level of private saving, even in those countries where there is a desire to sharply increase saving. Reform has focused on the allocation of saving and investment in a more efficient manner, rather than on the level of saving and investment.

The general direction of these tax reforms has been to reduce tax discrimination between the different forms of saving instruments. Generally, this has taken the form of broadening the personal income tax base by reducing or abolishing concessions in the more privileged areas of saving, but sometimes it has taken the opposite form by creating new tax incentives in the less privileged areas of saving, generally savings through financial assets. This relates to the issue touched on in Chapter 1 and discussed more fully at the beginning of Chapter 10, of whether the personal income tax should have a more comprehensive base or rather approach a progressive expenditure tax by allowing deductions from the base for all forms of savings. (Chapter 10C3c is also relevant to the present discussion.)

C. Taxation and income distribution

1. General remarks

As already indicated in Chapter 6, high taxation is in most countries correlated with high expenditures on social welfare programmes, some of which redistribute income from the rich to the poor and help to alleviate poverty. This section is confined to summarising the effect of taxation *per se* on income distribution and redistribution.

Commentators in most OECD countries are generally in agreement that the tax system as a whole does not greatly affect income distribution. In most OECD countries it is believed that the relatively mild progressivity of the personal income tax is offset by the relatively mild regressivity of consumption and payroll taxes.

Commentators are also broadly in agreement that the tax system is generally an inappropriate instrument to attempt to change income distribution. To the extent that governments desire to reduce inequalities and poverty, this is more effectively done by operating on differentials between before-tax incomes (e.g. income policies and minimum wages) and by social welfare measures. The main objective of taxation is to raise government revenues to finance expenditure *inter alia* on social welfare programmes. Attempts to achieve income redistribution objectives through the tax system are likely to conflict with other objectives such as economic and administrative efficiency and horizontal equity. The relative importance attached to income redistribution objectives through the tax system may in practice depend on how far they are taken care of through the social welfare system and income policies.

Nevertheless, the potential for changes in direct taxes on income distribution, especially if combined with changes to social benefits, should not be underestimated. Chart 7.1 taken from J. Hills (1988) provides a practical example of just how considerably income was redistributed regressively in the United Kingdom between 1979 and 1988 through the tax/benefit system.

A distinction should be made between the two income redistribution objectives of making the very poor less poor and making the very rich less rich. Tax provisions can do nothing to promote the former objective. It is true that non-wastable tax credits as used in Canada and the United States do relieve poverty but these are essentially social transfer provisions which use the taxation system as a delivery mechanism. On the contrary, the only way of making the very rich less rich is to tax their income, capital gains and capital quite heavily. This is done to some extent in all OECD countries, but rather mildly in many of them. At the ideological level, the retreat from socialism during the eighties in a number of countries, has reduced the popularity of soaking the rich and at the enforcement level, the presence of so many highly paid entertainers and sportsmen in tax haven countries illustrates the difficulty of taxing the mobile rich and many of the immobile rich undoubtedly hide much of their taxable income and capital in other countries.

Like capital and capital gains taxes, the personal income tax may make the rich less rich. In the case of the income tax this may be done through a progressive rate schedule and/or through standard tax reliefs, of which the most important are a threshold below which no income tax is payable and reliefs of various kinds for children and other dependants. Another factor affecting the progressivity of the income tax is whether reliefs are given by way of tax allowances (the value of which is a function of the marginal rate of tax) or tax credits (a fixed amount deducted from tax payable). Similar degrees of progressivity can be achieved by steeper rates combined with tax allowances and less steep rates combined with tax credits. In all OECD countries the overall progressivity of the personal income tax is reduced by the prevalence of non-standard tax reliefs for particular expenditures which benefit most higher income groups, and in most OECD countries by social

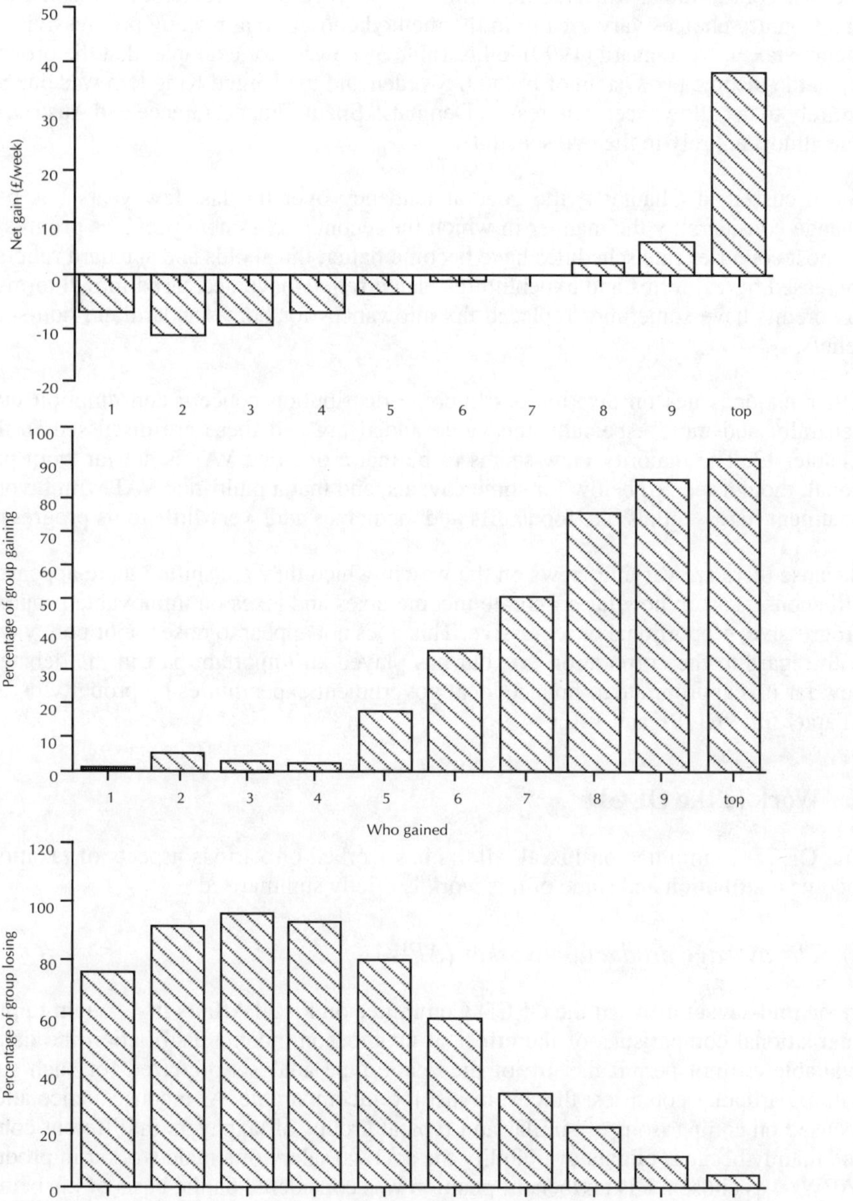

Chart 7.1: The effect of direct tax and benefit changes between 1979 and 1988 in the United Kingdom

Source: *Changing tax: how the system works and how to change it,* J. Hills, London 1988.

security contributions which some commentators regard as a regressive personal income tax. Country choices vary greatly in the method chosen to apply any progressivity to the income tax. J. Nørregaard (1990) in his Table 3 showed, for example, that the progressivity in the income tax system of Ireland, Sweden and the United Kingdom was due almost entirely to tax allowances, whereas in Denmark, Spain, France, Greece and Austria, it was due almost entirely to the rate schedule.

As discussed in Chapter 1, the general tendency over the last few years has been to change considerably the manner in which the income tax system provides progressivity: in most countries rate schedules have become flatter, thresholds and standard reliefs have increased in real terms and expenditure-related reliefs have decreased in real terms: also tax credits have sometimes replaced tax allowances for both standard and non-standard reliefs.

Other major issues on taxation and income distribution concern consumption taxation generally and more especially the value added tax and these are discussed further in Chapter 13. The majority view seems to be that a one-rate VAT is not far from proportional, though see 2d) below for some caveats, and that a multi-rate VAT with favourable treatment for essentials like foodstuffs and medicines adds very little to its progressivity.

Because there are varying views on the way in which they are shifted there appears to be little consensus on how far corporate income taxes and taxes on immovable property are progressive, proportional or regressive. This does not appear to raise major policy worries with regard to the corporation tax, but has played an important part in the debate as to how far it is appropriate to finance local government expenditures by property taxes (see Chapter 5E, 9E1, 9F and 14C).

2. Work in the OECD

The OECD Committee on Fiscal Affairs has worked on various aspects of taxation and income distribution and some of this work is briefly summarised.

a) The average production worker (APW)

In the mid-seventies when the OECD Committee on Fiscal Affairs first sought to provide international comparisons of the effect of taxation on income distribution the data then available did not permit the use of the decile type analysis preferred for such surveys within particular countries: they were just too incomparable. As a consequence attention focused on comparisons of similar and typical groups of taxpayers in different countries and mainly because of data availability the average salary of a male worker in production (APW) was chosen. His tax/benefit position was considered on the basis of his being single and married with two children after he had paid his income tax and social security contributions and in the latter case received family benefits, and the results are still published annually. Of course, there are many limitations on the comparability of APW in different countries duly recorded in OECD APW 1991 and earlier editions, but there are in most OECD countries a number of people with a wage around that of the APW and these comparisons have helped to provide valuable insights (e.g. see Chapter 10D as regards the relationship between income tax payments and social security contributions).

One interesting sociological phenomenon is that though the APW began as a 100 per cent male, he was transformed around 1980 into a hermaphrodite (two-thirds male, one-third female) to reflect the growing participation of women in the labour force, the lower wages earned by women and most crucially that earnings statistics were available in more and more countries on the basis of total work-force and not male work-force. (Gross APW wages were accordingly adjusted downwards which provided some discontinuity in the series.)

b) Income tax schedules

Towards the end of the seventies some internationally comparable data became available on a decile basis and in 1981 the OECD published an analysis of the central government income tax schedules of 18 OECD countries (other than Finland, Iceland, Luxembourg, New Zealand and Spain) for various years between 1975 and 1981 under the title *Income tax schedules: distribution of taxpayers and revenues*. Data availability entailed that the information had to be based on the schedule rates applying to taxable income. This meant that conclusions could not be drawn about the relation between gross earnings and the tax paid at different income levels, but the publication provided a great deal of information about tax rate schedules of which most people were and remain unaware. Since this analysis has not been updated, Table 7.2 summarises some of its results. The main findings (some but not all of which can be derived from Table 7.2) may be summarised as follows:

- In all 18 countries except Belgium the marginal rate for 80 per cent of taxpayers was less than 36 per cent.
- Less than 0.5 per cent of taxpayers were subject to the top rate in all 18 countries except Ireland (5 per cent), Denmark (4.2 per cent), France (0.8 per cent) and Sweden (0.6 per cent), and the second highest rate was often much lower than the top rate.
- The percentage of taxpayers liable only to the lowest rate of tax varied from 90 per cent or more in Australia and the United Kingdom to less than 6 per cent in Austria, Belgium, France, Turkey and the United States and in Canada it was only 1 per cent.
- Usually, top rate taxpayers accounted for well under 10 per cent of income tax revenues but in Denmark and Turkey it was over 20 per cent and in Ireland nearly 30 per cent. However, the yield from the 10 per cent of taxpayers with the highest income accounted for from around 35 (Canada and Italy) to 70 (the Netherlands) per cent of the total income tax yield.
- In nearly all countries taxpayers subject only to the lowest rate of tax accounted for a very small proportion of the total income tax yield, exceptions being the United Kingdom (76 per cent), Australia (68 per cent), Denmark (30 per cent) and Germany (20 per cent).

c) The personal income tax base

Improved data availability and analytical techniques rendered possible the publication in 1990 of a much more sophisticated report on the personal income tax base covering 17 OECD countries (other than Iceland, Japan, Luxembourg, New Zealand, Portugal, Switzerland and Turkey) for various years between 1982 and 1988. The main improvement was that countries could be compared on the basis of a much wider income base

Table 7.2: The distribution of taxpayers over the income tax schedule[1]

The table shows the schedule rate applicable at different percentage points of the cumulative distribution of taxpayers over the schedule (Central government income tax)

Cumulative percentage of taxpayers	10	20	30	40	50	60	70	80	90	95	96	97	98	99	100
Countries with joint or family taxation – Schedule rate %															
Belgium	21	25	30	37	37	37	39	44	44	46.75	46.75	46.75	46.75	57	60
France	15	15	15	20	20	25	25	25	40	40	40	45	45	55	60
Germany	0	22	22	22	22	23	29	32	38	43	45	46	48	50	56
Ireland	20	25	25	35	35	35	35	35	45	50	60	60	60	60	60
Italy	10	10	10	10	13	16	16	19	22	25	27	29	31	33	72
Norway[2]	6	11	11	11	16	16	22	28	33	38	38	38	42	42	48
Portugal[3,4]	4	4	4	4	4	6	6	6	8	14	20	20	20	34	80
United Kingdom	34	34	34	34	34	34	34	34	34	34	40	45	50	60	83
United States[3]	16	19	19	22	22	25	28	28	36	42	42	48	50	53	70
Countries with individual taxation – Schedule rate %															
Australia	33.5	33.5	33.5	33.5	33.5	33.5	33.5	33.5	33.5	47.5	47.5	47.5	47.5	47.5	61.5
Austria[3]	23	28	28	28	28	28	28	33	33	38	38	43	43	52	62
Canada	18	18	19	19	21	21	23	25	28	32	32	32	32	36	43
Denmark	14.4	14.4	14.4	14.4	14.4	14.4	28.8	28.8	28.8	28.8	39.6	39.6	39.6	39.6	39.6
Greece	5	7	9	11	14	17	23	23	34	42	42	46	46	50	60
Japan[5]	na.	na.	na.	na.	na.	na.	na.	na.	<25	<25	<25	<25	<25	<30	75
Netherlands	20	20	25	25	25	31	31	31	39	49	49	58	58	63	71
Sweden	2	4	5	11	14	20	26	29	33	48	48	48	53	53	58
Turkey	15	20	20	25	25	25	35	35	46	55	55	55	60	60	60

1. The table is constructed as follows: first, the distribution of taxpayers ranked by the highest bracket in which they are subject to tax is determined; secondly, the tax bracket in which each percentage point of this distribution falls is ascertained; the table then shows the tax rate applicable to that bracket.
2. In Norway there is an option between joint and individual taxation.
3. The figures refer to pre-credit tax liability but this does not significantly influence the results.
4. Figures refer only to the complementary tax paid by high income taxpayers.
5. The figures given for Japan indicate the upper limit of the schedule rate at selected cumulative percentage of taxpayers.

Source: *Income tax schedules: distribution of taxpayers and revenues* (OECD 1981).

than before (generally "income subject to tax", and in a few countries on "gross income" instead of "taxable income" which meant that, subject to the usual numerous caveats, for the first time it became possible to say something meaningful *inter alia* about the relative progressivity of OECD countries' income tax systems. To summarise this 250-page publication here is not possible, but some details from it are provided in Chapter 10B2, 10C2 and Table 10.1.

d) The impact of consumption taxes

In 1981 the OECD published a study limited to seven countries (Belgium, Finland, France, Germany, the Netherlands, Norway and the United Kingdom) under the title *The impact of consumption taxes at different income levels*, where the conclusion broadly was that the impact of VAT was mildly progressive in most of these countries if related to consumers' expenditures and roughly proportional if related to consumers' income with some reservations on the reliability of the results – taken from sample surveys – for the highest and lowest income groups. This question was examined again in *Taxing consumption* (OECD 1988) when the overall conclusion was rather proportional to consumers' expenditures and mildly regressive if related to consumers' income. However, as noted in greater detail in Chapter 13, the empirical data were scanty, not comparable between countries and generally too fragile to reach confident conclusions. For the most part, the income distribution effects of the excises on alcoholic drinks, cigarettes and petrol were even less clear than those of VAT.

D. Taxation and energy policy

1. Summary of developments between 1973 and 1992

Following the sharp upward revisions in energy prices during the seventies and the insecurity of oil supplies, energy policy became a central concern of nearly all OECD governments. The objectives then set for energy policies were summarised as improving the security and stability of energy supplies, encouraging a greater use of indigenous energy supplies, developing renewable energy sources and encouraging the conservation of energy and a more rational use of oil (OECD Inventory, 1982).

A number of non-tax instruments were used to achieve these objectives including, for example, grants, subsidies, loans on favourable terms, price regulation of public utilities, government sponsored research and development programmes, consultation and publicity programmes. However, virtually all OECD governments during the seventies implemented new tax provisions, usually in the form of tax incentives or tax penalties, to encourage the production of indigenous sources of energy and the conservation of energy. Some reviewed their existing tax legislation because provisions implemented for social,

Table 7.3: Percentage of taxes in gasoline prices, 1978-1991

	1978	1980	1982	1984	1986	1988	1989	1990	1991
Australia	27.7	18.7	17.0	24.6	41.0	47.0	48.4	44.9	53.1
Austria	54.1	41.6	44.8	49.9	57.3	61.7	58.5	56.0	58.1
Belgium	61.7	53.3	52.2	55.2	63.8	65.3	65.2	65.4	66.5
Canada	29.4	24.5	26.3	25.0	33.0	39.2	42.7	42.4	44.2
Denmark	63.7	58.8	53.3	57.3	71.0	76.2	73.0	69.1	67.8
Finland	46.8	36.1	32.2	34.0	46.7	52.4	49.4	51.1	61.3
France	63.2	58.0	52.7	57.3	73.9	77.0	74.6	74.2	75.0
Germany	57.9	48.7	48.1	48.7	61.5	64.3	65.0	63.1	67.6
Greece	58.6	41.8	34.6	47.1	68.1	67.4	55.8	63.8	n.a.
Ireland	55.0	48.1	50.1	56.5	65.8	70.7	69.1	67.1	66.2
Italy	71.2	61.4	59.5	65.6	78.2	78.7	75.9	75.0	76.0
Japan	43.4	36.7	32.9	37.2	43.9	46.6	47.9	46.4	45.7
Luxembourg	n.a	43.8	43.0	44.2	53.5	57.7	54.9	54.4	54.9
Netherlands	60.5	52.3	48.8	56.0	66.7	70.6	67.6	66.0	70.0
New Zealand	44.4	27.6	21.9	21.5	30.9	50.3	47.0	47.5	45.7
Norway	58.6	51.7	48.1	50.3	60.6	67.0	62.7	62.9	67.4
Portugal	70.6	61.4	57.5	53.7	67.6	68.6	65.0	67.8	72.2
Spain	22.3	34.6	30.8	39.2	67.6	65.9	64.3	63.0	65.4
Sweden	51.9	49.3	42.8	42.7	56.7	62.2	59.1	65.9	67.7
Switzerland	63.2	51.1	48.2	49.5	61.3	64.7	60.7	59.2	59.5
Turkey	n.a.	n.a.	n.a.	n.a.	n.a.	n.a.	52.2	53.0	56.1
United Kingdom	50.9	46.3	54.2	54.9	63.9	67.1	63.6	61.9	66.0
United States	19.2	11.2	12.0	23.8	32.7	31.2	29.3	26.7	32.9

Source: *Energy prices and taxes* (OECD 1991, fourth quarter).

economic or revenue-raising purposes were found to be inconsistent with their overall energy objectives.

Special considerations applied to the tax treatment of oil producers in those relatively few OECD countries which have important oil resources (Australia, Canada, Norway, the United Kingdom and the United States) where generally governments ensured through various forms of tax legislation that they received revenues from this source and that the windfall gains of the oil producers due to the increase in world prices were limited.

Not only has energy policy been one of the most important government concerns over the last two decades and especially between 1973 and around 1985, but it provides an excellent example of OECD governments' preference for tax interventionism over tax neutrality when matters are considered to be sufficiently important and also illustrates the wide range of tax instruments at governments' disposal if they wish to influence taxpayer behaviour. It is for these reasons that the taxation of energy has been singled out for special treatment. There are equally a large variety of tax instruments which can and have been used to promote many other policy objectives, for example, in the field of agricul-

Table 7.4: Percentage of taxes in automotive diesel oil prices, 1978-1991

	1978	1980	1982	1984	1986	1988	1989	1990	1991
Australia	29.7	20.9	19.5	26.6	47.8	57.5	56.1	52.7	54.9
Austria	42.8	32.5	38.7	39.3	46.8	49.3	49.3	45.5	46.5
Belgium	53.4	33.5	23.7	26.6	36.5	41.0	42.9	46.6	45.2
Canada	n.a.	n.a.	n.a.	23.3	28.9	33.7	34.9	34.5	34.7
Denmark	0.0	0.0	0.0	0.0	0.0	0.0	0.0	0.0	20.9
Finland	43.5	32.1	29.1	28.8	41.0	49.7	49.3	49.9	51.8
France	54.2	47.4	40.5	41.2	53.2	59.4	57.7	55.2	54.3
Germany	53.1	41.4	38.1	38.5	51.0	57.5	53.5	50.8	52.8
Greece	19.6	12.6	11.9	27.9	42.3	39.7	21.4	26.7	n.a.
Ireland	32.6	27.9	34.1	37.6	49.8	54.8	52.7	51.4	49.8
Italy	17.4	7.6	6.8	19.5	40.0	56.4	55.5	60.5	63.3
Japan	n.a.	23.5	20.3	23.1	28.6	35.3	37.7	35.1	35.1
Luxembourg	n.a	17.3	21.1	27.2	31.9	36.8	34.5	32.5	31.9
Netherlands	35.4	22.7	19.4	19.6	29.9	41.4	38.6	44.5	45.6
New Zealand	2.4	2.6	7.8	12.0	20.8	42.3	n.a.	30.2	11.8
Norway	1.1	1.3	0.9	1.0	3.4	12.6	12.1	15.1	24.3
Portugal	16.8	7.2	18.2	29.3	54.1	52.0	50.3	52.3	56.3
Spain	16.5	24.7	20.0	20.7	50.9	51.7	48.1	48.8	50.0
Sweden	7.7	8.4	14.3	18.3	22.7	33.1	31.8	27.3	30.3
Switzerland	n.a.	50.6	48.5	48.3	60.7	65.5	61.3	59.1	58.6
Turkey	n.a.	n.a.	n.a.	n.a.	n.a.	n.a.	48.8	51.8	52.6
United Kingdom	45.0	39.5	41.6	43.1	51.9	57.8	54.9	52.8	56.5
United States	25.9	14.8	13.1	23.8	35.5	34.0	32.0	27.9	34.1

Source: *Energy prices and taxes* (OECD 1991, fourth quarter).

ture, education, research and development, but over the period under consideration, taxation has been used much less in these areas than in the area of energy policy.

During the periods immediately following the two high increases in the price of imported crude oil, governments were evidently inhibited from raising the tax on refined oil products. A. Tait and D. Morgan (IMF 1980) showed that the excise tax on gasoline sharply declined in real terms in the seventies and especially after 1973, while Tables 7.3 and 7.4 show a large decline in the percentage of taxes in the prices of gasoline and automotive diesel oil in nearly all OECD countries between 1978 and 1982, which followed automatically from the combination of rising oil prices with no or little change in tax rates. Following the decrease in the price of imported crude oil the percentage of tax in oil prices increased rapidly and by 1986 was higher than the 1978 percentage in nearly all countries (see Charts 7.2 and 7.3) and higher still in 1988. Between 1988 and 1990 this percentage tended to fall in most OECD countries, but in 1991 to increase, in many countries to its highest ever recorded level (see Table 7.4 and Charts 7.2 and 7.3). Further analysis (doubtless already undertaken) is necessary to demonstrate how far this increase in the tax percentage in prices is due to falling net of tax prices, and how far to increases in tax rates.

In *Energy conservation in IEA*[1] *countries* (OECD 1987) it was noted that even in the current easy energy markets it is important to maintain the momentum of energy conservation, because:

- energy conservation will extend the availability of energy resources that are depletable;
- there is likely to be a return to tightening energy markets before the end of the century; energy conservation will delay and lessen its impact;
- energy conservation reduces the environmental consequences on energy production and use in a way which is consistent with energy policy objectives;
- investment in energy conservation at the margin provides a better return than investment in energy supply;
- investment in energy conservation can often be undertaken in small increments and is therefore flexible at a time when the energy outlook is uncertain.

2. Taxation and the two oil shocks

a) General considerations

Reflecting the concern of OECD governments, the OECD Committee on Fiscal Affairs set up one Working Group in 1975 after the first oil crisis and another in 1980 after the second, each with a mandate to report back within two years on, *inter alia*, international issues relating to the taxation of energy and measures introduced by OECD governments with the specific aim of influencing taxpayers' demand and supply for energy. In 1981 the Committee issued a generally available, but unpublished report of nearly 200 pages, which provided an inventory of tax provisions which may have had a direct impact on the supply and demand for energy.

This sub-section summarises certain provisions described in the 1981 OECD inventory. It refers generally to tax provisions which were introduced after the two oil crises with the deliberate intention of influencing taxpayer behaviour. Since 1981 some of them may have been discarded and new ones introduced, and as I am unaware of the current position, they are always referred to in the past tense as something introduced at a particular period, whether or not they still exist. For similar reasons the summary is not country specific, since the objective here is not to exhibit country practices which may be out of date, but rather to give a general picture of the use of tax expenditures and tax penalties in the energy sphere. Much of the inventory was devoted to the general provisions of taxation, which also could influence the demand and supply for energy (e.g. rates of VAT, depreciation provisions) but this summary is limited almost entirely to tax expenditures or penalties introduced specifically in the energy sector to influence supply or demand. Finally,

1. The International Energy Agency (IEA) is an associated body of the OECD, comprising all the 24 OECD countries (listed in the footnote to the Preface at the beginning of this book) except Iceland, though Finland and France joined only during the last two years.

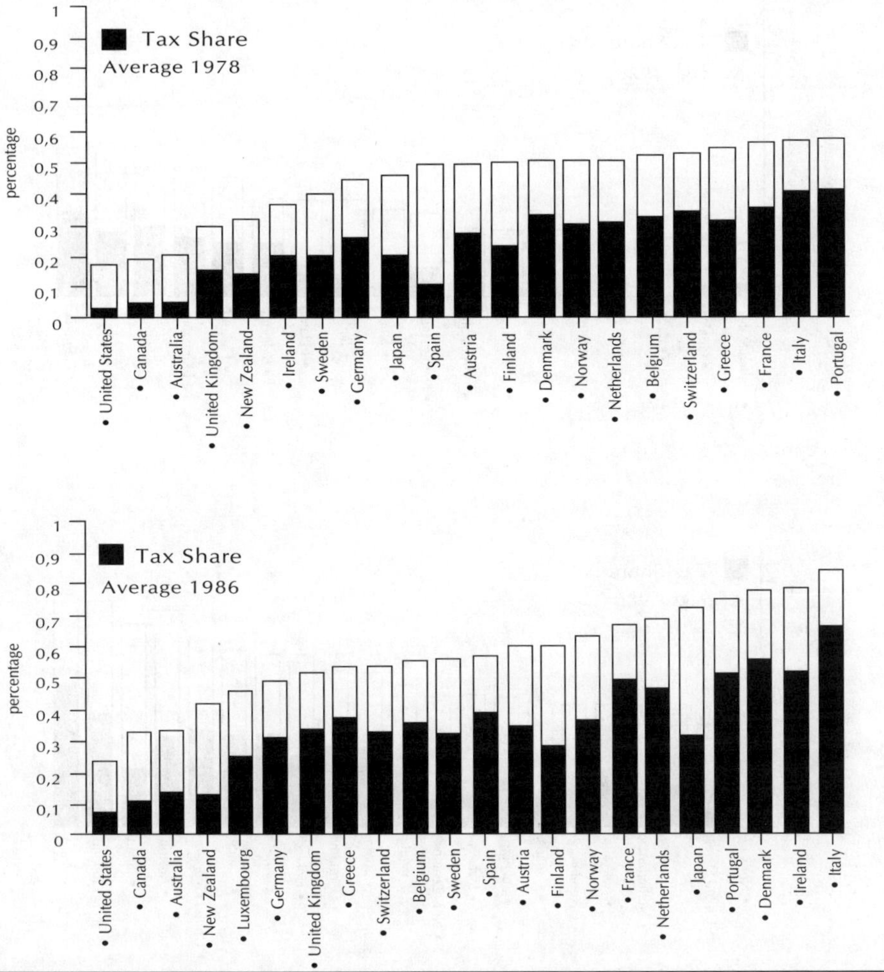

Chart 7.2: Gasoline prices and taxes, 1978 and 1986

Source: *Energy prices and taxes* (OECD 1987).

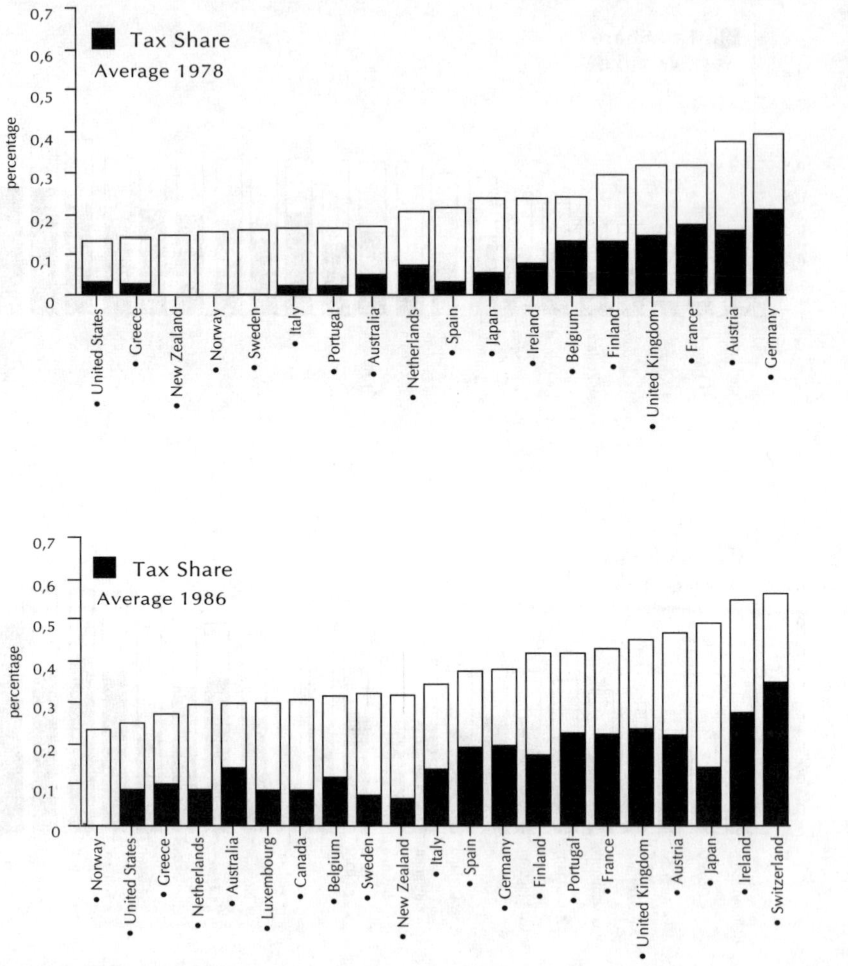

Chart 7.3: Automotive diesel oil prices and taxes, 1978 and 1986

Source: *Energy prices and taxes* (OECD 1987).

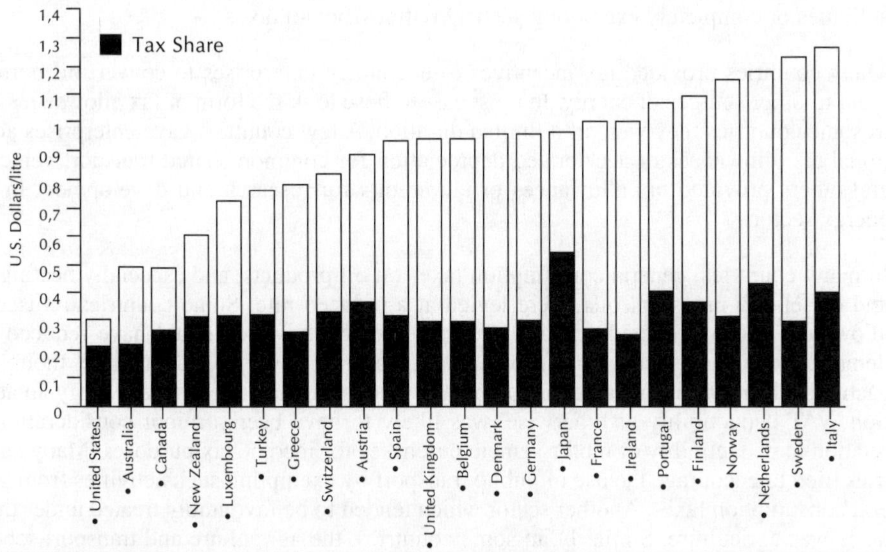

Chart 7.4: Gasoline prices and taxes, end 1991
Source: *Energy prices and taxes* (OECD 1991).

the inventory covered a very wide area, including all forms of energy, but for the purposes of this book, it seems sufficient to confine the summary to those areas which seemed most important and likely to be most relevant to the energy policy issues of the nineties.

b) Tax provisions designed to influence the demand or supply for oil or gas

There were few special personal income tax incentives for individuals, although a number of countries provided favourable tax treatment for income derived from oil and gas exploration/exploitation activities which may have increased the funds available for such activities. A few countries tried to encourage employers to provide common transport facilities for their employees by excluding such fringe benefits from the taxable income of employees. Limits on work-related travel expenses, which may discourage suburban sprawl, also existed in a few countries.

Measures applying to incorporated and unincorporated enterprises were more prevalent. On the supply side, many countries allowed an immediate expensing of exploration and development expenditure – a means of taking into account the high costs involved in the search for oil and gas – and some provided depletion allowances, in recognising that part of the assets of natural resource producers are exhaustible. A few countries permitted oil companies to build up tax-free reserves, a few provided accelerated depreciation for investments in oil storage facilities, and a few others tried to encourage the exploration for oil in their territories by either substantially reducing the domestic tax burden on such activities or completely exempting such activities from all taxes.

Many countries provided tax incentives to encourage enterprises to convert oil burning plant to other sources of energy. In most cases, these took the form of tax allowances and in some countries they were of a limited duration. A few countries gave enterprises additional tax allowances or accelerated depreciation for common shared transport vehicles, and others provided tax allowances or tax credits for research and development in the energy sector.

In many countries, general consumption taxes on oil products, and especially heating oil and diesel and industrial oils, were levied at a reduced rate. Some countries refused to allow VAT to be deducted on cars used by enterprises, which could have reduced the demand for such vehicles, and in others, VAT on petrol was not deductible, though in each case the motive was rather to combat tax avoidance than to conserve energy. In addition, VAT deductibility or otherwise, was likely to have been a minor consideration in relation to deductibility of motor vehicle purchases for income tax purposes. Many countries tried to encourage the use of public transport by exempting such activities from general consumption taxes. Another sector which tended to be favourably treated under these taxes was agriculture. Similarly, in some countries, the agriculture and transport sectors were favourably treated under excises. There was a tendency to apply a lower rate of excise to diesel and heavy industrial oils than to other oil products and, again, public transport tended to be subject to a reduced rate. A few countries provided tax exemption for conservation equipment and electrically powered motor vehicles, or to encourage the use of liquid petroleum gas in motor vehicles by exempting it from specific taxes.

Differential consumption taxes on motor vehicles were also used to influence the demand for oil. Taxes on their purchase and annual registration fees sometimes varied according to the weight, size, power or cubic capacity of the vehicle and tax distinctions were made in a number of countries between household and commercial vehicles. Favourable tax treatment was frequently given to public transport vehicles. However, sometimes these differentials had nothing to do with energy policy, but rather reflected the damage of vehicles to roads (e.g. tax differentiation by weight of vehicle).

c) *Tax provisions designed to encourage the conservation of energy*

Under the income tax, a number of countries introduced provisions to encourage (mainly households) to conserve energy. These usually took the form of tax allowances to encourage the improvement of home insulation or tax credits for energy conservation equipment. Various limits were applied to these provisions which varied according to such factors as the age of the house and whether rented or owner-occupied.

Tax incentives to enterprises took the form of favourable depreciation or tax credits tied to the installation of energy conservation equipment or improved insulation of plant. Again, there were various conditions attached to these reliefs. In a few countries, property taxes on enterprises were reduced on the installation of energy conservation equipment or hydro-electric plant. A few countries reduced general consumption tax rates applied to conservation and insulation material, but in most countries they remained subject to normal rates of tax.

Also of relevance was the tax treatment of energy related grants to incorporated enterprises, which always followed the normal tax treatment of grants under corporate income tax systems. This, however, varied in that in just under half of the countries, capital grants were included in taxable income and were offset against the base used to calculate depreciation. In the remaining countries they were excluded from taxable income, but country practices as regards their effects on the depreciation base differed.

d) Tax provisions designed to encourage the use of alternative energy sources

The types of alternative energy sources that are referred to are: solar energy; wind-powered equipment; biomass energy; peat and wood; geothermal energy; heat pumps and heat-recovery equipment. Reference was also made to co-generation or district heating schemes and solid waste recovery plants. Some of these relate rather to extracting more energy from existing sources than using new sources.

A number of countries introduced personal income tax reliefs for the use of solar power and heat recovery equipment in the taxpayers' principal place of residence. These were usually subject to a ceiling and varied according to the family circumstances of the taxpayer.

Special tax incentives were introduced for enterprises to install alternative energy equipment in a number of countries. Such provisions were usually intended to encourage a greater use of solar or geothermal energy, solid wastes, co-generation and heat-recovery equipment. They took the form of favourable depreciation provisions or additional tax reliefs.

Fewer countries provided a favourable treatment of alternative energy equipment under general consumption taxes. Where such provisions existed, they took the form of exemption for solar heating equipment and for marginal sources of energy (e.g. timber, peat). A few countries exempted from excises and customs duties energy produced from certain alternative energy sources (e.g. peat, wind, solar) as well as geothermal equipment.

3. Relative taxation of gasoline and automotive diesel oil

Over the years there has been tax differentiation in nearly all countries between these two fuels, as indicated by Tables 7.3 and 7.4 and Charts 7.2 and 7.3. In Switzerland there has been little differentiation and this is so nowadays in Australia which in the past gave favourable treatment to gasoline, as the United States has done consistently. In all other OECD countries, gasoline is taxed at a higher rate than diesel oil and frequently the differential is substantial. Doubtless the main reason for taxing diesel oil at relatively low rates is to reduce the costs of industry and to maintain international competitiveness with neighbouring countries, but the greater efficiency of diesel oil in terms of kilometres per litre may be another reason (see also Section E3 below on environmental aspects).

4. Tax policy and energy policy

The foregoing paragraphs have suggested that at least between the early seventies and mid-eighties energy conservation objectives have played a much greater part than most other economic and social objectives in influencing tax provisions. Energy policy experts see the situation somewhat differently. IEA (OECD 1987) stated:

> There is no country where taxation and energy objectives are brought together in a systematic and well-balanced fashion. IEA countries could do more to improve integration of general taxation and energy objectives and to develop the necessary internalisation of externalities related to the supply and consumption of energy.
>
> There are some instances of distortions in tax policies which act against energy conservation. Examples include tax regimes that do not give equal treatment to supply and conservation options, for example in the United Kingdom, where a value-added tax is charged on insulating material, but not on electricity and natural gas. Another example is the tax regime for company cars in Sweden, the United Kingdom and – to a lesser extent – other countries, which favours the purchase of larger cars and more profligate car use than would be the case without such tax incentives. Other examples of tax regimes which could be improved to enhance energy efficiency are motor car purchase and ownership taxes that collect vehicle charges on the basis of technical car characteristics (e.g. weight or engine size), regardless of vehicle use. These exist in most IEA countries. Such charges could be collected as a tax on fuel use thus making the user pay and promoting energy conservation.

At the same time the IEA Report does recognise that:

> Tax policies have much broader concerns than energy objectives, in particular, fiscal and different macroeconomic, social, regional and industrial considerations. Generally, the need for governments to raise revenue in a convenient and effective way is the primary consideration in virtually all Member Countries. As a result there is a wide variation among Member Countries and among energy commodities in the proportion of final energy prices represented by taxation. Taxes are heavily concentrated on petroleum products, particularly gasoline, where they are easy to collect and where there is an easily explained justification – the need to construct and maintain roads.

The last few words from the quotation, possibly inserted for political reasons, raise the earmarking or hypothecation issue discussed in Chapter 8 in connection with financing social security benefits and would seem irrelevant to tax policy makers in most OECD countries. Whilst the proceeds or some small proportion of the proceeds of energy taxes are sometimes earmarked for transport-related activities, in most OECD countries in acknowledgement of the fact that their purpose is to raise revenues for general government, they are not so earmarked.

E. Taxation and the environment

1. Some general remarks

Until very recently, pollution taxes as such did not exist, even if a number of taxes were likely to have some effect on the environment – sometimes favourable, sometimes the reverse. The primary reason for the imposition of such taxes was to raise revenues for government, and sometimes to further economic (including energy) and social objectives, but rarely, if ever, to promote environmental objectives. In recent years governments have increasingly taken into account the environmental consequences of taxation and are likely to continue to do so in the future. However, for the time being, pollution taxes exist in relatively few countries and mostly at low rates.

Unlike other taxes, pollution taxes are not intended to raise revenues for governments but only to reduce pollution and usually they do not raise substantial revenue. The potential exception would be the carbon tax, which it is generally agreed could succeed in reducing carbon dioxide emissions only if the rates imposed were sufficiently high to raise considerable amounts of revenue. What governments do with any such extra revenues is one issue, but the immediate effect would be to change relative revenue reliance on the different fuels (oil, gas, electricity, coal, peat) something which would also have repercussions on energy policy as well as economic and social policy.

Taxation and the environment raises important international issues: cross-frontier environmental problems, including atmospheric or water pollution by sources near to national boundaries; multilateral problems affecting a group of countries, such as acid rain in Europe; and global problems such as the greenhouse effect. In all these cases the levying of pollution taxes on a national basis is likely to have implications for international competitiveness. Industries in countries seeking to maintain high standards of environmental quality will tend to be disadvantaged in international trade, in comparison to industries permitted a free choice of production processes. This disadvantage is likely to be particularly severe where environmental policies take the form of taxes or charges rather than regulations, since industry in the country setting higher standards will not only use more costly production techniques (as a result of the tax incentive), but also has the additional burden of the environmental taxes or charges. Though the revenue from the environmental taxes may be used to reduce other taxes, including taxes on industry, and exchange rate movements may partly offset any initial loss of competitiveness, it is likely that pollution intensive industries would experience a worsening of their competitive position vis-à-vis those in neighbouring countries where similar taxes were not levied. As noted later, international co-ordination would appear to be a prerequisite for the introduction of a major new pollution tax such as the carbon tax. Even so, national administrations are likely to continue to differ in introducing minor pollution taxes or adapting existing taxes to meet environmental objectives. Preferences for environmental quality over other objectives vary between countries and there are also likely to be important differences as regards vulnerability to environmental damage.

As a last general remark it may be mentioned that there is a close relationship between environmental taxation and energy and transport taxes in that over 95 per cent of tax receipts that could affect environmental objectives derive from these energy and transport taxes. This is not to say that the relatively small pollution taxes outside the energy field are unimportant in their impact on environmental objectives. For example, it has been reported (D. Williams, 1992) that the Italian tax on plastic bags has halved their use. Whilst there could be future scope for new important pollution taxes with regard to agricultural pesticides and waste for example, for the time being a discussion of taxation and the environment has to concentrate on energy and transport taxation. In some areas environmental and energy policy may be identical (e.g. the reduction of the consumption of gasoline) and in others they may conflict (e.g. the encouragement or discouragement of high pollution forms of energy like coal and peat). Whilst energy economists have tended to follow traditional cost-benefit analysis with economic growth being the main desideratum, environmental economists have argued that such analysis cannot be accurately applied over the time scales with which they are concerned and the main objective should be not economic growth but 'sustainable development' or sharing environmental resources in an equitable way with future generations.

2. The polluter pays principle (PPP)

Environmental policies began to be formulated in the late sixties when it was generally agreed that polluters should pay for the costs of pollution. In economic terms the starting point of PPP was that the price of goods and services should fully reflect their cost of production and resources used, *including* environmental resources. Environmentalists argued that the free use of such resources as air and water is a prime cause of environmental degradation and it was held that ideally the polluter should pay the full cost of damages caused by the pollution activities. In practice, it is often not easy to identify the cost of the damage caused by individual polluters and a further complication is that environmental controls would become a source of distortion of international competition, if some countries were to take different decisions with regard, for example, to the subsidisation or taxation of private investment in pollution control.

Taxation is but one of a number of economic or other instruments that may be used to influence environmental objectives and the question for the tax policy maker is in what circumstances it is appropriate to use taxation rather than these other instruments whether by introducing new kinds of taxes (henceforth 'pollution taxes') or by modifying existing tax provisions. Alternative instruments include tradeable emission permits, deposit-refund systems, enforcement incentives and financial aids. Direct regulations may provide permits for certain levels of emissions which polluters may buy and sell, so that those who perform above requirements may receive supplementary permits to be stored for later use or sale to other polluters. Under deposit-refund systems a rebate is applied to the return of anti-pollution usages. An example would be returnable bottles for beer, wine and soft drinks which may be combined, as in Denmark, with a tax on plastic containers for such drinks. Enforcement incentives include non-compliance fees for polluters exceeding prescribed environmental standards or the requirement of deposits to be refunded if such standards are not breached. Financial assistance to aid producers to reduce their pollution is yet another option and finally there is the possibility of user charges on particular polluters.

The choice of tax expenditures or tax penalties to achieve environmental objectives raises the general questions discussed in Chapter 6 and in many other chapters of this book. First, it has to be decided from a technical point of view whether tax expenditures or penalties are superior to other instruments for achieving the desired objectives and secondly, whether such tax expenditures or penalties would conflict with other policy objectives. Evidently they would clash with the currently favoured neutrality objective of taxation (however much, some environmentalists – see Chapter 5C – have argued otherwise) but this hardly seems a decisive factor in the choice between tax and other kinds of government instruments, all of which involve government intervention and non-neutrality.

Financial deterrents to pollution may take the form of user charges on particular polluters, the proceeds of which are normally designed to cover costs. However, they may contain a 'penalty' charge in excess of costs, generally earmarked to defray the particular pollution costs in question. Alternatively, such deterrents may take the form of increased general taxation, the proceeds of which usually accrue to general government revenues and are not earmarked.

User charges may be technically superior to taxation when it is possible to measure emission charges from particular polluters, or when the extent of pollution varies over different areas or particular periods, since in the latter case general tax provisions cannot take into account such variations. However, it often happens that there are many emission sources and no single point at which monitoring equipment could be used. In these circumstances, user charges are not feasible and taxation has to be used. One such example is the very many emission sources of carbon dioxide (motor vehicles, domestic heating appliances, industrial energy combustion, as discussed in the next sub-section) and another is contamination of water supplies by excessive use of agricultural fertilisers.

If PPP is to be sought through the tax system, adaptation of existing tax systems offers a number of possibilities. In particular, environmental restructuring of the indirect tax system provides a route for the introduction of market-based incentives for pollution control. Rather than directly charging for each unit of pollution emitted, using the existing tax system to pursue environmental objectives would involve indirect incentives, making use of the relationship between polluting activities and the various transactions which are currently taxed. For example, instead of taxing the pollution output from car exhausts, additional tax may be levied on petrol purchases, on the assumption that the amount of this form of pollution is closely correlated with the amount of petrol used. In some cases, however, it seems that only new kinds of pollution taxes can be utilised effectively for PPP purposes, because adaptation of existing tax provisions cannot be sufficiently targeted.

Another possibility is to use the direct tax system, particularly accelerated depreciation provisions under corporate taxation, to subsidise installation of certain types of pollution control equipment, etc., but as argued in Chapters 6 and 12, this would clash more importantly with the objectives of neutrality and transparency sought by tax policy makers.

3. Environment policy and taxation in the energy and transport area

This is the area where taxation could play the greatest part in promoting environmental objectives and in recent years it has begun to do so in a few countries. Until recently, however, environmental considerations have not played an important role in the design of energy and transport taxes and where energy or transport objectives have clashed with environmental objectives, the former have invariably taken precedence. An obvious case is the favourable tax treatment accorded to coal and peat in relation to other energy sources even though they pollute the most. Of course, in many areas of taxation, energy and environmental objectives coincide. Higher taxes on gasoline help to conserve energy, reduce pollution and raise additional revenues, even if they are unpopular with motoring voters and increase inflationary pressures.

Road transport in particular is an area where the taxation practices of most OECD countries have taken little account of environmental objectives. *Environment and economics* (OECD 1992) states that:

> In industrialised countries, transport is a major sector of the economy. Users' expenditure, including the use of infrastructure, represents 4 to 9 per cent of GDP in OECD countries. Transport provides 2 to 4 per cent of employment and accounts for about 30 per cent of total energy consumption (of which road transport alone consumes 82 per cent). Between 1970 and 1989 the number of cars multiplied by a factor of 2.0 in Western Europe by 1.6 in North America and by 2.7 in Japan; there are about 150 million cars (plus 44.5 million goods vehicles) in North America and 130.3 million cars (plus 14.5 million goods vehicles) in Western Europe. Furthermore, road traffic volumes have almost doubled. This share of transport in the economy is still expected to increase in the future.

It then goes on to remark that transport is a major cause of environmental disruption, most importantly through air and noise pollution and that many government interventions have detrimental environmental effects. Among taxation measures are cited

> ...fiscal concessions inducing car over-use, e.g. in the United Kingdom, 2 million cars (10 per cent of total car stock) are company cars purchased with tax concessions. In Sweden, income tax deductions for commuting from home to work by car attain approximately 9 billion SK per year. In Germany, income tax deduction for commuting by car were estimated to increase both accident cost and air pollution by about DM 1 billion/year each. In France, the annual tax on cars is halved for older vehicles (5 years or more), thus contributing to a greater number of older and less environmentally efficient cars.

Leaving aside new pollution taxes, there are a number of ways in which existing consumption taxes on transport and energy can be adopted to promote environmental objectives. Taking first taxes on transport which include VAT and excises on the purchases of new cars and annual registration taxes, differentiation could be made according to how environmental goals are affected. To some extent this is already done in that annual registration taxes are sometimes related to measures such as horsepower which could have some deterrent effect on buying cars consuming more fuel. Among consumption taxes on vehicles it has been suggested that since excises and VAT tend to be charged only on new cars, there is an incentive to keep old environmentally inefficient cars and that one environmentally favourable measure would accordingly be to shift the tax burden from VAT and excises to annual registration taxes. More important adaptations seem possible in the taxation of energy, including a move from the various taxes on cars to higher taxes on gasoline, in order to reduce fuel consumption.

In recent years various measures have been introduced to adopt transport and energy taxes to meet environmental objectives. These include:

- providing a lower rate on unleaded than leaded petrol (as now occurs in most OECD countries);
- providing a reduced rate of tax on cars equipped with a catalytic converter as occurs for example in Australia, Belgium, Finland, Germany, the Netherlands and Sweden (in Denmark, Norway and Switzerland and the United States their use is mandatory);
- a 'gas guzzler excise' on cars that do not meet specified fuel efficiency standards (the United States);
- tax incentives to scrap very old cars, which most pollute the environment (Greece);

- replacing (in part) general energy taxes by specific taxes on carbon and sulphur emissions (Sweden in 1991).

Although existing for many years, and not designed to discourage pollution, the severance taxes in many states of the United States on the extraction of petroleum and other mineral resources may have the effect of reducing and postponing the exploitation of inferior types of deposits.

The tax differential between gasoline and diesel oil, in almost all countries in favour of diesel oil (see Section D3 above) has almost certainly not been made for environmental reasons. It appears that these two kinds of fuel pollute partly in similar ways, partly in different ways. For example, diesel has no lead and virtually no carbon monoxide or hydrocarbon emissions, but has particles, while gasoline has lead and CO emissions, but no particles; but both have nitrous oxide emissions.

Finally, to put matters in perspective, transport taxation probably has to play a minor role in promoting environmental objectives. For example, a mandatory requirement for catalytic converters on new cars is more effective than a tax preference, and mandatory standards regarding not only safety but also pollution for old cars are more effective than the tax measures referred to above. (For a whole series of other non-tax measures to reduce transport pollution see the summary of J. Short (1992).)

4. Carbon taxes

As noted by S. Cnossen and H. Vollebergh (1992) from which some of the descriptive part of this section is drawn, the International Panel on Climate Change (IPCC) recently submitted its report on the scientific assessment of climate change (IPCC 1990). The build-up of greenhouse gases (GHGs) – the main ones being carbon dioxide (CO_2), chlorofluorocarbons (CFCs), methane and nitrous oxide – suggests a rise in global mean temperatures in the range of 0.2°C to 0.5°C per decade over the next century. According to the IPCC, slowing down the rate of warming to 0.1°C per decade would require more than a halving of GHG emissions from current levels. At the first World Climate Conference in Toronto in 1988, it was suggested that CO_2 emissions should be reduced by 20 per cent in the long run. An Intergovernmental Panel on Climate Change (IPCC) was established – bringing together more than 3,000 scientists from 35 countries – to report on the causes and consequences of global warming and on possible remedies. Its reports were adopted at the second World Climate Conference held in 1990. In the same year, the EC Commission proposed to stabilise man-made CO_2 emissions at their 1990 levels by the turn of the century. Finally, a framework convention on climate change was prepared by an Intergovernmental Negotiating Committee for the June 1992 United Nations Conference on Environment and Development.

In recent years, some OECD governments and international agencies such as the United Nations and the European Community have taken the view that a substantial tax on the emissions of CO_2, by far the most important of these ozone-depleting emissions, is likely to be a necessary measure to reduce global warming or the so-called greenhouse effect. Despite these international pressures very few (Denmark, Finland, the Netherlands, Norway, Sweden and the United States at the last count) have introduced such taxes and then, at rates well below those estimated to preserve, let alone reduce CO_2 emissions. Estimates of the level of taxation necessary to stabilise or reduce demand vary considerably. One example is that OECD simulations by Hoeller and Wallin (1991) suggest that the carbon tax needs to rise to something like $300 per ton of carbon in order to reduce CO_2 emissions in the developed countries to 20 per cent below their 1990 level by 2020. Such a tax would be equivalent to a price increase of about $36 on a barrel of oil and would imply tax revenues ranging from 3 to 7 per cent of GDP for different OECD countries, though of course the introduction of carbon taxes could be accompanied by a reduction of other energy taxes, as took place in the Swedish 1991 tax reform, or indeed by a general reduction in rates of (say) corporation income taxes.

A carbon tax is an excise levied per unit of CO_2 emitted. The carbon content of different gasoil fuels varies and the imposition of a carbon tax would raise prices considerably for coal, less for oil and even less for gas. In designing the structure of the carbon tax, the implicit carbon tax has evidently to be taken into account.

Table 7.5 shows the carbon excise equivalent of current excises in fossil fuels as well as current emission prices. Given approximately similar pre-excise world oil prices, it appears that implicit carbon excises and emission prices are closely correlated. The implicit carbon excise on oil products is well over $200 in most OECD European counries (much higher in France and Italy) and Japan, but is only $65 in the United States. In all OECD countries natural gas is taxed at much lower rates and except in Sweden and Switzerland coal is not taxed at all and is sometimes subsidised.

Table 7.6 indicates the mechanical effect on fuel prices of a new tax of $100 per ton of carbon and panel C of that table shows that end-use prices would increase most in the United States and least in Japan in the three largest OECD countries with regard to the fuels selected.

Chart 7.5 shows that the United States is responsible for more CO_2 emission per head than any European country save Luxembourg and Chart 7.6 indicates the source of these emissions.

The main reason why adequate carbon taxes have not so far been introduced is that it would make little sense for countries to introduce large carbon taxes unilaterally. A single country, even if it phased out its emissions completely, would not affect global warming. In addition, export competitiveness would suffer, at least in the short run, and imports of energy-intensive goods – if untaxed – would increase sharply. If energy-intensive production were to shift location to countries with no carbon taxes, global emissions could even increase. Other arguments that have been voiced against a carbon tax have been that it would be market-distorting, could switch demand to the energy sources which might be equally environmentally damaging and would require large costs for its implementation. Some have even been sceptical as to whether the greenhouse effect has actually been scientifically established.

At the international level there are formidable obstacles to agreement to a co-ordinated carbon tax. So far the European Community has been making most of the running, in proposing a combined energy/carbon tax, provided Japan and the United States agree to do likewise, but many objections have already been made to such an EC carbon/energy tax.

Table 7.5: Implicit carbon excise, 1988 (US$ per ton)

Country	Emission price	Implicit carbon excise			
		Coal	Oil	Gas	Total
United States	208	0	65	0	28
European Community					
Belgium	319	0	162	35	86
Germany	351	0	212	23	95
Netherlands	359	0	221	27	89
Spain	373	0	176	19	112
Denmark	391	0	297	110	147
United Kingdom	399	0	297	0	106
Portugal	441	0	205	131	150
Ireland	446	0	177	4	138
Italy	506	0	317	80	223
France	556	0	351	38	229
Canada	301	0	108	0	52
Finland	402	0	189	0	107
Japan	431	0	130	2	79
Austria	487	0	267	39	150
New Zealand	517	0	235	0	117
Sweden	578	0	268	13	214
Norway	623	0	258	0	182
Switzerland	640	0	224	18	198

Sources: *Energy prices, taxes and carbon dioxide emissions,* P. Hoeller and S. Wallin (OECD 1991). Figures are not available for Australia, Greece, Iceland, Luxembourg and Turkey.

Within the EC doubts have been raised about whether a harmonised carbon tax makes sense when existing energy and transport taxes are so unharmonised; second, there is a fear that such a tax could accentuate competitive distortions among EC countries, since the more seriously obligations are taken by governments to ensure the tax is properly collected, the greater the competitive disadvantage of their industries vis-à-vis other EC countries; third, it has been estimated by a committee of the European Coal and Steel Community that one projected carbon tax would raise the price of coal by 58 per cent and of gasoline by only 6 per cent – with serious economic and social consequences. In relation to non-EC countries, whereas the totality of EC countries account for only 13 per cent of carbon emissions, the United States with its much lower taxes on explicit and implicit carbon emissions accounts for 23 per cent, and more importantly it is argued that the effects of an EC global tax on global warming would be negligible, since the largest increases in CO_2 emissions over the next years are expected to take place outside the OECD area, especially in Eastern Europe and China. Others take the view that, nevertheless, it is for the richer OECD countries to set an example.

Table 7.6: The mechanical effect of a $100 tax per ton of carbon on energy prices, 1988

A. Carbon content and carbon mission coefficient[1]

	Gram of carbon per megajoule	Ton of carbon per ton of oil equivalent
Heavy fuel oil	20-21	0.80-0.84
Light fuel oil		
Gasoline	19-20	0.76-0.80
Diesel		
Petrol		
Coal	24-25	0.96-1.00
Gas	14-16	0.56-0.64
Cooking gas	50	2.00
Liquid gas	17	0.68
Peat	18-30	1.10-1.20
Wood	29-33	1.20.1.30
Wastes (solid)	30-45	1.20-1.80

B. Price effect on primary energy sources

	Crude oil	Coal	Natural gas
Unit of measure	**Barrel**	**Ton**	**Ton of oil equivalent**
Tons of Carbon/Unit of fuel	0.12	0.61	0.60
World market price ($)	14.9[2]	44.0[3]	95.0[4]
Absolute tax ($)	12.0	60.5	60.0

C. Price effect on end-use prices (per ton of oil equivalent

	Gasoline			Steam coal			Gas price for household		
	United States	**Japan**	**Germany**	**United States**	**Japan**	**Germany**	**United States**	**Japan**	**Germany**
End-use price($)	299.5	1084.5	720.4	58.4	110.7	252.3	234.2	1086.7	353.2
Price increase, per cent	26.04%	7.2%	10.8%	167.8%	88.5%	38.8%	25.6%	5.5%	17.0%

1. One ton of carbon corresponds to 3.7 tons of CO_2.
2. IEA country average import price.
3. OECD average steam coal import price.
4. EEC average import price by pipeline.

Sources: *Estimation of greenhouse gas emission and sinks* (OECD 1991), Paris.
Energy prices and taxes (OECD 1991), Paris.

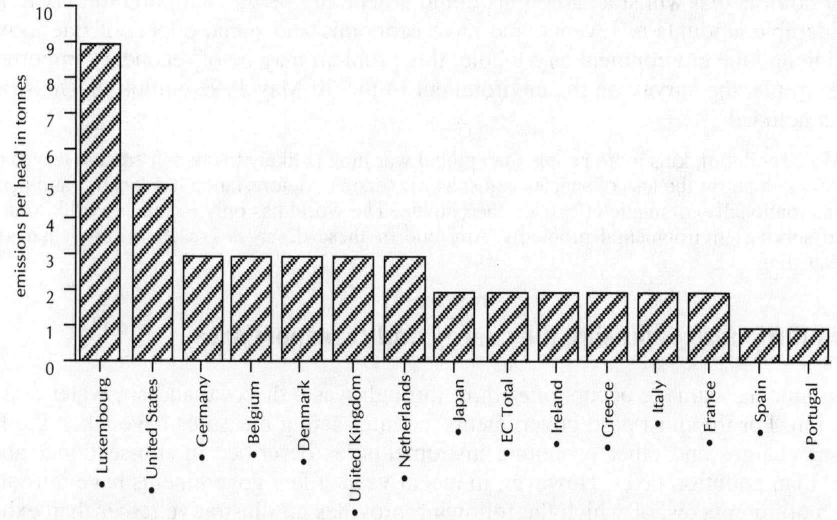

Chart 7.5: Carbon emissions per head in EC countries, Japan and the United States (latest year)

Source: Commission of the European Communities as adapted by *The Economist* 9 May 1992

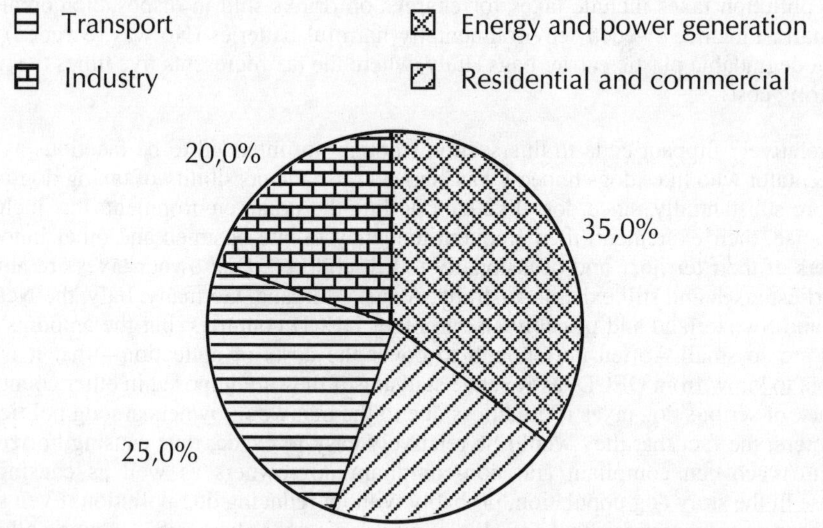

Chart 7.6: Source of carbon emissions in EC countries, Japan and the United States (latest year)

Source: Commission of the European Communities as adapted by *The Economist* 9 May 1992

A last point is that whilst a carbon tax could potentially be the first pollution tax to raise considerable amounts of revenue and have economic and social effects, if one looks at taxation and the environment as a whole, this problem may be of secondary importance. For example, the survey on the environment in the 30 May 1992 edition of *The Economist* concluded:

> Water pollution kills more people than global warming is likely to do; soil erosion leaves more people hungry; the loss of species is just as irreversible; deforestation has locally (and perhaps internationally) dramatic effects on the climate. The world has only so much wealth to devote to solving environmental problems. Any one of these deserves greater priority than global warming.

5. Pollution taxes outside the energy and transport area

Environmental damage occurs *inter alia*, through waste disposal and air, water and soil pollution. For the most part, governments' counter-acting measures have taken the form of user charges and other economic instruments, as described in sub-section 2 above, rather than pollution taxes. However, in recent years a few governments have introduced some pollution taxes, of which the following provides an illustrative rather than exhaustive list:

Taxes have been recently introduced on chemical agricultural fertilisers and/or pesticides in Austria, Denmark, Finland, Norway and Sweden, the proceeds of which are usually earmarked and are perhaps more akin to user charges than taxes. Other recently introduced pollution taxes include taxes for charges on drinks sold in disposable containers (Denmark, Finland, Sweden) environmentally harmful batteries (Norway, Sweden) and non-biodegradable plastic carrier bags (Italy, where the tax represents five times the manufacturing cost).

As a relatively flippant coda to this section (though not intended to be facetious as one commentator who likes dogs hoped I was being) I raise the possibility of taxing dog-owners more substantially, since dogs like cars pollute the urban environment: this includes their noise, their excrement, their frequent tendency to bite postmen and other innocent invaders of their territory and occasionally to kill children. Dog-owner taxes are among the earliest taxes and still exist in Australia, Austria, Finland, Germany, Italy, the Netherlands and Switzerland and possibly also in other OECD countries, but the amounts collected are so small – often not enough to cover the costs of collection – that it is not possible to know from OECD tax revenue statistics if they are imposed in other countries. The lack of serious dog taxes is doubtless due to the many dog-owners among politicians and voters, the fact that they would be relatively easy to evade, thus causing horizontal inequities between compliant and non-compliant dog-owners as well as causing an increase in the stray dog population, probably without reducing dog pollution. Even so, it does seem somewhat unfair that non-dog-owners have not only to suffer canine pollution but also to subsidise it.

F. *The taxation of small to medium enterprises*

This section is very brief, because little internationally comparative work has been done on the taxation of SME's outside value added taxation. However, the OECD is currently preparing a comprehensive study on this topic and it is understood that a report is likely to be published in 1993.

As in many other areas governments have the choice of intervening or not intervening to aid or penalise SME's and if they decide to intervene there are a variety of measures both outside the tax system and within it by which they may do so.

From the point of view of economic efficiency SME's have various advantages and disadvantages in relation to larger enterprises, but how far there is a case for governments to provide special assistance on economic or social grounds to SME's is a question outside the scope of this book. It is of relevance, however, to record that there are various ways of doing this outside the tax system and the criteria for choosing between non-tax measures and tax expenditures do not differ generally from those already discussed in Chapter 6C, apart from the fact that SME's may be discriminated against under tax laws as noted in the introduction to this chapter.

Governments' possibilities of helping SME's outside the tax system include, firstly assistance for starting-up in the form of availability of capital at low rates of interest and provision of training and information facilities; second, improving the technological environment, including supporting know-how, research and development, but also using a wide variety of other possible measures; third, reducing financial and administrative obstacles to SME's though continuing loans at favourable rates and financial guarantees to lenders. This last category of aid extends also to reduced formalities in the taxation field as recorded in detail in Chapter 13C3 in relation to value added taxation.

Within the tax system, leaving aside the relaxation of formalities generally and other measures in respect of value added taxation recorded in more detail in Chapter 13C, favourable income tax treatment may take various forms. A first point is that SME's will normally be subject to progressive rates of personal income tax if unincorporated and to what is usually a flat rate corporation income tax if incorporated. Like other enterprises they generally have the choice of whether or not to seek incorporation, though tax factors are by no means the only influence on this decision.

As described in Chapter 12C1 and Table 12.5 favourable corporation tax rate treatment is rarely given to SME's, and in the few countries where it is so given this may be a by-product of lower rates for enterprises making small profits, which are not necessarily SME's. Some countries provide other concessions which largely, but not always necessarily, will be targeted on SME's; (e.g. Belgium, Canada, France, Germany, Japan, the Netherlands). These include tax credits, tax deferrals and favourable depreciation allowances. Tax concessions for unincorporated SME's subject to the personal income tax frequently take the form of applying a flat rate rather than the normal progressive rate to them (e.g. Belgium, France, Greece, Portugal, Spain, the United Kingdom) and less frequently favourable treatment of the tax base vis-à-vis the normal situation. Simplified accounting methods are permitted in many OECD countries for the purposes of both the personal and corporation income tax.

Chapter 8
Financing social security benefits

A. Introduction

A first question could be why devote a chapter to financing social security benefits? One view (as reflected in the practices of Australia and New Zealand) is that social security is a public good, like education, defence, law and order, industrial infrastructure, and that insofar as it is considered that benefits should be provided by government, they should be financed out of general government revenues. However, that is not the way that most OECD governments see things, and some of them even prefer to regard social security contributions as quasi-social insurance premiums and not at all as taxes. These two extreme views, together with the various compromises between them, provide the main theme of this chapter, for the view that governments take is bound to influence how they decide social security benefits should be financed.

Social security contributions (hereafter referred to as "contributions" or when the context requires as "earmarked payroll taxes") are in most OECD countries the main way of financing social security benefits. For reasons discussed in Chapter 2 and the Annex to Section E of that chapter, these contributions are taken to be taxes, but the question remains to be discussed further to what extent they should be regarded as special kinds of taxes, in view of the fact that they are the only major earmarked tax, that their payment confers rights to benefits and that they may be perceived differently from other taxes by those who pay them.

As in the case of financing local government expenditures, financing social security benefits raises economic and social issues going beyond tax policy questions and these are discussed in this chapter only in so far as they could be relevant to the ways of financing benefits. Thus nothing is said about the optimal amount of social expenditures and revenues that should be raised in any particular country at any given point in time or the effect of social security programmes on the level and composition of savings. Where, however, the method of taxing contributions may have an influence on taxpayers' social and economic behaviour, in particular their labour supply patterns, this is commented on. A particularly important tax/expenditure policy issue, briefly referred to in Chapter 10D6 and in this chapter is the possible integration of the personal income tax with the social security system as a whole, including benefits as well as contributions and encompassing ideas that have been experimented with on a small scale but never been put fully into practice, such as negative income tax systems. In addition, this chapter and Chapter 10E4 do cover specific expenditure issues, like the financing of aid to parents, to whom relief may be given through the spending side as well as through the personal income tax or employers' contributions.

Social security benefits may be financed partially outside the tax system. Possibilities include compulsory levies to be paid to the private sector, in some countries quite considerable, and voluntary payments by employees to the government, in most countries very small. Another important source of funding equivalent benefits to those under social security programmes which are provided by the private sector is the revenues governments forgo when they give taxpayers income tax relief in respect of contributions to pension funds and to health and other insurance. So far, it has not been possible to quantify these on an internationally comparable basis. Another area where quantitative information is lacking is the relative importance of revenues raised by contributions and those from general government revenues or deficit financing when security benefits exceed the funds available to finance them. However, some information is available on the funding of pensions for the years 1960 to 1984, the most important component of social security benefits, and this is reproduced in Chart 8.1.

OECD RS collects information (pages 154-7 of the 1991 edition) on the relative importance of compulsory contributions to the private sector and voluntary contributions to general government, but most OECD countries have been unable to provide this information. The following shows the percentage of these non-tax payments as a percentage of contributions plus other earmarked taxes, plus compulsory contributions to the private sector plus voluntary contributions to government for the years 1980 and 1989 in those countries which were able to supply the information:

	Compulsory contributions to the private sector		**Voluntary contributions to government**	
	1980	**1989**	**1980**	**1989**
Austria	n.a.	n.a.	less than 1	less than 1
Denmark	5	13	1.4	2.8
Finland	49	52	n.a.	n.a.
Germany	less than 1	less than 1	9	8
Iceland	28	35	n.a.	n.a.
Netherlands	21	13	3.2	less than 1
Switzerland	36	40[1]	1.6	1.4[1]
United Kingdom	50	40	less than 1	less than 1

1. For 1988, not 1989.

Earmarked taxes for social security benefits other than contributions are shown in OECD RS as existing only in Finland, France, Iceland, Portugal and Switzerland. In Iceland they are much more important than contributions, in Finland about half as important, and in France, Portugal and Switzerland, very small indeed. More detailed revenue statistics on contributions have already been provided in Chapters 2 and 3.

A definitional point that should be mentioned is that there is a lack of consensus among countries and international organisations on what should be the coverage of social security benefits and, *a fortiori*, contributions earmarked for such benefits. Table 8.1 which provides information on country practices in Section E follows the source (US 1989) in confining data to a) old age, invalidity and death; b) sickness and maternity; c) work injury; d) unemployment and e) family allowances. This does not always correspond to what is shown in Chapters 2 and 3 since in some countries these revenue data may include contributions for other benefits which, however, are of negligible revenue importance. A more serious difference is that the OECD classification of taxes regards universal family allowances as welfare benefits (benefits in respect of actualities) and not as social security benefits (benefits in respect of contingencies) so that receipts from employers' contributions to universal family allowances are shown as taxes on payroll and workforce (3000) and not as employers' social security contributions (2000). However, payroll taxes earmarked for family benefits occur only in a very few countries (see Table 8.1, column 7). (Unearmarked payroll taxes are discussed in Chapter 12E along with taxes on business other than corporation taxes.)

B. The compulsory social insurance versus the income support approach

1. A comparison of the two approaches

a) *The compulsory social insurance approach*

Social security schemes, first introduced by Bismarck in Germany in 1880 and subsequently followed by nearly all the other OECD countries, were based on the compulsory social insurance approach, which requires that benefits are provided only if sufficient contributions are made and that such benefits are paid only in the event of certain contingencies, such as old-age, sickness, maternity, industrial injury and unemployment, actually taking place. A similar approach was taken in the 1942 Beveridge Report in the United Kingdom and after the 1939-1945 war there was a massive increase in contributions and benefits based on the compulsory social insurance approach in most West European countries.

This approach continues to have much support among many commentators and governments, some of whom prefer to maintain that contributions are not taxes but quasi-insurance premiums (quasi because they are concerned with social insurance and not

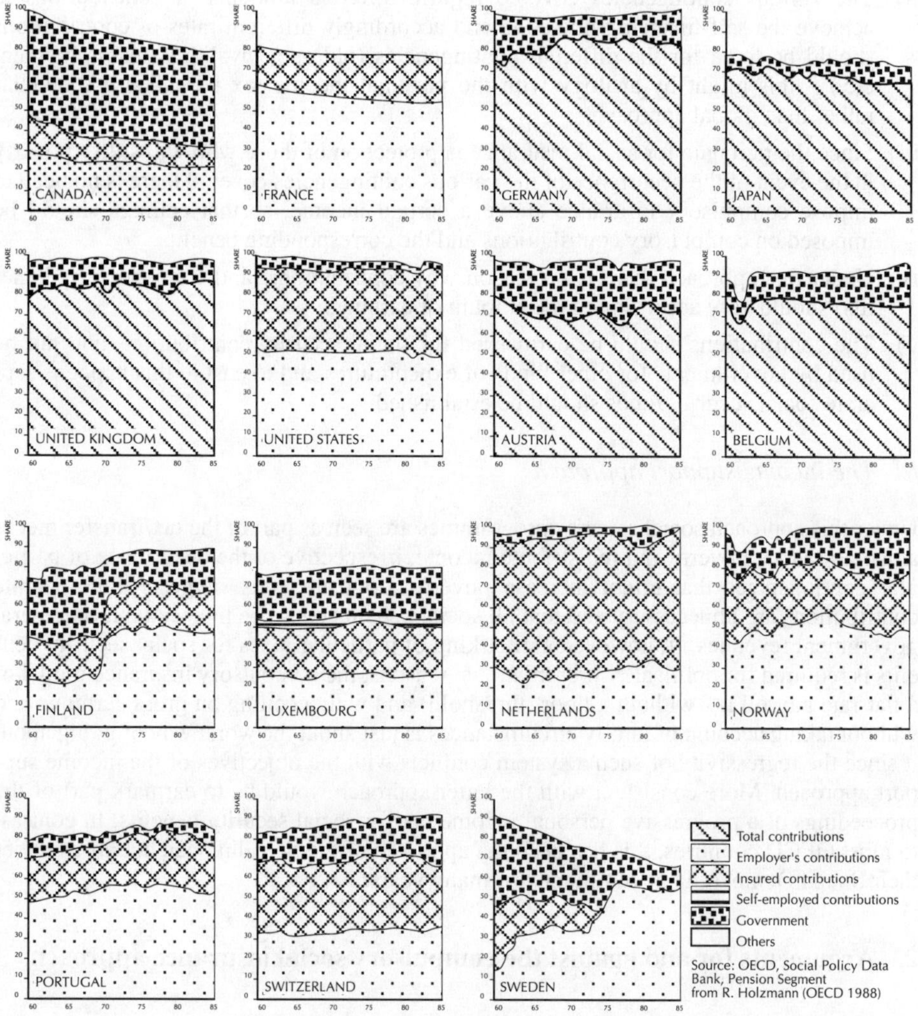

Chart 8.1: Revenue structure and development of general public pension schemes in OECD countries

individual insurance and because insurance is not normally compulsory, even though it may be for some contingent risks such as motor accidents or accidents in dwelling places which could incur costs for neighbours). Adherence to a strict compulsory social insurance approach would imply the following:

i) The scheme is jointly funded by the insured persons and their employers and contributions should entirely finance the benefits to be paid.

ii) The various contingencies covered require different amounts of contributions to achieve the self-financing objective and accordingly different rates of contributions should be fixed for the different contingencies (old age, invalidity, unemployment etc.) – this might by analogy with the personal income tax be called a schedular rather than global approach.

iii) Since the rationale for social insurance is protection of those who will suffer poverty in the event of the occurrence of the various contingencies covered there is no need to impose compulsory insurance above a certain income, so that ceilings should be imposed on compulsory contributions and the corresponding benefits.

iv) Under this approach there is no reason why contributions (and corresponding benefits) should vary according to the amount of earnings.

v) The contributions should be earmarked for social security contributions and not be used by governments for other kinds of expenditures and to ensure this happens separate social security funds should be established.

b) The income support approach

Under this approach social security programmes are seen as part of the tax/transfer mechanism to reduce poverty and redistribute income, irrespective of the occurrence of particular contingencies that might increase poverty. Logically, this suggests that separate contributions are unnecessary and that all social benefits could be financed out of general government revenues. If, however, earmarking of particular taxes for social security benefits is required for political or presentational reasons, the compulsory insurance model of a flat-rate payroll tax without a floor (threshold) and with a ceiling on gross earnings and without taking account of family circumstances is just about the worst way of going about it since the regressivity of such a system conflicts with the objectives of the income support approach. More consistent with the latter approach would be to earmark part of the proceedings of a progressive personal income tax for social security benefits. In contrast to most OECD countries, this has been the approach of the Scandinavian countries under their Social Democratic governments for many years.

2. Arguments for and against the compulsory social insurance approach

a) For

The appeal of the compulsory insurance approach has been summarised by J. Kay (1990), referring especially to the time when compulsory contributions were first being phased in:

> For the political right, their attraction is that they appear to give protection against poverty and its consequences without explicitly involving the State in the distribution and redistribution of income. Historically, this is in fact the way in which the social insurance concept gained at least partial adoption in so many countries: it provided a device by which growing concern for social problems could be reconciled with prevailing attitudes of laissez-faire. For the political left, the appeal of social insurance is that it seems to entrench redistribution as an entitlement, rather than as the outcome of a political process which may choose to be more, or less, generous at particular times.

I remember being impressed in the early eighties at two separate conferences where both left and right preferred to regard contributions as quasi-insurance payments rather than taxes: the predominantly left International Social Security Association, favouring high social expenditures, feared that if contributions were regarded as taxes, the receipts would be annexed by governments for other expenditures, such as defence, infrastructure, law and order, and the predominantly right public finance economists at the International Institute of Public Finance, who favoured lower expenditures on social benefits, considered that the insurance concept provided a market discipline on the demand for greater welfare expenditures.

b) *Against*

The most important argument against is bound up with the changing social consensus that it is desirable to protect the underprivileged not only from the poverty arising as a result of such contingencies as old age, sickness and unemployment, but also from poverty not related to these contingencies. The large growth of one-parent families over the last three decades has possibly been the greatest cause of such poverty, and it is difficult to see how a compulsory social insurance approach can improve matters there. Second, causes of poverty change considerably over the years and the insurance approach is a somewhat inflexible way of coping with this. For example, unemployment was an important cause of poverty in the thirties, of negligible importance between 1950 and the late seventies, and since then has become more and more important. Third, the insurance approach entails benefits to be paid to all those who can afford to make the qualifying amount of contributions, irrespective of their income and wealth, and though the imposition of ceilings and benefits was designed to reduce these costs, this is a reason why in almost all OECD countries contributions have been insufficient to finance benefit payments. Finally, since for any particular taxpayer there is no necessary connection between contributions and benefits received, the latter depending both on contingencies which may or not arise and sufficient contributions having been paid to qualify for any benefits, a number of commentators prefer to speak of the "insurance illusion" or "insurance myth" rather than the "insurance approach".

3. Arguments for and against the income support approach

a) *For*

Most of the arguments for the income support approach have been stated in the last paragraph in criticising the alternative compulsory social insurance approach. In addition, it may be argued that it is irrational for governments to pursue contradictory and uncoordinated policies through the income tax on the one hand, and through contributions on the other.

b) *Against*

The arguments against the income support approach take two separate forms: the defence of the integrity of the compulsory social insurance principle and the "pie in the sky" attack from the radical right, which emphasises the intergenerational problem. The first line of criticism might accept the need that governments should use the tax/transfer system to reduce poverty whether by universal measures such as minimum wages and family benefits or by selective income support schemes for the most needy, but would claim that this is a separate issue from the need to safeguard the sound insurance principles which should prevail with regard to the contingencies that social security schemes are designed to cover. The radical right goes somewhat further in asserting that young workers financing income support may never recuperate their contributions. J. Buchanan, (1968), always one of the most eloquent supporters of this approach said:

> Once the tax-transfer terminology begins to be used, and once the nation's policy makers come to think of the whole system as one that is based on taxes and transfers, levied and provided at the whims of the national government, rather than on sound insurance principles, a Pandora's box is opened. Liberal policy advocates immediately ask, and understandably, why regressive payroll taxes need be used. Why should these not be replaced by general taxes levied on more equitable grounds? More importantly, they will also ask why benefits should be earnings related. Why should those in need be excluded, even if they have not been prior contributing participants in the systems? Why should we not add other features to the tax-transfer systems such as Medicare? Recent experience makes clear that the sophisticated defense for the indirect insurance scheme, using intergenerational taxes and transfer as surrogates for real investment in order to secure the possibly higher rates of return promised by economic growth, will not likely produce a politically viable institutional structure. If and when he recognizes all this, and if he should be given the opportunity for effective choice, the young worker would almost certainly choose the straightforward insurance scheme over the current system. The "pie in the sky" aspects of existing institutions loom larger, and he can, in fact, foresee that increasing political gimmickry can produce a collapse of the whole structure.

C. Arguments for and against earmarking revenues and taxing payroll

1. The link between earmarking and payroll taxes

Although in most OECD countries payroll taxes are the only important tax to be earmarked, the arguments for and against earmarking any kind of tax for specific expenditure purposes are different in many respects from the arguments for and against raising revenues through payroll taxation rather than through income taxation or consumption taxation. Also payroll taxes are not always earmarked for social security benefits. Hence the two issues are discussed separately. However, because the compulsory social insurance approach requires both earmarking and payroll taxation, the arguments are discussed in the same section.

2. Arguments for and against earmarking

a) *For*

The main argument in favour of earmarking taxes for certain expenditures is that tax payers may be more willing to pay if they know what they are getting in return for the taxes that they are obliged to pay. Taxpayers may find a rough justice of using, for example, some of the proceeds of motor taxes to pay for road repair, or tobacco and alcohol taxes for health care. In the more important context of social security, earmarking might also help to stabilise the revenue resource in that social security administrations would not be obliged to indulge in annual bargaining with other government spending departments for their share of funds. It has also been argued that earmarking may help to promote taxpayer choice between higher benefits and higher contributions or lower benefits and lower contributions, though one may be sceptical as to whether this often happens in practice.

b) *Against*

The main argument against earmarking is that it imposes rigidities on governments' possibilities of re-allocating expenditures to areas where they are most urgently required. This rigidity becomes especially important in countries, where not only over a third of tax revenues derive from earmarked contributions but, in addition, there is separate earmarking for each social security benefit that is being financed. Just as the arguments for earmarking parallel those referred to in the last section in favour of the social insurance approach, so some of those against earmarking parallel those in favour of the income support approach. For example, it is no use having an under-utilised unemployment fund in times of low unemployment when poverty is mainly due to the growth of one-parent families.

c) *Evaluation*

It is not easy to evaluate the arguments for and against earmarking and doubtless they assume different weights in different countries and over different periods of time. As already suggested at the end of Chapter 5, the greater acceptability of earmarked contributions than other taxes to those who pay them may be due to a mixture of two separate kinds of illusions, the insurance illusion that they can expect to receive benefits in some relation to their contributions and the shifting illusion that their employers are bearing some part of these contributions. (In practice, it often happens that employees do not receive benefits corresponding to their contributions and young and mobile employees may not qualify for any benefits at all, and the shifting illusion is the unawareness of employees that they themselves will in the medium- to long-term be paying their employers' contributions in the form of lower wages and salaries or higher prices of the goods and services which they themselves consume.) However, even complex illusions come to an end eventually and also where the same withholding system is applied to both income tax payments and contributions, taxpayers may be generally unaware of how much of the deductions from their gross pay are due to their contributions, and how much to income tax, so in these circumstances the one levy is likely to be as acceptable or unacceptable as the other. Though growing unemployment levels are probably the main reason why in recent years receipts from earmarked contributions have ceased to grow as a percentage of total tax receipts or GDP, the reduction in taxpayer innocence may be another.

3. Arguments for and against payroll taxes as a means of financing benefits

a) For

One argument for payroll taxes is their relative invisibility except in times of recession and high unemployment: at other times employers, though probably resenting any increase in their own contributions as an extra short-term non-wage labour cost, realise that in the longer-term they are likely to be absorbed by lower wages whereas voting householders may be barely aware of increases in employer contributions; second, the use of payroll taxes follows the principle that taxpayer discontent is reduced if revenue sources are diversified; third, they are simple to collect; fourth, they are relatively simple to vary for conjunctural purposes either by changing rates generally or by providing special concessions for certain regions, certain industries, certain groups of taxpayers, such as youths, part-time workers or first-time employees; fifth, in some countries they represent a pragmatic proxy for a personal income tax which for administrative or political reasons it is too difficult to collect in sufficient quantities to meet revenue needs. However, their main justification is that payroll taxes are the only coherent taxing method of implementing the compulsory social insurance approach.

b) Against

The arguments against payroll taxation centre on their unfairness and their economic inefficiencies, or a mixture of the two. Many of their defects in this regard can, and have been, modified by various adjustments to the rate structure, but as with other taxes, such adjustments increase their complexity and may create other kinds of distortions. Employers' payroll taxes encourage them to substitute capital equipment for labour and provide a tax incentive for requiring their existing staff to work overtime as against taking on additional full or part-time employees. Also, employers who have to shed labour may take into account that the low or zero thresholds generally prevailing increase the relative non-wage labour costs of low paid compared to high paid employees. Moreover, the relatively heavy contribution burden on the low-paid, because of low or zero thresholds, provides an inducement to them to work part-time or even full-time in the underground economy.

4. Evaluation of earmarked payroll taxes

These merits and defects of earmarked payroll taxes are perhaps best evaluated in the light of the more specific rate and base issues discussed in the next section. As with unearmarked taxes, it seems that their defects assume greater importance in times of recession and growing unemployment, but earmarked payroll taxes continue to be levied on employees in 18 of the 24 OECD countries (all except Australia, Finland, Iceland, the Netherlands, New Zealand and Sweden) and on employers in 21 OECD countries (all except Australia, the Netherlands and New Zealand).

D. Policy choices under earmarked payroll taxes

1. Introduction

As with other taxes, a number of policy choices arise in deciding upon the rate structure of payroll taxes and the base to which it should be applied. Country practices are discussed in the next section from which it will be seen that there has been a universal retreat from the pure compulsory social insurance approach. The retreat has been much greater in some countries than others and earmarked contributions at variable rates according to contingencies covered remains in force in most countries. But the insurance desiderata with regard to the appropriate rate structure and base, as set out in Section B above, have in all countries been modified to accommodate the income support approach.

2. Rate issues

a) Schedular versus global rates

The social insurance principle requires separate (schedular) rates to ensure that each risk is self-financed, but fiscal principles of flexibility and simplicity favour a single rate to cover all benefits, so that expenditures can be switched from over-funded to under-funded benefits in the event of changes in priorities of governments. (Schedular rates still obtain in most OECD countries.)

b) Floors or thresholds below which contributions are not required

The social insurance principle requires that contributions should be paid on all earnings and that there should be no exemption for earnings below a certain amount. On an income support approach to contributions, this would be inequitable and some threshold should be set below which contributions are not payable as in the case of the personal income tax. (In practice, a number of countries do provide thresholds, but these are usually low and much lower than those set for the personal income tax.)

c) Ceilings above which contributions are not required

Under the social insurance principle compulsion is necessary only to protect the potentially poor from the extreme poverty that might occur in the event of certain contingencies arising. Beyond a certain level of earnings there is little risk of such extreme poverty and, accordingly, no rationale for making such contributions compulsory, so that any additional benefits required by such higher paid employees should be effected through private insurance. From a fiscal point of view ceilings create a number of anomalies and distortions: they are regressive, they increase the relative cost to employers of low-paid labour below the ceiling in relation to high paid labour, and in interaction with progressive income tax schedules contribution ceilings produce unintended effects: for example, the combined marginal income tax and contribution rates may decrease at income levels just above the ceiling. (Contribution ceilings remain in most countries but they have frequently been increased or abolished either for all benefits or for some of them.)

d) Flat rates versus percentage of earnings or payroll

Under the social insurance principle the employees' income is irrelevant to the cost of the contingencies for which they are being insured and so the same flat rate should be charged on all employees for a particular benefit (assuming risks are similar). Under the income support approach such a flat rate offends against vertical equity and would place too great a burden on the low paid. (This is one area where the income support approach has been universally accepted and flat rate contributions, commonplace in a number of OECD countries twenty years ago now exist only in Denmark for employees in respect of a small part of their pension entitlements.)

e) Single rates versus progressive rates

The same song continues. Progressive rates would be irrelevant on an insurance approach, necessary on an income support approach. (In all OECD countries, save the United Kingdom, rates are not progressive).

f) Relative rates of employees' and employers' contributions

A priori, it would seem that the social insurance principle has little to say on what should be the relative contributions, though the conventional line has been 50-50 for most benefits, the employer bearing the total cost of workers' injury assurance. Public finance economists claim that it does not matter in the medium to long run because the employee will bear both in the form of either lower wages or higher consumer prices – depending on the market situation, but it does matter in the short run when increases in employers' contributions may have to be borne by themselves. Also, those governments relying heavily on contributions could not get the amounts of revenue they require only from employees, and in practice they have to impose much heavier rates of tax on employers, which may be considered as a rough proxy for an unprogressive income tax, to the extent that they are shifted into lower wages or higher prices. (Greater revenues were received in 1989 from employers' contributions than those from employees in all OECD countries, except Denmark, Greece, the Netherlands and Switzerland.)

3. Base issues

a) Gross earnings versus income tax base

A social insurance approach would presumably find the fiscalisation of social insurance through integration with the income tax more objectionable than using gross earnings as a base. The income support approach would see no point in using one base for contributions and another for the income tax. (In practice, most OECD countries have a much wider base, approaching to gross earnings, for contributions than they have for the income tax base on earnings, but there has been a movement towards an income tax base on earnings in a number of OECD countries, and in a few they coincide.)

b) Contribution expenditures

This returns to the neutrality versus interventionist approach discussed several times earlier. Over the last twenty years, favourable contribution treatment has been given as a means of encouraging the development of certain regions (France, Italy), certain labour intensive industries such as textiles (Finland, Italy), young employees (France, Spain), female employees (Italy), etc. However, as indicated by the above examples, contribution expenditures do not occur in most countries. It may be relevant that over most of the last two decades employers' contributions in France, Italy and Spain have been much heavier than in any other OECD country, since in other countries their economic impact may be of insufficient importance to justify special concessions of this kind.

E. Country practices

1. A classification of practices

OECD countries can, with the usual reservations about borderline cases, be divided into three categories:

- 5 1/2 countries have predominantly adopted the income support approach where the financing of social benefits becomes part of the tax/transfer mechanism (the half is Sweden, for employees only, the others being Australia, Denmark, Iceland, the Netherlands and New Zealand).
- 5 countries have adopted hybrid systems with elements of the income support and elements of compulsory social insurance approach, where contributions remain an important source of finance but with one global rate instead of several schedular rates for the various benefits. (Norway, Portugal, Spain, United Kingdom and to a lesser extent Ireland which has two rates).
- 13 1/2 countries continue predominantly to follow the compulsory social insurance approach in that benefits are mainly financed out of schedular payroll taxes with no or low thresholds and separate ceilings for most of the various contingencies covered (the half is Sweden in respect of employers' contributions, the other 13 being those countries not mentioned under (a) and (b) above).

a) Countries adopting the income support approach

This is usually done by abolishing or almost abolishing the earmarking of particular taxes for benefits, or financing them entirely or almost entirely from general government revenues. This is what happens in Australia, Denmark, Iceland, New Zealand, and for employees only in Sweden. In Australia there is a surcharge on personal income tax payable for sickness benefits. In Denmark (1989) there are contributions from employees and employers for pensions covering less than 10 per cent of their cost and for unemployment insurance. In Iceland (1989) there are employers' contributions of 2 per cent for pensions and maternity and 1 per cent for unemployment, while employees pay 2 per cent of income subject to local income tax for sickness benefits. In 1990 the Netherlands introduced a practice previously followed in Denmark and Norway of converting employees' contributions to the rates and base applied to the personal income tax (with some minor differences) and earmarking a portion of the proceeds from this enlarged income tax for social security benefits. In addition, in the Netherlands employers' contributions have been abolished and the amounts previously paid added to the gross remuneration of employees.

b) Countries adopting a hybrid approach

The situation may be summarised as follows:

Countries		**Employees' contributions % of earnings**	**Employers' contributions % of payroll**	**Floor below which contributions not payable**	**Ceiling above which contributions are not payable**
Norway	(1990)	7.8 (wage) 12.8 (other)	about 15.6	17 000 Nkr. per year	None
Portugal	(1990)	11.0	24.5	None	None
Spain	(1990)	6.0 variable	29.4 variable	275 820 Ptas. per month	Variable
United Kingdom	(1990)	2 to 9	5 to 10.45	£46 per week	£350 per week
Ireland	(1989)	Sickness and maternity 1.25	1.25	None	(for employee only) IR£15 500
		All other 6.5	12.33	None	IR£16 200

- In Spain the variability relates to 12 different occupation classes.
- In the United Kingdom there is the possibility of contracting out of a government supplementary pension scheme, when there is a reduction of 2 percentage points for employees and 3.8 percentage points for employers in respect of incomes between £46 and £350 per week.
- In Ireland there is a ceiling for contingencies other than sickness and maternity of IR£16 200 for employers and above IR£16 200 the rate for employees is 1 per cent instead of 6.5 per cent.

c) Countries continuing to rely predominantly on schedular payroll taxes

Whilst most OECD countries fall into this category, in all cases the desiderata of a strict social insurance approach have been relaxed, though to varying degrees. Such relaxations take the following forms:

- contributions are insufficient to fund benefits in nearly all OECD countries;
- modifications have been made to gross wages to bring them nearer to an income tax base;

- floors (thresholds) have been introduced and ceilings increased in real terms and sometimes abolished;
- flat rate contributions have been replaced by percentages of payroll, wages and salaries.

2. The financing of particular benefits under schedular payroll taxes

a) General observations

Table 8.1 provides some information as to what was happening in 1989. The source of this information is US (1989) which warns the reader that the data reproduced has been simplified. Table 8.1 contains greater simplifications, for example:

- the contributions of the self-employed are ignored altogether;
- for certain benefits in certain countries different rates apply to wage earners and salary-earners and categories of each: the data in Table 8.2 refer to a typical wage-earner;
- no information is provided on the amount of the various ceilings for different kinds of benefits;
- workers' insurance is treated very summarily, because not all countries can provide average rates that employers have to pay and rates vary considerably according to the kind of occupation of the insured person.

With the problem of varying ceilings, varying rates of employers' contributions to workers' injury insurance, special agreements for overtime and holidays, special treatment for particular sectors or kinds of work, or age, or sex, it is impossible under these schedular systems to provide a meaningful international comparison of overall effective payroll tax rates. Probably the revenue statistics provided in Chapters 2 and 3 give a better indication of the relative weight of contributions, even if these too have their limitations. All one can say from the data provided in Table 8.1 is that statutory rates on wage earners tend to be between 9 per cent and 18 per cent of earnings and that the statutory rate of employers' contributions vary much more being over 30 per cent in France and Italy, but below 20 per cent in most other countries.

b) Pensions (old age, invalidity and death)

The contributions of employees to pension schemes are heavier than those to any other benefits in all countries: this is also the case for the contribution of employers, except in France and Sweden where employers' contributions to sickness and maternity are more important. Of the 13 countries covered in Table 8.1, there are ceilings to pension contributions in all countries, except Sweden (where only employers are involved), Belgium, Italy and Switzerland.

c) Health and maternity benefits

Contributions to health and maternity benefits are usually the next most costly for both employees and employers. As with contributions to pension funds there is a ceiling in most countries for both employees and employers, but not in Belgium and France, nor in Sweden where again only employers are involved.

d) Unemployment

Employees do not contribute at all to unemployment insurance in Italy, Japan, Turkey and the United States and not through payroll taxes in Luxembourg and Sweden. In Austria, Belgium, Canada, France, Germany, Greece and Switzerland where employees do contribute, there is a ceiling on the contributions, except in Belgium. Employers contribute in all countries with schedular payroll taxes to unemployment insurance, except in Luxembourg and Turkey and ceilings are imposed on such contributions in all these countries, except Belgium, Italy, Japan and Sweden.

e) Workers' injury insurance

It seems that all OECD countries require this to be funded fully by employers, but while those operating schedular payroll taxes (Canada and Switzerland apart) fix rates of contributions, sometimes up to a ceiling, sometimes not – see column 8 of Table 8.1, other countries generally allow the employer to cover these costs by private insurance.

f) Universal family allowances

Employers are required to contribute towards universal family allowances in 8 OECD countries and both employers and employees in Greece. In the other 16 countries (with the exception of the United States, which confines family allowances to low-income parents) such allowances are paid entirely by governments out of general revenues. Table 8.1 (column 7) indicates the rates on employers and that only in France, Greece (for employees also) and Luxembourg are there ceilings on these contributions. Information is lacking on the relative amounts of contribution of governments and employers towards the cost of family allowances, except in Japan where employers bear around 70 per cent of the total cost. (Family allowance benefits are also discussed in Chapter 10E4 since a number of countries provide relief from personal income tax for parents, in addition to the universal cash payments referred to above.)

Table 8.1: Simplified summary of rates of social security contributions in 13 countries with traditional schedular systems, 1989 (as percentage of wages of employee or payroll of employer)

	Old age invalidity and death		Health and maternity		Unemployment		Family allowance	Worker insurance paid by employer	
	Wage-earner	Employer	Wage-earner	Employer	Wage-earner	Employer	Employer	Average	Range
Countries	**(1)**	**(2)**	**(3)**	**(4)**	**(5)**	**(6)**	**(7)**	**(8)**	**(9)**
Austria	10.25 C	12.55 C	3.15 C	3.15 C	2.6 C	2.6 C	4.5 NC	1.4 C	none
Belgium	7.5 NC	8.86 NC	3.7 NC	8.78 NC	0.87 NC	2.9 NC (plus sup-plements)	7.0 NC	2.6 NC	?
Canada (federal)	2.1 C	2.1 C	–	–	1.95 C	2.73 C	–	private insurance	
France	7.6 C	8.2 C	5.9 NC	12.6 NC	2.47 C	4.43 C	8.0 C	3.73 C	?
Germany	9.35 C	9.35 C	6.41 C (variable)	6.41 C (variable)	2.47 C	2.15 C	–	1.38 NC	?
Greece	4.75 C	9.50 C	2.25 C	4.5 C	2.15 c	2.0 C	2.0 (also em–ployers)	1.0 NC	none
Italy	7.15 NC	18.06 NC	0.9 C	9.6 C	1.0 c	0.4 NC	6.2 NC	5.78 NC	0.6 to 16
Japan	6.2 C	6.2 C	4.15 C	4.15 C	–	1.61 NC	0.09 NC	? NC	0.5 to 14
Luxembourg	8 C	8 C	4.2 C	4.2 C	–	–	1.8 C	2.45 C	0.68 to 15.6
Sweden	–	9.45 NC	–	10.1 NC	flat pay-ment co–vering 23% of cost	2.16 NC	–	0.9 NC	
Switzerland (federal)	4.8 NC	4.8 NC	variable	variable	0.3 C	0.3 C	1.2 to 2.5 NC	private insurance	
Turkey	9 C	11 C	5 C	6 C	–	–	–	2.5 C	1.5 to 7
United States (federal)	6.06 C	6.06 C	1.45 C	1.45 C	–	0.8 Cc	–	2.0 (1982)	

C: ceiling NC: no ceiling ?: not known.

Country notes:

Finland : Is excluded because there are so many wide variations for different kinds of contributors.

Greece : Has (a) a higher rates in columns (1) and (2) for hazardous work; (b) uniquely a contribution by wage-earners of 1 per cent towards family allowances, which also uniquely are subject to a ceiling.

Japan : a) The 6.2 in columns (1) and (2) is for males: the corresponding figure for females is 5.8; (b) the 0.09 rates column (7) represents 70 per cent of the cost.

Luxembourg : There is a special solidarity surcharge of 5 per cent on employees for unemployment insurance.

Netherlands : Is excluded, since though having such a system in 1989, moved in 1990 to semi-integration with the personal income tax.

Sweden : (a) The traditional schedular system applies only to employers; (b) Column (4) 10.1 NC represents about 85 per cent of cost.

United States : Figures in columns (3) and (4) refer only to hospitalisation.

General notes:

It is recalled that this table provides no information about what happens at state and local levels in Canada, Switzerland and the United States. Nor does it show general government revenues earmarked for social security benefits, which are provided in most, but not all OECD countries (e.g. not in the United States). The table summarises *only* compulsory payroll taxes paid by employers and employees to central/federal government.

Source: *Social security programmes throughout the world*, US Department of Health and Human Sciences, 1989.

Chapter 9
Financing sub-central government expenditure

A. Introduction

Before discussing anything else, it is convenient to devote a paragraph to the terminology question, which is apt to be confused, especially because different considerations apply to federal and unitary countries. In this chapter, *central government* is the expression normally used when referring to what is sometimes called "national government", i.e. federal government in federal countries and central government in unitary countries, but in the context of comments relating only to federal countries, "federal government" is sometimes used. *Sub-central government* is the expression used to cover both state and local government. *State government* is reserved exclusively for intermediate levels of government in federal countries and so comprises Australian states, Austrian Länder, Canadian provinces, German Länder, Swiss cantons and the states of the United States. *Local government* refers to the third tier of federal countries and the second (regional level) plus third (municipal level) tier of unitary countries, no distinction normally being made between the second and third tier of unitary countries. Other expressions related to finance sources used in this chapter are defined ostensively in Table 9.1.

This chapter deals with the domestic tax policy issues involved in the financing of expenditures of sub-central levels of government. It does not cover international tax policy issues, such as the sharing of tax revenues between supranational authorities and Member Countries in the European Community or other international groupings. Domestic tax policy issues in this area cannot be rationally discussed, however, without reference to certain non-tax matters, such as the degree to which expenditure functions should be centralised or the relative advantages and disadvantages of financing the expenditures of sub-central levels of governments other than through taxation.

The structure of this chapter is the following: Section B deals with the so-called fiscal federalism issue, what should be the relative spending and taxation powers of different levels of government? It describes the conflict between the agency and local autonomy approaches, discusses the arguments for each and concludes by summarising overall developments during the eighties. Section C examines the various ways that local governments may be and in practice are financed whether by taxes or by other means and if by taxes whether by shared taxes or own taxes. Section D discusses the questions of relevant criteria for assigning taxes between different levels of government and for determining what constitutes a good state or local tax. Section E surveys the various taxes which are actually used in OECD countries to finance state and local expenditures. Section F provides some evaluations of what constitutes good state and local taxes.

Throughout the discussion that follows it should be borne in mind that federal state governments usually have more spending functions and taxing powers than local governments in unitary governments, especially when the state governments in federal governments control large geographical areas. However, this is not necessarily the case. Among federal countries, though Australian state governments have important expenditure functions, they have little fiscal autonomy relying on federal grants to meet their expenditure requirements and the Swiss cantons have as much, if not more, fiscal autonomy than the Canadian provinces or the states of the United States. Also the tax raising powers of local governments in the Scandinavian unitary countries are considerably greater than those of the states in most federal countries.

Table 9.1: A ranking of sources by the degree of fiscal autonomy normally provided to state and local government[1]

Own taxes:	Base and rate under local control.
Overlapping taxes:	Nationwide tax base, but rates under local control.
Non-tax revenues:	Local government is able to determine the fee to be charged, although central government may specify whether such a charge can be levied and the provisions that have to govern the calculation of such a charge.
Shared taxes:	Nationwide base and rates, but with the lower level of government able to exert some influence on either the proportion of revenues attributed to it or the amount that each level of government receives.
General purpose grants:	Local government share is fixed by central government (usually with a redistributive element), but local government is free to determine how the funds should be spent.
Specific grants:	The amount of the grant may be determined by central government or may depend upon the spending decisions of a lower level of government, but in either case central government specifies how the funds should be spent.

1. In practice most of these revenue sources are subject to detailed controls by central government. For example, own taxes are almost always subject to constraints on the base and rates and the amount of general purpose grant received by local authorities sometimes depends upon the rates fixed for their own taxes.

Source: *Local government, an international perspective,* ed. J. P. Owens and S. Panella, North Holland 1991.

B. Fiscal federalism: the agency versus the local autonomy approach

Fiscal federalism encompasses the assignment of expenditure functions and taxing powers between different levels of government. At the extreme a distinction can be made between countries where virtually all taxing powers and spending functions rest with central government and those where sub-central governments take the leading role and where central government functions are confined to defence and foreign policy. Of OECD countries, only Switzerland approximates to the latter situation. Outside the OECD, this question was a main political issue during the last years of what was the former Soviet Union, Czechoslovakia and Yugoslavia. The debate on fiscal federalism issues has also taken place in a number of OECD countries.

On the one hand, sub-central authorities can be seen simply as agents of central government which can more conveniently, from an administrative point of view, provide local services: on the other hand, state and local authorities may be seen as independent bodies elected by local people to provide certain services in accordance with their wishes. It is beyond the scope of this book to go into the various arguments for and against what have been respectively called "the agency" and "the local autonomy" approach, and as is ever the case, approaches vary considerably between countries and change over time within countries. Previously, but less so more recently, it could be said that the middle ground between the agency and local autonomy approaches would be that sub-central governments are best placed to judge local preferences for private versus social goods but that re-distribution and stabilisation policies are more efficiently carried out at central government level. However, currently local government functions are not restricted to the provision of social goods. The unsatisfactory macroeconomic performance in the seventies and eighties has led a number of countries to involve state and local governments more actively in the pursuit of full-employment, in view of their higher level of expertise concerning the structure and functioning of local labour markets. In addition, in many countries, local governments also carry out programmes which have important redistributional effects, particularly social welfare programmes. More generally, the rationale for this move towards decentralisation is the welfare gain that follows from the possibility of varying levels of government provided services according to local preferences.

Over the last fifteen years or so, a number of OECD countries have been moving towards greater decentralisation or the local autonomy approach (e.g. see Table 9.2). The decentralisation reaches extreme forms in Switzerland and the Nordic countries and in an interesting description and evaluation of the Nordic situation L. Söderström (1991) notes that local governments are big in the Nordic countries accounting for up to 70 per cent of all public consumption and about 25 per cent of the labour market, which makes them as large as all industries together. He concludes his article by saying:

> At the same time local governments live in a sort of fantasy world. Economic activities undertaken by them are based on prices not reflecting real costs and revenues are obtained from sources which are difficult to identify at the local level.

This last sentence from L. Söderström provides a reminder of the constraints on any move towards decentralisation that have resulted from the changing economic climate and the relative lack of buoyancy of local government sources of revenue. As in so many other areas of tax/expenditure policy, the transition from the expansionist economies of the sixties and early seventies to the more constrained circumstances since prevailing in many OECD countries, has led to a reversal of earlier attitudes: generous spending by local governments was looked upon happily in earlier years, but in recent years the tendency has been to curb public expenditure, including that of local government. In a number of unitary countries, especially for the last 15 to 20 years, central governments have been concerned by the absolute growth of local and regional public expenditure which has become a source of increasing strain on macroeconomic policy. If financed from local taxation, expenditure allegedly contributes to inflationary pressures and generates discontent with the burden of taxation, if financed from borrowing, it contributes to the volume of deficit financing, and if financed from grants, it becomes a source of increasing budgetary strain for national aid to different areas. On the other hand, it may be argued that central governments have been transferring their deficits to the local level by shifting more expenditure functions to local authorities than revenues and that local governments contribute to inflationary pressures only insofar as the central bank validates their deficits by issuing more money (assuming velocity constant).

Another problem is that local taxes tend to be less buoyant than those levied by central government. For example, local income tax schedules are usually at a flat rate, or at rates much less progressive than central government income taxes. In addition, there tend to be more mechanisms directly available to the public for influencing local taxes than non-local taxes: personal pressure on local politicians, sometimes the right to impose a referendum on a proposed tax increase, and always the right to migrate from one tax jurisdiction to another. Furthermore, local governments generally have access to far fewer tax sources than has central government. There are also limits to the possibility of increasing non-tax revenues, partly because the deterrent effect of user-charges can be just as important as the revenue-generating effect (e.g. public transport); partly because certain public services are intended to be subsidised and not revenue-raising (services for special groups, children, the aged and the handicapped); and partly because many services are indivisible in the sense that their costs cannot be allocated to individual users (e.g. police).

The constraint on decentralisation caused by the combined effect of the changing economic climate and the sluggishness of local tax revenues has been augmented by other government concerns. For example, as already noted, central government may prefer to give priority to controlling the growth of the public sector or to avoid any conflicts with macroeconomic goals and may take the view that lower levels of government should not be involved in distributional issues; local tax rate increases may enter into published price indices; central governments may wish to prevent the creation of state and local tax havens and other forms of taxpayer segregation regarded as undesirable as a matter of national or regional policy; central government may wish to maintain the right to determine the base for a state or local tax where the same base is used for a central tax (e.g. the property tax base may be used to calculate central government capital taxes, as in Denmark and Germany).

Thus there is likely to remain a conflict between the agency and local autonomy approach, with government choices varying between countries, and since this is also a political question, changing over time according to the predilections of newly-elected governments, especially at central level but to some extent at local level. To explore this issue further is outside the scope of this book. However, the following trends covering the eighties which were identified by J. Owens and J. Nørregaard (1991) are reproduced here.

- Local and intermediate government expenditures per capita increased, reflecting the social and fiscal consequences of continued labour mobility, suburbanisation and the spread of welfare programmes.
- Local and intermediate government expenditure growth slowed down, although it generally remained positive in real terms.
- Grants to lower levels of government increased in importance in most countries during the seventies, though during the eighties this trend was reversed in some countries. The structure of grants also changed quite dramatically, with many countries increasing their relative reliance on general grants in order to increase local autonomy.

- The increased importance of grants caused a growing disparity between the real costs of providing local public services and the perceived costs (in terms of local revenues sources) from the point of view of the local electorate, though in recent years this trend has been reversed in a number of countries.
- Local and regional finances have increasingly been involved in central government conjunctural policies, for example, in a number of countries the squeeze on grants was seen as an easy option in cutting back on central government expenditure.

C. The various ways of financing state and local government expenditures

1. Own taxes, overlapping taxes and shared taxes

As noted in Table 9.1, central governments normally impose limits on the powers of local governments to vary the base or rates of own and overlapping taxes levied by local governments and may further punish them by reducing grants, if a particular central government regards the local levy as excessive. One of the main reasons why central governments impose these limitations is to prevent local governments from imposing their own distribution policies through varying the base or rates. Nevertheless, there does remain some element of choice for sub-central authorities under own taxes and overlapping taxes that is absent under shared taxes, except to the extent that they have had some say in how the tax revenues were originally shared and more importantly in any future revision of the sharing formulae. However, while reducing local tax autonomy, the shared tax solution has the advantage of avoiding all the complications that arise when different local jurisdictions apply different rates and/or different bases to particular taxes, from which a part of the proceeds also accrue to central government.

2. User charges and other non-tax revenues

User charges include those for the provision of such services as fire protection and litter collection and disposal, though the provision of other public services such as education, health and housing, may be unsuitable for this kind of financing. Other non-tax revenues include fees, fines and sale proceeds of public assets.

Bird and Wallich (1992) have suggested the following threefold classification of such charges:

Service fees such as license fees (marriage, business, dog, vehicle) and various small charges levied by local governments essentially for performing specific services – registering this or providing a copy of that – for identifiable individuals. In effect, such fees constitute cost reimbursement from the private to the public sector: indeed, in some budgetary systems, such cost recoveries are netted out and only net (of recoveries) expenditures are shown.

Public prices are the revenues received by local governments from the sale of private goods and services (other than the cost-reimbursement just described). All sales of locally-provided services to identifiable private individuals – whether public utility charges or admission charges to recreation facilities – fall under this general heading.

Specific benefits taxes in contrast to such general benefit taxes as fuel taxes levied on road users as a class or local taxes in general viewed as a price paid for local collective goods (see below) – relate to the specific benefits supposedly received by specific taxpayers. Examples include : special assessments, land value increment taxes, improvement taxes, front footage levies, supplementary property taxes related to the provision of sewers or street lighting, development exactions and charges, delineation levies, and so on. Usually such charges are imposed either on the assessed value of real property or on some characteristic of that property – its area, its frontage, its location.

Bird and Wallich (1992) conclude:

> Much as there is to be said in principle for charging for local government expenditures, experience to date in most countries is not very encouraging. Even where the common philosophical objections to pricing in the public sector can be overcome, the prices charged are seldom those needed for efficiency. The potential for improved user charge finance as a means of financing local government thus remains more potential than reality.

3. Intergovernmental transfers (grants)

These may be defined as unrequited, non-repayable, non-compulsory payments from higher to lower levels of governments (or in the case of some former Communist countries from lower to higher levels). They are of two kinds: those providing general budget support (not so different from shared taxes) and those given only for projects defined by central governments, whether taking the form of current expenditures or capital outlays. Often specific grants are matching in that central government contributes to particular expenditures on condition that local government also contributes.

The most frequently cited rationale for grants by central to sub-central levels of government is the need to equalise the different taxable capacity and expenditure needs of different local jurisdictions to prevent the migration of citizens from one tax jurisdiction to another simply to reduce their tax burden. Further details on the equalisation issue are outside the scope of this book, but recent interesting analyses of the problems involved may be found in D. King (1991) and N. Tatsos (1991). Other rationales cited by Bird and Wallich (1992) are to provide local governments with sufficient resources to enable them to provide some bundle of public services and to respond adequately to incentive grants, to face local decision-makers with (socially) correct prices with respect to externalities arising from their actions and to maximise the impact of central expenditures in certain areas by inducing local governments to spend from their own resources as well.

Bird and Wallich note that in addition to the various economic rationales for intergovernmental transfers, there are also important political arguments, since it may be necessary, for example, to transfer some resources to jurisdictions that do not, strictly speaking, need them in order to make it politically feasible to transfer needed amounts to other jurisdictions. It may also be essential to transfer resources simply in order to keep some economically non-viable local governments alive for political reasons – to salvage regional pride, to provide jobs for local supporters, or for some other reason.

4. Borrowing or deficit financing

Except in Canada and the United States and perhaps a few other OECD countries, borrowing by state or local government is strictly controlled by central governments who generally consider that state and local governments should not be allowed to incur deficits which could undermine their stabilisation policies or crowd-out private sector borrowing which could sometimes be more economically efficient than local government borrowing. Also to the extent that central governments wish to avoid the bankruptcy of particular local governments, they often implicitly guarantee local government debt, which raises the possibility that local government borrowing could become a large and destabilising claim on budgetary resources. To prevent this, central governments impose in practice a number of restrictions on local borrowing including (i) permitting it only for approved capital projects; (ii) requiring prior approval of local taxpayers for borrowing above a certain amount; (iii) requiring prior approval of central authorities for borrowing; (iv) restricting the amount of debt to some percentage of local revenues; (v) permitting borrowing only from a central "municipal fund", and (vi) providing other restrictions regarding the role of interest or period of repayment. Thus, leaving aside the few exceptions, local government borrowing represents a last resort of own resources for sub-central government and is not an important source of their revenues.

5. Allocation of revenues between central and subordinate levels of government

a) Allocation of different revenue sources

Table 9.2 indicates governments' relative reliance for the years 1980 and 1988 on their state and local main sources of revenue: tax revenues, non-tax revenues and grants. Unfortunately, available data do not permit further disaggregation of these results between own taxes, overlapping taxes and shared taxes or between general and specific grants. The table shows considerable variation between relative use of these various sources of sub-central government revenues. With the reservation mentioned above that shared taxes are more akin to grants than taxes, but have in this table to be treated as taxes, own taxes plus shared taxes are the most important revenue source for sub-central government of all federal countries save Australia (at state level) and grants are the most important revenue source in all unitary countries except Denmark and France. Non-tax revenues usually represent a small proportion of local government revenues, but account for over a third of them in Australia and Germany and nearly a third in Austria and Switzerland. Table 9.2 shows also that between 1980 and 1988 state and local tax revenues and state and local total revenues increased in nearly all countries, Austria, Germany and Denmark providing exceptions with regard to the latter ratio.

Table 9.2: Revenues received by state and local government

	A: as a percentage of GDP								B: as percentage of total tax revenue receipts					
	Tax revenue		Non-tax revenue		Grants		Total		Tax revenue		Non-tax revenue		Grants	
	1980	1988	1980	1988	1980	1988	1980	1988	1980	1988	1980	1988	1980	1988
Federal countries														
Australia														
State	4.10	5.14	1.97	2.34[1]	7.63	7.59[1]	13.70	15.07	29.9	33.1	14.4	15.7	55.7	51.1
Local	1.09	1.03	0.46	0.92[1]	0.46	0.47[1]	2.00	2.42	54.2	43.2	22.8	37.6	23.0	19.2
Austria														
State	4.17	4.43	1.16	1.25[1]	3.50	2.72[1]	8.83	8.39	47.3	58.5	13.1	13.0	39.6	28.4
Local	4.58	4.52	2.64	2.71[1]	1.39	1.34[1]	8.60	8.58	53.2	52.7	30.6	31.6	16.1	15.7
Canada														
State	11.49	12.09	2.63	2.69	4.07	3.91	18.19	18.70	63.2	64.7	14.5	14.4	22.4	20.9
Local	3.11	3.09	1.29	1.19	4.06	3.62	8.46	7.89	36.8	39.1	15.2	15.1	48.0	45.8
Germany														
State	8.58	8.20	1.44	1.49	2.20	1.81	12.22	11.49	70.2	71.3	11.8	12.9	18.0	15.7
Local	3.47	3.26	3.26	3.22	2.89	2.39	9.62	8.87	36.0	36.7	33.9	36.3	30.1	27.0
Switzerland														
State	7.01	7.15	2.31	n.a.	3.46	n.a.	12.78	n.a.	54.8	56.0	18.1	18.4	27.1	25.6
Local	5.47	5.13	3.27	n.a.	1.61	n.a.	10.34	n.a.	52.9	52.7	31.6	31.2	15.6	16.1
United States														
State	5.25	5.59	1.85	2.87[1]	2.42	2.17[1]	9.51	10.63	55.2	52.9	19.4	26.8	25.4	20.3
Local	3.30	3.63	1.57	2.11[1]	3.84	3.37[1]	8.70	9.11	37.9	34.8	18.0	23.2	44.1	37.0
Unitary countries														
Belgium	1.81	2.23	0.51	0.38[1]	4.19	3.96[1]	6.50	6.57	27.8	34.5	7.9	5.8	64.4	59.7
Denmark	13.77	15.64	3.31	3.12	18.38	12.75	35.46	31.51	38.8	49.6	9.3	9.9	51.8	40.5
France	2.96	3.93	1.29	1.84	2.98	3.11	7.23	8.88	40.9	44.3	17.8	20.7	41.2	35.0
Italy	0.51	0.65	n.a.	1.31	n.a.	16.26	n.a.	18.23	5.2	5.9	12.7	12.7	82.2	81.4
Netherlands	0.89	1.04	2.18	2.24	14.13	14.33	17.20	17.61	52.4	57.3	37.8	15.6	9.8	27.1
Spain														
Local	1.15	3.72	0.83	0.93[1]	0.22	1.61[1]	2.20	6.26	–	–	9.4	6.6	90.6	93.4
Regional				0.26[1]										
United Kingdom	3.72	3.93	2.96	2.52[1]	5.86	5.81[1]	12.54	12.26	29.6	32.6	23.6	20.4	46.7	47.0

1. 1987, not 1988.

Source: OECD RS 1990.

b) Allocation of tax revenues between different levels of government

Table 9.3 shows how tax revenues are allocated between levels of government. Country practices vary greatly: among federal countries, central government receives 80 per cent of tax receipts in Australia and less than 30 per cent in Switzerland and among unitary countries, central government receives over 90 per cent of tax receipts in New Zealand and over 80 per cent in Ireland, but less than 50 per cent in France and Japan. Changes over the last 15 years in this allocation are not very great in most countries, but between

1955 and 1975 the share of federal and central government declined in all OECD countries except New Zealand, and often substantially.

Table 9.3: The share of tax revenues allocated to different levels of government,[2] 1955, 1975, 1980, 1989[1]

A. Federal countries

	Central government				State			Local			Social security			
	1955	1975	1980	1989	1975	1980	1989	1975	1980	1989	1955	1975	1980	1989
Australia	86	80.1	81.8	80.2	15.7	14.4	16.4	4.2	3.8	3.4	–	–	–	–
Austria	57	51.7	50.5	50.6	10.6	10.1	10.4	12.4	11.1	11.00	20	25.3	28.2	27.9
Canada	67	47.7	43.3	42.5	32.5	36.3	35.7	9.7	9.8	8.8	4	10.1	10.5	13.0
Germany[2]	47	33.8	32.8	31.9	22.4	22.6	22.2	9.1	9.1	8.7	25	33.5	34.4	36.3
Switzerland	41	27.3	28.6	28.9	24.0	22.8	22.0	19.5	17.8	16.3	21	29.2	30.9	32.7
United States	63	43.0	44.8	40.0	18.4	17.8	18.7	13.9	11.2	12.1	11	24.6	26.2	29.2
Unweighted average	60	47.3	47.0	45.7	20.6	20.7	20.9	11.5	10.5	10.1	14	20.4	21.7	23.2

B. Unitary countries

	Central government				Local				Social security			
	1955	1975	1980	1989	1955	1975	1980	1989	1955	1975	1980	1989
Belgium	70	63.4	65.1	61.0	4	4.7	4.2	4.7	26	30.5	29.0	32.8
Denmark	73	68.5	67.6	66.6	22	29.8	30.3	30.4	4	1.2	1.4	2.3
Finland	71	59.6	60.6	61.9	25	26.8	25.8	26.4	3	13.7	13.6	11.8
France	n.a.	51.2	49.6	46.6	n.a.	7.6	7.1	8.9	n.a.	40.6	42.7	43.9
Greece	n.a.	67.1	65.1	66.3	n.a.	3.4	2.2	1.4	n.a.	29.5	32.7	31.2
Iceland	n.a.	81.3	82.8	78.8	n.a.	18.7	17.2	21.2	n.a.	–	–	–
Ireland	80	77.4	81.8	82.5	15	7.3	3.4	2.6	5	13.1	12.9	13.1
Italy	57	53.2	59.9	64.1	11	0.9	1.7	2.2	32	45.9	38.0	33.2
Japan	62	45.4	45.4	46.3	25	25.6	25.5	25.8	13	29.0	29.1	27.9
Luxembourg	n.a.	57.6	58.5	62.1	n.a.	12.6	12.2	11.6	n.a.	29.1	28.8	25.8
Netherlands	82	58.9	58.5	55.2	2	1.2	1.9	2.2	16	38.4	38.1	41.0
New Zealand	70	92.3	92.8	92.9	4	7.7	7.2	7.1	22	–	–	–
Norway	60	50.6	58.3	53.5	33	22.4	18.8	21.1	7	27.0	22.9	25.5
Portugal	75	65.4	66.9	68.6	7	–	3.6	5.1	17	34.6	29.5	26.3
Spain	n.a.	48.2	47.7	54.4	n.a.	4.3	4.8	10.8	n.a.	47.5	47.5	34.3
Sweden	66	51.3	39.3	55.6	29	29.2	31.9	28.0	5	19.5	28.8	16.4
Turkey	n.a.	n.a.	79.7	74.3	n.a.	n.a.	6.3	10.0	n.a.	n.a.	14.0	15.6
United Kingdom	82	70.6	71.5	70.7	8	11.0	10.5	10.6	10	17.4	16.6	17.6
Unweighted average	71	62.5	63.0	63.9	16	12.5	12.2	12.9	13	24.5	24.2	22.5

1. Data are unavailable for Turkey for 1955 and 1975, and for France, Greece, Luxembourg, Spain and Turkey for 1955.
2. Excluding payments to supranational government (European Community) which generally represent between 0.5 and 2 per cent (unweighted average 1 per cent for 1989).

n.a. = not available.

– = no such state or local tax.

Sources: Table 122 for 1975, 1980 and 1989 of OECD RS 1991. Table 11 for 1955 of OECD RS 1981. Figures for 1955 are to nearest percentage point and breakdowns between state and local government are unavailable.

Table 9.4: Tax revenues of the main state and local taxes as a percentage of total tax revenues of these levels of government[1], 1975, 1980, 1989

	Personal income tax 1100			Corporation tax 1200			Payroll 3000			Property 4000		
	1975	1980	1989	1975	1980	1989	1975	1980	1989	1975	1980	1989
Federal Countries												
Australia												
State	–	–	–	–	–	–	35.3	34.1	28.3	26.6	26.9	31.0
Local	–	–	–	–	–	–	–	–	–	100.0	99.9	99.8
Austria												
State	42.7	45.1	41.4	1.6	1.5	2.9	–	–	–	1.8	1.7	1.0
Local	33.8	34.5	31.0	5.1	4.4	6.9	11.5	11.9	11.4	11.2	11.2	9.1
Canada												
State	32.4	36.0	41.3	11.2	9.9	8.1	–	–	–	2.3	2.0	3.8
Local	–	–	–	–	–	–	–	–	–	88.5	89.5	85.0
Germany[2]												
State	55.2	52.7	53.2	7.5	9.3	9.5	–	–	–	6.2	5.6	6.2
Local	58.3	64.1	67.6	11.1	13.8	14.8	9.0	1.7	–	20.3	19.5	16.6
Switzerland												
State	63.6	64.8	62.6	14.2	11.0	12.6	–	–	–	14.3	15.5	17.4
Local	73.2	75.6	74.0	13.4	10.1	12.2	–	–	–	81.9	75.9	74.3
United States												
State	n.a.	26.9	31.2	n.a.	9.7	8.4	–	–	–	4.1	4.3	4.0
Local	n.a.	5.0	4.9	n.a.	0.7	1.0	–	–	–	81.9	75.9	74.3
Unweighted Average												
State	32.3	37.6	38.3	5.7	6.9	6.9	5.9	5.7	4.7	9.2	9.3	10.6
Local	27.5	29.9	29.6	4.9	4.8	5.8	3.4	2.3	1.9	52.5	51.0	49.7
Unitary Countries												
Belgium[2]	60.6	63.5	60.3	12.3	10.8	15.1	–	–	–	–	–	–
Denmark[2]	84.8	87.7	90.5	1.6	1.6	1.7	–	–	–	13.2	10.5	7.6
Finland	91.4	91.3	89.4	8.4	8.6	9.7	–	–	–	–	–	0.8
France[2]	23.0	18.2	14.6	–	–	–	–	–	–	23.1	29.3	33.8
Greece[2]	11.0	10.8	–	–	–	–	–	–	–	6.6	7.1	–
Iceland	62.0	62.3	55.3	3.1	2.8	2.1	–	–	–	15.3	15.3	14.4
Ireland[2]	–	–	–	–	–	–	–	–	–	100.0	100.0	100.0
Italy[2]	48.0	15.4	13.4	32.0	22.1	9.0	–	–	–	17.5	0.5	–
Japan	26.3	27.6	28.7	28.5	29.6	34.7	–	–	–	24.9	22.7	23.1
Luxembourg	37.2	37.7	32.7	39.5	43.5	52.4	–	–	–	4.9	4.6	3.4
Netherlands[2]	15.4	–	–	–	–	–	–	–	–	54.2	75.3	73.4
New Zealand	–	–	–	–	–	–	–	–	–	89.1	92.6	93.1
Norway	86.3	87.1	80.7	5.7	5.6	7.5	–	–	–	5.2	4.5	8.2
Portugal	n.a.	n.a.	9.3	n.a.	n.a.	1.9	–	–	–	50.0	1.6	24.0
Spain	43.0	40.9	15.1	–	2.8	4.6	–	–	–	8.5	3.8	27.9
Sweden	91.5	94.5	99.6	8.2	5.2	–	–	–	–	–	–	–
Turkey	n.a.	34.6	37.2	–	3.3	9.9	–	–	–		12.3	2.5
United Kingdom[2]	–	–	–	–	–	–	–	–	–	100.0	100.0	100.0
Unweighted Average[3]	40.0	37.5	34.7	8.2	7.8	8.2	–	–	–	30.1	27.5	30.0

Table 9.4(cont.): Tax revenues of the main state and local taxes as a percentage of total tax revenues of these levels of government,[1] 1975, 1980, 1989

	General consumption taxes 5110			**Specific goods & services 5120**			**Taxes on use etc. 5200**			**Other**[1]		
	1975	**1980**	**1989**	**1975**	**1980**	**1989**	**1975**	**1980**	**1989**	**1975**	**1980**	**1989**
						Federal Countries						
Australia												
State	–	–	–	16.1	17.1	14.3	22.0	21.9	26.4	–	–	–
Local	–	–	–	–	–	–	–	0.1	0.2	–	–	–
Austria												
State	33.9	36.3	37.6	13.5	8.2	6.4	4.4	3.9	5.2	2.2	3.2	4.1
Local	19.7	20.9	22.3	14.1	11.3	10.8	1.0	1.3	2.0	3.7	4.4	5.5
Canada												
State	19.6	16.9	21.6	16.8	13.5	15.4	17.8	21.7	9.8	–	–	–
Local	–	–	0.2	–	–	0.1	2.1	1.3	1.5	9.3	13.2	13.2
Germany[2]												
State	21.8	25.0	24.3	2.8	2.2	1.9	6.4	5.2	4.8	–	–	–
Local	–	–	–	0.5	0.3	0.4	0.4	0.3	0.4	0.4	0.2	0.3
Switzerland												
State	–	–	–	1.5	1.8	1.4	6.4	6.9	5.9	–	–	–
Local	–	–	–	0.2	0.3	0.3	0.1	0.1	0.1	–	–	–
United States												
State	30.8	31.4	32.8	23.6	18.3	15.9	10.0	9.4	7.7	–	–	–
Local	7.1	9.4	10.4	3.6	4.6	4.7	3.1	4.3	4.6	–	–	–
Unweighted average												
State	17.7	18.3	19.4	12.4	10.2	9.2	11.2	11.5	10.0	0.4	0.5	0.7
Local	4.5	5.1	5.5	3.1	2.7	2.7	1.1	1.2	1.4	2.2	3.0	3.2
						Unitary Countries						
Belgium[2]	–	–	–	–	–	–	20.4	17.2	17.1	6.8	8.5	7.5
Denmark[2]	–	–	–	0.2	0.1	0.1	0.1	0.1	–	–	–	–
Finland	–	–	–	0.1	–	–	0.1	0.1	–	–	–	–
France[2]	–	–	–	4.8	5.4	4.9	3.2	3.0	8.5	46.0	44.1	38.2
Greece[2]	9.0	6.7	4.2	32.9	24.3	21.2	18.7	13.0	11.6	16.3	37.9	63.0
Iceland	–	–	6.0	7.9	6.4	6.0	–	–	–	11.7	13.2	16.2
Ireland[2]	–	–	–	–	–	–	–	–	–	–	–	–
Italy2	–	–	–	–	–	19.7	2.5	–	0.2	–	27.9	35.7
Japan	–	–	–	15.1	14.0	8.6	4.9	5.2	4.0	0.2	0.9	0.9
Luxembourg	9.0	7.7	10.3	0.2	0.2	0.4	1.1	0.9	0.9	8.0	5.4	–
Netherlands[2]	–	–	–	2.7	1.0	1.2	27.7	23.7	25.4	–	–	–
New Zealand	–	–	–	6.7	3.3	0.9	4.2	4.2	6.8	–	–	0.8
Norway	–	–	–	–	–	–	–	0.2	0.7	2.9	2.6	2.9
Portugal	–	10.0	17.4	–	16.4	11.3	50.0	9.6	3.0	–	2.4	0.3
Spain	31.0	41.2	12.4	3.2	0.4	14.8	–	–	8.6	–	–	4.6
Sweden	–	–	–	0.3	0.3	0.3	0.1	0.1	–	–	–	–
Turkey		–	20.9		–	7.8		–	0.4		49.8	31.1
United Kingdom	–	–	–	–	–	–	–	–	–	–	–	–
Unweighted average	2.9	3.9	3.0	4.4	4.2	5.3	7.8	4.6	5.1	5.4	8.4	9.9

1. Including social security contributions allocated to local government (Austria, Belgium); taxes on net wealth (Norway); death taxes (Finland and Portugal); and some residual taxes mainly on business (Austria, Canada, Denmark, France, Germany, Greece, Italy, Netherlands, New Zealand, Norway).

2. Payments to the European Community are excluded.

3. Turkey is excluded.

– = no such state or local tax.

n.a. = not available.

Source: Tables 126 and 128 of OECD RS 1991.

c) *Contributions of different tax revenues to state and local government*

Table 9.4 indicates the extent to which various taxes contribute to state and local government revenues, but as already noted it is not possible to distinguish between receipts from "own taxes", "overlapping taxes" and "shared taxes", as defined in Table 9.1. Country positions vary greatly and change in different ways. It may be noted that the general tendency of unitary countries is for sub-central governments to rely predominantly on one source of revenue, usually local income taxes, sometimes property taxes, whereas in federal countries there is a tendency to rely more equally on several sources.

D. The assignment of taxes between different levels of government

1. Criteria for assignment

Much of the pioneering work on assignment theory, as in so many other areas of public finance, has been done by R. Musgrave. In *The Theory of Public Finance* (1959), he began to explore relevant criteria for assigning taxes between different levels of government under the title "Multilevel finance". More recently (ANU Press, 1983) after taking his readers on a tour to a yet unknown galaxy called Fiscalia, he elaborated his analysis, a summary of which is reproduced as an introduction to this section.

Based on his criteria of fair entitlement and efficient resource use, Musgrave set out the following general principles of tax assignment:

- Taxes suitable for economic stabilisation should be central; lower-level taxes should be cyclically stable.
- Progressive redistributional taxes should be central.
- Personal taxes with progressive rates should be levied by the jurisdictions most capable of implementing a tax on a global base.
- Lower-level governments should tax bases with low mobility between jurisdictions.
- Tax bases distributed highly unequally between jurisdictions should be centralised.

He noted also that benefit taxes and user charges might be appropriately used at all levels of governments.

Based on these principles, Musgrave assigned broad categories of taxes as follows:

Central level: integrated income and expenditure taxes and natural resource taxes.

Middle level: income taxes, consumption taxes and natural resource taxes.

Local level: property and payroll taxes.

In summarising the conclusions of R. Musgrave and other contributors (R. Gordon, C. Brennan and J. Buchanan and R. Mathews) on the normative assessments of the tax assignment problem, C. McLure, the editor of the publication, noted that their views do not all conveniently point in identical directions. He went on to add, however:

> But they do appear to have certain important conclusions in common. First, taxes on highly mobile factors are best reserved for use by central governments, whereas those on totally immobile factors often make ideal sources of revenue for local governments. This is likely to be true for both administrative and economic reasons. Second, residence-based taxes, such as personal income taxes and retail sales and other indirect taxes, are more likely to be appropriate for subnational governments than are source-based taxes, such as origin-based value added taxes and corporation income taxes. Third, even though the base is geographically immobile, source-based taxes on natural resources that are not distributed more or less uniformly across the country can cause economic distortions, in addition to horizontal inequities, because unequal access to revenues may allow resource-rich jurisdictions to attract excessive amounts of labour and capital, via lower taxes and/or greater public services. It may be necessary to redress such an imbalance (if it is not simply eliminated by reservation of the base to the federal government) through horizontal or vertical grants intended to equalize the fiscal positions of subnational governments. Fourth, and more generally, the fiscal capacity of subnational governments may be sufficiently unequal that horizontal equalization is deemed to be appropriate. Of course, such equalization is often implemented through the federal government. Finally, revenues assigned to various governments may not conveniently match expenditure needs. In particular, federal governments may be better able to raise enough revenues than are subnational governments. If this is true, vertical grants may also be required.

2. Criteria for good state and local taxes

The guidelines for assignment of local tax rules suggested above provide a starting point for judging what might be efficient and equitable taxes at state and local government levels. They need, however, to be amplified. The following list provided by Owens and Nørregaard (1991), slightly modified as a result of my discussions with the authors, provides a starting point. The following criteria were suggested:

- The tax base should not be very mobile, since otherwise taxpayers will re-allocate from high to low tax areas and the freedom of tax authorities to vary rates will be constrained.
- The tax should be visible, thereby encouraging local government accountability.
- The tax should be able to raise sufficient revenue to meet the needs of local government. The yield should be stable and predictable over time and preferably buoyant.
- It should not be possible to export a large part of the tax, thereby weakening the link between local taxes and benefits (i.e. the tax should not be easily shifted to non-residents).
- It should be seen by taxpayers as being reasonably fair.
- The tax should be easy to administer.

- A local tax, in particular, should not be too progressive since this may encourage rich taxpayers to migrate out of localities using such forms of taxation.

It is one thing to set up criteria, quite another to interpret them. As a non-expert in the tax assignment literature, I proposed a "local tax panel game" to three specialists in this field, R. Bird, J. Owens and J. Nørregaard where independently each of us would evaluate the suitability of particular taxes for financing state and local expenditures, under the headings: very good; good; fair; bad; very bad. Here was the proforma:

Taxes	(1) Mobility of base	(2) Visibility and local accountability	(3) Steadiness and buoyancy of yield	(4) Non-exportability of tax	(5) Perceived fairness of tax	(6) Ease of administration
a) Immovable property						
b) Personal income tax						
c) Business income tax						
d) Payroll tax						
e) Financial and capital transactions		Our very different evaluations are not reproduced for the reasons set out in the following paragraph				
f) General consumption tax						
g) Selective excises						
h) Ownership and permission taxes						
i) Poll taxes						

I had assumed that probably our assessments would not greatly differ, but in practice they did. How they differed is much less interesting than why they differed and here are some of the reasons:

- It was not made clear whether one was talking of rational applications of the taxes under (a) to (i) or how they were utilised by governments in practice (for example "visibility" (2) and "perceived fairness" (5) may be good in theory, but bad in practice.
- Evaluations may vary according to whether sub-central levels referred to federal or unitary countries, the size of geographical areas and the extent of the powers of sub-central authorities to vary tax rates and the tax base.
- The distinction should have been made between taxes on residential and non-residential immovable property.
- A distinction between criterion (1) and criterion (4) was unclear, and whilst it was believed they were not identical, how they differed was interpreted in different ways by different participants.

All this suggests that it might be more useful to focus on what happens in practice as regards own taxes of state and local government and this is done in the next section.

E. A survey of existing state and local taxes

1. Taxes on immovable property

a) Some general considerations

Revenue from these taxes, which are levied in nearly all OECD countries accrue almost exclusively to sub-central levels of government and above all to local government. As at 1989, this tax accounted for 100 per cent or nearly of local government revenues in Australia, Ireland and the United Kingdom, over 90 per cent in New Zealand and over 70 per cent in Canada, the Netherlands and the United States. There are good reasons for this. First, the base of the tax is immovable property which, by definition, cannot leave the locality, so that the property provides security for the tax which cannot be evaded. Second, the rates of a local property tax can generally be varied within limits without much risk of migration of residents, labour, trade or capital. Third, it is usually clear which local government is entitled to the tax. Fourth, the tax yield is in principle predictable and stable, even though this depends on regular revaluations being carried out, something which for political reasons rarely happens in practice in a number of countries. Finally, at least as regards residential property, these taxes fulfil well the criteria of local accountability since voting taxpayers have the choice between higher taxes and better services and lower taxes and reduced services. However, such taxes also have drawbacks as a local tax revenue source, even if some of these drawbacks are a consequence of the way that they function. For example, local businesses without voting power to control expenditures often provide the bulk of these revenues; households find them very visible, painful to pay and regard them as unfair for the reasons elaborated on in Chapter 14.

Policy problems pertaining to taxes on immovable property as such are discussed in Chapter 14. This sub-section is concerned only with those aspects of the tax affecting relationships between different levels of government. These take three forms: first, the degree of discretion that state or local government has over the tax base and tax rate; second, the general distribution of administrative responsibilities and, third, the arrangements for coordinating revaluations.

b) Property taxes in practice

While authorities at the state level in federal countries are typically given some power to vary the tax rates or base, local discretion is generally much limited in unitary countries. In some countries there is a choice between two or three tax bases, which must be applied to all properties in their jurisdiction. Local authorities more often have some discretion over the tax rates to be set, but in a number of countries there are limitations on the power to vary rates. For example, local authorities may be required to obtain prior approval of central government for rate increases, be limited by the rate of inflation, by the earmarking of taxes for specific expenditure purposes, or by the reduction of central government grants if rates exceed the amount prescribed by central government. Table 9.5 sets out the limits on the discretion of the authorities of state and local government in six federal and seven unitary countries.

The distribution of administrative responsibilities for property taxes is set out in Table 9.6. Although most of these taxes accrue to state or local governments, the central government is usually involved in their administration, with the exception of Australia, Japan, and the United States. Even where the central government is not involved in the administration of these taxes, it does not necessarily follow that the beneficiary government has complete responsibility. In some cases, for example, the beneficiaries are local governments but administration is done by state government, for example in New South Wales, as regards valuations for local property taxes. Also there are usually various devices to co-ordinate valuation procedures where they involve both state and local authorities.

The valuation of the tax base is usually the responsibility of state authorities or central government (see Table 9.6). Central governments may maintain responsibility for valuation because the base of the property tax may be related to the base of other taxes, such as net wealth taxes or taxes on imputed rent. Even where there is no such relationship, it is often the case that the central government is responsible for the valuations or that there are more or less formal institutional arrangements designed to secure some co-ordination of practices in different areas, and hence equality of treatment for owners of similar types of property.

2. State and local personal income taxes

a) *Some general considerations*

In the majority of OECD countries personal income taxes at subordinate levels of government are either non-existent or are relatively unimportant when compared to the yield from central government income taxes. However, in Switzerland, Sweden and Norway, they are far more important than central government taxes, in Denmark, Finland and Iceland of about equal importance, and in Canada, Japan and the United States not insignificant. (See the first two columns of Table 9.4.) It would accordingly not make sense to discuss income tax policy without some reference to state and local income taxes, since trends in central governments' income tax, tax yields, tax rates, etc. may be reinforced or offset by trends in those of state and local governments. Issues relating to the personal income tax as a whole are discussed in the next chapter where it is noted, for example, that the almost universal heavy fall in statutory income tax rates of central governments between 1985 and 1990 was not matched by a corresponding fall in the rates of state and local income taxes.

In those countries without local income taxes, the argument has been largely that they would involve too many administrative complications. This argument is not discussed here but may be found unconvincing in the light of the analysis, for example, of the 1976 Layfield Report in the United Kingdom and of Bird and Wallich (1992). Of course, from a political point of view, certain governments have a basic objection to any increase in personal income taxation and would rule out introducing local income taxes for that reason, even if others find it a necessary prerequisite for a well-functioning local democracy.

A more important argument against local income taxation is that individuals are more mobile than property and that income tax differentials could therefore lead to a transfer of the wealth from high-tax to low-tax jurisdictions. In commenting on this argument J. Lotz (1981) observes:

> In the Scandinavian countries, the income tax is supplemented by equalization schemes intended to support low-income authorities and in some cases also to place the burden on high-income municipalities. This means that a certain reduction of tax rate differentials took place. It may have helped to prevent tax-induced migration. Also, some capitalization of rate differentials may have taken place, which should have tempered the incentives to move to low-tax authorities. Of course, there are tax-haven municipalities, where taxes are low and services high. There are municipalities which find themselves in a resource-squeeze too, and migration is certainly a problem. This is, for instance, felt by the city of Copenhagen. However, other location considerations and imperfections are so important that the problem of mobility, in spite of the considerable rate differentials, has not been of magnitude as to derogate income taxation.
>
> A fear is sometimes expressed that local government expenditures will increase in an uncontrolled manner if they have recourse to income taxation. Experience seems to indicate that taxpayer awareness is strong enough to prevent such an increase.
>
> There are certain administrative complications of a local income tax. Without local tax rates, annual statements by every taxpayer may not be needed. The Layfield report stresses this point. Also, a system with cumulative assessments, and with tax tables to be used by employers, become nearly impossible if many authorities can set their own tax rate. Modern techniques should be able to provide a solution to this problem if there is the political wish to do so, and if it is possible to overcome public resistance against registration in centralized income tax files with information on residence.
>
> In summary, the income tax seems to be working better than is suspected. A local income tax on personal income can work with large inter-authority variations of rates. The jurisdictions should be based on the site of residence, and tax sharing arrangements with authorities of temporary residence or of employment should be avoided....

b) *Sub-central personal income taxes in practice*

Table 9.7 sets out the main features of countries where subordinate levels of government have some control of the state and local rate and/or base of their income taxes. It does not include countries like Austria, Germany, Luxembourg and Spain where state and local authorities automatically receive a fixed percentage of the overall income tax receipts, but where they have no say in the choice of rate or base. Aside from these tax sharing formulae, state and local income taxes may take one of three forms:

Table 9.5: Discretion of state and local governments over the property tax base

Country	Tax	Beneficiary government	Degree of discretion for the beneficiary government	Level of governments which specifies discretion
Australia (New South Wales)	Land tax Rates	State Government Local authorities	Unlimited Limited	– State government
Denmark	Land tax Service tax	Municipalities & counties Municipalities & counties	None None	Central Government Central Government
France	Land + land & building taxes Property tax	Local Authorities Local Authorities	None Limited	– Central Government
Germany	Real property tax (Grundsteuer)	Local Authorities	None	Central Government
Japan	Fixed assets tax City planning tax Special land-holding tax	Local Authorities Local Authorities Local Authorities	None None None	Central Government Central Government Central Government
Netherlands	Municipal tax Contributions to Polder Boards	Local Authorities[2] Local Authorities[2]	None[1] None	Central Government State Government
New Zealand	Rates	Local Authorities	Limited	Central Government
Spain	Rural land tax Urban land tax	Local Authorities Local Authorities	None None	Central Government Central Government
Sweden	Municipal guarantee tax	Local Authorities	None	Central Government
United Kingdom (England & Wales)	Rates	Local Authorities	None	Central Government
United States (Wisconsin)	Property tax	State Government & Local Authorities	Variable[3]	State Government

1. As from 1992 role of central government to be abridged.

2. Polder boards.

3. Representing central government and local authorities.

Source: *Local government, an international perspective,* ed. J. P. Owens and S. Panella, North Holland 1991.

- *Separate tax rates.* Intermediate and local governments have the right to decide within limits upon the rate of tax to levy on the taxable income or tax paid as determined under the central government income tax system, though the tax base remains identical or almost identical to that of the central income base. This is the system operating in Belgium, Canada (except Quebec), and Denmark.
- *Separate rate and allowance structures.* Although the income subject to tax is for the most part the same for central and local income taxation, the tax reliefs available to local taxpayers are not the same as those available under the central government income tax, though whether such reliefs are fixed by central or local government may vary. Each unit of local government applies its schedule rate to the taxable income so determined. These systems are used in Finland, Japan, Norway and Sweden.
- *Separate tax systems.* Under these systems, subordinate levels of governments determine both the base and the rate for income tax. In practice, however, the base is usually similar to that of the central government income tax. Separate tax systems are used in Switzerland, the United States and the Canadian province of Quebec.

The main distinction regarding the tax base is between those countries where it corresponds to that of the central government income tax system and those where it differs (column 2 of Table 9.7). The main difference between countries as regards the rate schedule is that in the majority of countries, lower levels of government use a flat rate, which

Table 9.6: Administrative responsibilities of different levels of governments under property taxes

Country	Tax	Beneficiary Government	Valuations	Assessments	Collection
Australia (New South Wales)	Land tax Rates	State Government State Government & Local Authorities	State Government State Government	State Government Local Authorities	State Government Local Authorities
Denmark	Land tax Service tax	Municipalities & counties	Central Government Central Government	Municipalities & counties	Municipalities & counties
France	Land + Land & building taxes Property tax	Local Authorities Local Authorities	Central Government Central Government	Central Government Central Government	Central Government Central Government
Germany	Real property tax (Grundsteuer)	Local Authorities	Central Government	Local Authorities & States	Local Authorities & States
Japan	Fixed assets tax City planning tax Special land-holding tax	Local Authorities Local Authorities Local Authorities	Local Authorities Local Authorities Individuals	Local Authorities Local Authorities Individuals	Local Authorities Local Authorities Local Authorities
Netherlands	Municipal tax Contributions to polder boards	Local Authorities Local Authorities[2]	Local Authorities Local Authorities[2]	Central Government & Local Authorities[1] Local Authorities[2]	Central Government[1] Local Authorities[2]
New Zealand	Land tax Rates	Central Government Local Authorities	Central Government Central Government	Central Government Local Authorities	Central Government Local Authorities
Spain	Rural land tax Urban land tax	Local Authorities Local Authorities	Joint agencies[3] Joint agencies[3]	Joint agencies[3] Joint agencies[3]	Joint agencies[3] Joint agencies[3]
Sweden	Municipal guarantee tax	Local Authorities	Central Government	Central Government	Central Government
Turkey	Immovable property tax	Central Government	Central Government	Central Government	Central Government
United Kingdom (England & Wales)	Rates	Local Authorities	Central Government	Local Authorities	Central Government
United States (Wisconsin)	Property tax	State Government & Local Authorities	State Government & Local Authorities	State Government & Local Authorities	State Government & Local Authorities

1. As from 1992 role of central government to be abridged.

2. Polder boards.

3. Representing central government and local authorities.

Source: *Local government, an international perspective*, ed. J. P. Owens and S. Panella, North Holland 1991.

usually varies from locality to locality, though in three countries (Japan, Switzerland and the United States) there exist progressive schedules at state and/or local levels (column 3 of Table 9.7).

Virtually all of the ten countries referred to in Table 9.7 use tax reliefs in their state or local income tax systems (see column 4). The use of these reliefs is a means of introducing a degree of progressivity into flat rate state and local income tax systems if they take

Table 9.7: Features of state and local government personal income taxes, 1990

(1)	(2)	(3)		(4)	(5)
Country	**Tax base**	**Rate schedule used (per cent)**		**Tax reliefs available under the state and local income tax**	**Responsibility for assessment and collection**
		Single rate	**Separate progressive rate schedule**		
Belgium	Central government income tax paid	7 (average)		None	Central government
Canada (excluding Quebec) [1]	Central government income tax paid before allowance for general tax credit	43-61 (av.= 55)		Some provisions provide tax credits for low income groups	Central government
Denmark	Central government taxable income	23-33 (av.= 29.6)		Yes	Central government for collection and local for assessment
Finland	Central government tax base and separate tax relief structure	14-19.5		Yes	Central government
Iceland	Central government taxable income	7.07		Central government tax credits apply to local income taxes	Central government
Japan	Central government tax base and separate tax relief structure		3.8 and 11 + fixed amount (municipalities)	Yes	Local government
Norway	Central government taxable income (minus dividend deduction)	2 and 4 + fixed amount (av. = 26.6)		Yes	Central government
Sweden	Central government tax base and separate tax relief structure	26-33 (av. =30.8)		Yes	Central government
Switzerland	Separate tax base in each Canton		2 to 13 [2]	Varies	Cantons
United States	Separate tax base in most States		4 to 7.9 [3]	Yes in some States	States

1. Quebec operates a separate provincial income tax system.
2. Zurich.
3. New York.

Source: *Local government, an international perspective,* ed. J. P. Owens and S. Panella, North Holland 1991.

the form of tax thresholds or tax credits rather than tax allowances or if they take the form of standard rather than expense-related reliefs.

The last column of Table 9.7 shows that in Japan, Switzerland and the United States subordinate levels of government are responsible for the assessment and the collection of income taxes, whereas in Belgium, Canada, Finland, Norway and Sweden they are both assessed and collected by central government. In Denmark they are assessed by local government but collected by central government.

Table 9.8: Relative importance of state and local income taxes, 1980 and 1988)

	State and local government income taxes as a percentage of:					
	Personal income taxes at all levels of government (heading 1100)		Total taxes		Gross domestic product	
	1980	1988	1980	1988	1980	1988
Belgium	7.5	9.6	2.6	3.1	1.1	1.4
Canada	38.4	37.3	13.1	13.7	4.1	4.7
Denmark	51.3	53.2	26.6	27.1	12.1	14.1
Finland	52.7	49.7	23.5	22.9	7.8	8.7
Iceland	50.9	52.1	10.7	11.7	3.3	3.9
Japan	28.9	32.3	7.0	7.4	1.8	2.3
Norway	58.4	60.7	16.4	16.9	7.7	7.9
Sweden	73.5	70.8	30.1	27.4	14.8	15.2
Switzerland	79.2	75.2	28.2	25.7	8.7	8.4
United States	14.5	18.1	5.4	6.3	1.6	1.9

Source: OECD RS 1990.

Apart from the information given in the table it may be added that, with the exception of the United States, state and local income taxes are not deductible from central government taxable income. On this issue, J. Lotz (1981) notes that arguments in favour of it have been provided in the United States by J. Due (1977) as a way of reducing opposition to increases in local income taxes and in ensuring that the combined rate of central and local income tax cannot exceed 100 per cent, and in Sweden to prevent excessive progression of local income tax rates. However, Lotz observes that even with deductibility the legal rate can exceed 100 per cent and actually did so in Denmark before 1968 when there was deductibility and in commenting on the J. Due paper, C. McLure remarks that: "Besides being inequitable, [deductibility] is undesirable because it involves unwarranted federal interference in state fiscal decisions in a way that runs directly counter to the lesson of the layer-cake model that income redistribution should be primarily a federal function."

Table 9.8 summarises the relative importance of yields from state and local income tax for the years 1980 and 1988 in relation to total income tax yields, total tax yields and GDP. The predominant but by no means universal trend was an increase between 1980 and 1988 in state and local income tax yields, which is in contrast to that of central government income tax yields.

3. State and local government corporate and business taxes

Four OECD countries (Canada, Norway, Switzerland, the United States) levy a corporate tax at state level, while eleven countries (Austria, Finland, Germany, Italy, Japan, Luxembourg, Norway, Portugal, Spain, Switzerland, the United States) levy a corporate or other business tax at the local level. In some countries (Austria, Canada, Finland, Germany, Japan, Luxembourg, Norway, Switzerland, the United States) the rates at the state level and local level vary from jurisdiction to jurisdiction. In unitary countries the tax base is usually determined by central government. In most federal countries state levels of government can determine both the base and rate, though in practice the state corporate tax base generally remains closely linked to the federal tax base.

Apart from the corporation tax, there are a number of other taxes levied on businesses, which for the most part, are often largely but not entirely related to business profits of which the most important examples are the Austrian, German and Luxembourg Gewerbesteuer, (largely related to profits) and the French "taxe professionnelle" (not at all related). These hybrid taxes are discussed at the end of Chapter 12. As noted there, they tend to be unpopular among both local businesses and economists because they are seen as distorting competition between businesses in an inefficient and unfair way and are not at all transparent.

4. Unearmarked payroll taxes

Unearmarked payroll taxes are relatively rare in OECD countries and in most cases they accrue exclusively to central government. Exceptions are Australia where they accrue entirely to state government and represent nearly 30 per cent of state government revenues, Austria where they accrue entirely to local government representing around 11 per cent of such revenues, Greece where a large portion of the payroll tax finances local government, and France where a small portion does (apart from the "taxe professionnelle" which is in part a payroll tax). Unearmarked payroll taxes and their defects are discussed in Chapter 12E6.

5. Taxes on financial and capital transactions

These various levies, often in the form of stamp duties mainly on the transfer of shares and immovable property are levied in most OECD countries, and usually accrue entirely to central government. However, they accrue in varying degrees to subordinate levels of government in Austria, Japan, Portugal, Spain, Switzerland and the United States. They are invariably of slight revenue importance and there has been a tendency to reduce or eliminate them (Switzerland and the United Kingdom).

6. State and local consumption taxes

a) General consumption taxes

In most countries, general consumption taxes are inappropriate as a source of finance for local government because of the risk of cross-border shopping if rates and coverage vary significantly and are viable only when geographical distances are great. It is accordingly no accident that they exist only in Canada and the United States, the large amounts shown for Austria and Germany in Table 9.4 referring to shared taxes – there being no local variation in the general consumption tax rates or base between subordinate levels of government.

Nine of Canada's ten provinces levy retail sales taxes at rates varying from 5 to 12 per cent and they accounted for around 22 per cent of Canadian state tax revenues in 1989. Retail sales taxes are levied by 45 of the states of the United States, the district of Columbia and about 7 000 local governments, and in 1989 accounted for around 31 per cent of all state revenues. In the United States, the rates of the states range from 2.0 to 7.5 per cent and if local rates are added, from 4.25 to 8.25 per cent.

Under the German tax sharing formulae, 65 per cent of value added tax revenues currently accrue to the federal government and 35 per cent to the state governments, the latter apportioned mainly according to the relative number of inhabitants which is regarded as a proxy for the amount of consumption. Whether or not this is the most appropriate revenue-sharing criterion between states has been much discussed and is another interesting tax policy issue that cannot be pursued here.

b) Excises etc.

A number of countries obtain significant revenues from excises at subordinate levels of government and in fact Germany and Switzerland are the only federal countries not to do so (see Table 9.4). These revenues derive mostly from taxes on alcohol and tobacco, but information is lacking on what discretion, if any, subordinate levels of government have to vary rates and base.

c) Permission and ownership taxes

These are applied in all federal countries and most unitary countries. In most countries they raise little revenue for subordinate levels of government, but account for over a quarter of the revenues of Australia's state government and of the Netherlands' local government, and nearly a fifth of Belgium's local government. Most of the revenues derive from motor vehicles licences. As noted elsewhere (Chapter 2 and the Annex to Section 2E) there is a grey area between these taxes and fees and user charges and what was said earlier in this chapter about user charges applies also to these taxes.

7. The poll tax

Though it is perhaps irrational to devote much space to a local government tax that existed in only one OECD country (the United Kingdom), it has bizarre aspects and has raised some interesting policy issues as well as much passionate political debate. There are three bizarre aspects: first, in the 20th century only Papua New Guinea (formerly) and some African countries (still) have levied such a tax; second, the English (as they then were) imposed a similar tax in 1379, which is recorded by historians as being the major cause of a peasants' revolt; third, the United Kingdom poll tax introduced in Scotland in 1989, in England and Wales in 1990 and repealed in 1991 is believed by many to be a major cause of the demise of the Prime Minister of the time who had gone on record as stating that there was no other valid way of financing local government.

Turning to the more serious policy issues, it would seem that the introduction of the poll tax can be explained only by three particular problems worrying the British government. The first was that successive governments had not carried out property revaluations since 1973 and when these were carried out in Scotland in the mid-eighties, the resultant changes in relative tax burdens caused much taxpayer discontent; second, this discontent was perhaps felt especially by single-occupancy households, who, receiving fewer local government services than multi-occupant households, nevertheless paid the same amount of tax; third, much of the property tax fell on businesses, which had no votes and which accordingly were unable to influence the tax/expenditure decisions taken by local governments. The rationale was thus to increase local accountability by ensuring that voters deciding in favour of increasing local government expenditures would have to bear their fair share of the burden. Unfortunately for this rationale, a fourth and overwhelming factor, which contradicted local accountability, was that central government had decided for macroeconomic reasons that local governments should *not* have the right to spend more, so if they raised the poll tax beyond certain limits, their more important grants would be reduced. In addition, the evident unfairness of the poll tax, under which a pauper paid as much as a millionaire, had to be alleviated by rebates to lower income groups, which were increased several times as complaints became more vociferous and the administrative complications for local government authorities became ever greater with each successive change. Moreover, the poll tax was relatively easy to avoid or evade. Some did it publicly as a matter of principle and got penalised under the law, but most did it by hiding their existence (for example by not registering or changing their abode). The consequence was that local authorities were only able to collect something like three quarters of their estimated revenues and accordingly had to increase their demands on compliant taxpayers for subsequent years.

It was accordingly decided in 1991 to abandon the poll tax, though the phasing-out process will not be completed before 1993. The poll tax has been replaced by a "council tax" which combines various features of a property tax, a household tax, a poll tax and an income tax, and which likewise has never been contemplated by any other OECD country. (For a good summary and negative evaluation of the council tax, see J. Hills and H. Sutherland (*Fiscal studies*, November 1991).

F. An evaluation of taxes used for financing state and local expenditure

In assessing the relative advantages of the different kinds of taxes for financing state and local government it is always necessary to recall the conflicting objectives that have to be resolved. To repeat briefly, the first conflict is between local autonomy where subordinate levels are given at least some discretion over their taxing and spending decisions and the shared taxes route which certainly creates fewer administrative complications and impedes less central governments' overall macroeconomic and distributional choices. Secondly, each particular kind of tax has its own particular advantages and disadvantages and usually to try to correct one disadvantage is apt to create another (for example to make the property tax fairer generally involves complicating its administration).

However, this is an area where some taxes seem better suited than others to fulfil the criteria for a good state and local tax referred to in Section D. Before elaborating on this, it may be observed, first, that own taxes versus shared taxes is one aspect of the local autonomy versus agency argument and its resolution is essentially a political decision, which could also be affected by the prevailing economic conditions, but perhaps more importantly by priorities of governments and their voters in the local freedom versus national security choice. Second, even if some taxes are less effective than others, it may be prudent to diversify sources of revenue to reduce taxpayer discontent which may arise if too much revenue is being collected from one source. The United Kingdom provides an example. One of the reasons why the former property tax (rates) was so unpopular was the large amount that British taxpayers had to pay (as a proportion of GDP property tax receipts were far higher in the UK than in any other OECD country) but instead of diversifying own tax revenues of local government, the British government chose to move from the rates frying pan to the poll tax fire and subsequently to what may well be the council tax furnace.

Apart from having the function of diversifying revenue sources, sub-optimal local taxes like business property and payroll taxes may have some justification just because they are less visible and so more acceptable than personal and property taxes, at least if the tax take from them is relatively slight. Of course, this raises another conflict already referred to in earlier chapters between the relative importance of transparency and other goals.

Turning now to the relative efficacy of the various own taxes where subordinate levels of government have at least some say in fixing the local tax burden, it has already been noted that general consumption taxes are not practicable outside countries like Canada and the United States and even in these countries, as mentioned in Chapter 13, their existence has inhibited the adoption of VAT, which might be desirable on other grounds. However, other consumption taxes, such as excises and ownership and use taxes (especially motor vehicle licences) are capable of providing some contribution towards state and local government revenues. Employers' payroll taxes, business property and other taxes – whether or not linked entirely, partially or not at all to profits – have the disadvantage that differential rates could drive employers, and so jobs, from one local jurisdiction to another and the business taxes may additionally create administrative complications if the enterprises have different branches in different jurisdictions.

To the extent that there is agreement with the above evaluations, it is clear that with the exception of excises and ownership and permission taxes, whose revenue raising capacity is somewhat limited, immovable property taxes, especially on households, and local income taxes seem the most efficacious way of raising revenue for state and local government and in practice they are by far the most used in OECD countries. There seems a lot to be said for the use of both these sources not only because of the practical advantages of diversification referred to above, but because the local income tax with appropriate reliefs for family circumstances embodies the ability to pay principle and the property tax the benefit principle. It does seem even possible to combine the two without too much difficulty as in the French "taxe d'habitation", where the tax base is the rental value of the dwelling, but allowances are deductible from this base to take account of personal (family) circumstances. A local property tax without a local income tax element is likely to be unfair and a local income tax without a local property tax infringes local accountability in inviting those below the income tax threshold to vote for higher local spending in the knowledge that they would not be contributing to its costs. However, the disadvantages of property taxes resulting from their low buoyancy, visibility and perceived unfairness (see Chapter 14) may suggest that they should play a subordinate role to local income taxes in raising revenue for local government expenditures.

PART III
THE DESIGN AND REFORM OF PARTICULAR TAXES

Chapter 10
The personal income tax

A. Introduction and overview

1. Organisation of the chapter

Of all the particular kinds of tax surveyed in Chapters 10 to 14, the personal income tax is the most important and complex. It is used to promote many, not always compatible goals, such as vertical equity, horizontal equity, economic efficiency, neutrality towards various kinds of social and economic decisions. There are also a variety of instruments at governments' disposal for promoting their priority objectives, such as different ways of giving tax relief, aggregation or non-aggregation of spouses' income, different degrees of progressivity of rate schedules, offsetting wholly, partially or not at all the impact of inflation. All these instruments interact with each other in determining the tax burdens of different categories of taxpayers, and it seems clear that policy makers have not always appreciated how they interact.

Thus the problems to be discussed are more complex and wide-ranging than those discussed with respect to the other major taxes in Chapters 11 to 14. Although the aim in this chapter, as in Chapters 11 to 14, is to highlight the main policy issues that emerge in designing or reforming the tax in question, to discuss the arguments in favour or against various possible options and to record the decisions that have been taken and how they have changed over time, the layout of this chapter differs from Chapters 11 to 14 in two respects.

First, because so many (often very detailed and lengthy) tables are provided and because the logic of their ordering (for which see Section B2 to B6) does not always follow the textual exposition, they are inserted at the end of the chapter rather than at the appropriate point in the text, as is done in Chapters 11 to 14. Second, this brief introduction does not attempt to summarise the contents of the chapter, for there would be too much to summarise and too much repetition. An attempt has been made, however, to guide the reader through the income tax maze, by providing first a detailed list of contents, second an introductory summary to most of the main sections and third cross-references between one section and another where this seems to be useful.

2. The contribution of the personal income tax to government revenues

Much information has already been provided in Chapters 2 and 3. Charts 10.1 and 10.2 briefly summarise the most recent situation and developments since 1955. What they do not show (see Tables 2.2 and 2.3) is that currently the personal income tax remains the most important source of government revenue in three quarters of the OECD countries, the remaining six being Austria, France, Greece, Iceland, Portugal and Spain. Chart 10.1 displays the considerable dispersion in OECD countries' reliance on the personal income tax, varying from 52 per cent to 12 per cent of total tax receipts and 26 per cent to 4 per cent of GDP.

Chart 10.2 indicates the continuing rise in the unweighted average of income tax ratios between 1955 and 1980 and thereafter a levelling-off as regards tax ratios and a mild decline as regards tax share. An important remark on this chart is that for 1955 and 1960, data are lacking for France, Iceland, Luxembourg, Spain and Turkey – all below average countries as regards income tax ratio and share – so that the chart overstates 1955 and 1960 income tax ratios and shares in relation to later years.

To illustrate more strikingly the rise in the relative importance of the personal income tax share and its transition from an elite tax to a mass tax between 1913 and 1970, here are some numbers taken from R. Goode (1976) with regard to the United States *federal* personal income tax.

US federal income tax revenues as percentage of total federal tax revenues								
1914-16	1917-20	1921-29	1930-40	1941-45	1946-49	1950-59	1960-69	1970-75
6.2	18.4	22.8	17.8	33.4	39.6	42.9	43.8	45.0
Percentage of population covered by the US federal personal income tax								
1913	1918	1926	1939	1945	1950	1960	1970	
less than 1	7.7	4.2	5	74.2	58.9	73.1	80.8	

These fluctuations were evidently largely influenced by the wars of 1914 to 1918 and 1939 to 1945.

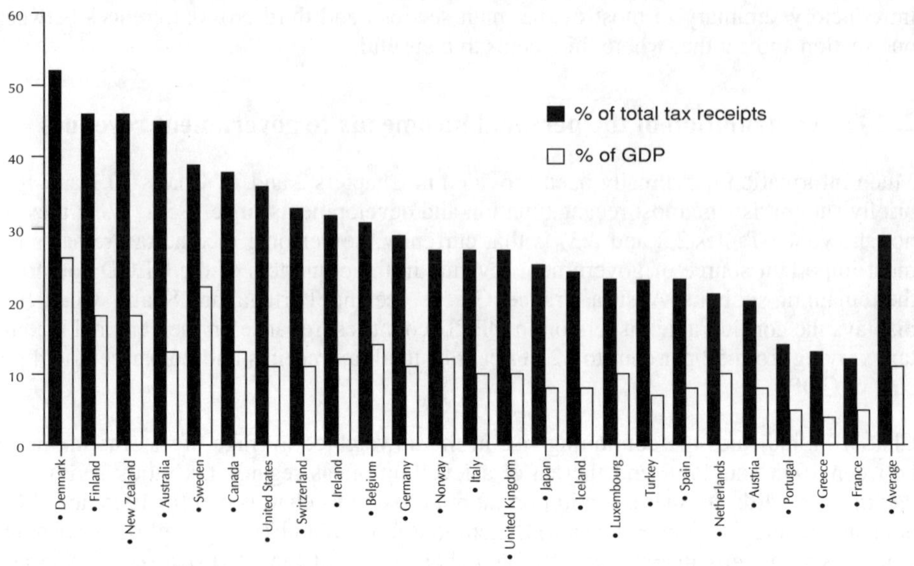

Chart 10.1: Personal income tax revenues as a percentage of total tax revenues and GDP, 1989 (Source: OECD RS 1991.)

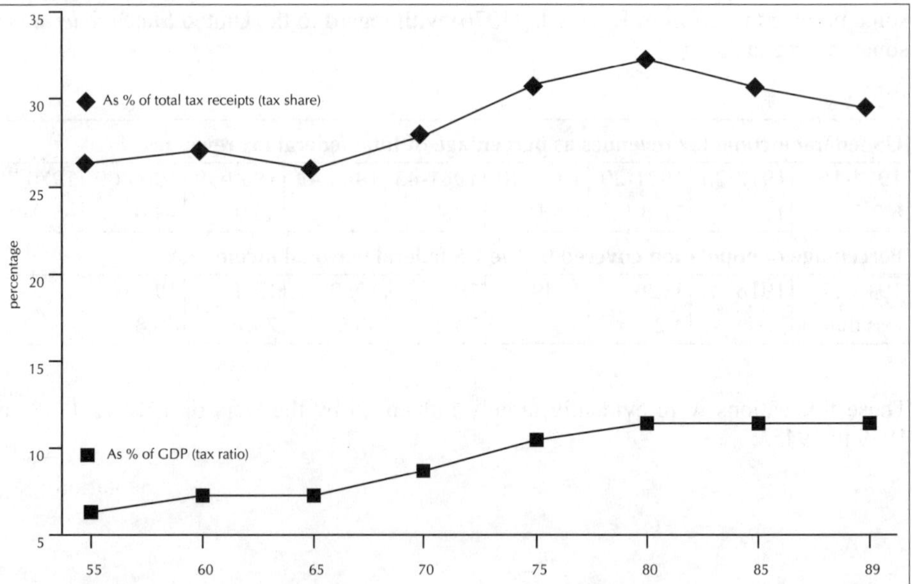

Chart 10.2: The unweighted OECD personal income tax ratio and share, 1955-89 (Source: OECD RS 1991.)

3. The income tax until now

In "*The individual income tax*" R. Goode (1964, revised 1975) records that:

> The belief that the individual tax is the fairest of all taxes arises from the conviction that it accords best with ability to pay. Net income is a measure of a person's capacity to command economic resources, and, intuitively, it seems to be a good indicator of ability to help finance government.

He indicates later that many American experts have accepted as the ideal starting point for defining income for tax purposes (as laid down by Schanz, Haig and Simons in the nineteenth century) the increase or accretion in the power to satisfy one's wants in a given period insofar as that power consists of money itself or anything susceptible of valuation in terms of money.

Thus the objective of supporters of the personal income tax as the main means of raising government revenues is to apply a progressive rate schedule to as comprehensive an income tax base (CIT) as is feasible in practice. Its most well-known academic supporters after the 1939-45 world war were Americans, R. Goode, J. Pechman and (with some reservations) R. Musgrave and its philosophy was totally endorsed by the well-known Canadian Royal Commission (Carter) Report of 1966. In the literature it is frequently referred to as embodying the ability to pay or accretion principle.

However, a number of conceptual and practical difficulties prevent any country from adopting anything like a CIT base and this failure to do so creates economic distortions, complexities and horizontal inequities. For example, it is generally considered not feasible (and by many not desirable) to take into account all accrued changes in the value of assets and liabilities. Accordingly, the income tax has to be limited to realised income, so that unrealised capital gains are not taxed, for example. Other conceptual problems arise for a progressive CIT income tax, such as the distinction between personal consumption which depends mainly on goods and services yielding direct satisfaction and intermediate goods and services contributing to a final product, as well as the measurement of change in net wealth and capital gains and losses when price levels and interest rates vary.

Partly for these reasons a number of theorists have expressed preference for a progressive expenditure tax as a replacement for or supplement to the personal income tax. Thus, citing Thomas Hobbes, N. Kaldor (1955) the most well-known 20th century supporter of an expenditure tax observed that it may be just and expedient to tax people with reference to what they take out of the common pool rather than what they contribute, so that consumption may be a better tax base than income. As already indicated in Chapters 1E and 7B, a detailed theoretical discussion of the arguments for and against the existing personal income tax and the non-existent expenditure tax is outside the scope of this book, but the next paragraphs, in the form of two extended, though slightly abridged quotations, summarise what has been happening in the past and also the present situation. Though the two views expressed are not incompatible – and in many respects similar – their different emphases suggest that the debate on the future of the personal income tax is likely to continue into the 21st century.

The first is from R. Bird and S. Cnossen (1990):

> The most important feature of tax policy in the twentieth century has unquestionably been the rise of the personal income tax to a predominant position in the revenue structure of most western countries. In several countries, the income tax was introduced during the First World War, remained in place after the war primarily as a relatively modest tax on higher incomes, became a mass tax during or soon after the Second World War, and rose to prominence during the next three decades of unparalleled increases in real and, especially, nominal incomes.
>
> During the 1970s and early 1980s, however, popular and academic discontent with the income tax rose, undoubtedly fuelled by the effects of inflation coupled with markedly slower economic growth. In at least some countries, the populace at large seemed to have lost faith in the fairness of the income tax. Striking evidence of this may be seen in the periodic surveys conducted by the US Advisory Commission on Intergovernmental Relations. Over the course of the 1970s the personal income tax moved from being perceived as the 'most fair' to the 'least fair' of taxes in the United States.
>
> Many students of taxation argued that the personal income tax had failed in terms of equity, efficiency and simplicity – the sacred trinity of the tax specialists. With respect to equity, although allegedly progressive, the tax in most countries, it was held, was so full of holes in practice that it blatantly favored recipients of capital income and discriminated against wage- and salary-earners. With respect to efficiency, empirical work indicated that the income tax distorted saving, investment, financing and production decisions, with resulting adverse effects on personal and corporate incentives, on business efficiency, on employment, on economic growth and on the rate of inflation. Finally, with respect to simplicity, the tax had become so complex and incomprehensible that certainty had been lost.

Bird and Cnossen conclude this introduction by saying that:

> The personal income tax has, it seems, risen from the recent fires of criticism and the ashes of tax reform like a phoenix. For the moment, at least, the challenge of the consumption base seems to be in abeyance. What remains unclear, however, is whether the future of income tax reform, lies in a return to the Holy Grail of Schanz-Haig-Simons purity. On the basis of the discussion in this volume, we think it more likely that what lies ahead is the continued evolution of a considerably muted and imperfect hybrid tax incorporating some consumption tax elements both by choice and necessity and less progressive in its rate structure than once seemed feasible and desirable, but still clearly something that may legitimately be called a personal income tax.

The second is from J. Pechman (1992):

> The federal income tax has been under attack by the economics profession for more than a decade. The attack comes from two directions: supply-siders who believe that progressive income taxation impairs economic incentives and more traditional economists who would substitute a progressive expenditure tax for the income tax... Today it is fair to say that many, if not most, economists favour the expenditure tax or a flat rate income tax...
>
> Despite an incessant barrage from both groups, no country in the world is planning to abandon the income tax or is even considering a personal expenditure tax. A wave of tax reform, beginning with the US reform in 1986 has been sweeping the world, aiming at improving the income tax, not eliminating it. Tax preferences formerly regarded as sacrosanct are being removed and there is a distinct movement towards comprehensive income taxation. However, individual income tax rates are being cut, tax progressivity has been declining almost everywhere and reliance on the income tax has been diminishing... I approve of the base broadening feature of the current tax reform movement, but I believe that the reduction in the redistributive effect of the income tax has gone too far. In this paper, I shall show that the progressivity of the US tax system – never very pronounced, except during and immediately after the two world wars – has been declining for more than two decades and that the Tax Reform Act of 1986 reversed this

> decline, but only slightly. Consequently, we have a long way to go to improve the equity of the tax system. I believe this can be done without punitive tax rates that will hurt economic incentives.

S. Cnossen and I concluded our 1990 survey of personal income tax reforms in OECD Member Countries by remarking *inter alia* that:

> The survey suggests that though much was changed, much has remained the same. The scope of the rate reductions and the changes in the tax base, provoked to a large extent by the income tax reform in the United States, are unprecedented. They reflect the growing internationalisation of the tax policy debate. That much has remained the same reflects the fact that systems of democratic countries have a given constitutional character. In other words a high degree of stability and certainty is desirable and whilst there may remain some some scope for further base broadening in some countries, attempts to move closer to the theoretical concept of income are likely to pose political and technical problems. Moreover, the personal income tax is only one stone in the tax and expenditure building. Conflicting priciples, practices and perceptions must be balanced....

There would appear to be no need to modify what we wrote in 1990, but a look at country trends in income tax systems does suggest some further generalisations, which evidently will not apply to a number of countries and the timing will be somewhat different as between those countries to which it does apply. Three broad periods may be identified:

- *1960-1975*. Income tax ratios increased mainly through fiscal drag (both bracket creep and erosion of the value of thresholds and other standard allowances) and the bracket creep effect was accentuated as rate schedules frequently became more progressive. On the other hand non-standard allowances proliferated for particular expenditures which had the effect of narrowing the income tax base.
- *1975-1980*. Income tax ratios remained stable mainly because governments took legislative measures to offset fiscal drag – which they had rarely done in earlier years – but there was little structural change to income tax systems.
- *1985-1992*. Income tax ratios remained stable and sometimes even declined as a result of continued offsetting of fiscal drag together with a restructuring of income tax systems, the rate lowering and base broadening phenomenum already discussed in Chapter 1F.

One country which has followed quite closely the above scenario is the United States and this sub-section concludes with the summary of J. Bakija and E. Steuerle of their 1991 article on "Individual income taxation since 1948":

> Since 1948 individual income taxes have undergone a variety of significant, sometimes dramatic, changes. On occasion the principal focus of domestic legislation, individual income tax rates were often lowered and never raised directly exept during the Korean and Vietnam wars. Until the 1980s, however, tax rates did rise because inflation and real income growth continuously pushed taxpayers into higher brackets. State individual income taxes also increased because of bracket creep and the expansion ot this type of tax to a greater number of states.
>
> Since the early 1950s, both average individual income tax rates and average tax rates for all federal, state, and local taxes have varied only moderately as a percent of total income. These average rates were also little different in 1990 than in 1980.
>
> Components of the tax base and marginal tax rates, however, are very different today from those of prior decades. A decline in the value of the personal exemption, and a related reduction in the income of non-taxable individuals, is by far the most significant change over the postwar period. Together they resulted in an expansion of the tax base by about one-quarter of total per-

> sonal income. The decline in the personal exemption also helps to explain why tax-exempt levels of income fell dramatically relative to average income and why households with dependents increasingly paid a greater share of the tax burden. Large expansions of exclusions and itemized deductions, and the restoration of the value of the standard deduction, can also be viewed as being financed by this decline in the personal tax exemption.
>
> In the mid- to late-1980s, the direction of change in many parts of the tax base was reversed. The personal exemption and standard deduction were both increased moderately in the Tax Reform Act of 1986, while itemized deductions were curtailed....
>
> While the top tax rate fell from 91 percent in the early 1960s to about one-third of that level by the late 1980s, few taxpayers were affected. By the end of the 1980s, base expansion had allowed marginal individual income tax rates to be lower for most taxpayers without significant effects on average rates. For the majority of taxpayers, the individual income tax in 1960 was a flat rate tax on income over exempt amounts. It was restored to that position by the Tax Reform Act of 1986.

4. Possible future trends

Whilst the direction towards less progressive rates looks like being irrevocable as well as justifiable on a number of grounds (see Mathews' quote in Chapter 1C) this need not reduce the overall progressivity of the personal income tax system, if the threshold is increased in real terms and if the base moves in a CIT direction rather than in the direction of exempting savings from income tax or giving preferential rate treatment for income from capital over wage and salary income. In practice, movements in the tax base appear to be occurring in both these directions and often in the same country. In many countries the income tax base has been widened by bringing in capital gains and fringe benefits and taking a more restrictive view on the deductibility of mortgage and other interest as well as of expenses on entertainment and company cars, from income subject to tax; but on the other hand, there has been a tendency in some countries to move towards a backdoor kind of expenditure tax by exempting or giving preferential treatment to all forms of savings (which has the incidental merit of greater neutrality towards different forms of savings – see Chapter 7B) and in a number of countries income from capital has recently become subject to lower rates of tax than wage and salary income as a proxy for an imputation system (see Chapter 12D).

Thus it seems safe to predict that most OECD countries will remain with hybrid personal income tax as their main source of revenue with a continuing tendency which has persisted from 1985 to 1992 for rates to drop and the base to widen. Within this general scenario country changes will doubtless vary according to the nature of their present system and the political, social and economic preferences of their governments. Much of the trend in recent years has reflected the presence of governments of the radical right in the United Kingdom and United States and the replacement of social democratic regimes in Scandinavia. If the retreat from socialist ethics continues, one can expect the trend to continue, especially as regards rate lowering: if parties of the left take over government during the nineties, a different scenario would emerge, including some (probably modest) increases in statutory rates for higher income groups and the reversal of any preferential treatment of unearned income.

In either event, whether or not higher marginal rates will continue to fall will depend to some extent on whether the income tax base can be broadened. For while the revenue-neutral constraint is not paramount – it can be relaxed in either direction to meet government policy choices, and also recourse may be had to other revenue sources – this constraint is evidently of relevance. In a few countries (Australia, Iceland, Italy and Spain) there is little room for base broadening, but this is not the case in most OECD countries (see Table 10.1). Section C comments in more detail on the scope for base broadening in its survey of income tax base issues.

Doubts on whether there is likely to be any future increase in the contribution of the personal income tax to government revenues, at least in most countries, have been referred to in Chapter 6B4.

B. The mechanisms of the personal income tax

1. Summary

This section refers briefly to certain mechanisms, techniques or instruments that together determine the different tax burdens, applied to different categories of taxpayer. They are discussed in more detail in subsequent sections of this chapter as follows:

- *Income subject to tax*: this relates to the tax base, which is discussed in Section C.
- *The tax unit*: the main issues are discussed in Section E3 under the relative tax treatment of single persons, one-earner and two-earner couples.
- *Global and schedular taxation*: the main discussion is to be found in Section D2.
- *Tax reliefs*: standard tax reliefs are discussed in Sections D and E: non-standard in Section C.
- *The tax schedule*: various aspects are discussed in Section D as indicated in the list of contents.
- *Tax collection methods* are discussed only in this section.

2. Income subject to tax

Certain income sources are generally excluded from total income to arrive at the income subject to tax which may be defined as all sources of income liable to tax without taking account of tax allowances. ("Taxable income," the base to which the rate schedule applies, represents "income subject to tax" minus "tax allowances".) Table 10.1 summarises the sources of income subject to tax in OECD countries. It shows that all countries include employment income (i.e. wages and salaries), net business income, rent income and public pensions as income subject to tax. These income sources taken together constitute the major part of total income in all countries. The table also shows a substantial variation in country practices with respect to other income sources, such as social transfers and capital gains. Nearly all countries exclude employers' contributions to sickness and all countries private pension schemes from income subject to tax.

3. The tax unit

Table 10.2 classifies countries according to whether or not they aggregate for personal income tax purposes the earned income of spouses where both are gainfully employed. In countries using joint taxation, tax liability is calculated by applying the appropriate rate schedule to the aggregated taxable earned incomes of the spouses; under individual taxation tax liability is calculated by applying the appropriate rate schedule to the taxable earned income of each spouse. Table 10.2 also summarises changes in country tax unit practices over the last two decades and the results are commented on in Section E3d.

4. Global and schedular tax systems

Over most of the period under review the OECD trend has been to move away from schedular taxation under which each source of income is subject to a separate treatment of rate and base towards a global taxation where all income from whatever source is aggregated and one rate schedule is applied. Portugal, the last OECD country to retain a schedular system, abandoned it in 1989. Before that Belgium (1963), Italy (1973) and Spain (1978) moved to global systems. In most recent years a number of Eastern European governments (e.g. Czechoslovakia, Hungary and Poland) are following this trend, and a number of Latin American countries have also moved to global systems over the last two decades. Until recently there has thus been a one-way move towards global taxation.

However, OECD tax systems have been only *relatively* global in that pension funds and capital gains are sometimes not taxed at all, different kinds of allowances may be given to the employed, the self-employed, farmers and the liberal professions and different schedule rates may apply to earned, investment and agricultural income (see Table 10.10). Moreover, in recent years certain aspects of schedular taxation have been introduced in the North American and Scandinavian countries, as discussed in Section D2 below.

5. Tax reliefs

OECD Member Countries provide tax reliefs in a variety of ways as shown in Tables 10.3 to 10.10. The main distinctions between types of relief can be summarised as follows:

a) Standard and non-standard reliefs

Standard tax reliefs are reliefs unrelated to the actual expenditure incurred by the taxpayer and are available to all taxpayers who satisfy the eligibility rules. Examples include the basic reliefs available to all taxpayers, irrespective of their marital or family status and the reliefs available for dependent children and other dependants and country practices are summarised in Tables 10.3 to 10.7. Non-standard reliefs, on the other hand, are reliefs the amounts of which are wholly determined by reference to the actual expenses incurred and information on these is provided in Tables 10.8 to 10.14. There are two borderline cases: work-related expenses which may be a fixed amount (standard) or according to costs actually incurred (non-standard); and in a different sense, deductability for social security contributions when allowed is available universally (standard) but relates to the amount of the contribution (non-standard). Leaving aside these borderline cases, there are very important differences between standard and non-standard reliefs: the former are most appropriately considered as part of the tax schedule and as an alternative to steep rates for achieving progressivity, especially when relating to the tax threshold or taking the form of tax credits: the latter are generally regressive and entail a narrowing of the tax base. In other terminology the latter are clearly tax expenditures, whereas it is arguable whether the former are (see Chapter 6C).

b) Forms of tax reliefs

Tax reliefs may take the form of tax allowances, tax credits, zero-rate brackets, quotient systems, income-splitting and separate schedules. *Tax allowances* are the most frequently used and take the form of deductions from income subject to tax. *Tax credits* are lump-sum deductions from tax payable, with rare exceptions being unaffected by the taxpayers' income. In Canada, France, New Zealand and the United States, but not in other countries, certain tax credits may be permitted to exceed tax liabilities and the difference paid out to the taxpayer. In a number of countries, the basic relief takes the form of a *zero rated first bracket*. In some circumstances the effect of substituting a zero rate for a positive rate in the first bracket is to produce the same effect as a tax credit. The increase of an existing zero rate bracket, however, has the same effect as increasing a tax allowance (i.e. it gives greater relief to top-rated taxpayers) unless the extension is balanced by a reduction of the next higher bracket or brackets.

In most countries family status is generally taken into account by the use of tax allowances or tax credits but reliefs in respect of family status may also take the form of:

Income-splitting systems: Germany, Ireland, Portugal, the United States;
Family quotient systems: France, Luxembourg;
Separate schedules: Norway, Switzerland, the United States.

Under income-splitting systems, whatever the actual income of the two spouses, for tax purposes it is deemed to be equal so that the schedule rate is applied to half their total income. Under family quotient systems, taxable income is divided by further amounts to take account of the existence of certain dependants most importantly minor children. The third alternative is to apply different rate schedules to single and married persons.

6. Tax rate schedules

Table 10.15 indicates the changes which have been made in the rate structures between 1975, 1986 and 1990. The main features brought out by the table are that top marginal rates have almost invariably declined, brackets have been reduced and that lowest rates have more often than not been increased.

These tax rate schedules are the statutory (or nominal) rates applied to taxable income. As already noted they provide a very poor guide to effective tax rates, but may provoke important behaviourial reactions among the many taxpayers who are unaware of this fact. To convert nominal rates to effective tax rates is a complicated business, though Table 10.16 gives some idea of how this can be done by comparing average effective rates and the income level of an average production worker with two children.

Included in the section on tax rate schedules are the indexation of income tax schedules and reliefs (Table 10.17) and the link between the income tax and social security contributions (Table 10.18).

7. Collection procedures

Tax is normally charged by reference to income of a particular year, which may be the calendar year or some other period of 12 months. In some cases the tax is charged on the actual income received or accruing in the year, and in others it may be charged on an amount calculated by reference to the income of the previous years. This process may vary not only from country to country but also, within the same country's tax system, from one source of income to another. The method of collecting income tax affects, *inter alia*, the amount of tax revenues, the speed with which tax is collected, the collection costs to yield ratio and the attitudes of taxpayers to the system.

The bulk of income tax revenues is provided by wage and salary earners, and in OECD countries, other than France and Switzerland, tax is withheld along with social security contributions by the employers on income currently earned. In Switzerland, employees (and employers) pay tax to the federal government on the average income earned in the previous two years. In France, employees pay tax subsequently on the income earned in the previous year. The French system puts employees in a similar position to the self-employed and employers as regards collection methods but this system does involve a considerable delay in collecting revenues and provides greater possibilities for evasion and an alternative would be to make provisional assessments for the self-employed, so that everyone would be on a current basis. Nor is it evident that the withholding system is more unpopular with employees, who, though they pay earlier, may pay it less painfully – i.e. in weekly or monthly instalments rather than as a yearly lump sum.[1]

Collection procedures are not further discussed in this chapter, but it is worth pointing out that they do appear to have an important effect on personal income tax revenues. For example, when Denmark in 1970 and Italy in 1977 moved to Pay As You Earn systems, personal income tax revenues substantially increased: the fact that France has the lowest personal income tax ratio of all industrialised countries is almost certainly not unconnected with France's collection procedures.

For completeness, though not further discussed, it may be mentioned that there are differences in the Pay As you Earn systems. For example, under the British system there is cumulative withholding with no periodical adjustment. Under the American and most

1. France provides taxpayers with the option of payment by monthly instalments, but most French taxpayers pefer to delay their payment.

other systems there is an end-year adjustment to take account of tax underpaid, or more usually overpaid. Also in some countries the tax authorities (usually via employers) assess the taxpayers' liability whereas in others the taxpayer makes a self-assessment.

C. The income tax base

1. Summary

Sub-section 2 surveys the differences in the tax base in OECD countries for various years ranging from 1982 to 1988. It provides a comparative quantitative survey from two main points of view, first by indicating the major sources of income that are subject to tax and second by indicating the quantitative importance of those tax allowances (i.e. expense related, non-standard) that limit the tax base. Attention is also drawn to the different tax treatment of different income sources prevailing in all OECD countries.

Sub-section 3 discusses five specific cases where tax base issues have been debated in recent years in a number of OECD countries and where changes have frequently been made. It would have been conceptually appropriate to refer here to a sixth issue, the tax treatment of capital gains, but because of the length of the discussion on this topic and because a number of problems of capital gains taxes relate also to capital taxes, capital gains taxes are discussed along with capital taxes in Chapter 11. The five categories which are discussed (in random order) are:

- The favourable tax treatment of fringe benefits, defined as "all advantages, other than monetary salary and wages, in consequence of services rendered or to be rendered, by an employee" (OECD 1988), has resulted in a proliferation of this form of wage and salary payment.
- The deductibility of premiums for retirement and insurance schemes has provided a large conversion of current income into future income.
- The favourable treatment of imputed income from owner-occupied property (generally by exempting the gross income of the asset while permitting the deduction of mortgage interest from other income) is augmented by the favourable capital gains tax treatment usually accorded to sales of dwelling-places.
- The deductibility of interest related to consumer credit expenditure still prevalent in a few countries has the effects of a negative consumption tax and discourages saving;
- The frequent exemption from income tax of unemployment and other welfare payments could have work disincentive effects and seems unnecessary since they could be grossed up to whatever level considered appropriate and taxed like other sources of income.

In their different ways all five of these kinds of tax concession may distort consumer choices, discriminate against certain taxpayers and lead to a non-optimal allocation of resources.

2. A comparative survey of the income tax base

a) The relative importance and tax treatment of different income sources

Table 10.1, taken from the *Personal Income Tax Base* (OECD 1990) gives an indication of what income is subject to income tax and the following sub-table taken from Table 5.3 of the same publication gives some idea of the relative importance of the five main income tax sources as a percentage of income subject to tax.[1] Leaving aside fringe benefits and capital gains which for most countries cannot be separately identified, other sources of income usually represent very small amounts: also identifiable fringe benefits always constitute less than 1 per cent of income subject to tax as do identifiable capital gains, except in the United States (4.5 per cent), Canada (2.5 per cent), Spain (2.4 per cent) and Sweden (1.3 per cent). The only other income sources to exceed 3 per cent of income subject to tax are rental income in Greece which accounts for nearly 7 per cent and for over 3 per cent in Italy and Spain (also over 2 per cent in France and the United States) and private pensions, annuities and life insurance which account for nearly 7 per cent in the Netherlands and over 4 per cent in the United Kingdom. The sub-table shows that in all countries employment income predominates varying from 60 per cent of income subject to tax in the Netherlands to 98 per cent in Ireland.

	Employment	Net business income	Interest income	Public pensions	Social transfers
Australia	72	11	5	6	
Austria	89	n.a.	n.a.	11	
Belgium	61	10		16	6
Canada	71	5	6		7
Denmark	68	8	4	7	6
Finland	72	7		16[1]	
France	63	10		21[1]	
Germany	80	n.a.	n.a.	n.a.	
Greece	71	21			
Ireland	98				
Italy	77[2]	19			
Netherlands	60	8		9	9
Norway	71	10		12	
Spain	75[3]	13	6		
Sweden	65	3		18[1]	6
United Kingdom	73	9	5	8	
United States	76	3	6	5[1]	

1. Includes private pensions etc.

2. Includes pensions, social transfers and alimony.

3. Includes pensions.

Blanks indicate less than 3 per cent.

n.a. = not available.

---

1. 14 sources were identified in all, the 9 other being: fringe benefits, dividend income, other investment income, rent income, imputed rent, private pensions, annuities and life insurance, alimony, capital gains and other sources.

By indicating the different kinds of preferential treatment for income from different sources, Table 10.10 shows that neither global taxation, nor a level playing field is realised in practice in OECD countries. It does not include labour income (see Tables 10.3 and 10.5) where yet other regimes apply.

b) The relative importance of non-standard tax allowances

Examples of favourable tax treatment found in many personal tax systems are:

- deductibility of mortgage interest payments combined with a preferential treatment of imputed rent;
- deductibility of contributions to private pension schemes and a favourable treatment of the income of the pension fund and/or the pension payment;
- deductibility of premiums on life assurance policies combined with a partial exemption of the proceeds;
- exemption of interest payments received on national savings arrangements, post office savings and bank deposits;
- tax exemption of interest received on government bonds;
- tax exemption or reduction on small investments in equities;
- tax incentives for private investments in equities to provide capital for productive investment;
- tax incentives for the purchase of employee participation shares;
- tax incentives for businesses starting up or expanding.

The scope for widening the tax base by reducing or abolishing these tax expenditures varies considerably from country to country. Table 5.4 of OECD 1990 showed that these expense related tax allowances varied from 22 per cent of income subject to tax in Denmark to 2 per cent in Spain (see Chart 10.3). Generally mortgage interest relief represented the most important of these tax expenditures, being as a percentage of income subject to tax nearly 14 per cent in Norway, over 10 per cent in Denmark and between 4 and 6 per cent in the Netherlands, Sweden, the United Kingdom and the United States. Non-mortgage interest relief represented over 5 per cent of income subject to tax in Denmark and 3 per cent in Sweden.

3. Five tax base issues

a) Fringe benefits

A generous attitude by the tax authorities in respect of the valuation of fringe benefits and the deductibility of mixed expenses, such as entertainment, travel and accommodation, which may relate to employment, but have an element of personal consumption, results in discrimination in favour of people who enjoy a higher-than-average amount of fringe benefits or who can deduct a higher-than-average amount of mixed expenses (or who can obtain a higher-than-average non-taxable reimbursement of mixed expenses). Favourable treatment of fringe benefits and mixed expenses will induce people to look for

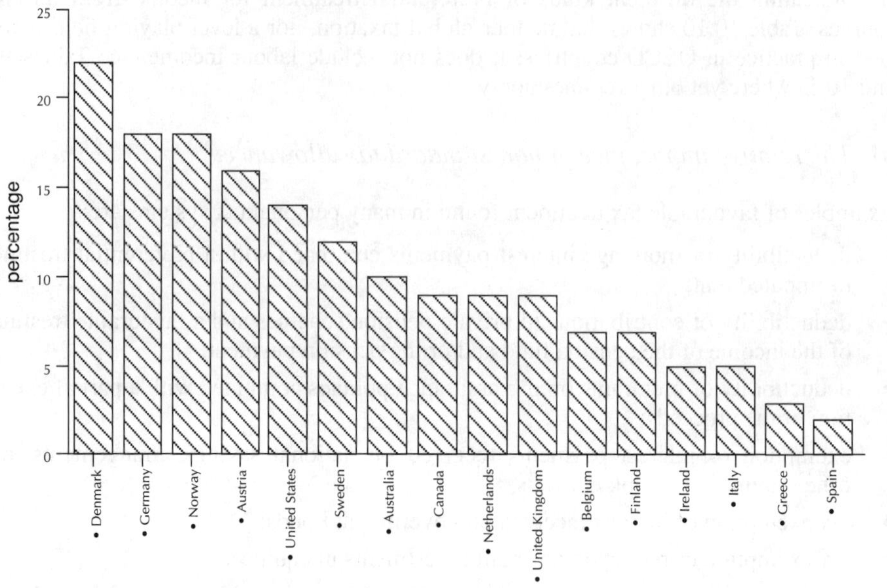

Chart 10.3: Non-standard income tax allowances as a percentage of income subject to tax

Note: In the source table Austria shows 5, but the 11 for social security contributions there described as a standard relief is counted here as a non-standard relief as in the case of Germany.

Source: Table 5.4, Item 6 of *The personal income tax base* (OECD 1990) with a few adaptions.

employment whereby, given the same gross wage, a larger portion of the income is received in the form of fringe benefits or a larger portion of the receipts are deductible as costs of earning income. Similarly, such treatment will induce firms to provide as large a portion of the remuneration in the form of fringe benefits or expense reimbursements as possible. This will distort the optimal allocation of labour, particularly since the income tax rates will have to be higher to ensure the same yield.

The most widely used fringe benefits in OECD countries are food discounts, transportation, leisure facilities, accommodation, medical and dental insurance, financial assistance and education expenses. Nearly all countries treat fringe benefits under their income tax legislation. Exceptionally, Australia and New Zealand impose a separate fringe benefits tax on employers. Nearly all countries tax the benefit of employer-provided motor vehicles and accommodation, but the tax treatment of other fringe benefits differs widely, as illustrated by Table 10.11.

Lacking from this table, because so many complications arise, is the tax treatment of what is probably the most important and widespread fringe benefit, that is employer-provided motor vehicles, which all OECD countries, except Greece, tax to some degree. As regards the taxation of other fringe benefits not summarised in Table 10.11, the benefit of employer-provided accommodation is taxed nearly everywhere. Low interest loans for housing are generally exempted, but similar loans for other purposes are usually taxed. Of course, whether or not the difference between the market rate of interest and the actual rate should be taxed also depends on the general rule regarding interest deductibility. If interest is fully deductible, the taxation of the benefit associated with a low interest rate makes little sense because the amount so taxed would also be a tax allowance against income. Finally, education expenses for employees are generally exempt, although often subject to the condition that the education must be employment-related. Similar expenses for dependants, however, are nearly always included in income.

Various reasons may be given for the existence of fringe benefits depending on whose views are solicited. Employees may find it convenient to eat on the employer's premises, feel pleased with receiving discounts or gifts, enjoy the added status of a company car, like to meet their colleagues at a physical work-out or appreciate the financial support provided by the employer. Presumably, employers try to encourage productivity by making their employees more content in the workplace and by making salary structures more flexible. Also, fringe benefits which receive favourable tax treatment permit them to reduce taxes in respect of gross wages and social security contributions.

On the other hand, governments may react against the erosion of the tax base and the loss of revenue that follow from the favourable treatment of fringe benefits. However, some fringe benefits, such as canteen or recreational facilities, may be so much a part of accepted working conditions that it would be considered unfair to tax them at their full value. Generally, the same reasoning applies to staff discounts and gifts. In other instances, e.g. the payment of education expenses or medical and dental insurance premiums, governments may consider that a worthwhile policy objective is being served. As the use of fringe benefits proliferates, however, governments become increasingly aware of the revenue cost as well as the distributional implications of the favourable tax treatment of fringe benefits.

One of the main issues in the taxation of fringe benefits concerns the monetary value that should be attached to the advantage enjoyed by the employee. Broadly, four methods may be followed: the value to the employee, the cost to the employer, the fair market value or the standard value established by the tax administration. Presumably, the value to the employee is the most difficult to ascertain. Gifts might be valued on this basis. The cost to the employer is readily ascertainable, but difficulties arise if a case can be made for taking incremental rather than total costs for valuation purposes. Airline tickets are an example. Market value would be the most satisfying criterion for the theoretically inclined mind, but its rigorous application might be regarded as inequitable or defeat the purpose of most fringe benefits. Standard values are commonly used for meals, company cars and accommodation. In practice, as this brief summary shows, different fringe benefits are valued in different ways.

One way to avoid some of the subjective and contentious aspects of the valuation of fringe benefits is to tax them at the level of the employer, either by disallowing their cost in computing taxable profits or by subjecting them to a separate tax. Since this approach obviates the need for attributing the value of fringe benefits to individual employees, significant administrative savings may be realised. Moreover, the revenue effects or distributional implications may be minimised if the top marginal income tax rate is set close to the rate of the corporation tax.

In recent years, a separate fringe benefits tax has been introduced in Australia and New Zealand. The New Zealand tax is confined to employer-provided cars, low interest loans and free or discounted goods and services. The Australian tax has a much broader coverage, including board, accommodation and air travel. The value of canteen and recreational facilities is excluded from the coverage of the tax. Employers' surveys in Australia indicate that there is expected to be a significant reduction in the provision of travel and holiday expenses. In New Zealand employers expect an increase in cash payment remuneration. This may be a possible route for other countries to take.

b) Contributions for income maintenance purposes

Most OECD countries do not include in income or provide a tax allowance for contributions which employers, employees or individuals make to social insurance schemes, pension and provident funds or life insurance and annuity schemes. These schemes have in common that they set aside current income for income-maintenance purposes at a later date, generally retirement but also unemployment, sickness or disability. Such tax treatment is of relevance to two issues already discussed, the tax treatment of household savings in Chapter 7B and the financing of social security benefits in Section 8A.

The exemption or provision of a tax allowance for the contribution made to these schemes, in conjunction with the later taxation of the benefits has the effect that the tax on the income set aside is deferred. It follows that the income tax discriminates against individuals who pay tax on their savings out of current income as well as on the interest earned thereon. In other words, employees and others who are permitted to make tax-free contributions for income-maintenance (retirement) purposes enjoy an interest-free loan from the government equal to the amount of tax that should have been payable.

Table 10.12 provides particulars of the tax treatment of social security contributions, pension contributions and life insurance premiums in OECD countries. Seven countries with separate levies do not allow the contributions as a deduction in ascertaining taxable income; accordingly, some of these countries exempt subsequent payouts. In 14 countries contributions are deductible, employer contributions are excluded from employee income and payouts are taxed.

Employer pension contributions are rarely included in income (Belgium and France are the only exceptions) and generally a tax allowance is granted to employees paying into pension funds. Nearly all countries impose a limit on the amount of the contribution for which an individual may obtain a tax allowance, the exceptions being Belgium, Luxembourg, the Netherlands and Turkey. A few countries (Austria, Canada, Germany, Japan and the United States) also impose a limit on the amount of the allowance for employer contributions (see Table 10.12).

The income tax treatment of life insurance premiums differs widely from country to country. The relief for employer-paid premiums is much less generous than the relief for employer pension contributions. Fourteen countries tax employers' premiums, while nine countries exempt the premium from tax, although some of them do set limits on the size of the premium or the amount of coverage for which relief is given. In some countries these limitations are the same as those imposed on pension contributions paid by the employer. Generally, the treatment of individually paid life insurance premiums is much more generous. Presumably, the philosophy is that the self-employed cannot join pension funds. Sweden, which has a comprehensive old age social security system, does not provide any relief. The United Kingdom abolished the allowance for life insurance policies issued after 1984. To limit the tax saving of high income groups, four countries provide the relief in the form of a tax credit.

The tax reliefs for retirement benefits have changed from an incidental phenomenon in the first half of this century to become a massive tax deferment mechanism, at least in respect of private schemes. As in other cases, legislators have attempted to adjust for the tax deferral benefit that some groups of taxpayers enjoyed by extending similar tax advantages to other groups. Reliefs for life insurance premiums and government contributions to public pension funds were followed by reliefs for private pension funds, professional retirement plans, the tax-free conversion of profits upon cessation of a business into an annuity and other reliefs. The equal treatment rule readily implied that voluntary contributions to private schemes should be treated on a par with compulsory contributions to public schemes. As a result, the income tax legislation became more complex, the corporate form of doing business was tax-preferred, tax avoidance schemes proliferated, and more generally, savings and investment decisions were distorted.

Another issue is whether contributions should be deducted from the tax base. If the view is taken that employees' social security contributions are equivalent to a (regressive) income tax, there seems no rationale for deducting them from gross income. Such a practice renders less transparent the taxpayer's relative income tax and contributions bill. More progressivity would be achieved if the revenue gained from non-deductibility were used to reduce contributions, especially at low levels of income. If, however, the view is taken that employees' social security contributions are quasi-insurance premiums, essentially different from income tax payments, there are a number of arguments for deductibility: to tax more or less the same income twice looks like economic double taxation; employers' contributions are deductible anyway as business expenses; and tax relief is generally given for voluntary and quasi-voluntary contributions. It may be that the lower-paid young tend to regard these contributions as taxes and the wealthier middle-aged as a contribution to savings.

To some extent, these considerations also apply to quasi-voluntary employer and employee contributions which are paid into pension and superannuation funds. Tax relief for contributions and full taxation at the time of payout have the advantage that income is averaged over the lifetime of the employee. Moreover, in most cases the amount of the contribution paid out of current income would not equal the increase in the discounted value of the future benefits which ideally should be included in income under the accretion concept. In fact, that increase cannot be determined accurately. The size of the benefits is uncertain because they usually depend on the length of service, the average income during the last years of employment, the outcome of wage negotiations and other incalculable factors. These arguments apply even more strongly in respect of employee insurance schemes that provide income support in case of disability, sickness or accident.

If relief is provided for voluntary contributions to pension and superannuation schemes, it could be argued that the equal treatment principle requires that the same relief be given to premiums paid for annuities or life insurance. However, an element of discrimination vis-à-vis the conventional saver remains to the extent that no tax is levied on the interest which accumulates on pension and life insurance reserves. Ideally, the employee or policyholder should be taxed annually on the interest. Alternatively, the pension fund or insurance company might be taxed in respect of its investment income.

c) *Owner-occupied dwellings*

In theory, the owner-occupier should be taxed on the net rental value of his dwelling, i.e. the rent his residence would fetch in the market place minus the costs incurred for interest on mortgage debt, depreciation, repairs and maintenance, property taxes and casualty insurance. The economic position of a home-owner does not differ from that of someone who invests his money in stocks or other income-yielding assets and who is assessed on the net income thereof, nor from that of someone who rents a house and whose rental payments are included in his income as consumption. The home-owner may be said to derive a return from his property (income) which he simultaneously offers himself as housing services (consumption).

In addition to the equity case, there are economic arguments for taxing the net rental value of owner-occupied dwellings. The exemption or less than full taxation of the gross rental value constitutes a tax saving which lowers the effective price of the housing services or, what is the same, increases the after-tax rate of return. Under some plausible assumptions, this means that more funds are invested in owner-occupied housing than in, say, business assets. In short, equity is violated and resources are misallocated. For various reasons these arguments are not accepted in the real world.

Table 10.13 shows that 12 countries tax the imputed rental income of owner-occupied dwellings on a presumptive basis, but also that they do so at very low rental rates. Moreover, these rates are applied to capital values which may be out of date or which are reduced before the rate is applied, and from which maintenance expenses and property taxes may be allowed as a deduction. Sweden appears to be an exception since the rental rate may be as high as 8 per cent of the capital value of the house. However, most home-owners in Sweden still report negative incomes from their investment. Japan, the United States and nine other countries do not impute any income in respect of owner-occupied housing.

Nearly all countries, whether or not they impute rental income, permit a deduction for interest on mortgage debt, generally against income from all sources, Canada, Germany and Turkey being the only exceptions. New Zealand also used to deny the relief, but in 1982 it changed to a credit system up to a ceiling. The relief in countries that tax rental values seems to be more generous than the relief in countries that do not tax such values. It appears as if the inclusion of a nominal rent in income is a pretext for providing greater relief. Sometimes the relief is confined to associated income (Belgium), or the relief is given in the form of a tax credit (Australia, France, Japan, New Zealand) which limits the benefit for higher income home-owners. Spain provides a limited tax allowance for mortgage interest, as well as a tax credit for investment in new residences.

Nearly all countries that tax rental values also provide relief for mortgage interest in respect of secondary residences, generally under the same conditions. Countries that do not tax rental values deny the relief. The United States is the only exception and its government has made it clear that it does not intend to abolish the relief for the purchase of a principal or secondary residence.

In principle, the line of reasoning that the imputed return of owner-occupied dwellings should be taxed also applies to the capital gain realised on the sale of private residences. As Table 10.18 indicates, however, the favourable treatment of such gains is even more widespread than the leniency shown in respect of the taxation of imputed rents. All OECD countries save Switzerland exempt the gain, although in some countries the gains are exempted only within limits and Portugal, Spain, Sweden and the United States stipulate that the proceeds of the sale must be used for the purchase of another house. Most countries, however, provide an unqualified exemption from capital gains taxation of owner-occupied residences. Usually, the argument is that in nearly all cases the owner's house is the only major asset he possesses. If he sells the house, he is likely to reinvest the proceeds in a new dwelling and his mobility might be impaired if he were taxed on the gain. The gain represents an accretion of economic power, but if he buys a similar house he does not acquire more dwelling space. If the owner moves into a smaller abode or, instead, rents a house, this event may coincide with his retirement and he may wish to use part of the proceeds of his previous residence to supplement a possibly inadequate pension.

These arguments do not apply to gains realised on the sale of secondary residences. Table 10.13 shows that half of all OECD countries tax those gains. The underlying argument is that secondary residences are less of a necessity than principal residences. Most countries, therefore, have opted for second-best solutions by disallowing all costs, except mortgage interest (and property taxes). In the late seventies and early eighties several countries limited the deductibility of interest. Ireland restricts the relief to the principal residence. Australia and New Zealand confine the relief to the first purchase of a dwelling, and Finland and Italy impose ceilings on hitherto unlimited deductibility. The United Kingdom has deliberately left the ceilings on mortgage interest deductions unchanged so that their real value has eroded. Japan denies the relief to taxpayers with income over a certain amount. Finally, Australia and France have replaced tax allowances with tax credits which provide the same nominal relief to taxpayers in all income brackets. These solutions appear to improve equity, because mortgage holders (and renters) are more numerous than equity holders in dwellings. The solutions are more illusory than real to the extent that rich mortgage holders can more easily effect changes in their debt portfolio than poor mortgage holders. Whatever the equity effects, efficiency in resource allocation should improve.

The proper taxation of imputed rental income, of course, has more angles to it than that of horizontal equity. Thus, first, in many countries, tenants also enjoy considerable untaxed benefits in the form of rent controls and housing subsidies. Second, it is not unlikely that the tax advantage associated with low imputed rents has been capitalised in the form of higher prices that new owners have had to pay for their house. This may be deduced from the low net returns that real estates fetches. Third, the property tax, to the extent that it is borne by owners and tenants, may be viewed as a substitute for the income tax that should be levied on the difference between (imputed) market rents and (imputed) actual rents.

Of course, this argument applies only to the extent that property tax payments exceed the benefits derived from government services provided in the form of roads, sewage facilities and parks, for example. Fourth, the objective of many governments that home ownership should be encouraged in view of the positive externalities that it generates has nothing to do with horizontal equity.

On the other hand, as already argued in Chapter 7B, there is a strong case, on both equity and economic efficiency grounds, for phasing out any mortgage relief and such a move is under discussion in many countries. The case seems much stronger for eliminating the mortgage interest relief for secondary residences. Even though work obliges certain taxpayers (e.g. US Congressmen) to have two residences, exception could be made for such taxpayers, rather than extending the relief to all taxpayers with secondary residences.

d) Deductibility of interest for consumer expenditure

At a time when most governments are anxious to promote household savings, it is somewhat surprising that a number of countries (Austria, Denmark, Finland, Luxembourg, the Netherlands, Sweden, Switzerland) still grant tax allowances for interest payments in connection with consumer expenditures – thus providing the equivalent of a negative consumption tax and an incentive to borrow rather than save. As indicated in the last column of Table 10.8 most OECD countries do not allow such deductions, which were abolished quite recently in Ireland, New Zealand and the United States. The reasons why such generous tax treatment nevertheless continues in some countries has been commented on in Chapter 7B3.

e) Unemployment and sickness benefits

On neutrality and equity grounds, a case can be made for taxing unemployment and sickness benefits and perhaps child allowances. Unemployment benefits are taxed in 14 OECD countries for which information is available, but not in Austria, Germany, Ireland, Japan, Portugal, Spain and Turkey. The tax treatment of sickness benefits generally follows that of unemployment benefits, except that in Canada, New Zealand and the United States sickness benefits are not subject to tax and in the United Kingdom they are only partially taxed. In most of the countries that tax them, unemployment and sickness benefits have been brought into the tax net only since the mid-1970s. On the basis of the information which is available, child allowances are taxed only in Canada and Spain.

In theory, all these benefits should be taxed and policy makers should be deciding what their value should be in net terms without regard to taxation. The work-incentive argument in favour of taxing unemployment benefits is, for example, irrelevant, since any work-incentive effect can be equally obtained by reducing the gross amount of the benefit. In the real world the situation is probably less simple, since taxing and spending decisions are taken and administered by different people and emotive arguments may be advanced for and against taxation of these benefits, which may influence governments at the political level. Another practical point is that in countries such as France where the tax threshold is high unemployment benefits may be too low to attract tax. Whilst it still seems eminently logical to tax unemployment and sickness benefits and look only at their net-of-tax level, other considerations apply to child allowances which explain why in almost all countries they remain untaxed. Collection costs in some countries would be high and little revenue recouped, and in a number of countries child benefits are paid to mothers, whose taxable income is frequently below the tax threshold or even non-existent.

D. The income tax schedule

1. Summary

What issues should be discussed under the heading "income tax schedule" is a matter for semantic debate not worth pursuing here, since topics are included or excluded in somewhat arbitrary fashion to make the chapter as a whole more coherent. Clearly of relevance to the schedule are the tax unit chosen (individual, joint, family) and tax relief for dependants, but it is more convenient to treat these topics in the next section as part of a wider approach of the tax/benefit system to marriage, two-earner families, parenthood, etc. On the contrary, the potential integration or partial integration of income taxes and social security contributions is not self-evidently an income tax schedule issue but is treated here as such. This section covers five separate topics:

- sub-section 2, alternative minimum and supplementary gross income taxes (relevant also is section B4);
- sub-section 3, rate schedules (with a number of subdivisions);
- sub-section 4, standard tax reliefs (non-standard reliefs having been dealt with in Section C);
- sub-section 5, progressivity through the rate schedule and through standard tax reliefs (see also Chapter 7C);
- sub-section 6, the relationship between the personal income tax and social security contributions (see also Chapter 8).

2. Alternative minimum and supplementary gross income taxes

As already noted, there has been a one-way move over the last few decades in both OECD and non-OECD countries from what were unambiguously schedular systems (each source of income being treated to a separate tax regime) towards ambiguously global systems (differentiation according to income sources being limited but not all that limited – see Table 10.10). What this sub-section notes is a return in certain ways to schedular-type income taxation in North America and Scandinavia with an indication of why this route appears to have been taken.

In its 1986 Tax Reform Act the United States introduced an alternative minimum tax under which higher income taxpayers were obliged to pay whichever is the greater of 21 per cent of their gross income or the normal rate schedule applied to their taxable income. Similar provisions exist in Canada. Norway has recently adopted what is colloquially known as a "top tax" (since its high threshold entails that it is payable only by those with very high incomes). It was levied in 1989 at 8.5 per cent on gross income. "Top tax" is payable in addition to the central and local government income taxes. Similar provisions were introduced under the 1986 tax reform in Denmark where there is a 12 per cent supplementary tax on "personal income" (which is roughly gross income minus income from capital) and where again a high threshold applies.

Alternative minimum taxes or supplementary gross income taxes may be introduced for a variety of reasons, including:

- to ensure high income groups pay a reasonable amount of tax and to counter tax avoidance (horizontal and vertical equity objectives);
- to prevent arbitrage through taking out of loans with the main purpose of obtaining deduction of interest on such loans from income subject to tax (horizontal equity and economic efficiency objectives);
- to reduce the tax advantage of borrowing compared with savings (economic efficiency objective);
- to avoid having to make a distinction between deductible interest for business expenses and non-deductible or limited deductible expenses for interest for house purchase or consumer credit, which the taxpayer may find it easy to camouflage as a business expense (administrative efficiency).

Such provisions do, however, complicate the tax system and it seems worth exploring further the relative advantages and disadvantages of the alternative approach of achieving similar objectives by further limiting the deductibility of interest payments from income subject to tax (e.g. in Austria interest on borrowing for business is deductible only against associated income and in the United States there is a ceiling on such deductibility). However, it seems that in practice there may be less political resistance to imposing such complicated schemes as alternative minimum or supplementary gross taxes than to cutting back on interest deductibility.

The second objective of attempting to achieve greater neutrality between various forms of unearned income has led Austria, Belgium and Denmark to impose a lower rate of tax on dividend income than on most other kinds of income. This issue is discussed in Chapter 12D on corporate tax systems, because such preferential treatment may be seen as a means of attaining the main objectives of an imputation system without taking on its complexities.

3. Tax rates

a) The variety of OECD country rate schedules

Whilst the statutory rates applied to taxable income have little relationship to the effective rate which depends upon the base to which they apply, it is nonetheless surprising how much they vary among OECD countries. Chart 10.4 illustrates this by indicating 1988 rate schedules converted by purchasing power parities.

b) *Top tax rates*

Though paid by few, the large decline in top tax rates over the last six years has attracted a lot of attention because it has been an almost universal trend in OECD countries, as illustrated by Chart 10.5 and Table 10.15. The latter shows that top rates vary substantially between countries (from over 70 per cent to under 30 per cent) and that since both 1975 and 1986 they have declined in nearly all OECD countries. In some countries, (Belgium, Japan, New Zealand, Norway, Sweden, the United Kingdom and the United States) this decline represents around 17 to over 40 percentage points and in most others it has been considerable. Very moderate declines since 1986 (less than 4 percentage points) occurred only in Germany and Luxembourg (see Chart 10.5). Also there was no change in Switzerland where the federal tax of 13 per cent is too low to be shown.

c) *Rate flattening*

The first columns of Table 10.15 indicate that the number of brackets has been reduced in most OECD countries since 1986 and often drastically so, but that there has been little or no change in the number of brackets in a few countries. France, Luxembourg and Spain are now the only countries with more than 10 brackets, but in 1991 Spain moved from a record 34 to 16 brackets.

The reduction of the number of brackets has an appearance of simplicity, but it is unlikely in most countries to have much practical effect. For example, fewer brackets will probably have little effect on tax administrative or taxpayers' compliance costs, since taxpayers will refer directly to details of liabilities at different income levels and in different family circumstances, which are made available by governments and published in newspapers, rather than calculate their liability from the legal schedule.

d) *Thresholds, zero rate brackets and first positive rates*

Thresholds, zero rate brackets and first positive rates should logically be discussed together, for while most countries simply have a threshold and then a first positive rate, others have a threshold and a zero rate before a positive rate is reached. Tax reforms generally involve adjustments to both thresholds and first positive rates which, in combination, will have varying effects on the relative burdens of low income taxpayers. Unfortunately data are not at present available to treat the two together on an internationally comparable basis. The last columns of Table 10.15 show that, like top rates, first rates vary considerably between countries (sometimes around 5 per cent, sometimes around 25 per cent) and that in recent tax reforms the tendency has been for them to increase considerably in most countries – especially in Canada, Finland, Greece, Iceland, New Zealand, Norway, Spain and the United States. As regards the last two countries, however, the increase in first positive rates was accompanied by a new zero rate in Spain and a large increase in the threshold in the United States. A large decline in first positive rates is to be found only in Austria, Luxembourg, the Netherlands and the United Kingdom. The reason for the increase in first positive rates is presumably – in at least some countries – to recoup some of the revenue lost from the reduction in higher rates and/or increases in thresholds.

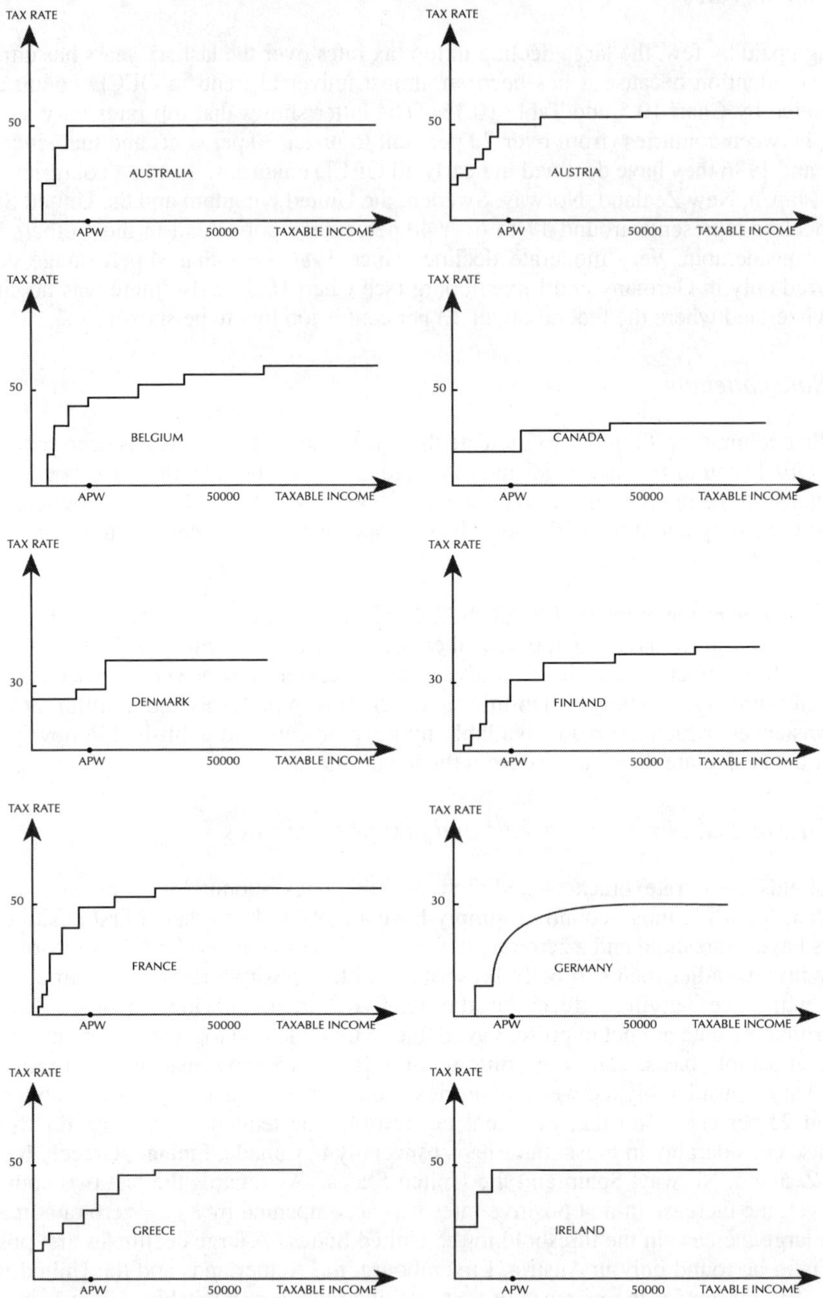

Chart 10.4: OECD rate schedules converted by purchasing power parities, 1988

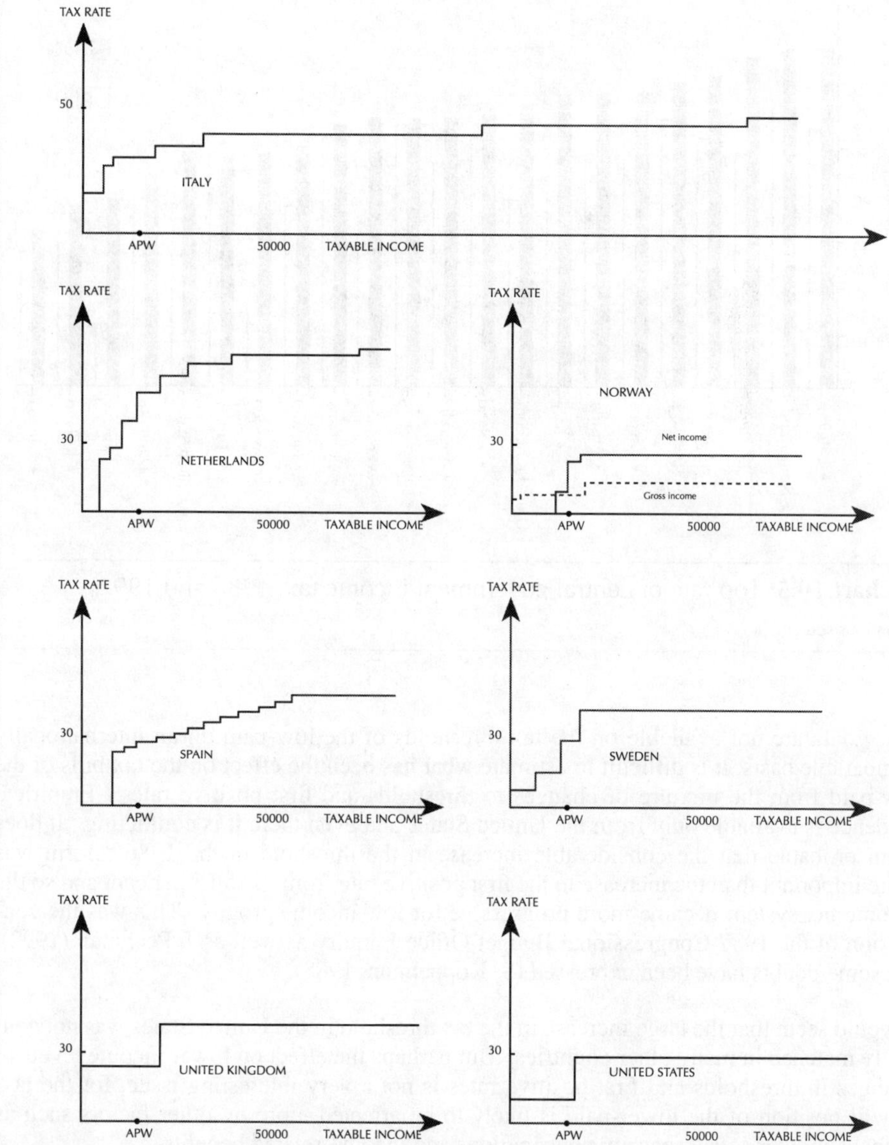

Chart 10.4(cont.): OECD rate schedules converted by purchasing power parities, 1988

Source: *The personal income tax base: a comparative survey* (OECD 1990).

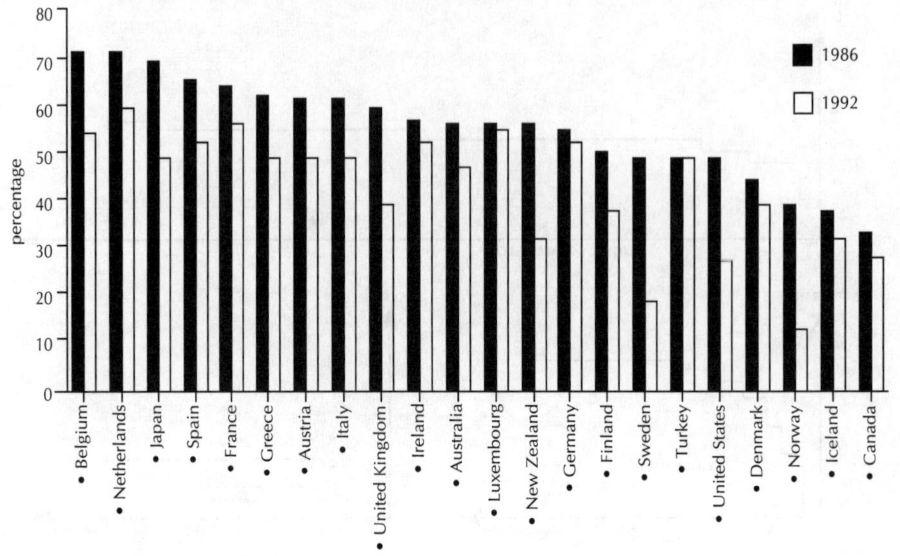

Chart 10.5: Top rate of central government income tax, 1986 and 1992

Various sources.

Since data are not available on the tax thresholds of the low-paid on an internationally comparable basis, it is difficult to estimate what has been the effect on the tax bills of the low-paid from the mixture of changes to thresholds and first positive rates. Empirical evidence is available only from the United States and even there it is conflicting. It does seem probable that the considerable increase in the threshold in the 1986 reform was more important than the increase in the first positive rate from 11 to 15 per cent and so the income tax system became more progressive for low income groups. This was the conclusion of the 1987 Congressional Budget Office Enquiry as well as J. Pechman (1992), but some doubts have been expressed (S. Koppelman, 1988).

It would seem that the large increase in the tax threshold in the United States was not generally matched in many other countries. But perhaps the effect on lower income levels of changes in thresholds and first positive rates is not a very interesting issue, for the tax/benefit position of the lower-paid is likely to be affected more by other factors such as changes in their social security contributions and income-related benefits.

There are varying philosophies about income tax thresholds. At one extreme the view is taken that under the ability-to-pay principle those around subsistence level should not be expected to pay income tax. This approach is adopted by France (where nearly half the population is below the threshold), Japan, the Netherlands and Norway. At the other extreme is the view that for reasons of accountability or solidarity nearly all citizens should be expected to pay tax, even if at the lower end of the income scale the taxpayer may be a net beneficiary of the tax transfer system (e.g. Denmark, New Zealand and Sweden). In favour of high thresholds, it can also be argued that it reduces the poverty and unemployment traps discussed elsewhere in this chapter and that the elimination of a substantial proportion of the population from the income tax simplifies tax administration, though this latter argument has much less force in these days of increased computerisation. A main argument against high thresholds is the important amount of revenue thereby forgone, which may require what on other grounds may be seen as excessively progressive rate schedules to make up the loss (cf. France). Another argument voiced by J.K. Galbraith (1958) in his *The Affluent Society* was that the modern liberal rallies to protect the poor from the taxes which in the next generation, as a result of a higher investment for their children, would eliminate poverty.

A final point regarding thresholds is that it would be misleading to look at particular countries' income tax thresholds without regard to their thresholds for social security contributions and even more misleading for the purposes of international comparisons.

e) *State and local income taxes*

State and local taxes have already been discussed in Chapter 9. Here it is recalled that some of the information provided early in this section and in Table 10.11 would be very misleading if account is not taken of the existence of state and local income taxes which are very much more important than central income taxes in Norway, Sweden and Switzerland, about as important in Denmark, Finland and Iceland, and quite important in Canada, Japan and the United States (see Table 9.9, first column).

It is also of relevance to note that the almost universal decline in central income tax rates, as summarised in Table 10.15, has not been accompanied by a similar decline in rates of state and local income taxes, as the following sub-table demonstrates.

Rates of personal income tax at subordinate levels of government to nearest percentage point

	1985	**1990**
Belgium	Flat 7 per cent minimum	Flat 7 per cent minimum
Canada	Between 43 and 60 per cent of federal tax	Between 43 and 60 per cent of federal tax
Denmark	22 to 31 flat rates with average of 28	23 to 33 flat rates with average of 30
Finland	14 to 19 with average of 16	14 to 20 flat rates with average of 16
Norway	22.5 flat rate	26 flat rate
Sweden	Various flat rates with average of 30	27 to 33 flat rates with average of 31
Switzerland	Various progressive rates (Zurich 2 to 13)	Various progressive rates (Zurich 5 to 34)
United States	Various progressive or flat rates (Michigan and Detroit flat 6 and 3 respectively)	Various progressive or flat rates (Michigan and Detroit 5 and 3 respectively)

Source: *The tax/benefit position of workers,* Table D (OECD 1986 and 1989). Comparable information is not available for Iceland and Japan.

4. Standard tax reliefs

Standard tax reliefs are given for specified characteristics of a taxpayer, e.g. family circumstances, age, health, source of income – and unlike non-standard reliefs, they do not usually depend of expenditures actually made, except in the case of deductions for social security contributions and work-related expenses which may relate to actual expenses. They represent a major determinant of the relative tax bills of different categories of taxpayers, they vary greatly in size and kind as between countries and frequently change within countries.

The basic threshold available to all taxpayers takes a variety of forms. Countries are almost equally divided between those that use fixed tax allowances, tax credits and zero rated tax brackets. The additional basic relief for earned income may take the form of a lump-sum allowance for work-related expenses, allowances for actual costs of certain work-related expenses, tax allowances related to earned income up to a ceiling or a tax credit, and again the choice varies greatly between countries, which often change their form and amount (see Table 10.3). Standard tax reliefs for the aged, the disabled and dependants other than children usually take the form of tax allowances, though a number of countries give tax credits for dependants other than children and a few for the aged and disabled (see Table 10.7).

Table 5.4 of *The Personal Income Tax Base* (OECD 1990) provided quantitative data on tax allowances. Most important is the basic allowance available to all taxpayers. It amounts to over 30 per cent of income subject to tax in Ireland and Canada and over 20 per cent in France, Greece, the United Kingdom, Denmark and Finland, though less than 10 per cent in Norway, Germany and Spain. As earlier mentioned, the classification into standard and non-standard allowance is somewhat arbitrary with regard to work-related expenses and social security contributions, both of which tend also to be quite important. Table 5.4 of OECD 1990 gives the following aggregate figures as a percentage of income subject to tax according to the classification provided by countries.

Tax Allowances			
	Standard	**Non-Standard**	**Total**
Australia	0	10.3	10.3
Austria	16.7	5.3	22.0
Belgium	20.8	7.1	28.0
Canada	32.6	9.3	41.9
Denmark	1.8	21.6	23.4
Finland	23.5	6.4	29.6
France	29.3	0.1	29.5
Germany	7.1	17.6	24.7
Greece	27.6	3.0	30.6
Ireland	37.3	5.0	42.3
Italy	0	5.0	5.0
Norway	8.4	18.0	26.4
Spain	5.1	2.1	7.2
Sweden	13.3	12.4	25.7
United Kingdom	34.5	9.0	43.5
United States	26.3	14.5	40.8

5. Fiscal drag and indexation

In the absence of any changes to the tax legislation, inflation (and real growth) has the effect under progressive income tax systems of pushing taxpayers into higher rate brackets, and also to bring into the tax net those whose income was previously too low to pay tax and in addition inflation erodes the real value of tax reliefs. This enables governments to increase their yields from the income tax without doing anything and provided inflation is not too rampant most taxpayers may be unaware of what is happening.

Fiscal drag has been much discussed over the last two decades and country choices as to whether to offset it and, if so, how, have varied greatly and have frequently changed over time. Two separate questions are involved, though the arguments for the choice between the policy options are very much interrelated: the first is should governments offset fiscal drag by legislative changes; the second is, if yes, should this be done by ad hoc changes to the tax rate schedule and/or tax reliefs, or should it be done by formal indexation which would link automatically the schedule and reliefs to some measure such as the consumer price index or hourly earnings?

On the first of these two questions it is argued in favour of regularly adjusting the income tax schedule and allowances that otherwise the relative tax burden of different categories of taxpayers is arbitrarily redistributed by inflation, infringing tax equity and frustrating the legislatures' original intention and also that without such adjustments the greater ease in securing extra receipts may obscure the choice implicitly made to allocate more funds to the public sector; against, it has been argued that to abandon or reduce the fiscal dividend resulting from fiscal drag would have undesirable economic consequences regarding the automatic stabilisation features of the income tax and would have regressive income distribution effects.

On the second issue of formal indexation versus ad hoc adjustments, numerous theoretical arguments have been found for both courses as set out in OECD 1986 (pages 65-67). To summarise some of these arguments very briefly: in favour of indexation is the government undertaking to protect taxpayers from the hidden effects of inflation within a specified period, the transparency it provides, its possibility of acting as a brake on increases in public expenditure and favourably influencing wage negotiations, and finally by compelling small regular adjustments it may avoid the more destabilising larger adjustments that may be necessary without indexation; against indexation, it is argued that it reduces the margin of discretion left to governments to adapt to economic circumstances, it may lead to increased public deficits, it is inappropriate to index a part of the tax system (income tax schedules and reliefs) without applying it to the tax base (interest income, business profits or capital gains) or to specific taxes on alcohol, petrol and tobacco, where, without indexation, yields decline in real terms. Indexation also creates a host of technical problems: what index to choose? over what period? whether or not to take account of indirect taxes and subsidies and price effects resulting from changes in terms of trade?

Table 10.17 summarises formal indexation provisions over the last two decades. It shows that about half of OECD countries have had such provisions and that many of those countries have either abandoned or modified them. At present they exist in Belgium, Canada, France, Greece, Italy, Luxembourg, the Netherlands, Sweden, Switzerland, the United Kingdom and the United States. Governments, whether with or without formal indexation provisions, generally make annual adjustments to the tax schedule and to tax reliefs to take account, *inter alia*, of rates of inflation. The evidence suggests that there is not much difference in the extent to which fiscal drag has been offset as between those countries with and those without formal indexation provisions (OECD 1986, Ch. 4). In the sixties and early seventies fiscal drag was rarely offset, but between 1975 and 1985 it was largely offset in most if not all OECD countries. There is no direct evidence on what has happened in most recent years, but the stagnation of income tax yields already reported in Part I, suggests that fiscal drag continues to be offset.

Indexation tends to occur after rapid rises in income tax yields (Canada and Denmark in the early seventies, the United Kingdom mid-seventies, Belgium, Greece and Italy in recent years) or as a political announcement of an intention to reduce income tax (United States 1985). Indexation is abandoned (Australia, Sweden) or modified (Canada) when countries get worried about their budget deficits and feel the need not to be committed to offsetting fiscal drag totally. It thus seems that the indexation issue has more to do with political attitudes and government relations with taxpayers than with the extent to which fiscal drag is offset in practice.

In more recent years with lower rates of inflation and rate flattening, with governments making important changes to tax reliefs and the rate schedule for other reasons, formal indexation seems to have little, other than rhetorical rationale. On the other hand, in the interests of transparency there is a case for arguing that when governments make their annual proposals for changes in tax reliefs and the rate schedule, they should make it known what would be the revenue gain from unadjusted fiscal drag deriving from both the erosion of the value of tax reliefs and bracket creep.

6. Relationship with employees' social security contributions

In most, though not all OECD countries, a very different base, schedule and threshold are applied to employees' contributions from those applied to the personal income tax. The contributions base is usually something approximating to gross income, no account being taken of family circumstances, etc. Rates are mostly flat and not progressive but usually become zero at a ceiling, generally somewhat higher than the earnings of an average production worker. Thresholds are either non-existent or very low and invariably much lower than income tax thresholds. All this means that employees' contributions are much less progressive than their income tax payments and that because countries vary greatly in relative reliance on these two levies, it would be misleading to ignore employees' contributions in any survey designed to achieve international comparability. This is confirmed by Table 10.18 which shows that when one of these levies is high, the other is usually low[1] and that when one of them increases, the other usually decreases. Charts 10.6 and 10.7 show graphically how countries' ranking positions change with regard to an APW's payment to the government if social security contributions are taken into account.

1. See also Chart 2.3 and commentary thereon in Chapter 2D.

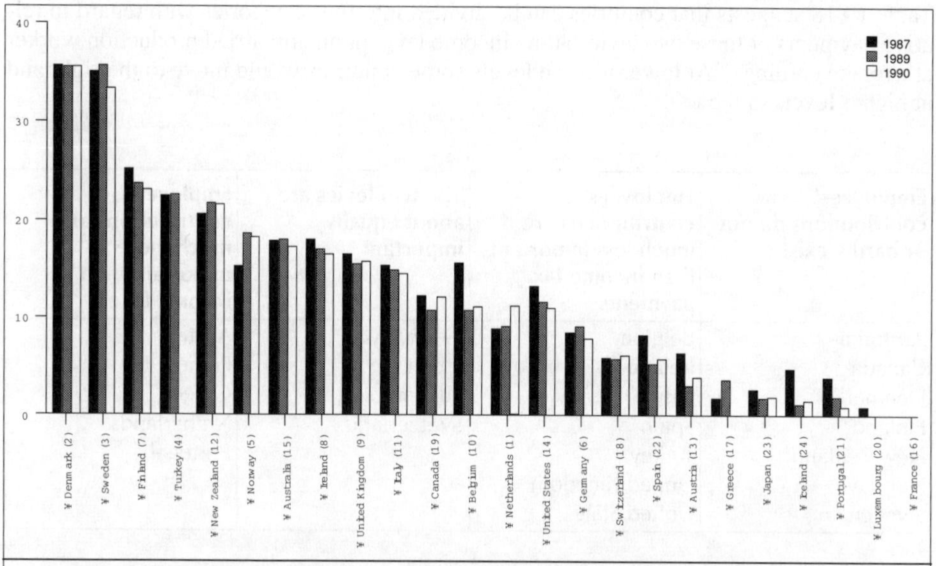

Chart 10.6: Income tax paid by a married APW with two children as a percentage of gross earnings[1], 1987, 1989 and 1990.

1. Countries are ranked by 1990 figures except for Greece and Turkey 1989. Figures in parentheses show ranking order, if employee's social contributions are added – see Chart 10.7 for details.

Reproduced from *The tax/benefit position of production workers 1987-1990* (OECD 1991).

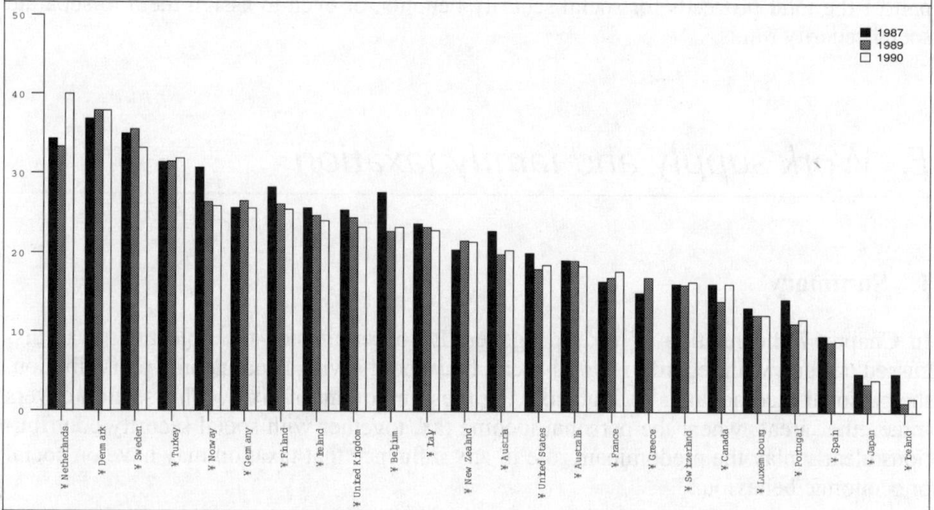

Chart 10.7: Income tax plus employees' social security contributions paid by a married APW with two children as a percentage of gross earnings[1], 1987, 1989 and 1990.

1. Countries are ranked by the rate of income tax and employees' contributions paid in 1990, except for Greece and Turkey 1989.

Source: as Chart 10.6.

Table 10.18 suggests that countries can be divided into four categories with regard to relative payments of these two levies at the income level of an unmarried production worker at average earnings. At lower income levels some countries would move to the right and at higher levels to the left.

Employees' contributions do not or hardly exist	**Employees' contributions are much less important than income tax payments**	**The two levies are about equally important**	**Employees' contributions are much more important than income taxes**
Australia	Belgium	Germany	Austria
Canada	Ireland	Japan	France
Denmark	Italy	Luxembourg	Greece
Finland	Spain	Switzerland	Netherlands
New Zealand	Turkey		Portugal
Norway	United Kingdom		
Sweden	United States		

As discussed earlier in Chapter 8, a number of commentators find that it is illogical to combine in an uncoordinated way the ability to pay (progressive) approach to the income tax and the insurance (regressive) approach to contributions, since unintended results are bound to arise. Integrating the two levies does seem a promising area for future tax reform, even if for psychological and political reasons it remains necessary to earmark a part of the total proceeds for social security benefits, or even to assign them to separate social security funds.

E. Work supply and family taxation

1. Summary

In Chapter 7 the relation of taxation generally to certain non-tax objectives was discussed, though with regard to two of them, household savings and income redistribution, the personal income tax is undoubtedly the most important of taxes. This section covers three other areas, where the personal income tax, together with social security contributions clearly play the predominant role in any influence that taxation may have on social or economic behaviour.

Sub-section 2 deals very briefly with the influence of income taxation and social security contributions on the supply of labour. V. Halberstadt (1977) the rapporteur of a 1976 conference at the Institute of Fiscal Studies noted that: "We do not seem to have come all that much further in the last ten years in measuring the relationship between taxation and the incentive to work.", and with two main reservations, the same would appear to be true of the following 13 years (see F. Bourguignon, 1990). The two main reservations are, first, at lower income levels the combination of income tax, social security contributions and income related benefits can create a poverty and unemployment trap which discourages taxpayers to work overtime or even to take on employment in the formal economy; the second is that there is a consensus that tax may have a negative effect on the labour supply of secondary earners (usually married women). A declared objective of many reforms to tax systems has been to reduce any disincentive effects on work supply. Yet, the theoretical and empirical evidence is ambivalent and conclusions may vary according to the methodology employed. It is generally agreed, however, that different types of taxpayers – the rich and poor, young workers and the elderly, primary and secondary earners of a family, part-time, full-time workers and overtime earners – are likely to respond in different ways to tax changes, and also that different measurements of work supply are appropriate for different types of taxpayers. This is not simply a question of hours worked, but includes readiness to change work location and age of retirement. In addition, a number of changes in income tax provisions taken primarily for other reasons, such as horizontal equity or sex equality, could have effects on work supply. Finally, taxation may affect not only the work/leisure decision, but influence the form work takes, especially in encouraging participation in the underground economy. Evidently taxation is not the only and probably not the most important factor affecting work supply. For example, the decisions of wives to enter the labour force may be influenced more by the availability of cheap child care facilities and cultural attitudes than taxation provisions. While it remains open to question whether tax changes over the last three decades have been taken primarily to improve work incentives, this has remained an avowed objective of governments.

Sub-section 3 deals more extensively with a basic problem of any income tax system: what should be the relative treatment of taxpayers in different working and family situations. It is necessary to distinguish between ends and means. Governments have varying possible conflicting ends such as to remain neutral or to encourage couples to get married, to influence their single or joint participation in the labour force, to determine what would be the most equitable, economically efficient and popular distribution of the tax burden between single persons, one-earner married (or unmarried) couples and two-earner married (or unmarried) couples. To complicate matters neutrality towards these decisions at one income level may entail non-neutrality at other income levels. Governments also have at their disposal a variety of means to achieve their preferred differentiation: earned income of couples (and their unearned income) may be aggregated for tax purposes or each member of the couple may be taxed separately; reliefs may be given in the different ways already described and rate schedules may be more or less progressive. The debate on the means or instruments has focused mostly on the choice of tax unit which has changed in most OECD countries over the last two decades from compulsory joint or family aggregation of income to separate taxation of couples or the option for separate taxation. OECD empirical studies have suggested that the choice of tax unit has relatively little importance for the relative tax burdens of different categories of taxpayers (generally separate taxation favours high income two-earner couples and penalises low-income two-earner couples) and that the rate schedule and the relief structure play a more important part in such determination. However, even though the choice of tax unit may have a relatively small influence on what many would regard as the paramount issue of relative tax bills of different categories of taxpayers, it has a great deal of social significance in other respects. First, whilst in theory the privacy of each spouse (in practice almost always the wife) as to his/her amount of income, could be equally protected under either system, in practice it is generally much less protected under aggregated taxation; second, joint or family systems are theoretically incompatible with the aim of giving similar reliefs to couples outside wedlock as are given to married couples, and whilst it would be possible to adapt them to achieve this objective, in practice no country with joint or family taxation does so.

Sub-section 4 discusses the less complex but very interesting policy question of whether or not preferential treatment for parents should be given under personal income tax systems and if so in what form. A "taxable capacity" approach would favour tax allowances and a "social welfare" approach, either non-wastable tax credits or cash payments outside the income tax system. Over the last two decades there has been much disagreement among theorists and many changes of mind among governments on the kinds of preferential treatment to parents which they have chosen to give.

2. Income tax and work supply

A rise in marginal income tax rates induces a substitution of leisure for work (the substitution effect), a rise in average income tax rates induces more work effort to compensate for lost income (the income effect). The overall effect of income tax on work supply is believed to depend on the relationship between the marginal and average rates of tax and on the relative strength of the resulting substitution and income effects. Since it is not possible to predict the outcome of this conflict between the substitution and income effect on purely theoretical grounds, empirical studies have been carried out in a few countries. They have taken three forms:

a) surveys to obtain opinions on whether income tax provided a disincentive effect;
b) cross-section data on household income, work effort and other household characteristics which permit the estimation of labour supply functions;
c) social experiments carried out in the United States to test, *inter alia*, the labour market response to the introduction of temporary negative income tax schemes.[1]

The earlier theoretical literature (summarised in Godfrey 1975) suggested that each of these approaches supported the conclusion that taxation does not have a large and significant effect on the total supply of work effort, and that in particular the net effect on the labour supply of "prime males" (an expression often used to reflect an earlier situation when the husband was more often than not the only earner) is likely to be very small.

1. Negative income tax or NIT is a system under which cash benefits are paid to persons in households whose income is below a certain prescribed level. In the late sixties and early seventies they were examined in a number of countries as a means of alleviating poverty and reducing work disincentives, but outside some temporary experiments in North America never adopted, though non-wastable tax credits may be regarded as a partial NIT. *Negative Income Tax* (OECD 1973) gives some reasons why NIT was not adopted.

Moreover, there is some evidence that taxation has little influence on the choice of occupations.

Summarising later literature OECD 1986 noted that:

> Recent empirical work on the estimation of labour supply functions has concentrated on more careful modelling of the income tax system and the application of more refined econometric techniques which permit, among other things, account to be taken of variations in individual preferences across the population. These 'second generation' studies of labour supply suggested that supply elasticities for both groups are larger than those derived from earlier studies but confirm earlier findings that female labour supply is more responsive to taxation measures than male labour supply.

Most of the literature has concentrated on the effects of taxation on the behaviour of the lower paid, for example, the choice of prime males to increase their work effort through overtime or to seek secondary work, usually in the underground economy, or to adopt the increased leisure option and the choice of secondary earners (usually working wives) to remain in or enter the labour force, both at the time of marriage and after their children no longer require full-time care.

As noted above, the second generation studies generally conclude that high tax rates have disincentive effects on the supply of labour. But some scepticism has been expressed on their validity on the grounds that they have been carried out in relatively few countries (mostly the US and the UK) and their findings have not always been corroborated by empirical sample surveys based on replies to questionnaires addressed to particular taxpayers . [See C.V. Brown and P.M. Jackson (1978) and Brown (1983)]. The effect of taxation, as such, on the supply of low-paid labour accordingly remains debatable.

Also of relevance is that the empirical surveys have shown that taxpayers are frequently unaware of their effective average and marginal rates of tax and generally overestimate it. As OECD 1981 noted:

> ...reference is frequently made to the rates shown in the income tax schedule and their work disincentive effects, perhaps because taxpayers are usually very much more aware of these schedule rates, which are readily available (e.g. they appear in newspapers and often accompany annual tax forms), than they are of their average and marginal rates of tax which, being dependent on the interaction of tax reliefs and the rate schedule, may be difficult to calculate. It thus seems likely that schedule rates play an important part in determining taxpayers' attitudes towards the payment of tax and in their work-leisure decision.

Taxation may have various behaviourial effects on high-income earners, but it is generally considered unlikely to have much effect on the *quantity* of their work supply. Business and industry executives are the most important numerically and it may be that high taxation inhibits risk taking, innovation and commitment and therefore the quality of their work supply. It is generally believed that the "brain drain" of successful academics is less due to tax regimes than to gross differences in salaries and in research opportunities. A third class of highly paid successful entertainers and sportsmen appear frequently to change their fiscal domicile to tax haven countries as a result of high taxation, but their work supply is unlikely to be significantly affected by the amount of extra travel entailed.

3. The relative tax treatment of single persons, one-earner and two-earner couples

a) Some conflicts

Governments have to decide, what should be the relationship between the taxes paid by single and married taxpayers with the same level of pre-tax income. For a long time, the major criterion for deciding on this point involved taking as a reference base the income level required to meet necessary expenditures and, so the argument usually ran, as married couples enjoy certain "economies of scale", the non-discretionary income which they require is less than twice that of a single person with a similar pre-tax income. The logic of this position entails considering that the members of a family effectively pool their incomes and consider their expenditures as being met out of a common budget. Today, this view has to be reconciled with the attitude, becoming increasingly accepted, that men and women have a right to be considered as independent persons vis-à-vis the fiscal authorities and from other legal and socio-economic points of view as well, and therefore should not be forced to adopt any particular attitude towards their habits of earning and spending even if, in practice they may follow a joint approach to them.

It is not easy to translate into a workable personal income tax scheme a compromise which recognises continued validity for the view that married couples enjoy certain advantages in spending their income compared with single persons and the newer approach that sees a need for marriage to be "fiscally neutral" in the sense that two earners pay more tax after marriage than before, or than two single partners with the same combined income. Again, for taxpayers in income brackets where tax is charged at higher, progressive rates, unless there are different rate schedules for single and married couples, substantial differences in marginal rates of tax can result between the tax positions of single and married persons at similar income levels.

The comparison of taxes paid by single persons and married couples is closely related to the further question of what the tax paid by two single persons in gainful employment should be if they marry and continue to work? If there is no tax advantage or disadvantage between the position of the two taxpayers before and after marriage, the tax system is neutral in this regard. Such neutrality can be seen as desirable to avoid influencing attitudes towards marriage and divorce. Alternatively, it may be considered desirable to make it more advantageous to marry from the tax point of view, whether one income earner or two are concerned.

The objective of tax neutrality with respect to marriage may require a reduction in the progressivity of the income tax system, unless the latter is to produce unequal treatment of taxpayers in different personal circumstances, but with the same income. Also, it may be difficult simultaneously to achieve tax neutrality with regard to the decision to marry of two single persons, only one of whom is working, and of two persons, both in employment and who wish to continue working after marriage.

Another problem is that a progressive income tax paid by a couple cannot satisfy the two criteria that the income tax paid by a couple should be based on total income, regardless of how much each contributes, and that the total amount of tax paid by two persons should not change in the event of their getting married or divorced.

b) Working wives

"Working wives" is used here as an abbreviation for those in gainful employment and something has already been said about them in the last sub-section, namely that taxation is believed to reduce their labour supply more than other categories of taxpayer. In a minority of cases the wife is the principal earner, but to avoid complicating the exposition it is here assumed that she is not.

There is no general consensus as to what would constitute equal tax treatment for working wives. Many of the considerations already noted above are relevant – the notions of discretionary income and of "economies of scale" when two people live together, of expenses due to working, of the imputed income of wives who do not work outside the home and so on. It is not self-evident to whose tax benefit situation that of the working wife should be compared: her husband's, that of a single gainfully employed woman, that of a wife not in the labour force? Comparisons here have mostly focused on the relative situation of one-earner and two-earner couples. Another point is that relative tax treatment of a working wife vis-à-vis other categories will vary not only according to income level, but whether her choice is to enter the labour force, remain in the labour force after marriage, work overtime or re-enter the labour force. (OECD 1977 and 1980 provide some quantitative illustrations, but as they are extensive and rather out of date they are not reproduced here.) Two questions concerning the relative tax treatment of one-earner and two-earner couples are discussed further. The first is the taxation of the imputed income of unpaid domestic services provided by wives who stay at home, the second is the tax treatment of additional costs incurred by working wives, especially in relation to child care.

On the first of these issues it has been argued by P. Musgrave (1981) that the non-taxation of the imputed income from the work performed in the home by a wife who does not go out to work may encourage married women to stay at home. This might be true, but would apply equally to work performed in the home by all categories of households – single, one-earner, two-earner couples – who provide themselves with such services. The issue is really about the allocation of time between paid work, unpaid work and leisure and how taxation affects this choice. Whilst it might be argued that married women have the greatest possibilities of choice in their work decisions, the extent to which they have a meaningful choice between working at home or in the labour market probably depends upon the couple's income level. At low income levels, both spouses may need to work to achieve an acceptable standard of living, whereas at high income levels, financial considerations may be secondary to the desire on the part of the wife to pursue a career.

The taxation of such imputed income would present almost insuperable difficulties of correct calculation. Where one and two-earner households at the same level of joint earnings consume the same level of self-provided domestic services, the only difference between their taxable capacity would be due to the difference in the time available for leisure, which would be difficult to measure. In any case, the taxation of this one form of imputed income could hardly be justified as long as other forms of imputed income go untaxed. Consequently, imputed income from domestic services is nowhere taxed. Some countries, however, do give two-earner couples additional tax reliefs. These may take the form of an earned income allowance to working wives or specific work related expense deductions. Against this, it is sometimes argued that the two-earner family is already treated too generously compared with one-earner families with the same total earnings in certain countries using joint taxation, insofar as the earning wife gets the same basic allowances as her husband and the couple also retain their marriage allowance.

The second issue relates to the extra costs incurred when both spouses are in paid employment in terms of child care expenses. In many countries such expenses are reduced by state subsidised child care facilities or cash transfers to mothers (see subsection 4) and since most governments allow taxpayers to deduct from income subject to tax unavoidable costs directly incurred in earning income, it could be argued that child-care expenses are an unavoidable cost of working for married women with children. On the other hand, it has been argued that such costs are also incurred by the wife who stays at home, where they take the form of an opportunity cost, which is expressed in terms of a loss of leisure rather than an explicit money payment. In a much-quoted passage, M. McIntyre (1977), said in support of this latter view:

> No-one would suggest that the costs of caring for a pet elephant are deductible, simply because it is impossible to go to work and leave the elephant alone. What made child care different was that a parent, after making the quintessential personal choice to have a child, could not undo that decision by giving the child to the local zoo. This difference, however, is not sufficient to convert child care into a business expense within the meaning of Section 162 of the US Internal Revenue Code.

Thus the question arises whether or not the income tax system should take account of the cost of bringing up children, and whether any such relief should apply equally to one- and two-earner families.

c) *The choice of tax unit*

Countries are generally classified mainly according to whether or not the earned income of spouses is aggregated for tax purposes, joint or family taxation being used for aggregation and separate or individual for non-aggregation. This distinction is not altogether unambiguous. Some countries classified as using individual taxation may tax jointly in some circumstances or even take the married couple as the legal tax unit and some countries classified as using joint taxation may permit spouses to be taxed individually or to introduce separate schedules for spouses which reduce the effect of the cumulation of earned income under joint systems. Most but not all countries with joint taxation adopt income splitting under which each of the spouses is deemed to have the same income, whatever their actual earnings may be, so that under progressive taxation this reduces their tax liability.

OECD publications have given two instances of a shift of opinion from joint to separate taxation. The first compared a 1955 resolution adopted by the International Fiscal Association advocating joint taxation with a 1972 resolution by the same body which considered that the choice between joint and individual taxation must be decided within each country, consideration being given to such factors as way of life, traditions and internal conditions of a social, economic and political kind. The second gave the following contrasting quotations from the 1966 Carter Commission in Canada and the 1975 Asprey Committee in Australia:

The Carter Commission states:

> We believe firmly that the family is today, as it has been for many centuries, the basic economic unit in society. Although few marriages are entered into for purely financial reasons, as soon as a marriage is contracted, it is the continued income and financial position of the family which is ordinarily of primary concern, not the income and financial position of the individual members. Thus, the married couple itself adopts the economic concept of the family as the income unit from the outset. In Western society, the wife's direct financial contributions to the family income through employment is frequently substantial. It is probably even more true that the newly-formed family acts as a financial unit in making its expenditures.

The Asprey Committee, on the contrary, gave its view:

> ....that the adoption of a compulsory family unit basis must be rejected on grounds of general social principle. The right to be taxed as an individual has always been accorded in Australia. At a time when women are playing an ever greater role in the economic and other affairs of society, the withdrawal of this right would certainly be regarded as a retrograde step. And objections would come not only from women: men too might take exception to a universal and compulsory commingling of their tax affairs with those of their wives. This would, in the Committee's view, make a change in this direction politically unacceptable irrespective of whether married women (or married men) paid more or less tax after the change than they do now: social attitudes to the separate status of the sexes, rather than purely economic considerations, are involved here.

Unmodified individual taxation produces a lower tax bill for two-earner couples at high income levels but (because of the usual method of tax reliefs by way of tax allowances) increases it at lower income levels relative to two-earner couples under joint taxation. An advantage of individual taxation is that it helps to protect the privacy of each spouse and may provide an inducement to the second spouse to enter the labour force. These were the main motives for the introduction of individual taxation in so many countries during the 1970s, when it was desired for both social and economic reasons to encourage female participation in the work-force. A consequence of unmodified individual taxation is that the tax bill of a two-earner couple whose joint earnings equal, say, $ 10,000 per year will vary immensely according to the individual composition of their incomes (e.g. $ 8,000 and $ 2,000 versus $ 5,000 and $ 5,000), because of the interaction of different marginal rates applicable to different levels of income with the amount and nature of the marriage allowance for each couple. This problem has recently become generally less important with the flattening of rate schedules and has been resolved earlier in some countries by the lower-earning spouse being permitted to transfer any basic tax relief and/or any additional marriage allowance to the higher-earning spouse.

The combination of the tax unit, the rate schedule and basic and married tax reliefs could equally provide the same kinds of horizontal inequity under joint taxation, e.g. between the $ 8,000/$ 2,000 couple and the $ 5,000/$5,000 couple, and for this reason most joint taxation countries base tax liability on the so-called income-splitting principle, i.e. $ 5,000/$ 5,000 is assumed, whatever actual earnings are.

There are also other relevant arguments about the various advantages and disadvantages of individual and joint taxation. For example, some social benefits (e.g. low income family benefits, child care expenses) may have to be based on the family and so (especially if the tax/benefit system becomes more integrated) there could be a mismatch between tax and benefits under individual taxation. On the other hand, for administrative simplicity, individual taxation probably has the advantage, especially if it is wished to avoid tax discrimination between married couples and informal unions.

It seems likely that the tax unit in determining the relative income tax bills of taxpayers in different family circumstances has little practical significance, first because the rate schedule and the extent and nature of tax reliefs are probably more important determinants, second because the two extreme systems have in practice been modified in the ways described above and third because rate schedule flattening and base broadening have reduced the tax differential between the various tax units.

Finally, it has been presumed that the different tax bills of unmarried, one-earner and two-earner couples at the same and at varying levels of income are settled in somewhat haphazard fashion by the interaction of tax unit, tax relief and rate schedule. This presumed "haphazard" effect should not be construed as a criticism of government policies, because the use of income tax differentiation in the wider sense to promote greater economic efficiency and horizontal and vertical equity seems much more important than getting what happens to be considered the optimum degree of fine tuning as between the relative tax bills to be paid by different family units at similar and different income levels, especially as the latter is apt to vary according to fashions in morality.

d) Country practices

Country practices regarding the tax unit in respect of earned and unearned income, reliefs for marriage, the effect on such reliefs if both spouses are gainfully employed, the possibility of transferring allowances between spouses, as well as changes to the tax unit are set out in detail in Table 10.2. This sub-section provides an indication of preponderant practices and trends. It also summarises country practices regarding responsibility for signing the tax form and payment of the tax and the tax treatment of informal unions.

Choice of tax unit

Within the OECD 15 countries have chosen the individual as the unit of taxation for earned income, five have joint or family taxation and four give married taxpayers a choice between either joint or individual taxation.

The major trend in recent years has been a move away from joint taxation and towards individual taxation. Since 1970, nine countries have moved from joint to individual taxation, six before 1980 (Austria, Denmark, Finland, Italy, the Netherlands and Sweden) and three since 1980 (Belgium, Iceland and the United Kingdom). Only Portugal (1989) has moved in the opposite direction.

Relief for marriage

Only four OECD countries have no tax relief for marriage. Seven countries provide relief through credits, five through allowances, and eight provide relief in the form of income splitting or different tax schedules.

Reduction of reliefs for marriage if both spouses are gainfully employed

Reliefs for marriage are reduced or lost in eight of the 20 OECD countries granting them if the second spouse either becomes gainfully employed or if his or her income exceeds a fixed amount. In some cases the relief tapers off according to the amount of earnings of the second spouse.

Transferability of allowances

Nine countries (Australia, Belgium, Canada, Denmark, Greece, Iceland, Ireland, the Netherlands and the United Kingdom) have provisions which enable certain unused allowances to be transferred between spouses. In Belgium, Denmark, Greece, Ireland and the Netherlands any unused portion of the basic reliefs are transferrable, in the United Kingdom the unused portion of the married couple's allowance can generally be transferred to the wife; in Australia only the pensioner credit is transferable; in Canada transferrable credits include the age, disability, education, medical expense and charitable contribution credits; in Iceland, the other spouse can use up to 80 per cent of the unused part of the basic credit.

Taxation of unearned income

As a general rule, the unit of taxation for unearned income is the same as that for earned income. In countries using joint taxation, unearned income is aggregated along with earned income. In countries using individual taxation, four countries provide a treatment different from that applied to earned income. In Iceland and the Netherlands unearned income is taxed in the hands of the spouse with the highest earned income and in Belgium and Denmark such income is taxed jointly. However, in the case of Denmark, the tax is divided between spouses according to their respective shares of total capital income. Until quite recently most countries with individual taxation for earned income required joint taxation for unearned income to avoid tax avoidance by couples artificially splitting their unearned income, but with the flattening of tax rate schedules this has become a less serious problem.

Responsibility for signing the tax form and payment of tax

Responsibility for both signing the tax form and for the payment of the tax follows closely the structure of the tax unit. Thus if the unit of taxation is the individual then responsibility for both signing the tax form and paying tax rests generally with the individual. Similarly, in the case of joint or family taxation both spouses sign the tax form and are jointly responsible for the payment of tax. In the case of optional taxation, the individual is responsible if individual taxation is chosen and both spouses are responsible if joint taxation chosen. Two exceptions are Greece, where only the husband signs the tax form, unless the wife also reports income in which case both sign and Luxembourg, where either spouse is able to sign the tax form in the name of both spouses.

Tax treatment and verification of informal unions

Six OECD countries, all with individual taxation, (Australia, Austria, Iceland, the Netherlands, New Zealand and Sweden) have provisions which enable informal unions between individuals of different sex to be treated in the same way as legally married couples. In all six countries the basic test for verifying informal unions is residence together, but the Netherlands requires registration as a joint household. Similar provisions for informal unions between members of the same sex occur only in Denmark and New Zealand. In Denmark, which does not recognise for tax purposes informal unions between individuals of different sexes (since unlike those of the same sex they can marry), registration as a joint household is required and in New Zealand residence together for two years is required. Of the above seven countries, it is recalled that there is no relief for marriage in Denmark, New Zealand and Sweden and there is compulsory separate taxation but the recognition of informal unions may enable transfer of other allowances as well as having significance for inheritance tax treatment.

4. Aid to parents through the tax/benefit system

It is pointless to consider aid to parents through the income tax in isolation because cash transfers represent an alternative and competing form of aid. Most governments use both forms of aid and have frequently varied their relative reliance treatment over the last twenty-five years. It should also be added that in many countries cash transfers take many varying forms (e.g. universal or income-related, or available only to one-parent families) and that such matters cannot be dealt with here.

Four normative positions may be taken towards the relationship between the tax/benefit system and the treatment of parents thereunder, but nowadays the first two command so little support that they are not discussed further. On the contrary, the relative merits of the last two approaches remains a much debated issue.

- *The elitist approach* holds that government should encourage the rich to procreate since the cost to society is less as they can self-finance the costs of child rearing and produce better-educated children for the next generation. The family quotient system without a ceiling, as formerly practised in France, is the most obvious way of implementing this approach, but tax allowances also do so to a lesser degree. (Theoretically cash transfers to parents positively related to their income could achieve the same effect, but proponents of the elitist approach have realised that this is politically not feasible.)
- *The children as a consumption good approach.* This takes the view that children are a form of consumption good which couples choose to indulge in and derive pleasure from, and in OECD countries where social pressures to reproduce are less and the means to avoid reproduction widely available, there is no reason for preferential treatment for parents unless governments wish to encourage this form of consumption. Of course, such a view ignores the ability to pay principle as well as the need for a future work-force to support future pensioners. It may be added that different considerations apply in a number of developing countries, where there is a social and economic need to limit population growth.

- *The taxable capacity approach*, as discussed by R. Musgrave (1959) and defended, for example, by G. Brennan and E. Morss (1973) which emphasises the need to preserve horizontal equity under income tax systems, may be summarised as follows. Under income tax systems based on the principle of ability to pay, the taxable capacity of parents is considered to be lower than that of childless couples because of the additional expenditure needs associated with having children. The advocates of the taxable capacity approach argue that the fact that tax allowances are worth more to taxpayers with higher incomes than to taxpayers with lower incomes is merely due to the progressivity of tax systems. This result cannot, on a taxable capacity approach, be considered inequitable: it follows from acceptance of the ability to pay principle as applied to a progressive income tax schedule. According to this approach, what is relevant is the appropriate differentiation between taxpayers having different sized families at given income levels and that the issue is not one of how taxpayers at different income levels should be treated. Thus, a report by the 1976 Committee on Income and Transfers in France, in defending the French family quotient systems questioned whether the concept of an "advantage" in this context was even applicable since, by taking account of the number of children, the aim of the family quotient was simply to maintain the family's taxable capacity at a constant level as the family itself increases. The fact that the incidence of the family quotient varies according to income level merely reflects the differences existing in this connection prior to the birth of an additional child. In short, proponents of the taxable capacity approach are concerned with the internal logic of a progressive income tax system based on the ability to pay principle. They might well accept the need for cash transfers to parents with below subsistence income, but would argue that this should not be done through the income tax system.
- *The social welfare approach* is more concerned with alleviation of poverty, which tends to be positively correlated to the number of children than with horizontal equity, and its proponents consider that the main rationale for subsidising parents is their need for such aid. Under this approach there is no place for tax allowances which benefit rich parents more than poor, or even wastable tax credits which are of no use to those whose income is below the income tax threshold. Under such an approach the appropriate method of aiding parents is either by cash transfers (for preference taxable) or by non-wastable tax credits. One country example of such an approach was Australia in 1976 which changed rapidly from tax allowances to tax credits to cash transfers. The change from tax reliefs to cash transfers provided assistance to low-income families whose incomes were insufficient to enable them to take full advantage of the wastable tax credits for dependent children. The tax credit system had not adequately provided for some 800,000 children in low-income families who paid little or no taxation. These included the children of widows and invalid pensioners, of workers close to the minimum wage or in intermittent employment, or self-employed people unable to earn an adequate income, and of many aborigines, recently-arrived migrants and other disadvantaged groups. It was estimated that the family allowance system provided greatly increased assistance to 300,000 such families. Large families also benefited significantly.

Supporters of the "taxable capacity" approach point out that if the fixed amount were equal to that needed to support a child of a taxpayer in the lowest income bracket, its value (being equal to that amount multiplied by the lowest marginal rate of tax) would be insufficient to compensate a higher income parent who would require relief equal to the subsistence costs multiplied by his marginal rate of tax. Conversely, if the tax credit were sufficient to free the highest rate taxpayers from tax on the subsistence costs of their children, the reduction in tax liability would be too great for low income parents. In other words, to provide a tax credit of the lower amount would, under the taxable capacity approach, be held to penalise rich parents unduly in relation to rich childless couples, and to grant a tax credit of the higher amount would be held to favour poor parents unduly in relation to poor childless couples.

Supporters of the "social welfare" approach also oppose tax credits as not going far enough to meet their objectives. Apart from the fact that tax credits for parents which exceed tax liabilities are wasted outside Canada, credits are received usually by the father and cash transfers usually by the mother who needs them most, and also cash transfers are in some countries taxable which meets progressivity objectives. Even on the "social welfare" approach, however, subsidies through the tax system have one great advantage over (even universal) cash transfers: the take-up ratio is likely to be much greater.

There are no objective criteria to support the choice between the taxable capacity and social welfare approaches. It is a matter of value judgment and, in particular, the importance that is attached to maintaining the internal integrity of the income tax system. On a taxable capacity approach, it may be seen as perfectly normal that tax allowances exist side-by-side with cash transfers, and most governments finding some validity in both approaches, operate aid to parents simultaneously through the two systems. However, (see Table 10.4B) a number of governments over the last twenty years have opted to aid parents exclusively outside the tax system.

Government choices on how to aid parents may in practice be more influenced by practical and pragmatic considerations than by the philosophical attitudes discussed above. Three of these considerations are of relevance:

- the general advantages and disadvantages governing the choice between tax expenditures and direct expenditures concerning transparency, effects on total ratios, degree of take-up, etc;
- the fact that *usually*, though not necessarily, the father benefits most or entirely from tax reliefs and the mother from cash transfers (at the last verification many years ago, cash payments for parents were paid to mothers in all OECD countries, except Austria, France, Italy, the Netherlands and Switzerland, where they were paid to fathers, and in Germany and Japan, where they were paid to the legal guardian);
- administrative convenience.

The first of these three factors has already been discussed in Chapter 6C. On the second, a move from tax reliefs to cash transfers will usually reduce the take-home pay of the husband, although the disposable income of the family may be more or less unchanged. Such a move may lead the husband to increase his wage demands to compensate for the heavier tax burden (tax-push inflation). Conversely, a move from cash transfers to tax reliefs may be resisted by the wife without paid employment as family allowances may be the only source of income over which she has control. OECD 1980 provided the following examples of how this affected certain OECD government decisions during the seventies.

In the United Kingdom, much of the debate over the move from tax allowances to cash transfers centred upon the distribution of assistance between the spouses. The change was announced at a time when the Government was operating an incomes policy and there was some concern that the husband would ignore the increase in cash transfers, which was paid to the wife, and try to compensate for his increased tax payments by higher wage claims. The Government chose gradually to phase in this move over a period of two years. Similar problems arose in New Zealand at the time when cash transfers replaced tax reliefs. Whilst the family as a unit was in almost all cases better off, there was a substantial number of ordinary workers who did not look beyond the fact that their personal tax had increased (by reason of the loss of the allowances) and who did not take into account that overall the family was better off by reason of the increased cash transfers to the wife. In due course this dissatisfaction died away. Some countries (Australia, Germany) have tried to overcome this problem by reducing income tax rates at the same time as they moved from tax reliefs to cash transfers. In Australia, for example, in the Budget speech introducing the move, it was stated that: "As endowment was usually paid to the mother and tax rebates usually reduced the tax liability of the father, family allowances involved redistribution of income within two-parent families in favour of the mother.". The visibility of this redistribution was reduced to some extent, in practice, by the simultaneous reduction in tax rates as a result of tax indexation. In Canada, the decision to pay the non-wastable tax credits to the mother, irrespective of whether or not she has earned income, was partly influenced by these considerations.

Governments' choices between aiding parents through tax expenditures and direct expenditures may also be influenced by administrative considerations. For example, in the late seventies, Germany preferred cash transfers to tax credits because the latter would have increased the number of taxpayers and the cost of collection, since farmers and students would have been required to file a return. In Canada, however, it was felt that such an increase would have very little impact on costs and the desire to relate assistance to income influenced the choice of the tax system as the instrument to achieve this aim, since income tax returns provided the most reliable measurement in this regard. The United Kingdom's choice of cash transfers was influenced by the fact that under a PAYE system, non-wastable tax credits would have been difficult to administer, especially if they were on a weekly or monthly basis. In Australia, the tax allowance system involved little more in the way of administration than had been required for the payment of cash transfers. On the taxation side, the change resulted in a small increase in the number of taxpayers (those who came within the tax net as a result of the changed arrangements) but against this many taxpayers were no longer required to lodge dependant declaration forms for PAYE purposes. A somewhat similar situation was found in New Zealand, where the personal and spouse allowances were converted to tax credits in 1974 partly as a means of simplifying the income tax self-assessment system.

These country examples show that the administrative feasibility and costs of different systems very much depends upon the method used to collect income tax receipts and the general coverage of income tax systems. In particular, the level of tax thresholds and the proportion of families with children who pay tax seem to be two factors which determine how costly it is to move from one system to another. It also seems likely that moves between tax reliefs and cash transfers will be more difficult in federal than unitary countries, at least if different levels of government are responsible for different programmes. The introduction of tax credits into the income tax system may be more difficult in those countries which operate weekly or monthly withholding systems, because of the administrative problems attached to incorporating these into the withholding tables, especially if the credits are non-wastable. A government may not wish to pay these credits at the end of the year as this would impose an undue burden on low-income families. In the United Kingdom, administrative difficulties were one of the arguments put forward against the introduction of the Tax Credit Scheme proposed in 1974. In New Zealand, however, the tax credits for families were incorporated into the PAYE tables so that the qualifying tax-payer gained the benefit very quickly.

Table 10.4B indicates how OECD governments have recently aided parents through the tax/benefit system and how things have changed over the last two decades. It shows that eight countries provide parents with tax allowances and another two apply the tax quotient with similar effects; five provide tax credits, of which only Canada's is non-wastable and nine do not give aid to parents through the tax system.

The last column of Table 10.4B indicates a growing tendency to confine aid to parents outside the income tax system as since 1976 cash-transfers have replaced tax reliefs in six countries. Canada introduced non-wastable tax credits in 1978, another way of implementing the social welfare approach. However, there have been some moves in the opposite direction. Germany abolished tax allowances in 1975, re-introduced them in 1983 and considerably increased their value in 1986 and Greece switched from tax allowances to tax credits in 1984, but back to tax allowances in 1988. The only other recent change has been the recent introduction of wastable tax credits in Norway, where formerly no tax reliefs were given to parents.

Thus the predominant tendency has been to increase the progressivity of aid to parents which in many countries would counter the reduced progressivity of rate schedules and the move from joint to individual taxation.

One last point is that though the foregoing has indicated the direction of government choices, without quantative examples one is left with a rather vague impression of how these choices affect the relative tax/benefit position of parents at different income levels and in different countries. For example, how much is the tax relief and the cash transfer and do they vary as between age of children, and as between first, second or subsequent children? Although the annual APW report of the OECD gives some information at that income level, to my knowledge, no internationally comparable quantitative work on the tax/benefit position of parents has been undertaken since *The tax/benefit position of selected income groups* (OECD 1980).

F. The 18 comparative tables

Notes to Table 10.1 on summary of income subject to tax

1. Income source dealt with in more detail in *The Personal Income Tax Base* (OECD 1990).
2. Refers to personal accounts only, i.e. accrued interest in pension funds is excluded.
3. Or I at the choice of the taxpayer.
4. Interest from future issues is taxable.

I = Income source subject to tax. P = Some components of income source subject to tax, others not.

N = Income source not subject to tax. N.A. = Information not applicable.

[ ] The situation as of 1 January 1989.

Source: Table 4.1 of *The personal income tax base: a comparative survey* (OECD 1990).

Table 10.1: Summary of income subject to tax in OECD countries

		Australia	Austria	Belgium	Canada	Denmark	Finland	France	Germany	Greece	Iceland
		(1987/88)	(1982)	(1987)	(1986)	(1987)	(1985)	(1987)	(1987)	(1987)	(1989)
1.	Employment income	I	I	I	I	I	I	I	I	I	I
2.	Fringe benefits[1]										
2.1	Employers' contributions to sickness schemes	I	N	N	N	N	N	N	N	N	N
2.2	Employers' contributions to private pension schemes	N	N	N	N	N	N	N	N	N	N
2.3	Other benefits	I	I	I	I	N	I	P	P	I	I
3.	Net business income	I	I	I	I	I	I	I	I	I	I
4.	Interest income										
4.1	Government bonds	I	N	P[3]	I	I	N	I	I	N	N
4.2	Certain savings accounts	I	I	P[3]	I	I	N	I	I	N	N
4.3	Pension savings accounts[2]	I	I	P[3]	I	N	N	I	I	N	N
4.4	Other bank accounts[1]	I	I	P[3]	I	I	N	I	I	N	N
4.5	Others	I	I	P[3]	I	I	I	I	I	I	N
5.	Dividend income	I	I	P[3]	I	I	I	I	I	I	I
6.	Other investment income	N.A.	N.A.	N.A.	N.A.	N.A.	N.A.	N.A.	N.A.	N.A.	N.A.
7.	Rent income		I	I	P	I	I	I	I	I	I
8.	Imputed rent[1]	N	N	P	N	I	I	N	N	I	N
9.	Public pensions	I	I	I	I	I	I	I	I	I	I
10.	Private pensions, annuities and life assurance										
10.1	Private pensions	I	I	I	I	I	I	I	I	I	I
10.2	Annuities	P	P	I	I	I	I	I	I	I	I
10.3	Life assurance–periodical	I	N	I	N	I	N	N	N	N	I
10.4	Life assurance–lump sum	N	N	I	N	N	N	N	N	N	N
11.	Social transfers										
11.1	Unemployment	I	N	I	I	I	I	I	N	I	I
11.2	Sickness	I	N	I	I	I	I	I	N	I	I
11.3	Invalidity or injury	P	P	I	I	P	I	N	P	N	I
11.4	Strike pay	I	I	N	N	I	N	I	I	N.A.	I
11.5	Family allowance	N	N	N	I	N	N	N	N	N	N
11.6	Dwelling allowance	N	N	N	N	N	N	N	N	N.A.	N
11.7	Others	N	P	N	N.A.	N	P	N	N	N	N.A.
12.	Alimony and maintenance receipts	N	N	I	I	I	I	I	N	N	N
13.	Capital gains[1]										
13.1	Short-term	P	I	P	P	P	P	P	P	P	P
13.2	Long-term	P	P	P	P	P	N	P	N	P	P
14.	Others										
14.1	Foreign earnings	I	I	I	I	I	I	I	P	I	I
14.2	Foreign pensions	I	I	I	I	I	I	I	P	N	I

Table 10.1(cont.): Summary of income subject to tax in OECD countries

		Ireland (1985/86)	Italy (1985)	Japan (1990)	Netherlands (1988)	Norway (1987)	Spain (1987)	Sweden (1987)	Turkey (1990)	United Kingdom (1986/87)	United States (1988)
1.	Employment income	I	I	I	I	I	I	I	I	I	I
2.	Fringe benefits[1]										
2.1	Employer's contributions to sickness schemes	N	N	N	I	I	N	N	N	N	N
2.2	Employers' contributions to private pension schemes	N	N	N	N	N	N	N	N	N	N
2.3	Other benefits	I	I	P	P	P	I	P	P	P	P
3.	Net business income	I	I	I	I	I	I	I	I	I	I
4.	Interest income										
4.1	Government bonds	I	N[4]	I	I	I	I	I	I	I	I
4.2	Certain savings accounts	I	I	I	I	I	I	I	I	I	I
4.3	Pension savings accounts[2]	I	I	I	I	I	P	I	I	I	I
4.4	Other bank accounts	I	I	I	I	I	I	I	I	I	I
4.5	Others	I	I	I	I	I	I	I	I	I	I
5.	Dividend income	I	I	I	I	I	I	I	N	I	I
6.	Other investment income	N.A.	N.A.	N.A.	N.A.	N.A.	I	N.A.	N.A.	N.A.	N.A.
7.	Rent income		I	I	I	I	I	I	I	I	I
8.	Imputed rent[1]	N	I	N	I	I	I	I	N	N	N
9.	Public pensions	I	I	I	I	I	I	I	N	I	I
10.	Private pensions, annuities and life assurance										
10.1	Private pensions	I	I	I	I	I	I	I	N	I	P
10.2	Annuities	I	I	I	I	P	I	P	I	I	P
10.3	Life assurance–periodical	I	N	I	N	N	I	N	N	N	P
10.4	Life assurance–lump sum	N	N	I	N	N	I	N	N	N	P
11.	Social transfers										
11.1	Unemployment	N	I	N	I	I	N	I	N	I	I
11.2	Sickness	N	I	N	I	I	N	I	N	P	P
11.3	Invalidity or injury	P	N	N	I	P	N	N	N	N	P
11.4	Strike pay	N	N.A.	I	I	N	I	N	N	N	P
11.5	Family allowance	N	N	N	N	N	N.A.	N	N	N	P
11.6	Dwelling allowance	I	I	I	I	N	N.A.	N	P	N	P
11.7	Others	P	P	N.A.	P	N.A.	N.A.	N	P	P	P
12.	Alimony and maintenance receipts	I	I	N	I	I	I	P	N	I [P]	I
13.	Capital gains[1]										
13.1	Short-term	I	N	I	N	I	P	I	P	P	I
13.2	Long-term	I	N	I	N	P	P	P	P	P	I
14.	Others										
14.1	Foreign earnings	I	P	I	I	I	I	I	I	P	P
14.2	Foreign pensions	I	P	I	I	I	I	I	P	P	I

Table 10.2:
Tax units for earned and unearned income, 1992, and changes since 1970

Country	Changes since 1970 in respect of earned income	Reliefs for marriage	Reduction in marriage reliefs if spouse gainfully employed	Can unused allowances be transferred between spouses?	Treatment of unearned income
	(1)	(2)	(3)	(4)	(5)
			Individual Taxation[1]		
Australia	–	Credit	Credit tapers-off as spouse's income exceeds fixed amount	Yes[2]	Separate
Austria	From joint in 1973	Credit	Yes	No	Separate
Belgium	From family in 1989	Both spouses receive married persons allowance	No	Yes	Aggregated
Canada	–	Credit	Credit is reduced if the spouse's net income exceeds fixed amount	Yes	Separate
Denmark	From joint in 1970	No relief	n.a.	Yes	Aggregated but divided between spouses according to their relative share of total capital income
Finland	From joint (separate schedules) in 1976	No relief	n.a.	No	Separate
Greece	–	Allowance	No	Yes	Separate
Iceland	From joint in 1980	Credit	Yes	Yes	Total of unearned income added to income of spouse with higher earnings
Italy	From family in 1977	Credit	Yes, provided the spouse's income does not exceed 4 500 000 lire	No	Separate
Japan	–	Allowance	Yes	No	Separate
Netherlands	From joint in 1973	Allowance	Yes	Yes	As Iceland
New Zealand	–	No relief	n.a.	No	Separate
Sweden	From joint in 1971	Credit	Yes	No	Separate
Turkey[3]	–	No relief	n.a.	No	Separate
United Kingdom	From joint to optional in 1972 and to individual in 1990	Allowance	No	Yes[4]	Separate
			Joint (J) or Family (F) Taxation[1]		
France[F]	–	Income splitting	No	No	Aggregated
Luxembourg[J]	–	Income splitting	No	No	Aggregated
Portugal[F]	From mixture of family and individual in 1989	Income splitting	No	No	Aggregated
Switzerland[5J]	–	Different schedules	No	No	Aggregated
United States[J]	–	Different Schedules	No	No	Aggregated
			Optional taxation[1]		
Germany	–	Income splitting	No	No	Aggregated
Ireland	Full income splitting in 1980	Income splitting with option for aggregation	No	Yes	Aggregated
Norway	–	Different schedules	No	No	Aggregated
Spain	From family in 1989[6]	Credit	No	No	Separate or aggregated

1. Countries are classified according to the taxation of earned income.
2. Holds only for the unused portion of the pensioner's rebate.
3. Joint above a ceiling.
4. Holds only for the unused portion of the married couple's allowance.
5. At federal level; varies at cantonal level.
6. With effect for income for the year 1988.

– = no changes since 1970, n.a. = not applicable.

Source: *The tax benefit position of production workers* (OECD 1991) with some modifications.

Table 10.3: Methods of giving standard basic reliefs, 1990

Tax allowance unrelated to income	**Zero rated first bracket**	**Tax credit**	
	A. Basic reliefs available to all taxpayers		
Austria	Australia	Austria	
Belgium	Finland	Canada	
Germany	France	Denmark	
Greece	Germany	Greece	
Ireland	Luxembourg	Iceland	
Luxembourg	Norway	Italy	
Japan	Spain	New Zealand	
Netherlands	Sweden	Portugal	
Portugal	Switzerland	Spain	
Sweden	United States		
Turkey			
United Kingdom			
United States[1]			
	B. Basic reliefs for earned income		
Lump-sum tax allowance for work-related expenses	**Tax allowance for actual costs of certain work-related expenses**	**Tax allowance unrelated to earned income**	**Tax credit for earned income**
Austria	Australia	Denmark	Austria
Belgium	Belgium	Finland	Iceland
Germany	Canada	France	Italy
Luxembourg	Denmark	Japan	Spain
Sweden	Finland	Netherlands	
Switzerland	Germany	Norway	
	Greece	Portugal	
	Ireland	Spain	
	Italy		
	Luxembourg		
	Netherlands		
	Norway		
	Sweden		
	Switzerland		
	United Kingdom		
	United States		

1. Certain allowances phased out at high income levels.

Source: *The role of tax reform in Central and Eastern European economies* (OECD 1991).

Table 10.4A: Methods of giving standard reliefs for marriage and children, 1990

A. Relief for marriage					
Income splitting system	**Quotient**	**Different schedules**	**Tax allowance**[1]	**Tax credit**[2]	**No relief**
Germany Ireland Portugal United States	France Luxembourg	Norway Switzerland (federal varies cantonal) United States	Belgium (for both spouses) Greece Ireland Japan Netherlands United Kingdom	Australia Austria Canada Iceland Italy Spain Sweden	Denmark Finland New Zealand Turkey

Table 10.4B: Methods of giving standard reliefs for marriage and children, 1990

B. Reliefs for dependent children[2]			
Quotient	**Tax allowances**[1]	**Tax credits**[1]	**No relief through tax system but cash transfers available to parents**
France (ceiling imposed in 1981) Luxembourg	Belgium Canada Finland Germany[3] Greece (since 1988) Japan Switzerland United States	Canada[4] (introduced 1978) Italy Norway (recently introduced) Portugal Spain	Australia (tax credit abolished 1976) Austria (tax credit abolished 1978) Denmark (no recent change) Iceland (earlier years unavailable) Ireland (tax allowance abolished 1986) Netherlands (tax allowance abolished 1978) New Zealand (tax credit abolished 1987) Sweden (no recent change) United Kingdom (tax allowance abolished 1978-9)

1. Unrelated to income.

2. All OECD countries give cash transfers to parents irrespective of their income, except Japan (for first child only), Switzerland and the United States (both at federal levels). The United States gives cash transfers to parents on low income levels.

3. Reduced to almost zero in 1975, re-introduced in 1983 and considerably increased in 1986.

4. In Canada, unlike the other countries, the credit is non-wastable. Canada is also unique in having both a tax allowance and a tax credit.

Source: as Table 10.3

Table 10.5 : Standard reliefs (basic, marriage and children) under individual taxation, 1990[1]

Country	Basic relief for each tax unit	When wife has no earned income, husband receives:		When wife has earned income the position is: Difference in couple's relief:	
		Married persons' relief	Relief in respect of children	for married person	in respect of children
Australia	Zero rated first bracket	Tax credit of fixed amount	An additional tax credit of fixed amount for one-parent family	Tax credit tapers off to zero as spouse's income exceeds a fixed amount	Total amount of fixed tax credit and additional tax credit reduces with respect to income of spouse
Austria	Fixed allowance and tax credit of fixed amount	Tax credit of fixed amount for sole earner	None (cash transfers)	Husband loses sole earner's tax credit when spouse's income exceeds fixed amount	No difference
Belgium	Fixed allowance	Fixed allowance, also 30 per cent of husband's income is attributed to the wife (subject to a ceiling)	Fixed allowance	Both husband and wife receive married person's allowance	No difference
Canada	Tax credit of fixed amount	Additional tax credit of fixed amount	Fixed allowance plus an additional refundable credit of fixed amount	Husband gradually loses credit for wife as wife's income increases	Additional refundable credit reduces as family income exceeds fixed amount
Denmark	Fixed personal relief (but used in such a way as to achieve the effect of a tax credit)	Basic personal tax relief doubled and unused portion of a spouse's relief may be transferred to the other spouse	None (cash transfers paid in respect of children)	No difference	No difference
Finland	Zero rated first bracket	None	Fixed allowance	No difference	No difference
Greece	Allowance of fixed amount	Additional fixed allowance	Allowance of fixed amount	No difference	No difference
Iceland	Tax credit of fixed amount	Additional tax credit of fixed amount	None (cash transfers)	Husband loses wife's tax credit if she becomes employed. However, 80 per cent of wife's tax credit is transferred to husband	No difference
Italy	Tax credit of fixed amount	Additional tax credit of fixed amount	Tax credit of fixed amount	Husband's spouse credit is not given if wife's income exceeds fixed limit	Tax credits halved if spouse's income exceeds fixed amount
Japan	Fixed allowance	Additional fixed allowance (higher allowance still for wife over 70)	Fixed allowance	Husband's spouse allowance is not given if wife's income exceeds fixed limit	No difference

Table 10.5(cont.): Standard reliefs (basic, marriage and children) under individual taxation, 1990[1]

Country	Basic relief for each tax unit	When wife has no earned income, husband receives:		When wife has earned income the position is: Difference in couple's relief:	
		Married persons' relief	Relief in respect of children	for married person	in respect of children
Netherlands	Fixed allowance	Husband receives higher fixed allowance than that for single person	None (cash transfers)	Husband loses spouse allowance if spouse becomes employed. If the income of the spouse is less than the basic standard allowance the entire standard allowance can be transferred to the husband.	No difference
New Zealand	Income-related credit	None	Credit allowable to child only	No difference	No difference
Sweden	Fixed allowance	Additional tax credit of fixed amount	None (cash transfers)	Husband's tax credit tapers off to zero as spouse's income increases	Fixed allowance
Turkey	Fixed allowance	None	None	No difference	No difference
United Kingdom	Fixed allowance	Married couple's allowance	None (cash transfers)	Broadly no difference but the husband is entitled to transfer some or all of the married couple's allowance to the wife if his income is insufficient to absorb it all.	No difference

1. It is assumed that the wife is the secondary earner and has no unearned income, though it is recognised that this is not always the case.

Source: As Table 10.3.

Table 10.6:
Standard reliefs (basic, marriage and children) under joint taxation, 1990[1]

Country	Basic relief for each tax unit	Married person's relief	Relief in respect of children
France	Zero rated first bracket	Quotient system	Quotient system
Germany	Fixed allowance and zero rated first bracket	Income splitting system, effective doubling of basic allowance	Fixed allowance
Ireland	Fixed allowance	Additional fixed allowance. Income splitting system	None (cash transfers)
Luxembourg	Fixed allowance and zero rated first bracket	Quotient system	Quotient system and income-related allowance
Norway[2]	Income-related allowance and zero rated first bracket	Different tax schedules	Tax credit of fixed amount
Portugal	Fixed allowance and fixed credit	Income splitting system	Fixed credit
Spain[2,3]	Zero rated first bracket, tax credit of fixed amount	Additional tax credit of fixed amount	Tax credit of fixed amount
Switzerland	Zero rated first bracket	Different tax schedules	Fixed allowance
United States	Fixed allowance	Different tax schedules. Income splitting system	Fixed allowance

1. Except in Spain (see footnote 3) reliefs are unaffected if both spouses have earned income.

2. Taxpayers may opt for individual taxation.

3. Subject to certain conditions there is an additional tax credit where the wife has earned income and a joint return is filed.

Source: As Table 10.3.

Table 10.7 : Other standard reliefs, 1990

Country	Relief for social security contributions	Special reliefs for the aged	Housekeeper or childminder relief	Dependant other than children	Special relief for disability
Australia	No social security contributions	Tax credit for age, pensioners, tapers to zero as income exceeds fixed amount.	Tax credit of fixed amount is given in respect of a housekeeper wholly engaged in keeping house for the taxpayer and in caring for a child of the taxpayer	Tax credit of fixed amount for invalid relative, parent or parent-in-law	Invalid pension is exempt
Austria	Deductible subject to ceiling	Fixed tax credit	None	None	
Belgium	Fully deductible	None	Proportion of expenditure deductible subject to certain conditions	Tax credit of fixed amount	Fixed allowance
Canada	Tax credit of 17% of contributions	Fixed tax credit	Deduction of actual expenditure subject to a ceiling	Tax credit of fixed amount	Tax credit of fixed amount
Denmark	Fully deductible	Tax credit of fixed amount			
Finland	Not deductible	None	None	None	Tax credit of fixed amounts varying with degree of disability
France	Fully deductible	Fixed allowance	Tax credit for proportion of childminding expenses subject to a ceiling		Fixed tax allowance
Germany	Fully deductible (subject to a ceiling)	Additional fixed tax allowance	Deduction of expenses subject to a ceiling		Fixed tax allowance
Greece	Fully deductible	None	Allowance for 50 per cent of expenses subject to a ceiling	Fixed tax allowance for each person living with and maintained by the taxpayer	Fixed tax allowance
Iceland	Not deductible	None	None	None	None
Ireland	Fixed tax allowance	Fixed tax allowance. Also higher general exemption	Fixed tax allowance for incapacitated taxpayer or his/her spouse who employs person to care for him/her	Additional fixed tax allowance for dependent relative	Additional fixed tax allowance for blind person and/or spouse
Italy	Fully deductible	None	None	Tax credit of fixed amount	Tax allowance for deambulation and locomotion means
Japan	Fully deductible	Additional fixed allowance	None	Fixed tax allowance (larger if dependant 70 years old or more)	Additional fixed tax allowance for handicapped taxpayer, spouse, children and other dependant
Luxembourg	Fully deductible	None	None	None	None
Netherlands	Not deductible	None		Support payments to close relatives deductible	Expenses arising from disablement deductible

Table 10.7(cont.): Other standard reliefs, 1990

Country	Relief for social security contributions	Special reliefs for the aged	Housekeeper or childminder relief	Dependant other than children	Special relief for disability
New Zealand	No social security contributions	None	Tax credit subject to a ceiling		
Norway	Not deductible		Deduction, from the lower of the two spouses incomes, of childminding expenses (subject to a ceiling)	Fixed tax allowance for each dependant	
Portugal	Deductible subject to certain conditions	None	None	None	Tax credit increased by 50 per cent in the case of a handicapped taxpayer, spouse, child and other dependant.
Spain	Fully deductible	Tax credit of a fixed amount for any taxpayer or dependant aged 70 years or more	None	Tax credit of a fixed amount for ascendants	Tax credit of fixed amount
Sweden	No social security contributions paid by employees	Tax allowance related to income	None	None	Tax allowance related to income (in some cases)
Switzerland	Fully deductible	None	None	Fixed allowance	None
Turkey	Fully deductible	None	None	None	Additional allowance for wage earners (varies according to disability)
United Kingdom	Not deductible apart from relief given for 50% of the class 4 National Insurance Contributions paid by sole traders and unincorporated partners	Higher rates of fixed allowance for those aged 65 and over.	None	None	Additional fixed tax allowance for blind person
United States	Not deductible	Additional fixed tax allowance for aged person and/or spouse	Tax credit related to expenses subject to a ceiling	Additional fixed tax allowance	Additional fixed tax allowance for blind person and/or spouse

Source: as Table 10.3.

Table 10.8: The deductibility of interest payments, 1990

Country	Interest on loans for: Investment or business purposes	Home purchases or improvements: Principal residence	Home purchases or improvements: Secondary residence	Consumer purchases
Australia	TA(B)	ND	ND	ND
Austria	TA(O)	TA(C)	ND	TA(C)
Belgium	TA	TA(O)	TA(O)	ND
Canada	TA	ND	ND	ND
Denmark	TA	TA	TA	TA
Finland	TA	TA(C)	TA	TA(C)
France	TA(B)	TC(C)	ND	ND
Germany	TA	ND	ND	ND
Greece	TA	TA	TA(C)	ND
Iceland	TA(B)	TC(C)	ND	ND
Ireland	TA(B)	TA(C)	ND	ND
Italy	ND	TA(C)	TA(C)	ND
Japan	TA	ND[1]	ND[1]	ND
Luxembourg	TA	TA(C)	TA(C)	TA
Netherlands	TA	TA	TA	TA
New Zealand	TA	ND	ND	ND
Norway	TA	TA	TA	TA
Portugal	TA	TA(C)	TA(C)	ND
Spain	TA	TA(C)	TA(C)	ND
Sweden	TA	TA	TA	TA
Switzerland	TA	TA	TA	TA
Turkey	TA(B)	ND	ND	ND
United Kingdom	TA(B)	TA(C)/TC(C)[2]	ND	ND
United States	TA(O)	TA(C)	TA(C)	ND

1. In Japan there is a provision which allows a tax credit against income tax liability corresponding to 1% of outstanding loans related to home acquisition at the end of each year for a certain period.

2. There is no relief for home improvement loans taken out after 5 April 1988.

TA = Tax allowance.

TA(B) = Tax allowance deductible for interest on loans for business purposes only.

TC = Tax credit.

ND = Not deductible (or creditable).

(C) = Subject to ceiling or maximum.

(O) = Fully deductible but only against associated income.

Source: as Table 10.3.

Table 10.9:
Main non-standard reliefs (other than deductibility of interest payments), 1990

Country	Pension Contributions	Life Assurance Premiums	Medical Expenses	Travelling Expenses to Work	Donations to Charities
Australia	TA(C)	ND	TC	ND	TA
Austria	ND	TA(C)	ND	ND	ND
Belgium	TA	TA(C)	ND	TA	TA(C)
Canada	TC(C)	ND	TC(C)	ND	TC(C)
Denmark	TA(C)	TA(C)	ND	TA	TA(C)
Finland	TA(C)	TA(C)	TA(C)	TA(C)	ND
France	ND	TC(C)	ND	ND	TC(C)
Germany	TA(C)	TA(C)	TA	TA	TA(C)
Greece	ND	TA(C)	TA	ND	TA
Iceland	ND	ND	ND	ND	ND
Ireland	TA(C)	TA(C)	TA	ND	ND
Italy	TA(C)	TA(C)	TA	ND	ND
Japan	TA(C)	TA(C)	TA(C)	ND	TA(C)
Netherlands	TA	TA(C)[1]	TA	TA(C)	TA(C)
New Zealand	ND	ND	ND	ND	TC(C)
Norway	TA(C)	TC(C)	–	TA(C)	–
Portugal	TA(C)	TA(C)	TA	ND	TA(C)
Spain	TC(C)	TC(C)	TC	ND	TC
Sweden	TA(C)	ND	ND	TA	ND
Switzerland	TA(C)	TA(C)	ND	TA	ND
Turkey	TA	TA(C)	ND	TA	TA(C)
United Kingdom	TA(C)	ND[2]	ND	ND	TA(C)
United States	TA(C)	ND	TA(C)	ND	TA(C)

1. In general life assurance premiums are not deductible, but a deduction is possible for annuity premiums up to a ceiling.
2. UK: relief for policies made before 13 March 1984.
TA = Tax allowance.
TA(C) = Tax allowance, subject to a ceiling.
TC = Tax credit.
TC(C) = Tax credit, subject to a ceiling.
ND = Not deductible or creditable.
– = no positive information.
Source: as Table 10.3.

Table 10.10 : Reliefs for specific sources of income, 1990

Country	Dividends	Interest	Pensions and Retirement income	Income of Farmers, Small Traders, Particular Trades or Businesses
Australia			Tax credit given in respect of certain social security pensions	Averaging system for taxing income of primary producers
Austria	Subject to tax at half the statutory rate which would be applicable on entire taxable income		Tax credit of fixed amount for pensions	
Belgium		Interest from certain savings accounts exempt up to a limit	Tax credit for retirement pensions	
Denmark			Higher personal reliefs for pensioners	
Finland		Fixed tax allowance	Tax allowance	
France	Fixed tax allowance	Interest on first savings account with postal services exempt	Proportionate deduction from pensions subject to a ceiling	Varying tax allowances for certain categories of employed persons up to a limit
Germany		Certain interest payments exempt, e.g. on government bonds	Tax allowance related to income	
Greece	Fixed tax allowance for dividends of stocks registered in stock market	Interest in bank accounts and on certain government bonds excluded from income subject to tax		Additional tax allowance for farmers
Iceland	Subject to a ceiling, dividend income up to 15% of total value of share is exempt	Interest generally exempt		
Ireland	Subject to certain conditions, 50 per cent of dividend income from manufacturing companies is exempt	Exemption for certain government interest		
Japan		Exemption for interest on small deposits and government bonds received by certain persons e.g. qualified aged persons.	Fixed allowance	
Luxembourg	Fixed tax allowance for certain dividend income	Fixed tax allowance for saving deposit or government bond interest		
Netherlands	First 1 000 Dfl. of dividend income exempt. For married couples the exemption is 2 000. Dfl.	First 1 000 Dfl. of interest income exempt. For married couples the exemption is 2 000 Dfl.		Fixed allowance (varying inversely with profits) for self-employed and entrepreneurs, and other provisions
New Zealand	First NZ$ 100 of interest and dividend income exempt in 1990 (this relief to be abolished from 1991)			

Table 10.10(cont.): Reliefs for specific sources of income, 1990

Country	Dividends	Interest	Pensions and Retirement income	Income of Farmers, Small Traders, Particular Trades or Businesses
Norway	Tax allowance for dividends and interest subject to a ceiling			
Portugal	Distributions from domestic portfolio investment funds are exempt		Tax allowance	Carrying back allowed where the taxpayer receives in one year income generated over the preceding 5 years
Turkey	Dividend derived by resident taxpayers are not taxable.		Public pensions generally exempt from tax	Set tax base for different categories of self-employed persons, based on a percentage of the minimum wage in the industrial sector
United Kingdom	Income from investment in a Personal Equity Plan exempt	Minor reliefs for certain savings bank and other government interest		Farmers allowed to average profits where there is a significant difference between the profits of two consecutive years. Income spreading for authors and artists in certain circumstances

Source: as Table 10.3.

Table 10.11: The tax treatment of certain fringe benefits, 1986

	Employers' contributions to		Medical insurance	Dental insurance	Life insurance premiums	Canteen facilities on employers' premises	Meal vouchers	Leisure facilities
	Public schemes	Private schemes						
Australia	n.a.	O	X[1]	X	X	O	X	O
Austria	O	OC	OC	X	OC	O	O	O
Belgium	O	X[2]	X	X	X	X	OR	X
Canada	O	O	OR	O	OC	OR	OR	OR
Denmark	O	O	X	X	X	X	X	X
Finland	O	O	O	O	OR	O	O	O
France	X	X	X	X	X	O	O	X
Germany	OR	OC	OR	OR	OC	O	OC	O
Greece	O	O	O	O	O	O	O	O
Ireland	O	OC	X[2]	X	X[2]	O	X	X
Italy	O	O	O	O	O	O	O	O
Japan	OC	OC	OC	OC	OR	OC	X[3]	OR
Luxembourg	O	OR	X	X	X	X	X	X
Netherlands	O	O	X	X	X	X	O	O
New Zealand	n.a.	OC	OC	OC	X	O	X	O
Norway	O	OC	X	X	X	O	X	O
Portugal	O	OC	X	n.a.	X	O	OC	X
Spain	O	OC	X[1]	X[1]	X	X	X	X
Sweden	O	O	O	O	OC	X	X	X[4]
Switzerland	O	O	O	O	O	X	X	O
Turkey	O	O	O	O	OC	O	X	O
United Kingdom[5]	O	OC	X[1]	X[1]	X	O	X	X
United States	O	O	O	O	OC	O	X	OC

1. Private schemes only.

2. But employee entitled to tax relief on payment.

3. Rarely encountered in Japan.

4. Except sports facilities.

5. Applies to higher paid whose total fringe benefits is £8 500 or more.

X = taxed. O = exempt. OC = exempt up to ceiling. OR = generally exempt but reservations on conditions. n.a. = benefit does not exist.

Source: This is a simplified version of Table A in *The taxation of fringe benefits* (OECD 1986) – simplified in that it does not reproduce the amount of the ceiling in OC or the reservations and/or conditions under OR.

Table 10.12: The tax treatment of pension and life insurance contributions, 1989

Country	Social security contributions (individual)[1]	Pension contributions		Life insurance premiums		
		Employer	Individual	Employer	Individual	Capital gains
Australia	None	E	TA(C)	T	TC	E
Austria	TA	E[2]	T	E[2]	TA(C)	E
Belgium	TA	T[3]	TA	T	TA(C)	E
Canada	TC	E	TA(C)	E[4]	TA(C)	E
Denmark	TA[5]	E	TA(C)	T	TA(C)	E
Finland	TA	E	TA(C)	E	TA(C)	E
France	TA	T	TA(C)	T	TC(C)	E
Germany	TA(C)	E[6]	TA(C)	T[6]	TA(C)	E
Greece	TA	E	T	E	TA(C)	E
Ireland	TA(C)	E	TA(C)	T[7]	TA(C)	E
Italy	TA	E	TA(C)	E	TA(C)	E
Japan	TA	E[8]	TA(C)	T[9]	TA(C)	T
Luxembourg	TA	E	TA	T	TA(C)	E
Netherlands	T[10]	E	TA	T	TA(C)	E
New Zealand	None	E	TA(C)	T	TA(C)	E
Norway	T	E	TA(C)	T	TC(C)	T
Portugal	T	E	TA(C)	T	TA(C)	E
Spain	TA	E	TA(C)[11]	T	TC(C)[11]	T
Sweden	T	E	TA(C)	E	T	T
Switzerland	TA	E	TA(C)	E	TA(C)	E
Turkey	TA	E	TA	E[12]	TA(C)	E
United Kingdom	T	E	TA(C)	T	T	E
United States	T	E	TA(C)	E[13]	TA(C)	E

1. The tax status of employers' social security contributions is not shown; nearly all countries do not include them in income.

2. If the contribution does not exceed 4 000 AS per annum.

3. But employee entitled to a tax deduction for the same amount.

4. If coverage does not exceed C$ 25 000.

5. Social security contributions are integrated with the income tax; therefore, exemption or deductibility has limited significance.

6. Statutory contributions or equivalent. Contributions to private pension and life insurance schemes are only tax-free up to 312 DM and for the equivalent of compulsory contributions if employee not subject to the compulsory schemes.

7. But employee entitled to tax relief on payment.

8. Assessable benefit if employer pays employee's contributions of more than Y 300 per month.

9. If paid to director.
10. The general social security premiums have been integrated with the income tax as of 1990; employees' social security premiums are still levied separately.
11. Fifteen per cent of pension contributions and life insurance premiums, subject to a ceiling (above the ceiling a tax credit is allowed).
12. If it does not exceed compulsory employees' contributions.
13. Up to $50 000 coverage only.

T = Taxed, not deductible, or included in income. E = Not taxed, exempt, or not included in income. TA = Tax allowance (contribution deductible from gross income). TC = Tax credit (contribution deductible from tax). (C): Subject to ceiling, maximum, or other conditions.

Sources: *Personal income tax systems under changing economic conditions,* (OECD 1986). *The taxation of fringe benefits* (OECD 1988). *Taxation of net wealth, capital transfers and capital gains of individuals* (OECD 1988).

Notes to Table 10.13:

1. Information on assessed rental rates is not available. Presumably, these are the same as for the principal residence.
2. Personal income taxes at the sub-national level which may include imputed income from owner-occupied property are levied in Belgium, Canada, Denmark, Finland, Italy, Japan, Norway, Switzerland and the United States.
3. Rental rates are assessed on various valuation bases, such as the value under the net wealth tax (e.g. Denmark, Spain), the cadastral value (e.g. Belgium, Italy), the capital value (e.g. Sweden, Switzerland), the market value (e.g. Greece, the Netherlands, Portugal) or the assessed value (e.g. Luxembourg, Norway).
4. Generally, the imputed income is wiped out by a lump-sum deduction.
5. Normally an exemption applies on the condition of occupation during at least two years. Gains on the sale of large estates are taxed in full if sold within three years of acquisition; thereafter gains on sale are reduced by 20 per cent for each additional year of ownership.
6. Subject to a ceiling of 800 000 Ptas. per annum. Additionally, an annual tax credit is provided of 15 per cent of the capital invested in the purchase of a principal residence.
7. Subject to repurchase of new residence and/or taxable on excess over repurchase of new residence.
8. Additionally, tax relief for house maintenance and energy insulation expenses.
9. Instead, an eight-year "amortisation allowance" applies with a maximum of 15 000 DM per annum.
10. First Y 30 million is exempt.

TA = Tax allowance (interest deductible from gross income).
TC = Tax credit (interest deductible from tax liability).
N = Interest not deductible.
(L) = Subject to ceiling, maximum or other conditions.
E = Capital gain generally exempt from tax.
T = Capital gain generally subject to tax.
n.a. = not applicable.

Sources: Assessed rental rates: updated from *European Taxation* (1986); deductability of interest: updated from Tables 1.7 and 2.1 of OECD 1986; treatment of capital gains: Tables 3 and 4 of OECD 1988b. Some information may not be complete or up-to-date.

Table 10.13: The tax treatment of income in respect of owner-occupied property, 1989

Country	Principal residence			Secondary residence[1]	
	Assessed rental rate (%)[2]	Deductibility of interest	Treatment of capital gains	Deductibility of interest	Treatment of capital gains
A. Rental value taxed[3]					
Belgium	4[4]	TA(L)	E	TA(L)	E
Denmark	2.5-7.5	TA	E[5]	TA	E
Finland	3	TA(L)	E	TA(L)	T
Greece	4	TA	E	N	E
Italy	...	TA(L)	E	TA(L)	E
Luxembourg	4-6	TA(L)	E	TA(L)	T
Netherlands	1.8	TA	E	TA	E
Norway	2.5	TA	E(L)	TA	E(L)
Portugal	...	TA(L)	E[7]	TA(L)	E
Spain	2	TA(L)[6]	E[7]	TA(L)	T
Sweden	2-8	TA	E(L)[7]	TA	T
Switzerland	varies	TA	T	TA	T
B. Rental value not taxed					
Australia	n.a.	TC(L)	E	N	T
Austria	n.a.	TA(L)	E	N	E
Canada	n.a.	N	E	N	T
France	n.a.	TC[8]	E	N	T
Germany	n.a.	N[9]	E	N	E
Ireland	n.a.	TA(L)	E(L)	N	T
Japan	n.a.	N	E(L)[10]	N	T
New Zealand	n.a.	N	E	N	E
Turkey	n.a.	N	E	N	E
United Kingdom	n.a.	TA(L)	E(L)	N	T
United States	n.a.	TA(L)	E(L)[7]	TA(L)	T

Table 10.14 : Main non-standard tax reliefs (including work-related expenses) received by an APW, 1987-1990[1]

Country	Average amount of each relief typically received by AWP (national currency)		Rate of income tax paid by an average production worker				Calculations refer to following taxpayers[2]
	Single people	Couples	Before taking into account these reliefs		After taking into account these reliefs		
			Single people	Couples	Single people	Couples	
Australia (1988)							
Union dues and expenses incurred in earning income	1 079	1 085					
Gift deductions (TA)	81	81	23.9	19.8	22.1	17.9	All non-business income earners around APW's income level
Belgium (1987)							
Work-related expenses (TA)	133 950						
Life insurance (TA)	4 169						
Work related pension contributions (TA)	786		23.5	15.6	17.2	10.3	
Mortgage invest (TA)	8 176						
Private pension contributions (TA)	4 809						
Canada (1989)							
Registered pension plan (TA)	1 201	884					
Registered retirement savings plan (TA)	226	269					APW type taxpayers
Union and professional dues (TA)	138	149	20.0	10.8	18.2	8.7	
Charitable donations (TC)	16	77					
Other (TA)	79	29					

Table 10.14(cont.): Main non-standard tax reliefs (including work-related expenses) received by an APW, 1987-1990[1]

Denmark (1987)							
Work related expenses (TA)	7 192	7 356					
Interest payments, net of imputed rent (TA)	20 060	32 193	44.0	35.7	35.6	23.9	APW-type wage earners
Contributions to pension schemes (TA)	520	1 152					
Other (TA)	1 880	846					
Greece (1988)							
Interest (TA)	8 500	8 500	5.1	2.7	1.6	–	All income earners around the APW's income level
Medical expenses (TA)	9 400	9 400					
Donations (TA)	1 480	1 480					
Family tax allowances (TA)	141 300	141 300					
Other (TA)	22 320	22 320					
Iceland (1990)							
Interest paid on personal dwellings (TA)	9 050	20 575	18.6	1.6	17.9	–	
Ireland (1987)							
Work-related expenses (TA)	28	}					All income earners in the range of £10 001-£12 500 of total income in manufacturing sector
Life assurance relief (TA)	74	}	27.9	17.9	25.6	16.2	
Medical insurance relief (TA)	41	}					
Interest paid in full (TA)	352	}					
Luxembourg (1989)							
Work expenses (5%) (TA)	52 000	52 000	13.5	–	7.6	–	All income earners
Special allowances (3.5%) (TA)	36 000	48 000					

Table 10.14(cont.): Main non-standard tax reliefs (including work-related expenses) received by an APW, 1987-1990[1]

Exceptions expenses (1.1%) (TA)	28 000	28 000					
Interest on personal dwelling (TA)	30 000	120 000					
Spain (1989)							
Mortgage interest (TA)	33 500	33 500	11.5	6.8	7.1	2.4	16% of all taxpayers around the APW's income level
15% house depreciation							
Switzerland (1989)							
Work-related expenses (TA)	1 000	1 000	10.8	5.8	10.6	5.4	All wage earners around APW's income level
United Kingdom (1989)							
Work-related expenses (TA)	19	19	19.0	15.6	16.6	12.8	All wage earners around APW's income level
Interest house purchase or improvement	1 296	1 296					

1. The reliefs refer to the non-standard tax reliefs received by taxpayers around the APW's income level. The value of each relief is calculated by dividing the total amount of the relief received by APW-type taxpayers by the total number of such taxpayers counting for this purpose both those who received the relief and those who do not. Calculated this way the amounts of all the separate reliefs are then added up to arrive at the total relief received by the APW.

2. Within APW's income range can be taken to mean in most countries within ± 5 per cent of APW's income. With the exception of Denmark, countries were unable to identify taxpayers with the characteristics of an APW.

TA = Tax allowance.

TC = Tax credit.

n.a. = not available.

Source: *The tax/benefit position of production workers 1986-1989* (OECD 1990) with additions from the 1991 edition where there is new or significantly different information.

Table 10.15:
Rate schedules of central government income tax[1], 1975, 1985 and 1992[2]

	Number of Brackets			Top rates			First positive rates		
				To nearest percentage point					
	1975	1985	1992	1975	1985	1992	1975	1985	1992
Australia[3]	6	5	7	65	60	48	20	30	22
Austria	11	10	5	62	62	50	23	21	10
Belgium[3]	20	22	7	60	72	55	17	24	25
Canada	13	10	3	47	34	29	9	6	17
Denmark[1]	3	3	3	40	40	40	14	14	22
Finland[1]	14	11	6	51	51	49	10	6	7
France[3]	12	13	12	60	65	57	5	5	5
Germany[4]	–	–	–	56	56	53	22	22	19
Greece[3]	18	18	9	63	63	50	3	11	18
Iceland[5]	n.a.	3	1	n.a.	38	33	n.a.	n.a.	33
Ireland[6]	6	3	3	77	60	52	26	35	29
Italy	32	9	7	72	50	50	10	18	10
Japan[1]	19	15	5	75	70	50	10	10	10
Luxembourg[3]	19	21	24	57	66	56	18	12	10
Netherlands	10	9	3	71	72	60	20	16	13
New Zealand	22	5	2	57	57	33	19	20	24
Norway[1,3]	10	8	2	48	40	14	6	3	8
Spain[3]	16	34	16	62	66	53	15	16	20
Sweden[1,3,6]	10	15	1	56	54	20	7	3	20
Switzerland[3]	8	6	14	13	13	13	1	1	1
Turkey	11	6	6	68	50	50	10	25	25
United Kingdom[7]	10	6	2	83	60	40	35	30	27
United States[1]	25	14	2	70	50	28	14	11	15

1. Countries with additional income taxes at subordinate levels of government typical rates for 1992 being *flat:* Belgium 7, Canada 17, Denmark 30, Finland 16, Iceland 7, Norway 25, Sweden 31; *progressive*: Japan 5 to 16, Switzerland 5 to 31, United States 2 to 4.
2. Comparison not possible for Portugal where system is completely changed.
3. Countries with a zero rate bracket (excluded from number of brackets). No zero rate in Luxembourg (1975) or Spain (1975 and 1985).
4. Germany: Number of brackets excluded because the tax schedule is based on a formula and does not have brackets.
5. In 1988, the personal income tax system was completely revised and withholding at source was introduced. Therefore the comparison of rates is not relevant for 1986 and 1992 and needs to be qualified.
6. Top rate reduced to 48 and bottom rate to 27 with no other rates in 1992 budget.
7. A 20 rate for first £2 000 of taxable income.
n.a. = not available, – = not applicable.
Various sources.

Table 10.16: Statutory and effective average tax rates at the level of an average production worker (APW) earnings: married couple with two children, 1989[1]

Country	APW's earning level		Schedule rate[2]			Average rate	
	Local currency	Purchasing power parities (US$)	Federal	State + local[3]	Total	Excluding Non-standard reliefs	Including Non-standard reliefs
Australia	27 212	18 386	39	–	39	17.9	n.a
Austria	223 288	13 699	32	–	32	3.0	n.a
Belgium	713 030	16 132	40	7.0[4]	43	10.8	n.a
Canada	27 198	21 586	17	55.0[4]	27	10.8	8.7
Denmark	192 700	18 709	22	30	52	35.6	n.a.
Finland	95 251	14 367	26	16	42	23.7	n.a
France	96 270	12 992	5	–	5	–	–
Germany	43 306	18 120	n.a	–	n.a	9.2	n.a
Greece	1 337 062	11 050	28	–	28	3.7	n.a
Ireland	11 100	14 939	32	–	32	17.0	n.a
Italy	22 280 000	15 054	26	–	26	14.8	n.a
Japan	3 467 800	17 083	10	5	15	1.9	n.a
Luxembourg	787 000	19 010	12	–	12	–	–
Netherlands	41 700	18 052	32	–	32	9.1	n.a
New Zealand	28 524	16 115	24	–	24	21.7	n.a
Norway	167 232	19 674	19	27	46	18.6	n.a
Portugal	712 280	7 217	16	–	16	2.0	n.a
Spain	1 513 095	13 510	26	–	26	6.8	2.4
Sweden	140 440	15 216	17	31	48	35.7	n.a
Switzerland	48 400	20 083	2	7	9	5.8	5.4
Turkey	4 247 774	9 048	30	–	30	22.1	n.a
United Kingdom	11 583	18 682	25	–	25	15.6	12.8
United States	22 208	22 208	15	7.6[5]	21	11.5	n.a

1. Turkey refers to 1988.
2. Rate which applies at the level of production worker earnings. No account is taken of non-standard reliefs.
3. Average state/local personal tax rate.
4 Percentage of central government income tax.
5. Detroit, Michigan.
n.a. = not available.
– = not applicable.
Source: *The tax/benefit position of production workers* (OECD 1990).

Table 10.17: Indexation of rate schedules and/or reliefs, 1978-1990[1]

Country	Year of legislation	Applies to rate schedules	Applies to main reliefs	Applies to local income taxes	Other comments and subsequent developments
Australia	1976	Yes	Yes	n.a	Not applied in 1979 Abandoned in 1982
Belgium	1987	Yes[2]	Yes[2]	n.a	
Canada	1974	Yes	Yes	Yes	Modified in 1983 and 1986. Now equals consumer price index minus 3 per cent
Denmark[4]	1975	Yes	Yes	Yes[3]	Abandoned in 1983
France	1969	Yes	No	n.a	
Greece	1989	Yes	Yes	n.a	As from 1990
Iceland	1965	No	Yes	Yes	
Italy	1989	Yes	Yes	n.a	As from 1990
Luxembourg	1968	Yes	No	n.a	
Netherlands	1971	Yes	Yes	n.a	Often only 80 per cent indexation
Sweden	1979	Yes	No	No	Abandoned in 1983. Reintroduced 1990
Switzerland	1985	Yes	Yes	In nearly all cantons	
United Kingdom	1978	Yes[2]	Yes[2]	n.a	Occasionally not applied
United States	1985	Yes	Yes	In some states	

1. During this period there was no formal indexation in Austria, Finland (except for pension income), Germany, Ireland, Japan, New Zealand, Norway, Portugal, Spain and Turkey.

2. For Belgium: rate schedules in 1987 and reliefs in 1990; for United Kingdom: rate schedules in 1981 and reliefs in 1978.

3. Reliefs only, since rates are flat.

4. Uniquely uses indexation to increase progressivity by usually indexing low income brackets, but not high income brackets.

n.a. = not applicable.

Source: *Personal income tax reforms in OECD countries*, S. Cnossen and K. Messere, North Holland, 1990.

Table 10.18: Income tax and social security contributions paid in April 1985 and 1990[1] by an APW

Country[2]	Income Tax Plus S.S. Contributions		Income Tax Payments at all levels of government		Social Security Contributions	
	1990	**1985**	**1990**	**1985**	**1990**	**1985**
Denmark	47	46	44	40	3	6
Netherlands	40	38	11	11	26	27
Sweden	35	36	35	36	0	0
Germany	35	35	17	18	29	17
Belgium	35	36	23	24	18	12
Finland	33	34	30	31	3	4
Norway	33	33	25	23	8	10
Ireland	33	35	25	27	8	9
Turkey[3]	31	31	22	23	9	9
United Kingdom	27	31	19	22	8	9
Italy	27	28	18	19	9	9
United States	26	30	18	23	8	7
Luxembourg	26	29	14	17	12	12
France	25	23	7	7	18	15
Canada	24	23	20	19	4	4
Austria	24	26	8	10	16	16
Australia	23	23	22	22	1	1
New Zealand	23	27	23	27	0	0
Switzerland	21	21	11	11	10	10
Greece	19	16	6	3	13	13
Portugal	17	17	6	5	11	12
Spain	17	19	11	12	6	6
Japan	15	16	8	9	7	7

1. Paid by an average production worker as percentage of gross earnings (unmarried earner) to nearest percentage point. These figures do not take account of expense-related reliefs, which even at this income level vary considerably from country to country as Tables 10.12 and 10.14 show. Most countries are unable to provide estimates of how much non-standard reliefs typically reduce the income tax bill of the APW, but they do so by around 8 percentage points in Denmark, 6 percentage points in Belgium and Luxembourg, 4 percentage points in Greece and Spain, 3 percentage points in UK, 2 percentage points in Finland and Ireland, and less than 2 percentage points in Australia, Canada and Iceland.

2. Ranking in order of highest combined percentage in 1989.

3. 1989 not 1990.

Source: *The tax benefit position of production workers* (OECD 1986 and 1991).

Chapter 11
Taxes on the net wealth, capital transfers and capital gains of individuals

a) Short- and long-term gains
b) The relative tax treatment of income and capital gains
c) Averaging
d) Treatment of gains at death and on gifts
e) Deemed realisations other than at death or on gifts
f) Exemptions and reliefs

A. Summary

1. Scope of chapter

Net wealth taxes are levied annually on certain assets minus debts in connection with such assets. Capital transfer taxes are taxes levied on the transfer of assets, whether at the time of death or earlier, and are more popularly known as death and gift taxes. Capital gains taxes are levied on some measure of the difference between the purchase and selling price of certain assets, most importantly equities, land and buildings.

This chapter deals only with such of those taxes that are levied on the capital or capital gains of individuals or households. The tax treatment of partnerships and other unincorporated enterprises and of trusts is omitted for reasons of space, though a brief reference is made in Chapter 12 to net wealth taxes and capital gains imposed on incorporated enterprises. Also omitted are the miscellaneous collection of taxes, often in the form of stamp duties, on financial and capital transactions. These are levied on both business and individuals, most importantly in connection with the transfer of equities or immovable property.

There are a number of reasons for treating net wealth taxes, capital transfer taxes and capital gains taxes together, even though conceptually capital gains taxes are more appropriately regarded as a part of the income tax system, being levied on the application of assets over a period of time rather than on a stock of assets at a point in time.

First, the objectives of taxing capital gains are largely similar to those of levying capital taxes – to promote horizontal equity and reduce inequalities of wealth and to protect or reinforce income tax yields. Second, there are a number of common choices under these three taxes, where in each case it has to be decided what should be the value of the assets or gains on which tax should be payable, what rate or rates should be applied to this value, which kinds of assets or capital gains should be included and which excluded from the tax base, how assets or gains should be valued and what allowance, if any, should be made for inflation. Third, these three taxes are often seen as complementary or alternatives to each other. For example, the Canadian government took the view in the seventies that with its new capital gains tax, including a clause imposing such a tax on gifts and bequests, there was no need for a separate federal capital transfer tax; and the 1975 Asprey Tax Reform Commission in Australia found a net wealth tax to be unnecessary if there were an effective estates and gifts tax plus a capital gains tax in force. In addition, as

Table 11.1 shows net wealth and capital transfer taxes were often introduced at roughly the same time – e.g. in the Nordic countries, Germany and Japan.

As observed later in more detail trends with respect to these three kinds of tax are very different. In nearly all countries net wealth taxes are old taxes and have hardly changed. Death and gift taxes are also generally old taxes formerly prevalent in all OECD countries but since the seventies no longer so in Australia and Canada. In contrast, capital gains taxes have been introduced quite recently in most countries and they have continued to expand in many countries in recent years as a part of the broadening of the income tax base.

A second sub-section of this summary comments on the contribution of net wealth and capital transfer taxes to government revenues (as summarised in Table 11.1), information being unavailable for capital gains tax revenues.

A last sub-section provides at the most general level the arguments for and against having these taxes and Table 11.2 provides an overall summary of capital and capital gains taxes in OECD countries. Section B, C and D cover in more detail the main policy issues and country choices pertaining respectively to net wealth taxes, capital transfer taxes and capital gains taxes. Important issues *not* discussed because they are more of a technical than a policy nature, are valuation questions, treatment of debts and losses, treatment of non-residents and the relationship between each of these taxes and other taxes. These and other matters are covered in the OECD 1979 and 1988 publications on these three taxes. These two books are the source of nearly all the descriptive material in this chapter and country practices usually refer to the situation in 1986.

2. The contribution of capital taxes on individuals to government revenues

Table 11.1 provides details of capital tax receipts as a percentage of total tax receipts for the years 1965, 1975, 1982 and 1989. As already remarked in Part I, such ratios give as much information about development in other sources of tax revenue as about the receipts of the taxes under consideration, but the numbers already very small would become exceedingly so, if GDP were selected as the denominator. The table also provides some quite interesting information about countries' relative reliance on capital taxes on individuals during the last twenty-five years.

First, nowadays, outside Switzerland, receipts from these taxes invariably represent less than 2 per cent of total tax receipts and in the great majority of countries less than 1 per cent.

Second, over the period 1965 to 1989, the relative importance of capital taxes has declined in all OECD countries, except France, Greece, Iceland and Japan. On the other hand, between 1982 and 1989, the decline in the share of these taxes has been halted and there have been significant increases in this share in Iceland, Japan, Norway and Sweden. Leaving aside the special case of Switzerland, in 1982 receipts from capital taxes reached 1 per cent of total tax receipts only in Greece, Iceland and the United States (in each case 1.1 per cent) whereas in 1989, there was Japan at 1.6, Iceland at 1.5, Norway at 1.3, France and Greece at 1.1 and the Netherlands at 1.0 (see Table 11.1).

Table 11.1: Receipts from capital taxes on individuals as a percentage of total tax revenues

Country	4120 Net wealth taxes on individuals				4300 Capital transfer taxes[1]				4210 + 4300 Total capital taxes on individuals[2]			
	1965	1975	1982	1989	1965	1975	1982	1989	1965	1975	1982	1989
Australia	–	–	–	–	2.7	1.5	0.1	–	2.7 (2)	1.5 (3)	0.1 (23)	– (23)
Austria	0.6	0.5	0.4	0.4	0.3	0.2	0.2	0.2	0.9 (18)	0.7 (15)	0.6 (11)	0.6 (11)
Belgium	–	–	–	–	1.2	0.7	0.7	0.6	1.2 (14)	0.7 (15)	0.7 (9)	0.6 (11)
Canada	–	–	–	–	1.5	0.3	–	–	1.5 (11)	0.3 (22)	– (24)	– (23)
Denmark	1.4	0.5	0.4	0.3	0.7	0.4	0.4	0.5	2.1 (6)	0.9 (9)	0.8 (8)	0.8 (8)
Finland	0.9	0.5	0.2	0.1	0.2	0.2	0.2	0.4	1.1 (16)	0.7 (15)	0.4 (17)	0.5 (15)
France	–	–	0.3	0.2	0.6	0.7	0.6	0.9	0.6 (22)	0.7 (15)	0.9 (5)	1.1 (5)
Germany	1.3	0.6	0.3	0.3	0.2	0.1	0.2	0.2	1.5 (11)	0.7 (15)	0.5 (14)	0.5 (15)
Greece	–	–	–	–	0.9	1.0	1.1	1.1	0.9 (18)	1.0 (7)	1.1 (2)	1.1 (5)
Iceland	–	0.4	0.9	1.3	0.1	0.1	0.2	0.2	0.1 (24)	0.5 (20)	1.1 (2)	1.5 (3)
Ireland	–	–	–	–	1.9	1.1	0.3	0.3	1.9 (8)	1.1 (5)	0.3 (18)	0.3 (18)
Italy	–	–	–	–	0.9	0.2	0.2	0.2	0.9 (18)	0.2 (23)	0.2 (21)	0.2 (21)
Japan	–	–	–	–	0.7	1.0	0.9	1.6	0.7 (21)	1.0 (7)	0.9 (5)	1.6 (2)
Luxembourg	0.7	0.2	0.2	0.3	0.5	0.3	0.4	0.2	1.2 (14)	0.5 (20)	0.8 (11)	0.5 (15)
Netherlands	0.8	0.5	0.5	0.5	1.1	0.4	0.4	0.5	1.9 (8)	0.9 (9)	0.9 (5)	1.0 (7)
New Zealand	–	–	–	–	2.3	1.6	0.3	0.3	2.3 (5)	1.6 (2)	0.3 (18)	0.3 (18)
Norway	1.4	0.9	0.6	1.1	0.3	0.2	0.1	0.2	1.7 (10)	1.1 (5)	0.7 (9)	1.3 (4)
Portugal	–	–	–	–	2.5	0.9	0.3	0.3	2.5 (4)	0.9 (19)	0.3 (18)	0.3 (18)
Spain	–	–	0.3	0.2	1.1	0.8	0.3	0.4	1.1 (16)	0.8 (12)	0.6 (11)	0.6 (11)
Sweden	0.9	0.5	0.3	0.6	0.4	0.3	0.2	0.2	1.3 (13)	0.8 (12)	0.5 (14)	0.8 (8)
Switzerland	3.3	2.8	2.5	2.3	1.1	0.7	0.8	0.8	4.4 (1)	3.5 (1)	3.3 (1)	3.1 (1)
Turkey	–	–	–	–	0.2	0.3	0.2	0.1	0.2 (23)	0.3 (24)	0.2 (21)	0.1 (22)
United Kingdom	–	–	–	–	2.6	0.8	0.5	0.6	2.6 (3)	0.8 (14)	0.5 (14)	0.6 (11)
United States	–	–	–	–	2.0	1.4	1.1	0.8	2.0 (7)	1.4 (4)	1.1 (2)	0.8 (8)

1. Where taxes on gifts can be identified separately they represent 0.1 or 0.2 per cent of total taxes except Greece 1982 and 1989 where they represent 0.3 per cent.

2. Numbers in brackets indicate ranking order.

Source: OECD RS 1991 and earlier editions.

Table 11.2: Forms of capital and capital gains taxation in OECD countries

	Net wealth tax		**Transfer tax on gifts at death**		**Capital gains taxation**	
	First introduced	**1 Jan. 1990**	**First introduced**	**1 Jan. 1990**	**First introduced**	**1 Jan. 1990**
Australia	–	–	1914	–	1986	I
Austria	1923	W	1850	H	–	B
Belgium	–	–	1936	H	–	B
Canada	–	–	n.a.	–	1972	I
Denmark	1903	W	1903	H	1958	C
Finland	1920	W*	1920	H	1920	I
France	1982[1]	W*	1978	H	1976	I
Germany	1923	W	1923	H	–	B
Greece	–	–	1919	H	–	B
Iceland	n.a.	W*	n.a.	H	n.a.	I
Ireland	1975	–	1894	HA[2]	1975	C
Italy	–	–	n.a.	EH	–	B
Japan	1951	–	1950	H	1946	I
Luxembourg	1944	W	1817	H	1979	I
Netherlands	1892	W	1917	H	–	B
New Zealand	–	–	1885	E	–	–
Norway	1918	W*	1918	H	1911	I
Portugal	–	–	1958	H	1965	C
Spain	1978	W*	n.a.	H	1978	I
Sweden	1910	W*	1914	H	1928	I
Switzerland [3]	various	W*	various	HE	various	various
Turkey	–	–	1959	H	–	B
United Kingdom	–	–	1894	E	1965	C
United States	–	–	1916	E	1913	I

1. Abolished in 1987. Reintroduced 1989.
2. Accessions tax: aggregate gifts and legacies from any donor to determine the rate of tax.
3. All taxes are cantonal with considerable variation between the cantons.

A = Accession tax.

B = Taxation of capital gains for businesses (whether or not incorporated) but no comprehensive or capital gains on individuals.

C = Capital gains tax (separate).

E = Estate-type transfer tax.

H = Inheritance-type transfer tax.

I = Comprehensive taxation of capital gains under income tax.

W = Single-rate net wealth tax. W* = Multi-rate net wealth tax.

– = No tax.

n.a. = Not available.

Various sources.

Third, there have been significant shifts in the ranking order of countries' shares of revenue from these taxes over the period as a whole. Thus, whilst Switzerland remains always by a long way at the top of the ranking order, a comparison of 1965 and 1989 shows, for example that Australia moves down from 2nd to 24th place, the United Kingdom from 3rd to 11th, and New Zealand from 4th to 18th, whereas Japan has moved up from 21st to 2nd, Iceland from 24th to 3rd and France from 22nd to 5th.

Fourth, not unexpectedly most of the countries at the top of the ranking order have both net wealth taxes and capital transfer taxes, Japan in 1989 being a notable exception, but the relative importance of these two sources of revenue varies greatly from country to country. In 1989 the net wealth tax was much the more important in Austria, Iceland, Norway, Sweden and Switzerland, the two taxes were of about the same importance in Germany, Luxembourg and the Netherlands, and capital transfer taxes were much the more important in Denmark, France and Spain. Intuitively, one would expect an annual net wealth tax to raise more revenue than a death tax which, by definition, is paid once in a lifetime, so it is for the last category of countries that the counter-intuitive results require explanation. In Denmark, they appear to be due to a large reduction in rates (compare 1989 with earlier years). It is perhaps more surprising that the recently enacted net wealth taxes in France and Spain yield so little revenue in view of their progressive rate structure and wide base: perhaps it is partly a matter of high thresholds and partly a question of not yet having provided an efficient collection mechanism.

Capital gains tax revenues are excluded from Table 11.1 for the reason already mentioned that very few countries are able to separate revenue receipts from capital gains and those from the personal income tax (except for gains from betting and gambling which are dealt with briefly in Chapter 13D4). It would appear from those that can, that such receipts are likely to be very slight, but as remarked earlier, the main revenue function of capital gains taxes is to protect income tax yields, since if capital gains are exempted or treated more favourably than income, the tax avoidance industry will transform income into capital gains.

3. General arguments for and against these taxes

It is not their slight revenue raising capacity but rather social considerations which provide the main rationale for capital and capital gains taxes, even if such social considerations cannot be divorced from the economic consequences of introducing or changing such taxes.

a) Social arguments

The argument about horizontal equity is that, if taxpayers whose taxable capacity derives mainly or solely from income are to be given the same tax treatment as those who also hold wealth in one form or another, capital as well as income must be taxed; for over and above any income derived from it, wealth gives its possessor independence, security and the opportunity to purchase advantageously or to spend on consumption goods.

Taxes on capital can, however, at best only approximate to the additional taxable capacity that wealth confers. Different types of capital tax make this approximation in different ways. An annual net wealth tax, seen as a regular supplement to income tax, can be expected to take account on a continuing basis of the advantages conferred by wealth. Capital transfer taxes provide an irregular supplement to the income tax by taxing wealth once (or more for gifts) in a generation. As for capital gains taxes, an appreciation in the value of assets is very much akin to income, and equal treatment of taxpayers requires that it be taken into account: the argument for taxing capital gains is strengthened if some taxpayers have the possibility of converting ordinary income into capital gains (by allowing profits to accumulate, for example).

In practice, for a number of reasons the capital taxes found in the OECD area achieve horizontal equity only imperfectly. Thus, under an annual wealth tax, for example, it is common for household and personal effects to be wholly or partially exempt; so also are works of art, life insurance policies, annuities, goodwill, patents and copyrights. Moreover, no country taxes the accumulated value of pension rights or the capitalised value of future earning power. Such exclusions can also affect vertical equity and create investment distortions.

Some proponents of capital taxation desire, on grounds of vertical equity, to see the wealthy meet a larger share of the expenses of governments; others believe that governments should pursue a deliberate policy to reduce inequalities in the distribution of wealth. In practice – as evidenced by the very low yields of these taxes – they probably do not play much of a role in redistributing wealth, though net wealth taxes do have the effect of making the very wealthy less wealthy than they would otherwise be, and capital transfer taxes have the same effect on the heirs of the very wealthy.

A social argument of a sort, applying to death taxes and still much employed in the market place, was summarised by Pliny the Younger in ancient Roman times when he said that the death tax is an "unnatural" tax augmenting the grief and sorrow of the bereaved. However, the argument from double grief of two different kinds has about as much validity as arguments from "economic double taxation" when the taxes in question are of different kinds.

b) Economic arguments

Various economic arguments have been advanced for introducing or increasing capital and capital gains taxes. For example, because the tax base is related only to past accumulations, both the net wealth and the death tax may have less of a disincentive effect on work than taxing current income. Moreover, an annual net wealth tax, particularly if it is introduced as a partial substitute for income tax, may be expected to encourage transfers from assets which yield nothing, such as jewellery, to investments offering high yields. High marginal rates of income tax may, for example, encourage a wealthy person to buy say a very expensive car, which yields a tax-free income of satisfaction rather than to invest in a taxable income-yielding asset. A wealth tax might counteract that tendency. It is sometimes argued that there is no guarantee that the heir of a business or farm is competent to carry it on and that, after the death of its creator, heavy capital transfer taxes may fulfil a useful economic function in forcing such enterprises onto the market where the enterprise may be bought by the most competent potential manager. A capital gains tax can also be justified on the grounds that investment patterns are less likely to be distorted by the diversion of savings into assets which offer the prospect of untaxed capital gains but yield little or no income.

On the other hand, capital and capital gains taxes may adversely affect savings, as well as work undertaken with an eye to saving, because accumulated savings – unless invested in assets which are exempt – are taxed. A heavy wealth tax imposed on top of an already heavy income tax might not only discourage saving but stimulate dis-saving – that is, consumption out of capital. In addition, the argument that an annual net wealth tax encourages more productive use of capital ignores the objection that, in the real world, capital is not perfectly mobile, and that high yield and efficiency are not invariably synonymous. Capital transfer taxes may also discourage savings to leave the maximum possible to one's heirs, if the heirs have to share this amount with the State. (There is rationally a conflict between the income and substitution effect of death taxes, but here one is talking of the irrational consequences of resentment that the State should benefit from one's death.) Finally, capital gains taxes may have the effect of locking in capital to avoid tax, since the tax usually applies only on realisations.

I would like to acknowledge my debt to Professors C.T. Sandford and J.R.M. Willis with whom I discussed the topics covered in this chapter at great length during the late seventies.

B. Net wealth taxes

1. To have or not to have a net wealth tax

The debate on whether or not to have a net wealth tax has focused primarily on equity and administrative issues, though economic efficiency arguments for and against have been invoked. Its revenue raising potential being so low provides an argument against its introduction, but the fact that it does raise *some* revenue is an argument against its abolition in those countries which have it.

A motive for some of the earliest net wealth taxes was the administrative convenience of taxing something which, unlike income, was visible. Especially when the bulk of wealth consisted of immovable property, problems of non-disclosure were minimised by a net wealth tax. With the greater sophistication of modern tax administrations, and the need for high standards of equity as tax burdens have risen, this simple administrative advantage has lost its force – indeed, many of the countries without a net wealth tax are deterred from introducing it by its anticipated administrative complications and costs. On the other hand, there remains a particular administrative advantage of having a net wealth tax, mentioned by a number of countries: in the course of administering a net wealth tax information collected on asset holding can be used to cross-check with income tax returns to help reveal inconsistencies and anomalies and to detect (and discourage) tax evasion.

The object of reducing inequality in the distribution of wealth was not given much prominence in countries' responses to the questionnaire which provided the input for the 1979 and 1988 OECD reports referred to above. But it figures rather more in the arguments of those countries which have introduced a wealth tax in recent years or have seriously contemplated so doing. To reduce excessive inequalities of wealth was one of several objectives given by France for introducing its net wealth tax. Spain indicated an objective of increasing the progressivity of the tax system. In Finland the equality aspects of a net wealth tax have figured in recent discussions. In the United Kingdom the reduction in inequality of wealth was presented as a major objective of wealth tax proposals considered in 1974-1975 but never enacted.

In most countries which have never had a net wealth tax there appears to have been little recent discussion of the possibility. In Australia the Asprey Committee (Taxation Review Committee – appointed 1972, reported 1975) considered the possibility of a net wealth tax but rejected it, primarily on grounds of administrative difficulty, preferring to recommend the improvement of the estate and gift tax and the introduction of a tax on capital gains. More recently the Australian government's draft White Paper on *Reform of the Australian Tax System* (June 1985) reviewed the arguments both for net wealth taxes and for capital transfer taxes, but concluded that: "The Government is not attracted to introducing any form of wealth tax." In Japan the *Report on the Overall Review of the Tax System* by the Tax Commission (October 1986) proposed that a net wealth tax be given further examination in the medium and long term. In New Zealand the idea has been raised from time to time both by economic analysts and by politicians, but it has not been the subject of widespread debate. In the United Kingdom in the mid-seventies the Labour government gave serious consideration to introducing a net wealth tax both to improve horizontal equity and to reduce inequality in the distribution of wealth. That government published a discussion paper and a Parliamentary Committee considered the issue. The matter was shelved during the life of the Parliament. The Conservative government which came to power in 1979 was opposed to a net wealth tax. In Belgium the possibility of a net wealth tax has been frequently raised in Parliament, but the Belgian government has shown no inclination to introduce it for fear of inducing a movement of capital out of the country. In Belgium, as in some other countries the idea of a tax on wealth generates opposition that is partly psychological. A tax on wealth is associated with confiscation, sometimes because of a confusion between the tax base, wealth, and the source of payment, which may be income. Moreover, a wealth tax is objected to because it may lead to inquisitorial activities by the tax authorities, seeking information on bank accounts and asset holdings of all kinds.

In practice, as already noted in Table 11.2 as at January 1990, half the OECD countries impose net wealth taxes and the other half do not. In ten of the twelve countries which have them, revenues accrue exclusively to central/federal governments, in Switzerland exclusively to the cantons, and in Norway revenues are shared between central and local government. Only two countries have recently introduced such taxes (Spain in 1978 and France in 1982), though a net wealth tax was introduced in 1975 in Ireland and abolished in 1978 and introduced in Japan in 1951 and abolished in 1953, whilst the French tax was abolished in 1987 and re-introduced with variations in 1989. In the other ten countries with such taxes, they were introduced towards the end of the nineteenth century or the first half of this century. Apart from the cases of France, Ireland and Japan, there has been no example of an OECD country with a net wealth tax subsequently abolishing it.

Also, as far as is known, the introduction of a net wealth tax is not currently contemplated in any OECD country, and its abolition is only contemplated in Sweden where in 1992 the two higher rates were abolished. It seems probable that if a net wealth tax were to be introduced or abolished in the future it would be in order to fulfil some election promise by an incoming government.

2. Main policy choices under net wealth taxes

a) *Flat versus progressive rates*

As with the personal income tax progressive rates refer to the imposition of higher rates on larger amounts of wealth. Here there is a typical conflict of goals in that administrative simplicity points to flat rates and vertical equity to progressive rates. Political considerations are likely to play a part, which is probably why the only two countries recently to have adopted a wealth tax – France and Spain – have chosen the progressive option. The OECD countries are about equally divided (see Table 11.2) between those with flat and those with progressive rates and there have been no changes from one to the other, except that Denmark in 1978 and Sweden in 1992 moved from progressive to flat rates.

b) *Rate structure and thresholds*

Table 11.3 provides information as at 1976, 1986 and 1991 of thresholds and rates of net wealth taxes. It shows considerable variation between countries regarding both thresholds and rates, extreme thresholds' differences representing around US$ 9,000 in Luxembourg to US$ 520,000 in France. Whilst information is not systematically available for later years it can be said that at January 1991 there has been little change in rates in most countries. The main changes are that Denmark's 2.2 per cent flat rate has been reduced to 1.0 per cent and that the top rate in France (it is recalled under different legislation: see penultimate paragraph of section B1 above) is 1.5 per cent instead of 2 per cent. 1991 thresholds appear to have been increased roughly in line with inflation in a number of countries (Denmark, the Netherlands), but information on this is incomplete: at the one extreme, between 1986 and 1991, the low thresholds of Austria and Luxembourg have remained unchanged, and at the other, the very high thresholds in France and Sweden have just about doubled in nominal terms (4 260 000 Frs. instead of 2 400 000 Frs. in 1986 and 800 000 Skr. instead of 400 000 Skr.).

Table 11.3 shows also that the combined income and net wealth tax is limited to 70 to 80 per cent of income in Denmark, Finland, the Netherlands, Norway, Spain and Sweden, but there is no such ceiling in Austria, France, Germany and Luxembourg. There are also ceilings in some, but not other, Swiss cantons. It should be mentioned that in the countries without ceilings top income tax rates are relatively low and combined income tax and net wealth tax liability is in any event unlikely to exceed 70 per cent of taxable income.

Two countries with net wealth taxes are excluded from Table 11.3. The reason for excluding Iceland is that 1986 details were not available. Switzerland is omitted because these are cantonal taxes and rates vary considerably between cantons as indicated by the following details for January 1991, in respect of a childless couple: Basle 0.4 per cent; Berne 0.377 per cent; Geneva 0.387 per cent; Lausanne 0.612 per cent; Zurich 0.147 per cent.

For reasons of space, Table 11.3 is much simplified as regards thresholds, ceilings, etc., but leaving aside the newcomers to the net wealth scene (France and Spain) it does point to a difference between some countries where there has been virtually no change in rates and thresholds for the last fifteen years (Austria, Luxembourg and Germany) and others where there has been much change (the Netherlands and the Nordic countries).

c) *Relevance of family status*

There is no difference in the allowance given to single persons, to childless couples and to parents in Denmark, France and Sweden. In Austria, Finland, Germany, Luxembourg, the Netherlands and Spain, parents receive a larger allowance than childless couples who receive a larger allowance than single persons. In Norway and Switzerland (Zurich) marriage but not parenthood increases the allowance. In all OECD countries the wealth of husband and wife is aggregated as is that of dependent children, except in Denmark and the Netherlands.

d) *Scope of tax base*

Table 11.4 gives some country details as to what in April 1986 was excluded and included in the tax base. The tax base seems to be somewhat wider in the two countries (France and Spain) recently introducing net wealth taxes than in the other ten having such a tax for many years, and of the latter ten somewhat wider in Switzerland (Zurich) than elsewhere.

Table 11.3: Rates and thresholds of net wealth taxes[1] 1976, 1986, 1991

	Rates: countries with flat rates (%)				Ceiling	
	1 July 1976	**Between 1976 and 1986**	**April 1980**	**January 1991**	**1976**	**1986**
Austria	0.75%	1 from 1.1.77	1.0	1.0	none	none
Denmark	multi-rate	0.5 as from 1.1.78	2.2	1.0	–	78
Germany	0.7%	abolished as from 6.4.78	0.5	0.5	none	none
Ireland	1%		–	–	80	–
Luxembourg	0.5%		0.5	0.5	none	none
Netherlands	0.8%		0.8	0.8	80	80

	Rates: countries with graduated rates (%)					
Denmark	0.9 and 1.1		single rate	single rate	70	–
Finland	0.7, 1.9 and 2.0	in 1978: 1.0, 1.4, 2.4 and 2.6	1.5 and 1.7	?	80	80
France	not yet in force		0.5, 1.0, 1.5 and 2.0	0.5, 0.7, 0.9, 1.2 and 1.5	–	none
Norway	0.4, 0.8, 1.2 and 1.6		0.2, 0.6, 0.9 and 1.3	?	80	80
Spain	not yet in force		0.2, 0.3, 0.45, 0.65, 0.85, 1.1, 1.35, 1.7 and 2.0	As 1986	–	70
Sweden	1.0, 1.5, 2.0 and 2.5		1.5, 2.0, 2.5 and 3.0	1.5, 2.5 and 3.0	80	75

	Thresholds		
	1 January 1976	**Between 1976 and 86**	**January 1991**
Austria	100 000 AS for each member of family. Raised to 150 000 AS on 1.1.77	As 1977	As 1977
Denmark	450 000 DKr. , irrespective of family circumstances	1 253 500 DKr.	1 452 700 DKr.
Finland	50 000 Fmk. single, 58 000 Fmk. married plus 3 000 Fmk. per child	800 000 Fmk. single 850 000 Fmk. married 10 000 Fmk. per child	?
France	not yet in force	3 600 000 Frs.	4 260 000 Frs.
Germany	70 000 DM for each member of family	As 1976	?
Ireland	£IR 70 000 plus £IR 30 000 for marriage and £IR 2 500 for each child	n.a.	n.a.
Luxembourg	100 000 Lfrs. for each member of family	As 1976	As 1976
Netherlands	59 000 Dfl. plus 15 000 Dfl. for each child	single 88 000 Dfl. married 112 200 Dfl. child 7 000 Dfl.	single 92 000 Dfl. married 117 000Dfl. child 7 000 Dfl.
Norway	75 000 NKr. single, 100 000 NKr. married	single 120 000 NKr. married 150 000 NKr.	? ?
Spain	not yet in force	6 000 000 Ptas. married 9 000 000 Ptas. children 750 000 Ptas.	
Sweden	290 000 Skr. irrespective of family circumstances	400 000 Skr.	800 000 Skr.

1. Excluded are Switzerland (many different cantonal rates) and Iceland (early details not available) – see text.

n.a. = not applicable.

? = not known.

Various sources.

Table 11.4: The net wealth tax base, April 1986

	Household and personal effects				Saving instruments				Other main assets			
	Jewellery	**Cars**	**Boats**	**Others**	**Small savings**	**Pension rights and annuities**	**Other commodities**	**Insurance policies**	**Works of art**	**Owner occupied houses**	**Patents**	**Goodwill**
Austria	T*	T	T	E	T*	E	T	T*	T*	T*	T	T
Denmark	E	T	T	E	TG	E	EG	E	E	T	ES1	E
Finland	T*	T	T	E	E	E	TG	E	T*	T*	ES1	ES
France	T	T	T	T	T	E	TG	T	E	T	ES1	T
Germany	T*	E	T*	E	T*	E	TG	T*	T*	T	ES1	E
Luxembourg	E	E	T*	E	T*	EG	EG	E	T*	T	ES1	EG
Netherlands	T*	T	T	E	T	EG	EG	EG	E	T	T	EG
Norway	T*	T*	T*	T*	T*	E	E	T*	T*	T	ES1	E
Spain	T	T	T	T	T	?	T	T	TG	T	T	T
Sweden	T*	T	T	E	TG	E	T	E	E	T	ES1	E
Switzerland (Zurich)	T	T	T	E	T	E	T	T	T	T	EG1	T

T = taxable.
TG = taxable generally.
T* = taxable over a certain level.
E = exempt.
EG = exempt generally.
ES1 = exempt generally if in the hand of the inventor.
Source: Tables 1.3, 1.4 and 1.5 of *Taxation of net wealth, capital transfers and capital gains of individuals* (OECD 1988).

e) Valuation questions

There are a number of important technical rather than policy questions to resolve. As an example to illustrate divergence in country practices, it may be mentioned that the valuation of life assurance policies is variously based on premiums paid, their redemption values, their surrender value, their capitalised value or some combination of all four.

f) Frequency of assessments

There is a short-term administrative and political convenience in opting for infrequent assessments, which could lead to administrative and political inconveniences if the gap between assessments is too long. In practice, in most countries tax is assessed annually, but the period is two years in some Swiss cantons and in Austria, Germany and Luxembourg it is three years.

g) Debts

Outstanding debts are generally deductible, but complicated technical problems arise, not dealt with in this book, in distinguishing between allowable and non-allowable deductions, and, as ever, country practices differ.

C. Capital transfer taxes

1. Terminology

Similar terms and expressions are used in different senses in writings on capital transfer taxes. In this section, the following terms and expressions have the following meanings.

"Capital transfer tax" is a generic term covering all taxes levied at death or on gifts.

An *"estate tax"* is a tax levied on a capital transfer as a result of a death, where the tax base and the rate of tax are governed by the amount transferred by the deceased (donor).

An *"inheritance tax"* is a tax levied on a capital transfer as a result of a death, where the tax base and the rate of tax are governed by the amount received by the beneficiary (donee).

An *"accessions tax"* is a form of inheritance tax, where the tax base and rate of tax is governed by the total amount received in legacies (and gifts) from all donors, not just from one donor.

A *"donor"* is the person making the transfer of capital, whether by gift or at death.

A *"donee"* is the recipient of the transfer whether by gift or legacy.

A *"death tax"* is a tax on a capital transfer at death whether estate tax, inheritance tax or accessions tax. A *"gift tax"* is a tax on such transfers made during lifetime.

A *"slice"* scale of tax rates is one in which the tax rate in respect of a particular band of wealth relates only to that band and does not apply to wealth below that band. The rates in a slice scale are marginal rates.

A *"slab"* scale of tax rates is one in which the tax rate in respect of a particular band of wealth relates to the whole of the wealth up to and including that band. The rates in a slab scale are average rates.

"Taxable wealth" is wealth which is subject to taxation over and above any threshold, exemption or zero rate band; it is thus the wealth to which the first positive tax rate is applied.

A *"threshold"* is the maximum amount of wealth which can be given or left at death (under an estate-type tax) or received by gift or legacy (under an inheritance-type tax) without the donor or the donee respectively incurring a tax liability. It includes any general zero rate band.

2. To have or not to have a capital transfer tax

All OECD countries have had such taxes and they are at present lacking only in Australia and Canada. In Switzerland they are imposed at cantonal level and in all other countries at central or federal level.

Death taxes have in most countries evolved over many years and in their replies which formed the basis of the OECD 1988 report most countries were unable to indicate the reason for their introduction. Among the reasons that were mentioned were the raising of revenue, the reflection of the ability to pay principle and the reduction of inequality in the distribution of wealth or undue concentration of wealth. The reasons for a gift tax is above all to prevent the erosion of the tax base of taxes on death. Their yield is invariably small compared to revenues from death taxes (see Table 11.1).

In Canada, the federal capital transfer tax was abolished in 1972 as part of a federal tax reform that included the introduction of a capital gains tax which applied to bequests and gifts (except to spouses). In Australia, the estate tax was phased out from 1977 on the grounds that it was causing hardship especially to the inheritors of farms and family businesses. Both these countries are federal states and, at the time of abolition of the federal death tax, almost all the provinces (in Canada) and the states (in Australia) had death and gift taxes. However, the abolition of the wealth transfer taxes at federal level was followed by the abolition of the wealth transfer taxes under the control of the provinces/states, so that there are now no death and gift taxes in either Australia or Canada.

3. Main policy choices under capital transfer taxes

a) *Estate versus inheritance taxes*

The main policy option for governments is whether the amount of the tax on the bequest should be determined by the amount left by the deceased (donor-based or estate tax) or by the amount inherited by the beneficiary (donee-based or inheritance tax). The main claims made for the estate tax are that it is simpler and easier to administer, that it is a better revenue yielder than inheritance tax and that for countries without a net wealth tax it may be a more suitable way of taxing wealth at least once a generation. For the inheritance-type tax it is argued that it is more equitable than the estate tax in that it accords more closely with ability to pay, can be more readily adjusted to the circumstances of the heir (by giving preferential rates to the immediate family) and is a better medium for encouraging a wider dispersion of wealth.

The administrative advantages of an estate tax seem undeniable, since the tax authorities are concerned only with the total property, and not as under an inheritance tax with shares in it, so that there are far fewer accounts to be dealt with. At first sight, it is less evident that the estate tax entails a larger revenue yield than an inheritance tax. It is obvious that if an estate tax and an inheritance tax had the same progressive rate schedule the estate tax would yield the larger revenue since it applies to the total estate and not just to the shares in it. Nevertheless, the rate schedules do not have to be the same, and to yield a revenue equivalent to any given estate tax, inheritance tax rates could be set higher. On the other hand, because of the tax advantage of dispersing property under an inheritance tax, there will always be a tendency for the revenue to be less.

Against the claim that an inheritance tax relates tax more closely to ability to pay than an estate tax it may be argued that under the latter the testator can vary the incidence of the tax among the beneficiaries by the manner in which he draws up his will. Nevertheless, the total burden cannot be varied under an estate tax, and where there are large families little can be done to lighten their tax load under such a tax.

The second advantage claimed for inheritance tax is the greater facility it offers for meeting the special circumstances of the heirs. The importance attached to the facility of the inheritance tax to encompass different rates according to relationship is reflected in the practices followed by countries with inheritance taxes; all except Japan have additional schedules or thresholds or both to allow for different relationships and Italy, with both an estate tax and an inheritance tax, had adopted the latter precisely in order to distinguish the tax treatment of the immediate family (not subject to the inheritance tax) from others. On the other hand, provisions for special treatment of spouses have sometimes been incorporated into estate-type taxes and sometimes, also, concessions for special categories of persons, such as minors. Undoubtedly, however, special treatments related to the circumstances of heirs fit more easily into an inheritance tax than into an estate tax, where their inclusion reduces the administrative simplicity which is the primary advantage of the estate-type tax.

The third advantage claimed for the inheritance tax, that it has a greater effect in reducing inequalities in the distribution of wealth than does an estate tax, may be true but is difficult to prove empirically. It may be that the total amount of death tax paid is more important than who pays it in this regard.

Heavy death taxes of either the estate or inheritance kind reduce inequality in the distribution of wealth (or, at least, check its growth), but they do so in different ways. Both reduce inequality insofar as a proportion of large fortunes or large legacies is taken by the State. This is not a redistribution of wealth amongst persons but rather a transfer from the wealthier persons in the private sector to the State, reducing inequality in the private sector by particularly reducing the wealth of the richest. However, the inheritance tax is more selective: it is large inheritances rather than large estates as such which perpetuate inequality and a progressive inheritance tax by relating tax to size of inheritance addresses more directly the problem of inequality resulting from the transmission of wealth between generations. Further, the progressive inheritance tax provides an incentive for the dispersal of property amongst persons, because the more widely property is dispersed the less the total tax paid, even if it is unlikely that tax considerations will deter most testators from leaving property to those whom they particularly wish to benefit. However, the existence of schedules for different degrees of relationship by which rates of tax are lighter on near relatives, heavier on more distant relatives and heaviest on strangers appears to limit the wealth-spreading characteristics of the inheritance tax, since the encouragement to disperse wealth is mainly restricted to dispersion within the immediate family. The advantages claimed for an inheritance tax appear therefore to conflict with each other.

The objectives of an inheritance tax concerned with taxing according to ability to pay and promoting the diffusion of wealth may be better fulfilled by a particular form of inheritance tax, an accessions tax. An accessions tax takes account of the ability to pay which the donee derives from all gifts and legacies, not just those from one source. Correspondingly, the incentive to the donor is not only to spread gifts and legacies widely, but to direct them towards those who have hitherto received little or nothing by way of gifts and legacies. A cumulative accessions tax reduces avoidance possibilities, but creates additional administrative complications and, of the OECD countries, only Ireland has adopted it (in 1984).

Whatever the merits of these arguments there has been over the last two decades a one-way move towards inheritance taxes, the United Kingdom apart. In 1970, all the OECD countries had death taxes: sixteen countries had inheritance taxes, six had estate taxes and two, Italy and Switzerland, had both. By the end of 1987, Australia and Canada had abandoned all death taxes and only New Zealand, the United Kingdom and the United States had just estate taxes; Italy remained with both, and most but not all Swiss cantons had inheritance taxes.

There are a few countries which have some features of an estate tax and others of an inheritance tax, even if their main classification is not in doubt. For example in the Netherlands and in Japan in a somewhat more complex way, the transfer tax is basically of the inheritance type, but the value of the property distributed is derived in general from the total value of the estate. In the United Kingdom, although the tax at death is called "inheritance tax" the tax rate is determined in relation to the estate left by the deceased and not the shares received by the beneficiaries (except that transfers between spouses are usually exempt). Further, liability for gift tax may fall on the donee; there is no general gift tax for gifts between individuals, but gifts made within seven years of death are taxed; the responsibility for any tax which may arise on these potentially exempt transfers primarily falls on the recipient. In the United States there is both an estate tax and a generation-skipping tax. The generation skipping tax was enacted to ensure that an additional transfer tax is imposed when a person transfers property to a person two or more generations below that of the transferor.

b) Rate structure and thresholds

As with the net wealth tax the income redistribution goal points to a relatively low threshold and a progressive rate schedule and administrative simplicity points to a high threshold and a flat rate schedule. A recent trend, which echoes that discussed in Chapters 1 and 10 concerning the income tax, is a reduction in the number of rate bands and a lowering of rates. In nineteen of the twenty countries which have death taxes at the federal or central level, the tax rates are graduated except that in several Member countries a single rate applies to certain limited classes of beneficiary. In the United States, the estate tax rate schedule is graduated but the generation-skipping tax is imposed at a flat rate equal to the highest estate tax rate. The one country where a single rate of tax applies throughout is New Zealand.

Comparisons of thresholds and tax rates are not very meaningful between estate-type taxes on the one hand and inheritance-type taxes on the other. The following tables of rates and thresholds therefore separate those countries with estate or donor-based taxes from those with inheritance or donee-based taxes. Italy, with both an estate-type and an inheritance-type tax, appears in both sets of tables.

To give meaningful comparative tables of rates and thresholds, even in simplified form, required twelve pages in OECD 1988. The following three, much more simplified, tables (Tables 11.5, 11.6, 11.7) lack much of the detail in OECD 1988 and are intended to give only a very rough idea of certain country choices on thresholds and rates of capital transfer taxes. Lacking in particular from these tables is information on the width of brackets for each rate and at what level of wealth the maximum rate becomes applicable.

c) *Consanguinity differentiation*

Under estate taxes the relationship between donor and donee is generally irrelevant except that bequests and gifts between spouses are exempt in the United Kingdom and the United States and so are pensions for minor children in New Zealand. On the contrary, under inheritance taxes there is considerable differentiation both as regards thresholds and the rate scale, and country choices vary greatly. Whilst bequests and gifts to spouses, to children and sometimes grandchildren receive the most favourable tax treatment, the relative capital transfer tax treatment of such bequests and gifts to parents, siblings, nephews and nieces and strangers in blood varies considerably from country to country for reasons which have to remain unknown.

Nevertheless, arguments have been advanced for various solutions. To differentiate the burden of taxation according to the closeness of relationship to the deceased reflects the policy that a deceased person's estate should be kept to a great extent within the family, though it may be that most people with capital would in any case be disposed to leave it mainly to the immediate family, in which case tax incentives to make the policy acceptable are hardly needed. On the other hand, the scale of the differentiation in some OECD countries is somewhat incompatible with the main argument which is put forward in favour of an inheritance-type rather than an estate-type tax, namely that the charge can take account of the beneficiary's ability to pay. A progressive inheritance tax does, of course, tax a large inheritance more heavily than a small one, but to charge one beneficiary five or six times more tax than another beneficiary is charged on an inheritance of the same amount can hardly be said to pay much regard to their respective taxable capacities.

These arguments are intriguing, but one wonders whether they have much to do with the real policy world, since these taxes have been existing for many years, generally without much structural charge, and one may suspect that the differentiation was not taken after much conceptual discussion. Indeed, there seems little rationale for differentiating between transfers to parents and those to grandchildren, between those to nephews and nieces and those to strangers in blood, and to this extent the very different choices of countries as exhibited in Table 11.5 is not too surprising. What is perhaps more surprising is the lack of any trend between 1976 and 1986, as indicated in Tables 11.5 and 11.6. In some countries thresholds were enormously increased, in others thresholds were decreased even in nominal terms; in some countries, rates were increased, in others rates were decreased. Attention is drawn to these phenomena, but no attempt is made to explain them. (To economise on space, thresholds in Tables 11.5 and 11.6 have been expressed only in US dollars, so that when the US dollar threshold is shown as changing only very slightly, this probably means that no change has been made to nominal thresholds, but the exchange rate of the US dollar to the currency of the country concerned has varied.)

Table 11.5: Rates and thresholds of death and gift taxes in countries with estate taxes, 1976 to 1986

Estate taxes (as at (a) 1.1.76 (b) 1.4.86)

		General threshold including zero rate ($)	**Spouse household**	**Minimum and maximum rates**		**Changes between April 1986 and 1986**
Australia	(a)	25 500	50 000	3	27.9	
	(b)	abolished	abolished		abolished	
Italy[1]	(a)	44 000	44 000	3	31	From July 1986 threshold $110 000 and top rate 27
	(b)	20 120	20 120	3	31	
New Zealand	(a)	24 000	60 000	7	40	
	(b)	234 791	234 791	40	40	
United Kingdom	(a)	30 000	exempt	10	75	From July 1987 threshold increased from £ 71 000 to £90 000
	(b)	104 106	exempt	30	60	
United States	(a)	60 000	deduction	3	77	From 1988 top rate reduced to 50
	(b)	500 000	of half estate exempt	18	55	

Gift taxes (as at 1.4.86)

	Exemption limit including any zero rate bonds and excluding small gift exemptions	**Spouse exemption limit**	**Minimum and maximum rates**	**As gifts grossed up for gift tax**	**Aggregation**		
					Gifts with gifts	**Gifts with estate**	**Gifts included in estate for deaths tax**
Italy	As death	As death	As death	No	Lifetime	Lifetime	not applicable[2]
New Zealand	14 087	As death	5–25	No	12 consecutive months	None	Within 3 years
United Kingdom		Exempt	Half death[4]	No	[4]		Within 7 years
United States	As death	Exempt	As death	No	Lifetime	Lifetime	Within 3 years

1. It is recalled that Italy has both estate and inheritence tax: see Tables 11.5 and 11.6.

2. The value of property sold in previous six months is included in gifts on tax base, unless proceeds are re-invested in taxable assets.

3. For gifts within 7 years of death, as death.

4. If a gift is immediately chargeable or becomes chargeable because of a death within 7 years, it is charged at the top slice of chargeable transfers in the previous 7 years (as is death estate).

Source: Tables 2.2 and 2.3 of *Taxation of net wealth, capital transfers and capital gains of individuals* (OECD 1988).

Table 11.6: Rates and thresholds in countries with inheritance taxes, a) January 1976 b) April 1986

		Spouse		Children		Grandchildren		Parents		Brothers and sisters		Nephews and nieces		Strangers in blood	
		US$	%	US$	%	US$	%	US$	%	US$	%	US$	%	US$	%
Austria[1]	a)	1 630	2 – 15	1 630	2 – 15	1 630	4 – 25	326	6 – 40	326	6 – 40	326	8 – 50	82	14 – 98
	b)	1 965	2 – 15	1 965	2 – 15	1 965	4 – 25	393	6 – 40	393	6 – 40	393	6 – 40	98	14 – 60
Belgium	a)	5 090	3 – 35	5 090	3 – 17	zero	3 – 17	zero	6 – 17	zero	13 – 65	zero	15 – 70	zero	20 – 75
	b)	11 188	3 – 25	11 188	3 – 25	zero	3 – 25	zero	3 – 25	zero	20 – 65	zero	25 – 70	zero	30 – 80
Denmark	a)	16 200	2 – 32	1 300	2 – 32	1 300	2 – 32	8	10 – 80	8	10 – 80	8	10 – 80	8	15 – 90
	b)	12 362	2 – 32	989	2 – 32	984	2 – 32	989	10 – 80	989	10 – 80	989	10 – 80	989	15 – 90
Finland	a)	2 090	3.5 – 11	520	3.5 – 11	510	3.5 – 11	520	7 – 22	520	3.5 – 11	520	7 – 22	520	17.5 – 55
	b)	7 396	6 – 14	2 959	6 – 14	2 959	6 – 14	2 459	12 – 28	2 959	6 – 14	2 959	12 – 28	2 959	18 – 42
France	a)	39 100	5 – 20	39 100	5 – 20	39 100	5 – 20	39 100	35 – 45	2 240	5 – 20	2 240	55 flat	2 240	60 flat
	b)	39 700	5 – 40	39 700	5 – 40	39 700	5 – 40	39 700	35 – 45	1 444	5 – 40	1 444	55 flat	1 444	60 flat
Germany	a)	96 100	3 – 35	34 600	3 – 35	19 200	6 – 50	3 850	11 – 65	3 850	11 – 65	3 850	11 – 70	1 150	20 – 70
	b)	115 101	3 – 35	41 436	3 – 35	23 020	6 – 50	4 604	11 – 65	4 604	11 – 65	4 604	11 – 70	9 604	20 – 70
Greece	a)	n.a.	n.a.	n.a.	n.a.	n.a.	n.a.	n.a.	n.a.	n.a.	n.a.	n.a.	n.a.	n.a.	n.a.
	b)	6 460	6 – 27	6 460	7 – 29	4 675	7 – 29	4 675	12 – 50	2 058	12 – 50	1269	16 – 61	745	19 – 72
Ireland	a)	300 000	25 – 50	304 000	25 – 50	30 400	5 – 50	30 400	5 – 50	20 300	10 – 50	20 300	10 – 50	10 150	20 – 60
	b)	exempt	exempt	200 000	20 – 55	20 000	20 – 55	20 000	20 – 55	20 000	20 – 55	20 000	20 – 55	13 387	20 – 55
Italy[2]	a)	exempt	exempt	exempt	exempt	exempt	exempt	exempt	exempt	5 100	3 – 19	2 930	3 – 24	1 470	3 – 29
	b)	exempt	exempt	exempt	exempt	exempt	exempt	2 347	3 – 19	1 341	3 – 19	1 341	3 – 19	671	3 – 29
Japan[3]		special system													
Luxembourg[4]	a)	510	2.5 – 11	510	2.5 – 11	510	2.5 – 11	510	2.5 – 11	510	15 – 33	510	15 – 33	510	15 – 33
	b)	1 119	2.5 – 8	1 119	2.5 – 8	1 119	5 – 16	1 119	5 – 16	1 119	15 – 48	1 119	15 – 48	1 119	15 – 48
Netherlands	a)	94 000	3 – 17	2 250	3 – 17	2 250	5 – 22	18 800	5 – 22	600	18 – 36	600	27 – 45	600	36 – 54
	b)	85 707	5 – 27	5 306	5 – 27	5 306	8.4 – 3.2	26 529	26 – 53	530	26 – 53	530	41 – 68	530	41 – 68
Norway[5]	a)	exempt	exempt	9 010	8 – 35	9 010	10 – 50	9 010	8 – 35	9 010	10 – 50	9 010	20 – 60	9 010	20 – 60
	b)	exempt	exempt	13 528	8 – 20	13 528	8 – 30	13 528	8 – 20	13 528	10 – 30	13 528	10 – 30	13 528	10 – 30
Portugal	a)	3 650	8 – 32	7 300	8 – 35	7 300	10 – 48	365	10 – 48	365	30 – 75	365	36 – 5	365	30 – 75
	b)	1 687	8 – 33	1 687	4 – 36	1 687	10 – 49	810	10 – 49	67	10 – 49	67	30 – 67	67	30 – 76
Spain	a)	168	3 – 21	168	3 – 21	168	3 – 21	168	3 – 21	zero	28 – 58	200	40 – 69	zero	58 – 64
	b)	71	3 – 21	71	3 – 21	71	3 – 21	71	5 – 26	zero	28 – 58	zero	40 – 89	zero	59 – 84
Sweden[4]	a)	6 850	5 – 65	3 430	5 – 65	3 434	5 – 65	640	8 – 72	640	8 – 72	690	8 – 72	690	8 – 52
	b)	7 019	6 – 70	3 509	6 – 70	3 509	6 – 70	702	10 – 75	702	10 – 75	702	10 – 75	72	10 – 75
Switzerland (Zurich)[5]	a)	exempt	exempt	11 450	2 – 6	11 450	2 – 6	11 430	4 – 12	1 910	6 – 18	zero	10 – 30	200	12 – 36
	b)	exempt	exempt	16 685	2 – 6	16 683	2 – 6	16 685	4 – 12	2 781	6 – 18	2 781	10 – 30	2 781	12 – 36
Turkey	a)	n.a.	n.a.	n.a.	n.a.	n.a.	n.a.	7 – 30	n.a.	n.a.	n.a.	n.a.	n.a.	n.a.	n.a.
	b)	7 473	3 – 20	7 433	3 – 20	zero	3 – 20	zero	3 – 20	zero	7 – 30	zero	10 – 44	zero	10 – 44

Notes to Table 11.6

1. Slab not slice scale.

2. Estate duty also – see Table 11.4.

3. For all beneficiaries there is a basic deduction of $ 118 681 plus $ 23 736 multiplied by the number of heirs; spouses and minor children receive a special tax credit. Rates are the same, whatever the relationship and range from 10 per cent to 75 per cent.

4. From 1987 increase in threshold for spouses to $ 14 038 for children and grandchildren to $ 7 019 and to others to $ 1 407.

5. From January 1987 a tripling of threshold value for children, grandchildren and parents and a doubling for other categories.

n.a. = not available.

Source: Table 2.4 of *Taxation of net wealth, capital transfers and capital gains of individuals* (OECD 1979 and 1988).

d) The relation between gift and death taxes

In most, though not all OECD countries, death and gift taxes are integrated in the sense that they are governed by a single code of law and, in most cases, the same or substantially the same scales of rates apply both to lifetime transfers and to transfers on death. There is, however, considerable variation in the extent to which lifetime gifts are aggregated with each other or with transfers on death for the purpose of determining the rate of tax chargeable on successive transfers.

The argument in favour of a fully integrated and cumulative tax on gifts and inheritances (or estates) is that it removes some of the advantage which could otherwise be gained by making transfers of property during life and places gifts and bequests on the same footing. Experience has shown that any death tax needs to be protected against avoidance through lifetime gifts. If, however, the period is too long it becomes difficult or impossible to trace all the gifts which should be taken into account, and better protection will be afforded by a specific tax on gifts which can be charged at the time the gift is made.

A tax imposed on each gift taken by itself will tend to be lighter than the tax which would be charged under a graduated death tax if the gift were included in the donor's estate at his death. Moreover, it will be open to donors to reduce its impact further by making their benefactions in a series of separate gifts instead of in one sum. Aggregation of gifts over a period and charging tax on a cumulative basis provide a remedy, the efficacy of which depends on the length of the aggregation period. For complete protection full integration of the gift tax and death tax, on a cumulative basis, would seem to be required.

On the other hand, even with full integration and cumulation, it may be neither necessary nor desirable to tax lifetime gifts as heavily as transfers on death. If the tax on gifts is regarded simply as the equivalent of the tax which would be payable on death if the gift were not made, it would be reasonable to charge it at a somewhat lower rate than would be applicable on death, on the grounds that the State is receiving the tax before the time of death and should allow some discount for payment in advance. The point has less force, however, if the view is taken that transfers of property as such, whether during life or at death, should be taxed and that the taxation of gifts is not required solely for the protection of the death tax.

Lighter taxation of lifetime gifts may also be adopted as a matter of policy, in order that wealthy people may be encouraged, as they grow old, to hand on their property to the next generation. This may be especially important where the property in question is a private business. If the tax consequences are the same whenever the property is handed on, the owner of the business may be tempted to keep it in his own hands as long as possible in order to postpone the time for payment of tax, although the interests of the business might be better served if it was transferred to a younger person. A preferential charge on a lifetime gift gives an incentive to the owner to dispose of the property before becoming too old to manage it properly, and in this way could help to promote business enterprise and efficiency. Again this is perhaps to overestimate the influence of taxation in decisions of this kind.

The tax treatment of OECD countries on gifts including integration and aggregation is provided in Table 11.5 for countries with estate taxes and Table 11.7 for countries with inheritance taxes, as of April 1986 in both cases. A more detailed description of countries' greatly varying practices would be out of proportion in a book of this size, and accordingly the interested reader is referred to the 1988 OECD publication.

e) Adjustments for inflation

Because capital transfer taxes are levied at irregular intervals of time rather than annually, because the time at which death taxes are levied is not within the control of the taxpayers, and because wealth transfer taxes may be very heavy, it could be argued that there is an especially strong case for providing for regular inflation adjustment if inequity between taxpayers is to be avoided. Since asset prices often change at different rates (and sometimes in different directions) from prices in general, it is not clear that indexation using the retail price index would provide an appropriate solution, and frequent ad hoc adjustment might be preferable. In practice, only the Netherlands and the United Kingdom together with one Swiss canton have adopted indexation. In Norway, thresholds are regularly increased in line with the retail price index. In countries where the adjustment is not automatic the position has varied. At one extreme, tax reforms (rather than simple inflation adjustments) have reduced the tax burden in real terms, as in the United States and New Zealand; at the other extreme, for example in Austria, Denmark and Germany, rates and thresholds have remained virtually unchanged between 1976 and 1986. For the majority of countries the adjustments of thresholds and rate bands have not kept pace with inflation.

f) Exemptions and reliefs

Details of country practices are not provided, but it should be mentioned that they vary widely. Most countries entirely exempt transfers, but a few (e.g. Austria, Belgium, Denmark, the Netherlands, New Zealand and Sweden) give favourable tax treatment. A few countries (e.g. Austria, Germany, Ireland, the Netherlands and the United Kingdom) also give favourable tax treatment to transfers to political parties. Practices vary also between

Table 11.7: Gift taxes in countries with inheritance taxes, April 1986

	Exemptions limit (including any nil–rate bonds and excluding small gift exemptions)	**Minimum and maximum rates**	**Aggregations**	
			Gifts with gifts	**Gifts with legacies**
Austria	As death[1]	As death	10 years	10 years
Belgium	None	As death	3 years	3 years
Denmark	$ 989	As death[5]	lifetime	Usually none
Finland	As death	As death	2 years	2 years
France	As death[2]	As death	Lifetime	Lifetime
Germany	As death	As death	10 years	10 years
Greece	As death	As death	Lifetime	Lifetime
Ireland	As death	75% at death rate[6]	Lifetime[7]	Lifetime[7]
Italy	As death	As death	Lifetime	Lifetime
Japan	$ 3 650[3]	As death	1 year (all donors)	3 years (same donor)
Luxembourg	None	1.8 to 14.8	None	Only for gift within one year of death
Netherlands	$ 1 554[4]	As death	2 years[8]	180 days
Norway	As death	As death	Lifetime[9]	Lifetime[9]
Portugal	$ 101	As death	Lifetime	Lifetime
Spain	None	As death	3 years	3 years
Sweden	$ 281	As death	10 years	10 years
Switzerland (Zurich)	As death	As death	Lifetime	Lifetime
Turkey	$ 75	As death	not available	not available

1. Except for $6 549 for lifetime transfer between spouses.

2. Except that special $ 1 144 for inheritance tax is not available for gifts tax.

3. $ 59 340 for gift of residential property allowed once only for spouses married for 20 years or more.

4. Additional allowances for gifts to children and grandchildren.

5. For gifts to spouse, children, parents, grandparents. Otherwise gifts count as income or are untaxed.

6. As death if within 2 years of death.

7. Applies to gifts from all donors, in all other countries, except Japan and the Netherlands only from same donor.

8. 1 year for gifts from parents to children.

9. For heirs and direct descendants Otherwise none for gifts with gifts and 6 months for gifts with legacies.

Source: Table 2.5 of *Taxation of net wealth, capital transfers and capital gains of individuals* (OECD 1988).

countries regarding exemption degrees of favourable treatment and no favourable treatment for transfers of certain categories of assets, including household effects, works of art and pension rights and life insurance, agriculture property and small gifts.

D. Capital gains taxes

1. To have or not to have a capital gains tax

In favour of taxing capital gains, it is argued that capital gains constitute an accretion of economic power that increases a taxpayer's ability to pay and on grounds of both horizontal and vertical equity, they should be included in taxable income, due allowance being made for the offset of capital losses. It is for these kinds of reasons that bringing capital gains into the tax net may be seen as part of the trend to widen the income tax base discussed in the last chapter, irrespective of whether taxation of such gains is integrated into the income tax or taxed separately. A second argument in favour of taxing capital gains is that it reinforces and protects income tax yields. Whilst it is probable that capital gains taxes raise very little revenue (and most countries are unable to estimate how much revenue they do raise because they generally form part of the personal income tax) it is probable that taxing them helps to protect the yield of the much more important income tax, since there are many tax avoidance devices for transforming taxable income into less highly taxed or untaxed capital gains. A third economic efficiency argument for taxing capital gains is that in the absence of such taxation, there could be investment distortions in encouraging investment to take forms which generate capital appreciation with little or no income yield.

The arguments against taxing capital gains flow mainly from the imperfections inherent in real-world capital gains taxation. The first problem is that with a few exceptions (deemed realisation on bequests, gifts and emigration – see later) it is not practically possible to tax accrued but unrealised capital gains and normally capital gains tax is payable only at the time of sale of assets. A capital gains tax is thus likely to have the effect of artificially locking in capital which could create economic inefficiencies. A second problem is the practical difficulties in confining a capital gains tax to real rather than inflationary gains and, if gains which are largely inflationary are taxed, horizontal equity is affected. Some of the main policy issues that arise if a capital gains tax is adopted have to address this issue (distinction between long- and short-term gains with tapering as an in-between possibility, indexation, lower rates than personal income tax etc.). An analogous problem is that capital gains may be very heavy in one year, but there may be no gains or even losses on the sales of similar assets in another year and the solution of averaging over a period adopted by a few countries creates technical problems. Lastly arguments against capital gains taxation can be employed independently of the way it works in practice: for example, like other taxes on income from capital it may stimulate consumption at the expense of saving, it may induce capital flight especially in small open economies, or it may be shifted ultimately into lower wages.

Whatever the merits of the arguments for and against capital gains taxes, there has undoubtedly been in recent years a one-way move in OECD countries to both adopting them if they previously did not exist (see Table 11.2) or extending their scope if they did (see Table 11.9). OECD 1988 noted that replies from only two countries gave reasons for not adopting such a tax: the Netherlands found after a 1980 debate in Parliament that the administrative costs would be too high in relation to the revenue yield, there would be too many technical complications and that it would have disadvantageous economic and financial effects; the New Zealand Minister of Finance referred to problems of introducing a capital gains tax which was both fair and practicable.

It is less easy to provide an unequivocal classification of capital gains practices than of net wealth or capital transfer taxes, because such practices frequently vary both according to the type of asset sold (equities versus immovable property) and to the length of time the asset is held. However, as indicated in Table 11.2 it is possible to offer a rough classification of country practices as at January 1990 on the following basis:

a) separate tax on capital gains: Denmark, Ireland, Italy (since 1991), Portugal, Switzerland (generally), the United Kingdom;
b) taxed within the income tax:
    i) comprehensively including long-term gains: Australia, Canada, Finland, France, Japan, Luxembourg, Norway, Spain, Sweden, the United States;
    ii) special provisions mainly confined to short-term speculative gains: Austria, Belgium, Germany, Turkey;
c) no special provisions: the Netherlands, New Zealand.

Revenues from capital gains accrue to federal/central government except in Switzerland where they accrue exclusively to the cantons and normally relate only to gains from immovable property and in Spain where there is a separate local tax on gains from urban immovable property.

2. Main policy choices under capital gains taxes

In determining an appropriate rate schedule and threshold, governments have to decide what should be the relative treatment of short- and long-term gains and what should be the relative treatment of capital gains and income. These two interrelated issues are considered first.

a) short- and long-term gains

Different arguments may be advanced for distinguishing between short- and long-term gains according to whether they are regarded as income. If they are so regarded, in principle they should be included in full in the income tax base, however long the period for which the taxpayer has owned the asset disposed of. However, if a large gain was accrued over a long period and were to be taxed at full income tax rates in the year of realisation, the charge under a progressive system of rates might be unduly burdensome. Further, in modern times inflation has produced gains which do not reflect any increase in the real value of the asset. It is considerations of this kind, together with possible adverse effects on investment if full income tax rates were imposed, which are held to justify either the inclusion of only a proportion of the gain as income or the application of a lower rate for long-term gains. If the capital gains are not considered to be income the case for differential treatment of short-term gains rests on other grounds that although they are not income they resemble income so closely that they ought on grounds of equity to be taxed as income, whether or not long-term gains are subjected to any form of taxation. These are often referred to as "speculative" gains – i.e. gains resulting from transactions which have been entered into with a view to making a quick profit, as distinct from gains arising on the disposal of an asset which has been held as an investment. Thus in Germany short-term gains are taxed as income, but there is no tax on long-term gains; and in the United Kingdom short-term gains were made liable to income tax some years before a general capital gains tax was introduced.

A case may also be made against differentiating between short-term and long-term gains on the grounds that it is inappropriate to attempt to tax real rather than nominal capital gains when other areas of taxation (e.g. interest, excises, earned income) are generally based on nominal values or income. Moreover, all attempts to avoid taxing nominal gains or to tax them more lightly than real gains meet with administrative inconveniences and theoretical drawbacks.

The simplest method of imposing a lower rate schedule (or lower tax base) for long-term gains creates an arbitrary dividing line with the possibilities of inequities between taxpayers whose disposals come just each side of it, as well as complicating the administration of the tax. The so-called "tapering" method, under which rates decline more gently according to the period that the assets have been held, renders the administration even more complicated and creates a number of inequities, in particular providing relief in proportion to the luck of the investor and not to the effect of inflation on the investment.

Another possible solution is indexation of thresholds which, however, creates the same kinds of problems already discussed in the last chapter with respect to the personal income tax. Also finding an appropriate index is even more difficult than with an income tax since different kinds of assets may appreciate at different rates, so that it may be difficult to find a single index to provide equitable treatment for all kinds of assets.

Attention now turns to what certain countries have been doing in practice to differentiate between short- and long-term capital gains. To begin with, the charge on non-business assets is limited to short-term gains in Austria and Germany. The narrowest charge is in Germany where gains on disposals of movable property are taxable as income if realised within six months of the acquisition of the asset, while disposal within two years attracts liability in the case of immovables. The corresponding periods in Austria are one year and five years. In Sweden there is no liability where movable property (other than shares) has been held for over five years.

Where both long-term and short-term gains are taxed, the charge may differentiate between them by imposing a lower rate of tax on long-term gains, or by imposing tax on less than their full amount or by indexing the cost base of long-term gains but not short-term gains. In Finland and Luxembourg, which only recently extended tax to long-term gains, a separate treatment of short-term gains has been retained. In Finland gains from property held for five years or less are subject to full income tax rates whereas gains from property held for over five years are more leniently treated. The short-term gains tax in Luxembourg (which, like the German tax, charged gains on disposals of movable property to income tax if realised within six months of the acquisition of the asset, and on immovables if held for less than two years) remains, but provisions for taxing longer-term gains in real property at reduced income tax rates have been added. In the United States where the asset was held for more than six months, only 40 per cent of the gain was formerly subject to taxation, but this distinction disappeared in 1987 when all gains were equally taxed at ordinary income tax rates. In Denmark business gains and gains on shares held for less than three years are taxable as ordinary income; other gains are subject to a separate capital gains tax, but in the case of real property gains from property held for more than three years are reduced by 20 per cent per year and exempted after seven years. In Ireland which has a separate capital gains tax, the rate of tax is reduced after one year in stages up to six years when it is half that for assets held for less than one year. In Australia, gains from property held for less than one year generally continue to be taxable as ordinary income under an existing provision, whilst longer-term gains, previously untaxed, are now taxed as income via the new capital gains tax, but only the real gain is taxable because of the indexation of the cost base.

A reduction of the chargeable amount is also applied in Sweden and in France. In Sweden only 40 per cent of the gain is chargeable where shares have been held for over two years; for other movables, including government securities, the chargeable gain is reduced annually after two years until after five years it is exempt. In the case of immovables, the acquisition price is indexed after the first four years. In France, the gain on movables disposed of within one year and on immovables within two years is taxable in full as income. Movables held from between one and twenty-one years and immovables between two and twenty-two years (thirty-two years for building land) are taxed on a reduced value, becoming exempt at the end of the period. In addition, long-term gains benefit from a "quotient" or top slicing system form of averaging. The tax payable on one fifth of the gain, treated as the top slice of the taxpayer's income, is ascertained, and this tax is multiplied by five to arrive at the tax payable on the gain as a whole. In this way the impact of a progressive tax schedule on a gain which has accrued over a number of years is modified; in broad effect the gain is taxed as if it has been realised in equal instalments over five years. A similar averaging system is adopted in the new Australian capital gains tax and also in Spain (where the period over which the gain is averaged depends on the length of time the asset has been held).

In Japan, in general, gains on disposals within a period as long as five years are treated as short-term gains and charged at full income tax rates. For property held for more than five years half the gain is subject to income tax.

In contrast, some other countries take little or no account of the differences in the length of time between the acquisition and disposal of an asset. In Norway, for example, all capital gains rank as ordinary income [though gains from shares are taxed at a separate rate of 30 per cent if held for under two years (exempt if held longer) and gains on the disposal of land may be charged at a flat rate if this is more favourable than the progressive scale]. In Canada, three quarters of any capital gain is taxable as income, but no distinction is made between long-term and short-term gains. In the United Kingdom capital gains, irrespective of the period for which the asset has been held, are charged at a flat rate on their full amount, but the United Kingdom (since 1982) is one of the minority of countries which update the acquisition value for inflation, as well as the threshold, according to the retail price index. (The other countries with similar practices with respect to valuation are Australia, Ireland, Luxembourg and Spain, and the Scandinavian countries for gains from immovable property.)

b) The relative tax treatment of income and capital gains

Whether a country opts for a separate capital gains tax or to tax capital gains through the income tax is perhaps primarily a matter of administrative convenience, but the relative tax treatment of income and capital gains raises more substantial issues, not unconnected with the relation between short- and long-term gains just discussed. In addition to the fact that inflation may erode the value of capital gains more seriously than income, another argument in favour of preferential treatment for capital gains is the bunching problem already referred to: whilst the problem of high and low income years also arises for the self-employed under income tax systems, heavy capital gains over one year combined with no gains or even losses on disposals over other years may be a more serious problem. Against preferential tax treatment for capital gains is the vertical equity argument that beneficiaries of capital gains are likely to be in the highest income groups, and the tax avoidance point that significant preferential treatment for capital gains over income is likely to induce artificial conversion of higher taxed income into lower total gains. Another equity argument against preferential treatment is that the asset-holder has already benefitted from the postponement of payment of the tax from when it accrued to when it is realised.

Table 11.8 summarises rates and thresholds of capital gains taxes as at 1 January 1990, indicating where the position was different in 1976. As regards countries with separate capital gains taxes, there has been a large increase in the rates in Ireland, a small increase in Portugal and no change in the other countries; thresholds have doubled in Switzerland since 1976, risen fourfold in Ireland and sixfold in the United Kingdom. Of countries where the capital gains tax is integrated with the personal income tax what cannot be seen from Table 11.8 (see rather Table 10.11 in Chapter 10) is that capital gains rates are generally much lower and much fewer: in the United States, for example, there was a reduction in the number of rates of rates in 1987 from 14 to 2.

Also since 1987, the United States has even given preferential tax treatment to income over capital gains by taxing both at more or less the same rate, whilst providing indexation for the income tax but not for capital gains tax, which has been a contentious political issue in that country over the last few years. Other countries generally afford either equal tax treatment or give preferential treatment to long-term capital gains. Table 11.8 shows that rates on long-term gains have been increased in Canada and Spain and reduced in Japan since 1976.

c) Averaging

In countries with progressive rates of tax, averaging may protect those whose capital gains are bunched within a particular tax year. A few countries permit averaging of capital gains tax payable over a number of years to meet this problem, but it does make for administrative complications and Canada and the United States are among countries

Table 11.8: Rates and thresholds of capital gains taxes, at 1 January 1990

	Rate of tax		General threshold per annum	Situation in January 1976
	Long-term gains	Short-term gains		
(a) Countries with separate capital gains tax				
Denmark	50 %	As long-term unless tax on income	No general threshold	Same rate 6 000 DKr. threshold
Ireland	Assets owned between 1 and 3 years 50% 3 and 6 years 35% Over 6 years 30%	60% (gains realised within a year)	IR£ 2 000 (double for married couple)	26% for both long- and short-term gains IR£500 threshold
Portugal	12% or 24% for sales of building land	As long-term	—	10 or 20% long- and short-term gains
Switzerland (Zurich)	Progressive scale 10-40%	As long-term	In general 2 000 Sfrs.	same rate scale 1 000 Sfrs. threshold
United Kingdom	30%	As long-term	£6 600	Same rate £ 1000 threshold
(b) Integrated with income tax				
Australia[1]	Real gain taxed as income.	Taxed as income	None	No such tax
Canada	Three quarters gain taxed as income	As long-term	Lifetime: C$ 100 000	Half gain taxed as income for both long- and short-gains. No threshold
Finland	40% of gain over 200 000 Fmk. taxed as income	As unearned income: reduction for immovables after 5 years	Long-term gains only	No tax on long-term gains
France	Depends on nature of asset and period held	Taxed more heavily than long-term gain	6 000 Ffrs.	Various rates. Same threshold
Japan	Half gain is taxed as income	Taxed as income if held < 5 years	Y 500 000	As income tax for both short- and long-term. Same threshold
Luxembourg	Half income tax rates	As income tax	1 250 000 Lfrs. over 10 years	No tax on long-term basis
Norway	As income tax (land: 30 %)	As long-term (shares: 30%)	None	As 1990
Spain[2]	As income tax	As long-term	None	15% long-term. otherwise as 1990
Sweden	Proportion of gain is taxed as income	As income tax	None	As 1990
United States	Taxed as income	As long-term	None	Long-term gains half taxed as income

1. Averaging provisions relate to a national 5-year period.

2. Averaging provisions relate to number of years held.

Source: OECD 1988 updated by Cnossen and Messere (1990) and OECD Secretariat (1991).

which have recently abolished averaging, partly in view of the reduction of number of rates and progressivity of the income tax schedule. Countries remaining with averaging provisions include Australia, France, Norway and Spain.

d) Treatment of gains at death and on gifts

When the owner of assets dies there are three possible ways of treating any gains which have accrued on the assets but have not been realised. First, the assets may be deemed to have been realised at the date of death; tax may then be charged on the resulting gains as if the deceased had actually disposed of the assets. Secondly, the accrued but unrealised gains may be recognised, but the liability to tax may be deferred until they are actually realised by the persons who succeed to the ownership of the assets (who may be either the personal representatives or the heirs of the deceased). Thirdly, they may be exempted, and escape tax altogether. All three treatments are found in OECD countries, as indicated in Table 11.9.

The objection to exemption is that otherwise the impact of the tax is uneven as between two persons with gains of the same amount, one of whom has realised his gains during life while the other has not. The former pays tax on the gains even if dying on the day after realising them; the latter escapes, if the choice is not to sell. In effect the tax burden is determined at the taxpayers' choice. Further, exemption has a locking-in effect in later life; because the gains will escape tax if they are held until death, the taxpayer may refrain from selling assets which, apart from tax considerations, it might have been considered sensible to sell.

On the other hand when, as in most cases, liability to capital gains tax at death coincides with the imposition at death duties, it might be thought that the double charge would constitute an excessive burden. The method of deferred liability meets both points; the tax is not charged until the gains are realised, and it is not charged at the same time as the death tax (though the deceased's executors may realise assets soon after the death in the course of administering the estate).

Subject to certain exceptions deemed realisation of death has been adopted in Canada and Spain – particularly understandable in Canada where there is no death or gift tax. Deferred liability at death is the normal rule in Australia, Denmark, Japan, Luxembourg and Sweden. Under this method the gains are not taxed at death, when there is no actual realisation, but they do not escape tax altogether. The deceased's successor is treated as having acquired the asset at the cost at which it was in fact acquired by the deceased, so that when it is disposed of, tax is payable on the whole of the gain arising since the deceased acquired it.

Exemption at death is the practice of the majority of countries. Where exemption on death applies the successor is treated as having acquired the asset at its market value at the date of death.

As to gifts made during the donor's lifetime, the same three treatments are found (see Table 11.9); but more countries treat lifetime gifts as taxable (Denmark and Ireland as

Table 11.9: Capital gains tax treatment regarding death and gifts, April 1986		
Countries	**Death**	**Gifts**
(a) Countries with separate capital gains tax		
Denmark	Deferred liability	Liable
Ireland	Exempt	Liable
Portugal	Non-taxable	Exempt (as from 1986)
Switzerland	Exempt	Exempt
United Kingdom	Exempt	Deferred
(b) Countries with comprehensive coverage within income tax		
Australia	Deferred liability	Liable
Canada	liable (deferred between spouses)	Liable (deferred between spouses)
Finland	Exempt	Exempt
France	Exempt	Exempt (provided donee does not sell within 5 years)
Japan	Deferred liability	Deferred liability
Luxembourg	Deferred liability	Deferred liability
Norway	Exempt	Exempt
Spain	Liable	Liable
Sweden	Deferred liability	Deferred liability
United States	Exempt	Deferred liability

Source: Table 3.3 of *Taxation of net wealth, capital transfers and capital gains of individuals* (OECD 1988).

well as Australia, Canada and Spain) and two countries, the United Kingdom and the United States, treat gifts as a deferred liability whilst exempting transfers at death.

e) Deemed realisations other than at death or on gifts

Outside the case of death and lifetime gifts just discussed, capital gains are usually taxed only when actually realised. There are, however, a few cases where gains are deemed to have been realised, generally as an anti-tax evasion measure. In Canada and Australia there is a deemed realisation of assets situated outside the State when a taxpayer becomes non-resident and Denmark has a somewhat similar provision treating as a deemed disposal the transfer abroad of business assets which have previously been used in the state. There are other examples of a more technical nature. Thus, Japan may treat the letting of a leasehold as a deemed disposal in certain circumstances; change of use of assets in Canada may give rise to a deemed disposal; and in Ireland and the United Kingdom there is deemed to be a realisation whenever the owner of an asset derives a capital sum from it.

f) Exemptions and reliefs

A major policy choice for governments is to decide which asset disposals to include, which to exclude from the tax base. Table 11.10 which sets out country practices in this regard gives some indication of the comprehensiveness of the tax system. However, the table should be interpreted with care, for the effective coverage of the capital gains taxation depends to an important extent on other factors considered above, in particular the period over which gains are taxable, the existence of any general threshold or exemption and the treatment of transfers at death and by gift (see Tables 11.8 and 11.9). Table 11.10 also shows by indicating changes between 1976 and 1986 the increasing coverage of capital gains taxes, not only in countries like Australia and Luxembourg which have introduced or widely extended capital gains taxes in recent years, but also in other countries, including Canada, France, Spain and the United States.

As can be seen from Table 11.10, exemptions or reliefs for gains on some classes of asset are provided in all countries whether on social or economic grounds or for reasons of practical administration. Probably the most important class in terms of revenue forgone is the principal private residence. The proceeds of life insurance policies and superannuation benefits are very commonly exempted; the latter, however, are usually received in the form of income and are taxable as such.

Table 11.10: Summary of capital gains tax treatment of some specific assets, April 1986

Country	Principal private residence	Other private residence	Life insurance and superannuation	Foreign currency	Unit trusts	Government securities	Wasting and deteriorating chattels	Small chattels (exemption limit)	Loans repaid in appreciating currency
(a) Countries with separate capital gains tax									
Denmark	Generally exempt	Generally exempt	Exempt	Exempt	–	Exempt[1]	Sometimes taxable	Sometimes taxable	Generally exempt
Ireland	Exempt subject to conditions	Generally taxable	Exempt	Generally taxable	Taxable	Exempt	Exempt	Exempt below IR£2 000[1] (4 000 for married couples)	Exempt
Portugal	Non-taxable	Non-taxable	Non-taxable	Non-taxable	–	Non-taxable	Non-taxable	Non-taxable	Non-taxable
Switzerland (Zurich)	Taxable	Taxable	Exempt	Exempt	–	Exempt	Exempt	Exempt	Exempt
United Kingdom	Exempt subject to conditions	Generally taxable	Generally exempt	Generally taxable	Taxable	Generally exempt	Generally exempt	Exempt below £3 000	Exempt
(b) Countries with comprehensive coverage within income tax									
Australia	Generally exempt	Taxable[1]	Exempt	Taxable[1]	Taxable[1]	Taxable[1]	Generally taxable[1]	Exempt below A$5 000 ($3 342)	Exempt
Canada	Exempt	Taxable	Exempt	Taxable	Taxable	Taxable	Taxable	Exempt below C$1 000 ($720)	Taxable[1]
Finland	Generally exempt	Taxable	Exempt	Exempt	Taxable	Taxable	Taxable	Taxable	Exempt
France	Exempt	Generally taxable	Exempt	Generally taxable[1]	Exempt subject to conditions	Exempt if total sales of stocks and bonds below a threshold	Generally exempt	Exempt below 20 000 ($ 2 887) Ffrs.	Exempt
Japan	First Y 30 million ($178021) exempt	Taxable	Taxable	Taxable if business activity	Generally exempt	Generally exempt	Taxable	Exempt	Taxable
Luxembourg	Generally exempt	Generally taxable	Exempt	Exempt unless gains from speculation	Taxable[1]	Taxable[1]	Taxable[1]	Taxable[1]	Exempt

Table 11.10 (cont.): Summary of capital gains tax treatment of some specific assets at April 1986

Country	Principal private residence	Other private residence	Life insurance and superannuation	Foreign currency	Unit trusts	Government securities	Wasting and deteriorating chattels	Small chattels (exemption limit)	Loans repaid in appreciating currency
Norway	Exempt subject to conditions	Exempt subject to conditions	Taxable	Taxable	Taxable	Taxable	Taxable	Exempt	Taxable
Spain	Exempt subject to re–purchase of new residence	Taxable	Taxable	Taxable[1]	–	Taxable	Taxable	Taxable	Generally exempt
Sweden	Taxable on excess over re–purchase of new residence	Taxable	Taxable	Possible taxable	–	Taxable	Taxable	Taxable	Exempt
United States	Taxable on excess over re–purchase of new residence	Taxable	Exempt	Exempt	Taxable	Taxable	Taxable	Taxable	Taxable[1]

1. Not taxable 1976.

Source: Table 3.4 of *Taxation of net wealth, capital transfers and capital gains of individuals* (OECD 1988).

Chapter 12
Corporation income taxes and other taxes on business

A. Summary

1. Scope of the chapter

The most important and complicated corporation income tax issues relate to the treatment of cross-frontier capital flows, but for reasons explained in the introduction, they are outside the scope of this book, except where these international considerations influence domestic choices.

Logically the first question to address is, should there be a separate corporation income tax at all, since though every OECD country has one, tax reform commissions and academics have recommended three alternative forms of taxation to replace it: in the early sixties the Canadian Carter Commission Report recommended that it be fully integrated with the personal income tax, so that corporation tax payments would simply represent a deduction at the company level of personal income tax payable by shareholders on their dividends; second, in the sixties British and United States sources investigated the possibility of replacing the corporation income tax by a value added tax; lastly, in the seventies and eighties consideration has been given in various countries including Ireland, Sweden, the United Kingdom and the United States to the replacement of the corporation income tax by a cash flow corporation tax.

These three attacks on the traditional corporation income tax concentrated on three quite different defects. The Carter approach saw it as being in conflict with the comprehensive income tax principle. Those who wished to replace it with VAT saw it as balance of trade disadvantageous, in a context where it was believed to be shifted partially into prices, exchange rates were fixed and under GATT rules there was no possibility of having export rebates and/or income equalisation charges to compensate for domestic corporation tax paid. The cash flow alternative attacks the inability of a corporation income tax to tax economic profits in a fair and neutral way. However, the corporation income tax has proved sufficiently robust to survive in all OECD countries at central level of government and in addition nearly half OECD countries impose such taxes or similar taxes at subordinate levels of government. The reasons why are discussed in the next sub-section of this summary, which then goes on to refer to a number of mixed base and rate issues. The summary concludes by referring briefly to issues considered in more detail later in the chapter – specific issues relating to the tax base and to statutory tax rates and the taxation of distributed profits as well as the taxation of enterprises otherwise than through the corporation income tax, and finally makes some remarks on the contribution of these taxes to government revenues and on the different ways in which governments collect these taxes.

2. The rationale for the corporation income tax and suggested alternatives

The formal justification for the corporation income tax[1] is that a corporation has the status of a legal person and, like physical persons, should therefore be liable to income tax. Sometimes the corporation tax is also seen as a payment for the legal privilege of limited liability or for cost-reducing public services to the corporate sector (e.g. the provision of infrastructure facilities). These arguments have been considered as theoretically weak, since there is hardly any systematic relationship between the corporate income tax and the benefits stemming from limited liability or from public services provided to the corporation. Also, corporations as such, cannot bear the burden of the corporation tax since a tax burden can be borne only by physical persons, in their capacity as employers, wage and salary-earners, or consumers and savers.

According to the traditional theory of taxation, the income tax should be levied on an individual's potential consumption, defined as the maximum amount which a taxpayer

1. Also known as "the corporation tax" or "the corporate tax" (See Annex to Chapter 12D).

would be able to consume without eroding his real stock of net wealth. To realise this ideal of so-called comprehensive income taxation, all corporate profits, whether distributed or retained, should in principle be allocated to individual shareholders and taxed as personal income. In other words, corporate-source income should be subject to the same tax treatment as income from partnerships or other unincorporated enterprises. Under such a full integration system there would be no room for a separate corporate income tax except as a withholding tax to be fully credited by shareholders against the personal income tax due on their imputed share of corporate profits. At the theoretical level it was argued recently by M. Gammie (1992) that it is only the absence of a comprehensive income tax (or instead a universal expenditure tax – see Chapter 10A) that renders it necessary for practical reasons to tax companies.

No country has attempted to implement a general system of full integration of corporate and personal taxation, because of the difficulties of taxing retained corporate profits at the personal level, in the context of a personal income tax progressive rate schedule, which applies in nearly all OECD countries. It would also be administratively cumbersome to impute corporate profits to individual shareholders since shares frequently change hands within the fiscal year. In theory, personal income tax on dividends plus full capital gains tax on shares, whether these gains have been realised or not, could be charged instead of imputing corporate profits to shareholders. However, in practice it would often be very difficult to evaluate non-realised capital gains on shares in unquoted private corporations, and even if this valuation problem could be overcome, a tax on non-realised gains could still impose a liquidity problem on shareholders.

The arguments for replacing the corporation income tax by VAT were never particularly convincing and since exchange rates ceased to be fixed nothing more has been heard of this proposal.

The third attack on the corporation income tax focuses on its non-neutrality and the inherent problems in measuring true economic profits and would seek to replace it by a cash flow corporation tax. Whatever view is taken of the arguments in favour of such a tax, its adoption would create practical problems at both the domestic and international level. As regards the former, there would be considerable implementational and transitional problems in adopting a cash flow corporation tax, accentuated by the fact that if it were to work properly it would require the simultaneous replacement of the personal income tax by a personal expenditure tax; and at the international level it would be difficult for one or a group of countries to adopt a cash flow tax in a world where the traditional personal and corporation income taxes remained in force.

Despite its imperfections the corporation income tax has certain useful functions. First, given that existing personal income taxes fail to tax on an accruals or integrated basis, the corporate tax enables revenue to be collected that would not otherwise be taxed at the personal level. Income taxes could be avoided at the personal level, because personal taxes can be deferred by companies retaining and reinvesting profits rather than paying them out as taxable dividends, thereby generating capital gains, realisation of which can often be postponed until a time chosen by shareholders, or because shareholders happen to be non-residents. A source-based corporation tax restricts shareholders' ability to defer (and thus to reduce) their tax liabilities. Secondly, the corporate tax has the function of taxing pure profit or economic rent (defined as firms' revenues in excess of the full opportunity costs of all inputs including capital, in other words, the excess of the amount of profit which the shareholder requires to make the investment worthwhile). Economists consider that this ought to be taxed, even if in practice the corporation tax tends to overtax it. Third, the corporate tax can be used for government stabilisation and structural policy purposes, since changes could influence the level and payment of interest in the corporate tax sector as well as its timing, whatever view is taken on whether it should be so used. Lastly, it enables source countries to tax all corporate income originating within their boundaries, including income accruing to foreign-owned corporations operating in their country, even though by taxing capital supplied by resident countries, it may reduce the supply of services and technology that might be otherwise supplied from such countries.

3. Statutory and effective rates of tax

Base and rates are necessarily interlinked, since nominal or statutory rates give no indication of corporate tax burdens without an indication of the base on which they are charged. To achieve a measure of *effective* tax rates as distinct from *nominal* tax rates on an internationally comparable basis requires heroic and simplifying assumptions, which have in fact been made in OECD 1991, the most comprehensive work in this area. Though international comparisons of effective tax rates yield interesting information which could influence government policies, because of their technicality and level of generality it is doubtful if they have yet done so. Nor, insofar as influences on business decisions go beyond statutory rates, would it be on the basis of a global analysis of effective tax rates but on much narrower parameters related to the tax treatment of their special situations. The empirical evidence as to whether or not business uses statutory rates in practice as a proxy for effective rates in taking their investment and location decisions is very confused. It seems inconceivable that sophisticated multinational enterprises would make such an equation, but it would seem that small and medium enterprises, according, for example, to evidence supplied to the 1992 Ruding Committee, often do. The OECD analysis does suggest that unintended distortions have been created both at the domestic level, for example between the depreciation of buildings and machinery, and at the international level where cross-border investment is usually treated less favourably from a tax point of view than investment within one country. However, because of their technicality and relative irrelevance hitherto to government domestic policy choices, effective tax rates are not further discussed in this book. Nor are any results reproduced, since these vary considerably according to the assumptions that are made. Many such results can be found in OECD 1991 and the Ruding Report 1992.

4. Base broadening and rate lowering: the general picture

The base broadening and rate lowering combination, already discussed in Chapter 10 in connection with the personal income tax, has also occurred in recent years with regard to the corporation income tax. Statutory rates have been reduced since 1986 in all OECD countries except Italy (where there was a slight increase in 1991), Spain and Switzerland. The corporate tax base may be widened in three separate ways: first, and perhaps of least importance, a stricter line could be taken with regard to the tax treatment of inventories, second, depreciation practices could be made less generous and, third, special allowances such as investment credits could be reduced or eliminated. There has been little change in the tax treatment of inventories over recent years while changes in depreciation practices have been, in various directions, more generous (France, Germany, Portugal), less generous (Ireland, the United Kingdom, the United States), ambiguous as regards generosity (Denmark, Italy, Japan), or they have undergone no or hardly any change (Belgium, Netherlands, Spain). However, France apart, the tendency has been overwhelmingly to reduce or to eliminate special allowances (see last column of Table 12.1) and at the level of generally applicable legislation the corporate tax base has probably widened even if less so than that of the personal income tax.

As indicated below most corporate tax systems remain non-neutral but governments have recently been placing more emphasis on providing a neutral tax structure under which investment patterns are primarily determined by non-tax factors. Nevertheless, there remain significant incentive provisions in most tax systems. Two approaches can be identified. First, some governments favour the provision of across-the-board investment incentives which apply to most sectors and types of activities. Here the objective is to increase the overall level of investment, but to leave the market to determine its allocation. A second approach, which is more prevalent, is to provide incentives for particular sectors or activities. The rationale behind this approach is that the government rather than the market may be better placed to "pick the winners", or that positive externalities may be associated with certain incentives, in particular, if incentives are limited in time to stimulate investment in times of recession.

A major influence on the trend towards lower statutory rates of tax is the need to ensure that a country's tax rate does not get too much out of line with that of its major trading partners. Statutory rates are important because they may influence taxpayers' perceptions of the effective tax rate, which is not always easy to measure and because they can influence how the worldwide tax base of a multinational enterprise is allocated between countries (by transfer pricing policies, for example). Thus, once the United Kingdom and the United States substantially reduced their rates in the eighties, many other countries also felt obliged to reduce their own rates. This in turn put pressure on them to widen the tax base so as to prevent erosion of the corporation tax yield.

5. Base narrowing and rate lowering in specific cases

In a few OECD countries there are some situations where the tax base has been narrowed and rates lowered to the extent that little or no corporation tax is payable. Two separate cases may be identified: first, special tax treatment to encourage certain domestic activities such as research and development and energy and environmental research or the economic development of particular regions, or small to medium enterprises; second, favourable tax treatment, such as that accorded to managerial and financial activities in Belgium, Ireland and Luxembourg, principally designed to create employment or to stop emigration by attracting inward investment from other countries. Such measures also have "beggar my neighbour" implications and raise international tax policy issues outside the scope of the present book.

Table 12.1: Corporate income tax changes and proposals between 1986 and 1992 relating to base and rate schedule[1]

Country	Base Broadening	Reduction of Rates	Various
Australia	1988 1991	1988	Removal of various incentives in 1988 and in 1991.
Austria	1989	1989	Removal of various incentives in 1989.
Belgium	1989/90	1989/90	
Canada	1988	1988	
Denmark	1990/91	1990/91	
Finland	1989 1990 1991	1990 1991	Limits to incentives in 1989–1991.
France		1989[2] 1990[2]	Introduction of new incentives relating to new firms in 1989 and to firms which reduce the working hours of their personnel in 1990.
Germany		1990	Limits to regional incentives in 1988.
Greece		1988	
Ireland	1988 to 1991	1988 1989 1991	Accelerated depreciation phased out. Tax rates reduced and rationalised. Export sales relief ended.
Iceland	1991	1991	Lowering of investment credits.
Italy[3]		1989	
Japan		1988 1989 1990	
Luxembourg		1987 1988 1989 1990	
Netherlands	1988	1988	
New Zealand		1988	
Norway	1992	1992	
Portugal	1989	1989	Removal of various incentives in 1989.
Spain			Limits to investment credit in 1989.
Sweden	1991	1991	
Switzerland			Flat rate proposals (June 1991)
United Kingdom	1986	1986 1991 1992	Reduction in rate for small companies in 1987 and 1988.
United States	1987	1987	Removal of various incentives and introduction of the new branch tax in 1987.

1. No major changes have been made or proposed in Turkey.

2. Only for retained profits.

3. Rate increase in 1991.

Various sources.

6. A brief summary of issues addressed in Sections B to E

a) Tax base issues

The issues involved are very technical and the discussion of policy issues in Section B is relatively brief. Subjects addressed are the definition and scope of the tax base, the definition and calculation of depreciation, the treatment of inventories and to what extent the tax base should be adjusted for inflation.

b) Tax rate issues

Section C covers the following two questions: first,is there any case for a multi-rate corporation income tax? Second, should the statutory rate of corporation tax be aligned to some rate or other on the generally progressive personal income tax schedule and, if so, should this be at the top rate or some other rate? (Whether or not a different rate should apply to distributed and retained earnings is discussed in Section D.)

c) The taxation of distributed profits

The taxation of distributed profits, first through the corporation tax system and second through personal income tax on shareholders' income has for many years been one of the most controversial issues in corporate tax policy. Many commentators claim that this double taxation discriminates against the corporate form of organisation, favours debt finance at the expense of equity finance, discriminates against finance by new share issues compared to finance by retained earnings and discourages corporate investment by raising the cost of corporate capital. Other commentators see few problems in the fact that distributed profits are subject both to corporation and personal income tax, either because they prefer to see the corporation as a separate entity distinct from its shareholders, believing that corporations should be taxed in their capacity as legal persons, or because they consider that the total amount of tax payable on distributed profits is more important than how much is paid by way of corporation tax, and how much by way of personal income tax on dividends. The second set of commentators may claim in addition that the double taxation of dividends does not seriously discourage investment in the corporate sector because only a minor part of that investment is financed by new share issues. Under debt finance there is no problem of economic double taxation, and in the case of investment financed by retaining earnings the return to shareholders accrues in the form of lightly-taxed capital gains on shares. On this basis it is concluded that abolition of the double taxation of dividends would yield an arbitrary windfall gain to existing shareholders and cause a loss of government revenue without significantly reducing the required rate of return on corporate investment.

Unfortunately, the discussion of these issues has been obscured by the misuse of language, as already examined to some extent in Chapter 5. Terms and expressions are used emotionally, rhetorically, ambiguously and also artificially in the sense that they have no relationship to the normal use of words in the English language, as is further discussed in the Annex to section D of this chapter. Abstracting from the more general issue referred to in Chapter 10 on what should be the relative income tax burden on earned income and income from capital, including dividend income, the substantive issues are, first, should any action be taken to offset the difference between distributed profits, subject both to corporation and personal income tax and retained profits which are subject only to the former? Second, if offsetting action is to be taken, should it be through relief for corporation tax on distributions, or for personal income tax on dividend income? Third, if such offsetting action is to be taken, which of the various available methods should be utilised?

d) Taxes on business other than corporation income taxes

These business taxes are briefly surveyed in Section E. Apart from the uniform business rate in the United Kingdom and payroll taxes in Australia and Austria, these very different kinds of taxes do not bring in much revenue and rarely raise important tax policy issues. Many of them exist today, only because they existed yesterday and to abolish them would require increases in other taxes which governments are reluctant to make. In particular, the mixed-base taxes are legitimately criticised as somewhat arbitrary, unfair and non-transparent and remain generally unpopular, but the fact that they generally represent own taxes for state and local government, which are even more constrained than central government in finding alternative sources of revenue, makes for their continuation. On the other hand, taxes on the net wealth of corporations or on their turnover can be defended on the ground that they represent a better proxy than profits as regards both ability to pay and under the benefit principle the advantages a corporation receives from government financed infrastructure, police protection, etc.

7. The contribution of business taxes to government revenues

The contribution of corporation tax revenues has already been illustrated and discussed in Part I (e.g. see Tables 2.2 and Charts 3.2 to 3.4). To recapitulate briefly, in 1989 the corporation income tax on average accounted for less than 8 per cent of total tax revenues, though the difference between countries is very great (e.g. 25 per cent of total tax revenues in Japan and less than 4 per cent in Austria, Iceland, Ireland, Portugal and Sweden). Over the last ten years average receipts have increased from 2.6 to 2.9 per cent of GDP and from 7.5 to 7.8 per cent of total tax receipts. As mentioned in Chapter 2, a better measure for purposes of international comparisons would be the ratio of corporate tax revenues to total profits but attempts to make such comparisons were considered too flawed to make the results worth publishing (OECD 1985).

Despite their relative unimportance in revenue terms compared with revenues from the personal income tax or social security contributions or consumption taxes, businessmen and hence politicians are keenly interested in their relative importance in their own country in relation to revenues collected from similar taxes collected in other countries. On the same lines, attempts have been made to compare total business tax receipts (including net wealth, property, payroll and mixed taxes as listed in Section E) as a percentage of GDP or total tax receipts. Such attempts seem doomed to failure and scarcely seem worth undertaking. First, it is virtually impossible to separate certain taxes from those levied on consumers and business inputs (e.g. excises on hydrocarbon oils); second, the various taxes unambiguously levied on business will be shifted to differing degrees and over differing periods into lower wages and salaries and/or higher prices; third, a number of these business taxes are in fact paid by businessmen from other countries. This therefore seems a blind alley into which there is no point in marching further.

8. Corporate tax collection lags

As with the personal income tax, it may seem somewhat incongruous in a book on tax policy to insert a paragraph on the essentially administrative problem of how the tax is collected. But these different methods of collection do affect cash flows to the state and effective rates of tax and, accordingly, could influence government decisions on statutory rates and coverage. These differences are summarised in Table 12.2, but nothing more is said about them.

B. The tax base

1. Definition and scope of taxable income

This sub-section records certain particular areas where the practices of OECD countries are generally similar and where they differ. Information on an internationally comparable basis is not always easy to come by and the list is by no means complete (for example, the tax treatment of reserves and of expenditures on research and development which vary between countries is omitted). In short the purpose of this sub-section is simply to provide some factual information on OECD country practices.

a) The relation between tax rules and financial accounting standards

Taxable income is calculated in similar ways under the different tax regimes. Income arising from all sources, including business or trading income, as well as non-business income, is normally included in the base. Although the concept of income is usually not defined, taxable income is, as a rule, computed under principles of "sound commercial accounting practice" and in most countries is based on the profits shown in the company accounts, though it varies as to whether accounting standards have derived from tax legislation or whether tax rules follow accounting practices. In some countries, however, such as Denmark, Ireland, the Netherlands, the United Kingdom and the United States, a number of adjustments are made to company accounts in arriving at income subject to tax.

b) Deduction of interest and other business expenses

Subject to restrictions in certain countries to prevent tax avoidance, all expenses (including interest) incurred wholly and exclusively in earning taxable income or in maintaining

Table 12.2: Corporation tax collection lags, January 1991

Country	Collection lag
Australia	85 per cent of the tax due must be paid within 28 days of the end of fiscal year. The remaining 15 per cent must be paid by the 15th day of the next month.
Austria	Taxes prepaid by quarterly instalment based on previous year's assessment.
Belgium	Tax is paid in quarterly instalments.
Canada	Monthly instalments. Balance of tax due two months after the end of the fiscal year.
Denmark	Lag will vary according to the company's own accounting period. Where the accounting period is the calendar year, the lag is $10^2/3$ months.
Finland	Lag will vary according to the company's own accounting period. However, where the accounting period is the calendar year, the first instalment (December) is paid in advance and the remaining instalments (February and March) within three months of the end of the fiscal year.
France	Tax is paid in four instalments during the fiscal year totalling 38 per cent of the taxable income of the preceding year. The balance must be paid no later than $3^1/2$ months after the end of the fiscal year.
Germany	Tax for the current year is paid in quarterly instalments. The final instalment is due when the final assessment is issued.
Greece	Tax is paid in seven equal instalments. The first instalment is due upon filing the tax return.
Iceland	Tax is paid in 10 monthly instalments in assessment year, the first five based on previous year's assessment, the last five on final assessment in July.
Ireland	Preliminary tax of not less than 90 per cent of the amount actually due is payable six months after the end of an accounting period. The balance becomes payable on submission of the tax return nine months after the end of an accounting period.
Italy	Tax is paid in two instalments: 39.2 per cent of the prior year's assessment is due when the prior year's return is filed and 58.8 per cent in the eleventh month of the company's financial year. The balance is due when the return for that year is submitted.
Japan	Tax must be paid at the same time the return is filed, usually three months after the end of the accounting period.
Luxembourg	Quarterly tax advances have to be paid. These are fixed by the tax authorities on the basis of the previous year's assessment.
Netherlands	Tax is paid in instalments during the year in which the income is earned on the basis of a provisional assessment. After the end of the accounting period, tax has to be paid within two months of the issue of a (provisional) assessment.
New Zealand	Tax is paid in instalments. Provisional tax on account of the current year's liability is payable in three instalments in the fourth, eighth and twelfth months of the taxpayer's income tax year. The balance is due in the eleventh month of the year following the assessment.
Norway	Companies are required to make advance payments on tax on 15 February and 15 April in the year following the income year. The balance must be paid in two instalments within two months of the assessment being issued.
Portugal	Tax is paid in four instalments. The first three, each equivalent to 25 per cent of the previous year's assessment, are due in June, September and December of the year in which taxable income arises. The final instalment is due upon filing the annual return in April of the following year.
Spain	Three payments on account of the current year's tax equivalent to 20 per cent of the previous year's tax are required to be made on 20 April, October and December. The balance is payable at the time of filing the return.
Sweden	Tax is collected during the year in which the income is earned under a preliminary tax system. Tax is paid in six equal instalments starting in March of the tax year. The balance is paid in the year after the assessment is made.
Switzerland	Tax is usually paid in two or three instalments based on the previous year's assessment.
Turkey	Tax is paid in three equal instalments in April, July and October of the year of filing. 50 per cent of the tax assessed in the previous year must be paid as an advance tax.
United Kingdom	Nine months after the end of the accounting period.
United States	Tax must be paid in full either by the time of the filing of the return or by the 15th of the third month following the close of the fiscal year, whichever comes first.

Source: Table 3.17 of *Taxing profits in a global economy* (OECD 1991).

the assets used in a company's activities are, in principle, deductible from income subject to tax, though there may be a variety of technical reasons why this principle is not fully

Table 12.3 : The treatment of corporate capital gains, January 1991

Country	Taxed at corporation rate	Tax at special rate	Inflation adjusted	Tax deferred if reinvested
Australia	Yes	—	Yes (holding period at least 12 months)	No
Austria	Yes	—	No	Yes[1]
Belgium	Yes (holding less than 5 years)	19.5% (more than 5 years)	No	Yes
Canada	75% of value	—	No	No
Denmark	Generally exempt	—	No	No
Finland	Yes [2, 3]	—	No	Yes
France	—	Less than 2 years 34%. More than 2 years 19% or 25%[4]	No	No
Germany	Yes	—	No	Yes
Greece	Yes	20% partition of business, 30% trade-mark, goodwill	No	No
Iceland	Yes	—	Yes	Yes
Ireland	—	Holding period / Rate Less than 3 years 50% 3–6 years 35% More than 6 years 30%	Yes	Yes
Italy	Yes	—	No	No[5]
Japan	Yes [3]	—	No	No
Luxembourg	Yes	—	No[6]	Yes
Netherlands	Yes	—	No	Yes[7]
New Zealand	Exempt	—	—	—
Norway	Yes [8]	—	No	Yes
Portugal	Yes	—	Yes[9]	Yes[10]
Spain	Yes	—	No	Yes
Sweden	Yes[11]	—	No	No[11]
Switzerland	Yes[3]	—	No	No
Turkey	Yes	—	No	Yes
United Kingdom	Yes	—	Yes	Yes
United States	Yes	—	No	No

Notes to Table 12.3

1. Under certain conditions (esp. 7 years minimum holding requirement, reinvestment in intangible assets).
2. Different rates for securities.
3. Special rates for real estate.
4. Must be reinvested, otherwise 34%.
5. Except in special cases.
6. Capital gains on buildings, in case of liquidation of a company, are corrected for inflation.
7. Subject to a four-year time limit.
8. For depreciable assets; other rules exist for other capital gains.
9. For depreciable assets and land.
10. Subject to a two-year time limit.
11. With respect to the special reserve provision based on corporate equity (see Table 3.4), the effective tax rate is 77% of the corporate tax rate.

Source: Table 3.4 of *Taxing profits in a global economy* (OECD 1991).

achieved in practice. Also, disputes may arise between businesses and the tax authorities in the interpretation of expenses incurred wholly and exclusively in earning taxable income.

c) *Treatment of trading losses*

All countries allow a company to carry forward trading losses and eight OECD countries (Canada, France, Germany, Ireland, Japan, the Netherlands, the United Kingdom, the United States) allow a carry back of trading losses, varying from one to three years. The number of years over which trading losses can be carried forward ranges from five years to indefinitely.

d) *Treatment of capital gains*

The rules governing the taxation of corporate capital gains are summarised in Table 12.3. Most countries provide for taxation of corporate capital gains at the full corporate rate, though a number of countries exempt capital gains which are reinvested in the corporation.

e) *General investment grants*

There are no general investment grants taking the form of cash transfers in OECD countries and tax credits exist only in Luxembourg (for investment exceeding the average of the last five years) and in Spain (for new fixed assets). Tax allowances, however, of varying amounts and under varying conditions are provided in Austria, Belgium, Finland, Greece, Iceland, the Netherlands, Sweden and Turkey.

2. Definition and calculation of depreciation

All countries provide tax allowances for the depreciation of assets but the way in which they do so varies considerably. Because of the complexity of depreciation provisions it is not easy to bring out these differences unambiguously but, with some simplifications and omissions, Table 12.4 does so for the depreciation of building and machinery. (Another contentious area not covered here is whether "goodwill" should be regarded as a depreciable asset and whilst most countries so regard it, some do not.)

Table 12.4: Depreciation systems, January 1991

Country	Depreciation		Switch–over[1]		Rate of depreciation in percent			
	Machinery	Buildings	Machinery	Buildings	Machinery	Buildings	Machinery	Buildings
					SL	DB	SL	DB
Australia	SL/DB	SL	No	No	12%	1.5 x SL	2.5	—
Austria	SL	SL	n.a.	n.a.	10	—	4	—
Belgium	SL/DB	SL/DB	Yes	Yes	20	2 x SL	3–5	2 x SL
Canada	DB	DB	n.a.	n.a.	—	25	—	4
Denmark	DB	SL	n.a.	n.a.	—	30	6/2	—
Finland	DB	DB	n.a.	n.a.	—	30	—	9
France	SL/DB	SL	Yes	n.a.	10–20	1.5/2.5 x SL	5	—
Germany	SL/DB	SL	Yes	n.a.	10	3 x SL	2.5–10	—
Greece	SL	SL	n.a.	n.a.	10–20	—	8	—
Iceland	SL	SL	n.a.	n.a.	12–20	—	2	—
Ireland	DB	SL	n.a.	n.a.	—	10–25	4	—
Italy	SL	SL	n.a.	n.a.	10	—	5	—
Japan	SL/DB	SL/DB	Yes	Yes	10	3 x SL	2.2–4.3	3 x SL
Luxembourg	SL/DB	SL	Yes	n.a.	10–20	3 x SL	2–4	—
Netherlands	SL/DB	SL/DB	Yes	Yes	10–15	2 x SL	3.3	2 x SL
New Zealand	SL/DB	SL	Yes	n.a.	10	1.5 x SL	2	—
Norway	DB	DB	n.a.	n.a.	—	30	—	7
Portugal	SL/DB	SL	No	No	12.5–25	1.5/2.5 x SL	5	—
Spain	SL/DB	SL/DB	No	No	8	2.5 x SL	3	2.5 x SL
Sweden	SL/DB	SL	Yes	n.a.	20	30	1.5–5	—
Switzerland	SL/DB	SL/DB	No	No	0.5 x DB	30–40	0.5 x DB	7–8
Turkey	SL/DB	SL/DB	Yes	Yes	20%	2 x SL	4	2 x SL
United Kingdom	DB	SL	n.a.	n.a.	—	25	4	—
United States	SL/DB	SL	Yes	n.a.	14.3	2 x SL	3.2	—

1. Switch over from declining balance to straight line but not vice versa.

SL = straight line.

DB = declining balance.

n.a. = not applicable.

Source: Table 3.9 of *Taxing profits in a global economy* (OECD 1991).

At a more general level this once again raises the question of whether tax neutrality or tax interventionism should prevail. Some countries, but not others, have chosen the neutrality route in attempting to keep tax depreciation as close as possible to economic depreciation (which takes into account the wearing out of assets as well as obsolescence) whereas others have intentionally provided tax rules which are more generous. Accurate measurement of economic depreciation is technically and administratively very difficult and most countries therefore utilise some standardised depreciation rules such as straight line depreciation (being equal allowances over the length of the tax life of the asset) or declining balance (being a fixed percentage of depreciated book value, where the actual allowance is larger in the initial year and gradually diminishes in subsequent years).

Incentives granted in this field generally take the form of accelerated depreciation, i.e. by allowing depreciation at a higher rate than is justified on purely technical or economic grounds in the early years of the useful life of the asset as operated in Germany (for small companies only), Italy, Japan, Luxembourg and Switzerland (for environmental and energy investment), and Portugal and Spain (only under certain conditions and in certain sectors). Apart from infringing neutrality, accelerated depreciation provisions have the disadvantage that they are not transparent, in that it is not clear how much tax revenue is forgone in any particular instance, and they are capable of manipulation for tax avoidance purposes.

3. The valuation of stocks

There are a variety of methods of valuing stock for tax purposes (e.g. actual cost, weighted average price, indexed FIFO, etc.) but basically these methods are variants of LIFO and FIFO. Under the FIFO method the first items purchased are assumed to be disposed of first, whereas under the LIFO method the items last acquired are assumed to have been disposed first when the cost of sales from inventories is evaluated. The principal difference between the two systems is that where FIFO is used, increases in the value of inventories solely due to inflation are taxed in the absence of indexation, whereas with LIFO, though they are taxed, the time at which they are taxed is deferred. Inventories can be valued under the FIFO method in all OECD countries with the exception of Germany and the LIFO method is allowed in thirteen countries (Austria, Belgium, Denmark, France, Germany, Greece, Italy, Japan, Luxembourg, the Netherlands, Portugal, Switzerland, the United States) although six (Austria, Belgium, Denmark, Finland, France, Luxembourg) impose some restrictions on the use of this method. All OECD countries allow actual cost valuation where this method is feasible.

4. Offsetting the tax base for inflation

To offset or not to offset the tax base for inflation is of relevance in a number of areas already discussed (i.e. interest deductibility, capital gains, depreciation provisions, and stock valuation). This is probably the most difficult and important policy issue with regard to the tax base and it is extremely difficult both because of conflicting objectives and the complexity of inflation adjustment in this area to come to any coherent solution – and no OECD government has (even if such solutions have been sought in countries outside the OECD with three-digit inflation such as Brazil and Chile). Fortunately, the combination of reduced rates of corporation tax and reduced rates of inflation in most OECD countries has rendered the problem less important than it seemed ten years ago. However, the problem remains of importance, especially as it cannot be assumed that inflation rates are permanently under control.

Leaving aside for a moment the practical complexities of inflation adjustment, the main problem is that while inflation may create all kinds of distortions between different types of assets and industries, adjustments for inflation to the corporate tax base in a situation where personal income and capital gains taxes and financial reporting systems are mainly geared to nominal rather than real income may cause other distortions, arbitrarily providing windfalls to some taxpayers and penalising others. For example, to the extent that stocks have been financed by debt and relief is given for interest, inflation adjustment could overcompensate corporations for inflation.

It is, however, mainly for practical reasons that OECD countries have adopted pragmatic ad hoc approaches to inflation adjustment. Systematic indexation against inflation would require great complexity in designing indexing procedures, defining a real interest rate and handling financial assets and liabilities within an international group of companies, as well as involving much more record keeping for both business and tax administrations. When rates of inflation (and tax rates) were high, devices like accelerated depreciation were introduced as corrective measures even if allowances were at the same time based on historical costs, taxes on capital gains were indexed in some countries (see Table 12.3) and the LIFO method provided some offset to the impact of inflation on the replacement of inventories.

C. Tax rates

1. One or more rates?

Table 12.5 sets out corporation tax statutory rules prevailing at 1 January 1991. Unless there is a strong case for progressive rates on equity, economic efficiency or simply grounds of voter-appeal, it is simpler to remain with a single rate, which also prevents the possibility of tax avoidance which multi-rates open up. The case for multi-rate corporate taxes is much less strong than that for the progressive personal income tax, since enterprises are not people and there is little rationale on equity grounds for taxing enterprises making large profits at higher rates than those making small profits. Austria and Portugal have recently abandoned multi-rates and like most OECD countries now have one single rate. On the other hand, Japan proposed the introduction of a special 2.5 per cent surcharge on corporation tax in excess of 4 million yen during the period 1 April 1992 to 31 March 1993. Belgium, Canada, Finland, Japan, Luxembourg, the United Kingdom and the United States levy lower rates either on firms making lower profits or for small or medium enterprises or for both, but only Switzerland remains with a progressive rate schedule throughout the range of profits. The Netherlands even imposes a regressive two-rate schedule to provide a threshold to incorporation by sole proprietorships and partnerships.

Nevertheless, there are pressures both to subject firms with large profits to higher taxation and firms with small profits to lower taxation. It may be held, perhaps mainly on political grounds, that on the assumption that corporate entities are accepted in some way as hav-

Table 12.5: Statutory corporation tax rates, at 1 January 1991 (in per cent)[1]

Country	Central Government	Intermediate Government	Local Government	Local Tax Deductible	Overall Tax Rate
Australia	39	—	—		39
Austria	30	—	12.9	Yes	39
Belgium[2]	39	—	—		39
Canada[2]	28.84(23.84)[3]	12.9(11.9)	—	No	41.74(35.74)
Denmark	38	—	—		38
Finland[2]	23	—	17.2	No	40.2
France	34	—	—		34
	42[4]	—	—		42[4]
Germany	50	—	13	Yes	56.5
	36[4]	—	13	Yes	44.3[4]
Greece	46(40)	—	—		46(40)
Iceland	45	—	—		45
Ireland	40(10)[5]	—	—		40(10)[5]
Italy	36	—	16.2	Yes[6]	47.83
Japan[2]	37.5	—	12 + 6.49	Yes	49.98
Luxembourg[2]	33.33	—	9.09	Yes	39.39
Netherlands	35[7]	—	—		35
New Zealand	33	—	—		33
Norway	27.8	—	23	No	50.8
Portugal	36	—	3.6	No	39.6
Spain	35[8]	—	[8]	Yes	35.34
Sweden	30	—	—		30
Switzerland	3.63–9.8[9]	4.32–12.96[9]	5.20–15.60[9]	Yes	13.15–38.36
Turkey	49.2	—	—		49.2
United Kingdom[2]	33	—	—		34
United States[2, 10]	34	6.5[11]	—	Yes	38.3

1. No account is taken in this table of reductions through imputation credits.
2. These countries apply lower rates to corporations with profits below a certain threshold or to small businesses.
3. 23.84 per cent for the manufacturing sector, otherwise 28.84 per cent.
4. On distributed profits.
5. In Greece 40 per cent for manufacturing, hotels and certain other sectors, otherwise 46 per cent. In Ireland 10 per cent primarily for the manufacturing sector, otherwise 43 per cent.
6. Holds for 75 per cent of local tax.
7. A higher rate of 40 per cent is applied on the first 250 000 Dfl. of profits.
8. In addition, a 1.5 per cent surtax levied by the Chamber of Commerce, see country chapter for details.
9. Progressive rate schedule.
10. Average rate for state and local taxes.
11. Includes average tax rate for local governments.

Source: Table 3.14 of *Taxing profits in a global economy* (OECD (1991).

ing an independent existence those with a higher taxable capacity, taking greater advantage from the infrastructure, depreciation allowances, etc. should be subject to heavier taxation in some form or other. Two alternatives are the imposition of net-wealth taxes on enterprises or the imposition of a lump sum addition to firms making higher profits, having greater net wealth or turnover. In France, there is an annual lump sum tax related to the turnover of corporations, ranging from 5 000 Ffrs. for those with less than one million francs turnover to 21 000 Frs. in excess of ten million francs turnover. However, in practice these devices do not impose a heavier burden on enterprises making higher profits, but rather on those with greater assets or larger turnover. The rationale is anyway doubtful and heavier taxation of larger or more profitable firms does not obtain in most OECD countries.

At the other end of the scale, reduced taxation is provided in the countries noted above through the rate schedule, either for firms making low profits or for small businesses, or both. From an interventionist view, some case can be made out for giving aid to both low-profit making firms and small businesses, especially as the latter at any rate are usually unlikely to be able to take full advantage of the various means of reducing effective tax rates via depreciation provisions, etc.; and it is also arguable that such enterprises are unlikely to make substantial distributions and are so unable to receive the advantage of any imputation on shareholder provision relief. On the other hand, a large proportion of these small businesses go bankrupt before they have even started to make profits and these blanket low rates for businesses taxable below a certain size encourage them to make themselves appear even smaller than they are to the tax authorities to obtain the benefit of the lower rate. In addition, it has been observed that these enterprises often pay virtually no corporation tax, because profits are generally withdrawn as salaries. From a government point of view such blanket relief has the attraction of appearing to encourage small enterprises at the cost of forgoing only potential revenues: but whether objectively such measures are the most effective way of aiding small to medium enterprises is another matter. (See Chapter 7A and 7F where the treatment of SME's has been discussed in more general terms.)

2. Alignment of corporate and personal income tax rates

One of the factors that may encourage those traders who have in practice the choice to incorporate and be subject to the corporate tax regime, or to remain unincorporated and be subject to personal income tax is the relative statutory rates of the two taxes, and accordingly there have been moves in certain countries (e.g. Austria and Finland) to align them for that reason. Of course, there are many factors other than the rates of the two taxes, including the tax base and various non-tax factors which could affect the incorporation decision. One problem is whether the corporation tax rate should be aligned to the top personal income tax rate (as is usually assumed) or some lower rate, a problem less acute than it was with the lowering of personal income tax rates and flattening of schedules, which over the last few years has had the incidental effect of bringing the two rates of tax in question closer together (see Tables 12.6 and 12.9).

Table 12.6: Changes in the rate structure of corporate income tax of central government[1] between 1986 and 1991 (Tax rates to nearest percentage point)

Country	**Basic rate[2]**	
	January 1986	**January 1991**
Australia	49	39
Austria[3]	30/40/50/55	30
Belgium	45	39
Canada[3]	36(15)	29(13)
Denmark	50	38
Finland[3]	33[3](17)	23(17)
France	45	34
Germany[3]	56	50
Greece	49	46
Iceland	51	45
Ireland	40/50	40
Italy[3]	36(10)	36(10)
Japan[3]	43[6](19)	37.5[6](19)
Luxembourg[3]	40	33
Netherlands	42	35
New Zealand	45	33
Norway[3]	28(23)	28(23)
Portugal[3]	42/47	36.5(3.65)
Spain	35	35
Sweden	52	30
Switzerland[3,4]	4–10	4–10
Turkey	46	49
United Kingdom	35[6]	34[6](33 from 4/91)
United States[3,5]	15/18/30/40/46	15/25/34

1. State/Local tax rates are shown in brackets where information is available. No information is available for Switzerland and the United States.

2. The table does not refer to the reduced rates for certain specified industries and qualified companies in a number of countries including Canada (now abolished), Greece and Ireland.

3. Countries with corporate taxes at subordinate levels of government.

4. The direct federal tax is imposed at rates of 3.63% to 9.8% of net profits. As a general rule, the maximum income tax rate on profit before tax for federal, cantonal and communal taxes is approximately 20% and 35% depending on the company's canton of residence.

5. A 5% surtax applies on taxable income between $100 000 and $333 000.

6. There is a reduced rate for small enterprises.

Source: Tables 3.24 and 3.19 of *Taxing profits in a global economy* (OECD 1991).

3. Corporate tax rate reductions in recent years

As already noted, corporate rates of tax have been substantially reduced in most countries over the last five years. Table 12.6 compares the central government corporate tax rates on retained profits in 1986 and in 1991.

4. Relative rates of tax on retained and distributed profits

This is a question discussed in the next section in the context of the taxation of distributed profits. Here it is simply recorded that apart from Norway (at central government level) and Greece which do not subject distributed profits to corporate tax, only Germany currently applies a lower rate to distributed profits, though between 1989 and 1991 France imposed a lower rate on *retained* profits.

D. The taxation of distributed profits

1. Terminological and classification questions

a) The meaning of words

> "When I use a word, Humpty Dumpty said, in a rather scornful tone it means just what I choose it to mean – neither more nor less." "The question is, said Alice, whether you *can* make words mean so many different things." "The question is, said Humpty Dumpty, which is to be master – that's all."
>
> Lewis Carroll *Through the looking glass and what Alice found there*.
> (p. 269, Penguin Edition, 1965)

There have been many "masters" staking their claim in the area of the taxation of distributed profits where words have been used in many different senses by different persons and frequently by the same person and often they bear no relation to how English terms and expressions are normally used. That is why some terminological spring cleaning seems necessary. However, as the general reader might find it a little tedious, it is relegated to an Annex to this section, but it should be noted that the terminology used in the rest of this section sometimes departs from that generally used.

b) A terminology for systems and methods currently in existence

The expression "classical system" (sometimes called "separate" or "separate entity system") is used to cover both cases where no tax relief is given at either company or shareholder level to distributed profits (unmodified classical system) and where it is given by way of limited shareholder relief provisions which bear no relation to the amount of corporate tax paid on the distributions (modified classical system).

"Imputation system" is used to refer exclusively to systems where there is a direct link between tax credit given to the shareholder in respect of income tax paid on dividends received and corporation tax paid by the distributing company, full imputation referring to the case where *all* the tax on distributed profits is taken into account in the shareholder's credit, and partial imputation where only some of it is.

In a number of countries favourable tax treatment is given to dividend income from domestic sources irrespective of what, if any, corporate tax has been paid. For the reasons discussed in the Annex to this chapter, these are referred to as a modified classical system or shareholder relief provisions. Such favourable personal income tax treatment may take a variety of forms which include:

- credit for some proportion of the dividend (Canada and previously Belgium and Denmark);
- taxing dividend income at the lowest rate applied to wage and salary income (Belgium now);
- a separate more favourable rate schedule for dividend income than that for earned income (Denmark now);
- no income tax at all on dividend income [United States Treasury, (1992) preferred proposal].

Other variants were also proposed during the discussions of the Ruding Committee, including a maximum rate on dividend income. These different methods of giving relief to dividend income have been described variously as imputation systems, tax credit systems and modified classical systems. The last approach is followed in this Chapter. The problem with calling these reliefs imputation systems is that "to impute" in the English language means "to attribute": where there is a defined relationship between corporation tax paid and personal income tax relief on dividends, it is the former that is being attributed, but where there is no such relationship nothing is being attributed. Moreover, it is misleading to describe preferential tax treatment for dividend income as a system. The problem with calling these provisions a tax credit is that while this used to be a fair description it is now so only in Canada (see previous paragraph).

As regards relief at company level, "dividend deduction method" is used to describe cases where a deduction is made from the corporate tax base in assessing tax to be paid on distributed profits and "split rate method" to describe cases where the preferential treatment for distributed over retained profits takes the form of a lower rate rather than a deduction from the base. The "zero rate method" is one in which no corporation tax at all is charged on distributed profits.

c) A classification of country practices

When it comes to classifying the various systems and methods to illustrate how country practices resemble or differ from each other, it has to be accepted that any classification is open to criticism, much depending upon what it is considered most important to emphasise. For example, if it is deemed more important to emphasise the fact that shareholders in some way get preferential treatment for their dividend income vis-à-vis other sources of income it is logical to classify imputation systems and shareholder relief methods together (as OECD 1991), but if it is considered more important to compare different *systems* and to regard shareholder relief methods in the policy context of distinguishing between the income tax treatment of different sources of income another classification is required (as in this chapter). This unusual classification is preferred because in practice shareholder relief provisions have generally been introduced not for reasons of offsetting the tax differential between distributed and retained profits as such, but rather to encourage citizens to invest in domestic equities (Canada and Denmark). Where it seems appropriate, however, to compare imputation systems with shareholder relief methods as a means of reducing shareholders' personal income tax on their dividends, they are so compared (see Section 7). Also, it has to be admitted that calling the Austrian system "modified classical" when the schedule rate on dividend income is as much as half that on other sources of income may seem odd: evidently the classification as "modified classical" would be completely inappropriate if the latest United States "dividend exclusion" proposal with total exemption for dividend income in the hands of the shareholder ever became operative (see sub-section 8 below). It is arguable whether small amounts of dividend relief as the 10 per cent credit in Spain should be ignored on *de minimus* grounds as is done in Table 12.7 or taken into account as is done in other classifications (e.g. Cnossen, 1992). Finally, country preferences also differ: Belgium considers its regime to be classical whereas the not so dissimilar regime prevailing in Denmark is considered by that country to be non-classical (see OECD 1991), all of which indicates the difficulties in producing a rational classification of the ways of taxing distributed profits.

Table 12.7 provides a classification of OECD country practices within the framework discussed above and reveals the great diversity among OECD countries' tax treatment of distributed profits. It does not take into account targeted shareholder relief provisions as distinct from general provisions, which for example exist in France and the United Kingdom. More importantly, Table 12.7 does not indicate how much relief is accorded under partial relief systems or methods. Calculations to establish this are quite complicated and different methodologies may yield different results. Annex 2 to OECD 1991 provides one methodology for calculating the amount of relief given, the so-called ACID test as used in the Ruding report provides another and the results between the two are fairly similar. However, these results require careful interpretation and the methodology is too technical to describe in a book of this kind.

2. Country practices

a) Developments over the last three decades

Changes in country practices over the last 30 years are provided in Table 12.8, though it may well be that some are missing. Subject to this possibility, it shows, first, that there have been only 21 changes in the OECD over the last 30 years and more than one change has occurred only in Austria, Belgium, France and the United Kingdom (last time 1973). Second, three separate trends may be identified: between 1965 and 1976 the move was universally towards offsetting the greater tax burden on distributed vis-à-vis retained profits; between 1976 and 1985 there were no changes at all apart from in Italy which followed the earlier trend. Between 1986 and 1991 there have been a number of changes, but no clear trend: sometimes the offset has been increased (Australia, Finland, New Zealand,

Table 12.7: A classification of the tax treatment of distributed profits at central government level[1], January 1992

Classical system		Imputation systems		Reduced taxation of distributed profits at company level		
(1)	(2)	(3)	(4)	(5)	(6)	(7)
Unmodified classical	Modified classical	Partial imputation systems	Full imputation systems	Split rate method	Dividend deduction method	Zero rate method
(no or little relief for personal income tax on dividends)	(shareholder relief of various kinds for personal tax on dividends unconnected with corporation tax paid on the distribution)	Partial credit is given for shareholder income tax liability in respect of corporation tax paid on distributed profits	Full credit is given for shareholders income tax liability in respect of corporation tax paid on distributed profits	A lower rate is applied to distributed profits than to retained profits	A deduction is provided from the corporation tax base for distributed profits	Corporation tax is not charged on distributed profits
Luxembourg[2] Netherlands Switzerland[2] United States[2]	Australia[2] Belgium Canada[2] Denmark Iceland Japan[2] Portugal[2]	France Ireland United Kingdom	Australia Finland[2] Germany[2] Italy[2] New Zealand	Germany[2]	Iceland Spain Sweden	Greece Norway[2]

1. Turkey is excluded because of too many contradictory reports about how the system operates. It would seem to belong in column 4 but with certain differences.

2. Countries with unmodified classical systems of corporation tax or other profit related tax at subordinate levels of government.

Country amplifications:

France	Between 1989 and end 1991 a *lower* rate on retained than on distributed profits. Now rates are identical.
Germany	Since 1976 has both full imputation and split rate.
Greece	Though formally providing total relief of corporation tax on distributions, there are withholding taxes ranging from 42 to 50 per cent, which exceeds the usual 35 per cent domestic corporation tax charge.
Sweden	The dividend deduction applies *only* to new share issues.
Iceland	Partial relief at company level plus partial relief on dividend income.
Spain	In addition to a dividend deduction there is a 10 per cent shareholder relief provision {considered too small to be shown under column (2)}.
Turkey	No personal income tax is charged on dividends distributed out of profits which have borne corporation tax: a withholding tax of 10 per cent is applied to profits exempt from corporation tax.

Various sources, but the classification is mine. Many different classifications have been published. The reasons for adopting this one are set out in Section 12D1.

Table 12.8: Country changes in the taxation of distributed profits, 1962 to 1991

1962:	Belgium introduces partial shareholder relief provisions.
1965:	United Kingdom removes partial shareholder relief provisions from its classical system.
1965:	France moves from classical system to imputation system.
1968:	Austria moves from classical system to split rate system.
1968:	Sweden moves from classical system to partial dividend deduction (for new issues only).
1970:	Norway moves from classical system to zero rate system.
1971:	Canada changes its form of shareholder relief provisions.
1973:	United Kingdom moves from classical to partial imputation system.
1976:	Germany moves from split rate to split rate plus full imputation.
1983:	Italy moves from partial to full imputation.
1986:	Austria adds partial shareholder relief to its split rate system.
1987:	Australia moves from classical to full imputation.
1988:	New Zealand moves from classical to full imputation.
1989:	Austria abolishes split rate system.
1989:	Portugal moves from split rate to partial shareholder relief.
1989:	France introduces lower rate for retained profits.
1989:	Finland moves from partial dividend deduction to full imputation.
1990:	Belgium changes its form of shareholder relief provisions.
1990:	Japan abolishes split rate system.
1991:	Denmark abandons a full imputation proposal in favour of changing its form of shareholder relief provisions.
Proposals from the Commission of the European Community	
1962:	Neumark Report recommends split rate system for the European Communities.
1970:	Van den Tempe Report recommends classical system .
1975:	EC Commission recommends adoption of partial imputation system.
1990:	EC Commission withdraws 1975 proposals, pending a further enquiry into the need and desirability of harmonising its Member Countries' systems, rate and base and establishes a group of independent experts to make recommendations.
1992:	Group of experts (Ruding Committee) whilst agreeing desirability of harmonised system in the long term, make no recommendations for any particular system in the short term.

Various Sources.

Table 12.9: Corporation tax rates compared to personal income tax rates on dividends and interest (all levels of government)

Country	Overall corporation tax rate*	Tax Rate on Dividends[1]		Tax Rate on Interest	
		Top Rate	Average Marginal Rate	Top Rate	Average Marginal Rate
Australia	39	48.3	39	48.3	39
Austria[2]	39	25	19.8	50	39.7
Belgium[3]	39	25	25	10	10
Canada	36–42	49.1	44.6	49.1	39.5
Denmark	38	45	37.6	57.8	51.1
Finland[4]	40.2	60	45.2	10	10
France[5]	34	57.9	45	18.1[6]	5.6
Germany	56.5	53	39.1	53	39.1
Greece	48	50	n.a.	25	0
Iceland	45	39.8[7]	15.8	0	0
Ireland	43	53	50(27)[8]	53	38.4
Italy	48	50	39.4	30	12.5
Japan	50	35[9]	35	20	20
Luxembourg	39	51.25	24.6	51.25	24.6
Netherlands	35	60	49[10]	60	42[10]
New Zealand	33	33	28.6	33	25.9
Norway	51	19.5	n.a	40.5	n.a
Portugal	40	25[11]	25	25	25
Spain[12]	35	56	28.4	56	31.5
Sweden	30	30	30	30	30
Switzerland	15–38	43.8	30.8	43.8	30.8
Turkey	49	10	10	10	10
UK	34	40	32	40	24
USA	38	36	31	36	28

1. Based on statutory rates prior to any gross-up and dividend tax credits.

2. The cost of newly issued shares is deductible from personal tax.

3. The 25% withholding tax on dividends and the 10% withholding tax on interest is the final tax paid.

4. Interest income from certain types of bonds is exempt from tax.

5. Including an additional tax of 1.1% introduced in 1991 (cotisation sociale généralisée).

6. Different withholding tax rates are applied to different sorts of interest income; the figure used reflects that in State bonds.

7. Iceland exempts dividends from personal tax up to 15% of total value of shares owned by the taxpayer. This exemption, however, is subject to an upper limit.

8. Figure in brackets is the average marginal rate on manufacturing dividends. This is lower than the overall average marginal rate on dividends because half of manufacturing dividend income is exempt from taxation (subject to not more than IR £7 000 being exempted in any tax year).

9. Japanese shareholders have a choice between a final withholding tax and personal tax. The above figures reflect the withholding tax.

Notes to Table 12.9 (cont.).
10. The dividend and interest exemptions have not been taken into account.
11. A withholding tax of 25% is levied on 80% of the value of dividends from shares quoted on the Portuguese Stock Exchange. Individuals may elect withholding taxes as the final tax they pay on the dividends.
12. Spanish interest income is taxed as ordinary income, 10% of dividends received can be deducted from the personal income tax.
* See Table 12.5 of this book for qualifying footnotes to this column.
Source: Table 3.14 and 3.19 of *Taxing profits in a global economy* (OECD 1992).

Turkey) sometimes reduced (Japan) sometimes increased in one sense and reduced in another (Austria, France), sometimes changed in form (Belgium, Denmark, Portugal). However, in quantitative terms, according to the ACID test, referred to in the last paragraph, the offsets have continued to increase in a number of countries during the last decade. Third, new fashions have emerged in recent years: whilst Australia, Finland and New Zealand have followed the German/Italian move to full imputation systems, other countries have abolished the split rate or dividend deduction method (Austria, Japan, Portugal) or have introduced shareholder relief provisions (Portugal) or substantially changed the method of giving the shareholder relief by moving from a tax credit to a separate schedule for dividend income (Belgium and Denmark). Another observation is that recommendations emanating from the EC Commission have so far had no effect on the practices of EC Member Countries. The bottom of Table 12.8 indicates the various suggestions of the Commission, and it can be seen that there was no change to a split rate system between 1962 and 1970, no change to a classical system between 1970 and 1975 and no change to partial imputation systems since 1975. On the contrary a number of EC countries have moved in other directions.

b) The relation between statutory corporate and personal income tax rates on dividends

In the various arguments about to be examined for and against the various ways of taxing distributed profits, it is not only the system but the statutory rates of corporation tax and personal income tax rates on dividends and interest income that are regarded as relevant and Table 12.9 accordingly provides details of these. In comparing statutory corporate rates with personal income tax rates on dividends it is arguable that what should be compared with the corporation tax rate is the average marginal personal rate of tax on dividend income[1], but that is not possible to calculate on an internationally comparable basis. Table 12.9 provides calculations of this average marginal personal rate, but without assurance that the results are altogether internationally comparable, and so as a proxy the maximum rate on dividend income is also included, which evidently in most countries is higher than the average marginal rates on dividend income. Table 12.9 shows that it is more often the case that the corporation tax rate is higher than the average marginal rate of income tax on dividends income than the reverse. Only in four countries (Australia,

1. This is based on the ratio between the total amount of increase in tax and the total amount of increase in dividend income, both aggregated over all taxpayers.

Denmark, Sweden and the United Kingdom) are the two sets of rates identical or almost identical. It may also be argued that the overall shareholder rate is the appropriate comparison, which atypically in the United Kingdom is close to zero because most dividends are paid to tax-exempt financial institutions.

Table 12.9 also shows the relative rates of personal income tax on dividend and interest income. Countries' treatment of these sources vary greatly, interest income being taxed at a lower rate in most, but by no means all, countries. However, the tax bias in favour of debt financing has much more to do with the deductibility of interest payments and non-deductibility of dividend payments from income subject to tax than with the differences in these rates.

3. Factors relevant to the choice of a system or method

a) Economic efficiency and neutrality

This is by far the most important consideration, for it is only if it is considered that significant improvements can be made to economic efficiency that it is worth undertaking the disrupting task of fundamentally changing a corporate tax system. The debate has focused mainly on the effects that different systems may have in influencing the choices of companies and shareholders with respect to the three main sources of financing investment – viz. loan capital, retained earnings and new share issues. Neutrality of income tax systems is the generally preferred benchmark since its absence could lead to tax arbitrage which in turn could result in an unfair distribution of tax burdens and a revenue loss to governments, but conflicting interventionist goals have also to be taken into account.

The tax system can be shown to be neutral towards corporate financing decisions if a given pre-tax flow of corporate profits produces the same after-tax income in the hands of the ultimate investors, whether the return of investors takes the form of interest payments, of dividends, or of capital gains on shares. This requires that the combined corporate and personal tax burden on a unit of distributed profits be equal to the combined tax burden on retained profits, and that the total burden on distributions or retentions in turn be equal to the effective tax rate on a unit of corporate interest payments. OECD corporate tax systems are generally not neutral towards corporate financing decisions, in that they tend to favour debt finance, because corporate interest payments are deductible from the corporate tax base and because effective tax rates on interest income are often low. If, as a consequence the corporations rely excessively on debt, this could threaten the financial stability of the corporate sector and make corporations too vulnerable to downturns of the business cycle, thereby destabilising the national economy. In several countries the debt-equity ratio of the corporate sector does indeed seem to have increased during the eighties, but at the same time there has been a development of new debt instruments which allow corporations, especially large firms, more flexibility in meeting their interest obligations.

One consequence of the fact that under most OECD tax systems the combined corporate and personal tax burden on distributed profits exceeds that on retained profits is that corporations usually – pension funds excluded – have an incentive to retain their earnings, thereby providing shareholders with a lightly taxed capital gain on their shares instead of paying out a more heavily taxed dividend. As with the tax incentive for debt finance, the tax preference for retentions over distributions has been criticised. It has been claimed that a high retention ratio makes it more difficult to reallocate funds from mature, slow-growing companies to more innovative and fast-growing corporations which have to rely on external sources of finance and that if the dividend-payout ratio were higher, funds would be more smoothly channelled to those firms and sectors where it can be invested most productively. On the other hand, it has also been held that a tax policy encouraging corporate retentions will help to aggregate savings and capital accumulation in the private sector, on the grounds that the marginal propensity to consume is likely to be higher out of dividend income than out of capital gains. Although the capital gains on shares produced by corporate retentions may stimulate household consumption, the evidence suggests that consumption usually does not increase by the full amount of an increase in retained corporate profits. Hence higher corporate retentions should in fact tend to increase aggregate private savings, and if this is an important policy goal, it may be found to justify some tax discrimination against corporate distributions. The lack of a generally accepted theory of corporate finance and disagreement on the effects of taxation on corporate financial policy are often the basic reasons for the conflicting views on the corporate income tax expressed in debates on tax policy. Three views, each of which is based on a specific assumption regarding the interaction of taxation and corporate financial policy, have been expressed: these are known as the "optimistic view", the "old view" and the "new view".

The "optimistic" view of the corporation tax assumes that companies typically use debt as their marginal source of investment finance and that the corporate income tax is approximately neutral or even beneficial to corporate investment. However, this view is not widely shared. Some critics observe that because the return to most corporate investment projects is uncertain, and because investors wish to avoid excessive risks of bankruptcy, corporations in practice often have to finance at least part of their marginal investments by equity. Others point out that in practice the interaction of accelerated depreciation allowances and limited loss offsets implies that corporations relying excessively on debt finance will often be unable to exploit all their deductions for depreciation and interest payments. However, these critics disagree on the relative importance of retained earnings and new share issues as marginal sources of finance.

The "old view" assumes that new share issues are or should be important as a marginal source of finance and, noting that dividends have been subject both to corporation tax and personal income tax, considers that this is likely to reduce this source of finance as a consequence of reductions in payment ratios of profits. Supporters of the "old view" hold that corporations will raise their dividend pay-out ratio to the point where the marginal benefit from extra dividends is just offset by the extra tax imposed on dividends relative to capital gains, so that a lower effective rate of tax on dividends will reduce the marginal tax cost of distributions and raise the optimal dividend pay-out ratio, thus stimulating corporate investments.

The "new view" assumes that retained earnings will inevitably account for the major part of equity-financed corporate investment and that, accordingly, the greater taxation of distributed profits in relation to retained profits has little distortive effect. Under the "new view" it is considered that shareholders should rationally prefer lightly taxed capital gains on their shares to heavily taxed dividends, so that companies should retain all profits for which they can find a profitable investment outlet, and reduce distributions.

OECD 1991 in adjudicating between the "old" and "new" view concludes that the evidence does not unequivocally favour either view, and that probably both contain important elements of truth: also that the difference in the policy implications of the two views should not be exaggerated. Whilst adherents of the new view would certainly consider reduction of the relatively greater tax burden on distributions to be of less importance than those favouring the old view, they would probably admit that this extra burden could distort the investment decisions of "immature" and rapidly expanding companies, where retained earnings are insufficient to cover their needs for equity finance.

As regards the tax treatment of debt, it is normal to allow corporations full deductibility for all nominal interest expenses, despite the fact that inflation erodes the real value of corporate debt. Under such circumstances the corporate tax system provides an artificial stimulus to debt-financed corporate investment unless the government offsets the privilege of full interest deductibility by levying full tax on all accrued nominal capital gains, and by restricting deductions for depreciation to the decline in the nominal value of business assets, which, in practice, it does not.

b) *Administrative considerations*

Administrative simplicity militates against both imputation systems and tax relief at company level, because these create a number of practical problems, as described in more detail by C. McLure (1979).

- Should tax preference income be passed through to shareholders on distribution or washed out (or treated as taxable income to the shareholder)? And what are to be the presumptive ordering rules? Should tax preferences be stacked first (against dividends) or last (against retained earnings)? Or should preferences be attributed proportionately to distributed and retained earnings? What technique should be used to achieve the desired tax treatment of tax preferences? Should there be a time limit within which income must be distributed if it is not to be considered preference income subject to corporate taxation (précompte) again, as in the French system?
- Should excess credits be refunded to both individual and corporate portfolio shareholders?
- Should credits be refunded to tax-exempt organisations, or would the answer depend on the nature of various organisations? (An analogous question in the case of the split-rate and dividend deduction method is whether integration should be joined with a tax on the dividends or investment income of such organisations).

Administrative simplicity, as already mentioned, also militates against any kind of major change in ways of taxing distributed profits, because of the need for new laws and administrative regulations, as well as transitional provisions to soften the impact of arbitrary gains and losses that would otherwise result.

c) *International considerations*

The international complications entailed by the departure by any country from an unmodified classical system provides one of the most important arguments for a classical system, but there is little evidence that this has had much influence on governments' decisions. On the other hand, it does seem clear that international considerations, in the form of tax treaty negotiations, have had a great deal of influence (see sub-section 5 below) on the majority preference of OECD countries for relief from personal income tax on dividends rather than from corporation tax on distributed profits.

d) *Equity*

Equity arguments can and have been advanced in favour of all kinds of systems and methods, but generally as a reinforcement to support choices made on other grounds. While the choice of system and method can have a significant impact on the distribution of tax burden on profits, what effect will depend on how profits taxes are shifted, something on which there is no agreement among theorists. However, it is generally acknowledged that the redistribution of income plays no important part in the choice of the appropriate way to tax distributed profits, as this can be more effectively done by other means. On the other hand, as remarked earlier, changes in the system or method of taxing such profits can entail arbitrary windfall gains or losses for different categories of taxpayers, even with more softening transition provisions. Because of the arbitrary windfall gains which would follow a move from a classical to a non-classical system, it has been suggested by W. Andrews (*inter alia* in C. McLure, 1979) that any such relief should be confined to new shares, as has been done in Sweden. CL, DIS.

e) *Budgetary constraints*

Budgetary constraints may require that governments cannot afford to reduce their revenues from the corporation income tax, and, other things being equal, providing tax relief either at company or shareholder level for distributed profits requires raising the rate of tax on retained profits to raise the same amount of revenue. A high rate of tax on retained profits may, however, be considered to have drawbacks (e.g. reducing the availability of funds for self-financing and encouraging multinational enterprises to shift their tax base from high to low tax rate jurisdictions). I ADO This is probably why a number of countries with imputation systems have preferred partial to full imputation and why in most countries with relief at company level some tax is charged on distributed profits. Thus, a 1984 United States Treasury report stated:

> Despite the advantages of full relief from double taxation of dividends, the Treasury Department proposal would provide a deduction of only one-half of dividends paid from income taxed to the corporation. This decision is based primarily on considerations of revenue loss, and can be reconsidered once the proposal is fully phased in.

f) *Tax compliance*

I ADO

An argument advanced in favour of imputation systems is that taxpayers are provided with an incentive to declare their dividend income in order to obtain their tax credit. Whilst the same effect could be achieved under other systems by use of withholding taxes, there may be other difficulties (including especially double tax treaty negotiations) in imposing them. However, this is certainly not a decisive reason for adopting such a system, and is generally employed as a subsidiary argument in favour of imputation systems which have been chosen for other reasons.

4. The choice between unmodified classical systems and alternatives

Unmodified classical systems are generally considered to have three main deficiencies, each bound up with a particular kind of tax non-neutrality, which they either cause or accentuate.

The first of the tax non-neutralities of an unmodified classical system is that it discourages the incorporation decision since enterprises incorporating will be potentially liable to two sets of taxes instead of only the personal income tax. However, insofar as the incorporation decision is influenced by tax factors, this will depend on how much total tax and not how many taxes they expect to pay and this depends primarily on the rates of corporation tax on retained profits and the marginal rate of personal income tax they would expect to pay. Table 12.9 gives details of these relative rates and indicates that in a majority of countries a classical system would increase rather than offset the tax distortion to the incorporation decision and that, accordingly for most countries this criticism of an unmodified classical system is valid.

Second, an unmodified classical system is clearly non-neutral between retained and distributed profits, thus discouraging distributions and encouraging investment through retained earnings at the expense of investment through new share capital. It is held that this is likely to reduce productive investment and to penalise new dynamic enterprises in relation to mature enterprises in encouraging the survival of the fattest rather than the fittest, as it has been expressed. In addition, firms may use these excessively retained profits to strengthen their market power through mergers thus worsening the competitive position of new firms. A number of commentators have found that the additional tax on distributed relative to retained earnings has led to a reduction in the pay-out ratio of earnings and that when this difference is reduced an increase in pay-out ratios follows, but there is still not much unanimity on whether the quality of investment is thereby affected. As noted above, much depends on whether the "old view" or "new view" is considered the more valid. Three other relevant points are first, that there may in certain circumstances for macroeconomic reasons be a case for tax incentives for retained earnings which are likely to be re-invested to a greater degree than distributed earnings; second, the more technical point that a full imputation or zero rate corporate tax on distributions would not necessarily achieve neutrality between the taxation of retained and distributed earnings, since relative rates of corporation and personal income tax may also be relevant in this regard; third, in countries, where there are heavy capital gain dues and/or net wealth taxes on enterprises, these are most likely to be borne predominantly by mature firms, which are accordingly in a tax disadvantageous situation in relation to new firms.

Third, an unmodified classical system widens the tax differential between debt financing and financing through new share issues. The main cause of this non-neutrality is the deductibility of interest, and of systems actually existing in OECD countries only full imputation or zero rate corporation tax remove this non-neutrality, the partial relief schemes merely reducing it.

Among the advantages of an unmodified classical system is its simplicity and its increased revenue-raising powers since any offsetting measure costs revenues which may have to be recouped by higher rates on retained earnings. However, its main advantage is that all other ways of taxing distributed profits create non-neutralities and complexities in relation to cross-border investment. It is outside the scope of this book to open the Pandora's box of these international complications, but it is not always even clear what would constitute neutrality between domestic and cross-border investment under non-classical systems. For example, under the split rate form of relief, it is arguable whether neutrality requires that (a) distributions by foreign subsidiaries should have the full benefit of the lower rate; (b) distributions by foreign branches should have the full benefit of the lower rate and (c) mirror image rates of withholding tax should prevail in double taxation conventions with countries which have classical or imputation systems. Under imputation systems the questions arise whether neutrality and non-discrimination imply that (a) the tax credit be given to all foreign investment; (b) it be given only to portfolio investment; (c) it be given only to portfolio investment under a double taxation convention; (d) it not be given at all. Even shareholder relief provisions within a classical system give rise to problems of discrimination against cross-border investment. In addition, in the context of double tax treaties, when one or both treaty partners do not operate an unmodified classical system there are problems in arriving at global principles to determine appropriate revenue sharing from the proceeds of cross-border investment. These problems would be accentuated if, as some have urged, the EC adopted some standardised form of non-classical system, both as regards tax relations between EC countries and those between EC and non-EC countries. It was because of the contrast between the uncertainty of the extent of any economic advantages of non-classical systems and their evident disadvantages on the international plane, that in commenting on an article which stated that "there is no case for concluding that the international (non-discrimination) tail should wag the domestic (integration) dog", I posed the question [Messere (1976)]: "Which really is the dog, which the tail?"

This is typically an area where criteria clash, and where improving neutrality of one kind may worsen neutrality of another kind. Accordingly, it is not surprising that views differ on whether or not other ways of taxing distributed profits should be preferred to an unmodified classical system. Suggested alternatives include a number of ways not yet practised in any OECD country. Of existing systems it is probably fair to say that most public finance economists place the greatest emphasis on the distortions to which unmodified classical systems undoubtedly contribute, and opt for full imputation or zero rate corporation taxes on distributions; most governments have for budgetary reasons chosen the half-way house of partial relief; those who give priority to the avoidance of complexities and of non-discrimination at the international level, especially now that rates of personal and corporate income tax have markedly fallen, prefer unmodified classical systems.

Personally, as intimated in the last paragraph, I subscribe strongly to this last point of view. In addition to the points about dogs and tails and the evident costs and doubtful benefits of non-classical systems already made, there is little evidence that favourable tax treatment for distributions has much effect on the overall distribution policies of corporations, even if it could have at the margin. It is noteworthy, for example, that the percentage of total profits retained in Germany is much higher than that in the United States, even though the German tax system has a pro-distribution bias and the United States system a pro-retention bias. This suggests that factors other than tax regimes may be more important in influencing the distribution policies of corporations, such as the relative demand in different countries by shareholders for dividend pay-outs, which itself may largely depend on the ratio of company and institutional shareholders to individual shareholders.

Whatever one's evaluation of the arguments may be, as already indicated most OECD governments currently prefer non-classical systems. Only Luxembourg, the Netherlands, Switzerland and the United States have completely unmodified classical systems and in January 1992, not for the first time, the US Treasury has recommended abandoning its classical system.

5. Relief at shareholder level versus relief at company level

Numerous examples have been provided to show that the same amount of shareholder cash flow as well as total taxes paid (personal plus corporation tax) can be provided at either company or shareholder level and Table 12.10 gives one such example. Nevertheless, arguments have been advanced for preferring either one or the other route. These relate to the possibility that because of conflicting interests of company directors and shareholders, equivalent relief at such level might result in different behaviourial responses with regard to pay-out ratios and investment and saving decisions of enterprises and shareholders as well as to the international implications of such a choice.

a) In favour of relief at shareholder level

Probably the most influential argument in persuading the majority of countries to adopt shareholder relief rather than company relief has been that a country adopting the latter solution has no bargaining power in negotiating double taxation conventions. In the days when the German tax rate on retained profits (51 per cent) was much higher than on distributed profits (15 per cent), Germany was unable to persuade its partners, and especially the United States, to let Germany levy a compensatory withholding tax at source on dividends distributed by the German companies to foreign shareholders. This loss of revenue from the proceeds of cross-border investment prompted Germany to amend its system in 1976 to introduce full imputation in addition to its split rate. And it was especially to avoid the same kinds of difficulty that France in the sixties and the United Kingdom in the early seventies chose a partial imputation system, though on other grounds the United Kingdom had earlier opted for the split rate method. Other arguments in favour of relief at shareholder level are:

Table 12.10: Comparison of a possible dividend deduction and partial imputation system

Example 1: Dividend deduction system

Corporation		Shareholder	Tax rate 20%	Tax rate 60%
Income	$100	Cash dividend	$40	$40
Dividend	40	Tax	8	24
Dividend deduction (50%)	20	After-tax cash flow	32	16
Taxable income	80	Total, corporate plus shareholder, tax	48	64
Tax (50%)	40			
After-tax income	60			
Retained earnings	20			
Dividend	40			

In this example, the corporation is entitled to a $20 dividend deduction, one-half of the actual dividend, pays $40 in tax, and is left with $20 in retained earnings. Shareholders are taxed at their individual rates on the dividend. A shareholder in the 20 per cent bracket would be left with after-tax cash flow of $32 and a 60 per cent shareholder with after-tax cash flow of $16.

Example 2: Shareholder imputation system

Corporation		Shareholder	Tax rate 20%	Tax rate 60%
Income	$100	$Cash dividend	$30	$30
Corporate tax	50	Gross-up (1/3)	10	10
After-tax income	50	Gross dividend	40	40
Retained earnings	20			
Dividend	30	Tax	8	24
		Tax credit	10	10
		After-tax cash flow	32	16

In this example, the corporation pays $50 in tax, distributes a dividend of $30, and is left with $20 in retained earnings. This imputation system provides for a shareholder gross-up and credit equal to one-third the cash dividend or $10. In effect, the corporation distributes a cash dividend of $30 and a shareholder credit of $10. A 20 per cent shareholder is left with $32 in cash, a 60 per cent shareholder with $16.

"Compared to the pre-integration regime, if the corporation maintains the same level of distribution under the dividend deduction systems, the entire increase in cash flow will accrue to the corporation. If it maintains the same cash dividend under a shareholder imputation system, the shareholder will receive the full benefit of integration. Examples 1 and 2 illustrate the dividend deduction and shareholder cash flow as well as total taxes paid. The two systems differ in terms of the amount of dividends declared and the amount of corporate after-tax profits. The corporation's cash dividend is lower under the imputation system, but this is because it also is distributing the right to shareholder credit. The corporation's after tax profits (but not the corporation's retained earnings) are higher under the dividend deduction system."

Source and quote: E. Sunley, *IBFD Bulletin* 1979.

- From the point of view of tax evasion and avoidance the credit under imputation systems, if available to non-residents, can be claimed only if the income is declared, which means that from the point of view of tax enforcement there is no need for a withholding tax. Whilst it is theoretically possible to achieve similar results by a higher withholding tax under split-rate systems, tax treaty negotiations may preclude such a solution (see above reference to the Germany-United States case).
- Under company level relief problems arise as to what is the appropriate rate to apply to the profits of branches distributed to their head office in other countries.
- Shareholder relief may achieve better the objective of increasing household investments in equities and have political appeal in fostering the idea of a share-owning democracy.
- Company directors have a well-known tendency to use company profits to award themselves heavy salary increases and company tax relief could provide further pretexts or temptations to exaggerate in this regard.

b) *In favour of relief at company level*

But for the international dimension, relief at company level would probably have been preferred by France, Germany and the United Kingdom to imputation systems because of its greater simplicity and transparency. It is true that if relief is given at company level administrative complications arise when the dividends are distributed from a subsidiary to a parent company and the latter does not redistribute them immediately to its own shareholders. This means that as the subsidiary has benefited unfairly from a reduced rate of corporation tax, the difference has to be "recouped" from the parent company in the form of a compensatory tax. But in other situations relief at the company level would appear to be administratively simpler than imputation systems (see 7a below, for the complications of the latter). Among arguments for relief at company level are:

- Relief at company level appears to address more directly and transparently the problems of tax discrimination against distributed profits.
- Capital import neutrality may be easier to achieve under a split rate system which gives the benefit of the lower rate to all shareholders, than under an imputation system which may, and in practice often does, apply only to resident shareholders.
- Relief at the company level is likely to reduce the motivation to indulge in thin capitalisation; (the tax avoidance device to disguise what is in reality a dividend as a loan).
- The amount of company tax relief can be varied according to the size of the firm; for example, it can be restricted to small- and medium-sized firms to allow them to raise capital more easily.
- Company tax relief may be more likely to influence the decision of corporations on how far to finance their investments through retained earnings, and how far through new share issues.

It was for these kinds of reasons that the United States Treasury Department recommended, in its 1984 tax reform proposals, that the corporate tax system should include a partial deduction of distributed profits. A proposal for a dividend deduction method was approved by the House of Representatives in 1986 but was subsequently abandoned partly because it would have led to the transfer of untaxed profits (or profits paying only the 15 per cent withholding tax) to non-resident shareholders. The Treasury Department's suggestion of a "compensatory" levy could have conflicted with double taxation agreements. (c.f. German case cited above.)

c) *Summary*

There appears to be a conflict between what is regarded as the advantages of company level relief at the domestic level and its disadvantages at the international level. In opting in 1984 for company tax relief, the 1984 United States Treasury Report took the view (vol. 2, pages 142-3) that:

> because dividend deduction and imputation systems are economically equivalent, it would be unwarranted to adopt an imputation system, rather than a dividend deduction system, merely to avoid technical treaty violations. Moreover, in the context of the United States economy and tax system, an imputation approach to dividend relief would be extremely cumbersome. A dividend deduction system, therefore, has been proposed.

However, the US Treasury (1992), whilst still rejecting the imputation system as too complex and unwieldy, rejected also the dividend deduction method and has favoured a dividend exclusion method (i.e. zero-rate on dividend income) with a comprehensive business income tax as its second choice (see sub-section 8 below for details).

The many arguments in favour of shareholder relief on the one hand and company relief on the other have been differently evaluated by the various commentators. The fact remains that two thirds of OECD countries now have shareholder relief of some kind and that for the last twenty years there has been a one-way move from company to shareholder relief.

6. Alternative methods of relief at company level

Relief at the company level can be given either by reducing the rate of tax on distributed profits (split rate method) or by reducing the base to which the rate is applied (dividend deduction method). As noted in Tables 12.7 and 12.8 some countries have chosen the first and others the second option. Although arguments have been advanced for or against the relative merits of these two systems [e.g. Van den Tempel (1970) much preferred the split rate method whereas the United States Treasury (1984) preferred the dividend deduction method], there would seem little to choose between them on policy grounds, for in principle it would seem that special problems (e.g. separating qualifying distributions from those to which governments consider that relief should not be given) arise under either method. It could be that the choice between the two methods is taken on grounds of which one can be more conveniently be adapted to the legal provisions or administrative machinery of a particular country.

7. Alternative methods of relief at shareholder level

As already noted it can be misleading to compare imputation systems, where shareholder relief is strictly linked to corporation tax paid on the relevant distributions, with shareholder relief provisions, where there is no such link. Another difference between these two approaches is that under imputation systems shareholders have the possibility of refunds from the government, if their tax credit exceeds their income tax liabilities, whereas such refunds are impossible under shareholder relief provisions. It is simpler, however, to continue with a separate discussion of first, imputation systems and then classical systems modified by shareholder relief provisions.

a) *Imputation systems*

What distinguishes imputation systems from other ways of taxing distributed profits is the link between corporation tax paid on distributions and tax credit given for dividend income, but there are almost as many variants of imputation systems as there are countries employing them. What imputation systems do have in common is their complexity. Table 12.11 gives an idea of some of these differences, which a fuller description would make more evident (for which, see Appendix B to US Treasury 1992).

A first main distinction made by the US Treasury (1992) is between the "compensatory tax method" as practised in Europe and the "credit limitation method" as practised in Australia and New Zealand. Under the compensatory tax method corporate tax on distributions is collected by advance payments and is refunded later as a credit in the hands of the shareholder whereas under the credit limitation method no advance payment is required on qualifying dividends. Compensatory tax methods also take two very different forms: under the United Kingdom's Advance Corporation Tax (ACT) the compensatory tax is imposed on *all* distributions, irrespective of the amount of corporate tax previously paid, with the compensatory tax allowed as a credit against regular corporate tax. Alternatively, as in France and Germany, the compensatory tax applies only to distributions of earnings that have not been taxed at the full corporate rate. An important administrative difference between these two variants is that under the French/German variant, but not under the British variant, corporations are obliged to determine the amount of corporate tax deemed to have been paid with respect to such distribution and to pay additional tax where earnings used to make distributions have not borne tax at the full corporate rate. Another complication of the non-British type of compensatory tax method is that stacking rules have to be established, but as noted in Table 12.11, distributions are generally assumed to have been first paid out of profits that have borne tax at standard rates, thereby minimising the disadvantage to companies investing in tax-favoured activities and those doing business in high-tax foreign jurisdictions. However, a compensatory tax approach may create an extra tax cost for corporations engaged in these activities especially under the British system where the avoidance of wastage of credit for ACT induces UK parent companies to take tax planning measures, which in practice has the effect of discriminating against investment in other countries.

Under the credit limitation method a different approach is applied. In Australia, for example, dividends distributed by resident companies qualify for full imputation credits, provided they are paid out of company income which has borne the full rate of company tax, so that such qualifying dividends are effectively relieved of any further income tax in the hands of the shareholder. Any credit, in excess of that required to relieve dividends from income to offset income tax on other income of the shareholder, is not refunded and no carry forward of imputation credits is allowed. Qualifying dividends are exempt from

Table 12.11: Summary of certain features of imputation systems for corporation tax paid, at 1 January 1991

Country[1]	Tax levied in respect of distributed profits not bearing "standard" corporation tax	Ordering rules for profit distribution	Tax credit for domestic corporate shareholders		Refund to domestic shareholder if tax credit exceeds income tax	
			Portfolio	Direct	Individual	Exempt entity
	(1)	(2)	(3)	(4)	(5)	(6)
Australia	Yes, at the shareholder level	Dividends required to be franked to the maximum extent possible	No	No	No	No
			But rebate of tax for domestic dividends received by resident companies (rebate equal to the tax on this income) except for unfranked dividends received by private companies			
Finland	Yes	Highest-in-first-out	Yes	Yes	Yes	No
France	Yes[2], also on profits retained more than 5 years	Current profit; previous four years, profit (FIFO); profits subject to equalisation tax	Yes	No[2], but dividends from 95% + holding exempt. Tax credit deductible from equalisation tax on redistribution	Yes	No
Germany	Yes	Highest-in-first-out	Yes	Yes	Yes	No
Ireland	Yes. Profits of manufacturing companies taxed at the special rate of 10% carry a reduced credit	Proportional to corporate tax rates	No, dividends exempt. Tax credit deductible from equalisation tax upon redistribution.	Yes	Yes	Yes
Italy	Yes[3]	Not necessary	Yes	Yes	Yes	No
New Zealand	Yes	Not necessary	No, dividends exempt	No, dividends exempt	No[4]	No
United Kingdom	Yes, through Advance Corporation Tax (ACT)	Not necessary	No, dividends not liable to corporation tax. Tax credit franks ACT on redistribution. No ACT on intra-group dividends.	No, dividends exempt. Tax credit deductible from ACT on redistribution. No ACT on intra-group dividends.	Yes	Yes

1. This table refers to the countries indicated in Columns 3 and 4 of Table 12.7.
2. As of January 1 1990, however, there is an exemption of equalisation tax for holding companies under the following conditions:
— the exclusive purpose of the companies is the holding of shares.
— 2/3 of their assets consist of a 10% or more participation in foreign companies.
— 2/3 of their income is derived from their foreign participation. As a consequence the shareholder shall not receive the imputation credit, but the companies transfer their tax credits to the shareholders.
3. The equalisation tax is withheld by the company from the dividends paid out of exempt profits or profits taxed at a lower rate.
4. But conversion of any excess imputation credit into a tax loss to be carried forward.
Source: Table 3.2 of *Taxing profits in a global economy* (OECD 1991).

dividend withholding tax when paid to non-residents; however, dividends paid to non-residents out of company income which has not borne company tax are liable for the existing 15 per cent withholding tax for dividends paid to countries with whom a tax treaty is in operation. Dividends received by companies from other resident companies continue to be free of company tax in the hands of the receiving company. Where dividends are paid out of company income which has borne company tax, they are relieved of further tax by imputation credits. Dividends paid out of such taxed company income are referred to as qualifying dividends (or "franked" dividends). A credit limitation method is apt to be more complicated to administer than a compensatory tax method, since shareholders are required to apply a different rate of gross-up to each corporation.

Another feature of imputation systems is that when a company collects dividends from a portfolio investment on which it is liable for corporation tax, it can, just like an individual shareholder, impute the tax credit to its tax liability on the dividends collected, and is entitled to a refund if the credit exceeds its actual tax liability. However, the situation is different if the dividends relate to direct investment. In most countries the dividends that a company pays to its parent company (or to a company that has a major stake in it) are exempted from corporation tax at the level of the parent company (under the so-called affiliation rule). When a company (and particularly a parent company) collects dividends on which it has not paid corporation tax and it then redistributes them to its own shareholders (who can impute the tax credit against their own tax) under the above-mentioned rule, it must pay tax. However, in France, Ireland and the United Kingdom, a company that redistributes dividends received can impute the tax credits to which it is entitled against the tax it pays in respect of dividends.

The above over-abbreviated account of how imputation systems operate, indicates that they are generally highly complex and ingenious with an internal logic of their own and it should be recorded that they seem to be popular among those countries which have adopted them both among the business community (apart from certain points of friction) and tax administrations. However, at the international level, the differences in the ways in which they operate augment the difficulty of reducing the tax non-neutralities that imputation systems generate as between domestic and cross-border investment and equitable revenue sharing among governments of the revenue proceeds of international investment: at the domestic level, as the United States Treasury has twice found, they do seem to represent an excessively complicated way of achieving their policy objectives.

b) Shareholder relief provisions within a classical system

Over the last few years certain countries have considerably modified the form that shareholder relief should take with consequent impact on savings incentives and income distribution. The traditional method of affording shareholder relief since the late sixties and early seventies, generally referred to as tax credit systems, has been to provide a percentage deduction from shareholders' personal income subject to tax as was the case in Austria, Belgium, Canada (no change) and Denmark. In Austria (1986) the tax credit was increased to 50 per cent, but expressed differently as a separate income tax schedule for dividend income. In Belgium (1980) the former credit was replaced by a flat 25 per cent tax rate on declared dividend income which is the bottom rate of the income tax schedule for earned income. In Denmark (1991) a separate progressive schedule (rates 30 per cent and 45 per cent) replaced the former tax credit and these rates are much lower than the personal income tax rates on earned income, especially when the heavy local income tax on earned income is taken into account. In Japan dividends are normally taxed at a flat rate of 35 per cent: alternatively the shareholder can deduct 10 per cent of his dividends from the personal income tax or 5 per cent beyond a ceiling. In Portugal, a withholding tax of 25 per cent on dividends normally applies. In Canada, which remains with the traditional method, a credit of around 25 per cent is allowed against personal income tax paid at federal and provincial level.

Shareholder relief provisions may be judged according to whether the incentive for domestic investment is worth the revenue forgone, or at what amount of relief is the ideal balance achieved. There is an obvious trade-off between, on the one hand, a possible increase in economic efficiency through greater investment in domestic equities and, on the other, a loss of revenue and international neutrality. At the domestic level, the advantage of shareholder relief provisions over imputation systems is their greater simplicity, their disadvantage is their random effect in taking no account of the amount of corporation tax, if any, paid by such firms on their distributions which also has disadvantages from a budgetary point of view. The form that these provisions have been recently taking in most countries also increases the formal regressivity of the tax treatment of dividend income vis-à-vis earned income on the generally accepted assumption that dividend income is predominantly received by higher income groups liable to top or near-top marginal rates of personal income tax on their other income sources. (To the extent that these concessions result in the reporting of dividend income previously unreported, this regressivity would evidently be less in practice.)

8. New proposals in the nineties

a) Introduction

Recent proposals over the last two years aimed at levelling the playing field between the taxation of the various financing resources have at any rate widened the playing field of systems to be considered. In accordance with the approach taken to other non-existent systems in this book, they are only briefly described. Since 1991, a number of members of the London-based Institute for Fiscal Studies have developed the ACE system, and the US Treasury (1992) is the source of two other proposals, the dividend exclusion prototype and the CBIT prototype, which are recommended in that order of preference. (The same report does not recommend full integration in the Carter sense which is referred to as the shareholder allocation type, nor an imputation system, nor a dividend deduction system as previously recommended by the US Treasury in 1984). Each has its attractions, though as argued persuasively by one of its creators (M. Gammie, 1992), ACE may have more than the others. The future of these candidate new systems may depend in the first instance on how they are regarded as possible harmonised European Community systems in the next ten years or so.

b) ACE (Allowance for Corporate Equity)

The ACE gives relief against tax based on the funds that shareholders have put into a business akin to that generally available for interest payments. Shareholders' funds for a given period would equal those in the last period *plus* total taxable profits (net of the equity allowance), the equity allowance, dividends received and net new equity issues *minus* tax payable, dividends paid and net new acquisitions of shares in other companies. It is argued that the ACE system retains the neutrality properties of an annual pure profits base, while avoiding most of its practical difficulties. Taxable profits could be calculated as under any current schedule, but companies would be given an allowance, reflecting the opportunity cost of equity finance. This new allowance would be reached by adding up the historical value of the funds put into the company by shareholders, and multiplying this figure by an appropriate nominal interest rate.

c) CBIT (Comprehensive Business Income Tax)

The CBIT would tax all but the smallest businesses on total earnings before payment of any interest or dividend but not tax dividends or interest received by shareholders or holders of debt. The objectives of this approach are to eliminate any tax incentive for companies to turn to borrowing rather than equity to finance their operations, to tax corporate and non-corporate business alike and to reduce significantly the tax differential between retained and distributed earnings. The CBIT would be self-financing and would permit the lowering of the corporate tax rate, but it was envisaged that it would take many years to phase in such a radical departure from the present classical system.

d) DEP (Dividend Exclusion Prototype)

This is to extend what has earlier been called shareholder relief provisions to the limit by exempting dividend income altogether from personal income tax, as currently happens in Columbia but not in any OECD country.

United States Treasury (1992) provides a useful comparative table of CBIT, DEP, shareholder allocation and imputation, which is reproduced as Table 12.12.

E. Taxes on business other than corporation income tax

The following taxes are specifically levied on enterprises and whoever may pay them in the longer run are believed by businesses to be burdens on themselves, which could put them at a competitive disadvantage with their competitors in other countries lacking such taxes altogether or paying less. Generally speaking they do not raise important issues which have not been dealt with in other chapters, so discussion here is very brief. In addition to specific taxes levied on business the much more important employers' social security contributions or earmarked payroll taxes discussed in Chapter 8 are also seen by

Table 12.12: A comparison of imputation systems with three non-existent systems

	Prototype			
Issue	**Dividend exclusion**	**Shareholder allocation**	**CBIT**	**Imputation credit**
Rates: a) Distributed[1] b) Retained	a) Corporate rate b) Corporate rate (additional shareholder level tax depends on the treatment of capital gains)	a) Shareholder rate[2] b) Shareholder rate	a) CBIT rate (31%) b) CBIT rate (additional investor level tax depends on the treatment of capital gains)	a) Shareholder rate[3] b) Corporate rate (additional shareholder level tax depends on the treatment of capital gains)
Treatment of non-corporate businesses	Unaffected	Unaffected	CBIT applies to non-corporate businesses as well as corporations, except for very small businesses	Unaffected
Corporate tax preferences	Does not extend preferences to shareholders. Preference income is subject to shareholder tax when distributed	Extends preferences to shareholders	Does not extend preferences to investors. Preference income is subject to compensatory tax or investor level tax when distributed	Does not extend preferences to shareholders. Preference income is subject to shareholders' tax when distributed
Tax exempt investors	Corporate equity income continues to bear one level of tax	Corporate equity income continues to bear one level of tax	A CBIT entity's equity income and income used to pay interest bear one level of tax	Corporate equity income continues to bear one level of tax
Foreign source income	Foreign taxes are creditable at the corporate level but shielded income is subject to shareholder tax when distributed	Foreign taxes are creditable at the corporate level and at the shareholder level	Foreign taxes are creditable at the entity level but shielded income is subject to compensatory tax or an investor level tax when distributed	Foreign taxes are creditable at the corporate level but shielded income is subject to shareholder tax when distributed
Foreign investors	Corporate equity income continues to bear tax at the corporate level and current withholding taxes (eligible for treaty reduction) continue to apply to distributions	Corporate equity income continues to bear tax at the corporate level and current withholding taxes (eligible for treaty reduction) continue to apply to distributions	A CBIT entity's equity income and income used to pay interest bear tax only at the entity level and no withholding taxes are imposed on distribution to equity holders or on interest payments	Corporate equity income continues to bear tax at the corporate level and current withholding taxes (eligible for treaty reduction) continue to apply to distributions
Treatment of debt	Unaffected	Unaffected	Equalises treatment of debt and equity	Unaffected (unless bondholder credit system adopted)

1. Assuming no dividend reinvestment plan.

2. Plus 3 percentage points of corporate level tax not creditable because the prototype retains the 34 per cent rate but provides credits at the 31 per cent shareholder rate.

3. See footnote 2. above.

Source: *United States Treasury Report on Integration* (31 January 1992).

enterprises as business costs for though they are probably shifted into lower wages, higher unemployment or higher prices in the longer run, any increase in them may be initially to provide additional costs for enterprises.

1. Taxes on the immovable property of business

These are imposed in virtually all OECD countries and revenues from them accrue to subordinate levels of government who usually have some say in fixing the rate to be charged. They are discussed further in Chapter 14, where some information is provided on them.

2. Net wealth taxes on corporations

These are imposed in eight OECD countries and could be regarded – and were so regarded in Canada – as an alternative to having a progressive corporation income tax. The base may vary from country to country (see Chapter 11 for the base of net wealth taxes on individuals). In descending order of rate percentage on the base they are as follows: Iceland (1.45), Austria (1 plus 0.5 surtax), Germany (0.6), Luxembourg (0.5), Switzerland-Zurich (0.439), Turkey (0.3 to 0.6), Norway (0.3) and Canada (0.2). Receipts from such taxes rarely exceed 1 per cent of GDP or 2 per cent of total tax receipts.

3. Local turnover tax

Iceland is the only OECD country to impose such a tax at roughly 1 per cent of the turnover of enterprises (whether or not incorporated).

4. The taxe professionnelle

This is a tax levied to finance local government in France, its base being a mixture of the rental value of enterprises' fixed assets and a proportion of salaries paid out. It brings in around one third of local government revenues and around 3 per cent of total tax revenues.

5. The Gewerbesteur

There are various English translations for the Gewerbesteuer which exists in Austria, Germany and Luxembourg, for example "enterprise tax", "trade and industry tax" as well as "local business tax". In all three countries the main base is enterprises' profits but in Austria there is an additional 0.2 per cent on the payroll of enterprises and in Luxembourg and Germany the net wealth of enterprises is included in the tax base. Proceeds are distributed to subordinate levels of government according to quite elaborate formulae and they represent around 3 per cent of total tax receipts in Austria, 4 per cent in Germany and 6 per cent in Luxembourg.

6. Payroll taxes on employers

These may be divided into three kinds:

i) by far the most important, those earmarked for social security benefits as discussed in Chapter 8;

ii) those earmarked for social welfare (family allowances), the distinction between these and the taxes of (i) again having been discussed in Chapter 8;

iii) unearmarked payroll taxes.

What these three kinds of payroll tax have in common is that it is generally believed that in the long term they are shifted into lower wages or higher prices but in the short term, when they are increased they can be a short-term non-wage labour cost for employers. Entrepreneurs in high payroll tax countries, whether earmarked or not, (e.g. France, Italy and Spain) often believe they suffer an international competitive disadvantage as a result of such high payroll taxes.

The arguments for and against imposing unearmarked payroll taxes are not dissimilar from those for and against imposing employers' contributions, with two important reservations. The absence of the underlying insurance philosophy that applies to contributions renders the arguments for them much less persuasive. Second, in contrast to employers' contributions their revenue importance is usually very slight (the 1989 OECD unweighted average for these taxes being 1 per cent compared to around 15 per cent for employers' contributions). They seem particularly inappropriate taxes to levy in times of recession and high unemployment and have recently been abolished in Finland, Germany and Luxembourg though introduced in New Zealand in 1985.

These taxes take different forms in different countries. In Austria, France, Germany and Luxembourg payroll has been, and in Austria and France still is, part of a composite local base of business taxes which are levied to finance local government. However, in Austria where in 1989 they represented a record 6 per cent of total tax revenues the greater part of this amount was to finance welfare benefits (family allowances) as distinct from social security benefits. Australia's long-established unearmarked payroll tax representing 5.7 per cent of total receipts finances state government expenditures. Otherwise significant revenues from unearmarked payroll taxes (more than 3 per cent of total tax receipts) nowadays exist only in Iceland and Sweden where they have been in force for many years. The only other important unearmarked payroll taxes over the last 25 years representing around 4 per cent of total tax revenues have been two separate, now abolished, taxes in the United Kingdom: the first, the selective employment tax was confined to employers in the service sector and was intended as a proxy for a tax on services which escaped the then wholesale sales tax ("purchase tax") on various goods then in force; it caused many borderline problems and was abolished when VAT was introduced. The second was the "national insurance surcharge", a surcharge on employers' contributions which was abolished in 1985.

Chapter 13
Consumption Taxation

A. Introduction

1. The mass conversion to VAT

It is generally accepted that the most striking development in the tax world over the last 25 years has been the spread of value added taxation (henceforth VAT). In the mid-sixties it existed only in France, and then in a not fully developed form. By 1991 VAT has become the general consumption tax system in 21 of the 24 OECD countries (see Table 13.1) as well as in 42 countries outside the OECD area. Consequently the greater part of this chapter is devoted to VAT, covering why countries have (or have not) adopted VAT, how it works in practice, what are the policy choices confronting governments with VAT and what are the solutions that they have adopted.

In the late sixties VAT was regarded with suspicion by governments, business and academics as a somewhat clumsy way of taxing consumption. The impetus towards VAT came from two independent sources: first, the original six signatories to the Treaty of Rome (Belgium, France, Germany, Italy, Luxembourg, the Netherlands) all happened to have had multi-stage general consumption taxes in the sixties and it seemed convenient to remain with such systems, but the cascade systems operating in all those countries except France had so many defects (see Section B2 below) that VAT constituted an evident improvement, and between the late sixties and mid-seventies they all moved to VAT; second, the Scandinavian countries saw VAT as potentially a greater revenue-raiser than their own single-stage wholesale (Denmark) or retail (Norway and Sweden) taxes, and their governments, who wished at the same time to spend more on social welfare and to reduce the large increase in reliance on personal income taxes that had been occurring in the late sixties, saw VAT as an answer to their needs, and adopted it between 1967 and 1970. In the seventies Ireland and the United Kingdom wished to join the European Community, for which the adoption of VAT was mandatory, and also recognised the defects of their

Table 13.1: General consumption tax systems, at 1 January 1967 and 1992

Country	1 January 1967	1 January 1992	Year VAT introduced
Australia	W	W	No VAT
Austria	C	VAT	1973
Belgium	C	VAT	1971
Canada	M[1] + R[2]	VAT[1] + R[2]	1991
Denmark	W	VAT	1967
Finland	VAT[3]	VAT	1990
France	VAT[4]	VAT	1954
Germany	C	VAT	1968
Greece	M	VAT	1987
Iceland	R	VAT	1990
Ireland	W + R	VAT	1972
Italy	C	VAT	1973
Japan	None	VAT	1989
Luxembourg	C	VAT	1970
Netherlands	C	VAT	1969
New Zealand	W	VAT	1986
Norway	R	VAT	1970
Portugal	W	VAT	1986
Spain	C	VAT	1986
Sweden	R	VAT	1969
Switzerland	R[5]	R[5]	No VAT
Turkey	None	VAT	1985
United Kingdom	W	VAT	1973
United States	R[6]	R[6]	No VAT
	Number of countries[7]	**Number of countries[8]**	
Single-stage			
M Manufacture	2	0	
W Wholesale	6	1	
R Retail	7	3	
Multi-stage			
C Cascade	7	0	
VAT	2	21	
No general consumption tax	2	0	
	26	25	

1. At federal level only.
2. At provincial level only.
3. Partial only. Full VAT in 1990.
4. Partial only. Full VAT in 1968.
5. W in certain cases.
6. At state and local level only.
7. Canada and Ireland counted twice.
8. Canada counted twice.

Various sources.

pre-existing consumption taxes which relied excessively on the narrow base of alcoholic drinks, tobacco and hydrocarbon oils. Both these countries joined the VAT club in 1972-73, about the same time as Austria. In the eighties Greece, Portugal and Spain were obliged to adopt VAT as a condition of entry into the European Community, and the Canadian, Japanese, New Zealand and Turkish governments came round to accepting the superiority of VAT over alternatives and, with much difficulty in the case of Canada and Japan, persuaded their voters to agree. Australia, Switzerland and the United States alone remain without VAT, though the Swiss government has tried three times to introduce it, and VAT still has a number of supporters in Australia and the United States.

The reasons for this mass conversion, elaborated on later in this chapter, may be summarised by the superiority of VAT to its alternatives in:

- making consumption taxes more neutral with respect to the choices of consumers and producers and in its ability to tax households and not business inputs;
- taxing services;
- reducing tax distortions in internationally traded goods;
- providing a superior defence against tax evasion;
- raising greater amounts of revenues from consumption.

2. Terminology

Consumption taxes are taken to be the taxes on goods and services of heading 5000 in the annual OECD Revenue Statistics Publication. The main subheadings of heading 5000 are reproduced in Table 13.2 with an indication of their relative importance in revenue terms in 1988 and how this has changed since 1965.

A general consumption tax is one levied on a relatively wide range of goods and sometimes services and is contrasted with selective taxes on consumption, of which by far the most important are those on the activities of drinking, smoking and motoring. Among general consumption taxes, a distinction first has to be made between single-stage taxes, where tax is charged at only one point in the production/distribution chain (i.e. whether on sales from manufacturers to wholesalers (MST) or on wholesalers to retailers (WST) or on retailers to consumers (RST), and multi-stage taxes, where tax is charged each time a product or its components is sold in the chain from manufacturer – assembler – wholesaler – retailer. Under multi-stage taxes, a further distinction has to be made between cumulative or cascade taxes under which traders receive no credit for tax paid on their purchases and non-cumulative taxes (VAT) where tax on purchases is generally refunded to traders who subsequently re-sell to other traders or consumers.

A useful expression in discussions of consumption tax policy is "taxe occulte" which may be defined as the hidden taxes on auxiliary materials, capital equipment and services used in the production, marketing or transportation of taxable goods. At the domestic level taxe occulte entails that consumption taxes become in part a tax on business inputs and at the international level a country with a system with much taxe occulte puts itself at a competitive disadvantage. As noted later taxe occulte is exceptionally heavy under cascade systems, quite heavy under MST and WST, less heavy under RST and least of all under VAT.

(I immodestly record that "taxe occulte", which I first used in 1964, has been my one contribution to expanding the English language.)

Table 13.2: Classification of consumption taxes and their revenue importance, 1989

			Unweighted OECD average as percentage of total consumption tax receipts		**Difference in percentage points between 1965 and 1988**
			1965	**1988**	
5000	Taxes on goods and services		100.0	100.0	–
5100	Taxes on products, sale, transfer, leasing and delivery of goods and rendering of services		93.9	94.0	+0.1
	5110	General taxes (e.g. VAT and sales tax)	32.3	53.3	+21.0
	5120	Taxes on specific goods and services	61.6	40.7	-20.9
	5121	Excises	40.0	29.5	-10.5
	5122	Fiscal monopolies	2.6	0.8	-1.8
	5123	Import duties	15.1	5.4	-9.7
	5124	Taxes on exports	0.1	0.1	–
	5125	Taxes on investment goods	0.0	0.3	+0.3
	5126	Taxes on specific services	3.2	3.8	+0.6
	5127-30	Other taxes (including those unallocable)	0.7	0.6	-0.1
5200	Taxes on use of goods, or on permission to use goods or perform activities		6.1[1]	5.6[2]	-0.5
5300	Unallocable between 5100 and 5200		0.0	0.3	+0.3

1. Of which 3.6 per cent represents revenues from motor vehicles taxes.
2. Of which 2.8 per cent represents revenues from motor vehicles taxes.
Source: OECD RS 1990. Numbers subject to rounding-up inexactitudes.

A distinction is made between tax-exclusive (or effective) and tax-inclusive (or nominal) rates of tax, the former indicating the amount of tax as a percentage of the selling price, excluding the tax itself, the latter the amount of tax as a percentage of the selling price, including the tax itself. In this book effective or tax-exclusive rates are invariably used, as is now the practice in all OECD countries, though in earlier days a number of cascade countries used tax-inclusive rates, as did Finland until very recently. (To convert nominal to effective rates the formula is: nominal rate divided by 100 minus nominal rate, multiplied by 100.)

Another distinction which applies only to VAT rates is that between zero rating and exemption. As A. Tait (1988) neatly summarised it:

> A linguistic quirk of the VAT is that 'exemption' actually means that the 'exempt' trader has to pay VAT on his inputs without being able to retain any credit for this tax paid on his inputs. 'Zero rating' means that a trader is fully compensated for VAT he pays on inputs and, therefore, generally is exempt from VAT.

Lastly, "first generation VAT countries" is an expression applied to those countries adopting VAT before 1974 and "second generation VAT countries" to those adopting VAT between 1985 and 1991. The main purpose of this distinction is to illustrate what happens to general consumption tax revenues when a country adopts VAT (see Table 13.5).

3. The internationalisation of consumption taxes – the EC dimension

As indicated in the introduction, international tax policy issues are outside the scope of this book, so nothing is said about border tax adjustment arrangements or amounts of duty-free alcohol and tobacco to be allowed to travellers between EC countries. What is relevant to this book, however, is the effect that membership of the European Community has had and is likely to have in the future on consumption tax developments in particular EC countries. It is recalled that the EC Commission's attempts to influence the consumption tax choices of its Member Countries have as their objective the abolition of fiscal controls at the frontiers without creating competitive distortions between EC countries or provoking tax evasion. From the Commission's point of view, the ideal would be a complete harmonisation of consumption taxes, but because of the greatly different reliance on such taxes among EC countries this has proved not to be a practical possibility.

The EC has already greatly influenced its Member Countries in first making adoption of VAT a mandatory condition of membership and then through the Sixth Directive which largely harmonised the VAT base. In 1987 the Commission of the EC attempted to impose a two-rate VAT system on all its Members with a standard rate of between 14 to 20 per cent and a reduced rate of 4 to 9 per cent on certain strictly defined merit goods. This retreat from harmonisation to approximation of rates still proved unacceptable for budgetary reasons to EC countries whose standard rates varied from 12 to 24 per cent. More recently the Commission has taken a much softer approach in two respects:

- *Standard rates*. A minimum 15 per cent rate has replaced the 14 to 20 per cent range, thus easing the budgetary problems of Denmark and Ireland with rates above 20 per cent.
- *Lower rates*. Instead of being *required* to have a lower rate of 4 to 9 per cent on a narrow range of products, Member Countries are now *permitted* to have up to *two lower rates* on a wider range of products, provided that the lower rate is at least 5 per cent after a transitional period where rates may remain below 5 per cent.

Judging by developments in the first half of 1992, this softer approach has been successful. Belgium and France[1] are both phasing out the forbidden higher than standard rate. In January 1993 Germany increased its standard VAT rate from 14 to 15 per cent, thus reach-

1. In France the higher 22 per cent rate was abolished as from April 1992 on everything exept tobacco, gambling and pornographic or violent publications and shows, and the intention is to abolish it altogether at the end of 1992.

ing the Commission's minimum (even if the main reason for the increase was to contribute to the costs of unification). Luxembourg has increased its standard rate from 12 to 15 per cent, but has also extended the coverage of its 3 per cent rate to include books, magazines, soft drinks, childrens' clothing and certain services, the 6 per cent rate on fuel, unleaded petrol, wine, milk products, and cleaning fluids, remaining unchanged. Ireland has recently increased its VAT rate from 12.5 per cent to 16 per cent on a number of goods and services. Portugal proposes to move from zero rating of food to 5 per cent while lowering the standard rate on other products. Spain has raised its 12 per cent to 13 per cent and reduced its luxury rate from 33 to 28 per cent as from 1 January 1992. Once these changes have been completed only Spain will have a standard rate below the 15 per cent desired by the Commission and only Greece, Portugal, Italy and Spain will remain with higher than standard rates on luxury goods, and Greece has recently announced its intention to abolish its luxury 36 per cent rate. The question of zero and lower than standard rates is more complex and is discussed further in section C2.

The EC influence on VAT rates has also extended to candidate member countries in that as from January 1992 Austria abolished its higher 32 per cent rate and in the same year Finland moved from its hybrid VAT (see B1 below) to an EC type VAT and expressed its rate as in EC countries on a tax-exclusive instead of a tax-inclusive selling price (see A2 above).

With regard to excise taxation, Article 95 of the Treaty of Rome states: "No Member State shall impose, directly or indirectly, on the products of other Member States any internal taxation of any kind in excess of that imposed directly or indirectly on similar domestic products." It follows that there should not be different methods of charge between home-produced and imported drinks of similar alcoholic strength. Article 95 goes on to add: "Furthermore, no Member State shall impose on the products of other Member States any internal taxation of such nature as to afford indirect protection to other products." Other issues affecting possible developments in the major excises are:

- the relative weight of specific and *ad valorem* taxation as regards tobacco products (discussed in Section D2 below);
- elimination of distortions of competition in the transport of goods by road through differential vehicles taxes, taxes on hydrocarbon oils and road tolls;
- levels of all the major excises should not be too disparate, especially between neighbouring States, in order to avoid cross-frontier shopping.

The problem with excise tax harmonisation is that it would entail extremely serious budgetary consequences for most EC countries, since not only are rates very different, but most of them are very far from an EC average. In 1987, the Commission, nevertheless, proposed excise harmonisation, suggesting that the four percentage points discretion on VAT could solve the budgetary problem. This, however, was never realistic since some countries (e.g. Denmark and Ireland) were both high excise and high VAT countries and others (e.g. Germany, Luxembourg and Spain) were both low excise and VAT countries. The Commission has had limited success in the field of alcoholic drinks persuading the French and British governments to adopt reasonable taxing practices between cognac and whisky and beer and wine respectively, but neither government seems ready to agree to tax cider at the same rate as wine; nor do Greece, Italy, Portugal and Spain show any inclination to have any excises at all on wine.

However, even if no progress has been made in the harmonisation of rates on wines or spirits, considerable progress has been made on that of other excises. Member states have agreed to apply the following rates as of 1 January 1993 with derogations for two years for Greece and Luxembourg in respect of certain hydrocarbon oils and Spain in respect of cigarettes:

Hydrocarbon oils per 1,000 litres in ECUs

leaded petrol:	237
unleaded petrol:	287
road diesel oil:	245
heating gas oil:	0
heavy fuel oil (1 000 kg):	13
kerosene:	To be set at a later date
LPG & methane:	To be set at a later date

Alcoholic beverages per 1,000 litres in ECUs

beer (finished product):	0.748 per plato or 1.87 per degree of alcohol
still wine:	postponed
sparkling wine:	postponed
alcohol for oral consumption:	postponed
intermediate products:	to be set at a later date

For small independent breweries producing less than 200,000 hectolitres per year, these minimum rates are reduced by 50 per cent.

Manufactured tobacco

For 100 cigarettes (global excise duty – specific and *ad valorem* without VAT) – 57 per cent of the retail sale price (all taxes included) of the price class of the most popular types of cigarettes.

Other manufactured tobacco	to be set a later date

4. Scope of the chapter

Section B examines in greater detail why VAT usually, if not invariably, is preferred to other forms of general consumption taxes. After an attempt to clarify what VAT means in theory and in practice, the universally acknowledged defects of MST, WST and cascade taxes are described. This leaves the choice between RST and VAT, and after a comparison of their similarities and differences, the two kinds of taxes are evaluated from a number of points of view. The conclusion is that VAT is technically superior but there remain obstacles of various kinds to countries' attempts to adopt VAT and the section concludes by discussing them. It may be mentioned here that the consensus that VAT is superior to RST has emerged very gradually and recently. Even in the early eighties, there remained a substantial body of governmental and academic opinion in favour of RST, but during the eighties the conversion to VAT has been almost complete (e.g. compare S. Cnossen (1983) and J. Due (1983) with S. Cnossen (1987) and J. Due and U. Brens (1986). Among governments recent converts to VAT include Canada (at federal level only), Iceland, Japan, New Zealand, and Turkey, leaving aside those countries which were obliged to adopt VAT as members of the EC.

Section C considers the main policy options facing governments which have decided to adopt VAT. It concentrates mostly on rate and base issues, of which the first is how many rates should there be? A single rate is favoured by most analysts, a standard and one lower rate by the EC Commission and a number of countries, and more than two rates of VAT have been chosen by a number of other countries. If it is decided that favoured treatment should be accorded to selected merit goods, such as basic foodstuffs, there is a choice between zero rating as in Canada, Ireland, Portugal and the United Kingdom and applying a lower rate as in most OECD countries, and if it is decided that certain luxury goods such as jewellery should be taxed at higher rates, there is a choice between separate excises, higher VAT rates or both. The remainder of Section C deals more briefly with some of the technical problems that countries with VAT have to confront with emphasis on the policy issues involved and governments' choices in practice.

Section D discusses some policy problems and country choices regarding the major excises on the activities of drinking, smoking, motoring and, to a lesser extent, betting and gambling.

B. The choice of VAT as a general consumption tax

1. VAT in theory and in practice

In the theoretical literature VAT is often referred to as a method of collecting tax which could apply to a personal or corporate income tax as well as to a consumption tax. In the mid-sixties there were even proposals in the United Kingdom and the United States to replace the corporation tax by VAT, but nothing since has been heard of such proposals (see Chapter 12A). In practice VAT has always replaced other consumption taxes.

Table 13.3 provides a classification of the main possible kinds of VAT mechanisms. Value-added can be calculated in two ways. It can be built up from its component parts (which, broadly, are the payments made by the firm to the factors of production it employs – wages, profits, rents and interest) – the so-called "addition method" of 2A; or it can be derived from the difference between the value of the firm's output (the price at which it sells its goods and services) and that of its inputs (the price it pays for the goods and services it buys from its suppliers) – the "subtraction method" of 2B. The direct subtraction method takes the aggregate value of sales and the aggregate value of purchases over a period and taxes the difference between them. The indirect subtraction method requires businesses to collect tax on their individual sales (outputs) and pay tax on their individual purchases inputs and pay to the revenue authorities the difference between the tax collected and the tax paid for each tax period.

With the addition method there may be problems in defining taxable profits or of making exact adjustments for imports and exports. Also, it is difficult to operate on any basis but a single rate and to relieve specified goods and services by exemption. However, there may be more opportunity for its use in respect of economic activities where inputs and outputs are difficult to measure, as in banking and finance. The direct subtraction method is in principle the simplest method but it is also difficult to operate if more than one tax rate is to be levied or if it is desired to exempt particular goods and services.

One reason why all OECD countries have now opted for net consumption-type tax systems with the indirect subtraction method is its greater possibilities for detecting tax evasion. Another reason is that only under such a system can cumulative taxation of investment goods be avoided.

Even though its Second Directive explicitly permits a tax credit for capital goods on a (pro-rata) depreciation basis (1B in Table 13.3), the European Community's harmonisation policy also influenced this decision, since, as already noted, subjecting capital goods to a quasi-consumption type tax could create international competitive distortions. Nevertheless, for a variety of reasons there may be some departure from the ideal VAT on final consumption only, of which the most important are:

- To prevent tax evasion, countries may disallow deductions for tax on certain business inputs, which introduces elements of a gross product type tax (1A) or a net income type tax (1B). Purchase of company cars which could be used for private purposes is a typical example, where deduction of VAT may be disallowed.
- Governments may introduce or continue separate taxes outside the VAT systems, which have similar effects to a VAT of type 1A or 1B. Two examples are the Swedish tax on energy and the Norwegian tax on investment goods.
- Countries with cascade taxes (1A type) were obliged for some years to retain a transitional and declining tax on capital goods before arriving at 3C type VAT, but these have long since been abolished.
- Some VAT countries (especially France) still impose delays and limitations on refunds of VAT on traders' inputs which entails that they bear part of the tax burden.

Nowadays, all OECD countries operate system 3C and some writers would prefer to restrict the expression "value added tax" to 3C type taxes. Over the years, Finland has moved from 1B to 1C and from 3A through 3B to 3C in 1990, and whilst the Finnish government preferred to call its system a VAT in OECD 1988, Tait (1988) called it a sales tax and Cnossen (1990) called it a business transfer tax (method 3A). Until 1990, the Finnish system was evidently a hybrid and it is a matter of taste how it is classified. For a time, largely due to the complicated relations with its provincial retail sales taxes, Canada contemplated a business transfer tax (method 3A) but finished with method 3C. The only deviant country from what might be called a "pure" 3C system, which requires the provision of invoices to obtain refund of input tax, is Japan where there is no such requirement. In Japan, the gross tax is calculated by reference to sales, but a credit is allowed for "qualifying purchases" including both taxed purchases as well as purchases from small and medium tax-exempt enterprises. This deviation reduces both the robustness of VAT against tax evasion and neutrality as between different enterprises and between exports and home-produced products. However, since Japan is the only country involved and its rate is atypically low, it scarcely seems worth complicating Table 13.3 by adding yet another category under 3C.

Table 13.3: A summary of possible types of VAT systems

1. Possible coverage of VAT systems		
A	**B**	**C**
A tax on all sales with no deduction at all for business inputs	Deductions for capital goods limited to their depreciation value	Deductions for business inputs immediately deductible (all OECD countries)
Gross product type VAT[1]	Net income type VAT	Net consumption type VAT

2. Possible methods of operating net consumption type VAT	
A	**B**
Identification of value added by the summation of all the elements of value added (wages, profits, rent and interest)	Identification of value added by the difference between inputs and outputs (all OECD countries)
Addition method[2]	Subtraction method[3]

3. Types of subtraction methods under net consumption type VAT systems		
A	**B**	**C**
Deducting the aggregate tax exclusive value of purchases from the aggregate tax exclusive value of sales and taxing the difference between them	Deducting the aggregate tax inclusive value of purchases from the aggregate tax inclusive value of sales and taxing the difference between them	Deducting tax on inputs from tax on sales for each tax period (all OECD countries)
Direct subtraction method[4]	Intermediate subtraction method	Indirect subtraction method[5]

1. Sometimes referred to as "gross" as distinct from "net type" VAT or "income-type" VAT. The second usage creates confusion with regard to the distinction between 1B and 1C in the terminology preferred in this table.
2. Sometimes referred to as "income approach".
3. Sometimes referred to as "product approach".
4. Sometimes referred to as "base on base" or "business transfer tax".
5. Sometimes referred to as "tax on tax" or "invoice method".

Source: *The role of tax reform in Central and Eastern European economies* (OECD 1991).

2. The inferiority of MST, WST and cascade taxes

Of single-stage general consumption taxes, MST and WST are generally regarded as bad taxes. Among the disadvantages of MST (which apply in somewhat mitigated form to WST) are the following:

- The amount of tax included in the price of similar goods selling at similar retail prices may vary greatly because of variations in manufacturers' prices to different trade levels (wholesalers, retailers, consumers) or thc inclusion in the prices of some manufacturers of costs such as advertising and transport that may be excluded by others.
- Profits at the wholesale and retail stages typically differ between products: valuable items like jewellery normally have higher mark-ups than mass-produced items like office furniture. An MST at a single rate will accordingly have a lower effective rate (i.e. tax expressed as a percentage of the retail price) on products like jewellery than on office furniture, and to vary rates creates other distortions.
- Manufacturers will refrain from undertaking such activities as packaging, transportation, storage, insurance and market research, which in the absence of an MST they might be expected to perform.
- It tends to involve the preferential treatment of imports, the value of which includes fewer distribution costs.
- If a tax is levied at the manufacturer level, its coverage has to be relatively narrow (e.g. it cannot include retail-type services) so it may prove inadequate to meet the revenue requirements of governments. Alternatively, to obtain sufficient revenues, rates may have to be relatively high, which enhances the distortive effects referred to above.
- To compensate for the narrowness of the base, MSTs often include certain producers' goods so that the tax becomes partially a tax on business inputs rather than on household consumption.

Cascade taxes also have a number of serious disadvantages, including some of those of MSTs. First, they create economic distortions by inducing firms to undertake manufacturing, assembling, wholesaling and retailing operations simply to avoid the tax which would be payable on sales between independent firms carrying out such activities separately. Second, because similar goods bear different rates of tax according to the number of times they and their components have been bought and sold, compensating levies at the border for imports and exports have to be an average, which even if roughly correct, will give an export subsidy to integrated firms, and insufficient compensation to unintegrated firms for tax already paid on their exports. Likewise, integrated firms will be paying less cascade tax and unintegrated firms more cascade tax than the average charged on imports of similar goods. Third, apart from variations on tax on similar goods according to the number of purchases and sales that have taken place, there will be variable amounts of taxe occulte on domestic transactions and on exports which will not apply (or apply much less) to imports from countries without cascade systems. It is impossible to quantify these taxes occultes on an individual basis and again rough averages have to be employed to calculate export rebates and import surcharges to avoid putting sales of domestic products at a tax disadvantage. These last two factors render the cascade tax as particularly unsuitable in a common market and they no longer exist in OECD countries (see Table 13.1).

3. Similarities and differences between RST and VAT

The main difference between the single-stage RST and the multi-stage VAT is that RST is essentially a suspensive system whereas VAT is a repayment system. Under RST primary producers, wholesalers and retailers are generally required to be registered and are accountable for tax on sales of goods to non-registered persons (usually consumers) but may buy and sell between themselves without liability to tax, provided that such goods are not for their own private use. Accordingly, payment of tax is suspended until the final stage when the goods are sold by registered traders to unregistered traders or consumers. In contrast, VAT operates an invoice or credit or repayment system, and not a suspensive system in that all traders buying goods are obliged to pay tax on their purchases (though if they are registered, tax on those purchases is reimbursed) and they are also obliged to charge tax on the value of their sales. Assuming equal coverage and rates between RST and VAT the same total amount of tax would be paid under RST and VAT. There is general agreement among commentators that apart from practical differences following from these different methods of collection, RST and VAT are economically equivalent since there has never been any serious suggestion that the different methods of collection have any substantial effect on the way in which the tax is shifted into final consumer prices.

The previous paragraph described the differences in the administrative mechanisms of RST and VAT as they affect the collection mechanism from particular traders. From the perspective of net revenue flowing to government from traders as a whole, however, such significant differences do not exist. Table 13.4 presents a simplified example showing a product sold by a manufacturer to a retailer (in one return period) and by the retailer to a final consumer (in another return period). Line 4 shows the calculation of the overall net payment of tax for each trader in relation to the product as described in the previous paragraph. Line 5 indicates the tax revenue flow from the perspective of the government and shows that because the tax collected by the manufacturer is paid to the retailer, no net revenue accrues to the government from that transaction. It follows that no net revenue accrues to government until a taxable sale is made to a person who is unable to claim a credit for the tax paid (e.g. final consumers and exempt traders). As is shown in line 6, this is the same result that arises under RST. In this example, therefore, differences would not normally arise as between RST and VAT as regards either the size or timing of net revenue flows from the private sector as a whole to the government.

Three separate but related questions have sometimes been confused in comparisons between RST and VAT:

- What are the different requirements *entailed* by the collection methods of RST and VAT?
- What are the minimum requirements under the collection methods of RST and VAT and what are the extra requirements that may be imposed?
- What do countries with RST and VAT do *in practice*?

Table 13.4: Illustration of RST and VAT collection mechanisms and revenue flows to the government

Manufacturer					**Retailer**		**Consumer**
1. Physical activity	Raw material Tree	Cuts, treats dresses	Product (sold in bulk) Timber	Product (bought in bulk) Timber	Advertises access-ability	Product (Sold singly)	Purchases product
2. Transactions: no tax	Cost $0		Sale at $100 each	Purch. at $100 each		Sale at $200 each	Purch. at $200 each
3. Transactions: VAT	Cost $0		Sale at $110 (inc. tax) Pay to govt. $10 Manuf. nets $100	Purch. $110 (inc. tax) Refund from govt. $ 10 Cost to retailer $100		Sale $220 (inc. tax) Pay to govt. $20 Retailer nets $200	Purch. at $220 (inc. tax)
4. VAT Calculation of each trader's net VAT liability			Manufacturer pays $10 to govern-ment (represents 10% of value added, i.e. sales less costs, 100-0) Government gets $10			Retailer pays $10 to govt. (i.e. 10% of value added, sales less costs 200-100) Govt. gets $10	Total govt. revenue is $20
5. VAT Net revenue flow to government	Government receives $0. pays $0. net $0.		Government receives $10. (from manuf.) pays $10. (to retailer) net $ 0.			Government receives $20. (from retailer) pays $ 0. net $20.	
6. RST Net revenue flow to government	Government receives $0. pays $0. net $0.		Government receives $0. (from manuf.) pays $0. (to retailer) net $0.			Government receives $20. (from retailer) pays $ 0. net $20.	
	May		August			November	

Source: Table 6.1 of *Taxing consumption* (OECD 1988).

With regard to the first distinction, the most important difference between RST and VAT is that under VAT the onus is always on traders to convince the tax authorities that their claims for tax credits or refunds of tax on their inputs are justified, whereas under RST there are no such claims to be made.

An important example of the second distinction is that the VAT credit mechanism obliges traders to keep detailed records of purchases as well as sales, in order to get their rebate of VAT paid on their inputs: such detailed records of purchases are not necessary under RST, but may nonetheless be required for RST or personal income tax control purposes by the tax authorities of a country operating RST. The relevance of this difference to the RST-VAT debate is that under RST systems the tax authorities may be unable to obtain these powers because of trader, judiciary, parliamentary, and/or public opinion resistance, whereas under VAT traders have to comply, if they are to have tax on their purchases refunded. Thus, any countries contemplating the adoption of RST or VAT or a change between them have to take into account whether the comparison is most realistically made between a minimum or a maximum control RST.

On the third distinction, what countries actually do under RST and VAT is to some extent a separate issue from the relative theoretical advantages and disadvantages of the two systems, since factors having no relation to RST or VAT as such, are involved. These include availability of trained tax inspectors and computer facilities; prevailing accounting standards; tax compliance attitudes by the public at large and the law courts; percentage of small traders and self-employed in relation to the taxpaying community as a whole; relative tax yields sought by the government from general consumption taxes. Thus, while sub-section b) below suggests that *in theory* VAT is more robust than RST against tax evasion, RST countries like Switzerland with an efficient tax administration and high taxpayer morality are likely *in practice* to suffer less tax evasion than some VAT countries.

4. RST versus VAT: technical aspects

a) Costs to governments and traders

It has been alleged that government administrative costs are likely to be less under RST than under VAT, since administrators of RST do not have to check purchase records as a matter of course, there being no need to pay out refunds. However, even if checking of purchases were not required, there are a number of other factors that suggest there is unlikely to be much difference in the administrative costs of the two kinds of taxes. First, the number of registered traders with whom the tax administration has to deal is unlikely to be very different under the two systems, since even under RST most traders prior to the retail stage have to be registered. Second, because VAT traders have to record purchase as well as sales data, there is likely to be a closer link with information required for income tax purposes and the exchange of information between VAT inspectors and income tax inspectors, and joint audits, or even joint control of the two taxes by the same inspector, have yielded additional revenue from both taxes by revealing evasion.

Taxpayers' compliance costs may be less in aggregate under RST than VAT because the records they have to keep can be less extensive, since under RST, unless the law or accounting practice prescribes otherwise, they are required to keep records only of their sales, but under VAT of both their sales and purchases. Though it is true that traders for other purposes (including income tax returns) will evidently need to have some record of their purchases, they may need to be more detailed under VAT than they would under RST. In addition, under VAT traders have to collate records of all their purchases over the appropriate accounting period which is not necessarily the case with RST. Under a single rate VAT most traders need not separately account for the VAT component of purchases – the tax element simply being a fixed fraction of the total value of taxed purchases. In practice, it will mainly be traders with less sophisticated accounting systems who will use this method. However, the compliance burden becomes greater if two or more rates of VAT are in operation since the tax included on each purchase and sale has to be separately recorded. If traders were required under RST to provide similar records than that entailed by the VAT system evidently this difference would disappear. (Regarding a trader's sales, the complications of two or more rates of tax are the same for both VAT and RST). Also under RST, traders' compliance costs additional to those under VAT may arise because of their need to verify whether or not their purchaser is entitled to tax-free delivery.

Compliance costs are likely to be relatively higher for small firms under both VAT and RST, since the requirements of the tax authorities may oblige small firms to keep records more elaborate than they otherwise would have kept, whereas larger firms would probably have kept them in any event. Accordingly, if more elaborate records are required under VAT than under RST, the compliance costs of small firms relative to large ones are increased. Under either tax, multi-rate systems of limited coverage increase not only absolute compliance costs but also the relative burden on small firms. Under both RST and VAT there are offsets to these compliance costs which take the form of cash flow benefits and managerial benefits. The cash flow benefit arises because firms collect tax from their customers over a specified period of time (the "collecting period") which they are then legally allowed to hold for a further period (the "grace period") before handing it over to the tax authorities. Assuming the same collection and grace periods, for the same revenue there is a similar aggregate cash flow benefit arising from both RST and VAT. The main difference is that the benefit is heavily concentrated on retailers with RST; with VAT it is spread across the whole range of production and distribution. The greater market power of large firms may enable them to demand payment from their customers more rapidly than can smaller firms, so that this offset probably increases the relative disadvantage of small traders under VAT. The second offset to compliance costs is the possible use for management purposes of data (e.g. better stock control) or records which firms have been required to compile for income tax purposes. This managerial benefit is particularly applicable to small firms, which otherwise might have kept much sparser records, whereas the larger firms would have anyway kept such records. To the extent that record-keeping for VAT is usually more extensive than that for RST, this benefit applies more strongly under VAT.

b) Robustness against tax evasion

One of the most contentious issues in the RST versus VAT debate has been how far, if at all, VAT is more resistant to tax evasion than RST. Again the discussion has been obscured because arguments have been advanced on different levels. The following three issues are discussed in turn:

- Which forms of tax evasion occur in common under the two systems and which are peculiar to one or the other?
- How much revenue is at risk under the two systems when successful evasion takes place?
- Which policing methods or built-in protection against evasion occur equally under both systems and which are possible only under VAT?

Among the kinds of tax evasion that would take similar forms under RST and VAT, are: concealment by enterprises of transactions through the underground economy, e.g. in the construction industry, ready-to-wear textiles, hotel and restaurant industries; unreported transactions by employees in the service sector (e.g. plumbing and painting) where payment is made by cash; under-reporting of sales of enterprises; non-reporting of secondary activities of enterprises. In certain instances the RST and VAT mechanisms offer scope for different types of evasion. Under VAT but not RST, traders can claim rebates of tax on purchases that they have not in reality made. Under RST, but not under VAT, non-registered traders may produce counterfeit registration numbers illegally to obtain tax-free goods and/or to sell them illegitimately free of tax. An important difference, however, between these two forms of evasion is that under VAT, but not under RST, the government actually hands out input tax to traders and large frauds of this kind have been detected in VAT countries. In short, under VAT revenue losses through fraud are likely to be more important, but the detection of fraud is likely to be more efficient.

It has been alleged that under RST the whole of the tax is at risk whereas under VAT only the tax on the value added by the retailer at the last stage is at risk, but as illustrated by Table 13.4 this is not necessarily the case. It is true that if a trader were able to operate entirely outside the tax system, then all the revenue would be lost under RST whereas under VAT at least some tax will have been collected on that trader's purchases, but such nomads usually represent a very small proportion of a country's population. Under either system it is difficult to imagine that a retailer with a permanent place of business could evade all the tax without attracting the attention of the tax authorities. Accordingly, in practice, evasion is more likely to take the form of the suppression of some sales and, to the extent that this goes undetected and the trader has claimed input tax, all the revenue on such sales is at risk under VAT. Under either tax therefore, in the context of slight under-declaration, the same amount of revenue is in practice likely to be at stake.

This leads to the third consideration of what RST and VAT have in common and where they differ as regards the detection of tax evasion. Taking first the possibilities of non-declaration or under-declaration by retailers referred to in the last paragraph, evidently under both RST and VAT the tax authorities have such methods of detecting this form of evasion as income tax records and normal profit margins of retailing firms selling similar goods. However, the requirement under VAT of retailers to request refund of tax on their purchases draws directly to the attention of the VAT authorities potentially dubious cases, so that at a very minimum an aid would be provided as to which retailers to subject to audit. If profit margins are high at the retail level and if the tax-evaders are not too greedy it seems likely that this would not necessarily provide a warning, but if profit margins were low and/or there were a multi-rate system and the retailers involved were selling lower or zero rated goods, so that they would be obliged to declare no tax liability or even claim tax credits in order to evade taxes, clearer signals might be provided to the tax authorities that investigation was necessary.

VAT has also a number of other built-in protective factors unavailable under RST and it is a matter of judgement how important these are in practice. The limitation on the time that tax inspectors have for cross-checking of invoices and the possibilities that traders have under VAT for issuing two separate sets of invoices may, in the absence of checking, render the following battery of anti-evasion devices under VAT less formidable than they might at first sight appear. These devices include: first, under VAT the taxpayer is obliged to prove entitlement to the credits claimed in the return; second, the VAT mechanism provides buyers and sellers an inducement to comply with the tax, because the buyer has an interest that the invoice shows a purchase price higher than that actually paid to obtain a high tax credit, whereas the seller wishes to keep the price as low as possible, in order to minimise his tax liability, and given these conflicting interests buyers and sellers are unlikely to agree on a false invoice; third, as observed above, since there are necessarily invoices for both purchases and sales, VAT provides more easily than RST the possibility of joint control by the tax administration with the income tax and only under VAT does such joint control occur in practice; fourth, it has been argued that registered firms are less likely to default on tax invoiced by their suppliers than on a tax payable directly to the tax collector; fifth, there may be slightly less risk of loss of tax on imports under the VAT credit mechanism than under the RST suspensive regime, since the former is collected at the border, and the latter on first domestic sale.

c) Ability to tax services

Whilst it is true that a few states of the United States have a wide RST coverage of services, these tend to be at rates of under 5 per cent rather than the typical 14 to 20 per cent VAT rates. The service sector is generally considered to be the most vulnerable to evasion and for the reasons elaborated below it may be difficult in practice to impose a high rate of RST on services. First, the bulk of services to consumers are provided by firms which also provide services to businesses and who would generally wish to be registered under VAT to get back tax paid on their inputs. However, all retail sales of services would appear to be equally prone to evasion under both RST and VAT, particularly those supplied by small self-employed traders such as builders, plumbers, electricians, painters and carpenters.

The second reason is that (as analysed by S. Cnossen) mixed-use services for business and private consumption pose far fewer problems under VAT than under RST. Services under VAT rendered to business firms are simply taxed in full. Identification of the purchaser, required under RST if cascading is to be avoided, is unnecessary. Whether or not the purchaser is subsequently entitled to take credit for tax is of no concern to the seller, but a matter between the purchaser and the tax office (which collects the corresponding tax from an upstream firm). To take a simple transaction such as the purchase of a train ticket for a business trip, whilst VAT does not require any consideration by the ticket office regarding the purpose of the trip, under RST it would be necessary to require not only the presentation of an exemption certificate, but also an inquiry into the purpose of the trip, and evidently the ticket office is not in a position to verify such information. This example could be multiplied many times over by others in the field of transportation, as well as communications, advertising, and the professions. Against this, it has been argued that a RST system with extensive coverage of services could be envisaged, where a registered trader would not be liable to tax, even if subsequently obliged to satisfy the tax authorities that the expenditure was for business, and not for private purposes. There would remain the difference, however, that under VAT the trader would be seeking a refund of tax paid, whereas under RST the onus would be on the tax authorities to recover the tax, if not satisfied with the trader's declaration. Also under RST verification of end-use falls on the supplier who cannot know whether the buyer is a trader or consumer, nor consequently the end-use; under VAT such verification falls on the purchaser who does know.

d) Ability to reduce taxe occulte

As already noted, it is generally agreed to be desirable to relieve producer goods of RST or VAT because the cascading effect of such taxes haphazardly distorts competition. As with the ability to tax services, a distinction should be made between what RST and VAT countries actually do and what the systems permit them to do. Among producer goods that may be taxed in the RST countries are agricultural and industrial machinery, transport vehicles, building materials, stationery used commercially, fuel, power and consumables. The VAT credit system permits a full credit for taxes paid on purchases of all investment goods and auxiliary supplies used by registered firms, even if most VAT countries in practice exclude certain dual-purpose consumer/business purchases such as motor vehicles to prevent tax avoidance by traders on their own consumption. In principle, RST systems permit the same relief for producer goods under its suspension system, but a problem arises with mixed-use goods which is likely to lead to some degree of cascade. Under RST it is necessary to verify the use which is made of such goods to distinguish those which should bear the tax and those which should not. This problem does not arise under VAT, where the seller need not be concerned with the use to which the goods are put, it being for the purchaser to claim credit, if he is a registered trader entitled to do so. (While such goods could be exempt under RST, the onus would be on the tax authorities to recover the tax if dissatisfied, whereas under VAT the onus is on the trader to get a credit for tax paid on his inputs), an analogous argument to that just referred to on the taxation of services. In addition RST systems tend to include producer goods to a much greater extent than do VAT systems, perhaps to raise required amounts of revenue, given the difficulties of taxing services. This drawback of RST applies not only to producer-goods as such, but to taxe occulte generally.

e) Neutrality towards exports and imports

In theory, the VAT credit mechanism under which exporters pay tax on their inputs and then have this tax credited against their sales has the advantage over the RST suspensive mechanism under which exporters never pay tax in that it is more transparent and renders it easier fully to relieve exports fully from tax but has also the disadvantage that it involves greater administrative and compliance costs. On the import side the VAT mechanism requires importers to pay VAT either at the time of importation or shortly afterwards and the RST suspensive mechanism requires that tax becomes due on most commercial importations only when a registered importer subsequently sells the goods in question to an unregistered trader or consumer. In practice, a number of VAT countries have adopted the RST suspensive method for registered traders. Under both RST and VAT imports by unregistered traders and consumers are taxed at the time of importation. Nevertheless, VAT has the advantage over RST in one respect as regards neutrality between domestic products and imports and exports: insofar as there remains a greater element of taxe occulte under RST, domestic transactions will be disadvantaged in relation to imports and exports from and to VAT countries.

f) Revenue capacity and buoyancy

The revenue raising capacity of a general consumption tax is a function of its rate and coverage. A comparison of the rates of the few RST countries with those of the many VAT countries shows that the latter are nearly always substantially higher. RST countries tend to charge around 4 to 6 per cent of the tax-exclusive value of goods, though in certain Canadian provinces the rate has reached 12 per cent; whereas standard VAT rates tend to vary between 14 and 25 per cent even if in a few countries (New Zealand, Spain, Turkey) they remain around 10 to 12 per cent, and for special reasons discussed elsewhere they are lower still in Canada (7 per cent) and Japan (3 per cent). Also in all VAT countries other than Canada and Japan which have just introduced VAT and France, Norway and Greece, 1992 rates were higher – often much higher – than those imposed when VAT was first introduced (see Chart 13.1).

An attempt was made to measure the tax base by comparing goods covered by RST and VAT as a percentage of total private consumption plus government purchases from the private sector, but it became apparent that the denominators provided by countries were inconsistent and it is not possible to standardise them. The data provided, however, did suggest that whereas over 70 per cent of total consumption was usually in the tax base of VAT countries, in RST countries the figure was between 30 and 50 per cent. The difference was due above all to the difference in coverage of services, but also to the greater tendency in VAT countries to include food, medicines, books, etc. in the base, even if at lower rates.

In conformity with these theoretical expectations, Table 13.5 indicates that VAT normally provides much more revenue than other general consumption tax systems and that over the years this revenue increases at a greater rate.

Table 13.5A compares general consumption tax ratios of first generation VAT countries (those introducing VAT before 1974) with these ratios in other countries. It shows that VAT receipts in 1975 were invariably higher as a percentage of GDP than those from other general consumption taxes (Greece excepted) and that in all countries (except France) they grew more as a percentage of GDP than did receipts from general consumption taxes in those countries without VAT. The unweighted average of general consumption tax to GDP of first generation VAT countries in 1975 and 1985 was around twice that of other countries and between 1975 and 1985 it grew by nearly twice as much. An update of the results to 1989 shows that among first generation VAT countries there is relatively little change between 1985 and 1989, but that in all second generation VAT countries, there was a considerable increase in the general consumption tax ratio and hardly any change (Canada excepted) in the general consumption tax ratio of those countries remaining without VAT during that period.

It may, however, be argued that consumption taxes should be looked at as a whole since non-VAT countries may be expected to rely more on selective consumption taxes to meet their consumption tax revenue needs and Table 13.5B does that. The picture is then somewhat modified. Most first generation VAT countries' total consumption tax to GDP ratios remain higher than those of other countries and have grown more rapidly, but there are many exceptions (e.g. compare Germany and Italy with pre-VAT Greece and compare Portugal as regards absolute amounts and Portugal and Spain as regards growth in total consumption tax ratios). The update to 1989 of total consumption tax ratios broadly reflects what had already been said about general consumption tax ratios except that Can-

Table 13.5: The revenue buoyancy of VAT compared to that of other general consumption taxes, 1975, 1985 and 1989[1]

A. General consumption tax ratios						
Country	**1975**	**1985**	**1989**	**1975-1989**	**1975-1985**	**1985-1989**
First generation[2] VAT countries						
Austria	7.7	9.0	8.7	1.0	1.3	-0.3
Belgium	6.6	7.5	7.2	0.6	0.9	-0.3
Denmark	7.0	9.8	9.7	2.7	2.8	-0.1
Finland[3]	6.3	7.9	9.3	3.0	1.6	+1.4
France	8.6	8.9	8.4	-0.2	0.3	-0.5
Germany	5.3	6.0	5.9	0.6	0.7	-0.1
Ireland	4.6	7.9	8.1	3.5	3.5	0.2
Italy	3.8	5.0	5.3	1.5	1.2	0.3
Luxembourg	4.7	5.6	5.9	1.2	0.9	0.3
Netherlands	6.3	7.3	7.5	1.2	1.0	0.2
Norway	9.2	8.7	8.7	-0.5	-0.5	0.0
Sweden	5.2	7.0	7.6	2.4	1.8	0.6
United Kingdom	3.1	6.0	6.2	3.1	2.9	0.2
Unweighted average	6.0	7.4	7.4	1.4	1.4	0.0
Other countries						
Australia	1.8	2.4	2.7	0.9	0.6	0.3
Canada	4.0	4.4	5.4	0.4	0.4	1.0
Greece[4]	4.7	6.0	8.6	3.9	1.3	2.6
New Zealand[4]	2.8	3.5	8.1	5.3	0.7	4.6
Portugal[4]	2.8	4.0	7.1	4.3	1.2	3.1
Spain[4]	3.0	4.2	5.8	2.9	1.2	1.7
Switzerland	2.3	3.0	3.2	0.9	0.7	0.2
United States	1.9	2.2	2.2	0.3	0.3	0.0
Unweighted average	2.9	3.7	5.4	2.5	0.8	1.7

B. Total consumption tax ratios						
Country	**1975**	**1985**	**1989**	**1975-1989**	**1975-1985**	**1985-1989**
First generation[2] VAT countries						
Austria	13.3	14.0	13.3	0.0	0.7	-0.7
Belgium	11.0	11.7	11.3	0.3	0.7	-0.4
Denmark	13.9	16.8	16.5	2.6	2.9	-0.3
Finland[3]	11.9	13.4	14.4	2.5	1.5	1.0
France	12.3	13.2	12.6	0.3	0.9	-0.6
Germany	9.7	9.7	9.7	0.0	0.0	0.0
Ireland	14.7	17.0	16.7	2.0	2.3	-0.3
Italy	7.7	8.7	10.2	2.5	1.0	1.5
Luxembourg	8.2	10.5	10.3	2.1	2.3	-0.2
Netherlands	10.6	11.5	12.0	1.4	0.9	0.5
Norway	16.9	17.8	16.5	1.4	0.9	0.5
Sweden	10.6	13.3	13.5	1.4	2.7	-1.3
United Kingdom	9.0	11.8	11.3	2.3	2.8	-0.5
Unweighted average	11.5	13.0	13.0	1.5	1.5	0.0
Other countries						
Australia	8.1	9.8	8.5	0.4	9.7	-1.3
Canada	10.4	10.5	10.4	0.0	0.1	-0.1
Greece[4]	11.9	15.0	15.0	3.1	3.1	0.0
Japan	3.6	3.9	3.9	0.3	0.3	0.0
New Zealand[4]	7.6	7.9	13.0	5.4	0.3	5.1
Portugal[4]	10.1	13.5	15.8	5.7	3.4	2.3
Spain[4]	4.7	8.3	9.9	9.2	3.6	1.6
Switzerland	5.9	6.1	5.9	0.0	0.2	-0.2
Turkey[4]	8.6	7.1	7.1	-1.5	-1.5	0.0
United States	5.4	5.2	4.9	-0.5	-0.2	-0.3
Unweighted average	7.6	8.7	9.4	1.8	1.1	0.7

1. Iceland is excluded for technical and data availability reasons. Japan and Turkey are excluded from Section A because of their lack of any general consumption tax before 1985, but are included in Section B.

2. First generation countries are defined as those introducing VAT before 1974 and second generation countries as those four introducing VAT between 1985 and 1987.

3. It is open to question whether Finland should be counted as a first generation VAT country (see Section B1).

4. Second generation VAT countries.

Source: OECD RS, various editions.

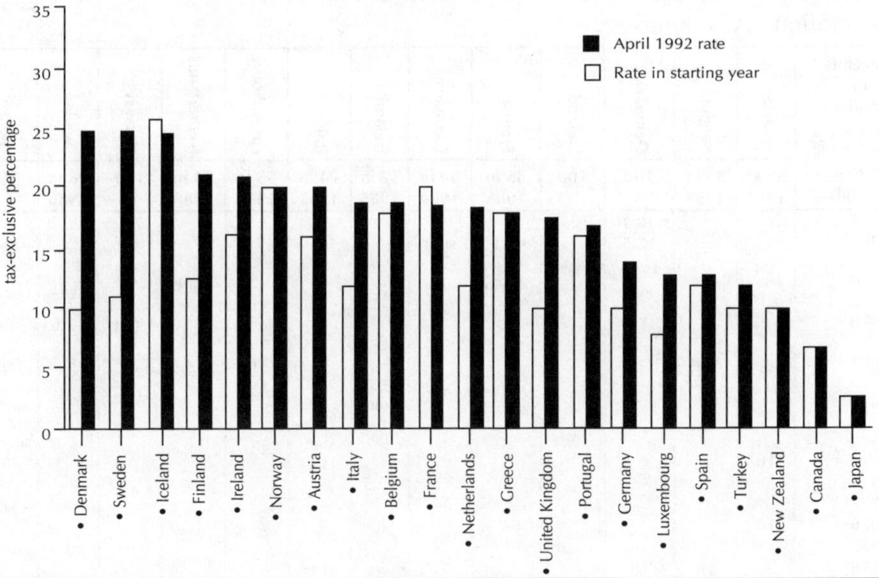

Chart 13.1: Standard rates of VAT, in starting year and April 1992

Various sources.

ada and Greece join the no-change countries, because of the decline in their excise etc. ratios during that period.

Table 13.6 provides one explanation for the increase in the VAT ratio of first generation VAT countries between 1975 and 1984 and its usual stagnation thereafter. Standard rate goods and services, as illustrated in the table for one particular year, account for the bulk of VAT receipts in all countries except Belgium and between 1975 and 1984 they increased in all such countries except France and Norway, whereas since 1984 they have been mostly stagnant and have even fallen in Ireland and the Netherlands. Another explanation is the extension of the tax base, especially to include more services, in accordance with the EC Sixth Directive in the seventies, has largely come to an end among first generation VAT countries, except recently in Sweden.

g) Conclusion on technical issues

The results of this examination of the relative advantages of RST and VAT in the light of the technical criteria discussed above suggest that there seems one slight advantage for RST regarding lesser complexity and consequent administrative and compliance costs, some slight advantages for VAT in greater neutrality towards imports and exports, but considerable advantages to VAT as regards robustness against tax evasion, ability to tax services, to remove taxe occulte and to provide more revenue. However, the technical superiority of VAT over RST is not a decisive reason for governments to choose it. In

Table 13.6: Development of standard rates[1] of tax in first generation VAT countries[2]

Receipts from standard rate as percentage of total receipts	Austria	Belgium	Denmark	Finland	France	Germany	Ireland	Italy	Luxembourg	Netherlands	Norway	Sweden	UK
	59 in 1985	**35 in 1984**	**100**	**100**	**86 in 1986**	**90 in 1984**	**57 in 1985**	**74 in 1987**	**55 in 1984**	**90 in 1986**	**100**	**96 in 1986**	**100**
1967			start 10	12.4									
1968			12.5		start[3] 20	start 10							
1969					23.45	11				start 12		start 11.1	
1970			15		23				start 8		start 20	17.6	
1971		start 18							10	14			
1972							start 16.4						
1973	start 16				20			start 12		16			start 10
1974							19.5						
1975													8
1976	18						20			18			
1977				16.28	17.6							20.6	
1978		16	18			12		14					
1979			20.25										15
1980						13	25						
1981		17	22					15				23.5	
1982							30						
1983		19		19.05	18.6		35	18	12				
1984	20					14				19			
1985							23						
1986							25						
1987										20			
1988													
1989							23						
1990								18		18.5			
1991													
April 1992	20	19.5	25	22	18.6	14	21[4]	19	15	18.5	20	25	17.5[5]

1. Rates are invariably expressed as a percentage of the selling price excluding the tax itself, and relate to the situation as at 1 January of each year.

2. Of second generation VAT countries there has been no change in the standard rate in Greece (18), but in New Zealand it has been increased from 10 to 12.5, in Spain from 12 to 13, in Turkey from 12 to 13.5, and in Portugal it has been reduced from 17 to 16. Percentage of yield from standard rate goods and services is 100 in New Zealand for all years, 70 in Portugal and 66 in Spain both in 1986. No information on percentage of yield from standard rate goods and services for Greece and Turkey.

3. Start in generalised form.

4. From March 1991.

5. From April 1991.

Various sources for updates.

practice, political and policy considerations are a more important determinant of governments' choices, as discussed in the next sub-section.

5. RST versus VAT: policy aspects

a) Summary

Governments unconstrained by EC membership, in choosing between RST and VAT may be influenced by a number of political and practical considerations concerning which of the two they perceive to be more acceptable to their voters, as well as by such contingent factors as what happens to be the prevailing view of influential politicians and civil servants, how strongly it is held and how persuasively argued. These points may be illustrated by the different choices in recent years by the Australian government for RST and by the New Zealand government for VAT.

The Australian government took the view that the advantage of VAT in combating evasion had been overstated. Whilst the Australians accepted that exports and intermediate goods could be more readily freed from tax under VAT than under RST, they were impressed by the lower administrative and compliance costs which they expected from RST. The Australian government, moreover, did not envisage a tax rate in excess of 12 per cent. An important consideration was the time needed to introduce each tax. The Commissioner of Taxation had estimated that it would take twelve months longer to introduce a VAT than a RST. Given a Parliamentary term of three years and the government's desire to see transitional problems resolved before the next election, this difference was seen as a significant factor in favour of RST. (In practice, the Australian government failed to achieve a RST and remained with its WST albeit somewhat reformed.)

The New Zealand government, on the other hand, took the view that VAT was definitely superior to RST in combating evasion. The relatively low level of RST everywhere suggested that VAT had a greater potential for revenue than RST. In regard to administrative and compliance costs, the New Zealand government took the view that these could be minimised by appropriate policy decisions, in particular exempting small taxpayers but otherwise having a comprehensive tax base with a single rate of tax. Their success in achieving this aim, was undoubtedly helped by having a powerful Minister of Finance strongly committed to this reform.

The conventional wisdom in the seventies, as endorsed more recently in Australia, was that the increased complexity of VAT makes it worth adopting in place of RST only if substantial yields were expected from it and that even with the potentially enlarged base, rates were imposed at least at 10 per cent to obtain such substantial yields. In recent years Japan has introduced a 3 per cent and Canada a 7 per cent VAT.

b) VAT as a money-making machine

The facts have been provided in Table 13.5 and they indicate that VAT has been a money-making machine for most of the countries which have adopted it. Of the first generation VAT countries this has not been the case in Belgium, France, Germany and Norway.

When Norway introduced VAT in 1970 its 20 per cent standard rate was higher than that of any other country except France, but this rate has remained unchanged since 1970 and the standard rate of France has declined. The classical pattern of countries moving to VAT (as has been followed by Austria, Denmark, Ireland, Italy, Luxembourg, the Netherlands, Sweden and the United Kingdom) is to start with a revenue-neutral profile and over the years to increase VAT rates (See Chart 13.1), widen the VAT base and so increase the VAT ratio. Not unnaturally VAT-watchers in countries without VAT have been observing this phenomenon, and whilst the potential money-making machine of VAT has attracted governments anxious to reduce budget deficits and income tax, it has incurred for the same reason the opposition of a number of other pressure groups, including politicians, business, academics and taxpayers on the grounds that it would be dangerous to give governments such a large revenue handle. In recent years the Japanese government which wanted to introduce VAT at rates of 5 per cent had to settle for 3 per cent, and then only after a political struggle. The Swiss government has tried twice in the seventies and then again in 1991 with the support of all political parties to introduce VAT, but in each case the proposal was defeated by referendum, Swiss taxpayers equating TVA with *taxe va augmenter.*

It seems that everyone can take comfort from the figures in Table 13.5 regarding the light they shed on the question "Is VAT a money-making machine?" The answer is it can be but does not have to be, and that sometimes it is, and sometimes it is not. However, it is fair to add that in most countries it does increase revenues with the consequence that OECD governments have become increasingly in agreement that they are handicapped in the absence of VAT to finance increasing expenditures, to reduce income or payroll taxes, to cut back deficits, or to achieve some mixture of these goals.

c) *Inflationary fears*

This has been a vital issue in the countries that have already introduced VAT systems as well as in those countries in which the introduction of a VAT is still under discussion. The evidence seems to indicate that in most countries the introduction of a VAT has had little or no effect on retail prices. Frequently countries have taken active measures to facilitate this objective when VAT was introduced or its rates were increased. Belgium and Italy delayed its introduction to the appropriate point in the business cycle; temporary price freezes occurred in France and Greece; monetary policy has also been utilised. An empirical survey by A. Tait (1988) showed that in 11 of the 13 OECD countries covered, the introduction of VAT had little or no effect on retail prices or simply had a one-time effect on the consumer price index. The exceptions were Norway, where the somewhat brutal increase in 1970 from a 12 per cent RST to a 20 per cent VAT fed a sustained price-wage increase, and Italy in 1973, largely on account of uncertainty and the widening of profit margins.

d) *The federal constraint*

It is probably no accident that the three countries still without VAT (Australia, Switzerland, the United States) are all federal states. Apart from the possibly greater resistance among states, provinces, cantons, etc. to giving the federal government a greater tax handle, complications arise when, as in Canada and the United States, there are already retail sales taxes in existence at subordinate levels of government. The relatively low 7 per cent rate in Canada is due to the co-existence of provincial RST at higher rates.

From the purely administrative efficiency point of view there is little doubt that the best solution would be a revenue sharing formula on the Austria-Germany lines, where the retail sales tax at the subordinate level would be abolished and this was the preferred solution of the Canadian government. However, this solution does limit local accountability and the Canadian government has so far been unable to sell it to the provinces, although it is understood that matters are still under negotiation. If a federal VAT were to be adopted in the United States, one imagines that the difficulties of persuading the states to forgo their autonomy to fix the rates and base of a general consumption tax would be even greater. Theoretically, it may be argued that consumption taxes are not an ideal vehicle for local government autonomy (because substantial differences in rates and base will encourage distortive cross-border shopping), except where local government jurisdictions are very large as in Canada and the United States. In such countries, the search becomes one for second- or third-best solutions. Probably, again from the point of view of administrative efficiency, the second-best solution would be to persuade the subordinate levels of government to replace their RST by VAT and have assessment and collections administered by one set of officials. A third-best solution, which takes into account a scenario which may well occur in the United States, if the Clinton administration introduces a federal VAT and the states prefer not to change their RST, is to co-ordinate the assessment/collection process of the federal income taxes and the federal VAT.

e) *Transitional problems*

Another reason why governments may feel reluctant to plunge into VAT is that any major change to a tax system involves complicated and costly transitional arrangements and inevitably some individual taxpayers are going to be penalised and will naturally be complaining to their political representatives. A transition to VAT from the WST or RST prevailing in those OECD countries without VAT will undoubtedly create problems of this kind. The main problem in this case is that where a trader has purchased capital equipment or trading stock prior to the introduction of the VAT, previous tax may have been paid on the equipment or stock. A similar purchase made after the VAT comes into effect will have a lower net cost to the trader as the VAT included in the purchase price of the equipment or stock is refundable. Clearly, any trader holding stock at the same time a VAT comes into effect is disadvantaged relative to the trader whose stock was purchased after that time. To remedy this and to avoid any potential distortions in buying patterns (e.g. by traders delaying stock and capital purchases until after the VAT is introduced), there are two possible solutions. Either traders can be reimbursed for the tax element on stock or assets on hand at the time the VAT comes into effect, or previous tax can continue to be levied and be phased out gradually. The first solution has been adopted in most OECD countries for trading stock and the second for capital equipment. Each, however, complicates the operation of the tax. However, these complications are much less serious if the transition is from single stage taxes than if they are from cascade taxes, and Australia and Switzerland have single stage taxes and the United States no general consumption tax at federal level.

C. Policy options under VAT

1. The impact of VAT on income distribution

The question of the impact of VAT on income distribution has much influenced the rate structure and coverage of VAT, as discussed in the next section; for even if the primary function of a general consumption tax is to raise revenue, its distributional effects have played – and still play – an important role in the design of such a tax, especially if it is being in part substituted for a more progressive personal income tax.

A first question is whether the progressivity of a VAT (or other general consumption tax) should be measured by reference to consumers' expenditure or gross income or disposable income (i.e. gross income minus income tax and social security contribution plus social welfare benefits). The choice depends largely on the purpose for which the analysis is being made and disposable income would evidently be the appropriate measure if the progressivity of VAT were being compared to that of the personal income tax. By definition a single rate VAT would be proportional to consumers' expenditures and sketchy empirical findings, based on sample surveys (considered to be very unreliable at the highest and lowest income levels) have borne out that a one rate VAT would be slightly regressive if related to disposable income and more so if related to gross income.

A second question is how far does zero rating or reduced rates for essential goods such as basic foods and higher rates on luxury goods increase the progressivity of VAT. The generally-held view is that multi-rate VAT has relatively little effect on its progressivity, because the rich tend to spend proportionately more on lower rate products. Unfortunately the empirical evidence that could be obtained in the two OECD consumption tax studies (OECD 1981 and 1988) was limited to few countries and the international incomparabilities were too great to come to any firm conclusions. Accordingly, the results are not reproduced. This does seem an area worthy of further empirical investigation, since the choice between a single or multi-rate VAT is strongly influenced by the perceptions of governments and voters concerning their relative effect on income distribution. (See also more general comments under Chapter 7C.)

2. Rate and base issues

a) *Single versus two or more rates*

Neutrality would require one single VAT rate on all goods and services that it is technically possible to tax, something – as Table 13.7 indicates – that rarely happens.

In addition to the basic argument about lack of neutrality, a multi-rate consumption tax system suffers from a number of other more practical problems. First, the goods and services in each rate category have to be clearly defined which – being difficult – may lead to ambiguities, economic distortions, tax evasion and higher administrative and compliance costs. Second, lower rates, zero rating or exemptions extend the tax relief to individuals and families with higher incomes. Due to the impossibility of precise targeting, the revenue cost of providing the relief may be relatively high, leading to a higher standard tax rate on most goods and services to provide sufficient revenue. In addition, favourable tax treatment for food and books entails government subsidies for luxury food and pornography, unless further complicated and costly dividing lines are drawn within these broad categories, which, as Table 13.8 indicates, does occur in a number of countries.

Table 13.7: VAT[1] rates in OECD countries, April 1992

Country	Zero rates[3]	Lower rates other than zero	Standard rates	Higher rates
Austria	–	10	20	–
Belgium	–	6, 12	19.5	–
Canada[2]	Yes	–	7	–
Denmark	–	–	25	–
Finland	–	–	22	–
France	–	2.1, 5.5	18.6	22[5]
Germany	–	5, 7, 8	14[4]	–
Greece	–	4, 8	18	36
Iceland	Yes	14	24.5	–
Ireland	Yes	2.3, 10	21	–
Italy	Yes	4,9	19	38
Japan	–	–	3	–
Luxembourg	–	3, 6	15	–
Netherlands	Yes	6	18.5	–
New Zealand	–	–	12.5	–
Norway	–	–	20	–
Portugal	Yes	8	16	30
Spain	–	6	13	33
Sweden	–	18	25	–
Turkey	–	1, 3, 8	13.5	15, 50, 60, 100
United Kingdom	Yes	–	17.5	–

1. Of countries without VAT, Switzerland has a standard rate of 6.2% of the retail sales price or 9.3% on sales from wholesalers to retailers. There are no higher or lower rates. In the United States, state plus local RST rates vary from 4.25 to 8.25% of the inclusive retail selling price according to state and municipality. Australia has a WST with a standard rate of 20% and others at 10% and 30%.

2. Canada has in addition a retail sales tax in nine of the 10 provinces at one rate only which varies between provinces from 5 to 12 per cent of retail selling price.

3. Excluding some minor zero rating, also exemptions which in some countries account for a substantial part of total consumption. Exports are zero rated in all OECD countries.

4. To be increased to 15% as from 1 January 1993.

5. To be abolished as from 1 January 1993.

– = non-existent, or nearly so.

Various sources.

The main argument in favour of multi-rate systems in spite of their distortive effects and consequent economic costs is that, by applying lower rates to basic necessities like foodstuffs and medicine consumed in relatively large proportions by low income earners, the tax burden on these families may be alleviated. Some countries, especially Canada, Ireland, Portugal and the United Kingdom, take this a stage further by zero rating such products. However, the income redistribution objectives inherent in such choices can be achieved without recourse to multi-rates. One possibility is to render other parts of the tax system more progressive, another is to follow the Canadian example of granting non-wastable credits against income tax payments (if any) in respect of VAT deemed to have been paid on essential taxable goods and yet another is to operate outside the tax system by increasing transfer payments to low income families as was done in the Scandinavian countries and New Zealand.

Even so, it is understandable that governments of countries, where citizens are unaccustomed to paying consumption tax on merit goods, such as food, medicines and books, will find too much political opposition to introducing them, particularly as there would be (a probably correct) perception among the electorate that the imposition of VAT on merit goods would be permanent, whereas the compensating social welfare payments on income tax reliefs may be less sure and durable, for example because they were not adjusted for inflation.

Additional problems confront governments with multi-rate VAT systems contemplating, as recently occurred in the Netherlands, a move to a single rate VAT. One is that such a move would provoke a change in relative prices which may have adverse effects on productivity and employment in certain sectors of the economy (e.g. agriculture), as well as increasing the general level of inflation, since price reductions when consumption taxes are reduced generally fail to match price increases when such taxes are increased. It is probably for these reasons that, New Zealand apart, there is no country that has moved from a multi-rate general consumption tax to a single-rate one. It should be added that no country with the technical advantages of a single-rate general consumption tax had moved to multi-rate VAT until Sweden at the end of 1991 increased the standard rate of VAT from 23.5 to 25 per cent and perversely introduced a reduced rate of 18 per cent for food, public transportation, hotels and restaurants and some tourist-related services as from 1 January 1992; perversely, because it is difficult to imagine that this narrow rate differentiation will have much economic effect and it will certainly complicate the administration of the VAT system as well as opening the way for other rate reductions demands from various pressure groups.[1]

b) *Reduced rates versus zero rate for merit goods and services*

Whether or not merit goods has meaning is one of those philosophical issues outside the scope of this book, and leaving aside cultural activities [see A. Tait (1988) for a good discussion of merit goods and cultural activities] favourable VAT treatment has generally been accorded in practice to the seven kinds of goods and services listed in Table 13.8. As

1. Sweden also proposes to reduce the standard rate from 25% to 22% as from 1 January 1993 without changing the 18% reduced rate. The loss of revenue will be partly offset by the abolition of a standard deduction of 4,000 Skr. allowed by wage-earners for income tax purposes.

Table 13.8: VAT treatment of merit goods and services, at 1 January 1991

Country	Basic foodstuffs	Other food	Drugs and medicines	Books and newspapers	Clothing and footwear	Electricity and fuel	Public transport
Austria	L	L	L	L	S	L	L
Belgium	L	L/S/H	L/S	L/Z	L/S	Z/L	L
Canada	Z	S	Z	S	S	S	S
Denmark	S	S	S	S/Z	S	Z/S	E
Finland	L[1]	L[1]	L[1]	S/Z	S	Z/S	E
France	L	S/H	L	L/S	S	L	L
Germany	L	L/S	S	L	S	L	L/S
Greece	L	L/S/H	L	L[1]	S	E/L	E
Iceland	L[2]	S	S	Z	S	Z/S	E
Ireland	Z	Z/L/S	Z/S	Z/L	Z/L	L/Z	E
Italy	L	L	L	L	L/S	L	E
Japan	S	S	S/E	S	S	S	S
Luxembourg	L	L/S	L	L	S	L	L
Netherlands	L	L	L	L	S	L	L
New Zealand	S	S	S	S	S	Z	E
Norway	S	S	S	Z	S	S	S
Portugal	Z	L	Z	Z	S	Z	L
Spain	L	L	L	L	S	L	L
Sweden	S	S	Z/S	Z/S	S	Z/S	E
Turkey	L	S	S	L	S	L	S
United Kingdom	Z	Z/S	E/Z	Z	Z/L	Z	S

1. Though nominally standard, the rate is reduced in practice through the use of the deduction technique.
2. Though nominally standard, the rate is reduced in practice through special reimbursement schemes at producer level.

S = Standard rates see Table 13.7.

L = Lower positive rate see Table 13.7.

H = Higher rate see Table 13.7.

Z = Zero rate.

E = Exempt or not taxed.

Source: Adapted from Table 6A, page 377 of *The role of tax reform in Central and Eastern European economies* (OECD 1991) and S. Cnossen (1992).

the table indicates, whilst the VAT treatment of basic foodstuffs is unambiguous, distinctions are made by a number of countries with respect to other food, drugs and medicines, books and newspapers, clothing and footwear, and electricity and fuel, which are bound to complicate VAT administration and increase government and business costs. Few countries extend preferential VAT treatment beyond those items, but national practices sometimes differ. As Cnossen (1990) nicely puts it: "South European countries consider wine a basic necessity (and indeed it is), Holland believes that flowers should be taxed at the lower rate (and who would want to quarrel with that?), and Belgium views soap as an indispensable consumer good (one smells the difference)."

The main policy issue is that if merit goods have to be treated more generously for VAT purposes than other goods, what are the relative advantages and disadvantages of a lower VAT rate and a zero rate. A distinction should be made between political/metaphysical arguments on the one hand, and technical arguments on the other.

Concerning the first, the EC Commission have consistently condemned zero rating as violating the important principle that all goods and services which can in practice be subject to VAT should be so. Similarly the British, Irish and Portuguese consider it a fundamental principle that certain merit goods should never be subject to VAT. One may find it difficult to sympathise with such fundamentalist arguments, but they are made and one can understand why, for presentational and political purposes, they are made.

On the technical level, it is arguable whether the distinction between a lower rate and a zero rate for basic foodstuffs, etc., is a difference of degree or of kind. To a large extent this depends on what is the lower rate. The smaller the lower rate, the greater the departure from neutrality. A somewhat more basic argument against zero rating is that it is technically perverse to require the setting-up of the complex mechanism that zero rating entails when no revenue is obtained and moreover that zero rating increases the risk of undetected tax evasion, since when net payments from governments to traders are commonplace as in the extensive zero rating of the British/Irish kind, there are not the same warning signals that occur under other VAT systems where net repayments to traders occur much less frequently.

c) *Higher VAT rates and/or nuisance excises for luxury goods*

As with merit goods, it is not clear what luxury goods should cover and opinions may differ about what should be covered by the expression. Leaving aside the major excises on drinking, smoking and motoring discussed in Section D of this chapter and pollution and environment taxes already discussed in Chapter 7, there are a number of products, as identified in Table 13.9, which are taxed either at higher VAT rates or with separate excises, or occasionally with both.

If for economic or social reasons governments wish to subject particular products or services to higher taxation, it would seem better to do so through a separate excise than through a higher VAT rate which unnecessarily complicates the VAT system. The argument for the higher VAT route is that this enables business expenses to be reimbursed but this has little force with regard to such products as caviar, perfume, jewellery and television sets which are the types of products normally subject to such rates. However, the main point is that while the extra taxation of luxury products may be a valid tax handle in primitive economies it has little rationale in industrialised countries, as recognised by the EC Commission, who wish to abolish both higher VAT rates and nuisance excises. As already stressed, consumption taxes are an inappropriate means of redistributing income and greatly complicate the administration of such taxes, whether by way of higher rates of VAT or separate excises, and even if it is higher income groups that mostly buy such luxury products, they can usually avoid the tax by purchasing these products in other countries, and it is also relevant that no OECD government has seriously tried to tax expenditure, mainly by higher income groups, on private health and education and holidays abroad.

The irrationality of governments does not stop with luxury products. Nuisance excises on such products as coffee, tea, salt, meat, imposed hundreds of years ago, may remain, even if the same products are subject to *lower* rates of VAT.

Table 13.9 shows that, in general Australia, Austria, Belgium, France, Greece, Italy, Portugal and Spain use higher rates of general consumption taxes and other countries (save Switzerland where there is no rate discrimination between different goods) use separate excises to subject certain goods to higher taxation. Only Belgium and France use both higher VAT rates and separate excises and then relatively rarely. Table 13.9 also reveals interesting sociological and historical differences between countries, sometimes easy, sometimes less easy to understand. For example, it would seem normal not to subject fur coats to higher rates of tax in cold climates like those of Canada and Northern Europe but to do so in the Mediterranean countries. Historical reasons apart, it is less easy to understand why sugar is not taxed in Australia, Canada, Ireland, Switzerland, and the United Kingdom, is taxed at higher rates than most products in Belgium, Finland, Italy, the Netherlands and Norway, and is taxed at standard rates in Austria, France, Germany, New Zealand, and Sweden. A similar variety of treatments is shown towards the taxation of non-alcoholic drinks and confectionery. Very small excises on matches and mechanical lighters (linked to smoking) and playing cards (linked to gambling) linger on in a few countries but have generally been abolished. The (probably incomplete) comparisons with 1967, also provided in Table 13.9 do not point to any consistent change in this area. A number of countries have abolished some nuisance excises but kept others. The Netherlands got rid of the higher rate of cascade tax on introducing VAT, France and Norway have introduced a number of new nuisance excises and Switzerland has exempted certain products formerly subject to RST.

d) The taxation of services

It is technically feasible to tax most kinds of services under VAT and rational to do so. They account for between a third and a half of consumer expenditures (see footnote 2 to Table 13.10) and in the absence of their taxation a higher rate has to be imposed on goods to raise the same amount of revenue. This entails a departure from neutrality towards consumer choices, and probably in a regressive way, since for the most part more is proportionately spent on services by higher income groups than lower income groups and less is spent on goods. The expansion of the VAT base over the last 15 years or so has in practice been largely an increase in the range of services covered.

This expansion of the coverage of the service sector was undoubtedly influenced by the EC Commission's Sixth Directive, which provided for the compulsory VAT taxation of most non-financial services, the exemption from VAT of a number of others (mainly in the cultural, welfare, social and religious areas but more irrationally postal services) with the option left to governments to subject or not to subject to VAT a number of financial services. The rest of this sub-section summarises OECD country practices first of non-

Table 13.9: Products[1] subject to separate excises and/or higher rates of general consumption tax, at 1 January 1991[2]

Country	Non-alcoholic drinks	Confectionery	Sugar	Video Radio, TV	Records and Record players	Clocks and Watches
Australia	O	O	X	H	O or H	H
Austria	O	O	O	O	O	O
Belgium	EO	O(E)	EO(HE)	H	H	H
Canada (Federal)	O	O	X(O)	O(EO)	O(EO)	EO
Denmark	EO(E)	EO(E)	O(E)	O(E)	O(E)	O
Finland	EO	EO	EO	O	O	O
France	EO(H)	O	EO(O)	O or H(H)	O or H(H)	EH(H)
Germany	O	O	EO	O	O	O
Greece	O	O	O	HE	HE	H
Iceland	E(EO)	E(EO)	E(O)	E(O)	E(O)	O
Ireland	EO	O	X(O)	EO(O)	EO(O)	O
Italy	O	O(EO)	EO	EO	EO	O(H)
Japan	O	O(X)	O(E)	O	O	O
Luxembourg	O	O	O(EO)	O	O	O
Netherlands	EO(H)	O(H)	EO	O(H)	O(H)	O(H)
New Zealand	O	O	0	O	O	O
Norway	EO	EO	EO(O)	EO(O)	EO(O)	O
Portugal	O	O	O(E)	O	O	O
Spain	O	O	O	O	O	O
Sweden	EO	EO	O	EO(O)	O	O
Switzerland	X(O)	X(O)	X(O)	O	O	O
Turkey	EO	O	O	O or H	O or H	O
United Kingdom	O	O	X	O	O	O
United States (Federal)	X	X	X(E)	X	X	X

1. Excluding the major excises on alcoholic drinks, tobacco products, mineral oils and motor vehicles which are in most countries subject to both excise or special taxes (e.g. motor vehicle oils, fiscal monopolies) and standard rates of general consumption tax. Exceptions are:

- *Wine, spirits and mineral oils* are liable to excises and higher rates of VAT in Belgium (liquified petroleum gas is only liable to the higher VAT rate while fuel for heating is liable only to the 17 per cent VAT rate).
- *Tobacco* is not liable to the Australian wholesale sales tax.
- *Wine* is not subject to excise in Australia, Greece, Italy, Portugal and Spain, nor is non-sparkling wine in Germany and home-grown wine in Luxembourg.
- *Tobacco and alcoholic drinks* are liable to both excises and higher rates of sales tax in Canada.
- *Mineral oils* are liable to lower rates of VAT in Spain.
- *Private motor vehicles* are liable to both separate taxes and higher rates of VAT in Austria, France and Spain and this is so for certain types of vehicles in Italy.
- Ordinary passenger vehicles and small 4-wheel drive passenger vehicles are liable to a higher rate of VAT in Japan until 31 March 1992.
- Certain types of motor vehicles are liable to both separate taxes and higher rates of VAT in Turkey.
- *Tobacco* is liable to both excises and the higher VAT rate in France.

For products liable to higher rates of general consumption tax see Table 4.3 and Appendix 2 to Chapter 5.

2. March 1967 position given in brackets when different. Information for 1967 unavailable for Australia, Finland, Greece, New Zealand, Spain and Turkey.

Table 13.9(cont.): Products[1] subject to separate excises and/or higher rates of general consumption tax, at 1 January 1991[2]

Country	Furs	Jewellery& precious stones	Playing cards	Mechanical lighters	Matches	Toilet goods and perfumery	Other products liable to separate excises and/or higher rates[3]
Australia	H	H	O	O	O	O	Various
Austria	O	O	O	O	O	O	Various
Belgium	H	H	O(H)	O(H)	O	H or O(HE)	Various
Canada (Federal)	O	EO	EO	EO	EO	O(EO)	Various
Denmark	O	O	EO	EO	EO	EO(E)	Various
Finland	O	O	O	O	O	O	Some foodstuffs
France	H	HE	O	EO(H)	EO	EH or O (H monopoly)	Various
Germany	O	O	O(E)	O	O(EO)	O	Various
Greece	HE	H	OE	OE	O	H or O	Various
Iceland	O	O	O	O	O	E(O)	Various
Ireland	O	O	O	O	O(EO)	OE(O)	None
Italy	H	O(H)	O(HE)	EO(HE)	EO	EO(H)	Various
Japan	O(H)	O(H)	O(E)	O	O	O	None
Luxembourg	O	O	O	O	O	O	None
Netherlands	O	O(H)	O	O(H)	O	O(H)	None
New Zealand	O	O	O	O	O	O	None
Norway	O(H)	O(EO)	O(EO)	O	O	EO	Various
Portugal	H(O)	H	H	O	O(E)	H	Various
Spain	O or H	H	O	O	O	O	Various
Sweden	O(EO)	O(EO)	O	O	O	EO	Various
Switzerland	O	O	O	O	O	O	None
Turkey	H	H	EO	O	O	H	Various
United Kingdom	O	O	O	EO(E)	EO(E)	O	None
United States (Federal)	X	X	X	X	X(E)	X	Various

3. List of other products

Australia:	Higher priced motor vehicles, cameras and other photographic equipment, and coin-operated gambling and amusement machines. In 1967 salt.
Austria:	Private motor vehicles, yachts, aircraft.
Belgium:	Coffee.
Canada:	Automobiles in excess of weight threshold, auto air conditioners. In 1967 smokers' goods.
Denmark:	Ice-cream, lamps, coffee extracts and substitutes, tea and tea extracts, certain retail packaging, certain pesticides, charter flights, disposable tableware, and electricity and coal.
France:	Meat, furniture, clothing, textiles, oil and forestry products. In 1967 coffee, tea, explosives.
Germany:	Coffee, lamps, salt, tea. In 1967 saccharine.
Italy:	Cocoa, coffee, fats, electricity and gas, lighting equipment. In 1967 quinine, salt.
Norway:	Various (unspecified).
Portugal:	Pharmaceuticals, coffee, textiles. In 1967 fish, pharmaceuticals.
Spain:	Pornographic movies.
Sweden:	Coal, coke, electricity, video tape recorders, cassette tapes, packages for beverages, charter flights, natural gas and LP-gas, combustible oils.
Turkey:	X-ray films, spirits, fuel oil, diesel oil, gasoline and LP-gas.
United States:	Higher priced jewellery, furs, boats, motor vehicles and certain aircraft, communication services, coal, certain vaccines, sport fishing equipment; bows and arrows and firearms; certain chemicals. In 1967 marijuana, opium, telephone (long distance).

E = Normally liable to excises or special taxes.

H = Normally liable to higher rates of general consumption tax.

O = Normally liable to ordinary or lower rates of general consumption tax.

X = Normally not subject to tax.

Sources: pp. 375-6 of *The role of tax reform in Central and Eastern European economies*, (OECD 1991) and *Border tax adjustments and tax structures in OECD Member Countries* (OECD 1968).

financial services and then of financial services and insurance. Because more akin to the sumptuary excises on drinking, smoking and motoring, taxes on betting and gambling are discussed in Section D on the major excises.

Table 13.10, which sets out the VAT treatment of a number of non-financial services, shows that standard rates of VAT mostly prevail and that outside Finland exemptions are relatively rare, though lower rates frequently occur in Austria, Belgium, Greece, Ireland, Luxembourg, the Netherlands, Portugal and Spain, these lower rates being probably due to the late taxation of services and pressure group persuasion from tourist, transport, entertainment, restaurant and hotel interests. There is little rationale for these lower rates, the coverage of which differs bewilderingly from country to country. The overall coverage of services in the VAT base may also be influenced by the choice to tax all services of a particular kind unless specifically exempt as is generally the case, or to tax only designated kinds of services as happens in Finland, Norway and Sweden. Naturally the latter group of countries are likely to have a less complete coverage of services, and this remains the case in Finland and did so until recently in Sweden.

Commentators are not in agreement on whether it is theoretically correct to apply VAT to financial services. Table 13.11 sets out OECD countries' tax treatment of financial services and insurance and shows that for the greater part they are not subject to VAT. A distinction is made between "core" and "secondary" services, as defined in footnotes 1 and 2 to the table. As a general rule, all OECD countries exempt "core" financial services and all countries except Finland, Norway and Sweden, subject "secondary" financial services to standard rate VAT. Finally, EC countries zero rate financial services exported to countries outside the European Community, but otherwise exported financial services are exempt.

The reasons for exempting "core" financial services are first that it is extremely difficult to identify the value added on each service provided by financial institutions (frequently defined by the differential between borrowing and lending rates) since financial services and their attendant costs are extremely flexible and it is not at all easy to untangle these bundles of services and costs. Second, the VAT actually payable on financial services would be only on retail sales to households, whereas the use of financial services by businesses, which are by far more important, would be deductible as a credit. Therefore, extending the VAT to include financial services would, in practice, not greatly increase either the VAT base or VAT revenues. In addition, VAT exempt financial institutions continue to pay tax on their inputs (e.g. buildings, computers, office equipment, stationery) and this VAT is not creditable. If these institutions were subject to VAT they would be able to claim these costs as credits against VAT on their sales. Also there are political implications in increasing the cost of borrowing to the private sector that may need delicate handling. Finally, both capital and the associated financial services are very mobile internationally, so that significant taxation could persuade residents to move their transactions to other countries. For all these reasons, despite the possible theoretical desirability of including financial services in the VAT base, on which much has been written, it seems sensible for pragmatic reasons not to do so.

Table 13.11 also provides information on the VAT treatment of insurance in OECD countries from which it can be seen that all OECD countries except New Zealand and, to a more limited extent Finland, exempt all forms of insurance and reinsurance from the

Table 13.10: VAT treatment of selected services, January 1991[1, 2]

Country	Transport of passengers by road	Telephone	Liberal professions,	Advertising	Entertainment (excluding betting)	Hotels/ restaurant
Austria	L	S	L	S[3]	L[3]	L
Belgium	L	S	E or S	S	L or H	L
Canada	S	S	S	S	S	S
Denmark	E or S	S	S	S	S	S
Finland	E	S	E	E	E	E or S
France	L or S	S	Various	S	Various	Various
Germany	L or S	E	S	S	S[3]	S
Greece	L	S	L or E	L	Various	L
Iceland	E	S	S	S	S	E
Ireland	E	L	S	S	E, L or S	L
Italy	E	L	S	S	S	L or S
Japan	S	S	S	S	S	S[3]
Luxembourg	L	E	L	L	L or S	L
Netherlands	L	E*	E, S or L	S or L	S or L	L
New Zealand	S	S	S	S	S	S
Norway	E	S	E or S	S	E	E or S
Portugal	L	L	S	S	L	L
Spain	L	S	S	S	L, S or H	L or S
Sweden	S	S	S	S*	E	S
Turkey	S	S	S	S	S	S
United Kingdom	Z	S	S	S	S	S

1. Australia and Switzerland do not tax services apart from repairs and cleaning in Switzerland. In the United States there is much variation between states, with most states taxing some but not many services.

2. Expenditures on services as a percentage of final domestic consumption of resident households for the year 1988 are reported by A. Tait as follows: Austria 47.2, Canada 46.0, Denmark 40.0, Finland 37.4, Greece 30.8, Japan 53.9, the Netherlands 43.2, New Zealand 44.8, Norway 33.5, Sweden 37.2, the United Kingdom 45.6, the United States 53.8.

3. Subject to selective consumption taxes.

Z = Zero-rate of tax.

L = Lower positive rate of VAT.

S = Standard rate of VAT.

E = Exempt or not covered by VAT.

H = Higher rate of VAT.

Source: A. Tait (p. 207) and OECD Secretariat (p. 378) of *The role of tax reform in Central and Eastern European economies* (OECD 1991).

Table 13.11: VAT treatment of financial services and insurance and reinsurance, January 1987

Country	"Core" financial services[1]	"Secondary" financial services[2]	Exported financial services	Life insurance	Fire and general insurance	Broker's and agent's services	Exported insurance services	Other indirect tax
Austria	Exempt	Standard rate	Zero rate	Exempt	Exempt	Exempt	Zero rate	Yes
Belgium	Exempt	Standard rate	Zero rate[3]	Exempt	Exempt	Exempt	Zero rate[3]	Yes
Denmark	Exempt	Standard rate	Zero rate[3]	Exempt	Exempt	Exempt	Zero rate[3]	Yes[6]
Finland	Exempt	Exempt	Exempt	Exempt	Standard rate[7]	Exempt	Exempt	No
France	Exempt	Standard rate	Zero rate[3]	Exempt	Exempt	Exempt	Zero rate[3]	Yes
Germany	Exempt[4]	Standard rate	Zero rate[3]	Exempt	Exempt	Exempt	Zero rate[3]	Yes
Greece	Exempt	Standard rate	Zero rate[3]	Exempt	Exempt	Exempt	Zero rate[3]	Yes
Ireland	Exempt	Standard rate	Zero rate[3]	Exempt	Exempt	Exempt	Zero rate[3]	Yes
Italy	Exempt	Standard rate	Zero rate[3]	Exempt	Exempt	Exempt	Zero rate[3]	No
Luxembourg	Exempt	Standard rate[5]	Zero rate[3]	Exempt	Exempt	Exempt	Zero rate[3]	Yes[8]
Netherlands	Exempt	Standard rate	Zero rate[3]	Exempt	Exempt	Exempt	Zero rate[3]	Yes
New Zealand	Exempt	Standard rate	Zero rate	Exempt	Standard rate	Standard rate[9]	Zero rate	No
Norway	Exempt	Exempt	Zero rate	Exempt	Exempt	Exempt	Zero rate	No
Portugal	Exempt	Standard rate	Zero rate[3]	Exempt	Exempt	Exempt	Zero rate[3]	Yes
Spain	Exempt	Standard rate	Zero rate[3]	Exempt	Exempt	Exempt	Zero rate[3]	No
Sweden	Exempt	Exempt	Exempt	Exempt	Exempt	Exempt	Exempt	No
Turkey	Exempt	Standard rate	Exempt	Exempt	Exempt	Exempt	Exempt	Yes
United Kingdom	Exempt	Standard rate	Zero rate[3]	Exempt	Exempt	Exempt	Zero rate[3]	No

1. Generally includes dealings in money, shares, stocks, bonds, or other securities, lending money or advancing credit (or the arranging thereof), and the operation of any current, deposit, or savings accounts.

2. Financial advice, safety deposit boxes, debt collection, and the keeping of securities.

3. Only if exported outside the EC.

4. Supplier can choose to have such services taxed where they are supplied to a trader for use in his business. The exemption also applies to the management of credit and credit guarantees, and the management and safe-keeping of securities.

5. Safe-keeping of securities is, however, exempt.

6. Applies only to insurance on boats.

7. Does not apply to credit and reinsurance.

8. Fire insurance only.

9. Life insurance brokers and agents are exempt.

Sources: Tables 10.3 and 10.4 of *Taxing consumption* (OECD 1988).

value added tax. Also included in these exemptions are related services provided by insurance brokers and agents. As with services, "exported" insurance services are zero rated in most countries – in the case of EC Member Countries only when exported outside the EC. In a number of countries (Austria, Belgium, France, Germany, Ireland, Luxembourg, the Netherlands, Portugal and Turkey) insurance services are generally subject to a separate indirect tax on gross premiums. As with financial services, it is difficult to value correctly insurance services provided, since insurance largely involves a group of people contributing to a pool, most of which is earmarked to meet claims, which are rather a transfer than a payment for services even if a proportion of this pool is required to meet administrative costs and a payment for services.

e) Real estate, building and construction

The OECD consensus is to tax building materials, repair and maintenance and the purchase of new buildings at the standard VAT rate, but to exempt the leasing for sale of commercial buildings from VAT, whilst frequently subjecting these latter transactions to a separate transfer tax or stamp duty. Table 13.12, extracted from OECD 1988, summarises main OECD practices regarding supplies of land and building, but as indicated in the final footnote the information is somewhat suspect in view of the various caveats and that somewhat different information is provided in certain cases by R. Conrad in World Bank (1990).

Table 13.12 shows that whilst the sale of newly constructed building is taxed at standard rates in most OECD countries (even if the alternative solutions of lower rate, exemption and zero rating are employed in some countries) sales of all other real estate are exempt from VAT, save in New Zealand and Spain. The rationale for this distinction is that whilst purchases of new houses are like the purchase of other consumer goods, on the sale of an existing old house which has not been taxed, the only taxable transaction under VAT is the service of the estate agent. However, as the last column of Table 13.12 shows most OECD countries apply a separate flat rate tax, apart from any stamp duties to which such transactions may also be subject.

A. Tait (1991) observes that:

> A useful way to think about the treatment of residential buildings is to consider the treatment of second-hand goods. After all, the largest stock of second-hand goods is in fact old buildings. The VAT is designed to tax the purchase of a good or service and should not tax the same good twice over. Thus, the original purchase of an item which may last a long time, e.g. a household durable, car, or residence, is the occasion for the levying of the VAT. What then must be created is a mechanism to avoid a further VAT liability if the item is resold.

This leads to a consideration of second-hand goods, the last category of goods and services which seem to require special discussion.

f) Second-hand goods

Some goods which at one stage have been sold to final consumers will eventually find their way back into the trading stock of registered traders as second-hand goods. This is commonly the case with motor vehicles, works of art, antiques, furniture, books and

Table 13.12: VAT treatment of supplies of land and buildings, January 1987*

Country	Lease of residential real estate	Lease of other real estate	Sales of newly constructed buildings	Sale of all other real estate	Alternative flat rate tax on exempt real estate sales
Austria	Low rate	Low rate	Standard rate	Exempt	Yes
Belgium	Exempt	Exempt[1]	Low rate[2]	Exempt	Yes, 12.5%[3]
Denmark	Exempt	Exempt[4]	Exempt	Exempt	No
Finland	Exempt	Exempt	Exempt	Exempt	No[5]
France	Exempt	Exempt	Standard rate	Exempt	Yes
Germany	Exempt	Exempt[6]	Exempt[6]	Exempt[6]	Yes, 2%
Greece	Exempt	Exempt	Standard rate	Exempt	Yes
Ireland	Exempt	Exempt[4]	Low rate	Exempt	No[5]
Italy	Exempt	Exempt[15]	Standard rate	Exempt	Yes, 10%
Luxembourg	Exempt	Exempt[4]	Exempt[4, 7]	Exempt[5]	No[5]
Netherlands	Exempt	Exempt[4]	Standard rate	Exempt[4]	Yes, 6%
New Zealand	Exempt	Standard rate	Standard rate	Standard rate	No[5]
Norway	Exempt	Exempt	Standard rate	Exempt	No
Portugal	Exempt	Exempt[4]	Exempt[4]	Exempt[4]	Yes, 8-10%[8]
Spain	Exempt	Standard rate	Low rate[9], standard rate	Standard rate	Yes, 6%
Sweden	Exempt	Exempt[4]	Low rate[10]	Exempt	No
Turkey	Exempt	Exempt[1]	Standard rate[11]	Exempt[11]	Yes, 4%[12]
United Kingdom	Exempt[13]	Exempt[13]	Zero rate	Exempt[14]	No[5]

1. Taxable where the building has been constructed for a commercial lessor.
2. There are three low rates in Belgium: 1 per cent, 6 per cent, and 17 per cent. The 17 per cent rate applies in this case.
3. This is the standard rate of the "registration tax", other rates may apply.
4. Supplier can apply tax at the standard rate if the purchaser agrees and is registered and the land and buildings are for use in a taxable activity.
5. Stamp duty only.
6. Supplier can apply tax at the standard rate if the recipient is a trader and the land and buildings are for use in his business.
7. This is, however, taxation at the standard rate on deliveries pursuant to a sales contract of buildings to be constructed to the extent they relate to non-existing buildings at the time of the conclusion of the contract as well as to deliveries pursuant to a rental contract of labour or industry.
8. This is not levied as an alternative to VAT.
9. Domestic housing only.
10. Low rate in effect results from the application of the standard rate to a reduced value of supply.
11. Exempt if the building is residential and does not exceed 150 square metres. Taxable where part of the real estate is part of the assets of an enterprise.
12. Imposed in all cases, even where sale is subject to VAT.
13. Leases in excess of 21 years granted by the original builder/developer are zero rated.
14. Sale or long lease of a protected building by a supplier who has carried out substantial reconstruction is zero rated.
15. The standard rate applies to lease of enterprises.
* This is a table which needs to be interpreted with care, given all the caveats in footnotes 1 to 15 alone. Moreover, other published sources sometimes give different results. For example, according to R.F.Conrad (World Bank 1990) the sale of both new and old buildings in Italy is taxable.
Source: Table 10.5 of *Taxing consumption* (OECD 1988).

records, and collectors' items. Under the normal value added tax treatment applicable to business sales and purchases, a dealer in such goods would receive no credit relating to the purchase price paid as the item would not have been purchased from a registered trader and no tax invoice held. Clearly, such a situation may result in tax being payable in excess of the traders' margin – a charge which may provide a significant incentive for private sales (which are generally not taxable). More importantly, as value added tax is most likely to have been paid when such goods were originally sold as new, imposing tax on the full price when sold second-hand results in double taxation. A similar potential exists in relation to purchases of second-hand goods for business use (rather than simple resale) from non-registered persons.

This potential for double taxation can be avoided by excluding from the taxable base of the purchaser the value added embodied in the goods at the time of purchase (represented by the purchase price paid). In the case of the dealer in such goods (i.e. a trader who purchases for resale), this can be achieved in one of three ways: first, by allowing a credit of tax at the time of purchase as would be the case if the article had been bought from another taxable trader; second, by taxing only the margin on sale (i.e. excess of sale price over purchase price); third, by taxing such sales at a reduced rate which would equal the standard rate applied to the margin. The first two methods, unlike the third, would not charge VAT on any increase in the value of second-hand goods. A fourth option would be not to tax second-hand goods at all (with no tax credit) perhaps with an exception for important items like motor vehicles.

Only the first option treats such transactions completely on a par with those involving new goods traded between registered persons in that the purchaser receives immediate recognition (by way of credit or refund) of the tax component included (albeit indirectly) in the purchase price. It is also the only option that can adequately alleviate the double taxation that potentially arises in respect of purchases of second-hand goods by registered traders for business use (other than for resale). As such goods will generally be in the form of assets, it would be impractical to apply either of the other options to the supply of goods and services to which those assets have contributed. Table 13.13 provides a summary of country practices.

3. The treatment of special categories of taxpayers and special supplies

This section covers briefly a number of predominantly administrative and technical issues on which governments introducing VAT have to make choices. They do, however, sometimes raise policy issues relating to equity and economic efficiency.

a) Concessions for small-scale traders and retailers

There are three kinds of concessions available for certain small traders and retailers:

- *Relief from the requirement to register.* This relieves a trader of the responsibility that would otherwise be imposed of furnishing regular returns, accounting for tax on sales and purchases, and keeping records etc. Such a concession usually takes the form of an annual turnover threshold below which traders can choose whether or not to register for the tax. The implications for those that do not register are an increase in the cost of purchases (since any tax component is not refunded) and an inability to charge tax (and issue tax invoices) on sales.

Table 13.13: VAT treatment of second-hand goods, January 1987[1]

Country	Tax on margin or full price	Type of second-hand goods	Type of trader	Margin taxed by[2]	
				Credit on purchase	Credit on sale
Austria	Full price	All	All	•	•
Belgium	Margin	Most[3]	Dealer	No	Yes
Denmark	Margin	Cars	Dealer	•	•
	Full price	All other	All		
Finland	Margin	All	Dealer	Yes	No
France	Margin	All	Dealer	No	Yes
Germany	Full price	All	All	•	•
Greece	Full price	All	All	•	•
Ireland	Margin	Trade-ins	Dealer	Yes[4]	No
Italy	Full price	All[5]	All	•	•
Luxembourg	Full price	All	All	•	•
Netherlands	Margin	Trade-ins	Dealer	Yes[4]	No
New Zealand	Margin	All	All	Yes	No
Norway	Full price	All[5]	All	•	•
Portugal	Margin	Most	Dealer	No	Yes
Spain	Margin	All	Dealer	No	Yes
Sweden	Margin	All	All	Yes	No
Turkey	Full price	All	All	•	•
United Kingdom	Margin	Most[6]	Dealer	No	Yes

1. Includes works of art and antiques.

2. • indicates that tax on the margin is not applicable, rather the sale is fully taxed.

3. Tax on the full price applies to motor vehicles and most other means of transport, antiques, original works of art, and collectors' items (e.g. stamps).

4. Credit effectively allowed on trade-ins by reducing the taxable value of the new goods sold by the amount of the trade-in.

5. Sale of traded-in in cars (all cars in Norway) exempt, therefore neither margin nor full price are taxed.

6. Tax on margin for cars, works of art, antiques, collectors' items, horses and ponies, boats, outboard motors, electronic organs, firearms, and aircraft.

Source: Table 10.6 of *Taxing consumption* (OECD 1988).

- *Reduction in net tax payable*. A number of OECD countries provide for the waiver of some or all of the net tax payable by certain traders. These concessions take two forms: those where the amount of tax waived is based on the amount of net tax payable by the trader, and those where the amount of tax waived is dependent on the trader's turnover. Typically there is an amount up to which full relief is given and beyond which the reduction in liability lessens.
- *Easing compliance through modified administrative requirements*. This is a broad category encompassing all concessions which directly or indirectly result in a simplification or reduction in the actions that have to be undertaken by a registered trader. Such concessions may involve the option to furnish returns less frequently or to account for tax on a cash basis.

Table 13.14 indicates that the majority of OECD countries provide concessions falling into at least two of these three categories.

For the most part the reasons for according or not according these alternative treatments under VAT are of an administrative/technical nature and so outside the scope of this book. However, it is perhaps worth enlarging a little on the various criteria that may be employed for qualification for relief from registration, since this gives some insights into the working of VAT as well as the influences on taxpayers to opt or not to opt for VAT. The basic trade-off for such small traders is that taking up the option not to register enables avoidance of the need to charge and account for the tax to the revenue authorities on the one hand, but forgoing the deduction of tax paid on their inputs on the other. The advantages and disadvantages of such a choice vary very much among different categories of small traders. For example, in the case of supplies of services to consumers (e.g. hairdressing) it probably pays to take up the option since taxable inputs are relatively slight in relation to other input costs such as wages, whereas small traders supplying mainly to registered traders or exporting or selling mainly low or zero rated goods will find it advantageous to remain a registered trader within the VAT network in order to recover input tax.

The exercise of the option not to register mainly by virtue of the exemption of their supplies that results may place such traders at an advantage vis-à-vis competing traders who are registered. For small-scale retail traders, particularly those selling goods, such an advantage may not be significant because of low margins and hence low value added. However, where personal services are supplied at the retail level, the potential advantage to the non-registered trader is likely to be greater. In order to reduce this distortion, Belgium and Spain generally subject such non-registered traders to a higher rate of tax on purchases (equalisation tax). Recognising the potentially greater distortion that can occur in the supply of personal services, Ireland, the Netherlands, and Portugal impose significantly lower registration thresholds for traders who supply services.

Optional registration for traders up to a certain size measured by annual turnover is generally the criterion for the right to exercise the option not to register. Only Finland and Spain use criteria other than turnover. In Belgium, Spain and Turkey the option not to register is given only to retailers. Table 13.15 summarises country practices regarding the option not to register.

Table 13.14: Small-scale trader and retailer concessions, January 1987			
Country	**Relief from registration**	**Reduction of tax liability**	**Modified administrative requirements**
Austria	Yes	Yes	Yes
Belgium	Yes[1]	No	Yes
Denmark	Yes	No	No
Finland	Yes[2]	Yes	Yes
France	No	Yes	Yes
Germany	Yes	Yes	Yes
Greece	Yes	No	No
Ireland	Yes	No	Yes
Italy	No	No	Yes
Luxembourg	Yes	Yes	Yes
Netherlands	Yes	Yes	Yes
New Zealand	Yes	No	Yes
Norway	Yes	No	No
Portugal	Yes	No	Yes
Spain	Yes[3]	No	Yes
Sweden	No	No	Yes
Turkey	Yes	No	Yes
United Kingdom	Yes	No	Yes

1. Some retailers only.
2. Sole proprietors with only family employees.
3. Individual retailers.

Source: Table 9.1 of *Taxing consumption* (OECD 1988).

b) Concessions for farmers and other primary producers

Apart from New Zealand, Sweden, and the United Kingdom, all OECD countries provide concessionary treatment to primary producers. These are generally traders involved in agriculture, animal husbandry, horticulture, viticulture, forestry, or fishing. Many of these concessions are on the lines already referred to for small traders and retailers, but the flat rate schemes referred to below benefit only primary producers. The predominant purposes of the bulk of concessions to primary producers are to reduce or eliminate the compliance costs of the value added tax and to compensate (at least partially) for the tax borne by the non-registered trader on purchases.

Under "flat rate" schemes primary producers can be relieved of most or all of the administrative requirements of the value added tax while being compensated in some way for the tax that they will bear as a result on their business purchases. Most commonly, such non-registered traders are compensated by increasing their selling price by a flat rate – their registered customers being able to obtain a deduction of the amount of that increase. However, France and Spain (the latter in the case of exporters only) do provide direct

Table 13.15: Concessions providing relief from registration, January 1987

Countries	Basis of concession		Qualifying criteria[1]			
	"Size" of trader	Trader type	Domestic currency	US Dollar Equivalent[2] ($)	Optional registration	Minimum registration period
Austria	Yes	No	TO up to 40 000 AS	2 918	Yes	5 years
Belgium	Yes	Yes	Some retailers[3]	-	Yes	irrevocable
Denmark	Yes	No	TO up to 10 000 Dkr.	1 362	Yes	None
Finland	No	Yes	Sole proprietor, only family employees	-	Yes	None
France	No	No	-	-	-	-
Germany	Yes	No	TO up to 20 000 DM	10 305	Yes	5 years
Greece	Yes	Yes	TO up to 1M Drs.[4]	7 207	Yes	None
Ireland	Yes	No	TO up to IR£ 25 000[5]	34 987	Yes	None
Italy	No	No	-	-		
Luxembourg	Yes	No	TO up to 200 000 Lfrs.	4 922	Yes	5 years
Netherlands	Yes	No	TO up to 4 150 Dfl.[6]	1 893	Yes	None
New Zealand	Yes	No	TO up to NZ$ 24 000	12 588	Yes	2 years
Norway	Yes	No	TO up to 12 000 Nkr.	1 622	No	2 years
Portugal	Yes	No	TO up to 800 000 Esc.[7]	5 475	Yes	5 years
Spain	No	Yes	Individual retailers	-	No	Irrevocable
Sweden	Yes	No	TO up to 30 000 Skr.	4 399	No[8]	None
Turkey	Yes	Yes	Varies with activity	-	No	None
United Kingdom	Yes	No	TO up to £ 20 500	30 074	Yes	2 years[9]

1. "TO" denotes total annual turnover (including any tax charged).

2. At end December 1986 (Source: *IMF Surveys*).

3. Small-scale retailers of food, clothing, shoes, books and periodicals, and druggists. For retailers of food, purchases must not exceed 4.5M. BFrs, for other traders 2.5M. Bfrs.

4. TO up to 250 000 Drs. (US$ 1 802) for suppliers of services.

5. TO up to IR£ 12 000 (US$ 16 793) for suppliers of services.

6. TO up to 25 000 Dfl. (US$ 11 405) for suppliers of services.

7. TO up to 500 000 Esc. (US$ 3 422) for liberal professions.

8. Option to register is provided to exporters and other suppliers of zero rated goods and services and to businesses in the development stage (i.e. high purchases and low turnover).

9. Does not apply in all cases.

Source: Table 9.2 of *Taxing consumption* (OECD 1988).

compensation payable to the farmer by the tax authorities calculated as a flat rate percentage of turnover. As with other concessions, it is not necessarily advantageous for primary producers to opt for them. In years of high capital expenditure, for example, some primary producers may gain an advantage by opting for the standard treatment under the value added tax in order to claim credit for the tax on that expenditure – the flat rate schemes only recognising an average level of inputs bearing tax. Similarly, some primary producers may find that they have, on an ongoing basis, a proportionally higher level of taxed inputs than that which would be accorded to them under the flat rate scheme and will opt for the standard treatment. The option for standard treatment under VAT will also be advantageous to those primary producers who export most of their output.

c) Inputs related to exempt supplies

The treatment of inputs related to exempt supplies, especially in relation to traders who are selling both exempt goods and those subject to VAT, which constitutes the usual case, poses complicated technical problems, as well as impinging on equity issues.

A trader selling both taxable and exempt goods may face the problem of identifying the extent to which purchases relate to each category of supply. Recognising the complexity of such an exercise, OECD countries provide traders with a simplified basis for determining the extent to which the tax on business purchases is creditable against the output tax arising from taxable supplies. Such simplified calculations can be on a turnover basis, a direct attribution basis for some purchases, or by using some indirect proxy.

The turnover basis simply divides the tax on purchases into deductible and non-deductible amounts in the same proportion as taxable and exempt supplies bear to total turnover. For example, a trader whose turnover from taxable supplies constitutes 80 per cent of total turnover would be allowed to deduct 80 per cent of the tax paid on business purchases. This turnover basis of apportionment is the simplest of the three forms, requiring no more of the trader in terms of record-keeping than that needed to identify separately taxable and exempt supplies for output tax purposes. Because of its relative simplicity, however, this method is more prone to yield a result which significantly departs from the actual attribution of inputs between taxable and exempt supplies. It will work to the advantage of a trader who, in generating exempt turnover, incurs a higher proportion of taxed inputs than is incurred in the generation of taxable turnover. In addition, the turnover method may be open to manipulation by traders artificially increasing the level of taxable supplies by engaging in a small number of high value-rated transactions (such as gold).

A trader will be disadvantaged where such inputs to taxable turnover are proportionately higher than those generating exempt turnover. The latter situation is likely to arise, for example, where the exempt supplies are services (such as financial services) and the taxable supplies are of goods. In such a case, the turnover from the exempt services may significantly restrict the deductibility of tax paid on inputs – even though those inputs still primarily relate to the generation of the taxable supplies. Consequently alternative methods are provided in most countries.

Table 13.16: Methods of apportioning inputs used for exempt purposes, January 1987

Country	Simple Turnover	Direct attribution	Other basis	Adjustment period capital assets/ land and buildings	De minimus rule[1]
Austria	Yes	Yes	No	5/10 years	No
Belgium	Yes	Yes	No	5/10 years[2]	No
Denmark	Yes	Yes	No	5/10 years	No
Finland	No	Yes	No	None	No
France	Yes	Yes	No	5/10 years	No
Germany	Yes	Yes	No	5/10 years	No
Greece	Yes	Yes	No	5 years[2]	No
Ireland	Yes	Yes	Yes	None	No
Italy	Yes	No	No	5/5 years	No
Luxembourg	Yes	Yes	Yes	5/10 years	Yes
Netherlands	Yes	Yes	No	5/10 years	No
New Zealand	Yes	Yes	Yes	Unlimited	Yes
Norway	No	Yes	No	None	No
Portugal	Yes	Yes	No	5/10 years	Yes
Spain	Yes	Yes	No	5/10 years	No
Sweden	Yes	Yes	Yes	None	Yes
Turkey	Yes	Yes	No	3/3 years	No
United Kingdom	Yes	No	No	None	Yes

1. A full input tax credit is allowed for all purchases where a registered trader makes minimal exempt supplies. See text for details.

2. Capital assets and buildings only, land is not subject to VAT.

Source: Table 10.1 of *Taxing consumption* (OECD 1988).

The "direct attribution" method increases the potential accuracy of apportionment by requiring the identification of those taxed inputs that can be associated uniquely with either exempt or taxable supplies. For those identified as being inputs related solely to exempt supplies no credit for tax paid thereon is allowed, a full credit being allowed for those inputs related solely to taxable supplies. The balance of inputs which cannot be isolated as contributing to only one class of output are usually apportioned on the simple turnover method.

While maintaining the relative simplicity of either of the above methods, the accuracy of apportionment can be considerably enhanced in certain cases if overhead costs are apportioned on some basis other than turnover. For example, such proxies as computer time and machine time can be used to improve, in a simple way, the accuracy of apportionments. Table 13.16 provides a summary of OECD country practices.

Table 13.17: Valuation of supplies for private use, January 1987

Country	**Goods**[1]		**Services**	
	Cost	**Market value**	**Cost**	**Market value**
Austria	No	Yes[2]	Yes	No
Belgium	Yes	No	No	Yes
Denmark	Yes	No	Yes	No
Finland	No	Yes	No	No
France	Yes	No	No	No
Germany	Yes[3]	Yes[3]	Yes	No
Greece	No	Yes	No	Yes
Ireland	Yes	No	Yes[4]	No
Italy	No	Yes	No	No
Luxembourg	No	Yes	Yes	No
Netherlands	Yes	No	No	No
New Zealand	Yes[5]	No	Yes[5]	No
Norway	No	Yes	No	Yes
Portugal	Yes	No	No	Yes
Spain	Yes	No	Yes	No
Sweden	No	Yes	No	Yes
Turkey	No	Yes	No	Yes
United Kingdom	Yes	No	No	No

1. Includes full or partial use of business assets.

2. Where a supply is the full or partial use of a business asset it is valued at cost.

3. Goods taken for a trader's private use are normally valued at acquisition, production or replacement cost. Goods supplied free to employees are assigned market value. Where a supply is the full or partial use of a business asset it is valued at cost.

4. Subsidised catering for employees only.

5. Lesser of cost or open market value.

Source: Table 10.2 of *Taxing consumption* (OECD 1988).

d) Supplies for private use

All OECD countries restrict the relief from tax paid on business purchases to the extent that they are used for the private purposes of a trader or a trader's employees or shareholders. In the absence of any special provisions, a self-employed trader could simply purchase goods through the business, claim the input tax and thus obtain them for private use free of tax. The trader would pay for such goods indirectly by way of a reduction in profit equal to the net of tax cost of the goods to the business. The same advantage can be gained by the full or partial private use of a business asset such as a motor vehicle or building, or the free supply of business services. The means of restricting such relief is essentially a technical valuation problem outside the scope of this book. Nevertheless, Table13.17 is provided to illustrate different practices among OECD countries.

e) Supplies by public sector bodies

The policy issue is to maintain VAT neutrality between supplies by public sector bodies and competing supplies by the private sector. In practice, OECD governments are generally consistent in their treatment of supplies made by public sector bodies (state, regional, and local government) under the value added tax. Countries generally apply the tax in relation to the activities of such bodies that are considered to be of a commercial or competitive nature. Where a public sector body is not conducting a taxable activity and is not registered, no relief is given in respect of tax paid on inputs.

D. The major excises

1. Introduction and orientations

a) Some general considerations

Selective consumption taxes are among the oldest forms of taxation in the world and remain the most important kind of consumption taxation in most countries outside the OECD area as well as in Australia, Japan and Portugal. This section is concerned with the *major* excises on the activities of drinking, smoking, motoring and, to a much less extent, betting and gambling. For organisational reasons it has been necessary to scatter around references to other selective consumption taxes, as defined in heading 5120 of Table 2.1, so this introduction recapitulates where references to these may (or may not) be found:

- Environment and/or pollution taxes have been discussed in Chapter 7, but there may be some overlap with what is said here on hydrocarbon oils and motor vehicles.
- Nuisance excises usually, though not always, on luxury goods have been discussed in connection with higher rates of VAT in Section C1c of this chapter and the conclusion was that there is little rationale for them.
- Selective taxes on services have been discussed in Section C1d of this chapter again in connection with the VAT treatment of services but the tax treatment of betting and gambling is briefly discussed here.
- Import and export taxes nowadays bring in minimal revenues and no longer appear to raise important tax policy issues in OECD countries, so they are not discussed in this book.
- Taxes on investment goods are reported in OECD RS 1991 to exist only in Norway, though the Swedish tax on energy consumption, classified as an excise, might well belong here, since it evidently has an impact on business inputs; as noted in Section B1 of this chapter, there seems little economic justification in imposing such arbitrary taxes on business inputs under what is supposed to be a consumption tax, but they may be regarded as environmental taxes.

The imposition of selective consumption taxes deliberately infringes the principle of neutrality of producer and consumer choices and often imposes additional administrative and compliance costs and, it has been argued, is difficult to justify except in the case of environment and pollution taxes and the major excises now discussed. The main justification for levying high taxes on drinking, smoking, motoring and gambling is that such taxes have for many years provided large and easily collectible sums of revenue, which governments cannot afford to forgo and in addition they involve low administrative costs. Also, this is an area where transactions are large, there is a relatively inelastic demand, precise definability and no close substitutes. Other economic efficiency and ethical arguments for imposing such excises which have been advanced include the aim of discouraging over-consumption of alcoholic drinks, tobacco, energy and gambling which inflict damage to both the consumer and others and to pay for the health and road-care costs associated with such over-consumption.

While taxes on alcohol and tobacco are relatively inelastic they are not entirely so and there is evidence that sufficiently high taxes on these products does significantly reduce overall consumption (e.g. Cnossen, 1977 and 1989). Another factor in the taxation of these sumptuary excises is that governments are aware that raising rates of tax on alcoholic drinks and cigarettes contributes to inflation in raising the consumer price index, even if the intent is merely to protect the revenue yield which may have been eroded by previous inflation. In addition there are powerful pressure groups in the alcohol and tobacco (and also motoring) industries arguing that insofar as higher taxation on these products results in lower domestic consumption there would be undesired repercussions on employment levels and export performance, while other pressure groups point to the regressive nature of some of these excises – tobacco everywhere, beer in some countries and wine in others. With so many conflicting objectives, it is difficult to provide unambiguous guidelines on what should be the appropriate tax take from drinking, smoking and motoring, a matter likely to be decided on pragmatic grounds relating to governments' needs for extra revenues and their perception of voters' reactions. If the primary objective is to get a fixed amount of revenue from the sumptuary excises on alcoholic drinks and cigarettes (which account for over 95 per cent of revenues from tobacco products) this may be achieved by the high duty/reduced consumption route as practised for alcohol in Norway and Sweden or the low duty/high consumption route as for example in France, though because of the relative inelasticity of demand, higher excise rates are likely in practice to provide higher revenues.

b) The contribution of the major excises to tax revenues

The contribution of all selective consumption taxes or "excises etc." to tax revenues has already been discussed in Chapters 2 and 3. Here it is briefly recalled that the excise etc. ratio declined considerably between 1965 and 1975, remained more or less stable between 1975 and 1985 and declined again between 1985 and 1989. Table 13.18 shows that in 1985 for nearly all countries for which information is available, identifiable selective taxes on drinking, smoking and motoring accounted for at least two thirds and often more than three quarters of revenues from all selective consumption taxes. Accordingly, the movement of the excise etc. ratio primarily reflects the movement of the ratio of the major excises. (It is also relevant not to the present discussion, but to the relative weight of taxation on the activities of drinking, smoking and motoring, to recall that the products

Table 13.18: : The relative importance of the major excises on drinking, smoking and motoring, 1985[1]

(Columns A to E receipts as percentage of receipts of 5000)

Country	A	B	C	D Motoring		E	F
	Taxes other than general consumption	Drinking	Smoking	1.Hydrocarbon oils	2. Vehicles (including licences)	B + C + D	Taxes on drinking + smoking + motoring as a proportion of specific taxes (B + C + D) / A
Australia	76	6	4	29[2]	7	46	61
Austria	36	3	6	9	3	21	58
Belgium	36	3	6	10	4	23	64
Canada	n.a.	n.a.	n.a.	n.a.	n.a.	n.a.	n.a.
Denmark	41	6	6	6	14	32	78
Finland	42	11	4	10	7	32	76
France	32	2	2	14	2	20	63
Germany	38	3	8	14	4	29	76
Greece	73[3]	2	13	0	13	27	37
Ireland	54	13	10	14	9	46	85
Italy	43	1	6	19	3	29	67
Japan	100	15	14	20	22	71	71
Luxembourg	n.a.	n.a.	n.a.	n.a.	n.a.	n.a.	n.a.
Netherlands	37	4	4	8	10	26	70
New Zealand	68	8	5	12	23	48	71
Norway	52	5	2	18	11	36	69
Portugal	50	1	6	20	4	31	62
Spain	48	3	5	(20)		28	58
Sweden	47	8	3	10	5	26	55
Switzerland	51	3	6	18	7	34	67
Turkey	n.a.	n.a.	n.a.	n.a.	n.a.	n.a.	n.a.
United Kingdom	50	10	10	15	8	43	86
United States	n.a.	n.a.	n.a.	n.a.	n.a.	n.a.	n.a.

1. In most countries alcoholics drinks, tobacco products, hydrocarbon oils and motor vehicles are also liable to general consumption taxes such as VAT, but it is usually impossible to isolate the amount of general consumption tax revenue obtained from such products.

2. Includes liquid petroleum gas.

3. Turnover tax is included. This tax was imposed on industrial products only and was abolished on 31 December 1986.

n.a. = not available.

Sources: OECD RS 1987 and Table 3.2 of *Taxing consumption* (OECD 1988).

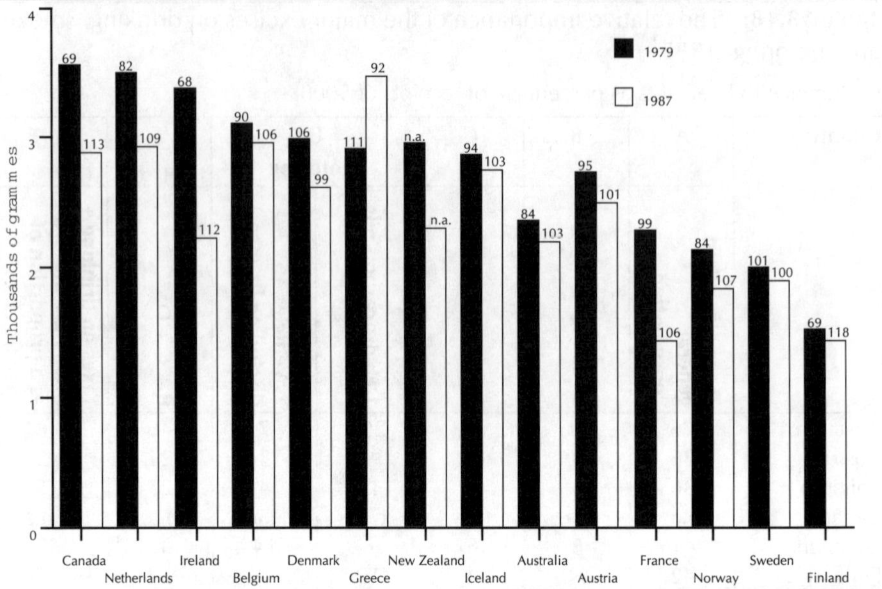

Chart 13.2: Consumption of tobacco per head, 1979 to 1987 (grammes per head of population aged 15 and over)

Source: OECD *Health systems, facts and trends* (OECD 1993 forthcoming)*.

* Some figures may be subject to revision. Relevant information lacking for other countries.

Note: Figures at the top of the columns show evolution of tobacco prices where 1985 = 100.

in question are usually subject to standard rates of VAT. See first footnote to Tables 13.9 and 13.18).

All governments have the desire to maximise revenues from, and to reduce the consumption of, alcoholic drinks and cigarettes. However, the effect of increased taxation and hence increased prices of alcoholic drinks and cigarettes on consumer demand should not be over-estimated. For example, it seems probable that non-tax factors such as social attitudes, goverment health warnings and anti-smoking campaigns will have a much greater influence on tobacco consumption than increased taxation. The data in Chart 13.2 suggest that there is little evidence of much correlation between changes in tobacco taxes and prices and changes in tobacco consumption. Of the 13 countries referred to in Chart 13.2, tobacco prices declined between 1979 and 1987 in real terms only in Denmark and Sweden where tobacco consumption also declined and in Greece where there was a very heavy increase in tobacco consumption. (Greece was the only country where there was any increase at all in tobacco consumption over this period.) Also, apart from Canada and Ireland, there seems little correlation between the amount of price increase and reduction in consumption: (for example, compare Belgium and the Netherlands). Other data reproduced in *The Economist* of 16 May 1992 show heavy falls in cigarette consumption between 1982 and 1990 only in Canada, the Netherlands and the United States where tobacco price and taxation trends were not greatly different from those in other OECD countries. (It is recalled that cigarette consumption represents over 95 per cent of tobacco consumption.)

Table 13.18 shows that in 1985 taxes on the activity of motoring, of which taxes on hydrocarbon oils are the most important, brought in more revenues than those on drinking and smoking. Revenues from taxes on drinking varied from 10 to 15 per cent of revenues from all consumption taxes in Finland, Ireland, Japan, and the United Kingdom to 3 per cent or less in Belgium, France, Italy, and Switzerland. There is also a similar divergence in the revenue importance of tobacco taxes relative to total consumption taxes: from 14 per cent in Japan and 10 per cent in Ireland and the United Kingdom to 3 per cent or less in France, Norway and Sweden.

Table 13.19 indicates that between 1965 and 1985 motoring has become increasingly a more important revenue source than drinking or smoking, and in 1985 –even leaving aside motor vehicle taxes – in most countries more revenue was derived from hydrocarbon oils than from alcoholic beverages or cigarettes. During the period 1965-1985 as a whole revenues from drinking and smoking declined in real terms in all countries except for very small increases from alcohol in France and tobacco in Belgium, whereas those from vehicles increased in real terms in all countries except Germany, Italy and Sweden. The increase in excise receipts to GDP between 1975 and 1985 was due entirely to the increase in taxes on motoring, since over that period taxes on alcoholic beverages and tobacco have declined in real terms, except for increases on tobacco in Austria and Belgium. Curiously enough, between 1980 and 1985 taxes on tobacco increased in real terms in many countries, though rarely by enough to offset their decline between 1975 and 1980, whereas during that same period revenues from alcoholic beverages continued to decline in all countries, except the United Kingdom. Table 13.20, using a different source, updates information on relative revenue yields from alcoholic drinks and tobacco products to 1988, this time as a percentage of total tax receipts. Those interested in the relative tax take from these two traditional vices may note that it varies very much not only between countries but also within a number of countries over time.

Table 13.19: Changes in reliance on revenues from the major excises, 1965-1985
(Receipts as percentage of GDP)

	1965	65-85	75-80	75-85	80-85	1985	1965	65-85	75-80	75-85	80-85	1985
Country	**Alcoholic beverages**						**Tobacco products**					
Australia	1.51	-0.93	-0.21	-0.44	-0.22	0.58	1.02	-0.62	-0.21	-0.32	-0.12	0.40
Austria	0.72	-0.14	-0.12	-0.18	-0.07	0.58	1.05	-0.28	-0.01	0.04	0.06	0.77
Belgium	2.00	-0.15	-0.02	-0.04	-0.02	0.36	0.63	0.02	0.00	0.08	0.07	0.65
Denmark	n.a.	n.a.	-0.35	-0.45	-0.11	0.97	n.a.	n.a.	-0.12	-0.29	-0.17	1.08
Finland	1.55	-0.01	-0.05	-0.20	-0.15	1.54	1.16	-0.62	0.01	-0.08	-0.09	0.54
France	0.24	0.04	-0.03	-0.09	-0.06	0.28	0.71	-0.38	-0.14	-0.09	0.05	0.33
Germany	0.57	-0.24	-0.08	-0.13	-0.05	0.33	1.02	-0.24	-0.10	-0.08	0.02	0.79
Ireland	2.94	-0.69	-0.11	-0.88	-0.76	2.25	4.08	-2.36	-0.58	-0.44	0.14	1.72
Italy	0.22	-0.15	-0.03	-0.04	-0.01	0.07	1.25	-0.71	-0.18	-0.15	0.03	0.55
Netherlands	0.54	-0.11	-0.03	-0.03	-0.01	0.43	0.94	-0.44	0.00	-0.05	-0.05	0.50
Norway	1.21	-0.40	-0.24	-0.35	-0.11	0.81	0.48	-0.34	-0.13	-0.07	0.06	0.44
Sweden	1.78	-0.74	-0.20	-0.41	-0.20	1.04	1.02	-0.58	-0.09	-0.24	-0.15	0.44
Switzerland	0.23	-0.04	0.00	-0.05	-0.04	0.18	0.50	-0.13	-0.02	-0.03	-0.01	0.37
United Kingdom	1.72	-0.54	-0.30	-0.21	0.09	1.18	2.79	-1.56	-0.32	-0.26	0.07	1.24
Country	**Hydrocarbon oils**						**Vehicles**					
Australia	0.95	1.92	1.63	1.57	-0.06	2.87	0.63	0.03	-0.04	0.04	0.07	0.66
Austria	1.41	-0.16	0.05	-0.11	-0.15	1.25	0.19	0.17	0.11	0.19	0.09	0.36
Belgium	1.34	-0.22	-0.35	-0.51	-0.16	1.12	n.a.	n.a.	0.02	0.06	0.05	0.45
Denmark	n.a.	n.a.	0.58	0.08	-0.50	0.95	0.69	1.70	-0.39	0.42	0.81	2.39
Finland	1.30	0.04	0.39	0.17	-0.22	1.34	0.79	0.22	0.03	0.18	0.16	1.00
France	2.01	-0.13	0.36	0.53	0.17	1.88	0.15	0.11	0.08	0.08	0.01	0.25
Germany	1.62	-0.28	-0.22	-0.33	-0.11	1.33	0.57	-0.17	-0.07	-0.12	-0.05	0.40
Ireland	2.54	-0.09	0.38	0.06	-0.32	2.45	1.45	0.08	0.35	0.43	0.08	1.53
Italy	2.00	-0.30	-0.54	-0.57	-0.02	1.69	0.29	-0.06	-0.04	-0.04	0.00	0.23
Netherlands	1.08	-0.14	-0.21	-0.31	-0.10	0.93	0.49	0.71	0.17	0.28	0.10	1.20
Norway	0.95	2.25	1.10	2.17	1.07	3.20	1.17	0.82	-0.04	0.58	0.62	1.99
Sweden	1.26	0.11	0.19	0.76	0.57	1.37	0.86	-0.19	-0.16	-0.30	-0.14	0.67
Switzerland	1.14	-0.05	-0.07	-0.28	-0.20	1.10	0.38	0.05	0.02	0.00	-0.02	0.42
United Kingdom	2.02	-0.23	0.05	0.39	0.34	1.79	0.65	0.27	-0.04	0.11	0.14	0.92

Sources: OECD RS 1987 and Table 3.3 of *Taxing consumption* (OECD 1988).

c) *Rates of excises on alcoholic drinks and cigarettes*

It is too complicated to follow tax rate developments in the numerous kinds of taxes on motor vehicles and it is recalled that rate developments have already been discussed in Chapter 7D on the taxation of energy. This sub-section is accordingly confined to developments in the rates of excises on alcoholic drinks and cigarettes.

Alcoholic drinks: Table 13.21 provides information on the approximate total tax burden on alcoholic beverages (i.e. beer, spirits and wine) for the most popular brands in each country. Except in a few countries, the highest rates are applied to spirits, medium rates to beer and the lowest rates to table wine. Among the exceptions are Japan and Portugal with lower tax rates on spirits and some Northern European countries which apply lower rates to beer than to wine. Over time the tendency has been for an increase in the tax rate on beer and a decrease of the tax rate on spirits.

Table 13.20: Receipts from excises on alcoholic drinks and tobacco products as a percentage of total tax receipts, 1965-88

	1965		1970		1975		1980		1985		1986		1987		1988	
	Alcohol	Tobacco	Alcohol	Tobacco	Alcohol	Tobacco	Alcohol	Tobacco	Alcohol	Tobacco	Alcohol	Tobacco	Alcohol	Tobacco	Alcohol	Tobacco
Australia	6.4	3.8(67)	5.1	3.2	4.2	2.8	3.5	2.0	2.8	1.7	n.a.	1.6	n.a.	n.a.	n.a.	n.a.
Austria	3.0	2.1	2.9	2.5	1.9	2.0	1.7	1.6	1.8	1.4	1.8	1.4	1.8	1.4	1.7	1.4
Belgium	2.0	1.4	1.8	1.0	1.4	0.9	1.3	0.7	1.4	0.6	1.3	0.6	1.3	0.6	1.2	0.6
Canada	0.4	n.a.	0.7	n.a.	0.5	n.a.	1.3	n.a.	1.4	1.0	1.3	1.1	1.3	1.0	1.2	1.0
Denmark	7.8(66)	6.5(66)	4.5	3.8	3.3	3.4	0.8	2.4	1.1	2.0	1.1	1.9	1.1	1.8	1.1	1.7
Finland	3.9	5.3	3.2	5.9	1.8	5.0	0.8	5.1	0.8	4.2	0.7	4.2	0.7	4.5	0.7	4.4
France	2.0	n.a.	1.6	1.1	1.1	1.0	1.9	0.8	1.5	0.5	1.4	0.5	1.5	0.5	1.4	0.5
Germany	3.2	1.8	2.9	1.6	2.4	1.3	2.0	1.0	2.1	0.9	2.0	0.8	1.9	0.8	1.8	0.8
Greece	7.5	1.4	6.1	0.9	4.7	0.8	3.1	0.5	3.3	0.4	3.4	0.3	2.1	0.3	2.8	0.3
Iceland	6.4	3.4	5.7	3.1	5.7	3.1	4.7	2.2	4.4	2.3	4.2	2.2	4.2	2.3	4.3	2.3
Ireland	15.7	11.3	8.9(71)	11.4 (71)	6.8	9.9	4.6	8.9	4.4	5.7	4.1	5.3	3.8	4.8	3.5	4.5
Italy	0.1	0.9	0.1	0.8	0.0	0.4	0.0	0.3	0.0	0.2	0.0	0.2	0.0	0.2	0.0	0.2
Japan	1.9	5.7	1.6	4.1	1.2	2.9	1.0	2.3	1.0	2.2	1.0	2.1	0.9	2.0	0.9	1.9
Luxembourg	0.0	0.6	0.0	0.3	0.0	0.3	0.0	0.4	0.2	0.8	0.2	0.7	0.2	0.7	0.2	0.5
Netherlands	2.8	1.6	1.9	1.5	1.3	1.1	1.2	1.0	1.1	1.0	1.0	0.9	1.0	0.9	0.9	0.8
New Zealand	3.3	3.7	3.7	3.0	2.3	1.8	1.3	1.1	1.1	1.8	0.9	1.8	2.1	2.0	1.9	1.7
Norway	2.3	3.6	1.6	3.1	1.1	2.6	0.8	2.0	0.9	1.7	1.0	1.6	1.1	1.9	1.0	1.8
Portugal	2.6	1.1	2.2	0.6	1.3	n.a.	3.4	n.a.	3.5	n.a.	2.7	n.a.	2.9	n.a.	2.8	n.a.
Spain	1.7	n.a.	1.6	n.a.	1.0	n.a.	2.8	n.a.	2.2	n.a.	2.1	n.a.	1.9	n.a.	1.8	n.a.
Sweden	2.9	5.0	2.4	4.2	4.2	3.3	1.2	2.5	0.9	2.1	0.8	1.9	0.7	1.8	0.8	1.7
Switzerland	2.4	1.1	3.0	1.1	1.5	0.8	1.2	0.7	1.2	0.6	1.0	0.5	1.0	0.5	1.0	0.5
United Kingdom	9.1	5.6	6.0	4.8	2.8	3.9	3.3	3.1	3.2	3.1	3.2	2.9	3.1	2.8	2.9	2.6
United States	2.0	2.9	1.6	2.3	1.3	1.8	0.4	1.2	0.3	0.8	0.1	0.8	0.0	0.8	0.0	0.7

n.a. = not available.

Source: *Health systems: facts and trends* (OECD 1992).

Tobacco: In Table 13.22 the total tax burden on popular cigarettes is shown as the percentage of tax in the retail price, broken down into specific excises (typically assessed per unit or on the basis of tobacco weight), *ad valorem* excises and VAT. It shows considerable variation between countries, but in most countries not much variation over time.

d) The uncertainty and relative importance of the impact of excises on income distribution

There is little evidence in most countries of the impact of the major excises on income distribution. Such limited evidence that is available would suggest taxes on cigarettes are invariably regressive, taxes on hydrocarbon oils mildly progressive and taxes on alcoholic drinks exhibit no clear distributional pattern, varying from country to country as between beer, wines and spirits and according to preferred drinking patterns, especially as between beer and wine. However, the income distribution impact is probably less important and relevant with respect to excises than any other area of taxation. The objectives of raising revenue and deterring over-consumption are far more important than income distribution effects of excises which, as already noted, are often uncertain.

2. Specific versus *ad valorem* rates of tax and indexing specific rates

Apart from certain taxes on tobacco products and motor vehicles the *ad valorem* element in the taxation of the major excise products is confined in nearly all OECD countries to the general consumption tax. It has sometimes been proposed that the usually subordinate or zero *ad valorem* element in the major excises should be increased, because specific taxes unrelated to the value of the product decline in times of inflation. There remains, however, strong arguments for applying specific rates of tax to alcoholic drinks, cigarettes and hydrocarbon oils, even if different arguments apply to the three kinds of products in question.

There is little, if any, support to move from specific towards *ad valorem* taxes for alcoholic drinks, where the specific tax may represent around half the retail sales price. At such levels sole reliance on *ad valorem* taxation would provide enforcement problems and where, as for example in the case of wines and spirits, the value varies greatly between products an *ad valorem* tax would make low quality products much cheaper in relation to those of high quality with the likely effect of shifting consumer choices to the former and the probability of increasing aggregate consumption of alcohol. Another argument against *ad valorem* taxation is that these very high *ad valorem* rates would apply not only to the products themselves, but also to packaging, advertising, brandmarks and other elements which go to make up the price of the product, thus arbitrarily increasing the differential in relation to other products where packaging, advertisement, etc. would be taxed much less. Finally, specific taxation represents the most practicable method for governments to achieve the social objective of taxing alcohol according to its strength and to protect consumers from product deterioration.

Though a number of the above considerations apply also, albeit with less force, to the taxation of tobacco products (e.g. the use of specific taxation to discriminate against the more dangerous forms of smoking), here the relationship between the *ad valorem* and

Table 13.21: Approximate total tax burden on alcoholic beverages as a percentage of retail price for home consumption

Country	1979			1982			1985			VAT Rates 1985		
	Beer	Spirits	Table wine	Beer	Spirits	Table wine	Beer	Spirits	Table wine	Beer	Spirits	Table wine
Australia	43	78-84	0	41	78	n.a.	46	72	16	n.a.	n.a.	n.a.
Austria	39	52-62	29	38	51-62	29	39	43	31	20	20	20
Belgium	25	63	37	29	74	30	34	69	31	19	25	25
Canada	45	70	45	45	72	54	52	84	60	n.a.	n.a.	n.a.
Denmark	46	80	40	47	80	36	49	82	43	22	22	22
Finland	34	65	61-65	39	65	65	41	66	66	19.05	19.05	19.05
France	18	63	17	18	63	17	21	46	18	18.6	18.6	18.6
Germany	20	54	12	20	52	12	20	64	12	14	14	14
Greece	n/a	n/a	n/a	n/a	n/a	n/a	n/a	n/a	n/a	n.a.	n.a.	n.a.
Ireland	53	88	54	54	82	49	53	62	55	23	23	23
Italy	14	22-41	6	19	26-36	7	21	29	8	18	18	6
Japan	44	17-35	13-24	49	26	14	49	14	27[1]	n.a.	n.a.	n.a.
Luxembourg	n/a	n/a	n/a	n/a	n/a	n/a	16	65	6	12	12	6
Netherlands	27	82	21	36	77	21	38	82	28	19	19	19
New Zealand	n/a	n/a	n/a	n/a	n/a	n/a	36	55	19	n.a.	n.a.	n.a.
Norway	48	87	47	53	87	53	55	87	55	20	20	20
Portugal	n/a	n/a	n/a	n/a	n/a	n/a	21	15	7	n.a.	n.a.	n.a.
Spain	6	45	45	13	35	4	13	25	5	n.a.	n.a.	n.a.
Sweden	40	90	63	40	91	63	41	92	70	23.46	23.46	23.46
Switzerland	11	49	5	n/a	n/a	n/a	15	44	6	n.a.	n.a.	n.a.
Turkey	n/a	n/a	n/a	n/a	n/a	n/a	n/a	n/a	n/a	n.a.	n.a.	n.a.
United Kingdom	35	70	50	40	65	44	39	56	35	15	15	15
United States	20	50	n/a	17	46	n/a	16	44[2]	n/a	n.a.	n.a.	n.a.

1. Sales (Commodity) tax.

2. Prior to October 1985 increase.

n.a. = not applicable.   n/a = not available.

Source: *Alcoholic beverage taxation and control policies, Brewers' Association of Canada*, Fourth, Fifth and Sixth Editions, Ottawa, 1980, 1982 and 1986.

Table 13.22: Taxation of popular cigarettes as a percentage of tax inclusive retail price

Country	1979				1985				1987			
	Specific excise	Ad valorem excise	VAT	Total tax	Specific excise	Ad valorem excise	VAT	Total tax	Specific excise	Ad valorem excise	VAT	Total tax
Australia	47.26	n.a.	n.a.	54.92[1]	35.19	n.a.	n.a.	46.05[1]	32.20	n.a.	n.a.	51.33[1]
Austria	n.a.	55.00	15.25	70.25	n.a.	55.00	16.67	71.67	n.a.	55.00	16.67	71.67
Belgium	3.6	62.05	5.66	71.31	4.23	60.70	5.66	70.61	3.66	60.70	5.66	70.02
Canada	n.a.	n.a.	n.a.	n.a.	n.a.	n.a.	n.a.	n.a.	n.a.	n.a.	n.a.	n.a.
Denmark	48.62	23.04	16.84	88.49	46.95	21.64	18.03	86.67	47.97	21.22	18.03	87.22
Finland	n.a.	n.a.	n.a.	n.a.	n.a.	n.a.	n.a.	n.a.	n.a.	n.a.	n.a.	n.a.
France	3.63	43.60	25.45	72.65	3.77	45.46	25.60	74.80	3.75	45.46	25.60	74.80
Germany	34.53	24.30	11.50	70.30	30.64	31.50	12.28	74.49	28.25	31.50	12.28	72.03
Greece	n.a.	n.a.	n.a.	n.a.	3.08	53.58	4.85	61.51	2.82	33.95	26.47	63.21
Ireland	33.70	20.20	9.09	62.97	40.68	14.89	18.70	74.33	40.21	13.61	20.00	73.82
Italy	1.73	56.20	15.25	73.18	3.76	53.25	18.00	75.00	3.38	53.39	15.25	72.03
Japan	n.a.	n.a.	n.a.	n.a.	n.a.	n.a.	n.a.	n.a.	n.a.	n.a.	n.a.	n.a.
Luxembourg	4.00	55.55	2.00	61.55	3.35	57.55	6.00	66.90	3.36	57.55	6.00	66.91
Netherlands	3.46	51.07	14.70	69.23	17.94	37.39	15.97	71.89	35.76	19.06	16.67	71.49
New Zealand	n.a.	n.a.	n.a.	n.a.	n.a.	n.a.	n.a.	n.a.	n.a.	n.a.	n.a.	n.a.
Norway	n.a.	n.a.	n.a.	n.a.	n.a.	n.a.	n.a.	n.a.	n.a.	n.a.	n.a.	n.a.
Portugal	n.a.	n.a.	n.a.	n.a.	n.a.	n.a.	n.a.	n.a.	6.99	51.03	13.79	71.81
Spain	n.a.	n.a.	n.a.	n.a.	n.a.	n.a.	n.a.	n.a.	4.79	28.00	11.94	44.70
Sweden	n.a.	n.a.	n.a.	n.a.	n.a.	n.a.	n.a.	n.a.	n.a.	n.a.	n.a.	n.a.
Turkey	n.a.	n.a.	n.a.	n.a.	n.a.	n.a.	n.a.	n.a.	n.a.	n.a.	n.a.	n.a.
United Kingdom	35.58	21.00	13.04	69.61	40.60	21.00	13.04	74.57	40.27	21.00	13.04	74.32
United States	n.a.	n.a.	n.a.	n.a.	n.a.	n.a.	n.a.	n.a.	n.a.	n.a.	n.a.	n.a.

1. In addition to the specific federal excise these figures include the Business Franchise Fee levied in New South Wales.

n.a. = not available.

Sources: 1979: *Report on the scope for convergence of tax systems in the community, Bulletin, Supplement 1180*; 1985: *EEC, Excise duty tables, 1985*; 1987: *EEC, Excise duty tables, 1987*.

specific element remains an important issue, especially in the context of European Community harmonisation. Generally, countries like France, Greece and Italy with cheap home-grown tobacco prefer *ad valorem* taxation which widens the difference between domestic and imported products, whereas countries like Denmark, Ireland and the United Kingdom who import their tobacco prefer greater reliance on specific taxes. In France, Greece and Italy the ratio of revenues from specific tax to those from total taxes on the most popular price category of cigarette was only about 5 per cent; in Denmark, Ireland and the United Kingdom, it was about 55 per cent (see Table 13.22).

In the case of hydrocarbon oil products where the pre-tax price has fluctuated sharply over the last twenty years, increased reliance on *ad valorem* rather than specific taxes has rarely been an issue, since such a change would have required frequent ad hoc adjustments to the rates to meet energy and anti-inflation policy objectives (see Chapter 7D).

Public finance theorists and governments other than those in countries with home-grown tobacco, have generally preferred specific to *ad valorem* rates, with the proviso that standard *ad valorem* rates of VAT should be applied to the products in question. Public finance theorists have also been attracted by indexing specific rates of excises to some price level measurement like the consumer price index, to offset negative fiscal drag and the reluctance of politicians in the face of the various pressures already noted to offset the revenue deterioration by ad hoc measures. However, in practice, only Australia, Canada and Denmark have adopted such a solution and even then only temporarily. The practical problems are that, first, it involves a number of difficult technical problems to get the index right given time lags; second, it could limit the flexibility of governments wishing for other reasons to vary the tax burden as between the excise products involved and, third, it is unlikely to be a popular measure with interested producers and consumers who are also voters. It is nonetheless somewhat irrational that the indexation of excises to offset negative fiscal drag so rarely happens, whereas the indexation of the personal income tax to offset positive fiscal drag frequently happens, and the difference can be attributed only to their relative electoral appeal.

3. Choices in taxing motoring

This sub-section briefly refers to some countries practices. A more general discussion of the energy and environmental policy issues involved was provided in Chapters 7D and 7E.

There are a variety of ways of employing selective taxes on the activity of motoring:

- *Excises on hydrocarbon oil products*. These are nearly always based on the volume of the fuels and rates nearly always vary as between gasoline and automotive diesel oil.
- *Excises on purchases of motor vehicles*. These are levied on an *ad valorem* basis in a number of countries often as an alternative to a higher rate of VAT (e.g. Denmark, Ireland, the Netherlands, the United Kingdom) but may be levied on a weight basis (Sweden).
- *Taxes related to the ownership or use of the motor vehicle*. These mostly take the form of specific motor vehicle licences which may be related to their weight (Denmark, Germany for non-passenger vehicles, the Netherlands, Sweden and Belgium

and the United Kingdom for certain commercial vehicles) or to horsepower (France, Italy) or to engine capacity of the vehicle (Belgium, Germany for passenger vehicles, Ireland and Luxembourg) or simply be based on a flat rate (the United Kingdom for passenger vehicles).

- *Higher rates of VAT or other general consumption taxes.* Usually standard rates on VAT are levied on hydrocarbon oils and private motor vehicles, but for certain country exceptions see footnote 1 to Table 13.9.

Non-tax revenues such as road tolls, parking fees and driving licences. These are generally designed only to cover administrative costs, but could be used to generate revenues.

4. Choices in taxing betting and gambling

Taxes on betting and gambling are of much less revenue importance than taxes on the activities of drinking, smoking and motoring, but probably of much greater revenue importance than any other selective tax on goods and services. Such levies may be collected in a variety of ways and this paragraph merely notes such possibilities rather than advancing arguments for and against them. In this area, control problems may be paramount and may govern, for example, the relative tax treatment of where the betting activity takes place (e.g. horse or dog racing courses or in other areas such as betting shops). The only selective consumption tax on these activities are taxes on the stake (5126) which occur in all OECD countries save Greece, Japan and the Netherlands, but other means of taxing the activity include subjecting them to general consumption tax, regarding the gain as liable to income tax as in the United States, imposing a separate tax on any winnings received as applied in Denmark and the Netherlands, levying a tax on the gross profits of enterprises carrying out such activities, the provision of a state monopoly for gambling activities, and compulsory transfers from licensed private enterprises. Typically the revenues from the specific consumption tax account for around 1 per cent of those from taxes on specific goods and services, but in a few countries they are more important: Spain (12 per cent), Australia and Finland (6 per cent), France (5 per cent), New Zealand and the United Kingdom (4 per cent).

Chapter 14 Recurrent taxes on immovable property

A. Introduction

1. Scope of the chapter

Taxes on immovable property or real estate (buildings and land) take many forms. Here is how they are treated in this book:

a) Recurrent (usually annual) taxes on immovable property (Heading 4100 of the OECD list at Table 2.1) is the subject of this chapter.
b) Transfer taxes on immovable property (Heading 4400) are not dealt with in this book, though the share of revenues from taxes on financial and capital transactions, of which those from transfers from immovable property provide an unidentifiable part, are shown in Table 14.1.
c) Other non-recurrent taxes on immovable property (Heading 4500) are likewise not covered in this book. They provide very little revenue and currently exist only in Canada, Greece and Spain.
d) Net wealth taxes (4200), death and gift taxes (4300) and capital gains taxes on individuals (1120) are all discussed in Chapter 11, where reference is sometimes, but not systematically, made to the treatment of immovable property under these taxes.

Recurrent taxes on immovable property almost invariably accrue to state or local governments and issues relating to the relations between central and local government – central control and local discretion – have already been discussed in Chapter 9. This chapter is accordingly restricted to other issues which arise in connection with these taxes.

Except for Table 14.1 which refers to all OECD countries this chapter covers only twelve countries. These include all countries with immovable recurrent property taxes of importance, except for Canada and Iceland which were not covered in the two OECD studies from which the material has been taken.

Unless ambiguity could be involved, recurrent taxes on immovable property are henceforth referred to in his chapter as "property taxes" or "the property tax", even though there are other property taxes and in some countries they are referred to as "the rates" or by other names.

2. The contribution of these taxes to government revenues

Table 14.1 (column 1) shows that nearly all OECD countries have recurrent taxes on immovable property, even if they make a negligible contribution to government revenues in Denmark, Greece and Spain, and are virtually non-existent in Belgium, Italy and Portugal. Only United Kingdom, United States, Canada, New Zealand and Japan raise significant amounts of revenue through this source, though Ireland used to do so before abolishing its tax on residential immovable property in 1978. Table 14.1 shows also that the share of receipts from immovable property taxes has declined between 1965 and 1989 in all countries except France, Ireland, Japan and the Netherlands.

Columns 2 and 3 of Table 14.1 show how these revenues are split between households and business, as further discussed in Section C2 of this chapter. Column 4 records receipts from financial and capital transactions, of which an unidentifiable, but probably quite large proportion, derives from the transfer of real estate. Financial and capital transactions exist in all OECD countries except Canada, but exceed 4 per cent of total taxation only in Australia.

3. To have or not to have a recurrent tax on immovable property

Over recent years a number of countries have been reconsidering what should be their relative reliance, if any, on the property tax. Ireland abandoned its tax on residential property in 1978, mainly because of criticisms of the fairness of the tax (rural areas contributed very little or sometimes even nothing and valuations were very much out of date – the last full scale valuation having taken place in 1850!). Whether or not what may be regarded as the bad administration of a good tax is a solid reason for abandoning the household property tax is still discussed in Ireland and the need for some revenue from residential property led the Irish government to introduce in 1983 a new tax which took the form of a tax on imputed income from residential property but of much smaller revenue importance. Some of the Swiss cantons (e.g. Zurich) decided in the early eighties to abolish the property tax. The main reasons given were that these taxes were very costly to administer in relation to the yield, which tended to be small in comparison to other cantonal taxes. (It is recalled – see Chapter 11 – that Switzerland has much heavier capital taxes than any other OECD country.) The reasons for the abandonment of a property tax for a poll tax in the United Kingdom in 1989 and 1990 and the subsequent abandonment of the poll tax in 1991 for a partial property tax has already been discussed in Chapter 9E7 and 9F.

On the other hand, Greece and Spain have recently introduced new property taxes or modified them substantially in order to raise more revenue as a part of a decentralisation policy already discussed in Chapter 9, but too recently to offset the low property tax yields shown in Table 14.1.

As discussed in Chapter 9, the property tax seems a particularly suitable method of financing local expenditures and is likely to continue to exist in nearly all OECD countries, even if its lack of revenue buoyancy means that the decline in their total share of tax revenues is also likely to continue in most countries.

B. The tax base and coverage

Three main issues are involved: first, the relative tax treatment of land and of buildings; second, the choice between annual rental values and capital values; third, exemptions from the tax base. Each of these issues is considered in turn.

1. Relative tax treatment of land and buildings

The use of differential rates on land and buildings has been advocated as a means of influencing land use development and has occasionally been implemented (e.g. in Australia). The argument for a heavier tax on land is to encourage its more intensive development (or by Henry George to achieve government control of land) and the argument for a lower tax on land is to slow down such development for environmental purposes. Whether such tax differentials are likely to have much practical effect is open to question, particularly in countries where there are no strong controls on land use. Even where such controls do

Table 14.1: Receipts from taxes on immovable property[1] as a percentage of total tax receipts

	Recurrent property taxes (1) 4100				Taxes on financial and capital transfers (2) 4400			
	1965	1975	1982	1989	1965	1975	1982	1989
Australia	6.8	5.3	4.8	4.7	2.0	2.1	2.3	4.1
Austria	1.5	0.9	0.8	0.7	0.6	0.5	0.5	0.7
Belgium	–	–	–	–	2.5	1.6	1.0	2.1
Canada	10.8	8.3	8.0	7.6	–	–	–	–
Denmark	4.9	4.0	2.7	2.4	1.0	1.1	1.0	1.2
Finland	–	–	0.2	0.2	2.0	1.3	1.7	3.2
France	2.0	1.5	1.7	2.2	1.7	1.2	1.1	1.3
Germany	1.5	1.1	1.1	1.0	0.7	0.6	0.6	0.7
Greece	0.2	0.3	0.4	0.2	8.5	8.2	1.9	2.1
Iceland	1.7	2.8	2.8	3.4	2.2	1.5	1.9	2.2
Ireland	12.2	7.3	2.3	2.6	1.0	1.0	1.2	1.9
Italy	1.7	0.2	–	–	4.6	2.9	2.8	2.1
Japan	5.2	5.8	5.4	5.4	2.2	2.3	2.6	3.1
Luxembourg	1.4	0.6	0.5	0.4	1.6	1.9	2.1	3.2
Netherlands	1.0	0.7	1.8	1.6	1.5	0.7	0.6	1.1
New Zealand	8.4	7.0	7.0	5.4	0.9	0.7	0.6	0.4
Norway	0.6	0.4	0.4	0.7	0.2	0.2	0.2	0.4
Portugal	–	–	–	–	2.5	1.6	1.2	1.2
Spain	0.4	0.4	0.4	0.1	2.5	1.6	1.2	1.2
Sweden	–	–	–	0.9	0.5	0.4	0.5	1.7
Switzerland	0.6	0.6	0.5	0.4	1.6	1.3	2.0	3.6
Turkey	5.1	1.6	0.0	n.d.	5.2	4.9	4.2	2.0
United Kingdom	11.2	11.1	11.3	10.8	0.7	0.7	0.8	1.1
United States	13.2	11.8	8.9	9.4	0.1	0.1	0.1	0.2

Table 14.1(cont.): Receipts from taxes on immovable property[1] as a percentage of total tax receipts

	Recurrent property taxes on households (3) 4110				Relevant property taxes on business (4) 4120			
	1965	1975	1982	1989	1965	1975	1982	1989
Australia	n.a.	n.a.	n.a.	n.a.	n.a.	n.a.	n.a.	n.a.
Austria	0.7	0.3	0.2	0.2	0.8	0.6	0.5	0.5
Belgium	–	–	–	–	–	–	–	–
Canada	n.a.	n.a.	n.a.	n.a.	n.a.	n.a.	n.a.	n.a.
Denmark	–	–	–	–	4.9	4.0	2.7	2.4
Finland	–	–	0.1	0.1	–	–	0.1	0.1
France	0.8	1.0	1.2	1.5	1.2	0.5	0.5	0.7
Germany	0.9	0.7	0.4	0.4	0.6	0.5	0.6	0.6
Greece	–	–	0.3	0.2	0.2	0.3	0.1	–
Iceland	0.7	1.1	1.0	1.2	1.0	1.7	1.8	2.2
Ireland	n.a.	n.a.	n.a.	n.a.	n.a.	n.a.	n.a.	n.a.
Italy	–	–	–	–	–	–	–	–
Japan	n.a.	n.a.	n.a.	n.a.	n.a.	n.a.	n.a.	n.a.
Luxembourg	n.a.	n.a.	n.a.	n.a.	n.a.	n.a.	n.a.	n.a.
Netherlands	n.a.	n.a.	n.a.	n.a.	n.a.	n.a.	n.a.	n.a.
New Zealand	n.a.	n.a.	n.a.	–	n.a.	n.a.	n.a.	–
Norway	n.a.	n.a.	n.a.	0.7	n.a.	n.a.	n.a.	–
Portugal	–	–	–	–	–	–	–	–
Spain	n.a.	0.4	0.4	0.1	n.a.	–	–	–
Sweden	–	–	–	0.4	–	–	–	0.5
Switzerland	0.6	0.6	0.5	0.4	–	–	–	–
Turkey	n.a.	n.a.	n.a.	n.a.	n.a.	n.a.	n.a.	n.a.
United Kingdom	5.4	4.3	4.8	4.7	5.8	6.9	6.6	6.0
United States	4.9	4.8	3.7	4.2	8.3	6.9	5.2	5.2

1. The other main taxes on property have been covered in Chapter 11. There remain non-recurrent taxes on net wealth on immovable property which exist only in Canada, Greece and Spain and which since 1975 have never exceeded 0.5 per cent of total tax receipts. – = Zero or near zero. n.a. = breakdown between households and business not available.

Source: OECD RS 1991.

exist (e.g. Australia, Germany and a few cities in the United States) there is little evidence to suggest that these tax policies have been effective in achieving their objectives. One reason is that in none of these instances is the tax rate differential sufficiently great to overcome other factors influencing decisions about land use, and a tax on land heavy enough to overcome such other factors could be regarded as confiscatory. Table 14.2 shows that nearly all countries include in the tax base the unimproved value of the land and most also any improvements to the land. In addition, it shows that buildings are usually, though not invariably, included in the tax base.

2. Annual rental value versus capital sales value

Under the annual rental value basis of property taxation, the base to which the tax rate is applied is the actual or estimated current annual rent of the real estate. Under the capital or sales value basis, the tax base is the amount for which the property has recently been sold or constructed or an estimate thereof. In the case of property which is ordinarily bought, sold, and used as rental property, such as residential apartment houses or office buildings composed of rental suites, it might be expected that the assessed values under either the annual or capital value basis would be closely related by current rates of capitalization, especially during periods of stable values and interest rates. In the real world, however, changing economic conditions and expectations about the future can lead to important differences in these two bases of taxation. A switch from rental to capital valuation may also involve some regional redistribution in rateable values and some redistribution of net income between households.

While the annual rental value basis uses actual or estimated current rents as the tax base, the capital value basis when applying the capitalisation of income method looks at the expected stream of future annual incomes. Since expectations about future rentals may differ substantially from current rentals, the resultant capitalised value will also differ from a capital value based upon the current rent and current long-term interest rates observed in the market, since in some areas there may be an increase in sales values and rental values, while other areas may be declining. Two properties having the same current rental income may have different sales values if there are different expectations with respect to he future stream of income of each of them.

Fast-growing areas may prefer the capital value basis to the rental value basis in order to keep the tax burdens tied as closely as possible to growth. Capital values may also be easier for the taxpayer to understand.

Other considerations, including rent controls, housing subsidies and administrative convenience may affect country choices. These are outside the scope of this book, but are fully discussed along with a number of other valuation issues in OECD 1983. Table 14.2 summarises country choices in this area.

It should be added that whatever system is adopted valuation inconsistencies are one of the main reasons for the unpopularity of the property tax. As R. Bird and C. Wallich (1992) note:

Table 14.2: The base and coverage of recurrent taxes on immovable property[1]

Country	Tax	Unimproved land value	Improvements to land	Buildings	Basis of Valuation
Australia (New South Wales)	Land tax	Yes	No	No	Capital
	Rates	Yes	In some local authorities	No	Capital
Denmark	Land tax	Yes	Yes	No	Capital
	Service tax	No	No	Yes	Capital
France	Land and building tax	–	–	Yes	Annual
	Land tax	Yes	Yes	–	Annual
	Property tax	No	No	Yes	Annual
Germany	Real property tax (Grundsteuer)	Yes	Yes	Yes	Capital
Japan	Fixed assets tax	Yes	Yes	Yes	Capital
	City planning tax	Yes	Yes	Yes	Capital
	Special land-holding tax	Yes	Yes	No	Capital
Netherlands	Municipal tax	Yes	Yes	Yes	Varies
	Contributions to polder boards	Yes	No	Yes	Varies
New Zealand	Land tax	Yes	Yes	No	Capital
	Rates	Yes	Yes	Sometimes	Capital or annual
Spain	Rural land tax	Yes	Yes	Yes	Annual
	Urban land tax	Yes	Yes	Yes	Annual
Sweden	Municipal guarantee tax	Yes	Yes	Yes	Capital
Turkey	Immovable property tax	Yes	Yes	Yes	Capital
England and Wales	Rates	Yes	Yes	Yes	Annual
United States (Wisconsin)	Property tax	Yes	Yes	Yes	Capital

1. Business assets are included only in Japan (tangible assets under the "fixed assets tax") and Turkey (machinery and livestock though may be taken into account in the Netherlands and New Zealand. A few minor items may be included in the United Kingdom and United States and infrastructure improvements may be taken into account in the Netherlands and New Zealand.

Sources: *Taxes on immovable property* (OECD 1983) and *Local government: an international perspective*, ed. J.P. Owens and S. Panella, North Holland, 1991.

As a rule, property is supposed to be assessed on the basis of its market value, usually defined as the price struck between a willing buyer and a willing seller in an arm's length transaction. In reality, however, discrepancies usually arise between assessed valued and market values within classes of property, between classes of property, and across municipalities for both political and technical reasons. Within-class inequity is perhaps the most significant from a policy perspective because it is the most visible. For example, two single-family houses each worth $100,000 may be assessed at very different ratios of market value depending on their location, the size of the lot, the age of the structure, and other factors. Centrally-located properties and older properties, for instance, are generally relatively under-assessed compared to suburban and newer properties. Since taxpayers can easily compare their property taxes with those of similar properties in their neighborhood, such discrepancies lead both to specific assessment appeals and to general pressure for tax relief. Single-family homes are usually under-assessed relative to apartments, and residential property generally *is* under-assessed relative to commercial and industrial property..... Assessed-to-market value ratios may be higher in one municipality than another, especially when assessment is done by the municipalities themselves. Some assessment biases result from problems inherent in the estimation of market value, where a property has recently been sold its market value may be easily determined, but where a property has not sold for several years and in particular where it has some unique characteristics, the determination of market value is an inherently difficult task. Moreover, when property values are changing rapidly even annual reassessment (which is too costly to be practical) would mean that assessed values are always out of date. Assessed values are thus at best only a rough estimate of true market value and hence always vulnerable to appeals.

3. Exemptions and concessions for certain properties

Many tax reliefs are available in all countries. Almost all countries exempt government-owned property from the tax base, though in many cases there are "in lieu" payments from central to local governments for the revenues so lost by the latter. Many countries also exempt from tax land used for highways, railways and other transport and communication facilities. Other common reliefs occur in the mining, agriculture, and forestry industries. In fact, almost all countries provide very favourable treatment of agricultural land and this subsidy to farmers has been much criticised. Also, many sports, social, religious, and education facilities receive favourable tax treatment, although this may depend upon whether they are owned by the public sector or by private institutions. Table 14.3 summarises some country practices in this area.

C. Economic and social issues

1. The influence of property taxes on urban development and investment decisions

Property taxes are designed to raise revenues for local government and are rarely used to influence urban development, although urban planners continue to examine ways in which these taxes can complement the effects of planning regulations. Nevertheless, the property tax may influence the use to which land is put and investment in property. Inter-locality differences in effective rates of tax may influence the location decisions of households and firms if they are large and are not fully capitalised into property values. In practice, however, other policy instruments, such as land control regulations and regional grants, may be of more importance.

The disincentive effects of property taxes on investment in property may give rise to concern, especially in urban areas with declining property values. *A priori*, it appears reasonable to assume that in the short to medium term a tax on property will to some extent discourage investment in real property. Also, property taxes could affect business location decisions, especially where the services provided by local government to the investing firms do not vary in proportion to the rate differentials. Where property taxes reflect payment for services to property desired by owners, there may be no net effect on property prices.

In practice, it may be that the potential effect of property taxes on decisions concerning the localisation of investment may have led to some reconsideration by governments of the relative weight of taxation on residential and business property.

2. The relative tax treatment of residential and business property

Property laws promulgated by higher jurisdictions may require or enable localities to tax business property differently from residential property. The resulting differentials in effective tax rates may range from zero taxation to full taxation and may influence the pattern of urban development within a jurisdiction. Those whose policy is to discourage the inflow of business property may implement that policy by heavier taxation of business, whereas those more concerned with job creation and development of land values may take the opposite approach. Moreover, in some countries, local jurisdictions may become quite selective in granting concessions to particular types of either business or residential property, businesses which attract highly-paid staff and residential property designed primarily for well-to-do childless families, may be favoured, especially in federal countries where there is greater local autonomy. In other countries such discrimination by local jurisdictions is not possible.

Different assessment standards may be applied to different types of residential or business property. Residential property may, for example, be sub-divided into single-family homes, two- or three-family homes, large multi-unit properties, etc., and business property may be sub-divided into commercial, industrial and utilities. Sometimes this is a result of difficulties in assessment, but sometimes it is deliberate and the differentials can be quite large.

In most countries, residential property is subject to more favourable tax treatment (through additional reliefs or lower rates) than business property. As may be noted from Table 14.1 where these taxes are levied on both households and business, the business component is more important in all countries except France, where the household component is twice as much, in Finland where the very small yield is equally shared and in Greece, Norway, Spain and Switzerland where property taxes are levied exclusively on household property. There appears no justification under the benefit principle for higher taxation of business property, because business generally uses few services than households and has no voting rights. Also the differential taxation of business property could induce moves to lower taxed localities.

The overall relative tax burden on residential and business property depends also upon whether payments may be offset against personal and corporation income taxes, on which country practices much vary (see last two columns of Table 14.4).

3. Responsibility for payment as between owner and occupier

In nearly all countries legal responsibility rests with the owner, though in practice the owner will usually shift all or some of the property tax into the rent charged to the tenant. Whilst transferring liability to the occupier of the property could make the cost of government services more visible to tenants and so improve local accountability, only France and the United Kingdom generally place the legal obligation wholly on occupiers, though the occupier may be legally responsible in Australia, Spain and Turkey.

4. The fairness of the property tax

The relevance of the progressivity of the property tax to its fairness is discussed in the last sub-section of this chapter. The particular issues arising on progressivity have been much discussed by public finance economists, and as will be noted there is no agreed view. If one were eventually to emerge, this could influence taxpayers' perceptions and government reactions, but for the time being there is little sign that this has occurred. This sub-section deals with taxpayer resentment of various features of the property tax and how governments have reacted.

a) Taxpayers' perceptions

A major reason why taxapayers frequently regard the proeprty tax as unfair is the necessary arbitrariness of valuation discussed at the end of Section 2B. In addition, the amount of property tax paid is in most, though not in all countries, decided by the capital or rental value of the property with little or no regard to the personal circumstances of the taxpayer, even though later adjustments may be made through rebates. Furthermore, to a nominal owner (i.e. someone with a large mortgage on the property) the property tax may seem like an exorbitant rent paid to local government. Taxpayers who are subject to little or no income tax because of low taxable income perceive the property tax as high in relation to their income, another reason for protest to the local government. More generally, the link between property tax paid and income may be perceived as being weak, which in some cases may be so, though mostly it is probably true that there is a strong correlation between the value of property owned and the income and wealth of the owners, so that a residential property tax is likely in practice to be a reasonable proxy for an income or wealth tax.

Taxpayers who hear about the ease with which others evade income taxes but who know that they themselves cannot evade the property tax perceive another level of unfairness, though many who pay the property tax may see this difficulty of evasion as an indication of the fairness of the tax. Taxpayers' perceptions may also be influenced by the fact that in a few countries property taxes have to be paid in one lump-sum and even in those countries which allow instalment payments these rarely exceed four per year. It could also be of relevance to taxpayers' perceptions that fundamental revaluations of value for purposes of the property tax are in practice undertaken very infrequently, so that when such revaluations do occur absolute and relative changes in taxpayers' bills are likely to be vary large. Another factor which could affect taxpayers' perception about the fairness of property taxes is whether or not such payments can be offset against their personal or corporate income tax payments, even if objectively this primarily reflects governments' relative reliance on these two sources of revenue.

Taxpayers' perceptions about the unfairness of property taxes can have serious political repercussions. Not only can voters express their discontent in elections both at central and local government level but in some countries can directly change matters through referenda, of which the Californian Proposition 13 referendum that resulted in a substantial reduction of property taxes in that state, is the best known example, especially because it resulted also in a reduction of local government services and an unforeseen increase in federal income tax revenues, since state property taxes were deductible from the income tax base.

b) Government reactions

The reactions of governments to these taxpayers' discontents have taken a variety of forms, for example, the introduction of personalised reliefs, or statutory limits on the proportion of income tax taken by property taxes or discretionary reliefs which the local authority can grant to taxpayers in reduced circumstances. For example, when the amount of the property tax payable for a year exceeds a stated percentage of an owner-occupier's income, then in some countries (e.g. Australia, France, the United States) legislation or administrative discretion enables local authorities to waive or rebate part of the excess, with higher levels of government usually reimbursing local governments for lost revenue. In the United States this type of measure is referred to as a "circuit breaker" and is intended to relieve hardship and to avoid reducing certain owners' or occupiers' net levels of income below acceptable levels. Such measures may be available to all who meet the income requirement or only to those above a certain age or having a certain family status in addition to meeting the income requirement.

Systems for deferring payment of the current property tax due may also be used as a means of providing personalised taxpayer relief. The unpaid tax liability may remain a lien on the property and may not be allowed to exceed more than a certain percentage of the capital value of the property after deducting existing mortgage loans secured by the property. Deferred payment may be available only to those who qualify on the basis of low income, age, or some other financial disability.

Governments have generally been reluctant to face the administrative costs (including taxpayers' appeals), which frequent revaluations would entail. The problem has accordingly been deferred with the results that when revaluation do eventually occur the problems are much greater. In principle, most OECD countries provide for revaluations of property every two to five years. In practice, while such adjustments are made, more important revaluations to take account of changing circumstances rarely occur. In most

Table 14.3 : Exemptions and concessions for some specific assets[1]

Country	Tax	Embassies	Property of government and its agencies	Transport and communi-cations	Mines	Agriculture and forestry	Public areas	Educational property
Australia (New South Wales)	Land tax	T	T	T	C	V	T	T
	Rates	EP	EP	T	T	T	E	E
Denmark	Land tax	EG	T	EG	T	T	EG	E
	Service tax	EG	T	EG	T	T	EG	E
France	Land and buildings tax	E	EP	T	T	E	EG	E*
	Land tax	–	E	E	T	V	EG	E
	Property Tax	E	E	–	–	V	EG	E
Germany	Real property tax (Grundsteuer)	E	EG	V	T	T	C	T
Japan	Fixed assets tax	E	EGP	VP	T	TG	TG	E
	City planning tax	E	EG	V	T	T	TG	E
	Special land-holding tax	E	EG	V	T	E	TG	E
Netherlands	Municipal Tax	E	V	V	T	E	V	T
	Contributions to polder boards	E	T	T	T	T	T	T
New Zealand	Land tax	EG	E	V	T	EG	EG	EG
	Rates	EG	V	V	T	T	EG	EP
Spain	Rural land tax	E	E	E or G	E	T	E	E
	Urban land tax	E	E	E or G	E	T	E	E
Sweden	Municipal guarantee tax	E	E	EG	T	C	V	EG
Turkey	Immovable property tax	E	E	E	T	T	E	E
United Kingdom (England and Wales)	Rates	E	EP	VP	T	E	V	C
United States (Wisconsin)	Property tax	E	EP	T	T	C	V	E

Table 14.3 (cont.): Exemptions and concessions for some specific assets[1]

Country	Tax	Hospitals	Religious buildings	Cemeteries	Charities	Historical property	Residential property
Australia (New South Wales)	Land tax	T	T	T	T	E	C
	Rates	E	E	E	E	E	T
Denmark	Land tax	E	EG	EG	E	E	T
	Service tax	E	EG	EG	E	E	T
France	Land and buildings tax	E*	E	–	T	T	–
	Land tax	–	T	E	T	T	V
	Property tax	–	E	–	V	T	T
Germany	Real property tax (Grundsteuer)	E	E	E	E	C	C
Japan	Fixed assets tax	T	E	E	T	E	C
	City planning tax	T	E	E	T	E	C
	Special land-holding tax	T	E	E	T	E	C
Netherlands	Municipal tax	T	E	EG	T	T	T
	Contributions to polder boards	T	T	T	T	T	T
New Zealand	Land tax	T	C	E	C	T	C
	Rates	EG	EP	EP	EGP	T	T
Spain	Rural land tax	E	E	E	E	E	T
	Urban land tax	E	E	E	E	E	T
Sweden	Municipal guarantee tax	E	E	T	E	T	T
Turkey	Immovable property tax	E	E	E	E	T	C
United Kingdom (England and Wales)	Rates	VP	E	T	C	T	C
United States (Wisconsin)	Property tax	E*	E	T	E	T	CP

T = Taxable TG = Taxable generally E = Exempt EG = Exempt generally.
C = Concessions V = Variable E* = If public or non profit.
P = Payments may be made to compensate subcentral government for loss of revenue on exemptions.

Sources: *Taxes on immovable property* (OECD 1983) and *Local government: an international perspective*, ed. J.P. Owens and S. Panella, North Holland, 1991.

countries the date of the last major revaluation was in the early eighties and in the seventies, or even 1964 in the case of the German Grundsteur (see Table 14.4).

Table 14.4 summarises different government provisions and practices in the areas referred to in this sub-section where there could be an influence on taxpayers' perceptions of the fairness of the tax.

5. The progressivity of the property tax

Two questions arise: first, is the property tax in itself progressive, proportional or regressive in relation to other taxes that could replace it; second, how relevant is the progressivity or otherwise of the property tax to its suitability as a means of financing local government expenditures? On both questions, opinions continue to differ. The more policy-oriented second question is first discussed.

a) The relevance of property tax progressivity to its use

The property tax is often held to exemplify the "benefit principle", under which the progressivity or otherwise of the property tax is irrelevant to its fairness. The argument runs that if revenues from the property tax is used largely to provide local government services relating to immovable property, such as land-use, planning, zoning, fire and police protection and maintenance of areas for pedestrians and cyclists, roads and local parks and other open and public space, then the level of effective property rates may be said to reflect the level of property-related local governmental services. In short, the tax may be considered as the price paid for the particular bundle of services supplied by that particular government. It is often held that this criterion of fairness – getting the benefit of what you pay for – is a better guide to local tax policy than considerations of ability to pay. In practice, as indicated in the previous sub-section, governments do not fully "buy" this argument and introduce various features into the tax to meet the ability to pay principle.

b) Conflicting views on the degree of progressivity of the property tax

The traditional view is that, especially in the absence of some of the measures referred to in sub-section 4 above, the property tax is a regressive tax. The correctness of this view depends primarily on how the property tax is shifted or who ultimately bears its burden. Ascertaining the incidence as distinct form the impact of the tax requires identifying who is worse off as a result of the tax and the possibility of its being shifted. This question remains unsettled, and there remain different views among academics. As noted, the traditional view was that property taxes are regressive, but under the so-called "new view" of property tax incidence based on a general equilibrium analysis of the whole economy of a country they have been considered even to be progressive, except for those at low income levels who may, however, receive rebates.

Table 14.4: Country provisions and practices affecting the fairness of taxes on immovable property

Country	Tax	Date of last revaluation	Reliefs (allowances and credits) usually for personal circumstances[1]	No of payments per year	Possibility of deferral	Property tax offset against personal income tax	Property tax offset against corporate income tax
Australia	Land tax	1979-81[2]	None	One	Limited	Yes	Yes
(New South Wales)	Rates	1979-81[2]	Some	One to four	Limited	Yes	Yes
Denmark	Land tax	1988	None	Usually 2 to 4	Very limited	No	Yes
	Service tax	1986	None	Usually 2 to 4	Very limited	No	No
France	Land + land & building taxes	Land 1967 buildings 1971-3	Some	One	Possible	No	Yes
	Property tax	1970-73	Some	One (monthly possible)	Possible	No	No
Germany	Grundsteuer	1964	Little	Four	Possible	No	Yes
Japan	Fixed assets tax	1982	Little	Four	Limited	Sometimes	Yes
	City planning tax	1982	Little	Four	Limited	Sometimes	Yes
	Special land holding tax	Revaluation not needed	Little	One	Limited	Sometimes	Yes
Netherlands	Municipal tax	1985-90[2]	Some	One or two	Possible	Owner prop. only	Yes
	Contributions to polder boards	Revaluation not needed	Little	One or two	Possible	No	Yes
New Zealand	Land tax	1977-81	Little	One	None	Yes	Yes
	Rates	1977-81	Some	One to six[2]	Possible	To some extent	No
Spain	Rural land tax	1986	None	One	Possible	Yes	Yes
	Urban land tax	1986	None	One	Possible	Yes	Yes
Sweden	Municipal guarantee tax	1981	None	Six	Limited	No	Yes
Turkey	Immovable property tax	1980	None	Two	Limited	No	No
United Kingdom (England and Wales)	Rates	1973	Some	Ten	Very limited	No[3]	Yes
United States (Wisconsin)	Property tax	Mostly early eighties[2]	Some	Several	Limited	Yes	No

1. Excluding reliefs for new residences which occur in France, Germany, Japan and Turkey.

2. Different dates for different local authorities.

3. Except for unincorporated businesses.

Sources: *Taxes on immovable property* (OECD 1983) and *Local government: an international perspective,* ed. J.P. Owens and S. Panella, North Holland, 1991.

APPENDIX

APPENDIX

A. Glossary of terms and expressions

This glossary is confined to terms and expressions used throughout the book. Other terms and expressions relating to particular taxes or issues are defined in the relevant chapter, for example, see:

- Table 2.1 and Annex to Chapter 2D for the classification of the various kinds of tax;
- Chapter 8B for compulsory social insurance versus income support approach;
- Chapter 9A and Table 9.1 for definitions regarding levels of government;
- Chapter 9B for the "agency" versus "local autonomy" approach;
- Chapter 10B for various terms used under personal income tax systems;
- Chapter 11C1 for various terms used under death and gift taxes;
- Chapters 12D1 and 8 for definitions of different kinds of corporate tax systems;
- Table 13A2 for definitions of different kinds of general consumption tax systems, and terms and expressions used in consumption taxation;
- Table 13.3 for terminology applied to the various kinds of value added tax systems.

In the glossary that follows, figures on the left hand indicate reference(s) to chapters where amplification may be found. A dash indicates lack of any amplification.

1, 6A, 10A	**Ability to pay or accretion principle**: shorthand for the view that taxes should be heaviest on those with highest income and or wealth.
7C 2a	**Average production worker (APW)**: an adult full-time production worker in the manufacturing sector, whose earnings are equal to the average of such workers.
–	**Average rate of tax**: tax payable as a proportion of income subject to tax over a given period.
10B	**Basic relief**: any income tax relief which is available to all taxpayers irrespective of their marital or family status or other personal circumstances. In a number of countries there is an additional basic relief applicable only to earned income.

1, 6A, 10A	**Benefit principle**: shorthand for the view that taxes should be levied in accordance with the benefits arising from the government services financed by the tax.
5C, 12	**Capital export neutrality (CEN)**: CEN occurs if taxation is neutraltowards the export of capital because investors in the capital exporting country are subject to the same marginal effective tax rate on income from similar investments, whether they are undertaken domestically or abroad.
5C, 12	**Capital import neutrality(CIN)**: CIN occurs when taxation is neutral towards the import of capital because domestic and foreign suppliers of capital to any national market obtain the same after tax rate of return on similar investments in that market.
10E	**Cash transfers**: unrequited payments by government.
6A, 10E	**Deadweight loss (or excess burden)**: the net welfare loss from a tax, equivalent to the total loss of welfare from a tax minus the welfare loss caused by raising the same amount of revenue in a way which does not disturb economic activity.
1, 6C, 12B	**Economic or true depreciation**: the actual year by year fall in value of an asset over its working (cash-generating) life.
5C, 12D (Annex)	**Economic double taxation**: the application by two different tax jurisdictions of similar taxes on the income of economically relaxed entities as contrasted to *juridical* double taxation where two different tax jurisdictions impose similar taxes on the income of some entity. (The expression is frequently used in a variety of other ambiguous senses, often for rhetorical purposes).
2, 3, 13D	**Excises, etc.**: a term used for the purposes of comparisons of revenue receipts to cover all the taxes of heading 5120 of Table 2.1 as distinct from excises without the etc. which refer only to heading 5121.
2C1, 10D5	**Fiscal drag**: the more than proportional increase in income tax liability corresponding to an increase in income as a result of real gains (real fiscal drag) or inflation (inflationary fiscal drag). (Under inflationary conditions the reverse situation applies to excises and this is referred to as fiscal boost or negative fiscal drag.)
–	**Flat rate tax**: an income tax system with only one schedule rate.
10D5	**Formal indexation**: regular and automatic adjustments made within the framework of specific legislative provisions.

10C3	**Fringe benefits**: benefits (usually non-cash) over and above wages and salaries received form employers by employees as part of their overall remuneration.
5B	**Horizontal equity**: the equitable tax treatment of persons with the same level of income or capital but who differ in other relevant respects.
10C3c, 10E3	**Imputed income**: income which is not in money form, such as the rental value of owner-occupied housing or the value of work done in the home by a non-gainfully employed spouse.
10B	**Income subject to tax**: all sources of income liable to tax without taking account of tax allowances (cf. "taxable income" as defined below).
–	**Marginal rate of income tax**: the additional income tax payable when income is increased divided by the increase in income.
3B3	**Marginal tax ratio**: the fraction of the increase in GDP absorbed by taxes.
10E	**Negative income tax (NIT)**: systems of welfare payments which are calculated on the basis of actual income usually of a family group, compared to what are deemed to be the minimum income levels for survival.
–	**Neutral taxes**: taxes that have no excess burden.
10B	**Non-standard tax reliefs**: reliefs from income tax where the amount is determined by reference to actual expenses incurred by the taxpayer.
10E	**Notch problem**: the sharp increase in the effective marginal tax/benefit rate that low paid persons may incur as their income increases as a result of the withdraw of income related benefits.
5C	**Persuasive definitions:** The process of defining, whether implicitly or explicitly, an emotive word in such a way that one can or does apply it to something one wants to be persuasively described.
10E2	**Poverty trap and unemployment trap**: the situation where increases in gross income have little or even a negative impact on disposable income because of reductions in cash and in-kind transfers and increased liability for personal income tax and employees' social security contributions. This provides a disincentive to increase work effort or even to take up employment.

– **Progressive tax**: A tax under which the average rate of tax increases with income.

– **Regressive tax**: A tax under which the average rate of tax decreases as income increases.

1, 6B **Revenue neutrality**: the constraint on tax reform that they should not (much) change revenues available to governments.

10B **Standard tax reliefs**: Reliefs from income tax unrelated to the actual expenditure incurred by the taxpayer.

1, 9, 12, 13 **Subsidiarity**: the approach under which taxing and spending (and other) functions should be assigned to the lowest level of government that can most efficiently carry them out. Most often used in practice in the context of allocations of functions between the European Community and its Member Countries.

10B **Taxable income**: The base to which the rate schedule applies, i.e. income subject to tax minus tax allowances.

10B5 **Tax allowances**: amounts deducted from the income subject to tax to arrive at taxable income under personal income tax systems. (Also referred to as tax deductions.)

2, 3 **Tax buoyancy and elasticity**: tax elasticity refers to the automatic effects over time of inflation, growth etc. on tax ratios in the absence of government intervention whereas tax buoyancy takes account of the effects of government intervention. Tax buoyancy is sometimes referred to as the dynamic tax elasticity.

3B3 **Tax buoyancy ratios**: The ratio of the change in total tax receipts to the change in GDP.

10B5 **Tax credits**: amounts deductible from tax due.

6C **Tax expenditures**: tax reliefs which involve a departure from the normal benchmark or generally accepted tax structure, and which produce a favourable tax treatment of particular types of activities or groups of taxpayers. (Also known as "tax aids" or more colloquially, as tax incentives.) The corresponding unfavourable treatment is referred to as "tax penalties".

13A **Tax-exclusive rate**: the rate of tax applied to the tax base exclusive of the tax itself.

2, 6B **Tax handle**: any means by which governments are able to raise more revenue (e.g. VAT which is also known as a money-making machine).

5E, 7C, 14C5	**Tax impact, incidence and shifting**: the tax *impact* is on those legally obliged to pay a tax, but such persons may be able to *shift* this tax to others who bear its *incidence*.
13A	**Tax-inclusive rate**: the rate of tax applied to the tax base inclusive of the tax itself.
5B, 5C	**Tax neutrality**: the situation in which tax considerations do not affect or hardly affect economic or social decisions. (Also used in several other senses.)
2, 3, 4	**Tax ratio**: the ratio of total tax receipts (total tax ratio) or particular tax receipts (income tax ratio, etc.) to GDP at market prices. (This ratio is used to compare the tax levels of different countries.)
–	**Tax reliefs**: a generic term to cover all the means of reducing tax liability, without regard as to how it is done.
2, 3, 4	**Tax share**: the proportion of the receipts from particular kinds of taxes to total tax receipts.
2, 3, 4	**Tax structure**: the relative reliance of a country on different kinds of tax expressed as the ratio between receipts from each tax to total tax receipts. (Also referred to as tax mix.)
10D3d	**Tax threshold**: the level of income at which a positive tax is first due.
13A2	**Taxe occulte**: the hidden taxes on auxiliary materials, capital equipment and services used in the production, marketing or transportation of taxable goods.
–	**Underground economy**: economic activity which hides income – e.g. through cash transactions or exchange of services – whether for the purposes of evading tax or because the activity itself is illegal.
–	**Unearned (or investment) income**: income from interest, dividends and rent.
1C	**Vertical equity**: the equitable differential tax treatment of persons who have different levels of income or capital.
10	**Wage inflation tax**: a surtax on wage settlements above a certain level as an anti-inflationary measure. (Though discussed during the seventies, it does not exist in OECD countries and is not covered in this book. It has been applied in a number of East European countries.)

13A2 **Zero rated goods**: the expression under value added taxation to describe the situation where a trader pays no tax on his sales but is compensated for VAT paid on his inputs (in contrast to *exempt* goods where there is no compensation for tax paid on inputs).

B. Annex to Chapter 2E on methodology and limitations

1. What is a tax?

The interpretative guide to the OECD classification notes that in this classification the term "taxes" is confined to compulsory, unrequited payments to general government and that taxes are unrequited in the sense that benefits provided by governments to taxpayers are not normally in proportion to their payment.

The significance of the words "confined to" in the definition is to convey the message that even though a levy may be compulsory, unilateral and paid to general government it will not *necessarily* be regarded as a "tax" . What was in mind were compulsory loans to government prevalent in a few countries, which it was agreed should not be counted as a tax, but it was also preferred that possible future government revenue-raising devices should be treated on their own merits as to whether they should or should not be counted as a tax.

The term "compulsory" creates problems, especially in the social security area. For example, although for the most part social security contributions are compulsory in the everyday sense that the payers have no choice as to whether or not they contribute, in practice, it can be difficult to distinguish between compulsory and quasi-compulsory contributions. Even where conceptually the treatment of these contributions may seem fairly self-evident, there remains the problem that it is not always easy to identify what amounts are in practice compulsory and what voluntary.

Both "compulsory" and "unrequited" raise problems in distinguishing between tax revenues and non-tax revenues such as fees, user charges and licence fees. Paragraph 9 of the interpretative guide to the OECD classification of taxes states :

> Apart from vehicle licence fees, which are universally regarded as taxes it is not easy to distinguish between those fees and user charges which are to be treated as taxes and those which are not, since, whilst a fee or charge is levied in connection with a specific service or activity, the strength of the link between the fee and the service provided may vary considerably, as may the relation between the amount of levy and the cost of providing the service, where the recipient of a service pays a fee clearly related to the cost of providing it, the levy may be regarded as requited and would not be considered as a tax. In the following cases, however, a levy could be considered as "unrequited" .
>
> a) where the charge greatly exceeds the cost of providing the service;
>
> b) where the payer of the levy is not the receiver of the benefit (e.g., a fee collected from slaughterhouses to finance a service which is provided to farmers);
>
> c) where government is not providing a specific service in return for the levy which it receives even though a licence may be issued to the payer (e.g., where the government grants a hunting, fishing or shooting licence which is not accompanied by the right to use a specific area of government land);
>
> d) where benefits are received only by those paying the levy but the benefits received by each individual are not necessarily in proportion to his payments (e.g. a milk marketing levy paid by dairy farmers and used to promote the consumption of milk).

Paragraph 11 of the guide indicates the normal treatment of the main charges in question: *Non-tax revenues*: court fees; driving licence fees; harbour fees, radio and television licence fees where public authorities provide the service. *Taxes of heading 5 200*: permission to perform such activities as distributing films, hunting, fishing and shooting; providing entertainment or gambling facilities; selling alcohol or tobacco; permission to own dogs or to use or own motor vehicles or guns; severance taxes.

"General government" also provides problems. In the OECD classification general government consists of supra-national authorities (in practice, the European Communities), the central administration and the agencies whose operations are under its effective control, state and local governments and their administrations, social security schemes and autonomous governmental entities, excluding public enterprises. One problem is that in some countries (e.g. Finland) the church is considered as part of government and performs certain services for government, such as registration of marriages. Yet it is questionable whether the church is "effectively under the control" of government. A second problem arises with separate social security agencies. For the most part, separate social security funds are clearly within general government but some funds are regulated by government though administered by the private sector. Some countries have separate funds for certain professions (e.g. Italy for doctors) where the control effectively rests with the profession, though the funds have to operate within the framework established by legislation. In practice separate social security agencies of this kind are treated as part of general government.

Though these borderline cases raise interesting conceptual issues, with one exception they relate to levies that raise relatively little revenues, so that any inconsistencies that remain will have little effect on the validity of international comparisons of tax levels and structures. The one exception is whether or not social security contributions should be regarded as a "tax", an issue which is now discussed.

2. Should social security contributions be regarded as a tax?

Broader aspects of the relationship between social security contributions and other compulsory levies paid to general governments are discussed in Chapters 8 and 10D6. Here the issue is simply should they or should they not be regarded as taxes when international comparisons of tax levels and structures are being made?

Examples have already been cited where certain types of social security contributions fit uneasily with the definition of taxes because they are not really compulsory or not unrequited or not paid to general government. They have also special features which make them arguably non-tax revenues:

- They are the only *major* source of revenue which is earmarked for a particular purpose.
- Contributions provide an entitlement to benefits and could therefore be considered as requited.
- Because of the insurance analogy, they may be perceived differently from other revenues by governments, politicians, employers and employees.

For these (as well as other reasons discussed in Chapters 8 and 10D6) some people prefer to regard social security contributions as other than taxes and to make a distinction between compulsory levies (including social security contributions) and taxes (excluding them). This appears to be the orthodox view in certain countries such as France and Germany.

Nevertheless, it would be inappropriate to exclude compulsory social security contributions paid to general government from international comparisons of tax levels, because countries rely to very differing degrees on them to finance similar kinds of social benefits. For example, in France, Italy and the Netherlands, social security contributions amount to more than 40 per cent of total revenues, whereas they are less than 3 per cent in Denmark and zero in Australia and New Zealand. Moreover, there exists the borderline case in some Nordic countries of levies on employees which could be regarded as either an income tax earmarked for social security contributions (to be classified as an income tax) or as social security contributions levied on an income tax base (to be classified as social security contributions). Finally, most of the arguments cited above for regarding contributions as other than taxes apply only to employees' contributions, which in most OECD countries are much less important than those of employers.

3. Borderlines between tax and expenditure provisions

The general problem of countries' varying reliance on tax and expenditure provisions to achieve similar objectives has already been discussed in Chapter 2E and Chapter 6C, but there are also particular cases where it is not evident whether a provision should be regarded as a tax expenditure, the receipts from which are to be deducted from gross tax receipts, or a direct government subsidy where no deduction is to be made.

In such borderline cases the principle of cash base reporting is used to distinguish between tax provisions and expenditure provisions. Insofar as a provision affects the flow of tax payments from the tax payer to the government, it is regarded as a tax provision and is taken into account in the data provided. A provision which does not affect this flow is seen as an expenditure provision and is disregarded in the data. Sometimes, however, this distinction is not always easy to interpret. The most important example is what are variously referred to as "non wastable" or "refundable" tax credits, where the taxpayer receives a payment from the government if the credit exceeds his income tax liability. In most countries tax credits are "wastable" in the sense that any excess over the liability is not refunded to the taxpayer. These credits are treated as tax provisions since they affect the flow of receipts to governments and are an integral part of the tax assessment process. In a few countries (e.g. Canada, France, New Zealand, the United States) there are non-wastable tax credits which can be offset against tax liability and any excess of the credit over tax liability is paid out to the taxpayer. The question arises of how should the payments of the excess credit be treated. It has been decided that the amount of credit offset against tax should be treated as a tax provision thus reducing tax receipts, but that payments made by governments should be regarded as a direct government expenditure provision and so would not affect tax receipts. However, arguments were put forward for treating non-wastable tax credits, both as entirely tax provisions and as entirely government expenditures.

4. Problems in comparing countries' tax structures

By definition, a valid comparison of countries' tax structures must ensure that like is being compared with like. There are two problems here. First, the name of the tax and national perceptions of what kind of tax it is have to be critically scrutinised before it is classified on an internationally consistent basis; second, there remain many borderline cases, because certain taxes have some characteristics of one category and others of another category of tax.

To elaborate on the first problem. When the OECD classification was first set up in 1971 on an experimental basis it became apparent that different tax administrations were classifying what was essentially the same kind of tax in different headings and what were different kinds of tax in the same heading. One reason for this is that the name given to a tax is often (deliberately or otherwise) misleading. In the United Kingdom, for example, the title "inheritance tax" is used to describe what in OECD terminology is an "estate tax" (i.e. it is donor based not donee based - see Chapter 11 on capital taxation) and the now-abolished unearmarked payroll tax was called a "national insurance surcharge" on the grounds that the base was the same as that of the employers' social security contribution. The latter case perhaps reflects politicians' belief that their electorate find "tax" a dirty three-letter word, as instanced recently in the same country where the about to be abolished levy on households to finance local government expenditures was referred to as the "community charge" by its supporters and the "poll tax" by its adversaries. The derogatory connotation of "tax" explains on a more important level why a number of commentators prefer to regard social security contributions as other than taxes. Other examples of country nomenclatures which could be confusing are provided by the multi-based local business taxes in *France* and *Germany.* In both countries the mixture of bases were changed, but in France the name was changed from "taxe patente" to "taxe professionnelle", whereas in Germany it continued to be called the "Gewebesteur" and (it is understood for constitutional reasons due to revenue sharing rules between different levels of government) even though the bulk of revenues from the Gewebesteur related to company tax profits, receipts from it in other international classifications were shown as indirect taxes.

In passing, it should be mentioned that the OECD classification deliberately refrains from using the expression "direct tax" and "indirect tax" on the grounds that its many areas (headings 2 000, 3 000, 4 000, 5 200 in the OECD classification) the criteria for dividing taxes into direct and indirect are conflicting and ambiguous and cannot be used operationally for the provision of data. This topic, together with the relationship between the OECD classification and other international classifications, are discussed in the interpretative guide to the OECD classification, but not further commented on in this book.

The second more serious problem of achieving international comparability is to resolve borderline problems when a tax has some of the characteristics of more than one heading of the OECD classification. Often, the appropriate classification would appear to depend on the purpose for which the comparison is being made. For example, in the case already cited under 2 above as to whether receipts from social security contributions levied on an income tax base should be shown as an income tax earmarked for social security expenditures under 1,000 or as social security contributions under 2,000 depends on whether the purpose is to compare the amount of income taxes paid in different countries or the amount of taxes earmarked for social security expenditures in different countries. In this particular case, it has been possible to get the best of both worlds by classifying these levies as income taxes while having a separate memorandum item which aggregates receipts from all taxes earmarked for social security expenditures together with certain non-tax levies such as voluntary payments to government and compulsory payments to the private sector.

However, in other borderline cases decisions have to be made which will evidently affect the published data on tax structures. For example: how to classify taxes levied on more than one base? How to classify taxes which have characteristics of both an income tax and property tax? At what stage does a collection of excises become a general consumption tax? Should taxes levied on tobacco and petrol when the ingredients are imported tobacco leaf or crude oil be regarded as an excise or an import duty? Decisions on these three questions will influence the relative importance of receipts respectively from income and property taxes, general and specific consumption taxes and excises and import duties.

Two solutions have been provided to meet this difficulty. First, as detailed a breakdown as possible is given from the receipts from each tax of each country, so that any reader who, for his or her own analytical purposes wishes to reclassify receipts from a particular tax and show it under some other OECD heading, has the possibility of doing so. Second, these borderline decisions are clearly set out in the Interpretative Guide to the OECD classification. Some of the more important ones are reproduced in the next section of this Annex.

5. Extracts from the interpretative guide to the OECD classification of taxes

"The main classification criteria

23. The classification of receipts among the main headings (1000, 2000, 3000, 4000, 5000 and 6000) is generally governed by the base on which the tax is levied: 1000 income, profits and capital gains; 2000 and 3000 payroll or manpower; 4000 property; 5000 goods and services; 6000 multiple bases, other bases or unidentifiable bases. Where a tax is calculated on more than one base, the receipts are, where possible, split among the various headings (see paragraphs 28 and 79). The heading 4000 and 5000 cover not only taxes where the tax base is the property, goods or services themselves but also certain related taxes. Thus, taxes on the transfer of property are included in 4400 and taxes on the use of goods or on permission to perform activities in 5200. In headings 4000 and 5000 a distinction is made in certain sub-headings between recurrent and non-recurrent taxes; recurrent taxes are defined as those levied at regular intervals (usually annually) and non-recurrent taxes are levied once and for all (see also paragraphs 45, 46, 48, 51, 52, 77 and 78 for particular applications of this distinction).
24. Normally, earmarking of a tax for specific purposes does not affect the classification of tax receipts. The only exception is that social security contributions earmarked for social security and levied as a function of earnings, payroll or number of employees are allocated to the 2000 heading. Levies on any other base and earmarked for social security are classified by the tax base (e.g. on an income base under heading 1000 or consumption base under heading 5000), though the revenues raised are identified separately in a memorandum item. This treatment has been followed to enable revenues earmarked for social security to be separated from revenues not so earmarked.
25. The way that a tax is levied or collected (e.g. by use of stamps) has no effect on its classification.

Classification of taxpayers

26. In certain sub-headings distinctions are made between different categories of taxpayers. These distinctions vary from tax to tax:

a) Between individuals and corporations in relation to income and net wealth taxes

The basic distinction is that corporation income taxes, as distinct from individual income taxes, are levied on the corporation as an entity, not on the individuals who own it, and without regard to the personal circumstances of these individuals. The same distinction applies to net wealth taxes on corporations and those on individuals. Taxes paid on the profits of partnerships and the income of institutions, such as life assurance or pension funds, are classified according to the same rule. They are classified as corporate taxes (1200) if they are charged on the partnership or institution as an entity without regard to the personal circumstances of the owners. Otherwise, they are treated as individual taxes (1100). Usually there is different legislation for the corporation taxes and for the individual taxes...

b) Between households and others in relation to taxes on immovable property

The distinction is between households as consumers (i.e. excluding non-incorporated business) on the one hand and producers on the other hand. However, taxes on dwelling-houses occupied by households, whether paid by owner-occupiers, tenants or landlords, are classified under households. This follows the common distinction made between taxes on domestic property and taxes on business property. Some countries are not, however, in a position to make this distinction.

c) Between households and others in relation to motor vehicle licences

Here the distinction is between households as consumers on the one hand and producers on the other.

Unidentifiable tax receipts and residual sub-headings

28. A number of cases arise where taxes cannot be identified as belonging entirely to a heading or sub-heading of the OECD classification and the following practices are applied in such cases:

a) The heading is known, but it is not known how receipts should be allocated between sub-headings: receipts are classified in the appropriate residual sub-heading (1300, 2400, 4520, 4600, 5130, 5300 or 6200).

b) It is known that the bulk of receipts from a group of taxes (usually local taxes) is derived from taxes within a particular heading or sub-heading, but some of the taxes in the group whose amount cannot be precisely ascertained may be classifiable in other headings or sub-headings: receipts are shown in the heading or sub-heading under which most of the receipts fall.

c) Neither the heading nor sub-heading of a tax (usually local) can be identified: the tax is classified in 6200 unless it is known that it is a tax on business in which case it is classified in 6100.

1000 – *Taxes on income, profits and capital gains*

29. This heading covers taxes levied on the net income or profits (i.e. gross income minus allowable tax reliefs) of individuals and enterprises. Also covered are taxes levied on the capital gains of v), and enterprises, and gains from gambling.

30. Included in the heading are:

a) taxes levied predominantly on income or profits, though partially on other bases. Taxes on various bases which are not predominantly income or profits are classified according to the principles laid down in paragraphs 28 and 79;

b) taxes on property, which are levied on a presumed or estimated income as part of an income tax (see also paragraph 45);

c) social security contributions based on net income after deductions and exemptions for personal circumstances. When such contributions are based on eligible earnings, payroll or the number of employees without deduction or exemptions for personal circumstances, they are normally included in heading 2000 (see paragraphs 37 and 38);

d) receipts from integrated schedular income tax systems are classified as a whole in this heading, even though certain of the schedular taxes may be based upon gross income and may not take into account the personal circumstances of the taxpayer.

2000 – *Social security contributions*

36. Classified here are all compulsory contributions which are:

a) paid to institutions of general government providing social security benefits;

b) levied as a function of earnings, payroll or the number of employees;

c) earmarked to provide social security benefits; and

d) made by insured persons or their employers.

A distinction should be made when the proceeds of taxes on payroll, etc. are earmarked to finance social welfare (as opposed to social security) benefits. Where there is normally no connection between the payment of the contribution and the entitlement to the benefits, as in the case of the Austrian tax earmarked for family allowances, receipts would be classified in heading 3000, as would also be contributions for financing government training schemes or general employment creation measures; where, however, there is a link between eligibility for benefits and the making of contributions, such receipts are shown under 2000, even though in some countries individuals may receive benefits without themselves or their relatives having made contributions.

3000 – *Taxes on payroll and workforce*

44. This heading covers taxes paid by employers, employees or the self-employed either as a proportion of payroll or as a fixed amount per person, and which are not earmarked for social security expenditure. Examples of taxes classified here are the United Kingdom selective employment tax (1966-1972) and the unearmarked national insurance surcharge (introduced in 1977), the Swedish payroll tax (1969-1979), and that part of the Austrian and German Gewerbesteuer based on payroll (1965-1978).

4000 – *Taxes on property*

45. This heading covers recurrent and non-recurrent taxes on the use, ownership or transfer of property. These include taxes on immovable property or net wealth, taxes on the change of ownership of property through inheritance or gift and taxes on financial and capital transactions. The following kinds of tax are excluded from this heading:

a) taxes on capital gains resulting from the sale of a property (1120 or 1220);

b) taxes on the use of goods or on permission to use goods or perform activities (5200) (see paragraph 74);

c) taxes on immovable property levied on the basis of a presumed net income which take into account the personal circumstances of the taxpayer. They are classified as income taxes along with taxes on income and capital gains derived from property (1000);

d) taxes on the use of property for residence, where the tax is payable by either proprietor or tenant and the amount payable is a function of the user's personal circumstances (pay, dependants, etc.). They are classified as taxes on permission to perform activities (5200);

e) taxes on building in excess of permitted maximum density, taxes on the enlargement, construction or alteration of certain buildings beyond a permitted value and taxes on building construction. They are classified as taxes on permission to perform activities (5200);

f) taxes on the use of one's own property for special trading purposes like selling alcohol, tobacco, meat or for exploitation of land resources (e.g. United States severance taxes). They are classified as taxes on permission to perform activities (5200).

5000 – *Taxes on goods and services*

53. All taxes and duties levied on the production, extraction, sale, transfer, leasing or delivery of goods, and the rendering of services (5100), or in respect of the use of goods or permission to use goods or to perform activities (5200) are included here.

Borderline cases between this heading and heading 4000 (taxes on property) and 6100 (other taxes on business) are referred to in paragraphs 45, 50 and 76. Residual sub-heading (5300) and (5130) are provided for tax receipts which cannot be allocated between 5100 and 5200 and between 5110 and 5120, respectively (see paragraph 28).

5100 – *Taxes on the production, sale, transfer, leasing and delivery of goods and rendering of services*

54. This sub-heading includes all taxes, other than import and export duties (5123 and 5124), levied on the production, leasing, transfer, delivery or sales of a wide range of goods and/or the rendering of a wide range of services, irrespective of whether they are domestically produced or imported and irrespective of the stage of production or distribution at which they are levied. It thus covers value added taxes, sales taxes and multi-stage cumulative taxes. Receipts from border adjustments in respect of such taxes when goods are imported are added to gross receipts for this category, and

repayments of such taxes when goods are exported are deducted. These taxes are subdivided into 5111 value added taxes, 5112 sales taxes, 5113 other general taxes on goods and services.

62. Excises are distinguished from:

a) 5110 (general taxes). This is discussed in paragraph 56.

b) 5123 (import duties). If a tax collected principally on imported goods also applies, or would apply, under the law by which the tax is imposed on comparable home-produced goods, the receipts therefrom would be classified as excises (5121). This principle applies even if there is no comparable home production or no possibility of it (see also paragraph 66).

c) 5126 (taxes on services). The problem here arises in respect of taxes on electricity, gas and energy. All of these are regarded as taxes on goods and are included under 5121.

5200 – *Taxes on use of goods or on permission to use goods or perform activities*

74. This sub-heading covers taxes which are levied in respect of the use of goods as distinct from taxes on the goods themselves. Unlike the latter taxes of 5100, they are not assessed on the value of the goods but usually as fixed amounts. Taxes on permission to use goods or to perform activities are also included here, as are pollution taxes not based upon the value of particular goods. It is sometimes difficult to distinguish between compulsory user charges and licence fees which are regarded as taxes and those which are excluded as non-tax revenues, and the criteria which are employed are noted in paragraphs 9 and 10.

75. Although the sub-heading refers to the "use" of goods, registration of ownership rather than use may be what generates liability to tax, so that the taxes of this heading may apply to the ownership of animals or goods rather than their use (e.g. racehorses, dogs and motor vehicles) and may apply even to unusable goods (e.g. unusable motor vehicles or guns).

76. Borderline cases arise with:

a) taxes on the permission to perform business activities which are levied on a combined income, payroll or turnover base and accordingly, are classified according to the rules in paragraph 79;

b) taxes on the ownership or use for property of headings 4100, 4200 and 4600. the heading 4100 is confined to taxes on the ownership or tenancy of immovable property and, unlike the taxes of 5200, they are related to the value of the property. The net wealth taxes and taxes on chattels of 4200 and 4600 respectively are confined to the ownership rather than the use of assets, apply to groups of assets rather than particular goods and again are related to the value of the assets.

6000 – *Other taxes*

79. Taxes levied on a base, or bases, other than those described under headings 1000, 3000, 4000 and 5000, or on bases of which none could be regarded as being predominantly the same as that of any one of these headings, are covered here. As regards taxes levied on a multiple base, if it is possible to estimate receipts related to each base (e.g. the Austrian and German Gewerbesteuer) this is done and the separate

amounts included under the appropriate headings. If the separate amounts cannot be estimated, but it is known that most of the receipts are derived from one base, the whole of the receipts are classified according to that base. If neither of these procedures can be followed, they are classified here. The sub-headings may also include receipts from taxes which governments are unable to identify or isolate (see paragraph 28). Included here also are fines and penalties paid for infringement of regulations relating to taxes but not identifiable as relating to a particular category of taxes (see paragraph 15). A sub-division is made between taxes levied wholly or predominantly on business (6100) and those levied on others (6200)."

C. Annex to Chapter 6C on defining and measuring tax expenditures

This annex, taken mostly from pages 16 to 21 of *Tax expenditures: A review of the issues and country practices* (OECD 1984), outlines some of the main problems in defining and measuring tax expenditures, which seem essential to an evaluation of the policy choice of whether governments should intervene in the economy through the tax or expenditure route.

Table 6.4 summarised country practices on defining and measuring tax expenditures as at 1983. Since then (as far as I am aware) there has been no systematic international comparison of country developments but a number of other OECD countries (including at least Belgium, Finland and the Netherlands) now systematically cost tax expenditures.

Defining tax expenditures

As already noted in Chapter 6, tax expenditure analysis and tax expenditure budgets presuppose that it is possible to define a normal tax structure, even if such a norm or benchmark is likely to differ between countries and within a country over time. The following paragraphs first provide some examples of countries which employ tax expenditure analysis and then give the reasons why some countries prefer not to do so.

The first report of the United States Secretary of the Treasury on tax expenditures defined them as "the major respects in which the current income tax base deviates from widely accepted definitions of income and standards of business accounting and from the generally accepted structures of an income tax...". In 1982, this definition of tax expenditures was modified to "departures from the basic structure of the existing tax laws which were expenditure programmes implemented through the tax system and which apply to a sufficiently narrow class of transactions or taxpayers so that their differential effects on particular markets can be identified and measured".

The Canadian Government tax expenditure account, first constructed in 1979, uses a similar definition, although more emphasis is placed on "neutrality" than on the "basic" tax structure: "The benchmark tax structure is one that provides no preferential treatment to taxpayers on the basis of demographic characteristics, sources or uses of income, geographic location, or any other special circumstances applicable only to a given taxpayer or to a particular group of taxpayers." Again, however, the Canadians qualified this definition by noting that the "benchmark" structure should not depart dramatically from the "public perception" of the current tax system and tax expenditures should form "a clear expenditure equivalent to a direct spending programme".

The definition of tax expenditures used in the first subsidy report of the German Government was: "Tax incentives are special deviations from the central concept of a tax norm, which involve a shortfall of receipts." In the sixth subsidy report published in 1977, the definition was restricted to subsidies given in the tax system which are intended "to preserve or adjust to new conditions, foster productivity and growth in the private sector, reduce the price of certain goods or services, or stimulate savings".

Austria uses a similar definition of tax expenditure: "Government income forgone due to exceptions from the general tax norm to the advantage of other agents with a view to their private activities performed in the interest of the general public." France uses the following definition: "Any legislative or administrative measure may be called a tax expenditure if its application entails a loss of revenue for the State and hence a lessening of taxpayers' burden in comparison to that which would have resulted under the "norm", that is, the general principles of French tax law." In Spain, tax expenditures are defined as departures from the normal tax structure which represent tax incentives or tax subsidies. Australia defines them as measures which could, in principle, be replaced by direct expenditures.

In each of the above countries the definition is qualified by criteria such as neutrality, applicability to a limited range of taxpayers, etc. and the relevant legislation may specify that the tax expenditures should be capable of being transformed into direct expenditure programmes. Each of the reports referred to above notes that difficulties exist in the implementation of the tax expenditure concept. It is often noted that the benchmark or norm may change over time. Most countries applying tax expenditure analysis found that the difficulties or borderline cases were relatively limited.

However, in other countries, such as Ireland, the Netherlands, Portugal and the United Kingdom, it was considered that over the whole range of tax reliefs, the problem of drawing a clear dividing line between the basic tax structure on the one hand and reliefs intended to support particular government programmes on the other is an intractable one. They have tried to by-pass these definitional problems by providing a listing of tax reliefs without any attempt to identify which are tax subsidies and which form part of the normal structure. Nevertheless, there remains the difficulty of defining what is a relief and what is part of the benchmark tax system, even under this listing approach.

For example, the question arises whether a progressive rate income tax with exempt thresholds and family allowances or a multi-rate VAT should be regarded as an essential part of the tax structure designed to implement the ability to pay principle so that lower rates and thresholds *should not* be regarded as tax expenditures (nor higher rates as tax penalties), or whether, on the other hand, rate variations and family reliefs should be regarded as an alternative to transfer payments to achieve the objectives of income redistribution and therefore *should* be regarded as tax expenditure. Another set of difficulties is that implementation of the criteria used to identify a tax expenditure requires decisions on a number of specific conceptual issues such as what is to be regarded as the benchmark or norm in respect, for example, of the family unit, relationship between individual and corporate income tax, inflation adjustment to the tax base, realisation versus accruals, since upon this will depend on what would and what would not count as a tax expenditure. In practice, each country takes its own system as the norm which renders the international comparison of tax expenditures of very limited use from any quantitative point of view. However, a listing of tax reliefs, whether or not in the framework of tax expenditure and even if the concept differs from one country to another, does enable comparison to be made of what kinds of tax concessions are provided in different countries.

Measuring tax expenditures

Since the costs of tax expenditures cannot be directly measured in the way in which most direct expenditure programmes can, a variety of statistical methods must be employed to estimate these costs. The techniques used and the problems encountered depend upon the structure of the tax administration, the data available and the complexity of the legislation (see Table 6.4). In some cases, computer simulations using tax models are used, in others more traditional estimating techniques.

There are three principal ways in which the costs or value of tax expenditures can be estimated: revenue forgone; revenue gain; outlay equivalence. All three methods are used within the OECD area (see Table 6.4).

i) ***Revenue forgone.*** This may be defined as the amount by which tax revenue is reduced because of the existence of a particular provision. It is an ex-post measure of the cost of a particular relief, based upon a comparison of the existing legislation and the legislation without the tax provision in question. The behaviour of taxpayers is taken as observed in the year for which the calculations are being made.

ii) ***Revenue gain.*** This is the increase in revenue that could be expected if a particular relief were to be abolished. To obtain an accurate estimate of the revenue gain that could be expected from the withdrawal of a relief requires, in principle, that the behaviourial or secondary effects associated with such a change be taken into account. These effects include:

• *The behaviourial effects of taxpayers.* Many tax subsidies are intended to encourage taxpayers to undertake certain activities: if they are successful, they will alter the taxpayer's behaviour which, in turn, may change his taxable income.

• *Feedback effect.* The elimination of tax expenditure provisions will have an impact on the overall level of economic activity and there will be a resultant feedback effect on government revenues.

• *The interaction between taxes.* A tax credit intended to encourage energy conservation, for example, will, other things being equal, have an impact on consumption tax receipts from energy products.

Nevertheless, in practice, most revenue gain estimates do not take into account these secondary effects because of the difficulties involved in measuring them.

iii) ***Outlay equivalence approach.*** This approach estimates what direct expenditure outlays would be required, in pre-tax dollars, to achieve the same after-tax dollar benefit if a tax expenditure were replaced by a corresponding direct expenditure programme, under which the direct outlay is accorded the tax treatment appropriate to that type of income in the hands of the recipient. This is essentially a resource cost measure which, for existing tax expenditures, takes the present behaviour of taxpayers as given and is, in practice, based upon the assumption of an overall unchanged budgetary situation.

Under all three approaches there is the problem that the costs of the different tax expenditures cannot meaningfully be added together. Under the revenue gain approach the revenue impact of simultaneously eliminating two tax expenditures is generally not the same as the sum of their individual revenue impacts. For example, the elimination of one tax relief may push many taxpayers into a higher bracket and thereby increase the value of the remaining reliefs they receive. Similarly, a change in one tax provision may encourage a greater use of another tax relief. This means that it is difficult to obtain an idea of the overall magnitude of tax subsidies within a particular area.

Two further variations in the ways in which estimates are made are:

- *Cash versus accrual estimates.* Estimates of tax expenditures may be made in terms of the impact on the cash flow to the tax authorities in a particular fiscal year or in terms of the impact on the tax liability accruing to the tax authorities within a fiscal year.
- *First-year versus long-run effects.* The first-year cost refers to the additional revenue that would be received during the fiscal year in which the tax relief was withdrawn. The long-run effect represents the additional revenue that would have been received during the first fiscal year when the withdrawal became fully effective. This distinction recognises that the full effects of certain tax reliefs (e.g. deferral provisions) will only occur after a time-lag of one or more years.

D. Annex to Chapter 12D on terminological aspects of the taxation of distributed profits

Terminological aspects of the taxation of distributed profits have already been discussed in Chapter 12D1, as well as in Chapter 5, and this Annex is provided for those who would prefer a more detailed analysis of what some consider to be an arid subject.

There is no need to be too pedantic or dogmatic in attempting to clarify terminology, for even if certain terms and expressions are used in a somewhat unusual sense, provided their meaning is clear and unambiguous, no harm is done and it is very convenient to have shorthand expressions. To take one example of an artificial use of an expression: "tax system" in the corporate tax context is usually confined to ways of taxing distributed profits, whereas with other taxes it has a much wider connotation covering, for example, the base and rate issues discussed in sections B and C of Chapter 12, but as it is a generally accepted convention that the expression "tax system" is used in this narrower sense, it is so used in this chapter. Again, if for reasons of euphony it is preferable sometimes to say "corporate", sometimes "corporation" tax no harm is done, nor to interchange on the same grounds "corporation" and "company" provided that it is realised that both are "incorporated enterprises" whereas "firms" or "enterprises" may or may not be incorporated. Similarly, "profits" and "earnings" of enterprises can be used in the same sense.

On the other hand, there are certain terms and expressions in this area that are used so ambiguously and artificially that it does seem necessary to comment on this, before rational analysis is possible. A number of them are so firmly entrenched in the literature that there is no hope of dislodging them, but at least it is possible to put out warning notices.

"Economic double taxation", as already indicated in Chapter 5C, is used indiscriminately in several different senses in the context of the taxation of distributed profits and it is used often as a shorthand propaganda slogan. There are other reasons also for objecting to its use in the present context. First the term "economic" which is used as a contrast with "juridical" in the transfer pricing context referred to in Chapter 5 is quite meaningless here. Second, there are two possible hypotheses about the relationship between corporate and personal income taxes: the first is that they are basically identical (see Carter and full integration as discussed in Chapter 12A) in which case it would be more consistent with normal usage to refer to a "distribution surcharge" rather than "economic double taxation", since most particular kinds of tax have different rates for different activities, different people, different goods, etc. On the more usually held hypothesis that the corporate and personal income tax are *different* taxes, the phrase "double taxation" is not normally used when the same income is subject to two *different* kinds of tax. For example, the fact that household income is subject both to personal income tax and social security contributions, to say nothing of consumption tax on their expenditures, is not normally referred to as economic double taxation. Nor does one normally talk of the economic multiple taxation of motorists who may be subject to one or more taxes on the purchase of the vehicle, tax on its fuel, an annual registration tax, a fee for the driving licence and toll charges on particular roads, as well as compulsory insurance.

In fact, the only other situation where the levying of two different kinds of tax has been referred to as economic double taxation is when corporations are subject to both corporation income tax and net wealth tax, though not when elements of these two separate tax bases are fused into one tax as in the German Gewerbesteuer. Yet one more reason for the inappropriateness of "double taxation" in this area is that both distributed and retained earnings may be subject to capital gains on disposals, so one could talk of triple taxation, as indeed some commentators do. In conclusion, the use of the expression "economic double taxation" in the present context explains nothing and confuses everything and in accordance the Occams' razor principle that entities should not be multiplied beyond necessity, the expression is avoided in the Chapter 12D analysis.

Two other terms that have been hijacked from the English language and which are now so firmly part of the literature that they are unlikely ever to be rescued are "integration" and "mitigation". These two terms are used both artificially (i.e. contrary to normal English usage) and ambiguously (it is sometimes unclear what they are meant to cover). Often the two terms are used synonymously to cover any measures reducing the tax differential between distributed and retained profits which occur as a result of the additional personal income tax charged in the hands of the shareholder. "Integration", according to English dictionaries, implies the addition of combination of parts towards some sort of completion and is appropriately used for imputation systems where there is a clear link between the corporation and personal income tax, but hardly applies in ordinary usage to a case where the corporation tax on distributed profits is reduced without regard to what happens to the personal tax, or where a reduction is made to personal income tax on dividend income without regard to what happens to the corporate tax. [C. McLure (1979) sensed that integration was being used in an artificial way when referring to relief for distributions at company level as "backdoor integration".] At least, no Humpty Dumpty has emerged, to my knowledge, to refer to the recent French reduction of tax on *retained* profits as a measure of "disintegration". "Mitigation", according to English dictionaries, means "alleviating or reducing severity" so that in normal language one can mitigate a burden but not a differential: for example, an increase in the rate of corporate tax on retained earnings would reduce the tax differential between retained and distributed profits, but it would be paradoxical in the extreme to refer to such an increase as a mitigation.

"Full integration" is sometimes used in the sense of eliminating that part of the tax differential between retained and distributed earnings due to the fact that the latter are also taxed at shareholder level, and sometimes in the wider sense of referring to the system recommended by the Carter report where retained earnings are also credited against shareholders' income tax on their dividends: "full mitigation" (itself a contradiction in terms according to the dictionary definition) is used in the former sense. In Chapter 12, "full integration" is used in the Carter sense, since full imputation or zero-rate corporation tax on distributions are sufficient to cover the first sense; otherwise, because of their artificiality and ambiguity, "integration" and "mitigation" are not used at all. The term "offset" is used to cover all measures reducing the tax differential between distributed and retained earnings which result from the additional personal income tax charge on the former, and "tax relief" is applied to the usual ways of doing this whether by reduction or elimination of the corporate tax on distributed profits or by reduction or elimination of personal income tax on dividend income.

It may seem unnecessary to make a distinction between system ("complex whole") and method ("form of procedure"), but the point of doing so is that while it is relatively easy for governments to modify their methods (e.g. a change in the relative rates of tax on distributed and retained profits or a change in the personal income tax schedule for dividend income) since limited repercussions follow from such modifications, a change in systems, for example from a classical to an imputation system, involves immense consequences and is normally not undertaken more than once in a decade. Consequently, a distinction is made in the classification in Table 12.7 between systems and methods.

E. Bibliography

1. INTRODUCTION

The objectives of the bibliography are first to acknowledge those sources which have been used and second to provide for the general reader additional material on particular topics, it being assumed that the specialist will already have an extensive reading list of books and articles relating to his or her particular interests.

The bibliography is divided into five sections, of which this Introduction is the first:

A list of main sources chapter by chapter of material used together with a few publications not used but likely to be of interest to the general reader (Section 2).

A list of OECD publications used (Section 3).
(As noted in the introduction, one of the purposes of this book is to provide a synthesis of many of these reports.)

A list of anthologies, from which many of the articles cited have been taken. These are in alphabetical order by author, by editor or institution (Section 4).

A list of books and articles in alphabetical order by author (or sometimes chairman or institution) (Section 5).

In Sections 3 to 5 most of the books or articles listed relate only to one or a few chapters or sections of chapters and where this is so numbers on the left hand indicate which chapter(s) or section(s) are relevant, a dash indicating relevance to several chapters.

In addition to the books and articles listed, there is usually something of general tax policy interest in a number of regular publications listed below, even if some of their contents will be very technical, whether on fine points of tax law or on econometric analysis.

Annual

- Proceedings of the Congresses of the International Institute of Public Finance (previously Cujas France and Wayne State University, US and currently Foundation Journal Public Finance, the Netherlands).

Quarterly

- National Tax Journal (National Tax Association – Tax Institute of America – US)
- Fiscal Studies (The Institute of Fiscal Studies – UK)

Monthly

- Bulletin for Fiscal Documentation (IBFD – Netherlands)
- European Taxation (IBFD – Netherlands)

There are many other specialised journals on the legal and economic aspects of taxation, but the ratio of articles of interest to a general reader to those for specialised accountants, lawyers, tax consultants and econometricians tends generally to be low.

2. MAIN SOURCES BY CHAPTER

In this section I have followed OECD practice of acknowledging outside contributors to official OECD reports. (See Chapters 11, 12, 13 and 14.)

Chapter 1 – An introduction to the recent waves of tax reforms.

Many sources have been used for this chapter, which covers not only tax reforms in practice but the rationale and philosophy behind tax reforms also referred to in subsequent chapters. The main sources are first, OECD reports taken from input provided by Delegates to the OECD Committee on Fiscal Affairs, second, comparative studies of tax reform, third, in-depth studies of particular countries, whether undertaken by government appointed or other tax reform commissions or by individual academics and fourth, theoretical works on the rationale for taxation in its varying forms.

Recent OECD Publications

1986	*Personal income tax systems under changing economic conditions*
1987	*Taxation in developed countries*
1988	*Taxing consumption*
1991	*The role of tax reform in Central and Eastern European countries*
1991	*Taxing profits in a global economy: domestic and international issues.*

Comparative studies in tax reform

1983	ed. S. Cnossen *Comparative tax studies*
1988	ed. J. Pechman *Comparative tax systems: Europe, Canada and Japan*
1989	ed. J. Pechman *World tax reform: a progress report*

Individual country studies

1966	Carter Report – Canada
1975	Asprey Report – Australia
1977	Blueprints Report – United States
1978	Meade Report – United Kingdom
1982	McCow Report – New Zealand
1982	O'Brien Report – Ireland
1985	*Fairness, growth and simplicity* – United States

Various editions	J.A.Kay and M.A. King – *The British tax system*
1989	H. Ishi – *The Japanese tax system*
Annual editions	J. Pechman – *Federal tax policy (United States).*

To understand the theoretical underpinnings of fiscal policy it would be necessary to read extensively from writers of at least two hundred years ago, eg. Adam Smith (1776) *Wealth of nations*, and perhaps even thousands of years ago. Three excellent studies provide a short cut. Of 20th century experts in public finance, along with many others, I believe that R.A. Musgrave is the most interesting and stimulating and of his many books I rate most highly the *Theory of public finance* (1959) though other later works listed in Section 5 are also rewarding. For a very readable article, which I came across very recently after finishing this book, there is J.A. Kay (1990) *Tax policy: a survey* which relates theoretical issues to current policy choices. Finally for a non-technical tour over 3 000 years there is C. Webber and A. Wildavsky (1986) *A history of taxation and expenditure in the Western world.*

Theory spills also into other chapters (eg. 6B, 7B, 10A) and two other books more relevant there that might be mentioned here are N. Kaldor (1955) *An expenditure tax* and R. Goode (1975), *The individual income tax.*

Chapters 2 to 4 – Tax Revenue Developments

The source for all statistical data is various editions of the annual OECD publications *Revenue Statistics of OECD Member Countries* (OECD RS). Mostly used is the 1991 edition which covers the years 1965-89, with provisional data for most countries for the year 1990.

Otherwise much of what is written is taken from my own earlier articles, of which most used is K. Messere and J. Owens (1987) *International comparisons of tax levels: pitfalls and insights.*

Other sources are:

R. Goode (1968)	*The tax burden of selected OECD countries*
C. Clark (1977)	*The state of taxation*
R. Bird (1979)	*Financing Canadian government: a quantitative overview*
S. Peltzman (1980)	*The growth of government*
R. Goode (1981)	*The limits of taxation*
OECD (1984)	*Tax expenditures: a review of the issues and country practices*
R. Rose (1985)	*Maximising revenues and minimising political costs: taxation by inertia*
P. Saunders and F. Klau (1985)	*The role of the public sector: causes and consequences.*

Chapter 5 – Irrationaltities

Apart from G. Orwell (1949) *Nineteen eighty-four*, of relevance also is C. Stevenson (1945) *Ethics and language* who pioneered the concept of "persuasive definitions" and I.D.M. Little (1950) who applied Stevensonian analysis in the area of welfare economics, which also has some bearing on tax equity considerations. F. Waismann (1968) is good on ambiguity and the law of the excluded middle and as noted in the text of Chapter 5, G. Ryle (1949) A. Rapoport (1960) and P.C. Wason and P.N. Johnson-Laird (1972) are all relevant in explaining the irrationalities of intelligent persons. Also relevant here, though quoted as an echo in Chapter 12D, is Lewis Carroll's *Alice's adventures in Wonderland and through the looking glass*. There are many editions, but the Penguin edition is recommended, because Martin Gardner's annotations are arguably more interesting than what is annotated.

Chapter 6 – Tax policy and public sector developments

On the first of the tax topics, higher government spending versus lower taxes, a number of references already cited under Chapters 1 to 4 have been used – Peltzman (1980), Rose (1985), Saunders and Klau (1985), Webber and Wildavsky (1986) and Cnossen (1982). Others are:

J. Lucas (1980)	*On justice*
R. Bird (1982)	*Closing the scissors or the real public sector has two sides*
H. Stein (ed)(1988)	*Tax policy in the twenty-first century* (articles by R. Bird, S. Cnossen, V. Tanzi)
OECD (1990)	*Taxpayers' rights and obligations*
L. Penner (1991)	*Federal government growth: leviathan or protection of the elderly*

On the second topic, tax expenditures versus direct expenditures, the main sources are:

C. Shoup (1975)	A survey of S. Surrey's *Pathways to tax reform* (1974) itself also used
R. Bird (1980)	*Tax incentives for investment: the state of the art*
OECD (1984)	*Tax expenditures: a review of the issues and Country practices*
S. Steinmo (1980)	*So what's wrong with tax expenditures? A revaluation based on the Swedish experience*

Chapter 7 – Some economic and social issues

This chapter covers five separate topics and the sources used are set out separately, no special sources other than the OECD publication on Taxing Consumption (1988) being used for the brief final section on small and medium enterprises.

Household savings

B.Bosworth (1984)	*Tax incentives and economic growth*
J. Hills (1984)	*Savings and fiscal privileges*
OECD (1986)	*Personal income tax systems under changing economic conditions*
V. Tanzi (1988)	*The tax treatment of interest income and expenses in industrialised countries*
R. Smith (1989)	*Factors affecting saving, policy tools and tax reform.*

Income distribution

OECD (1983)	*Taxes on immovable property*
OECD (1988)	*Taxing consumption*
OECD (1990)	*The personal income tax base: a comparative survey*
J. Nørregaard	*Progressivity of income tax systems* (1990)

Energy policy

OECD (1981, unpublished)	*An inventory of tax provisions which may have a direct impact on the supply and demand for energy*
OECD (1987)	*Energy conservation in IEA countries*
OECD (1987 & 1991)	*Energy prices and taxes*

Taxation and the environment

OECD (1992)	*Environment and economics: a survey of OECD work*
S. Cnossen and H.Vollebergh (1992	*Towards a global excise on carbon*
J. Short (1992)	*Transport growth in question*

In addition various sources have been used for the statistical information. These include:

OECD (1981)	*Income tax schedules: distribution of taxpayers and revenues*
United Nations (1987)	*United Nations national accounts statistics, 1985*
OECD (1987 & 1991)	*Energy prices and taxes*
J. Hills (1988)	*Changing tax: how the system works and how to change it*
P. Hoeller & M. Wallin (1991)	*Energy prices, taxes and carbon dioxide emissions*
OECD (1991)	*Estimation of greenhouse gas emissions and sinks*

Chapter 8 – Financing social security

The main sources are:

J. Buchanan (1968)	*Social insurance in a growing economy*
K. Olof-Faxen and G. Normann (1972	*The effects of payroll taxes*
L. Thompson (1983)	*The social security reform debate*
J.A. Kay (1990)	*The interrelationship between tax and benefit systems*
A. Dilnot and S. Webb (1991)	*A practical framework for the analysis of social security reform*

Statistical data are taken from:

U.S. Department of Health and Human Sciences (1989)	*Social security programmes throughout the world*
OECD (1991)	*Revenue statistics of OECD member countries*

Chapter 9 – Financing subcentral government expenditure

The three main sources are:

R. Musgrave (1983)	*Who should tax where and what?*
J. Owens and J. Nørregaard (1991)	*The role of lower levels of government: the experience of selected OECD Countries*
R. Bird and C. Wallich (1992)	*Financing local government in Hungary*

Also used were J. Lotz (1981), L. Söderström (1990), D. King and N. Tatsos (1991).

Statistical data were derived from *OECD RS* (1991) and the Owens and Nørregaard (1991) article cited above. For those wishing to study further in this field C.M Tiebout (1956) and P. Mieszkovski and G. Zodrow (1989) are recommended.

Chapter 10 – The personal income tax

The three main sources of the chapter are *Personal Income Tax Systems under Changing Economic Conditions* (OECD 1986) with various OECD internal and published updates, the *Personal Income Tax Base* (OECD 1990) and my joint article with S. Cnossen (1990) *Personal Income Tax Reforms.*

For section A3 the main sources were:

R. Goode (1985 and 1974)	*The individual income tax*

R. Bird and S. Cnossen (1990)	*Introduction to the personal income tax: phoenix from the ashes*
J. Pechmann (1991)	*The future of the income tax*
J. Bakija and E. Steuerle (1991)	*Individual income taxation since 1948*

Section B6 is taken from *Collection tax lags* (OECD 1983) and Section C3a from *The taxation of fringe benefits* (OECD 1988). Section D5 draws on *The adjustment of personal income tax for inflation* (OECD 1976), Section E2 from L. Godfrey (1975) *The theoretical and empirical aspects of the effects of taxation on the supply of labour* and OECD (1981) *Income tax schedules: distribution of taxpayers and revenues.* Sections E3 and E4 both use *The treatment of family units under tax and transfer systems* (OECD 1977) and *The tax benefit position of selected income groups* (1974-78) (OECD 1980).

Chapter 11 – The taxation of net wealth, capital transfers and capital gains of individuals

Virtually everything has been taken from two OECD publications (1979 and 1988) both with the same title as this chapter. Considerable input was supplied by J.R.M. Willis to the 1979 edition and by C.T. Sandford to both editions. There has been some, but not much updating from various other sources.

Chapter 12 Corporation income taxes and other taxes on business

The main source for the factual information is *Taxing profits in a global economy* (OECD 1991) to which much input was supplied by M. Devreux, M. Pearson, P.B. Sorensen and J. Visser.

Other sources directly used in this chapter are:

K. Messere (1976)	*Fashions in company taxation*
C. McLure (1979)	*Must profits be taxed twice?*
S. Cnossen (1992)	*Corporate taxes in the European Communities*
M. Gammie (1992)	*Reforming corporation tax: an evaluation of the US. Treasury integration proposals and other corporate tax systems in an international context* (as well as the 1992 U.S. Treasury Report itself).

Most of the literature of policy interest focuses on the question of the choice between the various tax systems. Here are some books and articles which have had at least an indirect influence on this chapter:

A.J. van den Tempel (1970)	*Corporation tax and individual income tax in the European Communities*
P. Mieszkowski (1972)	*Integration of the corporate and personal income tax: the bogus issue of shifting*

G. Whittington (1974)	*Company taxation and dividends*
J. Wiseman and M. Davenport (1974)	*Theoretical and empirical aspects of corporate taxation*
A. Bagachi (1990)	*Tax on dividends – the issues and non- issues*

Chapter 13 – Consumption taxation

The main source is *Taxing consumption* (OECD 1988) to which much input was provided by S. Cnossen and C. Sandford, and to which R. Bird also made useful suggestions. Use has also been made in the last Section of S. Cnossen (1989) *The role of excises in OECD Countries*. The other main source is A. Tait (1988) *Value added tax: international practice and problems.*

Another useful source was a number of articles from *Value added taxation in developing countries* (World Bank 1990) as listed below:

C.S. Shoup	*Choosing among types of VAT*
A.A. Tait	*Inflation and the foreign trade balance*
R.F. Conrad	*The VAT and real estate*
S.N. Poddar	*Options for a VAT at the state level*

Other input was supplied by articles by S. Cnossen especially *Key questions in considering a value-added tax for Central and Eastern European countries* (1991).

A fine general introduction to consumption taxation is J.F. Due, *Sales taxation* (1957). (I have always had a special affection for this book, since it was by virtue of reading it thoroughly, that I was able to convince OECD in 1964 that I was competent to write a report on border tax adjustments.) The VAT Monitor (IBFD) provides monthly information not only on VAT, but also on other consumption taxes.

On the statistical side a periodical publication, which has been used is the Canadian *Alcoholic beverage taxation and control policies* (Brewers Association of Canada). OECD *Health systems: facts and trends* provides annual information on both alcohol and tobacco taxes and prices as well as more frightening information on the consequences of absorbing too much alcohol and tobacco. IAE *Energy prices and taxes* provides quarterly information on energy taxation.

Chapter 14 – Taxes on immovable property

The main source is *Taxes on immovable property* (OECD 1983) to which substantial input was provided by D. King and to which O. Oldman also contributed.

Also used in this chapter as well as in Chapter 9 are J. Owens and J. Nørregaard (1991) and R. Bird and C. Wallich (1992) .

3. OFFICIAL OECD PUBLICATIONS

This list is confined to official OECD publications used in this book. Unofficial reports commissioned by OECD but under the responsibility of the authors are listed under the author's name in Section 5. Various OECD statistical publications have been referred to in the appropriate chapter in the last section and here it is appropriate to refer only to two annual statistical publications, the first very frequently and the second occasionally being used in this book. There are:

Revenue Statistics of OECD Member Countries (referred to as OECD RS)

The tax/benefit position of production workers (referred to as OECD APW)

The following publications are listed in chronological order together with the chapter or section of chapter to which they are relevant:

Chapter	Date	*Title*
12D	1973	*Company tax systems in OECD Member countries* *
10E	1974	*Negative income tax* *
10D	1976	*The adjustment of personal income tax systems for inflation* *
10E	1977	*The treatment of family units in OECD Member countries under tax and transfer systems* *
10E	1978	*The tax/benefit position of selected income groups in OECD Member countries 1972-1976*
11	1979	*The taxation of net wealth, capital transfers and capital gains of individuals* *
10E	1980	*The tax/benefit position of selected income groups in OECD Member countries 1974-1978* *
7C,13	1981	*The impact of consumption taxes at different income levels*
2,3	1981	*Long-term trends in tax revenues of OECD Member countries 1955-1980*
7C,10	1981	*Income tax schedules: distribution of taxpayers and revenues*
8B	1981	*The welfare state in crisis*
10B	1983	*Income tax collection lags*
14	1983	*Taxes on immovable property*
6C	1984	*Tax expenditures: a review of the issues and country practices*
10	1986	*Personal income tax systems under changing economic conditions*
–	1987	*Taxation in developed countries*
7D	1987	*Energy conservation in IEA countries*
11	1988	*Taxation of net wealth, capital transfers and capital gains of individuals*

13	1988	*Taxing consumption*
10C	1988	*The taxation of fringe benefits*
8	1988	*Reforming public pensions*
10	1990	*The personal income tax base: a comparative survey*
12	1990	*Taxation and international capital flows*
6B	1990	*Taxpayers' rights and obligations: a survey of the legal situation in OECD countries*
–	1991	*Taxing profits in a global economy: domestic and international issues*
–	1991	*The role of tax reform in Central and Eastern European economies*

* out of print

4. ANTHOLOGIES

Many of the articles listed in Section 5 are taken from the following 24 collections of articles, which are listed in alphabetical order by editor or chairman, or institution when there is no editor. To reduce repetition of publication details and to facilitate cross-reference, the publication details are inserted here with a cross-reference back from Section 5 when this is relevant.

–	(A) ed. AARON, Henry J. and PECHMAN, Joseph A. How taxes affect economic behaviour (Washington, D.C., Brookings Institution 1981)
1,10	(B) ed. AARON, Henry J. and GALPER, Harvey A. Assessing tax reform (Washington D.C., Brookings Institution 1985)
1,10	(C) ed. AARON, GALPER and PECHMAN Uneasy compromise: problems of a hybrid income-consumption tax (Washington D.C., Brookings Institution 1988)
–	(D) ed. BIEHL Dieter, ROSKAMP Karl W. and STOLPER Wolfgang F. Public finance and economic growth [Proceedings of 37th IIPF Congress (Wayne State University 1983)]
	(E) ed. CIANCONE, Aldo and MESSERE, Ken Changes in revenue structure [Proceedings of 42nd IIPF Congress (Wayne State University 1989)]
–	(F) ed. CNOSSEN, Sijbren Comparative tax studies: essays in honour of Richard Goode (Amsterdam, North Holland 1983)
–	(G) ed. CNOSSEN, Sijbren Tax co-ordination in the European Communities (Massachusets, Kluwer 1987)
10	(H) ed. CNOSSEN, Sijbren and BIRD, Richard M. (Amsterdam, North Holland 1983) The personal income tax: phoenix from the ashes? (Amsterdam, North Holland 1990)
–	(I) ed. EDEN, Lorraine Retrospectives on public finance (Durham, Canada, Duke University Press 1991)
13	(J) ed. GILLIS, Malcolm, SHOUP, Carl S. and SICAT, Gorado P. Value added taxation in developing countries (Washington D.C., World Bank 1990)
–	(K) INTERNATIONAL INSTITUTE OF PUBLIC FINANCE Inflation, economic growth and taxation [Proceedings of 29th IIPF Congress, (Madrid and Barcelona 1973)]

10E (L) INSTITUTE FOR FISCAL STUDIES
Fiscal policy and labour supply [Proceedings of a 1976 conference in Stirling (London, IFS 1977)]

8 (M) INTERNATIONAL SOCIAL SECURITY ASSOCIATION
Social security and taxation [Proceedings of a Jerusalem 1978 conference (Geneva, ISSA 1979)]

6C (N) ed. MACDANIEL, Paul and SURREY, Stanley
International aspects of tax expenditures (Massachusets, Kluwer 1984)

9D (0) ed. McLURE, Charles E. Jr.
Tax assignment in federal countries (Canberra, The Australian National University 1983)

9 (P) ed. OWENS, Jeffrey P. and PANELLA, S.
Local government: an international perspective (Amsterdam, North Holland 1991)

1,10A (Q) ed. PECHMAN, Joseph A.
Comprehensive income taxation (Washington D.C., Brookings Institution 1977)

1,10A (R) ed. PECHMAN, Joseph A.
What should be taxed: income or expenditure? (Washington D.C., Brookings Institution 1980)

1, 4 (S) ed. PECHMAN, Joseph A.
Comparative tax systems: Europe, Canada and Japan (Arlington, Virginia, Tax Analyses 1987)

1, 4 (T) ed. PECHMAN, Joseph A.
World tax reform: a progress report (Washington D.C., Brookings Institution 1988)

9 (U) ed. PRUDHOMME Rémy
Public Finance with several layers of government [Proceedings of 46th IIPF Congress (Netherlands, Foundation Journal Public Finance 1990)]

– (V) ed. RECHTENWALD, Horst Clauss
Secular trends of the public sector [Proceedings of 32nd IIPF Congress, Cujas 1978]

– (W) ed. ROSKAMP, Karl W. and FORTE, Francesco
Reforms of tax systems [Proceedings of 35th IIPF Congress (Wayne State University 1981)]

6B (X) ed. STEIN, Herbert
Tax policy in the twenty-first century (New York, John Wiley 1988)

5. INDIVIDUAL BOOKS AND ARTICLES

It is recalled that quite a large proportion of the articles that follow are taken from the 24 anthologies listed in Section 4. In such cases, references to publication details are to be found in that section.

1	AARON, Henry J. and GALPER, Harvey A., Assessing the reform (Washington D.C., Brookings Institution 1985)
1	ALLAN, Charles M., The theory of taxation (London, Penguin 1971)
1, 10A	ANDREWS, W.D., A consumption tax or cash flow personal income tax (Harvard Law Review 1974)
12D	BAGACHI, A., India: Tax on dividends: The issues and non-issues (Amsterdam, IBFD Bulletin 1990)
10A	BAKIJA, Jon and STEUERLE, Eugene., Individual income tax since 1948 (Massachusets, National Tax Journal, December 1991)
2, 6B	BIRD, Richard M., Financing Canadian government: a quantitative overview (Canadian Tax Foundation 1979)
1,2,6B	The tax kaleidoscope: perspectives on tax reform in Canada (Canadian Tax Journal September/October 1970)
1, 6B	A new look at benefit taxation (from 4(V) 1978)
6C	Tax incentives for investment: the state of the art (Canadian Tax Foundation 1980)
6B	Closing the scissors or the real public sector has two sides (Canadian Tax Journal December 1982)
12D	Corporate-personal tax integration (from 4(V) 1986)
6B	Experience from a century of choice (from 4(X)1988)
6B	Tax structure and the growth of government (from 4(I) 1991)
9	BIRD, Richard M. and WALLISCH, Christine, Financing local government in Hungary (Washington D.C., World Bank, March 1992, Working Paper 869)
7B	BOSWORTH, Barry P., Tax incentives and economic growth (Washington D.C., Brookings Institution 1984)
10C	BOURGIGNON François, Taxation of labour income (from 4(H) 1990)
1, 10A	BRADFORD, David F., The case for a personal consumption tax (from 4(R) 1980)
10E	BRANNON, Gerard M. and MORSS, Eliot R., The tax allowance for dependents: deductions versus credits (Massachusets, National Tax Journal 1973)

6B	BRENNAN Geoffrey, and BUCHANAN, James N., The power to tax (Cambridge University Press 1980)
6B	The tax system as social overhead capital: a constitutional perspective on taxes (from 4(C) 1988)
10E	BROWN, C.V., Survey of the effects of taxation on labour supply of low income groups (from 4(G) 1988)
10E	Taxation and the incentive to work (Oxford, OUP 1983)
–	BROWN, C.V. and JACKSON P.M., Public sector economics (Oxford, Martin Robertson 1978 and other editions)
8	BUCHANAN, James N., Social insurance in a growing economy: a proposal for radical reform (Massachusets, National Tax Journal 1968)
6B	Taxation in fiscal exchange (Amsterdam, Journal of Public Economics, North Holland 1976)
6B	BUCHANAN, James N. and FLOWER, Marilyn, An analytical setting for a taxpayers' revolution (Los Angeles, Western Economic Journal, December 1969)
12D	CARROLL, Lewis, The annotated Alice: Alice's adventures in Wonderland and through the looking glass: edited by GARDNER, Martin (Harmondsworth, Middlesex, U.K., Penguin 1965)
13D	CNOSSEN, Sijbren, Excise systems: a global study of the selective taxation of goods and services (Baltimore, Johns Hopkins University Press 1977)
13D	Specific issues in excise taxation: the alcohol problem (from 4(W) 1983)
12D	The imputation system in the EEC (from 4(F) 1983)
2,4B	Tax structure developments (from 4(G) 1987)
13B	VAT and RST a comparison (Canadian Tax Journal, March 1987)
6B	Day of reckoning approaches for the European Community (from 4(X) 1988)
13C	What rate structure for a goods and services tax? (Canadian Tax Journal, May 1989)
13D	The role of excises in OECD Member Countries (from 4(D) 1989)
13	Key questions in considering a VAT for control of Eastern European countries (Washington D.C., IMF Staff Paper, June 1992)
12	Corporation tax in the European Communities (IBFD 1992 forthcoming)
13D	Intrigues around the tobacco tax (Amsterdam, Intertax, February 1992)
10	CNOSSEN, Sijbren and MESSERE, Ken, Personal income tax reforms in OECD countries (from 4(H) 1990)

7E	CNOSSEN, Sijbren and VOLLEBERGH, H., Towards a global excise on carbons (Massachusets, National Tax Journal, March 1992)
13C	CONRAD, Robert F., The VAT and real estate (from 4(J) 1990)
8	DILNOT, Andrew W., KAY, John A. and MORRIS, Nick, The reform of social security (Oxford, OUP 1984)
8	DILNOT, Andrew W. and WEBB, Steven, A practical framework for the analysis of social security reform (London, Fiscal Studies, November 1991)
13	DUE, John F., Sales taxation (London, Routledge and Kegan Paul 1957)
10	Personal deductions (from 4(Q) 1977)
13B	DUE, John F. and BRENS, V., The controversial Norwegian value added tax (University of Illinois 1986)
1, 6B	FELDSTEIN, Martin F., On the theory of tax reform (Amsterdam, Journal of Public Economics, North Holland 1976)
1	GALBRAITH, J.K., The affluent society (London, Hamish Hamilton, 1958)
12D	GAMMIE, Malcolm (Chairman), Equity for companies: a corporation tax for the 1990s (London, Institute for Fiscal Studies 1991)
12D	GAMMIE, Malcolm, An evaluation of the U.S. Treasury integration proposals and other corporate tax systems in an international context (London, British Tax Review 1992 no. 3)
12	The Ruding Committee: An initial response (London, Institute for Fiscal Studies 1992)
10E	GODFREY, L., Theoretical and empirical aspects of the taxation on the supply of labour (Paris, OECD 1975)
10A	GOODE, Richard, The individual income tax (Washington D.C., Brookings Institution 1976)
2	The tax burden of selected OECD countries (The Annals of the American Academy of Political Social Science 1968)
2	The limits of taxation (from 4(W) 1978)
1, 10	Key issues in the reform of personal income tax (from 4(H) 1990)
10E	GOTTSCHALE, P., Deduction versus credits revisited (Massachusets, National Tax Journal 1976)
6B1	GRAPPERHAUS, Ferdinand H.M., Taxes, liberty and profits: the role of taxation in democratisation and national unity 511-1787 (Amsterdam, Meijburg and Co. 1989)
8,10E	HABIB, Jack, The relationship between social security and taxation: an overview (from 4(M) 1979)

10E	HALBERSTADT, Victor, Report on the proceedings in the tax working group (from 4(L) 1977)
–	HANSEN, Bent, Fiscal policy in seven countries 1955-65 (Paris, OECD 1969)
7B	HILLS, John, Savings and fiscal privileges (London, Institute for Fiscal Studies 1984)
7C	Changing tax: how the system works and how to change it (London, Child Poverty Action Group 1988)
4E	HILLS, John and SUTHERLAND, Holly, The proposed Council tax (London, Fiscal Studies, November 1991)
8	HOLZMANN, Robert, Reforming public pensions (Paris, OECD 1988)
–	ISHI, Hiromotsu, The Japanese tax system (Oxford, Clarendon Press 1989)
4, 10	KALDOR, Nicholas, An expenditure tax (London, Allen and Unwin 1955)
8	KAY, John A., The inter-relationship between tax and benefit systems (from 4(H) 1990)
–	Tax policy: a survey (Oxford, the Economic Journal, March 1990)
–	KAY, John A. and KING, Mervyn A., The British tax system (Oxford, OUP, various editions)
13C	KAY, John A. and DAVIS, Evan H., The VAT and services (from 4(J) 1990)
9	KING, David, Grants as a source of local government finance (from 4(P) 1991)
1,10,11	KING, Mervyn A., Tax reform: the next step (London School of Economics, Financial Markets Group, Division Paper no. 42 1988)
10D	KOPPELMAN, Stanley, Progressive effects of the Tax Reform Act of 1986 (Massachusets, National Tax Journal 1988)
4D	LAYFIELD, F. (Chairman), Local government finance (London, HMSO 1976)
5	LITTLE I.M.D., A critique of welfare economics (Oxford, Clarendon Press 1950)
1, 10	LODIN, Sven-Olof, Progressive expenditure tax: an alternative? (Report of the 1972 Government Commission on Taxation, Stockholm 1978)
9	LOTZ, Jorgen, Local government taxation: recent trends and issues (from 4(W) 1978)
6B	LUCAS, J.R., On Justice (Oxford, Clarendon Press 1980)
1, 10	MATHEWS, Russell, The mythology of taxation (the Australian National University 1984)

10E	McINTYRE, Michael J., Evaluating the new tax credit child care and maid services (U.S., Tax Notes, May 1977)
10E	Treatment of the family (from 4(Q) 1977)
10E	Implications of family sharing for the design of an ideal personal income tax system (from 4(H) 1990)
12D	McLURE, Charles E. Jr., Must corporate income be taxed twice? (Washington D.C., Brookings Institution 1979)
7C,9,13	Introduction to distribution and tax incidence under the VAT (from 4(J) 1990)
1,10A	MEADE, James E., The structure and reform of direct taxation (London, Allen and Unwin 1978)
2, 10	MESSERE, Ken, The impact of inflation on tax structures (from 4(K) 1973)
12D	Fashions in company taxation (Weekblad voor Fiscaal Recht, Kluwer, September 1976)
10E	Comment on C.V. Brown, (see 4(C) 1977)
3	Tax levels, structures, and systems: some intertemporal and international comparisons (from 4(V) 1978)
13B	A defence of present border tax adjustment practices (Massachusets, National Tax Journal, December 1979)
11D	Capital gains and related taxation in OECD Member countries (Canadian Tax Foundation 1981)
3	Quantitative developments in OECD tax levels and structures 1965-81 (Amsterdam, Intertax, August 1985)
1,2,3	Trends in tax revenues (from 4(F) 1983)
1	Overview to world tax reform (from 4(T) 1988)
12D	A personal view on certain aspects of the Ruding Committee Report and the EC Commission's reactions to it (European Taxation, January 1993)
10E	MESSERE, Ken and OWENS, Jeffrey P., The treatment of dependent children under income tax and social welfare (from 4(M) 1979)
2, 4	International comparisons of tax levels: pitfalls and insights (Paris, OECD Economic Studies no. 8, Spring 1987)
1,2,3	Long-term revenue trends and current tax reforms in OECD Member countries (from 4(D) 1984)
13	MESSERE, Ken and NØRREGAARD, John, Consumption taxes in OECD countries over the last two decades (Amsterdam, IBFD Bulletin 1989)
9,14	MIESKOWSKI, Peter and ZODROW, George R., Taxation and the Tiebout model: the differential effects of head taxes, taxes on land rents and property taxes (U.S., Journal of Economic Literature, September 1989)

10E	MUSGRAVE, Peggy B., Women and taxation (from 4(W) 1978)
–	MUSGRAVE, Richard A., The theory of public finance: a study in public economy (U.S., McGraw Hill 1959)
9	Fiscal systems (U.S., Yale University Press 1969)
	Who should tax where and what? (from 4(O) 1983)
–	MUSGRAVE Richard A. and Peggy B., Public finance in theory and practice (U.S., McGraw Hill 1984)
7C,10D	NØRREGAARD, John, Progressivity of income tax systems (Paris, OECD Economic Studies no. 15, Autumn 1990)
8	OLOF-FAXEN, Karl, and NORMANN, Görun, The effects of payroll taxes – a theoretical analysis (from 4(L) 1977)
5	ORWELL, George, Nineteen eighty-four (London, Secker and Warburg 1949)
9	OWENS, Jeffrey P. and NØRREGAARD, John, The role of lower levels of government: the experience of selected OECD governments (from 4(P) 1991)
6B	PEACOCK, Alan, and WISEMAN, Jack, The growth of public expenditure in the United Kingdom (Princeton University Press 1961)
7C	PECHMAN, Joseph A., Who paid the taxes 1966-1985? (Washington D.C., Brookings Institution 1985)
10A	The future of the income tax (U.S., The American Economic Review, March 1990)
–	Federal tax policy (Washington D.C., Brookings Institution, annual publication)
6B	PELTZMAN, Sam, The growth of government (U.S., The Journal of Law and Economics, October 1980)
6B	PENNER, Rudolph G. Federal government growth: Leviathan or protection of the elderly (Massachusets, National Tax Journal, December 1991)
13C	PODDAR, Satya N., Options for a VAT at the state level (from 4(J)1990)
10E	POGUE, Thomas F., Deductions versus credits: a comment (Massachusets, National Tax Journal, December 1974)
5	RAPOPORT, Anatol, Fights, games and debates (University of Michigan Press 1960)
6B	RAWLS, John, A theory of justice (Harvard University Press 1971)
6B	ROSE, Richard, Maximising revenue and minimising political costs: taxation by inertia (U.K., University of Strathclyde 1985)
12	RUDING, Onno, (Chairman), Report of the Committee of Independent Experts on Company Taxation (Brussels, Commission of the European Community 1992)

5	RYLE, Gilbert, The concept of mind (London, Hutchinson's University Library 1949)
13	SANDFORD, Cedric T., Costs and benefits of VAT (London, Heinemann 1981)
6B	SAUNDERS, Peter and KLAU, Friedrich, The role of the public sector: causes and consequences of the growth of government (Paris, OECD Economic Studies no. 4, Spring 1985)
10E	SCHMÖLDERS, G., Attitudes to taxation and their effect on work effort (from 4(L) 1977)
7E	SHORT, J., Transport growth in question: environment, global and local effects (Lisbon, European Conference of Ministers of Transport 1992)
6C	SHOUP, Carl S. Surrey's 'Pathways to tax reform': a review article (U.S., The Journal of Finance, December 1975)
7B	SMITH, Roger S., Factors affecting saving, policy tools and tax reform: a review (Washington D.C., IMF Staff Papers 1989)
9	SÖDERSTRÖM, Lars, Fiscal federation: the Nordic countries' style (from 4(T) 1988)
6C	STEINMO, Sven, So what's wrong with tax expenditures? A revaluation based on the Swedish experience (U.S. Public Budget and Finance, Summer 1986)
5	STEVENSON, Charles L., Ethics and language (U.S., Yale University Press 1944)
10E	SUNLEY, Emil, The choice between deduction and credits (Massachusets, National Tax Journal, September 1977)
12D	International aspects of integration (Amsterdam, IBFD Bulletin, July 1979)
6C	SURREY, Stanley S., Pathways to tax reform (Harvard University Press,1973)
11	TAIT, Alan A., Net wealth, gifts and transfer taxes (from 4(F) 1983)
13	Value added tax: international practice and problems (Washington D.C., IMF 1988)
1E,10A	Not so general equilibrium and not so optimal taxation (U.S. Public Finance, February 1989)
13	The value added tax: revenue, inflation and the foreign trade balance (from 4(J) 1990)
7D	TAIT, Alan A. and MORGAN, David R., Gasoline taxes in selected OECD countries, 1970-74 (Washington D.C., IMF Staff Papers 1980)
10	TANZI, Vito, Inflation and the income tax (Cambridge, U.K., Cambridge University Press 1980)

7B	The tax treatment of interest, income and expenses in industrialised countries: a discussion of recent crises (U.S., Proceedings of 80th annual conference NTA-TIA 1986)
6B	Forces that shape tax policy (from 4(X) 1986)
9	TATSOS, Nicolas, The choice between different sources of finance (from 4(P) 1991)
8	THOMPSON, Lawrence H., The social security reform debate (U.S., Journal of Economic Literature, December 1983)
9,14	TIEBOUT, Charles M., A pure theory of local expenditures (U.S., Journal of Political Economics, October 1956)
8	UNITED STATES DEPT. OF HEALTH AND HUMAN SCIENCES, Social security programs throughout the world (Washington D.C. 1989)
4,10	UNITED STATES TREASURY, Blueprints for basic tax reform (Washington D.C., U.S. Government Printing Office 1977)
4	Tax reform for fairness, simplicity and economic growth (Washington D.C. 1984)
12	Integration of the individual and corporate tax system: taxing business income once (Washington D.C. 1992)
12	VAN DEN TEMPEL, Arnold J., Corporation tax and individual income tax in the European Communities (Brussels, Commission of the European Communities 1970)
5	WAISMANN, Friedrich, How I see philosophy (London, Macmillan 1968)
5	WASON P.C. and JOHNSON-LAIRD, P.N., Psychology of reasoning: structure and content (London, Batsford 1972)
6B	WEBBER, Carolyn, and WILDAVSKY, Aaron, A History of taxation and expenditure in the western world (New York, Simon and Schuster 1986)
12B	WHITTINGTON, G., Company taxation and dividends (London, Institute for Fiscal Studies 1975)
–	WILLIAMS, David W., Trends in international taxation (Amsterdam, IBFD 1991)
12	WISEMAN, Jack, and DAVENPORT, Michael, Theoretical and empirical aspects of corporate taxation (Paris, OECD 1974)
12D	ZODROW, George R., On the 'traditional' and 'new' views of dividend taxation (Massachusets, National Tax Journal, December.1991)

[illegible]

F. Name index

G. Subject index

For reference to specific matters concerning the main kinds of taxes, including country practices, see detailed list of contents at the beginning of Chapters 10, 11, 12, 13 and 14. This index is confined to Parts I and II of the book, together with the more general aspects of Part III where there is interaction with issues discussed in the first nine Chapters. For minor or non-existent taxes, see specifically 'Unusual taxes' and 'non-existent' taxes. The Glossary at the beginning of the Appendix also constitutes a partial subject index. There are so many references to individual countries and to OECD that they are excluded from this index.

A

B

C

1. Some examples, there are many others.

D

E

H

I

L

M

N

O

P

R

S

T

U

W